The Social Psychology of Organizations

DANIEL KATZ

*Department of Psychology
and Survey Research Center
The University of Michigan*

ROBERT L. KAHN

*Survey Research Center
and Department of Psychology
The University of Michigan*

WILEY INTERNATIONAL EDITION

JOHN WILEY & SONS, INC.
New York · London

Library of Congress Catalog Card Number: 65-27660
Printed in the United States of America
ISBN 0 471 46041 9

WILEY INTERNATIONAL EDITION

10 9 8

The Social Psychology of Organizations

To Floyd Henry Allport

Preface

This book had its origin in the program of research on human relations in organizations launched by Rensis Likert in 1947 as one of the major programs of the Survey Research Center of The University of Michigan. From its inception, this series of researches has been concerned with problems of morale and motivation, productivity and effectiveness, power and control, and leadership and change processes in large-scale organizations. The research findings from the program and related work in the Institute for Social Research were well summarized several years ago by Rensis Likert, whose original work on organizational problems and whose contagious enthusiasm for research have been extremely helpful to us. This book is in part an effort to provide a more general theoretical treatment of some of the same issues which he considered in *New Patterns of Management* (1961), and we have drawn on some of the same materials and experience.

In our attempts to extend the description and explanation of organizational processes we have shifted from an earlier emphasis on traditional concepts of individual psychology and interpersonal relations to system constructs. The interdependent behavior of many people in their supportive and complementary actions takes on a form or structure which needs to be conceptualized at a more appropriate collective level. Classical organization theory we found unsatisfactory because of its implicit assumptions about the closed character of social structures. The development of open-system theory, on the other hand, furnished a much more dynamic and adequate framework. Hence, our effort, in the pages to follow, is directed at the utilization of an open-system point of view for the study of large-scale organizations.

Many individuals have provided ideas and approaches to the complex problems of organizational life, and we have benefited from

many. We are particularly indebted to Floyd H. Allport, whose original theoretical approach to problems of social structure inspired this
book even though it reflects but faint and distorted versions of his
thunder. Herbert Thelen and John R. P. French, Jr. have by means
of many discussions and through their own work improved the quality of ours. Others who have wrestled with problems of organizational
theory to our considerable advantage are Chris Argyris, Sidney Cobb,
Stanley Seashore, and Floyd C. Mann. They, along with Angus Campbell, Gerald Gurin, and Arnold Tannenbaum, commented on parts of
this manuscript, as did Ellen Baar and Shirley Ball. John DeLamater
provided valuable assistance in the preparation of the manuscript.

We are grateful for the support provided by the National Institutes of Health, by the Carnegie Corporation, and by the research
fund of the Horace H. Rackham School of Graduate Studies. We
want also to thank our colleagues in the Survey Research Center,
particularly Angus Campbell, for making possible occasional periods
during which the usual demands of ongoing research and administration could be eliminated in favor of writing. During the year 1960 to
1961 our work was greatly facilitated by the Ford Center for Advanced Study in the Behavioral Sciences. Daniel Katz spent the year
there as a Fellow (a fellowship supported by National Institutes of
Health) and Robert Kahn the summer as a visiting scholar. We are
glad to acknowledge the good effects of that unique environment and
to express our thanks to its director, Ralph Tyler, for having created
and sustained it.

Various people have typed and proofread numerous drafts of the
fourteen chapters of this book. Most of the work has been done, however, and done with excellence and unfailing good spirit, by Mrs.
Rita Lamendella. She deserves a share of whatever pleasure and satisfaction attend the completion of the book. Mrs. Nancy Abbey and
Marcia Kahn were her able assistants.

We also wish to thank the following publishers for permission to
use excerpts, tables, and figures in this book: American Psychological
Association, Basic Books, Dorsey, Doubleday, Free Press, Harcourt,
Brace and World, Industrial and Labor Relations Review, Industrial
Relations Research Association, McGraw-Hill, Mental Health Research
Institute, University of Michigan, Mentor, Pergamon, Tavistock Pub-
lications, and John Wiley and Sons.

DANIEL KATZ
ROBERT L. KAHN

September 1965

Contents

I

Point of Departure

The psychological approach to the study of problems in the social world has been impeded by an inability to deal with the facts of social structure and social organization. It is an elementary fact that societies in their very nature represent organized groupings of people whose activities are institutionally channeled. The exercise of power and control in a society is in good part a function of its institutional structure. Yet the dominant tradition in psychology has included the implicit assumption that individuals exist in a social vacuum. To fill this vacuum students of personality have recognized the importance of familial patterns of behavior for the development of character, but they have neglected the fact that people behave not only as grown-up children but as adult members of social systems. Social psychologists, too, have been guilty of negligence of the facts of social life. Again, however, it has not been possible for them to operate in a complete social vacuum. Their partial attempts to include social variables reflect a curious alternation between the most global of all influences, that of culture, and the most minute of group influences.

The great central area of man's behavior in organizations and institutions and the psychological character of such groupings has been ignored. Yet the individual in the modern western world spends the greater part of his waking hours in organizations and institutional settings. The usual text in social psychology consists of three parts—a restatement of the principles of laboratory psychology with some attention to their possible application to practical problems; a growing emphasis upon concepts and findings from small group experiments; and a section on personality recognizing the importance of child-rearing practices and the culture-bound character of personality traits and syndromes. This type of text, desirable as it is, generally leaves off at the point where the most important problems of social psychology begin. A second volume is necessary to move beyond the introduction to the field and to deal with the psychological aspects of social structures. The present work is an attempt to supply such a second book in social psychology, hazardous though the undertaking may be.

The modesty of psychologists in halting their study with the individual in the small-group setting is due in great measure to the lack of conceptual tools for venturing into more complex areas. Though the need for dealing with structure and organized forms has been acknowledged in all scientific disciplines, there have been basic weaknesses in most of the theoretical approaches popular in social psychology. Behaviorism, Freudianism, and field theory have been too individual in orientation and hence of very limited usefulness in dealing with social-structural problems. Nor have the older societal theories of the other social sciences provided the answers.

Behaviorism. Experimental and research-oriented social psychology in this country had its origins in the *behavioristic movement.* Group experimentation was launched in a systematic way by F. H. Allport and theoretically integrated in the first scientific text to appear in the field (1924). But behaviorism, based as it was on Newtonian mechanics, could not deal adequately with problems of organization and structure. The stimulus-response formula assumed too static, too constant, and too atomistic a psychological world. The relationships in a field of forces affecting the component elements were ignored. The constancies assumed between specific stimuli and specific responses produced descriptions of social phenomena which were not always accurate and were often inadequate.

Moreover, the very definition of the stimulus makes for difficulties in social application. The stimulus is a form of physical energy which can be manipulated and controlled in the laboratory. In the social situation, however, the dimensions of the stimulus can not be specified in comparable manner. Hence the behavioristic approach of F. H. Allport (1924) and later of Miller and Dollard (1941) soon ran into difficulties in identifying the social stimuli so important in their theoretical approach. In the laboratory we control the reinforcement administered for certain types of responses. But in the social situation we cannot predict satisfactorily from traditional learning theory because we generally cannot identify in advance of the outcome the nature of the reinforcement for the individual. This is less true in more restricted learning situations, such as the classroom or the home, but even here concepts of reinforcement present genuine difficulties of application in practice.

Field Theory. Field theory, the left wing of the Gestalt movement, did correct the elementaristic assumptions of behaviorism, but only at the individual level. The psychological field of the Lewinians is an individual field. Though field theory does utilize the dynamics of relationship and emphasizes the properties of a given structure no matter what its phenotypic history, it is still addressed to the problems of organization within the individual rather than within the collectivity. Power, as Cartwright conceptualizes it (1959), is the ability of individual A to influence individual B and not a function of social structure. And Festinger in the same tradition has moved from the problem of uniformity in the group to concepts of self-comparison (1954) and to cognitive dissonance (1957). The basic tenets of field theory are still clear in this development. Cognitive dissonance has the same properties no matter what the specific genesis of the imbalance. But again this is at the level of the individual.

The bold attempt of Brown (1936) to apply the theoretical concepts of the individual field to the social field was widely recognized as an unsuccessful tour de force. Brown took such constructs as barriers, locomotion, vectors, and valences and made them aspects of groups and social organizations—the familiar attribution to groups of individual characteristics. The more sophisticated approach of Asch (1952) in developing the doctrine of shared psychological fields has the merit of handling face-to-face interaction in social rather than individual terms without resort to analogy and within the logic of non-Newtonian mechanics. It falls short of handling larger social structures, however.

The field-theoretical approach has been responsible for the great progress in social psychology in the last twenty years. It made possible, moreover, full utilization of the knowledge of perception and cognition in social psychology in a way that was never possible on the basis of learning theory. But its primary contribution has been to give us a more adequate, sophisticated psychology of the individual. It necessarily breaks down with the social psychology of groups because its basic theoretical position is the psychological field of the individual.

Freudian Theory. The psychoanalytic school, and especially the neo-Freudians, have made great contributions to our understanding of the socialization process and of the personality types resulting therefrom. But Freudian theory, like field theory, has developed its concepts to deal with the psychology of the individual and not with the nature of social structures. Such structures are in part a product of the complex interactions of people, and not the simple reflection at the collective level of individual personality mechanisms. A society does not consist of people acting in parallel; it is not an additive model of the persons making it up. It consists instead of complicated interactions mediated by role systems; a nation declaring war is not reflecting the summation of the aggressive impulses of its individual citizens. Freud himself took account of social complexities in his customary insightful and penetrating manner, for example in discussing social-class conflict in his *Future of an Illusion* (1928). In such discussions Freud was not, however, applying the concepts of his own psychoanalytic theory, but was utilizing his interpretation of sociological knowledge.

Older Sociological Theories. Two types of sociological theory have dealt more directly with problems of social structure: the superorganic doctrine and the socioeconomic school. The superorganic approach is concerned with the collective level without reference to the psychological or social-psychological factors involved. It deals not with individuals or their interactions but with the products or outcomes of social processes. Culture in its many material and nonmaterial manifestations such as technology, art objects, linguistic forms, and social organization can be studied without recourse to the specific carriers of the culture. This was the position of Kroeber (1952) in his thesis that at the superorganic level one could work with cultural forms without dropping down to such intervening variables as perception, motivation, and learning. Similarly White (1949) argues that culturology is not exemplified by Malinowski, Mead, or Benedict, who often seek a social-psychological analysis of culture, but by those scholars who stay at their own level and treat culture as an emergent type of subject matter. The ecological school in sociology also follows this essential logic, and other sociologists embrace the superorganic doctrine but not with the consistency of the culturologists.

There is merit in the superorganic position in that collective products can be studied without regard to the psychology of their producers. Moreover, this approach avoids some of the logical difficulties of trying to bring different modes of conceptualization into the same framework. There are shortcomings, however, in the very limited generalizations which can be derived from dealing with outcomes rather than the dynamic processes responsible for the outcomes. This type of treatment approaches a closed-system conceptualization in that human inputs are ignored or regarded as constants. In small, primitive, stable societies it is possible to assume that the nature of the human inputs is constant. In larger, complex, dynamic societies this assumption is less tenable and knowledge of the changing character of various types of human inputs and of social interaction is essential for prediction and understanding. The superorganic approach contributes to our knowledge of the larger societal and cultural framework within which behavior takes place but it does not furnish an adequate analysis of that framework.

It is therefore an error to assume that the study of the social and cultural environment, of the institutions and organizations into which the individual is inducted, is solely the province of the social sciences at the superorganic level.

We psychologists sometimes assume that it is up to the other social sciences to describe and explain the social environment and identify its dimensions; then we, as psychologists, will try to account for the behavior of people in these social settings. This solution is a convenient one, but there are two basic difficulties with it. The social environment is not a parallel to the physical environment where we can turn to the physicists and chemists for the benefits of more precise analysis. The social environment merely consists of other people and their behavior and the products of their activities. Hence as psychologists we cannot absolve ourselves from the responsibility of making our own contribution to an analysis of the nature of the social environment and its dimensions. The second reason for the need of cooperative activity among all social scientists is that there is less justification at the social level than at the physical level for preserving the sanctity of specialized disciplines. Many of the different areas of study which differentiate the social sciences are more a result of their concepts than of the nature of the data at the empirical level of research and experimental manipulation. The physicist has a different level of phenomena to study than does the physiologist. Sociologists, anthropologists, and other behavioral scientists are not so much studying different levels of phenomena as they are utilizing different levels of generalization in their concepts for dealing with essentially the same level of phenomena, namely, the behavior of human beings.

Socio-Economic Theories. Perhaps the most systematic as well as challenging attempt to deal with social structure and its social-psychological aspects is Marxian theory. Because of its confusion with propagandistic doctrine, the theory itself has sometimes received summary treatment from social scientists. In some senses it was an effort at a field theory of society in which social relationships rather than individual characteristics were the determining forces and in which structural dynamics were expressed as the dialectic. It was not a theory of simple economic determinism but of complex socioeconomic determinism. Marx saw the social relations of production as the key institutional system of a society leading to its class stratification, its conflicts both internal and external, and their resolution. It was not so much the individual's self-interest which was the primary motivating factor as it was the role the individual played in the production process and the group interest of people playing similar roles. Behavior in common roles came first, then ideology developed as a weapon to handle common role interests. In other words, social stratification preceded class consciousness. Other subsystems of a society, such as the school, the church, and the state, were built around the social relations of production.

Thus the Protestant Reformation was the religious expression of the growth of capitalistic society and provided a free market in religious ideas as a counterpart to the free market for the exchange of commodities. Weber's thesis (1930) about the rise of the Protestant ethic accounting for capitalistic development was the reverse of the Marxian explanation.

The strength of the Marxian theory was its breadth and depth. It took account of societal organization, specified its apparent critical institutions, and yet related its structural analysis to the carriers, or human beings, of the system and their interactions. It proposed that the major determinant of ideas and values was not economic status as such but key economic roles, the way in which man related to his fellows in the productive process through selling his labor or some other commodity or buying the labor of others. The worker no longer owning his tools in a large factory system and being exploited in the sale of his labor power was alienated from the dominant values of the society. It asserted that social interaction among workers in urban factory centers would facilitate the development of ideology. It further claimed that overt behavioral conflict was necessary to crystallize group ideology. Hence demonstrations, strikes, and confrontation would facilitate such ideological development. Thus Marxian theory made assumptions about social interaction, social reinforcement, the playing of behavioral roles, alienation, and the conditions producing group solidarity.

The weakness of Marxian theory for social science purposes is twofold. In the first place, it was too specifically tied to certain conditions Marx had observed at one period in history and in certain localities. Thus Marx did not generalize his notion about the significance of role settings but narrowed it down to the one type of role relationship he considered primary, the social relations of production and the resulting class conflict. The facts are that social classes are not the significant groupings in American society whereas the type of organization setting in which the individual is socialized as a child and as an adult may be. In the second place, Marx was equally narrow in his conception of structural dynamics. There was but one basic dynamic process, the working out of the contradiction between collective, cooperative production and individual, exploitive appropriation. Again a more adequate structural dynamics would see a constantly changing pattern of forces since the social system responds to its own outputs, i.e., is continually receiving new inputs, many of them of its own making. Thus the contradictions of overproduction and economic cycles have been resolved, or at least compromised, in advanced industrial nations by new mechanisms for assuring widespread distribution and for keeping the economy on an even keel. The basic shortcoming of Marxian theory was a failure to understand the operation of structural dynamics over time, which means that structures change in character from time one to time two to time three. Finally, Marxian theory, though in advance of its time in dealing with social-psychological processes of group reinforcement, of confrontation, and of group cohesion, lacked a clear formulation of how a theoretician moved from the social structural to the individual level. The commonplace question, for example, is why people should take part in bringing about social change which Marxian dialectic would predict must result from the character of social structures.

A related approach is that of Durkheim (1947), who made the primacy of social structure his central doctrine. Durkheim looked at the economic role structure of a society and saw the division of labor as the major starting point for study. With little specialization of labor people play similar roles and internalize similar value systems. Under conditions of role homogeneity there is a mechanical solidarity based upon a common collective conscience. Criminal law is merely the codification of the outrage felt by people when actions of deviants violate the commonly held moral principles. With role diversification, people are no longer similar but their role interdependence produces an organic solidarity. Altruism and cooperation replace the specific moral code and civil law and restitution replace criminal and repressive law.

The Durkheimian analysis has something of the same strengths and weaknesses as Marxian theory. In one sense it was more general, in that it did not concentrate on one type of economic role. And it did call attention to the priority of existing social organization as far as individuals are concerned. It was weak, however, in its structural dynamics and gave little basis for predictions about social change save when a society moved toward complexity in its division of labor. It took less account of psychological variables than Marxian doctrines and also suffered from the lack of a systematic way of dealing with them. Though Durkheim talked a good deal about the social structural level, he did become involved in social-psychological problems when he differentiated between common and idiosyncratic values, between internalization of specific moral codes and a general altruism, and when he analyzed various types of anomie.

Open-System Theory. We are beginning to move toward a resolution of the dilemma of a social psychology concerned with social structure through the application of open-system theory. Three lines of development are apparently converging to indicate the type of approach necessary, though there is still not an elaborated theory available.

In the first place, since his early behavioristic formulation of the twenties, F. H. Allport has concerned himself with a structuronomic conception of social psychology. His early work was a vigorous attack upon the language of metaphor in the social sciences, upon the attribution of human agency to concepts referring to groups and institutions. He insisted that in any science the language of metaphor was not an adequate substitute for the language of data. Methodologically his position was correct, and Allport has not retreated from it. On the other hand, he also realized the inadequacy of the traditional behavioral concepts for dealing with problems of relationship and of social structure. His own theory (1954, 1962), still not completely formulated, conceptualizes structure as a cycle of events which return in circular fashion to reinstate the cycle. The events are the observable nodal points which can be conceptualized as structures. Instead of linear behavior of A stimulating B and B responding, as in the Newtonian model, Allport believes that there is a continuing series of events to complete a cycle before we have social structure. Moreover, cycles can crisscross or can be tangential to one another or can vary in size. These complex patterns need to be identified for an understanding of social behavior.

F. H. Allport's structural model is similar in type to that of the general-systems theorists. Miller (1955) and his colleagues have been applying open-system theory in general terms to embrace all levels of science from the study of a single cell to the study of a society. They are primarily concerned with generalizations which hold at all levels and so are willing to look at complex social behavior with respect to input, through-put, and output, with respect to methods for handling overload in any system, with respect to boundaries and coding subsystems, etc. Many of their hypotheses are suggestive for working at the level of social organizations, though they have not as yet directed a full-scale research attack at this level.

The third and for our purposes the most fully developed system approach is that of Parsons (1951). He, more than any other person, has utilized the open-system approach for the study of social structures. Before his writing and teaching most accounts of social systems followed closed-system theory as in doctrines of the superorganic. In Parsons' hands a considerable body of sociological thought has moved toward an open-system approach. Moreover he has provided the specific conceptual tools by delineating the various subsystems in a society and their functions. Much of the analysis in the chapters which follow borrows from his contributions.

The open-system approach seems to us to preserve many of the virtues of the older attempts to deal with social structures without being trapped by their oversimplifications and reifications. It has the advantage of allowing the facts at any one level to determine the specific theoretical formulation at that level. So much of the older thinking about social organization was analogical and relied heavily on biological and psychological metaphor. Though open-system theory can be utilized at all levels, as in the work of the Miller group, its major conceptions are general enough to demand the type of specific elaboration which Parsons has already begun to provide for social structures.

Open-system theory with its entropy assumption emphasizes the close relationship between a structure and its supporting environment, in that without continued inputs the structure would soon run down. Thus one critical basis for identifying social systems is through their relationships with energic sources for their maintenance. And human effort and motivation is the major maintenance source of almost all social structures. Hence though the theoretical approach deals with relationships, these relationships embrace human beings. If we are concerned with the specifics of the maintenance function in terms of human behavior we are at the social-psychological level. In open-system theory the carriers of the system cannot be ignored because they furnish the sustaining input.

On the other hand another major relationship encompassed by a system is the processing of production inputs to yield some outcome to be utilized by some outside group or system. The hospital meets the health needs of the community or the industrial enterprise turns out goods or furnishes services. These functions of given systems can again be identified through the input, through-put, and output cycle, but they may not be primarily psychological if we deal only with production inputs and exports into the environment, i.e., so many tons of raw materials and so many finished products. The moment, however, that we deal with the organization of the people in the system concerning the through-put, we are again at a social-psychological level. Thus open-system theory furnishes a useful framework for examining social structures from a social-psychological point of view.

Finally, open-system theory permits an integration of the so-called macro approach of the sociologist and the micro approach of the psychologist to the study of social phenomena. In looking at the actions of Castro and his followers overthrowing the Batista regime in Cuba social psychologists would talk about the deprivations and frustrations motivating people to take action against the visible sources of their difficulties. Sociologists might talk about an unstable social system in which a semifeudal society held together by military force collapsed when an agrarian revolution destroyed the military force. Two observations are immediately possible from this example. The sociological analysis is much broader in scope and attempts to bring into focus a much wider range of related facts. It can do this by the use of such concepts as semifeudal system, which refers to a societal patterning of economic, social, and power relationships. Moreover, the sociological frame of reference, broader in scope, calls attention not so much to a different level of phenomenal facts as to more and different facts of human behavior at the same phenomenal level. The narrower scope of psychological theory again would give us not so much facts of a different level, but more detail about facts that might be passed over very quickly in any sociological description. The trend in sociological research has been in the direction of using the same field methods of study as those of the psychologist, sampling and interviewing and the use of quantitative methods in the observation of behavior. The main difference is that the more global, more all embracing theories of the sociologist are directed at an understanding of the total pattern of events. The psychological theories are more concerned with finding some general aspects of all social situations even though they may be dealing with only a segment of the problem. This distinction between the macro and micro approaches is sometimes referred to as one of degree of abstraction and hence of generality. This formulation may be misleading in that it is the psychological approach that is more abstract in getting away from the content of specific situations and dealing with highly generalized forms of behavior. The sociological formulation may be no more abstract but is more comprehensive in dealing with the interaction of many variables.

The weakness of the macro approach is that the blunt or gross nature of its concepts does not contain sufficient specification of the psychological dynamics at work. We know in general that a nation in the process of shifting from secondary, or production industry, to tertiary, or service types of industry, will experience changes in the character of its political parties and of the voting behavior of its citizens. But precise predictions of the changes themselves will be dependent upon a knowledge of such factors as the nature of the fixation of people upon the identity and values of their old groups, of the conditions which facilitate realistic perception of the changes taking place, and of the attachment to group values which have no direct relation to occupational clustering. The macro approach is invaluable, however, in calling attention to the significant problem and directing our attention to areas in which variables need more careful formulation.

The weakness of the micro approach in the past has been twofold. It has dealt with too few of the significant variables in the total situation. It has often seized upon inappropriate variables and has pushed too hard in the direction of showing the universality of some fundamental principle such as reinforcement in the learning theory approach to social problems. This reductionistic emphasis in its very character tends to lose the problem with which it should be concerned. We are limited in our understanding of an organizational outcome such as a strike vote by a union when we try to reduce it to the principles of laboratory learning. We can use learning principles profitably, however, if we can identify the problem in the social system in which it arises.

It is the contention of the authors that these weaknesses in the micro approach are readily overcome if we combine this psychological attack with the concepts available from the macro approach. This procedure involves the translation of the sociological concepts into a host of micro concepts which are concerned with the same area of social behavior. The translation is made easier by the fact that the two levels by and large do not have different types of facts to worry about. The physiological and the psychological can be correlated but not translated; the sensation of blueness always remains distinctive as a factual datum from the neuro-chemical process upon which it may be dependent. A role system can, however, be translated into the interdependent and shared values and expectations of legitimate behavior of a group of people.

The macro approach thus describes the larger problem which needs detailed analysis in terms of the many interrelated behaviors of the actors in the scene. We know where to look and how to formulate the general lines of our attack. If we want to know more about why a union in a conflict situation voted to strike when it had not done so in a comparable situation in the past we would look at such system aspects as the industrywide conditions, the utilization of appropriate strategies by management and by the union for handling the cause of their differences, the power position of the labor leaders with respect to their followers, and the power positions of representatives of management with respect to the subsystems on which they are dependent.

To the extent that we can make any contribution to the knowledge of organizations it will be through a combination of the macro and micro approaches. The macro approach in itself will lack precise formulation of motivational dynamics to account fully for the behavior of people in organizations. The concern with the outcome and general properties of the system make for too global an approach to deal adequately with the host of causal psychological variables. On the other hand, the micro approach alone lacks direction and is apt either to deal with too few variables or with inappropriate variables. In other words if we want to understand why a nation is following a foreign policy of toughness, belligerence, and possible brinkmanship we need to know more than that the economy is a profit economy and that it is maintained at peak economic operation by a defense budget of billions of dollars. But the micro variables with which we need be concerned are not the belligerent character structure of the people or the leaders but the many detailed aspects of the political and social structure as they are expressed in the day-to-day behavior of the people.

SUMMARY

Past approaches to the study of social problems and social behavior have been limited by a lack of adequate conceptual tools. This limitation has been manifest both in psychology and sociology, although in different ways.

Psychologists have been characteristically unable or unwilling to deal with the facts of social organization and social structure. Societies and organizations consist of patterned behaviors, and the behavior of each individual is determined to a considerable extent by the requirements of the larger pattern. This context is not often incorporated into psychological theories. Some such theories—the psychoanalytic, for example—deal with the influence of the family on the individual. Others take some account of the small group as the individual environment, and still others are concerned with the influence of culture, that most global of environmental concepts. Even social psychology, however, has neglected the organizational and institutional level, and textbooks of social psychology typically conclude with some treatment of small face-to-face groups. This book is an attempt to extend such discussions by beginning where they leave off—with the behavior of people in organizations. It is in that sense a second book in social psychology.

The older sociological theories reflect a limitation complementary to the theories of psychology. Sociological theories treat the superorganic or collective level without reference to individual characteristics or to the attributes of transactions between individuals. They are concerned with the products of such interaction but not with the process. This general criticism must be modified for Marx and Durkheim, but is applicable nevertheless.

This book proposes that the resolution of such theoretical difficulties can best be achieved by means of open-system theory. This theoretical approach is not yet fully developed, but is exemplified by several important lines of work. These include the event-structure theory of F. H. Allport, the general systems approach of J. G. Miller and his colleagues, and the sociological theory of Talcott Parsons. Open-system theory seems to us to permit breadth without oversimplification. It emphasizes, through the basic assumption of entropy, the necessary dependence of any organization upon its environment. The open-system concepts of energic input and maintenance point to the motives and behavior of the individuals who are the carriers of energic input for human organizations; the concept of output and its necessary absorption by the larger environment also links the micro- and macro-levels of discourse. For all these reasons, open-system theory represents the point of departure for the chapters which follow.

2

Organizations and the
System Concept

The aims of social science with respect to human organizations are like those of any other science with respect to the events and phenomena of its domain. The social scientist wishes to understand human organizations, to describe what is essential in their form, aspects, and functions. He wishes to explain their cycles of growth and decline, to predict their effects and effectiveness. Perhaps he wishes as well to test and apply such knowledge by introducing purposeful changes into organizations—by making them, for example, more benign, more responsive to human needs.

Such efforts are not solely the prerogative of social science, however; common sense approaches to understanding and altering organizations are ancient and perpetual. They tend, on the whole, to rely heavily on two assumptions: that the location and nature of an organization are given by its name; and that an organization is possessed of built-in goals—because such goals were implanted by its founders, decreed by its present leaders, or because they emerged mysteriously as the purposes of the organizational system itself. These assumptions scarcely provide an adequate basis for the study of organizations and at times can be misleading and even fallacious. We propose, however, to make use of the information to which they point.

The first problem in understanding an organization or a social system is its location and identification. How do we know that we are dealing with an organization? What are its boundaries? What behavior belongs to the organization and what behavior lies outside it? Who are the individuals whose actions are to be studied and what segments of their behavior are to be included?

The fact that popular names exist to label social organizations is both a help and a hindrance. These popular labels represent the socially accepted stereotypes about organizations and do not specify their role structure, their psychological nature, or their boundaries. On the other hand, these names help in locating the area of behavior in which we are interested. Moreover, the fact that people both within and without an organization accept stereotypes about its nature and functioning is one determinant of its character.

The second key characteristic of the common sense approach to understanding an organization is to regard it simply as the epitome of the purposes of its designer, its leaders, or its key members. The teleology of this approach is again both a help and a hindrance. Since human purpose is deliberately built into organizations and is specifically recorded in the social compact, the by-laws, or other formal protocol of the undertaking, it would be inefficient not to utilize these sources of information. In the early development of a group, many processes are generated which have little to do with its rational purpose, but over time there is a cumulative recognition of the devices for ordering group life and a deliberate use of these devices.

Apart from formal protocol, the primary mission of an organization as perceived by its leaders furnishes a highly informative set of clues for the researcher seeking to study organizational functioning. Nevertheless, the stated purposes of an organization as given by its by-laws or in the reports of its leaders can be misleading. Such statements of objectives may idealize, rationalize, distort, omit, or even conceal some essential aspects of the functioning of the organization. Nor is there always agreement about the mission of the organization among its leaders and members. The university president may describe the purpose of his institution as one of turning out national leaders; the academic dean sees it as imparting the cultural heritage of the past, the academic vice-president as enabling students to move toward self-actualization and development, the graduate dean as creating new knowledge, the dean of men as training youngsters in technical and professional skills which will enable them to earn their living, and the editor of the student newspaper as inculcating the conservative values which will preserve the status quo of an outmoded capitalistic society.

The fallacy here is one of equating the purposes or goals of organizations with the purposes and goals of individual members. The organization as a system has an output, a product or an outcome, but this is not necessarily identical with the individual purposes of group members. Though the founders of the organization and its key members do think in teleological terms about organizational objectives, we should not accept such practical thinking, useful as it may be, in place of a theoretical set of constructs for purposes of scientific analysis. Social science, too frequently in the past, has been misled by such short-cuts and has equated popular phenomenology with scientific explanation.

In fact, the classic body of theory and thinking about organizations has assumed a teleology of this sort as the easiest way of identifying organizational structures and their functions. From this point of view an organization is a social device for efficiently accomplishing through group means some stated purpose; it is the equivalent of the blueprint for the design of the machine which is to be created for some practical objective. The essential difficulty with this purposive or design approach is that an organization characteristically includes more and less than is indicated by the design of its founder or the purpose of its leader. Some of the factors assumed in the design may be lacking or so distorted in operational practice as to be meaningless, while unforeseen embellishments dominate the organizational structure. Moreover, it is not always possible to ferret out the designer of the organization or to discover the intricacies of the design which he carried in his head. The attempt by Merton (1957) to deal with the latent function of the organization in contrast with its manifest function is one way of dealing with this problem. The study of unanticipated consequences as well as anticipated consequences of organizational functioning is a similar way of handling the matter. Again, however, we are back to the purposes of the creator or leader, dealing with unanticipated consequences on the assumption that we can discover the consequences anticipated by him and can lump all other outcomes together as a kind of error variance.

It would be much better theoretically, however, to start with concepts which do not call for identifying the purposes of the designers and then correcting for them when they do not seem to be fulfilled. The theoretical concepts should begin with the input, output, and functioning of the organization as a system and not with the rational purposes of its leaders. We may want to utilize such purposive notions to lead us to sources of data or as subjects of special study, but not as our basic theoretical constructs for understanding organizations.

Our theoretical model for the understanding of organizations is that of an energic input-output system in which the energic return from the output reactivates the system. Social organizations are flagrantly open systems in that the input of energies and the conversion of output into further energic input consist of transactions between the organization and its environment.

All social systems, including organizations, consist of the patterned activities of a number of individuals. Moreover, these patterned activities are complementary or interdependent with respect to some common output or outcome; they are repeated, relatively enduring, and bounded in space and time. If the activity pattern occurs only once or at unpredictable intervals, we could not speak of an organization. The stability or recurrence of activities can be examined in relation to the *energic input* into the system, the *transformation of energies within the system,* and the *resulting product or energic output.* In a factory the raw materials and the human labor are the energic input, the patterned activities of production the transformation of energy, and the finished product the output. To maintain this patterned activity requires a continued renewal of the inflow of energy. This is guaranteed in social systems by the energic return from the product or outcome. Thus the outcome of the cycle of activities furnishes new energy for the initiation of a renewed cycle. The company which produces automobiles sells them and by doing so obtains the means of securing new raw materials, compensating its labor force, and continuing the activity pattern.

In many organizations outcomes are converted into money and new energy is furnished through this mechanism. Money is a convenient way of handling energy units both on the output and input sides, and buying and selling represent one set of social rules for regulating the exchange of money. Indeed, these rules are so effective and so widespread that there is some danger of mistaking the business of buying and selling for the defining cycles of organization. It is a commonplace executive observation that businesses exist to make money, and the observation is usually allowed to go unchallenged. It is, however, a very limited statement about the purposes of business.

Some human organizations do not depend on the cycle of selling and buying to maintain themselves. Universities and public agencies depend rather on bequests and legislative appropriations, and in so-called voluntary organizations the output reenergizes the activity of organization members in a more direct fashion. Member activities and accomplishments are rewarding in themselves and tend therefore to be continued, without the mediation of the outside environment. A society of bird watchers can wander into the hills and engage in the rewarding activities of identifying birds for their mutual edification and enjoyment. Organizations thus differ on this important dimension of the source of energy renewal, with the great majority utilizing both intrinsic and extrinsic sources in varying degree. Most large-scale organizations are not as self-contained as small voluntary groups and are very dependent upon the social effects of their output for energy renewal.

Our two basic criteria for identifying social systems and determining their functions are (1) tracing the pattern of energy exchange or activity of people as it results in some output and (2) ascertaining how the output is translated into energy which reactivates the pattern. We shall refer to organizational functions or objectives not as the conscious purposes of group leaders or group members but as the outcomes which are the energic source for a maintenance of the same type of output.

This model of an energic input-output system is taken from the open system theory as promulgated by von Bertalanffy (1956). Theorists have pointed out the applicability of the system concepts of the natural sciences to the problems of social science. It is important, therefore, to examine in more detail the constructs of system theory and the characteristics of open systems.

System theory is basically concerned with problems of relationships, of structure, and of interdependence rather than with the constant attributes of objects. In general approach it resembles field theory except that its dynamics deal with temporal as well as spatial patterns. Older formulations of system constructs dealt with the closed systems of the physical sciences, in which relatively self-contained structures could be treated successfully as if they were independent of external forces. But living systems, whether biological organisms or social organizations, are acutely dependent upon their external environment and so must be conceived of as open systems.

Before the advent of open-system thinking, social scientists tended to take one of two approaches in dealing with social structures; they tended either (1) to regard them as closed systems to which the laws of physics applied or (2) to endow them with some vitalistic concept like entelechy. In the former case they ignored the environmental forces affecting the organization and in the latter case they fell back upon some magical purposiveness to account for organizational functioning. Biological theorists, however, have rescued us from this trap by pointing out that the concept of the open system means that we neither have to follow the laws of traditional physics, nor in deserting them do we have to abandon science. The laws of Newtonian physics are correct generalizations but they are limited to closed systems. They do not apply in the same fashion to open systems which maintain themselves through constant commerce with their environment, i.e., a continuous inflow and outflow of energy through permeable boundaries.

One example of the operation of closed versus open systems can be seen in the concept of entropy and the second law of thermodynamics. According to the second law of thermodynamics, a system moves toward equilibrium; it tends to run down, that is, its differentiated structures tend to move toward dissolution as the elements composing them become arranged in random disorder. For example, suppose that a bar of iron has been heated by the application of a blowtorch on one side. The arrangement of all the fast (heated) molecules on one side and all the slow molecules on the other is an unstable state, and over time the distribution of molecules becomes in effect random, with the resultant cooling of one side and heating of the other, so that all surfaces of the iron approach the same temperature. A similar process of heat exchange will also be going on between the iron bar and its environment, so that the bar will gradually approach the temperature of the room in which it is located, and in so doing will elevate somewhat the previous temperature of the room. More technically, entropy increases toward a maximum and equilibrium occurs as the physical system attains the state of the most probable distribution of its elements. In social systems, however, structures tend to become more elaborated rather than less differentiated. The rich may grow richer and the poor may grow poorer. The open system does not run down, because it can import energy from the world around it. Thus the operation of entropy is counteracted by the importation of energy and the living system is characterized by negative rather than positive entropy.

COMMON CHARACTERISTICS OF OPEN SYSTEMS

Though the various types of open systems have common characteristics by virtue of being open systems, they differ in other characteristics. If this were not the case, we would be able to obtain all our basic knowledge about social organizations through studying the biological organisms or even through the study of a single cell.

The following nine characteristics seem to define all open systems.

1. *Importation of energy*. Open systems import some form of energy from the external environment. The cell receives oxygen from the blood stream; the body similarly takes in oxygen from the air and food from the external world. The personality is dependent upon the external world for stimulation. Studies of sensory deprivation show that when a person is placed in a darkened soundproof room, where he has a minimal amount of visual and auditory stimulation, he de-

velops hallucinations and other signs of mental stress (Solomon et al., 1961). Deprivation of social stimulation also can lead to mental disorganization (Spitz, 1945). Köhler's (1944, 1947) studies of the figural after-effects of continued stimulation show the dependence of perception upon its energic support from the external world. Animals deprived of visual experience from birth for a prolonged period never fully recover their visual capacities (Melzack and Thompson, 1956). In other words, the functioning personality is heavily dependent upon the continuous inflow of stimulation from the external environment. Similarly, social organizations must also draw renewed supplies of energy from other institutions, or people, or the material environment. No social structure is self-sufficient or self-contained.

2. *The through-put.* Open systems transform the energy available to them. The body converts starch and sugar into heat and action. The personality converts chemical and electrical forms of stimulation into sensory qualities, and information into thought patterns. The organization creates a new product, or processes materials, or trains people, or provides a service. These activities entail some reorganization of input. Some work gets done in the system.

3. *The output.* Open systems export some product into the environment, whether it be the invention of an inquiring mind or a bridge constructed by an engineering firm. Even the biological organism exports physiological products such as carbon dioxide from the lungs which helps to maintain plants in the immediate environment.

4. *Systems as cycles of events.* The pattern of activities of the energy exchange has a cyclic character. The product exported into the environment furnishes the sources of energy for the repetition of the cycle of activities. The energy reinforcing the cycle of activities can derive from some exchange of the product in the external world or from the activity itself. In the former instance, the industrial concern utilizes raw materials and human labor to turn out a product which is marketed, and the monetary return is used to obtain more raw materials and labor to perpetuate the cycle of activities. In the latter instance, the voluntary organization can provide expressive satisfactions to its members so that the energy renewal comes directly from the organizational activity itself.

The problem of structure, or the relatedness of parts, can be observed directly in some physical arrangement of things where the larger unit is physically bounded and its subparts are also bounded within the larger structure. But how do we deal with social structures, where physical boundaries in this sense do not exist? It was the genius of F. H. Allport (1962) which contributed the answer, namely that the structure is to be found in an interrelated set of events which return upon themselves to complete and renew a cycle of activities. It is events rather than things which are structured, so that social structure is a dynamic rather than a static concept. Activities are structured so that they comprise a unity in their completion or closure. A simple linear stimulus-response exchange between two people would not constitute social structure. To create structure, the responses of A would have to elicit B's reactions in such a manner that the responses of the latter would stimulate A to further responses. Of course the chain of events may involve many people, but their behavior can be characterized as showing structure only when there is some closure to the chain by a return to its point of origin with the probability that the chain of events will then be repeated. The repetition of the cycle does not have to involve the same set of phenotypical happenings. It may expand to include more sub-events of exactly the same kind or it may involve similar activities directed toward the same outcomes. In the individual organism the eye may move in such a way as to have the point of light fall upon the center of the retina. As the point of light moves, the movements of the eye may also change but to complete the same cycle of activity, i.e., to focus upon the point of light.

A single cycle of events of a self-closing character gives us a simple form of structure. But such single cycles can also combine to give a larger structure of events or an event system. An event system may consist of a circle of smaller cycles or hoops, each one of which makes contact with several others. Cycles may also be tangential to one another from other types of subsystems. The basic method for the identification of social structures is to follow the energic chain of events from the input of energy through its transformation to the point of closure of the cycle.

5. *Negative entropy.* To survive, open systems must move to arrest the entropic process; they must acquire negative entropy. The entropic process is a universal law of nature in which all forms of organization move toward disorganization or death. Complex physical systems move toward simple random distribution of their elements and biological organisms also run down and perish. The open system, however, by importing more energy from its environment than it expends, can store energy and can acquire negative entropy. There is then a general trend in an open system to maximize its ratio of imported to expended energy, to survive and even during periods of crisis to live on borrowed time. Prisoners in concentration camps on a starvation diet will carefully conserve any form of energy expenditure to make the limited food intake go as far as possible (Cohen, 1954).

Social organizations will seek to improve their survival position and to acquire in their reserves a comfortable margin of operation.

The entropic process asserts itself in all biological systems as well as in closed physical systems. The energy replenishment of the biological organism is not of a qualitative character which can maintain indefinitely the complex organizational structure of living tissue. Social systems, however, are not anchored in the same physical constancies as biological organisms and so are capable of almost indefinite arresting of the entropic process. Nevertheless the number of organizations which go out of existence every year is large.

6. *Information input, negative feedback, and the coding process.* The inputs into living systems consist not only of energic materials which become transformed or altered in the work that gets done. Inputs are also informative in character and furnish signals to the structure about the environment and about its own functioning in relation to the environment. Just as we recognize the distinction between cues and drives in individual psychology, so must we take account of information and energic inputs for all living systems.

The simplest type of information input found in all systems is negative feedback. Information feedback of a negative kind enables the system to correct its deviations from course. The working parts of the machine feed back information about the effects of their operation to some central mechanism or subsystem which acts on such information to keep the system on target. The thermostat which controls the temperature of the room is a simple example of a regulatory device which operates on the basis of negative feedback. The automated power plant would furnish more complex examples. Miller (1955) emphasizes the critical nature of negative feedback in his proposition: "*When a system's negative feedback discontinues, its steady state vanishes, and at the same time its boundary disappears and the system terminates*" (p. 529). If there is no corrective device to get the system back on its course, it will expend too much energy or it will ingest too much energic input and no longer continue as a system.

The reception of inputs into a system is selective. Not all energic inputs are capable of being absorbed into every system. The digestive system of living creatures assimilates only those inputs to which it is adapted. Similarly, systems can react only to those information signals to which they are attuned. The general term for the selective mechanisms of a system by which incoming materials are rejected or accepted and translated for the structure is coding. Through the coding process the "blooming, buzzing confusion" of the world is simplified into a few meaningful and simplified categories for a given system.

The nature of the functions performed by the system determines its coding mechanisms, which in turn perpetuate this type of functioning.

7. *The steady state and dynamic homeostasis.* The importation of energy to arrest entropy operates to maintain some constancy in energy exchange, so that open systems which survive are characterized by a steady state. A steady state is not motionless or a true equilibrium. There is a continuous inflow of energy from the external environment and a continuous export of the products of the system, but the character of the system, the ratio of the energy exchanges and the relations between parts, remains the same. The catabolic and anabolic processes of tissue breakdown and restoration within the body preserve a steady state so that the organism from time to time is not the identical organism it was but a highly similar organism. The steady state is seen in clear form in the homeostatic processes for the regulation of body temperature; external conditions of humidity and temperature may vary, but the temperature of the body remains the same. The endocrine glands are a regulatory mechanism for preserving an evenness of physiological functioning. The general principle here is that of Le Châtelier (see Bradley and Calvin, 1956) who maintains that any internal or external factor making for disruption of the system is countered by forces which restore the system as closely as possible to its previous state. Krech and Crutchfield (1948) similarly hold, with respect to psychological organization, that cognitive structures will react to influences in such a way as to absorb them with minimal change to existing cognitive integration.

The homeostatic principle does not apply literally to the functioning of all complex living systems, in that in counteracting entropy they move toward growth and expansion. This apparent contradiction can be resolved, however, if we recognize the complexity of the subsystems and their interaction in anticipating changes necessary for the maintenance of an overall steady state. Stagner (1951) has pointed out that the initial disturbance of a given tissue constancy within the biological organism will result in mobilization of energy to restore the balance, but that recurrent upsets will lead to actions to anticipate the disturbance:

We eat before we experience intense hunger pangs. . . . energy mobilization for forestalling tactics must be explained in terms of a *cortical tension* which reflects the visceral-proprioceptive pattern of the original biological disequilibration . . . . *Dynamic homeostasis* involves the maintenance of tissue constancies by establishing a constant physical environment—by reducing the variability and disturbing effects of external stimulation. Thus the organism does not simply restore the prior equilibrium. A new, more complex and more comprehensive equilibrium is established. (p. 5)

Though the tendency toward a steady state in its simplest form is homeostatic, as in the preservation of a constant body temperature, the basic principle is *the preservation of the character of the system.* The equilibrium which complex systems approach is often that of a quasi-stationary equilibrium, to use Lewin's concept (1947). An adjustment in one direction is countered by a movement in the opposite direction and both movements are approximate rather than precise in their compensatory nature. Thus a temporal chart of activity will show a series of ups and downs rather than a smooth curve.

In preserving the character of the system, moreover, the structure will tend to import more energy than is required for its output, as we have already noted in discussing negative entropy. To insure survival, systems will operate to acquire some margin of safety beyond the immediate level of existence. The body will store fat, the social organization will build up reserves, the society will increase its technological and cultural base. Miller (1955) has formulated the proposition that the rate of growth of a system—within certain ranges—is exponential if it exists in a medium which makes available unrestricted amounts of energy for input.

In adapting to their environment, systems will attempt to cope with external forces by ingesting them or acquiring control over them. The physical boundedness of the single organism means that such attempts at control over the environment affect the behavioral system rather than the biological system of the individual. Social systems will move, however, towards incorporating within their boundaries the external resources essential to survival. Again the result is an expansion of the original system.

Thus, the steady state which at the simple level is one of homeostasis over time, at more complex levels becomes one of preserving the character of the system through growth and expansion. The basic type of system does not change directly as a consequence of expansion. The most common type of growth is a multiplication of the same type of cycles or subsystems—a change in quantity rather than in quality. Animal and plant species grow by multiplication. A social system adds more units of the same essential type as it already has. Haire (1959) has studied the ratio between the sizes of different subsystems in growing business organizations. He found that though the number of people increased in both the production subsystem and the subsystem concerned with the external world, the ratio of the two groups remained constant. Qualitative change does occur, however, in two ways. In the first place, quantitative growth calls for supportive subsystems of a specialized character not necessary when the system was smaller. In the second place, there is a point where quantitative changes produce a qualitative difference in the functioning of a system. A small college which triples its size is no longer the same institution in terms of the relation between its administration and faculty, relations among the various academic departments, or the nature of its instruction.

In fine, living systems exhibit a growth or expansion dynamic in which they maximize their basic character. They react to change or they anticipate change through growth which assimilates the new energic inputs to the nature of their structure. In terms of Lewin's quasi-stationary equilibrium the ups and downs of the adjustive process do not always result in a return to the old level. Under certain circumstances a solidification or freezing occurs during one of the adjustive cycles. A new base line level is thus established and successive movements fluctuate around this plateau which may be either above or below the previous plateau of operation.

8. *Differentiation.* Open systems move in the direction of differentiation and elaboration. Diffuse global patterns are replaced by more specialized functions. The sense organs and the nervous system evolved as highly differentiated structures from the primitive nervous tissues. The growth of the personality proceeds from primitive, crude organizations of mental functions to hierarchically structured and well-differentiated systems of beliefs and feelings. Social organizations move toward the multiplication and elaboration of roles with greater specialization of function. In the United States today medical specialists now outnumber the general practitioners.

One type of differentiated growth in systems is what von Bertalanffy (1956) terms progressive mechanization. It finds expression in the way in which a system achieves a steady state. The early method is a process which involves an interaction of various dynamic forces, whereas the later development entails the use of a regulatory feedback mechanism. He writes:

It can be shown that the *primary* regulations in organic systems, that is, those which are most fundamental and primitive in embryonic development as well as in evolution, are of such nature of dynamic interaction. . . . Superimposed are those regulations which we may call *secondary,* and which are controlled by fixed arrangements, especially of the feedback type. This state of affairs is a consequence of a general principle of organization which may be called progressive mechanization. At first, systems—biological, neurological, psychological or social—are governed by dynamic interaction of their components; later on, fixed arrangements and conditions of constraint are established which render the system and its parts more efficient, but also gradually diminish and eventually abolish its equipotentiality. (p. 6)

9. *Equifinality.* Open systems are further characterized by the principle of equifinality, a principle suggested by von Bertalanffy in 1940. According to this principle, a system can reach the same final state from

differing initial conditions and by a variety of paths. The well-known biological experiments on the sea urchin show that a normal creature of that species can develop from a complete ovum, from each half of a divided ovum, or from the fusion product of two whole ova. As open systems move toward regulatory mechanisms to control their operations, the amount of equifinality may be reduced.

SOME CONSEQUENCES OF VIEWING ORGANIZATIONS AS OPEN SYSTEMS

In the following chapter we shall inquire into the specific implications of considering organizations as open systems and into the ways in which social organizations differ from other types of living systems. At this point, however, we should call attention to some of the misconceptions which arise both in theory and practice when social organizations are regarded as closed rather than open systems.

The major misconception is the failure to recognize fully that the organization is continually dependent upon inputs from the environment and that the inflow of materials and human energy is not a constant. The fact that organizations have built-in protective devices to maintain stability and that they are notoriously difficult to change in the direction of some reformer's desires should not obscure the realities of the dynamic interrelationships of any social structure with its social and natural environment. The very efforts of the organization to maintain a constant external environment produce changes in organizational structure. The reaction to changed inputs to mute their possible revolutionary implications also results in changes.

The typical models in organizational theorizing concentrate upon principles of internal functioning as if these problems were independent of changes in the environment and as if they did not affect the maintenance inputs of motivation and morale. Moves toward tighter integration and coordination are made to insure stability, when flexibility may be the more important requirement. Moreover, coordination and control become ends in themselves rather than means to an end. They are not seen in full perspective as adjusting the system to its environment but as desirable goals within a closed system. In fact, however, every attempt at coordination which is not functionally required may produce a host of new organizational problems.

One error which stems from this kind of misconception is the failure to recognize the equifinality of the open system, namely that there are more ways than one of producing a given outcome. In a closed physical system the same initial conditions must lead to the same final result. In open systems this is not true even at the biological level. It is much less true at the social level. Yet in practice we insist that there is one best way of assembling a gun for all recruits, one best way for the baseball player to hurl the ball in from the outfield, and that we standardize and teach these best methods. Now it is true under certain conditions that there is one best way, but these conditions must first be established. The general principle, which characterizes all open systems, is that there does not have to be a single method for achieving an objective.

A second error lies in the notion that irregularities in the functioning of a system due to environmental influences are error variances and should be treated accordingly. According to this conception, they should be controlled out of studies of organizations. From the organization's own operations they should be excluded as irrelevant and should be guarded against. The decisions of officers to omit a consideration of external factors or to guard against such influences in a defensive fashion, as if they would go away if ignored, is an instance of this type of thinking. So is the now outmoded "public be damned" attitude of businessmen toward the clientele upon whose support they depend. Open system theory, on the other hand, would maintain that environmental influences are not sources of error variance but are integrally related to the functioning of a social system, and that we cannot understand a system without a constant study of the forces that impinge upon it.

Thinking of the organization as a closed system, moreover, results in a failure to develop the intelligence or feedback function of obtaining adequate information about the changes in environmental forces. It is remarkable how weak many industrial companies are in their market research departments when they are so dependent upon the market. The prediction can be hazarded that organizations in our society will increasingly move toward the improvement of the facilities for research in assessing environmental forces. The reason is that we are in the process of correcting our misconception of the organization as a closed system.

Emery and Trist (1960) have pointed out how current theorizing on organizations still reflects the older closed system conceptions. They write:

In the realm of social theory, however, there has been something of a tendency to continue thinking in terms of a "closed" system, that is, to regard the enterprise as sufficiently independent to allow most of its problems to be analyzed with reference to its internal structure and without reference to its external environment. . . . In practice the system theorists in social science . . . did "tend to focus on the statics of social structure and to neglect the study of structural change." In an attempt to overcome this bias, Merton suggested that "the concept of dysfunction, which implied the concept of strain, stress and tension on the structural level, provides an analytical approach to the study of dynamics and change." This concept has been widely accepted by system theorists but while it draws attention to sources of imbalance within an organization it does not conceptually reflect the mutual permeation of an organization and its environment that is the cause of such imbalance. It still retains the limiting perspectives of "closed system" theorizing. In the administrative field the same limitations may be seen in the otherwise invaluable contributions of Barnard and related writers. (p. 84)

SUMMARY

The open-system approach to organizations is contrasted with common-sense approaches, which tend to accept popular names and stereotypes as basic organizational properties and to identify the purpose of an organization in terms of the goals of its founders and leaders.

The open-system approach, on the other hand, begins by identifying and mapping the repeated cycles of input, transformation, output, and renewed input which comprise the organizational pattern. This approach to organizations represents the adaptation of work in biology and in the physical sciences by von Bertalanffy and others.

Organizations as a special class of open systems have properties of their own, but they share other properties in common with all open systems. These include the importation of energy from the environment, the through-put or transformation of the imported energy into some product form which is characteristic of the system, the exporting of that product into the environment, and the reenergizing of the system from sources in the environment.

Open systems also share the characteristics of negative entropy, feedback, homeostasis, differentiation, and equifinality. The law of negative entropy states that systems survive and maintain their characteristic internal order only so long as they import from the environment more energy than they expend in the process of transformation and exportation. The feedback principle has to do with information input, which is a special kind of energic importation, a kind of signal to the system about environmental conditions and about the functioning of the system in relation to its environment. The feedback of such information enables the system to correct for its own malfunctioning or for changes in the environment, and thus to maintain a steady state or homeostasis. This is a dynamic rather than a static balance, however. Open systems are not at rest but tend toward differentiation and elaboration, both because of subsystem dynamics and because of the relationship between growth and survival. Finally, open systems are characterized by the principle of equifinality, which asserts that systems can reach the same final state from different initial conditions and by different paths of development.

Traditional organizational theories have tended to view the human organization as a closed system. This tendency has led to a disregard of differing organizational environments and the nature of organizational dependency on environment. It has led also to an overconcentration on principles of internal organizational functioning, with consequent failure to develop and understand the processes of feedback which are essential to survival.

3

Defining Characteristics
of Social Organizations

System theory, as Kenneth Boulding (1956) has observed, furnishes the framework or skeleton for all science. It remains for the various disciplines to supply the flesh and blood, to provide a viable model for the understanding of phenomena at their own level of analysis. We are indebted to system theory for some useful general concepts and for the basic approach which emphasizes the principles of mutual influence in a fluid field of forces. But in the search for an all-encompassing dialectic, the essential character of the objects in the field of forces is often neglected as an important source of variance. Our discussion of the common characteristics of all open systems should not blind us to the differences that do exist between biological and social systems. The stuff of which a system is constituted—the cells of a biological organism or the human beings in the social system—needs careful study. Otherwise we could know all there is to know about the political state from the science of cytology.

THE NATURE OF SOCIAL SYSTEMS

Biological structures have a physical boundedness that social structures lack. The biological structures are anchored in physical and physiological constancies, whereas the social structures are not. The skin of the body, the walls of the cell, even the less visible boundaries of the magnetic field represent a kind of structural location and definition for which there is no close social analogue.

Social structures are of course not found in a physical vacuum. They are tied into a concrete world of human beings, material resources, physical plants, and other artifacts, but these elements are not in any natural interaction with each other. In fact the social system has considerable independence of any particular physical part and can shed it or replace it. The communication network of a social organization bears only a distant and figurative resemblance to the physical structures, such as the circulatory and nervous systems, by which the subparts of a biological organism are integrated. Too often such loose metaphors have prevented the sociologist or even the biologist, turned social theorist in his declining years, from grasping the essential differences between organism and society. The constancies of mutual influence among the subparts of a social system are fewer and less perfect than among the parts of a biological system.

A social system is a structuring of events or happenings rather than of physical parts and it therefore has no structure apart from its functioning (Allport, 1962). Physical or biological systems such as automobiles or organisms have anatomical structures which can be identified even when they are not functioning. In other words, these systems have both an anatomy and a physiology. There is no anatomy to a social system in this sense. When the biological organism ceases to function, the physical body is still present and its anatomy can be examined in a post-mortem analysis. When a social system ceases to function, there is no longer an identifiable structure. It is difficult for us to view social systems as structures of events because of our needs for more concrete and simple ways of conceptualizing the world. Hence we identify the buildings, the technological equipment, and the people they contain as the structure of an organization.

There has been no more pervasive, persistent, and futile fallacy handicapping the social sciences than the use of the physical model for the understanding of social structures. The biological metaphor, with its crude comparison of the physical parts of the body to the parts of the social system, has been replaced by more subtle but equally misleading analogies between biological and social functioning. This figurative type of thinking ignores the essential difference between the socially contrived nature of social systems and the physical structure of the machine or the human organism. So long as writers are committed to a theoretical framework based upon the physical model, they will miss the essential social-psychological facts of the highly variable, loosely articulated character of social systems. They will ignore in the future as they have in the past the significance of system openness with respect to maintenance and production inputs and will neglect the overriding importance of the maintenance input for the social system. They will see social organizations in terms of machine theory or reverse their field by interpreting social outcomes as individual decisions and equating roles with personalities.

PRODUCTION AND MAINTENANCE INPUTS

It follows from an analysis of the nature of social systems that special attention must be given to their maintenance inputs. All open systems, of course, require *maintenance* as well as *production* inputs. *Maintenance inputs* are the energic imports which sustain the system; *production inputs* are the energic imports which are processed to yield a productive outcome. In social systems, however, the maintenance problem is more complex than in biological systems in that the maintenance requirements are much less clearly specified in the former than the latter. Certain minimum nutritive and caloric input is necessary to keep the biological organism functioning. Science can specify these inputs with precision, and most organisms show a good deal of primitive wisdom about staying alive even without such specifications. By contrast, the motivations which will attract people to a social system and keep them functioning in it are varied, the relationship between organizational inducements and the required role behavior is indirect and mediated by many factors, and too little is known either at the practical or at the scientific level about maximizing productive output in relation to maintenance input. Moreover, physical and physiological systems with a given physical structure can lie dormant and still maintain their basic character when revived; the social system, once it ceases to function, disappears. This difference means that the social system is more open than physical systems; it must constantly import both production and maintenance materials.

Biological systems also require nourishment and maintenance. Food, water, air, and certain conditions of pressure and temperature are essential to life. But the preservation of the physical structure is not a problem from the point of view of the parts leaving the whole. Cells do not wander away from the organs in which they are imbedded, organs do not leave the body any more than the spark plug goes AWOL. Human beings do drift away from social systems, do go on strike, and do stay at home. Hence the social sciences must go further than natural sciences in order to take into account two types of system openness: openness with respect to production inputs and openness with respect to maintenance inputs. The trend in the social sciences, however, has been to focus as does the physical scientist upon one type of openness, namely the openness to production inputs. The natural scientist can concentrate solely upon the learning function of rats in a maze with the walls of the maze as a constant. In the social system the walls of the maze are not constant because they are made up of human behavior. Classic organization theory with its machine concepts has been concerned almost exclusively with the single type of openness and has attempted to develop principles of organizational functioning as if the production input and the methods of processing it were the only variables. Holding the human parts in the system and mobilizing their energies in prescribed patterns do not represent constant factors in the equation and cannot be ignored. The distinction we are emphasizing between production and maintenance inputs is similar to R. Cattell's (1951) differentiation between effective synergy and maintenance synergy in his discussion of the dynamics of groups. Synergy he defines as the sum total of the energy which a group can command. That part of the energy which is used up to keep the group in being is maintenance synergy and that part which is used to carry out the objectives of the group is effective synergy.

Studies of influence processes in unstructured groups also report a similar dichotomy in leadership functions. Specifically Bales (1958) has found that leadership activity is of two types: *socio-emotional* leadership supportive of group maintenance and *task* leadership oriented toward getting the work done. In general the individuals who contribute to group leadership are high in either socio-emotional support or task direction but not in both.

THE CONTRIVED NATURE OF SOCIAL SYSTEMS

Social structures are essentially contrived systems. They are made by men and are imperfect systems. They can come apart at the seams overnight, but they can also outlast by centuries the biological organisms which originally created them. The cement which holds them together is essentially psychological rather than biological. Social systems are anchored in the attitudes, perceptions, beliefs, motivations, habits, and expectations of human beings. Such systems represent patterns of relationships in which the constancy of the individual units involved in the relationships can be very low. An organization can have a very high rate of turnover of personnel and still persist. The relationships of items rather than the items themselves provide the constancy. Biological systems are also patterns of relationships but their constituent parts are sufficiently stable that the system itself can be readily identified and physically encountered. Our use of the term system, however, for describing a pattern of relationships is a conceptual definition rather than a term for a simply perceived or encountered aggregation of parts. It so happens that a biological system has the advantage, from the research point of view, of fixed physical boundaries and of sufficient smallness that it can also be perceived as a physical reality. Social systems thus are characterized by much greater variability than biological systems. Three aspects of this variability will concern us throughout this volume. (1) Social systems can be readily devised for a tremendous range of varying objectives, and any given system can acquire new and different functions during its life history. (2) The variable elements of the social system are not held in place by any set of biological givens, and many control mechanisms are introduced to hold the organization together. Much of the energy of organizations must be fed into devices of control to reduce the variability of human behavior and to produce stable patterns of activity. (3) The predictable growth curves of biological systems do not necessarily apply to social structures. Organizations are both more vulnerable to destruction and more long-lived than biological organisms. There is an internal determination of the life cycle of an organism based upon its genetic constitution. Built-in resources and forces for growth in the organism foster its survival and development in a normal environment. The social organization in its initial stages may or may not possess internal resources, and so may or may not survive its first few weeks or months of existence. The mortality rate of new enterprises and new organizations is significant, even in times of marked prosperity (Statistical Abstract of the United States, Bureau of the Census, 1963 and Survey of Current Business, U. S. Department of Commerce, September 1964). On the other hand, the social system has the great advantage of readily replacing elements or parts so that it can continue to operate within an unlimited future. All biological organisms have built-in entropy forces; their parts wear out and cannot be replaced.

Symbiotic Patterns versus Social Organizations

The contrived nature of social systems warrants closer examination, for the nature of human contrivances further specifies the system properties of social structures. Though all social systems are dominantly of a contrived character, they vary in the degree to which the interdependent patterning of behavior is culturally fabricated or biologically based. The reciprocal behavior of mother and child in the feeding process reflects some social learning, but it is maintained basically by the physiological satisfactions which both child and mother obtain in the process. The interdependence of sexual partners is another instance of the biological basis of a social institution. Social psychologists have traditionally made the family the basis of their theorizing because the social tie, the bond that maintains people in constant relationship, is most compelling in the symbiotic patterns of sexual behavior and mother-child interactions. In most social systems, however, the social tie is not reinforced by direct biological gratification deriving from the acts of responding to others. To what extent it has its basis in early family experience, to what extent it grows out of the incorporation of *significant others* into our self-conceptions, and to what extent it is instrumental to needs wholly removed from the interaction process will depend upon the particular social pattern in question. For the present, we will be content with pointing out the differences between the biologically sustained symbiotic pattern and the interrelated role activity in a socio-technical system maintained by sanctions and external rewards. In the symbiotic pattern, the person derives physiological gratification not only from his own responses, but from the reciprocal responses of his partner. In role relationships, there is also satisfaction from the mutual rewarding of expectations, but these gratifications are but a faint reflection of the intense rewards of the symbiotic relationships.

An example of two levels of systems can be seen in the biological history of the individual. Between the embryo and the body of the mother there is a fixed physiological interdependence. At birth the physical separation of mother and offspring has profound consequences for the relationship, which becomes increasingly psychological. At first biological ties persist in the symbiotic relationship of the nursing infant and the feeding mother. Soon, however, the ties between mother and child are wholly psychological in character and the social relationship is a far cry from the early biological relationship. The range and complexity of possible patterns of relationship between parent and offspring are great compared to the fixed regularities of the physiological tie between embryo and the body host of the mother. Some psychoanalysts have marred the understanding of adult relationships by failing to see their socially distinctive character. These theorists attempt to explain the behavior of adults as an extension of the symbiotic pattern of infancy, and sometimes they even push back into intra-uterine life for their interpretations. It is possible, of course, with adequate imagination to relate everything in this world to everything else, but the remote connections between the behavior of individuals in biological systems of early life and their behavior as members of social systems account for a negligible amount of the total variance. In other words, the major explanation of the malfunctioning of people in social systems is to be found at the level of social systems and not at the level of their infantile symbiotic patterns of nursing.

Types of Forces Reducing Human Variability

It is possible, as we have just indicated, to consider the basis of the patterning of social behavior in terms of symbiotic relationships or social demands. A more precise description of the control forces for reducing the variability and instability of human actions to the uniform and dependable patterns of a social system has been suggested by Thelen.° His model distinguishes between three types of control pressures: environmental or task requirements in relation to needs, demands arising from shared expectations and values, and the enforcement of rules.

1. *Environmental pressures.* The problem in the objective world requires a coordinated effort of people for its solution. The residents of a village without a fire department may work as a group to extinguish a fire in the home of any member. Division of labor arises naturally to meet the demands of the situation. A volunteer fire department may result in which activities are coordinated in relation to the task to be accomplished. Even in more complex organizations, the task requirements, or the pressures from the external environment, induce coordination of group effort.

2. *Shared values and expectations.* People have some goals in common and mutual expectations about how they should behave to achieve these common objectives. Some members of the community become convinced of the importance of flouridating their water supply. They discuss the problem, hold meetings, and form action committees. The cooperative activity engendered grows out of the shared values more than out of the imperative demands of an objective task. Voluntary groups are formed on this basis, and social organizations also depend upon this pressure though less exclusively than voluntary groups.

3. *Rule enforcement.* Variability is also reduced by rules, the violation of which calls for some form of penalty or negative sanction. Formal prescriptions develop in social systems in which the functions carried out are remotely and indirectly related to the needs of the members. People observe the regulations of the governmental agency or the company for which they work because they want to hold their jobs.

Variability of social behavior is brought under control by one or more of these mechanisms in all social systems. Community movements and voluntary groups are based much more upon the first two processes than upon the third. Large scale organizations employ all three. Sociologists have rightly called attention to the fact that organizations utilize cooperation based upon shared values much more than one would expect from studying their formal tables of work organization and work schedules. The concept of informal organization is sometimes used to call attention to this aspect of group functioning. Nevertheless, rules and their enforcement are also a very significant aspect of organizations. The essential difference between social organizations

° Personal communication to author, 1960.

and less structured social systems is the greater reliance upon formal prescriptions of acceptable as against unacceptable behavior in the organization. It is also true that in a voluntary movement the common values arise from sources prior and external to the association; like-minded people find one another. By contrast, the formal organization indoctrinates its members with its own system norms. We need then to describe the formal patterns of behavior achieved through rule enforcement, i.e., *roles* qua roles, and their ideological basis in *norms* and *values* for understanding social organizations.

MAJOR SOCIAL SYSTEM COMPONENTS: ROLES, NORMS, AND VALUES

The social-psychological bases of social systems comprise the *role* behaviors of members, the *norms* prescribing and sanctioning these behaviors and the *values* in which the norms are embedded. Roles describe specific forms of behavior associated with given tasks; they develop originally from task requirements. In their pure or organizational form, roles are standardized patterns of behavior required of all persons playing a part in a given functional relationship, regardless of personal wishes or interpersonal obligations irrelevant to the functional relationship. Norms are the general expectations of a demand character for all role incumbents of a system or subsystem. Values are the more generalized ideological justifications and aspirations. That the operator of a drill press should get blank stock from the man to his left, should drill holes in 240 pieces of such stock each hour, and should put the completed pieces on a moving belt at his right are examples of role requirements. The statement that all members of the organization shall follow to the letter the work instructions of their superiors or be penalized for insubordination is a norm; it is system-wide in its application, and it reinforces the role requirements. If the notion of obeying orders is embellished and elaborated as an expression of natural law and a means to national security, the appeal would be to values beyond the norms themselves, and an ideology would be in process of development.

Roles, norms, and values differ also with respect to degree of abstractness. There is relatively little problem about understanding what the role requirements are in most systems because of their specificity. Though the norms verbalize and sanction the role expectations, there are aspects of norms which are stated in sufficiently general terms as to lead to varying interpretations. This is even more true of such general values as equality and justice, which are subject to different translations.

Roles, norms, and values thus differ both with respect to generality and with respect to the type of justification mobilized to sanction behavior. At the level of role behavior it is simply a matter of expectancy about task performance; at the level of norms it is a matter of following the legitimate requirements of the system; at the level of values it is a matter of realizing higher moral demands.

THREE BASES OF SYSTEM INTEGRATION

Roles, norms, and values thus furnish three interrelated bases for the integration of social systems. (1) People are tied together because of the functional interdependence of the roles they play; for example, the worker in the production line depends on the appropriate activity of the man feeding him materials and in turn must add his contribution as the product moves to the next worker. Because the requirements of different roles are interrelated, people who perform them are bound together and, as a result, the organization achieves a degree of integration. (2) The normative requirements for these roles add an additional cohesive element; for example, the worker not only plays his part in the interdependent chain of activities but he accepts the norms about doing a satisfactory job. (3) Finally, the values centering about the objectives of the system furnish another source for integration; for example, the political activist may be dedicated to the liberal or conservative values of his party.*

Though role, normative, and value integration may be separated out for analytic purposes, they are interrelated in an ongoing organization. Nevertheless, the relative emphasis may be greater upon one component than another in different systems. The assembly line may give greater weight to task requirements or role performance, the research agency to the norms of rigorous scientific procedure, and the political party to saving the country from ruin. In primitive society, as Durkheim (1947) has observed, social integration was based upon a common value system. With little division of labor and few subsystems, there was a mechanical solidarity based upon a collective conscience or a common morality manifested by all societal members and appropriate to all situations. With a highly differentiated social structure containing many subsystems there is less in the way of a simple universal moral code, and societal integration is based more upon normative practices and role interdependence.

Before giving a more detailed description of roles, norms, and values as essential components of social systems, we shall examine the major subsystems in organized structures built around these components.

* Organizational leaders may epitomize system values, and identification with such leaders can be a powerful integrative force. The charisma of leaders also enhances and strengthens the integrative effects of roles and norms.

GENERIC TYPES OF SUBSYSTEMS

Social organizations like other systems have a through-put or a transformation of the energic input. Those activities concerned with the through-put have been called *production or technical subsystems* (Parsons, 1960). To insure existence beyond a single cycle of productive activity, there must be new materials to be worked on. *Supportive structures* develop in a surviving system to provide a continuing source of production inputs. They are of two kinds. One is the extension of the production system into the environment by activities which procure raw materials and dispose of the product. The second type is at the more complex level of maintaining and furthering a favorable environment through relations with other structures in the society—the institutional function, in Parsons' terms.

In addition to the need for production inputs, special attention must be given to the maintenance inputs, i.e., to insuring the availability of the human energy which results in role performance. If the system is to survive, *maintenance substructures* must be elaborated to hold the walls of the social maze in place. Even these would not suffice to insure organizational survival, however. The organization exists in a changing and demanding environment, and it must adapt constantly to the changing environmental demands. *Adaptive structures* develop in organizations to generate appropriate responses to external conditions. Finally, these patterns of behavior need to be coordinated, adjusted, controlled, and directed if the complex substructures are to hold together as a unified system or organization. Hence, *managerial subsystems* are an integral part of permanent elaborated social patterning of behavior.

Thus we can describe the facts of organizational functioning with respect to five basic subsystems: (1) production subsystems concerned with the work that gets done; (2) supportive subsystems of procurement, disposal, and institutional relations; (3) maintenance subsystems for tying people into their functional roles; (4) adaptive subsystems, concerned with organizational change; (5) managerial systems for the direction, adjudication, and control of the many subsystems and activities of the structure.

Production or Technical Subsystems

The production system is concerned with the through-put, the energic or informational transformation whose cycles of activity comprise the major functions of the system. Organizations are commonly classified according to their main productive process, e.g., educational, if concerned with training, political, if concerned with affecting power

relations, economic, if concerned with the creation of wealth. In the
chapter which follows we shall examine the operation of production
systems in more detail, especially with respect to their relationships to
the other subsystems of the organization.

Supportive Subsystems

Supportive subsystems are those which carry on the environmental
transactions in procuring the input or disposing of the output or aiding
in these processes. They are in part a direct extension of the production activities of the organization in importing the material to be
worked on or exporting the finished product. Or they may be indirectly
related to the production cycle but supportive of it in maintaining a
favorable environment for the operation of the system.

The relating of the system to its larger social environment in
establishing its legitimation and support would be an *institutional*
function. In general the top echelon of an organization, such as the
Board of Trustees, would carry this function and would often have
some degree of membership in outside structures. Thus supportive
systems concerned with environmental transactions include the specific
procurement or disposal structures as well as the more general high
level activities of securing favorable relations with larger structures.

Maintenance Subsystems

Maintenance activities are not directed at the material being
worked on but at the equipment for getting the work done. In most
organizations this equipment consists of patterned human behavior.
The arrangement of roles for interrelated performance does not guarantee that people will take or remain in these roles performing their
functions. Hence subsystems for recruitment, indoctrination or socialization, rewarding and sanctioning, are found in enduring social structures. These subsystems function to maintain the fabric of interdependent behavior necessary for task accomplishment. They tie people into
the system as functioning parts. They are cycles of activity which
are tangential to, or criss-cross, the production cycles. Individuals may
play both production and maintenance roles, as when members of a
college faculty move from their teaching roles to meet as an executive
committee to decide on promotions and salary increases for faculty
members. In many systems, however, the same individuals do not step
from one set of roles to another. The maintenance roles need not be
specific to the major differentiating function of the system. The person
functioning as an administrator in the maintenance structure is often
a generalist who can move from one organization or type of organiza-

tion to another. Indeed, a director of personnel or training in a given company probably could move more easily and with less strain to a functionally comparable position in another company than to a different subsystem in his own organization.

Whereas the supportive systems of procurement and disposal are concerned with insuring production inputs, i.e., materials and resources for the work of the organization, the maintenance system is concerned with inputs for preserving the system either through appropriate selection of personnel or adequate rewarding of the personnel selected. We have already noted the neglect of the maintenance function in traditional thinking which accepts social structures as objective and fixed in nature as biological relationships. The same neglect characterizes the world of practical action in which attention is centered on the production system and its inputs. Problems of personnel both on the recruitment and morale sides have received belated and inadequate recognition and the position of the director of these operations is generally low in the management hierarchy whether the organization is industrial or governmental.

Reward and sanctioning systems, utilized to maintain role performance, are major maintenance substructures. In social organizations rewards and sanctions are employed with respect to *specific* performances and infractions according to a set of rules. In feudal systems sanctions and rewards tended to be invoked in a more capricious manner. In the small agrarian community punitive actions towards a transgressor were based upon the outraged morality of community members and were not finely attuned to a set of particulars established about the transgressing act.

Social organizations, at least in our culture and era, move toward emphasis upon a reward system rather than a punishment system. To hold members in an organization and to maintain a satisfactory type of role performance means that people's experiences in the system must be rewarding, particularly if they have freedom to move in and out of organizations. Often one set of rewards develops to attract and hold members in a system and another to achieve some optimum level of performance.

In keeping with the relative neglect of maintenance functions is the blindness in most organizational theorizing to a significant characteristic of the reward system, namely its *allocation parameters,* or who gets what and why. The allocation of rewards in most organizations in western nations (and to a greater extent than is realized in communist countries as well) is highly differential between members of various subsystems. The problem is one of keeping people in the organizational system and keeping them motivated to perform when there are conspicuous differences in the amount of return to various subgroups in the organization. Rewards are not only monetary; they also include prestige and status, gratifications from interesting work, identification with group products, and satisfactions from decision making. The distribution of all these types of rewards is a basic dimension for understanding how an organization operates. There is a substantial correlation among the various kinds of reward; the members who are paid the most generally have the highest status, the most interesting jobs, and the opportunity to make decisions. Hence the differentials in rewards to subsystem members are even greater than the differences in monetary return would suggest.

Adaptive Subsystems

Nothing in the production, supportive, and maintenance subsystems would suffice to insure organizational survival in a changing environment. Except for the functions of procurement and disposal, these subsystems face inward; they are concerned with the functioning of the organization as it is rather than with what it might become. The risks of concentrating attention and energies inward are directly proportional to the magnitude and rate of change in the world outside the organization. External changes in taste, in cultural norms and values, in competitive organizations, in economic and political power— all these and many others reach the organization as demands for internal change. To refuse to accede to such demands is to risk the possibility that the transactions of procurement and disposal will be reduced or refused, or that the processes of maintenance will become increasingly difficult. In most formal organizations there arise, therefore, structures which are specifically concerned with sensing relevant changes in the outside world and translating the meaning of those changes for the organization. There may be structures which devote their energies wholly to the anticipation of such changes. All these comprise the adaptive subsystem of the organization and bear such names as product research, market research, long-range planning, research and development, and the like.

Managerial Subsystems

These systems comprise the organized activities for controlling, coordinating, and directing the many subsystems of the structure. They represent another slice of the organizational pattern and are made up of cycles of activities cutting across the structure horizontally to deal with coordination of subsystems and the adjustment of the total system to its environment. The functions of top management require actions affecting large sectors of organizational space, the formulation of rules rather than specific invoking of penalties for the recalcitrant member, or a change in policy to achieve better utilization of the system's resources. The exercise of the management function is observable, however, at all levels of the system. Two major types of managerial subsystems which deserve further description are *regulatory mechanisms* and the *authority structure*.

Our basic model of a social system is a structure which imports energy from the external world, transforms it, and exports a product to the environment which is the source for a reenergizing of the cycle. Substructures may develop which gather and utilize intelligence about the energic transactions. Such devices function to give feedback to the system about its output in relation to its input. Management in modern organizations operates in good part through such *regulatory mechanisms*. When a system operates without a specialized feedback or regulatory mechanism, we shall refer to it as a primitive group rather than a social organization. Voluntary groups, for example, may form from time to time and may carry on some cooperative activity. The degree of accomplishment will be the result of the number of members and their enthusiasm at the moment and will vary greatly from time to time. The group is not guided by any information about its impact upon the world or any intelligence about the contributions of its members. It may not even have a roster of its members and its new chairman may search in vain for the records of what was done under his predecessor, how it was done, and what the outcome was. A voluntary group becomes an organization when it acquires systematic methods for regulating its activities on the basis of information about its functioning. Operationally a voluntary group is identified as an organization when it has a permanent secretariat or some equivalent device for maintaining stability in the offices of secretary and treasurer with respect to membership rolls, finances, and records.

Regulatory mechanisms are highly developed in profit making organizations, and information about the market and the sale of the commodities of the enterprise is constantly used to control the productive activities of the enterprise and its actions with respect to its supply of raw materials. Regulatory mechanisms vary in complexity and sophistication, however, and very primitive mechanisms of regulation may direct the activity of large, complex systems. For example, a medical school may base its admissions upon the number of available microscopes or the size of its laboratories.

The dominant tendency is toward complexity in regulatory mechanisms. Industrial concerns utilize increasingly detailed estimates of economic trends in planning the capture of new markets. A highly significant development in modern industry is the use of electronic computers and automated devices to regulate the activities of the enterprise at two levels. Computers will be used to process all kinds of information about the internal functioning of the organization and about its environment, to guide decisions at the highest echelons about basic policies and procedures—even to help in assigning weights to various factors. Automated devices will be employed within subsystems to provide self-regulation for the performance of certain types of tasks.

The systematic use of information to guide organizational functioning is the sine qua non of an organization. The implications of such regulatory mechanisms are far-reaching. They include the elaboration of the role structure to provide for such a continuing function, and they imply the addition of other structures to coordinate the incoming information with the ongoing activities. The social system of feudalism rested more on status relationships than on highly developed role concepts and relied for stability on a combination of physical force and the mysticism of the masses. Modern role systems, however, need an intelligence function to maintain themselves.

Organizations need not be authoritarian in character, but they must possess an established and definitive form of decision making about organizational matters. The *authority structure* essentially describes the way in which the managerial system is organized with respect to the sources of decision making and its implementation. Decisions are accepted if made in the proper manner, whether by democratic vote or by an edict from duly constituted authority. The essence of authority structure is the acceptance of directives as legitimate, i.e., either the acquiescence or approval by people of rules of the game. The rules may be arrived at through a democratic process or they may be promulgated from above, but in either case they are binding upon the members of the system. They are properties of the system and not of the dominance-submission patterns of individual personalities. We recognize this when we say that a person has exceeded his authority. He has gone beyond the legitimately defined limits of his position. What has obscured this clear theoretical distinction in practice is that authoritarian personalities often select themselves or are selected for positions of power in social systems. Their personality traits may lead them to abuse this legal power in areas where it is difficult to check on their actions. The paradox is that the law enforcement agencies, whether local police, internal revenue agents, immigration authorities, or customs officials, are entrusted with carrying out the rules of the game, but often enjoy a reputation for officiousness or over-stepping their authority.

People tend to personalize relationships and often impute personal despotism to the orderly functioning of the social system, confusing the exercise of legal authority with authoritarianism. Since authoritarianism is a bad thing and is the opposite of the desirable qualities of liberty and democracy, there may be rebellion against any rules of the game which the individual does not relish.

Though in some organizations decisions are democratically arrived at, they are abided by until a change is effected through the legitimized channels for change. Or the organization may be authoritarian in character, but again decisions about given types of affairs are made by some appropriate officer. Even in the democratically constructed organization, minor decision making in keeping with lines of policy as determined by majority vote will be entrusted to representatives of the group. Such delegation of power creates a hierarchy of positions within the structure even though the elected official may have to validate his authority from time to time by standing for reelection.

Thus every organization has an *executive system* for carrying out policy or the implementation of administrative decisions. In a democratic structure there is, in addition, a separate *legislative system* with the power vested in the membership to select top executives, to set policy, to choose between alternative policies of the leadership, or to veto policy proposals. In an authoritarian structure a single system may include the *executive* and *legislative* functions, and the top executives do the legislating for the organization. It is also possible for an authoritarian structure to have separate legislative and executive systems, in which an appointed or self-perpetuating board of directors sets policy and a manager and his subordinates execute it. *The essential difference between a democratic and an authoritarian system is not whether executive officers order or consult with those below them but whether the power to legislate on policy is vested in the membership or in the top echelons.*

There is an interpenetration of the authority and reward systems of an organization. The authority structure allocates decision making, and decision making is rewarding in two senses; (1) its exercise is in itself gratifying to the needs of people for participation and autonomy, and (2) it is instrumental in its power potential for achieving other objectives. Hence an authority structure democratically based in a legislative system involving the membership has a built-in reward mechanism not found in an authoritarian system. There are other types of advantages to an authoritarian system but its problems of maintenance differ radically from the democratic system. Organization theorists apart from political scientists have given scant attention to this critical difference between organization forms. In the industrial world the appeal of the unions to workers is often a mystery to industrialists who have failed to grasp the significance of democratic structure and its reward character, even in imperfect manifestation.

Ordinarily the developmental processes by which groups acquire a regulatory mechanism and an authority structure are not independent but interactive. With a regulatory mechanism goes the need for decision making about the uses to which the information will be put. So long as a primitive group can operate in terms of the enthusiasm of its particular adherents at a given time and drop to another level of activity with less motivated followers at another time, it requires only task direction which can be generated within the group itself. But when it moves over to the utilization of information about maintaining some effective ratio of energy input to energy output and some stability in the level of its operations, it needs a more permanent and definitive form of decision making. Thus the authority structure grows in response to the development of a regulatory maintenance mechanism. And conversely, as authority comes to be vested in positions in the group, its exercise is dependent upon information feedback about its functioning. The officers charged with staffing an organization need information about the amount and causes of turnover, and about the kind of people who are lost relative to those who are retained. Some regulatory feedback mechanism is needed to maintain the quantity and quality of personnel which the operations require. The top officers are concerned with the total efficiency of the operations and they will institute cost accounting systems to aid them in the exercise of their authority.

There can be a power structure in primitive groups in terms of the superior personality force of a leader, whether because of physical prowess, mental alertness, or persuasiveness. This is not, however, the same as authority structure in which the order is followed because it comes from the legitimized position in the structure rather than from a certain personality. The soldier salutes the uniform of the superior officer, not the man. The informal group of teenagers on the corner may start as a primitive group with leadership a matter of the interplay of the strongest personalities in the group. After a time a leader may emerge and the group may develop norms about how his legitimate authority should be exercised. It becomes an organization when leaders and followers decide on membership and procedures for admitting novices to membership. This process is one of regulating group functioning through information about its component parts. The gang may, for example, vote to admit Joe Smith because he is a tough fighter, Bill Brown because he has a car, and to restrict other admissions indefinitely in terms of facilities available and activities planned for the future.

The authority structure in feudal and semi-feudal systems is clear and legitimized but is less a matter of role and more a combination of role and status and personality. The noble is obeyed because of his inherited status as a noble which is irretrievably mixed up with him as a person because of the confusion of biological and social inheritance. It is the modern bureaucratic organization, as Max Weber pointed out, which has developed an authority structure of the rational-legal type whereby the rules and prerogatives of authority are quite separated from the person and personality of the wielder of authority. Some structure of authority, some criteria for allocating it, and some rules for its exercise are, however, among the common characteristics of all human organizations.

DEFINING CHARACTERISTICS OF SOCIAL ORGANIZATIONS

Social organizations are a type or subclass of social systems. They possess more of certain system characteristics than do primitive social groupings. In the preceding sections we have laid the groundwork for their definition in describing their component subsystems. (1) Organizations possess a *maintenance* structure as well as *production* and *production-supportive* structures. Their activities are thus concerned both with a through-put and the preservation of the system. The maintenance subsystems operate to give them some degree of *permanence*. (2) Organizations have an *elaborated formal role pattern* in which the division of labor results in a functional specificity of roles. Thus social organizations, more than other groups, utilize roles as such, divorcing them from surplus elements of traditionalism, personal obligations, and charisma. (3) There is a *clear authority structure* in the organization which reflects the way in which the control and managerial function is exercised. (4) As part of the managerial structure there are well-developed regulatory mechanisms and *adaptive structures*. Hence the organization is guided by feedback or intelligence concerning its own operations and the changing character of its environment. (5) There is an explicit formulation of *ideology* to provide system norms which buttress the authority structure.

Bureaucratic structures are the clearest examples of social organizations. They carry out the formalization of roles in terms of functional specificity with minimal holdover of older institutional practices. The structure of authority in the bureaucracy is based upon the legitimacy of rational rules, and bureaucratic regulatory mechanisms are of a fairly elaborate type. Associations of people in which regulatory mechanisms are lacking we have termed *primitive groups*. Some voluntary groupings would fall into this category.

The small groups which are created in the laboratory are typically primitive groups. But there have been interesting attempts to create organizational structures in simulation demonstrations, as in the case of a hospital or a government agency set up with the intelligence functions of an operating enterprise. *Crowds* and *mobs* are primitive groups which not only lack a regulatory mechanism but also have no clearly defined authority structure and no firm role system.

The term *informal group* is sometimes used to describe certain types of primitive groupings. It has also been applied, since the Hawthorne studies (Roethlisberger and Dickson, 1939), to behavior in an organization which is outside role requirements and possibly opposed to their fulfillment, thereby equating informal systems with restriction of output. This usage seems to us parochial and confusing, since there may be informal systems that are uncodified supportive extensions of the formal structure, and all relevant cycles of behavior should be included for study and definition. To define as informal all acts which are unwanted by management has a certain pragmatic value, but it is a slippery base on which to construct organizational theory. The term *informal* has also been applied to well-developed structures which nevertheless lack the specialized substructures that characterize formal organizations, and it is this usage that we will follow. It locates informal groups somewhere between primitive groupings and formal organizations on the developmental scale.

The term *social institution* refers to a greater variety of social relationships than does social organization. An institution may have some organizational structure, but it also binds people together in many other ways. For example, the family is a combination of symbiotic patterns, personal interrelationships, the following of general roles based upon tradition, and a communal cooperative.

FURTHER SPECIFICATIONS CONCERNING ROLES, NORMS, AND VALUES

FORMALIZED ROLE SYSTEMS AND THE ROLE CONCEPT

The most general concept for describing the socially contrived stable patterns of interrelated behavior, as we have already noted, is that of the role system. For those situations in which complementary and reciprocal activities are not a direct function of complementary biological needs, men have devised the expedient of sanctioning certain forms of behavior which are required of people in their social relationships by virtue of their position in those relationships. Thus the person who calls the meeting to order and recognizes speakers does so by virtue of his role as chairman. One individual may play this role in a heavy-handed and partisan manner; another may be scrupulously fair and conscientious. But the role of chairman is the central fact for understanding the behavior of the individual presiding over the group. It makes incumbent upon him certain types of decisions and it also sets definite limits upon his behavior in the group meeting. Standardized or institutionalized behavior of this sort is termed *role behavior*. The person in a social system who plays a role is under the demands of that role to act in many of the ways he does.

Social organizations represent the clearest development of a pattern of interlocking roles in the sense that roles are employed without the encumbrances of socially inherited status or personality contamination. Moreover, the roles in a social organization represent prescribed or standardized forms of activity. The network of standardized role behaviors constitutes the formal structure of an organization. A *formalized role system*, then, is one in which the rules defining the expected interdependent behavior of incumbents of system positions are explicitly formulated and sanctions are employed to enforce the rules. Formalization or standardization of role performance is a matter of degree, but the individual in the organization has less freedom to transform his role to coincide with the expression of his personality than in other social settings. For example, a person may play his role as a citizen in a democratic state in a great variety of ways, from voting occasionally in a national election to running for an elected office. In fact, in nonorganizational settings, he is generally unaware of the social roles he plays. Within the organization, however, he is aware of the specific demands of the role.

A role abstracts the behavioral requirement from the satisfactions accruing to the individual for engaging in such activities. Whether or not the individual enjoys carrying out the expected task is irrelevant. What is relevant is that there are many other ways of making his behavior stable and reliable, ranging from the primitive man's reverence for or fear of his tribal chief to the modern organization man's generalized sensitivity and obedience to what is expected of him. Such mechanisms can be built into the processes by which the individual is socialized into his culture.

Roles are found in their purest form when they are the most completely divorced from the personalities of role incumbents and from any specific motivational tie which could encumber the role relationship. The slave and master who have reciprocal affection for one another interfere with the functioning of the system of slavery as such. *The general development of role systems has been in the direction of getting rid of surplus elements in role relations.* In some older societies role requirements became mixed with their sanctioning sources, as in the case of sanctity of economic practices; or with the personalities of role incumbents, as in the case of the semi-divine character of kings; or with the monopoly of physical force by the owning group, as in the case of slavery. The full utilization of roles came only with the development of bureaucratic structure where the role could be set up, abolished, or changed as part of the rules of the game—where it could be observed as a role and nothing more. The economic version of history, which makes the development of the free market the pivotal point in the development of modern western society, is only a partial statement of the facts of the matter. The free market was the economic expression of the discovery that roles could be developed as roles in all types of human endeavor.

The Concept of Partial Inclusion. At the individual level the role concept implies that people need be involved in system functioning only on a segmental or partial basis. Unlike the inclusion of a given organ of the body in the biological system, not all of the individual is included in his organization membership. The organization neither requires nor wants the whole person. Even where the person cannot withdraw physically from a social system, as in the case of military service, his psychological life space covers much more than his military duties. People belong to many organizations and the full engagement of their personalities is generally not found within a single organizational setting. Moreover, they frequently shift their membership in organizations. F. H. Allport (1933) developed the concept of *partial inclusion* to refer to the segmental involvement of people in social groupings.

The concept of partial inclusion helps us to understand many of the problems of social organization. The organizational role stipulates behaviors which imply only a "psychological slice" of the person, yet people are not recruited to organizations on this basis; willy-nilly the organization brings within its boundaries the entire person. The organizational demand on the individual to put aside some parts of himself for the sake of performing a role is literally a depersonalizing demand; in this sense the individual who joins with others to create an informal "organization within an organization" is fighting for his identity as a person.

The concept of partial inclusion is relevant also to the special boundary problems of social organizations. Since the individual is involved in a social system with only a part of himself, he might readily behave less as a member of any given organization and more in terms of some compromise of his many segmental commitments unless special circumstances make salient the demands of a particular system. There must be clarity of demands and constraints upon him so that he will give unto Caesar what is Caesar's. In other words, the boundary conditions which insure that behavior patterns within a system are appropriate to that system are largely psychological in character. The individual must not be confused about which system he is psychologically in at any given moment. The individual must realize that he has crossed over into an area where behavioral alternatives may be limited or nonexistent. The more time the individual spends in the boundary condition either because of frequent crossings, because this is his permanent place in organizational space, or because of competing cross pressures from two or more organizations, the more necessary it becomes for the organization to utilize mechanisms insuring his allegiance.

In trivial instances the failure of an individual to recognize when he has crossed an organizational boundary is mere gaucherie and provides a common kind of humor. For corporations with far-flung operations the boundary problem is by no means a subject of humor, and people are rotated from one location to another or brought back to the parent location at regular intervals as a way of preventing them from "going native"—that is, becoming influenced by people on the wrong side of the organizational boundary. When the analogous kind of thing occurs across a national boundary, we call it treason and it becomes a matter of life and death.

Organizations, as we have said, consist of patterned behavior; if members misperceive the organizational boundary and misbehave in terms of it, they threaten the very life of the organization.

SYSTEM NORMS AND VALUES

Social systems, as the patterned interdependent activities of human beings, are characterized by *roles,* which differentiate one position from another; they are characterized also by a set of *norms* and *values,* which integrate rather than differentiate; that is, they are shared by all (or many) of the members of the system. We shall use the terms *norms* and *values* to refer to the common beliefs of an evaluative type which constitute a coherent interrelated syndrome. System norms make explicit the forms of behavior appropriate for members of the system. System values or ideology provide a more elaborate and generalized justification both for appropriate behavior and for the activities and functions of the system. Norms and ideology shade into one another so that the distinction is one of emphasis rather than of uniqueness. Norms refer to the expected behavior sanctioned by the system and thus have a specific *ought* or *must* quality. In this they resemble roles. Values furnish rationale for the normative requirements. For a value to become a norm for a subsystem it must have an explicit formulation with specific reference to identifiable behavior of a systematically relevant character so that it can be enforced.

System norms and values (ideology) are a group product and may not be necessarily identical with the privately held values of a representative sample of the individuals involved in the system. They are the standards to which reference is made for judging acceptable and unacceptable behavior of relevance to the system. The foreman in a factory may give his workers instructions about a job. They may not like the directive but their criterion for accepting or not accepting it is based upon the system norm of whether it is within his area of jurisdiction as the legitimate spokesman of management.

System norms and ideology have the general function of tying people into the system so that they remain within it and carry out their role assignments. The more specific functions are twofold: (1) system norms and ideology furnish cognitive maps for members which facilitate their work in the system and their adjustment to it, (2) norms and ideology provide the moral or social justification for system activities both for members and for people formally outside the system.

Three Criteria for System Norms and Values. The participants in all social systems hold common beliefs and attitudes about some aspects of the system and its functioning. When these common beliefs are accompanied by the feeling that these ideas are the relevant and appropriate doctrine which specifies behavioral requirements for members of the group, they are termed *group norms* or *system norms*. In other words, three criteria define system norms: (1) there must be beliefs about appropriate and required behavior for group members as group members, (2) there must be objective or statistical commonality of such beliefs; not every member of the group must hold the same idea, but a majority of active members should be in agreement, (3) there must be an awareness by individuals that there is group support for a given belief.

To stipulate the degree to which each of these elements must be present in order to constitute a norm would be arbitrary; all three, however, are necessary to the definition. Thus where people have the same or similar beliefs and attitudes as a result of some ecological or demographic factor, such as occupation or geographical place of residence, they may still lack the feeling that there are such common and appropriate belief systems among people like themselves. (Elements 1 and 3 are lacking.) In such instances, where there is little consciousness of kind, we do not use the term *group norms* nor do we regard the grouping as a social organization. We speak rather of a public and its common attitudes. Advertisers and politicians often divide the nation into groups and publics, dealing with the publics as people of similar interests and trying to develop some consciousness of kind among them.

Similarly, we are not dealing with group norms where people hold differing beliefs even though each man may feel that his notions have group support. (Element 2 is lacking.) This is one of the most difficult of all conditions for the operation of any social system. People act on their own idiosyncratic beliefs as if there were a high degree of group support for them. If carried to a logical extreme, this would mean anarchy as each person plays the game according to his own rules. This condition is characteristically unstable and tends to be dispelled as individual actors come into collision. When the antagonists attempt to rally support, the objective amount of that support becomes visible to all. Conflict is almost inevitably clarifying.

There are also cases where group members may hold the same beliefs, be aware that the majority of their colleagues hold similar views, and yet regard these beliefs as inappropriate to their group membership. (Element 1 is lacking.) This can be found in some labor unions where most of the members are Democratic in political preference and are aware that this is the common preference of other union members. They may nevertheless reject the notion that the union should take a stand on political matters, repudiate the idea that the stand of the union leaders on political parties is relevant to their own wishes, and assert that it makes no difference how a union man votes; it is up to the individual to vote for the candidate of his choice. Such union members were just as likely to vote for Eisenhower in 1952 and 1956 as workers who were not union members. (Campbell, Converse, Miller, and Stokes, 1960.)

We should also recognize the situation in which the great majority of individuals have the same conflict between their own beliefs of proper group behavior and their own estimate of group support. They may favor one course of action but feel that the great majority oppose it whereas, in fact, the majority agree with them. This is the classic phenomenon labeled pluralistic ignorance by F. H. Allport, (see discussion in Katz and Schanck, 1938), and illustrated by the Andersen fairy tale of the king's imaginary garment which, of course, must be visible to others. Schanck (1932) confirmed the existence of pluralistic ignorance in his study of Elm Hollow, where he found a discrepancy between public and private attitudes of church members on such matters as card playing. The majority incorrectly thought they were the minority. Pluralistic ignorance is of particular significance in social organizations where the channels of communications are controlled from above and fictitious group norms therefore can be developed and fostered.

The reason for adding the dimension of objective consensus of common beliefs is our concern with the prediction of social behavior and system outcomes. The individual psychologist can be satisfied with the subjective conviction of a person that he has group support for his beliefs. The social psychologist who is interested in the common directions of group behavior must also take into account the actual amount of support in the social environment for a given system of beliefs. For the facts are that personal convictions and group support do interact, and most people over time bring their private beliefs into line with some of the social realities constituted by the opinions of others. Otherwise they may have little opportunity to put their beliefs into practice, since the structure for social action is based upon social systems which provide channels for certain forms of behavior and barriers for other forms.

Types of Values. The substantive justification of system behavior is essentially of two types. It consists basically of (1) transcendental, moral, or sacred values or (2) pragmatic values associated with functional outcomes. Both kinds may be involved in social relationships but many social systems give greater emphasis to one or the other. Values of the first type, with their emphasis upon some sacred quality, tend to imbue a symbol with properties over and above those of the reality it represents. Or to put it more precisely, these symbolic values often have little objective reference and so can be utilized by organizational leadership to support various programs. The tendency is to overwork these values, to allow them to creep into many specific means for meeting organizational objectives rather than reserving them for the objectives themselves. When this happens, rigidities in organizational behavior occur. What was a means to an end becomes an end in itself and, as Merton (1957) points out, the system becomes encrusted with ritualism.

An example of the pervasive character of symbolic values can be seen in the elaboration of the doctrine of organizational loyalty. Loyalty is applied to three types of behavior. In the first place, members should maintain their membership and should not desert to some rival organization. What is treason for the national state is diluted in its implications for organizations where the enemy character of competing systems is less pronounced. For union members, however, and for factory workers in general, the scab or strikebreaker is guilty of moral turpitude. Loyalty, then, is fostered as a moral value to keep people within the organization. In the second place, it is invoked as a supporting doctrine for the official purposes of the organization. Such purposes are not open to question; anyone who challenges them is guilty of heresy. This means of protecting the official ideology is easier to invoke in religious and political organizations than in other types of organized groups. Finally, loyalty, like other sacred values, may be used to protect the specific means for the attainment of organizational goals so that any criticism of accepted procedures is interpreted as a criticism of the organization itself.

Organizations which have direct commerce with their environment and rely heavily upon technology for turning out a product move in the direction of a pragmatic rather than a sanctified ideology. They must meet the changing demands of their clientele and so cannot afford to be ritualistic about their procedures. American automobile companies were slow to respond to public needs in the field of transportation, but they finally met the threat of foreign competition with smaller cars. A technologically oriented organization has its rationalized purposes geared to the world of empirical fact rather than to transcendental value. Absolutistic beliefs, unquestioning loyalty, and the excommunication of heretics just do not fit into a value system of pragmatic operationalism. Even such a sacred cow as the prerogatives of management is difficult to assimilate to concepts of consultative management and cooperative team effort. The technological system creates experts who are heavily task oriented, who fly no flags, and who are completely bored by ideological considerations. As experts in technology, they move into positions of leadership and pin on the walls their credo, "Data win."

THE CENTRAL ROLE OF ORGANIZATIONAL ACTIVITIES AND FUNCTIONS IN DETERMINING SYSTEM NORMS AND VALUES

Many studies in social psychology have demonstrated the power of the norms of the group over the individual (Newcomb, 1943). The rewards and sanctions which the group can use for conformity to its values and for deviance from its norms constitute a major source of compliance. Another is the gratification of affiliative needs through sharing beliefs and attitudes with others. A third and potent source of the strength of a system ideology is that it reflects and justifies the way of life of the group. Norms develop around the dominant ongoing functions of the social system. They give cognitive support and structure to the behavior in which people are engaged. Men do not possess universal minds familiar with all possible beliefs and values in this world. Their ideas and attitudes derive in good part from the input of information from their daily activities. The world of the coal miner is different from that of the farmer, or the man on the assembly line, or the nuclear research worker, or the diplomat in a foreign capital. The common behavior and interests of functional groups produce a common language, a common belief system, and a common way of thinking. In addition to this intellectual commonality there is a community interest in justifying and glorifying a common way of life. Group norms and ideology are influential in affecting the behavior of members not only because of conformity and affiliation needs but also because the ideology of the system gears into the very functions in which individuals are engaged and invests them with a significance and meaning they would not otherwise possess.

Organized groups differ in the types of tasks they perform and a key determinant of characteristic organizational norms is the type of activity in which the organization is involved. A major political party devotes its energies to getting its candidates elected to office and develops an important value system around the notion of winning elections. Every nominee proudly pledges himself to a winning campaign; every party official must maintain the public belief in victory for his side until the last shred of hope is gone. Professional politicians will make all sorts of compromises to insure a majority vote at the polls, and the political novice who has the magic of capturing votes is slated for a rapid rise in the party structure. In like fashion, the functions of a specific business enterprise determine its value system. And the Marine Corps, as the group with the task of pulling the military chestnuts out of the fire, develops a code of iron discipline, courage, and toughness.

The strength of system norms is due partly to their freedom from idiosyncratic patterns of genetic motivation. They derive their support from the common ongoing activities of the system. The severity of toilet training in early childhood is less relevant for system norms than the tribulations and rewards of adult behavioral requirements. The scientist's support of the value of freedom of inquiry is a necessity for his mode of operation. Individuals may have different reasons for following the same course of action, but in the organizational setting the means for reaching a variety of individual goals are reduced to a very few pathways. It is not necessary, therefore, to find a miniature reflection of the ideology of the system in the individual motivational patterns of most members in order to have an effective set of group values.

The Norm of Reciprocity. In his famous studies of the Trobriand Islanders, Malinowski (1926) came to the conclusion that their social structure was based upon the principle of reciprocity and mutual interdependence. A striking example of this principle of reciprocal rewarding relationships was the partnership between an island villager and a coastal fisherman. Each villager raising vegetables inland had a specific partner in the coastal village. Their many ceremonial and social relations comprised a superstructure for a basic exchange of gifts by which the fisherman was assured of a supply of fresh vegetables and his farming partner of a supply of fish. This same reciprocal principle, Malinowski found, pervaded all tribal life and could be considered the equivalent in social relationships of the symbiotic principle in biological relationships.

Homans (1958) and Gouldner (1960) have reinstated this concept of reciprocity in sociological thinking, and Gouldner has asserted that it is a universal norm. He believes it to be as universal and as important as the incest taboo and to be one of the principal components of all value systems. This norm in effect means that people should help those who have helped them and should not injure those who have helped them. Gouldner, moreover, feels that equivalence of return to both parties is not necessary in the operation of the principle. Berkowitz (1963) has generalized the notion still further by postulating a norm of obligation to those dependent upon us regardless of the return we achieve. In Berkowitz's experiments, subjects helped an individual who could not carry out his task without their assistance even though no rewards were offered them. This norm of helpfulness derives from the socialization process and, though it has some force in its own right, is undoubtedly of enduring strength because it does receive a considerable amount of reinforcement in adult life from specific acts of reciprocity.

The norms of reciprocity and helpfulness are major factors in *role readiness* (Chapter 5) which is so essential to large scale bureaucracy. We have given considerable attention in the preceding pages to the functionality of norms and values in various types of social systems. Here we are dealing with a general norm for all role systems which also is tied to a basic functional requirement. The essence of the social relationship, as Malinowski pointed out, is the give-and-take character of the social setting in which people are mutually dependent upon one another.

THE ORGANIZATION IN RELATION TO ITS ENVIRONMENT

Organizational functioning must be studied in relation to the continuing transactions with the supporting environment. The concepts of subsystems and supersystems, system openness, boundaries, and coding are all concerned with aspects of this relationship.

SYSTEMS, SUBSYSTEMS, AND SUPERSYSTEMS

Social systems as open systems are dependent upon other social systems; their characterization as subsystems, systems, or supersystems is relative to their degree of autonomy in carrying out their functions and to the particular interests of the investigator. From a societal point of view the organization is a subsystem of one or more larger systems, and its linkage or integration with these systems affects its mode of operation and its level of activity.

Where the interest is in the study of a manufacturing concern, the company in question can be considered as the system, its organizational activities of production, marketing, recruiting, and holding employees as the subsystems, and the industry and larger community as the supersystem. In spite of the high degree of autonomy implied by doctrines of national sovereignty, the dependence and openness of a social system does not necessarily stop at national boundaries. The student of national policy toward foreign affairs, as Singer (1961) points out, should consider international relationships as the revelant system. System theory dictates a strategy of research which is in basic opposition to reductionism or the immediate pushing to some more elementary level for an understanding of social-psychological phenomena. The first step should always be to go to the next higher level of system organization, to study the dependence of the system in question upon the supersystem of which it is a part, for the supersystem sets the limits of variance of behavior of the dependent system. More analytic study can then explore the contributions of subsystems to this limited range of variance. For example, if we want to study patterns of cooperation and conflict within an industrial company, our first step would not be to look at the informal standards in work groups but to study the position of the company in the industry as a whole. Its marginality or leadership position in the field, the position of its local union with respect to the larger organization of unions, and other such relationships will be reflected in the internal life of the organization.

Apart from the practical interests of the investigator, the characterization of systems can be specified relative to degrees and types of autonomy. There must be some degree of freedom for decision making on such key issues as fiscal policy, admission of members, type of product, or distribution of rewards to justify integrity as an organization. A practical criterion is legal responsibility. Corrections on the basis of the legal criterion may have to be made for those subsystems which are still under the complete control of the larger organization in spite of their nominal independence. For example, a manufacturing concern making parts for an automobile company may be completely under the domination of that company even though it is legally separate and independent. On the other hand, subunits of a larger organization which are legally bound to it may be granted considerable organizational autonomy. The establishment of "profit-centers" (subunits responsible and autonomous with respect to many organizational functions) exemplifies this assertion. The locus at which profits may be accrued and the locus at which decisions to use such profits may be made are additional criteria of obvious practical significance for assessing organizational independence from the supersystem.

A fully satisfactory set of theoretical criteria for such assessment is not available, but it might well include such factors as the following: power to stipulate sources of input rather than accepting sources prescribed by the supersystem; power to choose target populations for export of the organizational product; development of internal mechanisms for organizational regulation, including positive and negative feedback. It may be that many of these criteria will be reflected in a single aspect of organizational life: the ease or difficulty of moving across a boundary. The more difficult such a move and the more extensive the changes which it implies, the greater the degree of organizational autonomy.

SYSTEM OPENNESS, SYSTEM BOUNDARIES, AND SYSTEM CODING

These three concepts are interrelated and have to do with the relative autonomy of system functioning and with system differentiation from the surrounding environment. *System openness* is the most general of these concepts and refers to the degree to which the system is receptive to all types of inputs. Systems vary with respect to the general range of inputs that can be absorbed and with respect to openness to particular types of inputs.

Either of the major American political parties would be an example of a system open to a fairly wide range of influences. Many types of individuals can move into the organization, bringing with them different ideas and interests. The party accepts contributions and help from many sources. As a result, American political parties tend not to present distinctive action or ideological programs or distinctive candidates. They are not highly differentiated from one another or from the surrounding environment of community activities concerned with the exertion of influence. Eisenhower was sought as a presidential candidate by both parties. It has been proposed, and from an improbable source (Luce, 1964), that the history of American political parties can be understood as a cyclical process in which the tendency of the parties to become increasingly open and undifferentiated from each other is occasionally and dramatically interrupted by some historical issue that either polarizes them or creates a realignment of forces and a new pair of parties. On the other hand, the Communist Party in the United States is closed to a wide range of inputs but very open with respect to input from the international communist organization.

System coding is the major procedure for insuring specifications for the intake of information and energy, and it thus describes the actual functioning of barriers separating the system from its environment. One of the significant characteristics of any system is the selective intake of energy and information and the transformation of that input according to the nature of the system. Social systems develop their own mechanisms for blocking out certain types of alien influence and for transforming what is received according to a series of code categories. Though the coding concept can apply to the selective absorption and transformation of all types of input into a system, it is characteristically employed for the processing of information.

The procedure for excluding information may be deliberately and rationally developed. The judicial system, for example, has codified rules which define the nature of the evidence admissible. Hearsay evidence is excluded; so too are confessions obtained under duress; and in some states the results of lie detection tests are ruled out. Most organizations have not developed their rules for the exclusion of information in as systematic a manner, but they do possess *formal criteria* for rejecting some types of input. These criteria may specify that only information relevant to the questions posed by organizational leaders will be accepted, or that only members of a certain status or functional position will be heard on certain questions. More generally the practice is to have specialized structures for the reception of information so that any message will have to traverse and survive the "proper channels" in order to get a hearing.

System boundaries refer to the types of barrier conditions between the system and its environment which make for degrees of system openness. Boundaries are the demarcation lines or regions for the definition of appropriate system activity, for admission of members into the system, and for other imports into the system. The boundary constitutes a barrier for many types of interaction between people on the inside and people on the outside, but it includes some facilitating device for the particular types of transactions necessary for organizational functioning. The barrier condition is exemplified by national states with their border guards and customs offices which restrict the flow of people and goods across their boundaries. Within a national state, organizations are similarly characterized by boundaries, both physical and psychological, to maintain the integrity of the system.

Psychological separation is maintained by visible symbols, such as uniforms, dress, and insignia (e.g., fraternity pins), and even more subtly by speech patterns and other distinctive forms of behavior. Without such special provisions, organizational members at the boundaries would become susceptible to outside influence. The incursion of environmental influence would be uncontrolled and would vitiate the intrasystem influences. Where physical space can be employed to create separation, there is protection against such external forces. But since the organization must have interchange with its supporting environment, some of its members must occupy boundary positions to help in the export of the services, ideas, and other products of the system and in the import of materials and people into the system. Since these members face out upon the world and deal with the public, they are subject to the conflicting pressures of their own organization and the social environment. Because of their greater acquaintance with opportunities outside the organization as well as the conflicting demands of their roles, one would expect greater personnel turnover in these boundary positions than in the central production structure. Many other evidences of the stressfulness of boundary positions have already been produced (Kahn et al., 1964).

The boundary condition applies also to the process by which outsiders enter and become members of the organization. They may be physically within the organization for some time before they cross the psychological boundary and become part of the organization. Before foreigners are admitted to citizenship in the United States, they must have resided within its physical boundaries for five years, have passed required tests, and taken an oath of allegiance. Many organizations have formal induction and socialization procedures for instilling the behavior, attitudes, and values which differentiate the system from the outside environment. (Dornbusch, 1955)

We have been speaking mainly about the boundary condition with respect to maintenance inputs. Environmental transactions on the production side are also controlled by organizational boundaries. In system theory it is common to define the boundary as the area where a lower interchange of energy or information occurs than in the system proper. In social systems it is also a matter of qualitative breaks between the activity within the system and the activity on the outside.

FUNCTION AND STRUCTURE: INTRINSIC AND EXTRINSIC FUNCTIONS

We have already pointed out that at the social level there is no anatomical structure which can be encountered as at the physical or biological level. Structure is inferred as a relationship between events or nodal happenings—which can be directly observed and measured. Function is a shorthand description of social structure and refers to the outcome of structured activity. *Intrinsic function* refers to the immediate and direct outcome of a system or subsystem in terms of its major product. It should be distinguished from *extrinsic functions*, which are the system outcomes as they affect other systems or subsystems to which the structure in question is related.

A given system may have a number of extrinsic functions if it has different impacts on various adjacent systems. For example, the automobile factory has the intrinsic function of making automobiles. In relation to the stockholders it has the *extrinsic* function of making profits, in relation to the government the function of furnishing tax revenues, in relation to the union the function of providing gainful employment. This is not so much a matter of differential perception as of differential effect of its output as experienced by related systems. The intrinsic function is readily identifiable by observing the throughput of a system as it evolves into a product. Extrinsic functions call for assessment of consequences with respect to a larger systemic context.

Though there may be many specific consequences of an organization's outputs for the surrounding environment, the major extrinsic function is the part the organization plays as a subsystem of the larger society. We shall refer to this functioning in relation to the larger structure as the *genotypic function* of the organization. Thus the research organization has an adaptive function in furnishing information so that the larger system can survive in a changing environment. The political party has a representative and compromise function in aiding the governmental structure to make decisions about the allocation of resources; the manufacturing concern has a productive function in creating goods.

SUBSIDIARY CONCEPTS

In addition to the basic constructs for describing organizational components and subsystems, we shall utilize four concepts for characterizing the overall functioning and structure of social organizations: (1) leading systems, (2) organizational space, (3) organizational culture and climate, and (4) system dynamic.

Leading Systems

The subsystems within an organization, regardless of how essential they are to the organization as a whole, are not equipotential in their influence on the total system. Thelen (1960) uses the concept of leading system to designate "a component system whose output exerts the greatest influence on the inputs of other component systems, and through this, controls the interactions of the suprasystem." He further observes that subsystems may vary in this characteristic during periods of rapid organizational growth, though a coordinating system having inputs and outputs to most or all of the other systems in the organization may be permanently leading. During growth, the leading system may be the latest system to develop "in the sense that it tends to be the 'executive seat,' for it obtains feedback and stimulation from all the other systems; it is the system best able to mediate between internal and external demands, and thus to guide the locomotion of the organism as a whole."

The circumstances which make a certain subsystem leading are various. One of the most obvious is the possession of a technology or skill which assumes major importance because of larger developments in the organizational environment. In the decade of the 1940's population sampling represented such a technique for social research and the subsystem incorporating this function became the leading subsystem in the U. S. Bureau of the Census and in many other research organizations. More recently the development of computer technology has nominated a new kind of subsystem for leadership, with implications yet to be worked out.

Organizational Space

The complex set of interrelated activities comprising the social organization can be coordinated to a social map which we shall call organizational space. By organizational space we refer to the locus of the various organizational activities and the behavior distances between members in carrying out their many organization-related tasks. Sectors of organizational space can be identified objectively by observing the behavior of members. Organizational space is not identical with physical space, though physical space is one of its components. The head foreman of the foundry might be physically closer to the foundry workers than to the plant manager, yet his frequency and closeness of contact with the plant manager might be greater than with his workers. Inferences about behavioral distances can also be made from the psychological or perceived separations reported by organizational members.

Organizational space is the social transformation of physical or objective space that provides the topography of the organization. It is the use of physical space for social objectives. This is obvious in the business enterprise that not only has separate offices for its differing levels of officers but separate dining rooms for these levels, so that there is one dining room for the vice presidential level, another for the lesser managers, a third for other supervisory personnel, and a cafeteria for rank-and-file employees. Geographical spread and separation, moreover, must occur in organizational operations since they cannot be conducted in a vacuum. And such spread of activities over physical space tends to make for behavioral and psychological separation as well.

There are four types of separation of organizational members with respect to organizational space. The first derives from *geographical separation,* which makes constant communication difficult if not impossible. The workers in the foundry and the sales force in the field are so separated by geographical arrangements that each group can know little about the sector of organizational space occupied by the other. In addition to geographical separation, we have a *functional separation.* Even if the salesmen and foundry workers could have a common dining room, they would still eat with their own kind. Common interests, problems, and language of the occupation would pose barriers to communication just as great as physical separation.

A third type of separation has to do with the *status or prestige* of position and function. White collar workers may communicate more freely with other white collar workers than with blue collar workers because they do not want to lower their status in the eyes of other white collar workers. Or secretaries may sit by themselves in the lunch room rather than mingle with their bosses because it would be presumptuous to assume that they have equal status with the executives. Finally, there is a separation on the basis of *power,* which is related to status and prestige but not identical with it. The authority hierarchy of the organization sets a pattern for the flow of communication. The formal functioning permits a man to raise questions with his immediate supervisor but not with his supervisor's boss. The same pattern will carry over into informal patterns of communication, so that the hourly employee will not seek out the general manager for a luncheon date.

The reason for introducing the concept of organizational space is twofold. We do not encounter an organization in its entirety from any single observational point. Interpretations of a system tend, however, to be based on experiences within one sector of organizational space. The discovery of informal structure by the Mayo group, for example, called attention to some sectors of the organization as experienced at the floor of the factory (Roethlisberger and Dickson, 1939). However, Mayo followers have been occupied too exclusively with such limited segments of organizational space. Even more common is the error of the management consultant who perceives that sector of the organization most available to the level of management he is serving. There have been few attempts to study organizations by systematic observations which encompass the whole of organizational space.

Since top leadership in any large organization is remote in organizational space from many of its operating sectors, it is a fiction to expect that the intelligence and wisdom of the top officials can intuitively assess the impact of a change in one sector upon other sectors. One procedural device is to provide channels of communication from below so that policy makers do not become captives to the information provided by the official bureaucrats around them.

The second reason for introducing the concept of organizational space is that many of the internal problems of organization, such as intrasystem conflict and strain, can be understood by an appreciation of where people stand in terms of that space. Just as the outsider overgeneralizes his observations of an organization from his limited perspective, so the organizational member sees the organization in terms of the functioning of his sector. Studies show that even foremen are rather poor judges of the perceptions, attitudes, and motivations of rank-and-file workers, and that the phenomenon of differential perception becomes more pronounced as the intervening organizational space becomes greater (Kahn, 1958; Likert, 1961).

The tendency of any group of people occupying a given segment of an organization is to exaggerate the importance of their function and to fail to grasp the basic functions of the larger whole. Some of this may be defensive, and some of it is related to circumscribed visible horizons (Tannenbaum and Donald, 1957). Loyalties develop to one's own organizational sector rather than to the overall organization. Conflict between departments can become bitter and persistent because the members of each do not accept common organizational objectives but only the specific tasks which comprise their daily lives.

Organizational Culture and Climate

Every organization develops its own culture or climate, with its own taboos, folkways, and mores. The climate or culture of the system reflects both the norms and values of the formal system and their re-interpretation in the informal system. Organizational climate reflects also the history of internal and external struggles, the types of people the organization attracts, its work processes and physical layout, the modes of communication, and the exercise of authority within the system. Just as a society has a cultural heritage, so social organizations possess distinctive patterns of collective feeling and beliefs passed along to new group members. In an industrial concern with a long history of amicable union-management relations there may be no stigma attached to the union steward who becomes a foreman, no feeling that talking to a company officer is an attempt to curry favor, and no countenancing of sabotage or stealing of company materials. Educational institutions also show marked differences in climate and culture. Even a casual visitor can detect differences between the atmosphere of Antioch, Swarthmore, City College of New York, the University of Oklahoma, and Princeton University.

In spite of the obvious differences between the cultures of organizations performing essentially the same types of functions, it is not easy to specify the dimensions of such differences. Though the subculture of the organization provides the frame of reference within which its members interpret activities and events, the members will not be able to verbalize in any precise fashion this frame of reference. They will be clear about the judgments they make, but not about the basic standards or frames they employ in reaching a judgment. The many subtle and unconscious factors which determine a frame of reference are not susceptible to direct questioning. The technique of participant observation has thus been more revealing about organizational climate than the typical survey. What is needed ideally for the study of organizational climate is participant observation to supply the insightful leads and systematic depth interviewing of appropriate population samples within the organization to insure adequate coverage. Such work might also facilitate the development of adequate conceptual and operational definitions of organizational climate, so that this potentially valuable research concept might become more than a vague analogy from meteorology.

Research has neglected organizational climate, yet it can provide rich returns for the understanding of organizational functioning. The limited studies of informal structures within organizations (Belknap, 1954 and Sykes, 1958) have supplemented our knowledge of the realities of organizational life, but they have still not provided an adequate account of organizational culture or climate.

System Dynamic

Lacking the built-in stabilities of biological systems, social organizations resort to a multiplication of mechanisms to maintain themselves. We have already observed that they develop reward structures to bind their members into the system, norms and values to justify and stimulate required activities, and authority devices to control and direct organizational behavior. In other words, there is an overdetermination of the behavior necessary to preserve the organization. People are not only rewarded for taking their roles, they receive constant reminders from the incumbents of adjacent interdependent roles, and they share an ideological environment in which their role behavior is legally appropriate and morally right. In an effectively functioning system the field of forces determining the behavior of the members is not dependent upon one motivational source nor upon a single individual. There is a cumulative pattern of many reinforcements exerting pressure in a single direction. The occasional deviant, or the occasional failure of a single reinforcement, is not especially important. In inexact popular parlance we say that the system is greater than the individual.

In system theory we speak of *dynamic homeostatis* or the maintenance of equilibrium by constant adjustment and anticipation. We shall use the term *system dynamic* to refer to this same characteristic in social organizations. Both the major system and the component subsystems are characterized by their own dynamic or complex of motivational forces which moves a given structure toward becoming more like what it basically is. For example, a hospital for mental patients organized as a custodial institution tends over time to become more of a custodial institution unless it is subject to new inputs from its supporting environment, and even then the system dynamic may resist movement from the custodial homeostasis (Belknap, 1954).

The Acquisitive and Extractive Mechanisms. The operation of system dynamics can be seen in the acquisitive and extractive mechanisms employed by systems and subsystems. Much of the organizational literature on this subject is apolitical and antiseptic (with the exception of the work of such political theorists as Harold Lasswell). It is strangely silent, except in the case of the simple economic model, about how a social system acquires the input necessary to maintain itself and carry on its functions. Social organizations, however, employ many mechanisms for acquiring energic input besides the sale of their product in a free market. It is characteristic of any organization to try to place itself in an advantageous position with respect to environmental resources and competing groups. Even a charitable organization will struggle to get as favorable an allocation from the United Fund as possible or will go outside the Fund to conduct its own moneyraising campaign if this appears as the more effective way of securing an adequate budget.

In the beginning there is no guaranteed reservoir of energy for the social organization. If it is to survive it must secure some continuing supply of materials and men. Acquisitive and extractive procedures are thus the primitive mechanisms by which negative entropy is attained. The general law of entropy states that any system will tend to run down, lose its differentiated structure, and become one with its environment. These death forces are countered in the most direct and simple manner in social systems by taking over and exploiting natural resources and by taking away the possessions and even the labor power of other groups—whether by persuasion, guile, or force.

The mechanisms for acquisition of energic input are directed both at securing advantages with respect to obtaining raw materials and a ready market and at utilizing effectively as much of the energies of its man power with as little cost to the organization as possible. Such acquisition mechanisms include the obtaining of legal priorities or monopolies on sources of supply or on markets; the influencing of the public through persuasion, information, and propaganda; transactions or deals with leaders of other groups; developing distinctive capabilities which will place the organization in a monopolistic position; maneuvers and price wars to liquidate rivals; and the development of reward systems within the organization to maintain a favorable ratio between organizational costs and organizational gains. Within the national state, organizations compete through such mechanisms. Outside national boundaries, there is also the resort to threat, intimidation, and organized force. As has been noted, the acquisitive self-interest in organizations is not limited to profit-making institutions. Universities and colleges scramble to receive support from the federal government as well as from more traditional sources. And universities, like business organizations, raid one another for top talent.

Well-established organizations also develop protective mechanisms to guarantee their advantageous position with respect to energic input. They may acquire ownership of the sources of supply or they may invest a great deal in the maintenance of the status quo, which is favorable to them. Similarly, subsystems within an organization seek to perpetuate their favorable position vis-a-vis other subsystems. In the field of liberal education it took some fifty years before the sciences could obtain equality with the humanities because of the protective devices of required courses and the fixed budget allocation to various departments. It is tempting to regard these protective devices as defense mechanisms similar to the defense mechanisms of individuals. Though it is of interest to establish genotypical similarities between categories, the more specific the prediction, the greater the danger in jumping from the individual to the collective level. The organizational persistence in holding to its established pattern in spite of some social change can affect social reality in a manner in which the individual cannot. A strong, well-entrenched organization is in fact part of social reality, and the self-fulfilling prophecy holds at the collective level much more than at the individual level.

A good deal of organizational structure is built around the acquisitive or protective self-interest of the system. For the past fifteen years the major part of our national budget has gone to defense. In most organizational structures there are special units which concern themselves with procurement of materials, recruitment of personnel, public relations, and relations with outside elite groups. Top management and leadership, with special staff help, will devote considerable time to the full exploitation of environmental resources and organizational capabilities.

SUMMARY

All open systems share certain properties, but these are insufficient for adequate characterization of specific systems. It is useful therefore to create categories of open systems and to attempt some delineation of their distinctive properties.

Social systems, for example, lack the fixed physical structure of biological and other physical systems. Social systems have structure, but it is a structure of events rather than physical parts, a structure therefore inseparable from the functioning of the system.

This unique aspect of social structure as compared with physical structure implies great importance to *maintenance inputs* (which sustain the system), in addition to *production inputs* (which are transformed and exported as the system functions). This aspect of social structure reminds us also that social organizations are contrived systems, held together by psychological bonds. The contrived quality of social systems and their quality of event-structure mean that they can be designed for a wide range of objectives, that they do not follow the growth curves typical of the life cycle of physical systems, and that they require control mechanisms of various kinds to keep their component parts together and functioning in the required interdependent fashion.

Three types of forces are involved in reducing human variability to the patterns required for organizational functioning: environmental pressures generated by the direct, observable requirements of a given situation, shared values and expectations, and rule enforcement.

The formal patterns of behavior achieved through rule enforcement are *role* behavior, sanctioned by *norms*, which are justified in their turn by *values*. Roles, norms, and values thus furnish three interrelated bases for the integration of organizations.

The integration process is complicated by the different dynamics of the major organizational subsystems. These include the production or technical subsystem, primarily concerned with the organizational through-put; the production-supportive subsystems of procurement, disposal, and institutional relations; the maintenance subsystem for attracting and holding people in their functional roles; the adaptive subsystem, concerned with organizational change; and the managerial subsystem, which directs and adjudicates among all the others. The presence of these subsystems and the formal role pattern in terms of which they function are among the major defining characteristics of social organizations as a special class of open systems.

4
Development of Organizational Structures

The Classical Models of Organization

Traditional theory about social organizations gave primary attention to the character of their internal structures and so approached organizational problems much more in terms of closed-system than open-system thinking. The three classical models of traditional theory are: (1) the sociological description of bureaucratic structure of Weber (1947), (2) the public administration account of Gulick (1937), and (3) the scientific management approach of Taylor (1923). Weber's concern was with the more fundamental problems of the formalization and legitimation processes by which role systems are elaborated and sanctioned. The public administration school and the advocates of scientific management were more interested in the practical problems of the best methods of organizing for effective functioning.

Machine theory, to borrow a phrase from Worthy (1950), is the generic term that covers all three models. The organization, though consisting of people, is viewed by all three as a machine, and they imply that just as we build a mechanical device with given sets of specifications for accomplishing a task so we construct an organization according to a blueprint to achieve a given purpose. Some of the major concepts, explicit or implicit, in machine theory are the following:

1. *Process specialization of tasks.* Efficiency can be attained by subdividing any operation into its elements. These partial tasks can be taught, expertness in their execution can be readily attained, and responsibility for their performance can be easily fixed.

2. *Standardization of role performance.* As tasks become fractionated, their performance becomes standardized. There is one best way to assemble a gun. Such institutionalization of functions also protects against costly blunders. At higher levels in the organization the same logic is followed by prescribing not only the purpose of the role but the means for achieving this purpose.

3. *Unity of command and centralization of decision-making.* The organization, though conceived of as a machine, is not necessarily self-directing. To maintain the coordination of the whole, decisions must be centralized in one command, and to attain perfect coordination there should be *man-to-man responsibility* down the line. To further insure unity of command there must be *a limited span of control*, so that no person at any hierarchical level has more subordinates under his supervision than he can control.

4. *Uniformity of practices.* Not all behavior in the organization can be prescribed by task standardization. Much behavior must be controlled by the specification of uniform institutionalized practices. Thus the same personnel procedures should be followed with respect to all individuals in a given status.

5. *No duplication of function.* One part of the organization should not duplicate functions being performed by another. There should be one centralized set of operations for the whole organization. The army, navy, and air forces should not have separate purchasing departments. Different departments in an enterprise should not have their own travel and transportation units but should have their needs met by one centralized section.

These concepts are seen in their clearest application in military organizations and in railroads. Machine theory has also been especially applicable to large scale organizations engaged in the mass production of goods and commodities. The assembly line of the automobile factory is an example of the efficiency that is sometimes attainable through the use of this approach to organization. The concepts of machine theory have, however, infiltrated thinking about almost all types of organizations.

The scientific management approach probably pushed more strenuously than the other classical models toward specification of how tasks should be organized. It envisaged men, in the words of March and Simon (1958), as "adjuncts to machines." Time and motion studies were its principal tools. Rest periods during the working day were studied in terms of the optimum recovery from physiological fatigue. Wages and incentive pay as the sources of motivation were conceived of in terms of a model of economic man. Moreover, the scientific management approach dealt almost exclusively with the production structure of the organization and had little to say about the maintenance, institutional, and managerial structures, except that the same rational economic man was assumed to be operating across the board.

Machine theory, then, was sometimes wrong and sometimes right in its basic tenets, but it was almost always inadequate in dealing with the complexities of organizational structure and functioning. It lacked the power of open-system theory to deal with significant organizational variables. Specifically, (1) it took little account of the constant commerce of the system with its environment. The constantly changing environmental influences necessitate constant changes in the organization. (2) It neglected many types of input-output exchange with the environment. It restricted input to raw materials and labor power. That input also consists of the values and needs which people bring with them into the organization was ignored. That input, in addition, consists of the social support of surrounding structures and of the public was also ignored. On the output side there was a similar exclusion of all outcomes besides the physical product exported.

(3) The concepts of machine theory paid little attention to the subsystems of organization with their differential dynamics and their own interchange within the organization. Each subsystem in the process of interchange codes and filters its input according to its own characteristics. The mutual influencing of the different subsystems and the problems of their interrelationships are dealt with sparsely, if at all, in the older theories. (4) The semiformal and informal structures created within the formal organization, often as a reaction to institutionalization, were also conspicuously neglected. Merton (1957) and other sociologists have described the unintended and dysfunctional consequences of organizing according to machine principles. (5) Machine theory conceived of organizational constancy as a rigid, static arrangement of parts. Open systems, and all organizations are open systems, are indeed characterized by the maintenance of a steady state, but this maintenance is a dynamic process of preserving patterns of relationships by constant adjustments.

March and Simon (1958) sum up many of the weaknesses of machine theory when they state:

It is because activities are conditional, and not fixed in advance, that problems of organization, over and above the assignment problem, arise. For convenience, we may make the following specifications, without interpreting them too strictly:

(a) the times of occurrence of activities may be conditional on events external to the organization or events internal to the organization;

(b) the appropriateness of a particular activity may be conditional on what other activities are being performed in various parts of the organization;

(c) an activity elaborated in response to one particular function or goal may have consequences for other functions or goals. (p. 27)

A number of sociologists, following the lead of Robert Merton, have pointed out the inadequacies of machine theory with respect to the dysfunctional consequences of some unanticipated, yet logical, outcomes of bureaucratic structure. These theorists have made valuable contributions to our understanding of organizations but each writer has limited himself to a single, though different, aspect of organizational dysfunctioning. March and Simon have presented an incisive analysis of these models and the following account summarizes their analysis.

The Merton model (1957) starts from the problem, already described, of reducing the variability of human behavior to predictable patterns necessary for organizational functioning. From this demand for control comes the emphasis upon reliable behavior for which the resort is to rule enforcement. Standard procedures are outlined and supervision instituted with penalties for deviant behavior. The anticipated consequence is achieved when people follow role prescriptions and use categorization as a basis for making decisions. Problems are approached in terms of some ready organizational precedent rather than a thorough search for alternatives. The emphasis upon role and position decreases personalized relations (Figure 1).

The unintended consequences of such reliance upon rules and their enforcement include a rigidity of behavior which in turn increases the amount of difficulty with clients. The official follows the easily invoked rule even though it may not be the most appropriate response to the problem presented by the client. Rigidity reduces organizational effectiveness, and risks the support of clientele. It is no accident that the sales division of an organization tries to counteract this tendency by adopting the motto that the customer is always right. On the other hand, as long as rule enforcement continues to be the major emphasis in the organization, rigidity of behavior is fostered by the easy defensibility of individual action which adheres to the rules. The difficulty which this rigidity creates with clients only serves to reinforce the original pattern of lack of discriminating behavior on the part of the organization member. Since he is challenged in the performance of his duties his defense is to fall back upon some highly visible rule to prove that he has only been doing his duty as prescribed by statute. He is primarily concerned not with solving the problem of the client before him, but with the defensibility of his own behavior. Hence the client problem becomes aggravated.

The Merton model rightly calls attention to an important un-

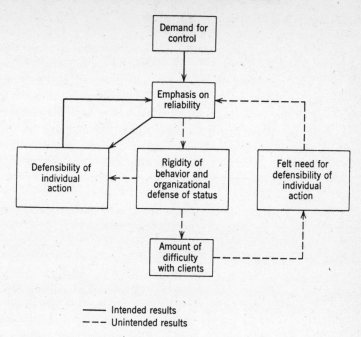

Figure 1   The simplified Merton model. (From *Organizations,* James G. March and Herbert A. Simon, New York: Wiley, 1958, p. 41.)

anticipated dysfunctional consequence of the heavy reliance upon rule enforcement to insure reliable patterns of behavior. But it is a simplified model dealing with one unanticipated consequence of one major type of control employed in organizations. The increased problems with clients growing out of rigidity of organizational behavior is a specific illustration of the failure to recognize the true character of organizations as open systems in constant interaction with a dynamic environment.

The Merton example applies primarily to the members on the boundaries of the organization who deal with the outside public. The same rigidity, however, can develop among the people on the inside of the organization in their observance of rules.* The unintended consequences can be similar to those Merton emphasizes with respect to clients. There can be increased problems of one subsystem of the

* The theories of Likert (1961) and McGregor (1960) emphasize the internal dysfunctional effects of conventional models of management, particularly in terms of motivational costs. These and other normative theories of organization, which will be discussed in later chapters, are in this respect complementary to the Merton model.

organization relating to another subsystem with resulting failures in cooperation, communication, and coordination. Another dysfunctional consequence within the organization itself is the lack of innovative and spontaneous behavior necessary for effective organizational functioning. It is impossible to prescribe role requirements precisely and completely or lay down rules with sufficient specification to cover all contingencies arising in a single week of work of a complex organization. An enterprise must rely both upon stable role patterns and the spontaneous actions of people directed toward the accomplishment of organizational goals. An almost exclusive emphasis upon rule enforcement, with its resulting rigidity, can destroy this innovative aspect of organizational functioning.

In Chapter 3 we pointed to three sources of patterned cooperation which account for the existence of organizations: (1) interdependence with respect to task accomplishment, (2) shared norms and values, and (3) rule enforcement. Machine theory neglects the *shared values* and makes inadequate use of *task interdependence*. Reliance on *rule enforcement* limits the attainment of organizational objectives either because it fails to call into play some of the needed types of behavior (it may in fact inhibit them) or because it leads to other types of dysfunctional consequence.

A similar attempt to spell out one type of dysfunctional effect of machine theory is found in the work of Gouldner (1954). The Gouldner model, like the Merton model, starts with the demand for control being met by the use of general, impersonal rules. Gouldner stresses the impersonal nature of the rules, which decreases the visibility of power relations within the group. (In a democratic society it is assumed that members of an organization will be more highly motivated when their supervisors are not arbitrary authority figures.)

The unanticipated consequence of the general, impersonal rules, however, is the creation of minimum acceptable standards of organizational behavior. The minimum standards of performance tend to become the common pattern for most organization members and thus become the maximum standards as well. The person who deviates in the direction of higher performance is the rate buster, the eager beaver, or the company man. Minimum performance, however, leads to a discrepancy between organizational goals (held by leaders) and organizational accomplishment. Pressure is put on supervisors to check more closely on subordinates. This increases the visibility of power relations within the group, leads to an increase of interpersonal tension, and disturbs the equilibrium of the system (Figure 2).

Again the Gouldner model correctly calls attention to some of the

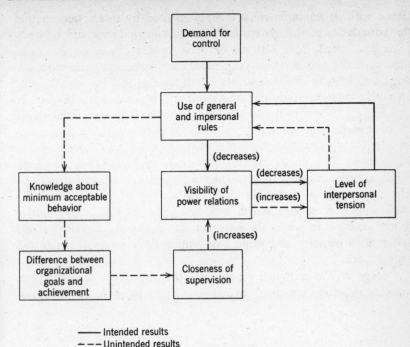

Figure 2 The simplified Gouldner model. (From *Organizations*, James G. March and Herbert A. Simon, New York: Wiley, 1958, p. 45.)

self-defeating effects of reliance upon rule enforcement. It does not, however, inquire into the psychological inputs into the organization which account for the dysfunctional outcomes. Nor does it deal with consequences other than the acceptance of minimal standards and the increased tension in the group growing out of close supervision.

The specific models described above have pointed out the deficiencies of machine theory in operation but have been too limited in scope to provide an adequate basis for the prediction of organizational behavior. Another approach to organizational theory is to abandon the closed-system approach of the machine model and to examine more directly the interrelationships between the subsystems of a structure and between the total system and its environment.

THE DEVELOPMENT OF ORGANIZATIONS

Utilizing the basic concepts of the previous chapter, we shall turn to applying an open system approach to the development of organizational structures.

The input and output transactions of the open system in commerce with its environment are supplemented by interactions within the boundaries of the system between role incumbents and between suborganizations. The patterns of these events constitute the functioning of the organization, take place in specific environmental settings, and involve specific people. These settings and the events going on within them are the determinants of subsequent events (Figure 3).

Stage 1. The two major sets of determinants in the initial stages of an organization are the *environmental pressures,* or the common environmental problem, and the *characteristics and needs of the population.* The environmental pressures generate task demands, which are soon met by appropriate *production or technical structures.* The requirements of the objective task thus exert pressures for the patterning of activities which will complete the task. A primitive system emerges in which the basis for the productive activities is the cooperative response of people based upon their common needs and expectations.

Stage 2. The primitive production structure which emerges from the task requirements does not necessarily constitute a social organi-

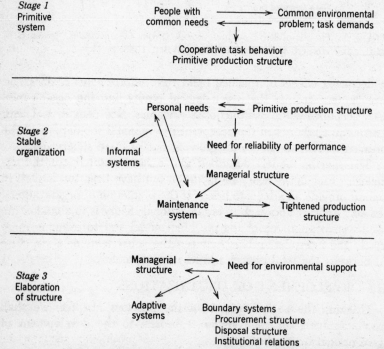

Figure 3   Stages in development of organizational structures.

zation. It is immediately dependent on the fit between the needs of people, their shared values, and their immediate cooperative effort in solving a common problem; as a result, it lacks consistent role performance and effective coordination of roles.

In addition to those common needs around which they cooperate, the people involved in the production system have their individual needs, aptitudes, and aspirations. Every step of the productive process of the organization, though carried out by human beings, is not necessarily going to coincide with their immediate needs. Moreover, the role requirements for stability and uniformity are not consistent with the facts of human variability. The closure of the first cycle of activities in task accomplishment does exert a pressure toward its repetition but there are the counter pressures of the many other interests and activities of the people involved.

The bases of the primitive production structure are the shared values and expectations of people dealing with a common problem. This is not enough to guarantee stability of socially patterned behavior. The urgency of the common problem and individual perceptions of urgency may vary over time. There will be idiosyncratic interpretations of the expectations about cooperative behavior. A host of individual decisions will arise about the kind of participation in the joint undertaking: precisely what each person is to do, how he should do it, when to do it, and the like. Around the first crude cooperative efforts will be built devices for formulating and enforcing rules—in other words an *authority structure*. As the source of binding pronouncements and the locus of decision-making process, the authority structure is the basis of the managerial system. People no longer merely do what the task demands of them; they follow the rules which are seen as binding on members of the system. We have emphasized the development of rules, but it often happens that variability in behavior is first brought under control by a strong personality. Many early groupings are held together by such individual leadership. Organizational progress comes, however, from a development of a system of impersonal rules.

Though the authority structure is the first manifestation of the managerial system, another major arm soon develops. This is the maintenance subsystem whose specialized function involves keeping track of the rules, socializing new members into the system and its regulations, and administering rewards and sanctions. This subsystem soon develops a life of its own.

The interaction between the primitive production structure and the variable character of human beings results in the development of patterns with a maintenance function. Considerable energy is expended to preserve the technical or production structures for task accomplishment. Special arrangements are required to insure that people will stay within the system and will carry out their roles in a reliable fashion. The maintenance structure develops and administers a reward system and mediates between the demands of the members and the requirements imposed by the technical structures. The maintenance structure thus faces toward the people in the system and toward task requirements.

The systematic use of rewards is ancillary to the establishment and operation of a set of rules prescribing certain forms of behavior. The maintenance structure relies heavily upon *rule enforcement*. Thus to the original *shared values* and *task requirements* is added the third and essential component for the stable social organization. With rules and rule enforcement the loose, primitive production structure becomes elaborated and tightened.

Informal Structures. Though the maintenance arm of the managerial system, if successful, does reduce the variability in performance, it does so at some cost to the personalities of the people in the system. Maintenance mechanisms generally do not seek to cope fully with the personal needs of people but only to effect some viable compromise between the task requirements and the psychological wants and gratifications of those on the job. The inevitable conflict between collective task demands and individual needs is sometimes erroneously attributed to the fact that human beings are inherently lazy and have to be bludgeoned into productive performance. The real reason is that the technical systems for getting work done are set up to insure predictability, efficiency, and coordination of the efforts of a great many individuals. The uniformity, the routinization, and the fragmentation of behavior run counter not only to the factor of individual differences but to the needs of people for self-determination, spontaneity, accomplishment, and the expression of individual skills and talents.

The compromises which are brought about by the maintenance structures are of two kinds. One type is the imposition of external rewards, especially money, to make the intrinsically unsatisfying job more desirable. The other is to introduce some minor reform in the character of the work itself. The first method keeps people performing but does not meet their basic needs; the second is too slight to affect many people deeply. The consequence of this organizational frustration is the development of an informal structure among the people in the system. They will interact, make decisions of their own, and cooperate among themselves, and so find gratification for their needs for self-determination and self-expression. To their work-oriented supervisor, they may be job holders, fillers of organizational roles; to their fellows they are personalities. Every group thus develops its own pattern of communication, interaction, and informal norms to meet the social and emotional needs of its members. Informal structure of this type is not necessarily in opposition to the basic objectives of the organization, but it frequently is in contradiction to the prescribed institutional paths for reaching those goals. One continuing problem for organization theory and practice is how to direct the enthusiasm and motivation of informal groupings toward the accomplishment of the collective task.

Stage 3. Supportive Structures at the Boundaries of the Organization. The fact that the organization is an open system means that it is constantly interacting with its environment to dispose of its product, to obtain materials, to recruit personnel, and to obtain the general support of outside structures to facilitate these functions. There is a constant need for environmental support. Hence subsystems develop within the organization to institutionalize environmental relationships and guarantee such support. An organization will often have separate departments for merchandising, advertising, and selling; for recruiting and selecting personnel; for procuring raw materials; and for public relations and contact with the larger society.

Though different organizations will assign different functions and names to these departments, three types of boundary systems can generally be identified.

The procurement operation is divided into the function of obtaining the input of materials to be converted and the input of personnel to get the job done. These two functions are characteristically found in separate bureaus or divisions of the organization. Theoretically part of the boundary subsystems, in practice the procurement of materials usually is tied into the production structure and the recruiting of personnel into the maintenance system. The basic condition for this allocation is a fairly abundant supply of materials and people in the external environment. When materials and personnel are difficult to obtain, the structures responsible for their procurement must face more completely toward the outside world and divorce themselves in part from the production and maintenance functions. Thus the securing of personnel for given periods of time in industrial organizations through contracts with unions is not handled through the personnel officer but through a vice president in charge of industrial relations.

The disposal function of marketing the product is found in its most exaggerated form in profit-making organizations with elaborate merchandising and sales systems. The primary emphasis is upon inducing the public to purchase the product of the organization, but feedback on the success of this effort will lead to changes in the product itself. Many nonbusiness organizations expend little energy in direct product disposal. They are not in the position of having their source of input support tied directly to the disposal of their output. For example, educational institutions have as their product the imparting of knowledge and the increase of knowledge, and they do little to market their graduates.

All organizations have as their essential boundary system what Parsons (1960) calls the *institutional system* or relations with the larger community or society. The operation of any organization depends not only upon the specific reception of its product but upon the support and legitimation of its activities by the larger social structure. Corporations deal with the federal government with respect to policy and practice on mergers and monopolies and tax laws, among other things. Corporations also relate to the general public regarding support for private enterprise and types of restrictions on private power. Awareness of this problem has led to concern with the image of the company in the public mind. In similar fashion, the public school interacts with the community it serves through its Board of Education. An educator named as president of a large university soon finds that little of his time is available for educational administration within the university. He is primarily its external representative, dealing with alumni groups, foundations, potential donors, governmental officers, civic and other public groups. The term *public relations* tends to be restricted to institutional advertising, and is not an adequate concept to cover this important function of relating the organization to the total social system of which it is a part.

Changing Environmental Pressures and Adaptive Subsystems. Organizations do not exist in a static world. The surrounding environment is in a constant state of flux and a rigid technical system, though preserved by an excellent structure, does not survive. The pressures for change are communicated most sharply to the organization when there is no market for its output. This is often too late for organizational survival and so many organizations develop *adaptive structures* whose function it is to gather advance information about trends in the environment, carry out research on internal productive processes, and plan for future developments. The maintenance activities are directed at survival in the limited sense of preserving the organization as it is. They are internally oriented and mediate conflicts between internal demands and existing production structures. The adaptive mechanisms face out upon the world and are concerned with solving the conflicts that arise between present organization practices and future environmental demands.

THE VERTICAL DIMENSION OF ORGANIZATIONS
Division into Subclasses with Varying Dynamics

We have described the articulated subsystems of organizations with respect to the flow of work and the specialized mechanisms for carrying it out, but we have neglected one basic aspect of organizational structure. In addition to the horizontal dimension according to which people are placed into production, maintenance, or adaptive systems, there is the vertical dimension associated with the managerial structure but not completely overlapping it (Figure 4). In Chapter 3 we referred to the allocation parameters of the reward system in organizations. Position in the vertical dimension is a matter of the differential power, privilege, prestige, and rewards enjoyed by the incumbent. In many industrial companies, for example, personnel are classified as hourly employees or salaried employees. In the army the major distinction is between enlisted men and commissioned officers; in universities between academic staff and non-academic personnel. Finer gradations are of course clearly visible in all three types of organizations but they merely emphasize the divisions of members according to this basic vertical gradient of privileged position. Though there is a correlation between power and the various perquisites of prestige, privilege, and reward, it is not a perfect correlation and we cannot equate the vertical dimension with the managerial system. Professional staff members, for example, may be well paid and may

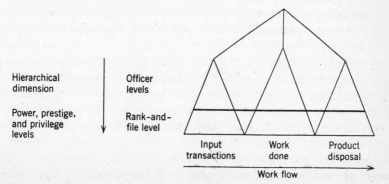

Figure 4 Two dimensions of organizational structure.

enjoy all the privileges of the organization and may still be low in the power hierarchy.

The reason for calling attention to this dimension of organizational structure is that it has implications for organizational functioning. Even though the members of a vertical organizational class, like the hourly workers in industry, do not represent an articulated subsystem of the organization, they do have attitudes, values, and interests in common with their fellows and at some variance with the salaried members of management. Since there is usually little formal representation of their interests within a firm, they often become members of an outside organization, namely the union, to represent their interests. The point we are making is, however, a general one. The vertical structure of an organization is not merely a gradient of reward; it frequently divides members of the organization into two or more classes. The *dynamic* or common motivation of a group of members is determined both by their work function and by their hierarchical position in the structure. A man is both carpenter and rated hourly worker, for example. Attempts at organizational change designed to improve organizational functioning frequently examine only the horizontal dimension of the organization, the flow of work. They do not inquire into the arrangements whereby the hierarchical distribution of rewards creates classes of varying patterns of motivation.

THE DYNAMICS OF THE SUBSYSTEMS OF ORGANIZATIONS

Formal structures, once created, generate pressures for their survival and enhancement. Organizations cannot be understood wholly in terms of the interaction of past, present, and future environmental requirements and personal needs of members. The very structures created to meet these demands exert a force in their own right. Once developed, a production system will exert profound influence upon the rest of the organization. Once developed, maintenance structures will be a powerful force for conservatism in the perpetuation of existing practices. One reason why the findings and concepts of small group experimentation within the laboratory are not adequate for an understanding of organizational functioning is that they deal with momentary pressures and not with the potency of formalized structures having historical depth and breadth. They dynamic of a structure derives, as we noted in Chapter 3, from the common interests of its members sharing a common fate, from the common norms for carrying out their functions, and from the common values which rationalize and provide a rationale for their activities. The dynamics contributed by different organizational subsystems will appear as we examine these structures in greater detail (Table 1).

PRODUCTION OR TECHNICAL STRUCTURES

The task requirements are met by the development of line operations in which the major responsibility of each role incumbent is directly related to some aspect of the major task of the organization. The organization of people to get the job done generally moves in the direction of specialization and fractionation of the component elements of the work process. More emphasis has been placed in the past upon breaking down a task into minute specialties than upon division of labor based upon functional units.

The scientific management school of Taylor (1923) addressed itself to the problems of rational analysis of the productive process and the appropriate forms of coordination. Standards for every piece of behavior were set on the basis of time and motion studies. Performance control was provided by records completed at the end of every day and transmitted up the line for the scrutiny of the higher offices. The foreman had daily records on the work of his men; the division chief had records on the sections under his foreman, and so on to the organizational summit. Similarly, the older industrial psychology was largely concerned with the efficiency of carrying out given tasks and devoted considerable attention to the physiology of fatigue, time and motion studies, and the influence of temperature and lighting on the work process. The modern extension of this approach can be seen in the concept of man-machine systems.

A comparable approach is the administrative theory of Gulick (1937). He examined the principles of organization of the work process and concluded that the basic factors for departmentalization were purpose, process, person, and place. Jobs could be allocated to a department on the basis of their general purpose, their similarity in terms of process, the people who would carry out the assignments, or the place and clientele to be served. Gulick's conclusions were that the factor most appropriate for a given system was contingent upon circumstances and upon the results desired. A small organization might have to forego purpose specialization in favor of process specialization. For example, if there is not enough work for a private secretary assigned to each officer, it is more efficient to have a central secretarial pool. In a large organization, however, a full-time secretary can be assigned to each officer. Moreover, no matter which factor is selected for primary organization, the other factors must be taken into account for secondary types of organizational structure. Gulick's

Table 1 FORMAL SUBSYSTEMS OF ORGANIZATIONS: THEIR FUNCTIONS, DYNAMICS, AND MECHANISMS

Subsystem Structure	Function	Dynamic	Mechanisms
I. Production: primary processes	Task accomplishment: energy transformation within organization	Proficiency	Division of labor: setting up of job specification and standards.
II. Maintenance of working structure	Mediating between task demands and human needs to keep structure in operation	Maintenance of steady state	Formalization of activities into standard legitimized procedures: setting up of system rewards; socialization of new members.
III. Boundary systems			
A. Production-supportive: procurement of materials and manpower and product disposal	Transactional exchanges at system boundaries	Specifically focused manipulation of organizational environment	Acquiring control of sources of supply; creation of image.
B. Institutional system	Obtaining social support and legitimation	Societal manipulation and integration	Contributing to community, influencing other social structure.
IV. Adaptive	Intelligence, research and development, planning	Pressure for change	Making recommendations for change to management.
V. Managerial	1. Resolving conflicts between hierarchical levels	Control	Use of sanctions of authority.
	2. Coordinating and directing functional substructures	Compromise vs. integration	Alternative concessions; setting up machinery for adjudication.
	3. Coordinating external requirements and organizational resources and needs	Long-term survival; optimization, better use of resources, development of increased capabilities	Increasing volume of business; adding functions; controlling environment through absorbing it or changing it; restructuring

early theoretical formulation has not been followed up by more refined analysis nor by systematic research to find the parameters of the relevant variables on the basis of which one organizing factor rather than another could be adjudged superior.

The production systems of organizations develop a *dynamic of technical proficiency*. The force field is generated by task requirements and the ideology is directed toward task accomplishment. The concentration upon getting the task done has the consequence of developing standards of skill and method. This does not mean, however, that the production structure will automatically move to the highest level of technical efficiency. It may well become arrested at a stage of development which falls far short of optimal functioning. Nor are the proficiency standards of the production department all-inclusive criteria for organizational costs as a whole. Technically proficient workers may be so negative in their attitude toward the company because of its enforcement of rules that they contribute heavily to turnover or do not step out of their technical roles to cooperate on matters of major concern to the organization. They may blink their eyes to stealing of company materials or other forms of cost and waste. In other words, though technical proficiency arises as a natural value from the production system, that fact does not guarantee overall organizational efficiency.

MAINTENANCE STRUCTURES

The maintenance structures are motivated toward *maintaining stability and predictability* in the organization. The dynamic here is one of preserving a steady state or equilibrium. This may take the form of a tendency toward organizational rigidity, the preservation of the status quo in absolute terms. Or it may take the form of preserving the pattern of existing relationships by adjustments of processes and parts according to some constant ratio of energic transaction. For example, the volume of business may be increased with no appreciable shifts in the patterning of activities. The maintenance dynamic in turn results in pressures toward formalization or institutionalization as the simplest method of achieving stability.

Many specific mechanisms are developed in the interests of preserving a steady state in the system. Selection procedures are employed to screen out applicants who do not seem likely to adapt to the system. Socialization or indoctrination practices are utilized to help fit new members into the organizational mold. System rewards are provided for membership and seniority in the system. Regulatory mechanisms are developed to give some automatic corrections to departures from the norm of organizational functioning. Rules are elaborated and provisions made for their policing. Decisions are made on the basis of precedent. Uniformity becomes the ideal, and standard operating procedures are worked out for human relations as well as for production requirements. A classic example of the psychology of the maintenance system is the sign on the wall of a railroad office: "Don't say it, write it. You can't file a conversation."

The most general statement that can be made about all the mechanisms for maintaining stability is that they seek to *formalize or institutionalize* all aspects of organizational behavior. If there is a standardized operating procedure which has been legitimized for all relevant human behavior in the system, then the problem of predictability and stability has been logically solved. All organizations move toward formalization and role prescription to insure appropriate selection from the vast realm of possible behaviors within the structure. Unfortunately this logical solution for decreasing variability and change is too much of a tour de force to be a complete psychological solution. It runs the risk of substituting organizational ritualism for genuine functionalism.

At most moments in organizational history the easiest way of insuring survival, at least for the short run, is to maintain things as they are and permit no changes. This is the characteristic tendency of the maintenance substructure. Moreover, its conservatism derives in part from the tendency to maintain itself as well as from the need to maintain the organization as a whole.

The conservatism of the maintenance structure is often a source of frustration to people in other subsystems of the organization. Among the agencies of the federal government, for example, the Civil Service Commission has often been encountered as an impediment to change, a source of information and edict regarding what may not be done. In years past this agency so diligently protected the old ways that the adaptation of the federal service to new demands—the demands of World War II, for instance—took place outside the usual jurisdiction of the commission.

There are times, of course, when the opposition of a maintenance structure to the demand of some other organizational subsystem appears as liberal and benign—protecting members of the organization from more strenuous effort or from the necessity of learning new ways. The maintenance stance is nevertheless conservative of the organization as it is, and the occasional proposals for organizational change which emanate from maintenance structures are likely to be superficial in nature, more designed to create increased satisfaction with what is than to create more satisfying alternatives. The reconstruction of General Motors by Alfred Sloan and his early colleagues into a close federation of quasi-competitive suborganizations is an example of change on a serious scale, change launched from the apex of the managerial structure involving the structure and policy of the entire organization (Drucker, 1964; Sloan, 1963). The "My Job Contest," launched in the same organization a generation later (Evans and Laseau, 1950), was the creature of the personnel division. Its effects on the structure and policy of the General Motors Corporation are unrecorded and difficult to discern, a fact which has occasioned no great surprise either within the organization or outside it.

Pressures to change often come from external demands which imply altering the character of the organizational task. These pressures are felt first by the sectors of the organization closest to the environment, the marketing and sales groups and the leaders who deal with the outside world. Next in sensitivity to external pressures is the production department concerned directly with the primary tasks to be done. The maintenance structures are the most insulated from such forces. The maintenance people face inward upon the organization. If the company cannot sell huge cars with nonfunctional body styling in large numbers, the production people may grumble but they will turn to changing their product. The secondary structures of maintenance are threatened in two respects. Some large segment of their activities may no longer be required, or demands may be made upon them for which they lack the resources to cope. In other words, the maintenance structures are as concerned with their own preservation as with the survival of the organization as a whole. In fact, the typical complaint from the production departments is that the administrative services do not facilitate the production operations but throw up road blocks to efficient functioning. Exaggerations in the criticism of administrative services are apparent, but there may also be some spark of fire which produces the smoke.

BOUNDARY SYSTEMS OF PROCUREMENT AND DISPOSAL

The functions of procurement and disposal, though directly supportive of production structures, have to do with transactional exchanges with the environment. They are directed at environmental manipulations of a specific and focalized kind and their function is largely unidirectional. The marketing and advertising divisions of an enterprise are concerned with influencing the buying public. Their attention is directed outward toward clients as malleable objects to be influenced. The primary job of the people in these structures is to break through whatever resistance the consumer may show. Public resistance and consumer need may affect the organization so that it will change its product or service, but decisions of this type are made in the managerial structure. Within fairly wide limits there is no easy method of determining in advance the exact outcome of a vigorous and ingenious production and sales campaign. Hence the initial push in the marketing and sales structure is toward influencing the client, not toward influencing the company to change its type of product. If these efforts are not attended by success, then management will evaluate the situation and will use as relevant data the reports from the marketing division about their difficulties with the public.

ADAPTIVE STRUCTURES

Since maintenance systems face inward upon the organization and even inward upon themselves, the survival requirements of the system in a changing world lead to the creation of units and departments concerned with problems of adjustment. For example, there may be a small planning group working closely with the heads of the organization, or small research units to gauge the needs of the outside market, or a large department of research and development engaged in experimentation on new processes, new products, and product improvement. These functions of planning, research, and development, which permit the organization to exploit a changing environment rather than to be exploited by it, are essentially the role responsibilities of the top leadership. In large organizations and especially in technical systems the governing group needs the help of specialists devoting their full time to research, development, and planning. A large enterprise like the General Electric Company will apportion a sizeable chunk of its resources to various forms of research with respect to increasing basic knowledge in the physical sciences, applying such knowledge to the manufacture of new and improved products, and investigating the needs of the changing world which the company serves. Sometimes these adaptive functions will be vested in the traditional departments concerned with maintenance functions; sometimes they will be adjuncts to existing task units either in production or sales; sometimes they will be located in new departments serving directly as one arm of top management.

The type of output and the type of dependence upon the external environment affect the form of adaptive activities. In contrast to General Electric, automobile companies deal with a single complex product which calls for little basic scientific research. They are, therefore, more concerned with the utilization of knowledge than with the development of new knowledge. Research and development are geared into existing production and sales units, and tend to lag behind the changing world instead of anticipating its changes. Former Secretary of Defense Charles Wilson, who had been president of General Motors and reflected well the culture of his industry, could never understand the need for basic research by the armed services. Basic research to him was just a name for the research of people who did not know what they were doing.

Most universities have relatively few and indirect transactions with their external environment and are poorly staffed for gathering information about changing demands and for determining how to utilize their resources to meet these demands. Though population increases and the trend of more young people from middle and lower income groups to go to college have been obvious since the end of World War II, few universities have developed systematic plans and policies for dealing with the cumulative impact of these developments. The general pattern among private colleges is to admit a slightly larger number of students each year until overcrowding becomes obvious and then to raise admission standards to prevent inundation. State universities and other public institutions which have less freedom in holding to arbitrary quotas for admission now face and will continue to face unusual problems of adjustment. To criticize educational institutions for failure to anticipate such foreseeable developments is to ignore the fact that they have lacked staff who could devote themselves to this type of research and planning. Universities have enjoyed considerable autonomy in their academic functioning and have not had to develop many specialized adaptive mechanisms. There are many ways in which education gains by being free from the "market test" with which industry is continuously confronted. An indirect and unintended effect of this freedom, however, is the poor adaptive response of educational institutions to those occasional massive demands which cannot be denied.

The adaptive function, like the maintenance function, is directed toward the survival of the organization. Although the maintenance function faces inward and the adaptive function faces outward, they are similar with respect to another basic tendency. Both move in the direction of preserving constancy and predictability in the conditions of organizational life. The maintenance function moves toward a constant set of internal structures. The adaptive function tends to achieve environmental constancy by bringing the external world under control. One method is to extend the boundaries of the organization so that it incorporates more of the external world. If rival companies can be swallowed up, the major company will have better control over what had been a competitive market. If raw materials present problems of fluctuation and unpredictability, the company will attempt to set up subsidiaries which own the sources and process the raw materials. In an older period of history public officials who might cause difficulty could sometimes be placed within the organization by the simple device of putting them on the payroll. Where it is not possible to incorporate pieces of the external world into the organization, the trend is to control external forces so that they lose their independence as external forces. Through public relations and advertising the company will attempt to create the need for its product. In the past the automobile industry has placed relatively little of its resources into market research, compared to the huge amounts allocated to advertising campaigns. The thrust has been toward molding public taste to fit the product, rather than changing the product to meet public taste and need.

The adaptive function can move, however, in both directions. It can strive to attain control over external forces and maintain predictability for its operations in this fashion, or it can seek internal modification of its own organizational structures to meet the needs of a changing world. Both tendencies will be at work in the same organization and the apparent illogic of organizational action is sometimes due to the compromises effected between these opposing trends. The hypothesis seems tenable that the dominant tendency in the powerful organization will be to seek control over the environment rather than to modify internal structures to accord with external changes. The organization thus will proceed on the principle that it is easier to make the world adjust than it is to adjust to the world, and the latter alternative will be adopted only if the first offers small hope of success.

The character of the social system is to impose its restraints and prescriptions on its members. If people spontaneously maintained a patterned form of cooperation, there would be little need of formal structure. A vital element in organization is the acceptance of basic role-patterning by members and leaders alike. When obvious malfunctioning occurs, it is easier to attack the external cause and attempt to control it than to give up the internal arrangements. If the public is not buying a product, a new sales campaign is more likely to be conducted than research to find out what the public really wants. If the new crop of students admitted to a college is not doing well in courses, it is easier to raise admission standards than to change the curriculum and teaching methods. A change of internal structure is a threat to the organization. To resolve an organizational problem by changing the environment constitutes no such threat. Indeed, if it can be brought off successfully, it affirms the power and rightness of existing organizational structure.

The limiting variable is the relative openness of the system to external influence. The American Medical Association, with its restriction of apprentices and its prestiged and privileged position in the body politic, is less open to outside influence than a political party constantly seeking the majority endorsement of a capricious public. Hence the American Medical Association will attempt to change society first and its own internal program second.

The choice between internal and external change does not only depend upon degree of openness; it also depends upon the extent of the needed modification. Sometimes the modification requires changing both people and organizational structure (the multidetermined patterns of interaction), and sometimes just people, or certain of their specific practices and ideas. If the problem can be met by changing people's specific behavior, that form of change is likely to be adopted in preference to a solution which involves changing both specific behavior and generalized institutional practices. Thus if an organization is confronted with the alternative of changing some preferences in its clientele or changing its own structure and personnel, it will take the former path. If, however, it must change outside structures and personal habits, as against a limited internal change in practice, it is more likely to seek the latter solution. In general, structural change means radical change in what is considered legitimate and proper; it implies new role prescriptions, new roles, and the task of getting people to accept their new roles and even to like them. This has been one of the reasons for the difficulty of achieving racial integration of schools in some southern states. Not only must many people come to accept a new pattern of legitimacy for Negroes, but some of them must also favor the changes themselves. Otherwise a tough minority of people who dislike the changes and who will not accept their legitimacy can exert more influence than a larger group moved only by a willingness to abide by a new law which they personally dislike.

Organizations sometimes do attempt to change their environment by seeking to modify existing external structures as well as people's preferences. They seek the passage of new laws or the revision of the economic or social structure in which they operate. Radical political movements are of this character. In this category also would fall the attempts of industrial concerns to smash the labor unions. Though such externally directed efforts at changes in social structure are sometimes attended by conspicuous success, their failures are even more notorious. Industrial companies were markedly unsuccessful in destroying organizations of labor either by direct attempts or by indirect efforts at undermining their morale. Radical movements have been less successful in effecting direct changes in the political structure than in furnishing ideas for change which have had a gradual influence on the major political parties.

Both the maintenance and the adaptive function have the effect of expanding the original organization. As the adaptive function is recognized, it leads to such new and specialized structures as departments of research and development. As it seeks control of the external world, it calls for bringing more of the outside into the organization, for developing activities to control the external forces, or at least for obtaining continuing information from outside. Hence it creates a powerful dynamic for organizational growth.

MANAGERIAL STRUCTURE

As we have already indicated, the managerial system cuts across all of the operating structures of production, maintenance, environmental support, and adaptation. It is the controlling or decision-making aspect of the organization and its parts. We have traced its origin to the need for stability and predictability in the cooperative efforts at solving a common problem. The first managerial function of maintaining the system occupied the major attention of management in the beginning and then became elaborated into the maintenance structure. The insurance of continuing inputs and a market for outputs were the next concerns of management, and again supplementary subsystems developed to implement top decision-making. Institutional relations remain, however, as a continuing concern of the management structure. The adaptive mechanisms were once the exclusive province of the men at the top of the hierarchy. Again organizational elaboration created specific groups to help in this function. The complexity of organizational structure implies that the functions of management are also complex. Three basic functions can be distinguished: (1) the coordination of substructures, (2) the resolution of conflicts between hierarchical levels, and (3) the coordination of external requirements with organizational resources and needs.

The four types of dynamics created by the substructures of the organization (the proficiency dynamic, the stability force, the push toward environmental manipulation, and the pressure for change) are often in conflict and must be resolved or kept in bounds by the managerial structure. Management not only has the function of coordinating current environmental pressures with internal organizational forces, but also adjudicates between the demands of the substructures of the system. Overall control is maintained by decisions which either resolve the differences between the subparts or keep them sufficiently localized and quiescent so that the organization preserves some semblance of unity. The adjudication function more often than not moves in the direction of *a dynamic of compromise*. It is much easier for management to meet conflicts on a day-to-day basis, making concessions first to one part of the organization and then to another part, than it is to attempt the thorough reorganization which abstract logic might dictate. The alternation of concessions in response to the mobilization of forces means that organizations often jolt along and move by jerks and jumps. They will be inactive about change too long and then move too rapidly on a single dimension of change. Movements in one direction will be counteracted by movements in another direction. Such jerky progress is often found in large complex organizations and is the result of compromises between the various substructures in the total system. To avoid some of the consequences of abrupt shifts in policy and to give continuity to decision-making, adjudication procedures will develop in organized groups. This is particularly true in political and labor organizations, is somewhat true of educational institutions, and is perhaps of less consequence still in industrial organizations.

The dynamic of compromise handles conflicts between hierarchical levels as it does between substructures. It is easier to meet the demands of one subclass with a concession than to try to solve the problem by organizational restructuring. In organizations in which representative democracy is not operative, the demands of those at the lowest levels tend to be muted in the long hierarchical passage to the top of the structure. What does reach top management are the indirect effects of the hierarchical conflict or the demands transmitted from outside organizations of employees.

In addition to its internal adjustment function the managerial structure has the major task of coordinating external requirements with organizational resources and needs, i.e., it must set and implement policy with respect to the problems under study by the adaptive structure. In some organizations there is no separate adaptive subsystem, and management either gathers its own intelligence or acts with little systematic information about external problems. Any overall consideration of the relationship between the organization and its surrounding environment generally leads to decisions which attempt to optimize this relationship. The optimization may be in the direction of insuring the stability of the system, of utilizing resources more effectively in its ongoing operations, or taking advantage of potential capabilities of the system to do additional things.

The dynamic for change generated in the adaptive structures must always be implemented through the managerial structure. This is so because change will affect the whole organization and top management cannot delegate the responsibility for modifications in basic policy without transforming the organization itself. When the adaptive substructure develops in an organization, the decision-making power with respect to adaptation remains with management; it is the intelligence function—the gathering and assimilation of data, and perhaps the making of recommendations—which is delegated to the new substructure. The implementation of proficiency for productive processes and of stability for the maintenance processes does not necessarily call for obvious changes in organizational structure, however, and so will often be carried out by the substructure itself.

At any given time management may be more influenced by one substructure than another. Top management positions, for example, may be held by people who have moved up from the production rather than the adaptive structure. In general, where the management structure has been more influenced by the production and maintenance subsystems than by research development and planning departments, it has met its problems by accepting the formalization dynamic of its maintenance unit and the technological way of thinking of the production people.

THE INSTITUTIONAL SYSTEM

Parsons (1960) has made an excellent case for distinguishing between the managerial structure concerned with internal administration and allocation of resources within the organization, and the decision-making centers occupied with broad problems of external relations. He reserves the term *managerial system* only for the former and adds the label *institutional system* for the latter. In addition he would subsume under a third level, *the technical system,* most of the functions we have described under the headings of production, maintenance, procurement and disposal, and adaptation.

In Parsons' words:

But not only does such an organization [a formal organization] have to operate in a social environment which imposes the conditions governing the processes of disposal and procurement, it is also part of a wider social system which is the source of the "meaning," legitimation, or higher level support which makes the implementation of the organization's goals possible. Essentially, this means that just as a technical organization (at a sufficiently high level of the division of labor) is controlled and "serviced" by a managerial organization, so, in turn, is the managerial organization controlled by the "institutional" structure and agencies of the community. (pp. 63–64)

Thus a business enterprise enters into the institutional system through its board of directors rather than its manager, the school system through the board of education rather than the school superintendent, and a university through its board of trustees and president rather than its deans and other internal administrators.

There has been a neglect of the institutional function in organizational theory because such theory has been dominated by an interest in business enterprises. And in the business field, Parsons points out, the institutional relations with the government are often carried by automatic controls and regulatory mechanisms. Support for business activity is so much a part of the accepted pattern in our culture that we tend to overlook the institutional aspect of organizational functioning. Even in the business world we find instances of very clear recognition of this function and heavy emphasis upon it. In some public utility companies, for example, the awareness of public power enterprises as dangerous competitors has resulted in top leaders directing a great deal of time to the institutional function. These leaders not only court the public with services going beyond the furnishing of electric power but also become integrated into the community structure through active participation in civic undertakings.

In small organizations, where the division of labor is not great, the same set of officers may operate at the technical, managerial, and institutional levels. The small college president may move from one to another of these functions as he deals with alumni, with internal managerial problems, and with technical problems of curriculum. These different types of activities, however, involve different kinds of information, different skills, and different problems.

One very significant derivation which Parsons makes from his analysis of the three system levels (the technical, the managerial, and the institutional) is the mythological character of an often-invoked principle: unity of the chain of command. Machine theory, it will be recalled, postulates a single chain of command with orders coming down the line from the top authority figure. Parsons, however, points out that there are significant breaks in the chain at the three system levels. For many problems the managerial executive is not competent to make decisions which his professional experts can make. He can hold them responsible for the consequences of their decisions. He can veto their recommendations. He may be utterly unable, however, to propose alternative or even meaningful changes. As a result many of the decisions in modern industrial plants with respect to production are made by research engineers and not by managerial executives. There is a similar break between decisions of internal management and problem solving at the institutional level. Even when the same persons try to handle both assignments, the unexpandable factor of time means that they are likely to neglect one function while dealing with the other.

As social structures grow with respect to these three levels of functioning, a genuine lag appears between the formal rules of the organization and organizational practice. A large university may have bylaws, going back to its days as a small college, which give the president and his board of trustees power and responsibility for making all decisions—from the addition of a new course in the curriculum or the promotion of an instructor to the building of a new library, the addition of a new school, or the launching of an endowment campaign. The board of trustees, however, lacks the knowledge to pass upon each new course or promotion, and if it concerned itself with such details it could never get through its agenda. Hence it merely functions as a rubber stamp for the technical problems, though on rare occasions it may exercise its veto power. In fact the technical decisions are made almost entirely in the academic departments themselves. What is to be taught and who is to teach it are professional decisions made by the professionals.

Acceptance of decision-making at these three levels by the appropriate people is perhaps found more frequently in American society than in many other countries, because division of labor and development of bureaucracy may have proceeded more rapidly in our country. Workers in international organizations such as the United Nations and UNESCO report that different nationals have different expectations with respect to organizational decision-making. Where the decision concerns technical problems, Americans turn to the professionally trained experts, readily accept their recommendation, and are not especially worried that the professionals are thus playing a leadership role. The English executives expect the staff under them to do a staff job but to come up with documented alternatives. The executive then goes through the form of making the decision, and the status relationships are preserved. The French prefer that decisions be made at the higher echelon, and staff members will not enter into the decision-making process unless specifically invited to do so by their superior.

Whatever the national differences are, there is much to be gained in understanding organizations by following Parsons' model. One practical implication is that where there is confusion in the upper echelons regarding the levels of system functioning, we would expect lowered organizational effectiveness and circuitous devices for maintaining organizational viability. The inadequacy of traditional organizational theory to deal with these problems of line authority stems from its static, closed system character. Parsons (1960) sums up his approach in these words:

I may generalize about the nature of the two main breaks in line authority which I have outlined by saying that at each of the two points of articulation between subsystems there is a *two-way* interchange of inputs and outputs. What has to be "contributed" from each side is qualitatively different. Either side is in a position, by withholding its important contribution, to interfere seriously with the functioning of the other and of the larger organization. Hence the *institutionalization* of these relations must typically take a form where the relative independence of each is protected. Since, however, there is an actual hierarchy, since in some sense, the "higher" authority must be able to have some kind of "last word," the problem of protection focuses on the status of the lower-order element. Accordingly, we find that such institutions as tenure serve, in part at least, to protect professional personnel from pressures exerted by management—pressures that are often passed on down from board levels. (p. 69)

THE MAXIMIZATION PRINCIPLE

The managerial structure, like all the substructures of the organization, has a self-maintenance dynamic. The structures which we have called maintenance systems (training and indoctrination, the administration of rewards and promotions, rule enforcement and morale building activities) seek to develop and preserve stable patterns for the whole organization. But every subsystem also attempts to maintain itself. The managerial structure, as the decision-making group for the whole system, is thus concerned with the preservation of the entire organization, though this sometimes is perceived as the preservation of the particular management group. Since the maintenance dynamic is all-pervasive throughout the organization, why is it not sufficiently potent to result in highly rigid and unchanging structures? Without question there is considerable resulting stability, but there is also growth, expansion, and change in almost all social systems. In fact, one of the basic properties of social systems of the bureaucratic type is that they move toward maximization, toward growth and expansion. Parkinson (1957), in noting this tendency, contends that increases in personnel and positions are not accompanied by increases in productivity.

The maximization principle can and frequently does override the maintenance dynamic for five basic reasons: (1) the proficiency dynamic leads to an increase in organizational capabilities; (2) expansion is the simplest method of dealing with problems of internal strain; (3) expansion is also the most direct solution in coping with problems of a changing social environment; (4) bureaucratic role systems in their nature permit of ready elaboration; and (5) organizational ideology encourages growth aspirations.

(1) The task requirements generate a proficiency dynamic for getting the job done well. Though maximum efficiency may not be achieved, the competitive pressures from outside the organization and the experience with the task within the organization will tend to produce some technological improvements in the work process. These improvements will result in increased capabilities of the plant for greater output with resulting increases in the sales and supportive functions. An example of such technological expansion in the steel industry was reported in the *Wall Street Journal* (January 31, 1961) as follows:

> "We don't particularly want to expand capacity, but we can't help ourselves, every step we take to raise efficiency seems to increase our capacity," one steel executive says. Equipping steel-making furnaces to use oxygen cuts costs but also lifts capacity. Pure oxygen is used in furnaces to speed the process.
> Bethlehem Steel Corporation is raising the capacity of its big Sparrows Point plant ten per cent to a million tons a year, mainly by equipping open hearths to use oxygen. (p. 1)

Even when the steel industry was operating at some 50 per cent of its total capacity because of lack of markets, it was still expanding capacity for more steel production. That such growth might have consequences of a harmful nature to the industry and lead to further reduction in operations did not prevent the development of increased capabilities. And the statement of the steel executive that they were operating in a situation beyond their control is highly significant. The maximization dynamic is not the expression of a few ambitious personalities at the top of the organization but the outcome of the total field of forces of the socio-technological system.

(2) The contrived character of a social system means that its subsystems are rarely coordinated so as to produce completely harmonious functioning of the whole. System strain inevitably occurs because of the inability of any mode of organization to meet all the demands placed upon the system. As Gulick (1937) pointed out, in the use of either purpose, process, person, or place as the basis of departmentalization, the selection of one criterion is made at the expense of other criteria. And as has been demonstrated in the above paragraphs, the

various substructures have their own characteristic dynamics which are often in conflict with one another.

The typical method of dealing with internal system strain is compromise. The compromise solution tends to make concessions to subsystems rather than requiring them to give up essential functions or resources. If one department brings pressure against a second department because the second unit seems overstaffed and overprivileged with respect to status and frequency of promotions, the tendency of management is not to cut back the one department but to upgrade the other. The compromise solution also makes for expansion when conflict between two departments is handled by setting up liaison offices between the two units. Because each subsystem will mobilize all its forces for self-preservation, it is easier for management to meet internal problems by adding rather than by subtracting. Forces for stability in the system thus generate forces for expansion. The more the system creaks, the more it requires patching to keep going.

Another method for dealing with the system strain evidenced by conflict between substructures is to create a larger structure which will absorb the subsystems and so reduce their identity and semi-autonomy. This was the solution attempted in the unification of the armed services. Though some duplication of functions was eliminated by defense unification, the total structure expanded to include an overall defense department above the three subsystems of the army, navy, and air force. Without entering into the controversy over the merits of unifying the armed services, we do want to point to the strength of the forces mustered by each subsystem to preserve its basic functions and to suggest that reorganization in the interests of streamlining operations can result in further expansion.

It is more probable that organizations will deal with internal problems by encapsulating them in expanded structures than by eliminating parts. The basic political maneuver is to create a new committee rather than to abolish the old one, or to increase the size of the committee and thus immobilize some of the old sources of strain. Speaker Rayburn saw the solution to the Congressional Rules Committee as one of increasing its membership, thus breaking the hold of its conservative members without removing them and without violating the doctrine of seniority. In most organizations it is notoriously more difficult to abolish an old committee or board than it is to create a new one.

To control the dissatisfactions of informal groups within the system, formal status may be accorded to some mechanism for their expression. Management may respond to the complaints of employees with a formal grievance committee or an elaborate suggestion system. Again internal strains of a system result in an enlargement of the structure.

(3) The third basic reason for the strength of the maximization principle is the strain on the organization resulting from the demands of the external environment. Since the organization is not self-contained, it attempts to control the sources of its energic input and the market for its output. It moves from an early condition of survival on a day-to-day basis by increasing its margin of reserves. One way to do this is by increasing the volume of business to obtain a greater absolute profit. At some point, however, sheer increase in volume may lead to diminishing returns, and organizational size may taper off until some modification of organizational functioning is effected, followed by a new spurt in growth.

This dynamic of expansion stems in part from the specialized roles in which responsibility for the organization is vested. In a small enterprise the head may have such a generalized role of handling all problems and of dealing with his small staff on a personal basis that he may be content with keeping the business small. In large organizations the top leaders are less concerned with personal satisfactions from a small retinue of faithful followers and more concerned with specialized roles of assessing and increasing the organization's capabilities in relation to the changing environmental forces. Their roles and careers are tied into the success of the organization and success is rarely associated with organizational suicide. In fact, in those organizations whose demise is assured by their accomplishment of their mission, there are special problems with respect to the motivation of leaders and followers as they approach their goal. Because of their special position with respect to knowledge of the functioning of the organization, the leaders are more likely to understand the advantages of increased capability of some substructures of their organization by relatively slight improvements and expenditures of energy.

In addition to expansion in the volume of business and in the structures for controlling the external environment, the organization may take on new functions and new structures to meet the new demands made upon it. It generally will do this, however, without abandoning its existing structures. Any existing structure represents an investment and has a maintenance dynamic of its own. It can be modified but not easily obliterated from the larger system. In all national emergencies the United States government has responded to changing needs not by the abolition of old line departments but by the creation of new agencies. Franklin D. Roosevelt, who had a profound understanding of the nature of bureaucratic structures, was a master in the creation of new agencies, many of which survived into the Republican administration. Since organizations do not drop activities and structures as readily as they acquire them, organizations which survive tend to expand. Almost any organized group which has survived over the years is the accretion of all sorts of activities and practices. The Protestant churches have added social service functions and perhaps these comprise their major activities. But the minister still gives sermons on Sunday, and Sunday school classes are held for children as if the theological function of the church were of significance. The oldest organization of them all, the Roman Catholic Church, is a remarkable collection of institutional techniques and organizational devices reflecting its long history of operation.

(4) Another reason for the expansion of organizations is the very nature of bureaucratic structure. Bureaucracy is a rational social device for dealing with problems by legitimizing a role system. The immediate response to any evidence of system strain or externally induced pressure is the creation of new roles and new rules. If management finds workers poorly informed about the company, the personnel department may be authorized to issue a house organ to remedy this gap in organizational communication. In governmental areas we pass a law, or issue an administrative edict, and in other organizations equivalent action is taken to legitimize new roles. So prevalent is this tendency that additional functions or roles are carefully scrutinized by the budget bureau, or its equivalent, to determine whether or not there will be additional expenses. Though the proposers of expansion generally answer in the negative, the additional activities will be used in another year as the basis for requesting additional budget. In universities academic departments will ask for new courses, hopefully stating that existing personnel can handle the task, only to find that the emergency arrangements for handling the extra work are no substitute for permanent additional budget.

It is customary to satirize our readiness to pass a law to solve any problem, but the facts of the matter are that every year our state and federal governments literally pass thousands of laws, many of them leading to some form of bureaucratic expansion either within or without the governmental structure. As a bureaucratic society we are likely to see more rather than less growth of organizational structure in the future.

(5) Finally, a factor making for maximization in organizations is the ideology generated to provide justification for the organization's existence and functions. This ideology not only suffers from inaccu-

racies as a scientific description of the organization but as ideology it is more pretentious than any specific organizational objective. The labor union may have the objective of advancing the interests of the workers in collective bargaining with the company, but the general ideology of unionism may support the functions of insurance, of recreational facilities, or even of political activities on a national scale. In America there is a positive cultural value placed on bigness and growth.

The conditions which facilitate organizational expansion follow directly from the underlying causes of the growth of structures in all open systems. In the first place, the greater the internal strains and the greater the impulsion to meet them with compromise, the greater will be the expansion of activities and of structures. The conditions productive of internal strain are many: the more complex the total structure, the greater the possibilities for some degree of dysfunctional relationships between the parts; the more autocratic and arbitrary the structure, the greater the strain between human needs and organizational demands; the greater the proportion of nonfunctional to functional channels of communication, the greater the strain between organizational parts. Among the conditions making for compromise rather than decisive solutions are the degree of authoritarian structure, the ambiguity of the information about the consequences of alternative solutions, and the strength of the maintenance dynamic in various substructures.

In the second place, the openness of the organization to environmental influence, its immediate dependence upon its external world for sources of energy input and for the disposal of its product, is an important determinant of growth. Though all organizations are open social systems, they vary in their degree of openness. Where a system is more self-contained and draws heavily upon the rewarding character of the activities of members, there is more opportunity to preserve the status quo. It also follows that openness of a system to environmental influence makes for change because the environment itself is in a state of flux. Where there is relative stability in the milieu upon which the organization depends, there is also less impulsion for change in the enterprise. The heavily endowed private college catering to an upper-class clientele preserves the classical college education of the past far better than the state universities. Even the privately endowed college, however, cannot help being affected by population pressures and the cumulative effect of a 5 per cent-a-year inflation.

Growth and expansion will occur more readily in enduring organizations whose energy cycles entail an immediate and direct transaction with the environment. Most forms of business enterprise are examples of this type of organization. They must market their output immediately and reconvert the money into materials and labor. Organizations which do not depend upon immediate environmental transactions can make more use of ritualism to build walls between themselves and their environments. The university which derives its support from alumni and from the general community is not faced with the immediate conversion of its output into renewable sources of energy. They are systems where the cycle of energy transformation is long and involved. Thirty years after graduation an alumnus may make a substantial contribution to his alma mater. Or the outcome of some university activity may result in donations remote in time and place from the activity itself. Technical or economic systems are subject, however, to much shorter and simpler energy cycles.

In the third place, the more the organization approaches the model of a pure bureaucracy, the more likely it is to move toward expansion. Organizations, though dominantly bureaucratic, can contain elements of feudal status or of personal charisma. In general, European organizations have not divorced themselves as completely from feudal remnants as have American institutions, which developed in a pioneering nation launched by a revolution against feudal barriers. The traditionalism and ritualism of the status type of authority gives stability to a social structure. Since they are not seen as rational devices for solving problems, the rules of the game are not changed to accord with internal strains or external pressures. In some European countries the hierarchy of society in prestige and privilege has carried over to some extent into industrial corporations. The effect of charisma on organizational expansion is less predictable. A strong personality can often develop a small organization into a far-flung enterprise through the vigor of his leadership. In larger organizations the strong leader may dominate his followers with his unchanging set of values and policies. In such instances any change in organizational growth may have to wait upon changes in top leadership.

In the fourth place, the ideology of the organization should be examined with respect to its aspirations and its absolutistic character. The grandiose nature of the system values may set goals which call for unlimited expansion, as in the Nazi ideology of the Third Reich. The absolutistic elements in the ideology of the organization (ours is the true religious faith or the correct political doctrine) impel its members toward proselyting rather than tolerance. Part of the conflict in the world today is based upon the assumptions of both communist and capitalist societies that, as carriers of the correct way of life, they must grow at a faster rate than their opponents. In addition to the ideology of a particular system or subsystem, the values of the society may explicitly equate growth and size with virtue and excellence. And if the society itself is a growing one, any organization that merely maintains its old rate of operations is losing its competitive position and is regarded as having reached "the sere and yellow leaf."

In addition to the general conditions which foster the maximizing principle in organizations, some social systems have a built-in device for maximization. If the transactions with the external environment can be so managed as to give the organization a greater return for its output than the energy required for its production, then the system will move toward maximizing this favorable type of exchange. The profit-making organization is the pure example of this sort of built-in maximization. In this case there is a measurable form of feedback and the trend is toward increasing the activities of the organization to insure greater profits. This is true whether the profits go to the managers, the absentee owners, or the members of a cooperative. The greatest profits in such organizations occur during a period of rapid growth, and stock market investors are constantly looking for such growth stocks. After the period of rapid growth and high profit, the organization is driven to further expansion and greater activity. This is due to the need to preserve absolute profits by a greater volume of business. Even where the profit motive is nonoperative, organizations with visible measures of feedback upon their operations are spurred toward maximizing their functioning. University departments in the various disciplines seek to attract more or better students into their courses this year than last, turn out more Ph.D.'s, improve the quality of their graduate training so they can place their graduates in better positions, or increase the research productivity of their staffs.

The maximizing principle operates differently, however, where the output system is not in competition with other systems and where restricting the number of members increases the privileges and powers they enjoy. Under this condition, there will be resistance to growth in size, as in the days when trade unions of skilled workers restricted the number of apprentices, or in the days of rapid population growth when the medical profession followed equivalent practices. But even in these instances the maximization principle is operative in directions other than membership growth. The monopolistic power position of the group is increased by the development of functions in the political spheres of life.

Not all the new functions and the expanded activities of organizations are effective devices for controlling their external environment. The maximization principle in itself cannot predict the efficacy of these attempts. But it does predict that organizations will attempt to control their environment not by subtraction but by addition of substructures and functions. They will also attempt to utilize available sources of energy efficiently in order to attain a better strategic position vis-à-vis outside forces as well as to provide a margin for any added functions.

In short, the maximizing principle means that the organization seeks to acquire more of the resources which will furnish energy for its activities, to utilize these energies more efficiently in its productive output, and to improve the ratio of return to the organization for the energy invested in its output. Maximization pushes in the direction of growth and expansion, of control over energy sources outside the organization both with respect to intake and output; it results in mergers and the assumption of more and more functions; it is the principle behind the attempt to create favorable social conditions for the organization in the external environment; it can be seen in the staff activities of research, planning, and development by which the organization controls the future as well as the present.

THE CONFLICT DYNAMIC

In keeping with the structural-functional approach, we have given emphasis to the factors which have to do with creating and maintaining a stable system. We have not viewed that system as static but as moving toward a closer approximation of its ideal form. Nevertheless, the effect of our analysis may be to reify organizational forms into absolutes of social behavior. Our interest in what ties people together in a system should not lead to the assumption that social ties, once explained, can thereafter be accepted as *fixed entities* in a study of organizations. The patterned relationships as the compromise outcome of antagonistic forces continue to reflect the essential conflicts which they have compromised. We have indicated that authority structure arises to maintain predictability but that informal structure inevitably arises to maintain the conflict between rules and regulations and human needs. We have also pointed out the fundamental cleavage in organizations based upon differentials in the hierarchical gradients of power, prestige, and reward. Though people in the lower ranks accept their lot to the extent of minimal conformity to organizational demands, they are often individually in rebellion against the organization, and sometimes they collectively attempt to modify it. Finally, there are competitive conflicts between the many functioning subsystems of the organization.

Dahrendorf (1958) has contended that the structural-functional approach in sociology, with its orientation toward problems of integration, neglects conflict processes. The facts of social disruption in general strikes or in race riots are too readily dismissed as unintentional and dysfunctional. Dahrendorf maintains that models of social structure must include recognition of built-in conflict associated with the dichotomy of positive and negative dominance roles—a dichotomy produced by the necessary authority structure.

The general point is that organizations are less integrated than biological systems; their patterns of cooperative interrelationships also represent constrained adjustments of conflict and struggle. The adjustment is not only the compromise of past antagonisms but also of immediate differences of feeling, belief, and interest. The contrived character of organizations means that by nature they contain built-in sources of conflict. Many facts of organizational life can be readily understood if the model of organizations is one which views social patterns not as fixed and rigid interrelations but as the outcome of a continuing tug of war. The implication of this model is that organizations are always in process of change and that the constancy attributed to the system is exaggerated by the fact that the verbal label for describing an organization remains the same even when the processes of organization do not. For example, the Democratic Party in the United States is the same organization from year to year, or from state to state, more in name than in the processes going on within the structure. Another implication of this approach is that the nature of the built-in conflicts in a given organization should be studied for an adequate understanding of its present functioning and future stability.

Conflict can have both dysfunctional and functional consequences, as Coser (1956) has pointed out. It can lead to heightened morale within a subsystem and it can lead to solutions which move more in an integrative than a compromise direction. Organizations generally develop mechanisms to handle internal struggles and devices to dull the sharp edges of conflict. As we have already noted in large complex organizations one of the main functions of top management is the adjudication of competing claims and conflicting demands.

SUMMARY

Three classical models of organization are considered: the bureaucratic theory of Max Weber, the public administration account of Luther Gulick, and the scientific management approach of Frederick Taylor. All three have elements in common, including an emphasis on process specialization of tasks, standardization of role performance, centralization of decision-making, uniformity of practice, and the avoidance of duplication of function. These emphases are descriptive in the case of Weber; they have the quality of advocacy in the theories of Gulick and Taylor.

None of the three models, even the Weberian, seems to us to deal adequately with the transactions between an organization and its environment. All three therefore offer no ready way for treating this major source of organizational characteristics and organizational change. Open-system theory is offered as a more adequate framework, and the development of organizations is described in open-system terms.

Three stages of organizational development are considered. At Stage 1 certain characteristics of a human population and some common environmental problem interact to generate task demands and a primitive production structure to fulfill them. At Stage 2 devices for formulating and enforcing rules appear. An authority structure emerges and becomes the basis for managerial and maintenance subsystems. Stage 3 sees the further elaboration of supportive structures at the organizational boundaries—structures for procurement, disposal, and institutional relations.

Each of these organizational subsystems develops its own dynamic tendencies—technical proficiency in the case of the production subsystem, stability and predictability in the case of the maintenance subsystem, external control and internal change in the case of the boundary and adaptive subsystems, and compromise, control, and survival in the case of the managerial subsystem.

These dynamic tendencies of subsystems are not always manifest in the same terms nor with the same strength. Moreover, there are tendencies which characteristically dominate in organizations. One of the most important of these is the maximization principle, which reflects organizational efforts at growth, insured survival, and environmental control. The tendency toward maximization, which solves at least temporarily many problems of internal strain and external threat, is often overriding in human organizations.

5

A Typology of Organizations

One can approach the study of organizations by asserting the uniqueness of every social structure and avoiding any generalization until empirical evidence of close similarity is in hand. This was the point of view urged on members of the research team of The University of Michigan by leaders in almost every organization studied. "Ours is a unique organization. We can't really be compared to any other setup." Railroad men saw their organizational problems as distinctive; so too did governmental executives. Insurance company officials reacted similarly, as did the managers of manufacturing concerns both large and small. The moment they started to talk about their problems, however, their claims to uniquenesss were invalidated. From an analysis of their problems, it would have been difficult to tell the railroad executive from the chief of a governmental bureau or the insurance vice-president from his counterpart in an automobile company. Though there are undoubtedly unique aspects in any social situation, there are also common patterns, and the deeper we go, the greater the genotypic similarities become. On the other hand, the global social theorist can become so involved in certain abstract dimensions of all social situations that he will be unable to account for the major sources of variance in any given situation. The common-sense approach to this dilemma is to create a typology. Organizations are assigned to certain types about which generalizations can be made. Thus there are voluntary and involuntary organizations, democratic and autocratic structures, centralized and decentralized hierarchies, expressive and instrumental associations. Organizations are classified even more commonly according to officially stated purposes such as education, profit-making, health, religion, social welfare, protection of the interests of labor, and recreation.

Most typologies of organizations, like most typologies of personality, tend to oversimplify the complexities of many interacting factors and to propose pure types based upon the presence or absence of a single characteristic. Typologies thus can be expanded indefinitely as some new factor is seized upon to indicate an additional class. The process is convenient but logically unsatisfying. The fact that a given organization possesses a characteristic that permits it to be classified as a particular type is less important and instructive than the *extent* to which this characteristic holds for the entire organization and what other factors also typify it.

One approach then is to regard the type-defining characteristic as a dimension along which organizations can be placed on the basis of having more or less of the attribute in question. In some instances, of course, a single continuous scale will not apply. For example, organizations either possess a democratic legislative structure or they do not. All organizations in which the legislative process is conducted by the body politic or by elected representatives are not equally democratic; they are, however, qualitatively different from organizations in which laws are made as well as administered by those at the top of the management hierarchy.

Moreover, parts of organizations sometimes show the same differences in kind which distinguish one entire organization from another. One part of an organization will possess a given characteristic and others will not. For the staff manning a penal institution the organization is a voluntary one; for the other inmates it is not. A further consideration is the fact that organizations represent the interaction of many factors, and the number of dimensions which could be used to describe them approaches the infinite. We shall follow the procedure of describing what seem to be the significant dimensions of organizational structure and functioning. Any organization can then be mapped into this set of dimensions and described as being high or low in each. The attributes of a given organization then consist of its position on each of the dimensions.

Not all characteristics are of equal importance in understanding the functioning of organizations. While there may be no one basic essence as called for by some type-theories, some attributes are of much greater significance than others. Accordingly we shall distinguish between *first order factors,* which describe the *genotypic function* of the organization, and *second order factors,* which in general are related to these basic functions.

GENOTYPIC FUNCTIONS

By genotypic function we refer to the type of activity in which the organization is engaged as a subsystem of the larger society. Thus we are concerned with the through-put or work that gets done in relation to its contribution to the surrounding social structure. Just as we considered the substructures of production, maintenance, adaptation, and management as they related to the total organization, so we shall describe organizations as they assume a production, maintenance, adaptive, or managerial role in the society.

Organizations then fall into four broad classes, though minor subtypes can be distinguished within each broad category.

(1) *Productive* or *economic* organizations are concerned with the creation of wealth, the manufacture of goods, and the providing of services for the general public or for specific segments of it. These organizations can be subdivided into the primary activities of farming and mining, the secondary activities of manufacture and processing, and the tertiary activities of service and communication. For the society as a whole they provide an instrumental integration. They provide the output—food, clothing, shelter, and the rest—for some of the most basic human needs. They also provide the rewards which are an inducement for people to keep the collective order working.

(2) *Maintenance* organizations are devoted to the socialization of people for their roles in other organizations and in the larger society. Organizations like the school and the church are the maintenance structures of the social order. Again a subdivision is possible between (a) the direct function of maintenance, as in education, indoctrination, and training, and (b) the restorative function, as in health and welfare activities and institutions of reform and rehabilitation. All these types of activities help to keep a society from disintegrating and are responsible for the normative integration of society. The groundwork for the maintenance structures has been laid in the early socialization process of the family.

(3) *Adaptive* structures create knowledge, develop and test theories, and, to some extent, apply information to existing problems. Universities (in their research activities) and research organizations carry on this adaptive function for society as a whole. Less directly adaptive activities can be found in artistic endeavor, in which there is an enriching of experience and the creating of new conceptualizations of experience.

(4) Finally, there is the *managerial* or *political* function, the organizational activities concerned with the adjudication, coordination, and control of resources, people, and subsystems. At the apex of political structures is the state, which provides a specific form of legitimation in its legal statutes and which has a theoretical monopoly

on the use of organized physical force for mobilizing the society against external enemies and internal rebels. The state is thus the major authority structure of society. In addition to the various formal governmental subsystems, there are such adjunct political structures as pressure groups, labor unions, and organizations of other interest groupings such as farmers, educators, manufacturers, and doctors.

Penal institutions as instruments of law enforcement are political organizations. They represent the repressive side of the law in their punitive and custodial aspects. As rehabilitation agencies, however, they have a socialization or normative function.

Society is sustained (1) through the rewards of its economic system, which provide powerful instrumental motivation toward socially-required behaviors; (2) by the maintenance structures of education and religion, which inculcate the general norms and specific behavioral codes; and (3) by the political structures which pass and enforce laws.

These three major types of integration are a more complex expression of the three bases of social systems: (1) task requirements in relation to needs, (2) shared values and norms, and (3) rule enforcement.

In brief, for a society to endure there must be economically productive activities which meet basic needs and provide basic services. There must be a central set of values and norms with socializing agencies to inculcate these belief systems and to provide general and specific training for social roles. To insure some viable integration or compromise among organized groups and interest publics, there must be an authoritative decision-making structure for the allocation of resources. Finally, in an advanced society specialized agencies develop for the creation of knowledge and for fostering artistic endeavor.

These major tasks are distributed among organizations which generally specialize in a single function but make supplementary contributions in other areas. Industrial organizations, for example, though concentrating on the economic function, make contributions to scientific knowledge; in the physical sciences they have their own laboratories concerned with increasing knowledge. Many business organizations develop political ways of dealing with their environment to insure a favorable allocation of resources. The manufacturing industries will press for high tariffs to rule out competition from foreign producers. The oil industry will seek favored tax treatment in depletion allowances. The airlines will try to acquire governmental subsidy through mail contracts or outright grants for the building of airports.

A single organization depends in part upon the contribution of other types of organizations to maintain itself. An industrial company depends upon the educational institutions for molding people for its operation, upon the political structure to preserve its position in the scheme of things, or upon health and welfare organizations to aid in the well-being of its personnel. In addition many organizations supplement the functions of outside agencies by special subsystems within their own boundaries. A company may extend the work of the public schools by developing its own procedures of socialization, extend the ethical system by developing its own values, and parallel the political system with internal mechanisms for self-protection and allocation of resources.

Some organizations take on two or more functions not in the above sense of supplementing a major task but in the sense of attempting more than one major job. Universities are concerned both with the training or socializing function and with the creation of new knowledge. Custodial institutions often attempt to rehabilitate their inmates as well as to remove deviants from the political scene. It may be noted in passing that organizations attempting more than one major function have special problems in integrating their tasks. Universities tend to split their research and teaching functions. Custodial institutions have great difficulty in rehabilitating inmates and still giving maximum emphasis to their custodial responsibilities (Goffman, 1961; Zald, 1962). It is difficult to be at one and the same time the punitive and repressive arm of the political system and the rehabilitation agency of the educational system.

At the level of the organization these same basic functions can be identified, even though the overall function of the organization is dominantly of one type. The industrial firm producing goods as its main function can still be differentiated into substructures of production, maintenance, and management. The same generalized frame of reference can be used at the level of the organization and at the societal level. Activities centering around the through-put are *productive*, around the human input *maintaining*, around coordination and control *managerial*, and around discovering solutions to problems *adaptive*. There will be some factors in common for people in a given type of organization because of its genotypical function. For example, members of an industrial enterprise, whether engineers in the plant, personnel people in the office, or managers around the board table, will all embrace in some degree the proficiency dynamic of getting on with the job, of turning out goods which can be sold in large quantities. There will also be factors in common between members of a substructure in one organization and their counterparts in another organization. A management person from industry might experience some difficulty in moving into a management position in a university but less difficulty than would a production engineer making the same move.

Recognition of these facts is widespread in the world of affairs. It is reflected in the frequency of individual moves from one organization or organizational type to another, but within the same functional substructure. We did not think it odd to find that the new president pro tem and chairman of the board of the Chrysler Corporation was a man whose industrial background was in coal mining; it was the function and experience in general management which made the move rational. Whether the degree of commonality within an organization is greater than the commonality between corresponding substructures of several organizations is difficult to predict unless we specify more about the organizations we are dealing with. In general the larger and the more complex the organizations, the greater will be the commonality of their management substructures.

SECOND ORDER CHARACTERISTICS

In addition to the genotypic function of the organization, we can describe organizations on many dimensions related to their specific structure, their transactions with their environment, and their internal transactions. The characteristics which can be listed seem limitless so we shall confine ourselves to some fundamental aspects related to (1) the nature of the through-put, (2) the processes for insuring the maintenance input of human personnel, (3) the nature of the bureaucratic structure, and (4) the type of equilibrium of the system. Finally we shall discuss the relationship of the genotypic functions already described to these characteristics.

THE NATURE OF THE THROUGH-PUT: TRANSFORMATION OF OBJECTS VERSUS MOLDING OF PEOPLE

A dimension of organizations which differentiates many economic from noneconomic structures is the nature of the work being done. The energy transformations may involve either the processing of objects or the molding of people.* The educational institution or the hospital is concerned with changing people who come within its boundaries and who become temporary members of the organization.

---

* We do not intend to imply that economic organizations can always be distinguished from noneconomic solely by this criterion. Many tertiary economic structures are concerned with molding people.

Human beings as objects of a change process require different organizational processes than materials transformed in a manufacturing plant, though hospitals have been slow to realize the implications of this distinction. Human beings are reactive, participating objects in any molding process, and their cooperation to enter many organizations must first be insured (Goffman, 1961). Moreover, their cooperation in an educational or even a therapeutic procedure is essential to its successful outcome. Parsons (1960) describes the educational organization as follows:

> The school class is a social system with an important degree of integration between teacher and pupils. Teaching cannot be effective if the pupil is simply a "customer" to whom the "commodity" of education is "turned over" without any further relation to its purveyor than is required for the settlement of the terms of the transfer—as in the case of the typical commercial transaction. . . . There must be a long-standing relation between a pupil and a succession of teachers . . . . This difference between the processes of physical production and various types of "service" has much to do with the fact that the *products* of physical technology in our society tend to be disposed of through the process of commercial marketing, while services—with many variations, of course—are much more frequently purveyed within different kinds of nonprofit contests. (pp. 72–73)

Two basic differences must be recognized in dealing with systems processing social objects as against physical objects. (1) The internal procedures and forms must attract and motivate temporary members who are to be trained or treated. To insure such cooperation there must be relative stability of personnel in the staff roles of the organization, the roles charged with the responsibility for training and treatment. In addition there must be a considerable area of discretionary power within these roles. The reactive nature of subjects or patients requires reciprocal spontaneity on the part of the staff. Open prisons, where such spontaneity is a basic aspect of the staff approach toward inmates, report significantly lower rates of escape and recidivism (Scudder, 1954).

(2) The external transactions of "people-processing" organizations are not those of the market place in any immediate or direct sense. The expense of the educational institution or the hospital is borne in part by the larger community through public subsidy, endowment campaigns, and exemption from taxation. Hence the institution is less open to the immediate influence of the market place and more concerned with long-range outcomes. This insulation from immediate external pressures, at least those of the market place, justifies and intensifies the insistence of the public that people-molding organizations such as hospitals and schools be guided by norms of somewhat

gentler, more individually oriented nature than might be imposed on an economic, object-molding organization. We make the same argument for occupations and professions concerned with training and therapy even when the test of the market place is also applied. For example, we expect medical doctors to manifest norms of truthfulness and benevolence in excess of television pitchmen, even though both market their services.

The contrast between object-molding and people-molding organizations is not absolute, because organizations concerned primarily with the manufacture of physical products must nevertheless deal appropriately with the human tools for getting the physical job done. In hiring, training, and motivating employees such organizations encounter many of the problems and are subject to much of the same logic which characterizes organizations whose product is wholly human. Employees are social objects and cannot be bought and sold like commodities. They are never passive role occupants with the same lack of reactivity as the machines which can replace them for many tasks. As has already been suggested, the mistake of the machine theory of organization is the assumption that people are tools for accomplishing a given purpose and that their work can be planned without consideration for human variability and reactivity. Machine theory is highly appropriate for the processing of material objects through the use of tools. Its weakness in applying the same logic to human instruments in factory production is often compensated for by its efficiencies in dealing with the processing of materials. Where the materials being processed are human beings, this compensatory factor is lacking.

COMMITMENT AND INVOLVEMENT OF PEOPLE IN ORGANIZATIONS

The Expressive versus the Instrumental Cycle

We noted in Chapter 3 that social systems have the dual task of self-maintenance and productive activity. The factory, for all its semi-automated machinery, ceases to run if the workers and technicians walk off the job. What, then, holds people to the performance of their roles? Their activities in the system must carry either some intrinsic rewards, some instrumental or extrinsic rewards, or some combination of the two. When the intrinsic rewards are part and parcel of the major productive activities of the system, we are dealing with an *expressive cycle;* when people perform in their roles because they will be paid or because they like their fellow workers or for other extraneous considerations, we are dealing with an *instrumental cycle.*

More formally, the energic input, through-put, and output constitute a cycle of events which return to the initial point so that the output provides the energy for renewing the cycle.

The simplest social system would consist of so-called expressive organizations in which the members meet for the purpose of self-enjoyment, as in the case of the bridge club, the bird-watching society, or the sports club. In these cases we are dealing primarily with a simple cycle of energic input and return which renews input. The club activity is rewarding in itself. It provides satisfactions directly, and these satisfactions are the basis of the continuation of the activity. In most organizations, however, the cycles of energy exchange are more complex. The product must be sold in an external market, and the money obtained is used to pay wages and purchase materials for the continuation of the production process. The organization and membership in it are instrumental for attainment of other objectives. In the expressive type of cycle we are dealing with a much simpler system, more self-contained in its activities and requiring little in the way of transactions with the external environment.

The expressive-instrumental distinction can perhaps be thought of as a dimension, with one extreme represented by the example of bird-watching or some other activity which provides an equally immediate and direct kind of satisfaction, and the other extreme represented by some job which offers no satisfaction beyond the paycheck —or even a job which offers negative satisfactions except for the paycheck. Among the jobs occupying intermediate positions on such a scale would be those that are neutral or dissatisfying in the most immediate sense but experienced as part of a more complex cycle which is expressive. For example, although dropping bombs is immediately satisfying only to a war lover, as John Hersey (1959) has reminded us, military service can provide such expressive satisfactions as demonstrating love of country, defending oneself against tyranny, and the like. Some managements, realistically recognizing the expressive limitations of the assembly line, have sought to inculcate identification with the organization as a whole in an effort to invest the most monotonous jobs with expressive value. The failure of most such efforts is not a failure of principle but a result of the feeble, over-economical devices used to accomplish the task.

Few organizations are pure types. In addition to the complex and indirect energy transactions in productive organizations which include the payment of workers, there are subcycles energized by satisfactions from the work process itself. Some members of industrial organizations do find expressive as well as instrumental satisfactions in their work. Similarly, the expressive organization may have to enter into commerce with the environment to insure adequate facilities and uninterrupted time for members to pursue their expressive activities; in the process it acquires a treasury and a paid staff and suffers consequent losses in its simplistic expressive character.

The expressive versus the instrumental cycle of activities is directly related to the three bases of organization: task requirements, shared values and expectations, and rule enforcement. Where the task generates its own motivation or where people are carrying out activities in accordance with their own shared values, the opportunities for expressive satisfaction are maximized. Where performance is in response to rules which must be followed to insure rewards (wages) and to escape penalties, the satisfactions tend to be instrumental. Almost every organization tends to employ all three bases to insure effective performance, but the relative emphasis upon them varies greatly from organization to organization, with industrial enterprises at one extreme and voluntary organizations at the other.

Voluntary organizations are often built upon an expressive cycle in which many of the members enjoy playing their roles or derive direct gratification from the success of the organizational mission. But such organizations may have many members who join for reasons which maximize their own satisfactions without incorporating organizational goals. Not all the members of a political party are there because they are fully rewarded by organizing and agitating for their beliefs. Many are there because of the social satisfactions associated with party work (Valen and Katz, 1964).

The expressive versus the instrumental cycle has to do with the character of the commitment of people to the system. Where the activity is intrinsically rewarding, it is directly expressive of the needs and values of the individuals involved. Members cannot be easily lured away by other organizations, since competing systems must furnish the same type of activity or offer extrinsic rewards in overwhelming amount. Where members are bound in by extrinsic reward, the possibility of defection increases.

Partial Inclusion, Potency, and Priority of Involvement

Another way of looking at the nature of maintenance inputs is in terms of the degree of inclusion of the individual's personality in the organization, the potency of his involvement, and the priority of his commitment to various social structures and personal value systems. Both partial inclusion and potency of involvement are concepts developed by F. H. Allport (1962) to describe the relations of the individual to social systems.

Partial Inclusion. We have already discussed the inclusion of the individual in the organization on a partial or segmental basis (see Chapter 3). Organizations require only partial inclusion of their human units; indeed the most powerful organization cannot command more. The individual as a personality generally does not need to enter into the role requirement with anything like his full potential of response. The worker on the assembly line and the nurse in the hospital have limited responsibilities which can be met while much of their mental energy is directed elsewhere.

Segmental involvement of individuals is the basis of organizational structure. Organizations and offices differ, of course, in the totality of involvement which they require, and individuals differ in the magnitude of involvement which they find acceptable. In general, however, only part of the individual's life space is occupied by his organizational role. Individuals can belong to many organizations, and this variety of organizational roles sometimes furnishes outlets for more of their personality needs. Of course top leaders, more than most organizational members, may be fully involved in roles which permit wide discretion and call for more responsibility. They will repress part of their personality, however, or restrict its expression in accordance with the particular type of organization and its demands. The executive in charge of a business does not necessarily bring his own individual conscience into play when he makes organizational decisions, nor can he give full expression to his artistic, scientific, or emotional interests when he is confronted with an economic problem. On the contrary he may act in ways which contravene such motives and values. Even custodial institutions, which are totally inclusive in a physical sense, are not necessarily so in a psychological sense. The prison has complete control in time and space over the physical activities of the inmate, but psychologically he struggles to make his responses to these demands as minor a fragment of his personality as he can.

The central fact that organizations consist of segments of people rather than an integration of their whole personalities has been consistently ignored both in popular thinking and in scientific theory. Theorists no less than men of affairs insist upon looking at this patterned arrangement of segmental responses of individuals as if it had a personal rather than a contrived collective existence. They endow it with purposes and with many of the qualities of human agency as if this pattern were capable of feeling, thinking, and acting. This misconception persists because we are trapped by language habits which make it difficult to communicate about organizations in any other fashion. Though the present writers are committed to a system approach which does not equate the contrived pattern of segments of individuals to a single whole individual, it has not been possible to escape the anthropomorphic language of organization entirely.

Potency of Involvement. Related to the concept of partial inclusion is the potency of involvement of individuals in any given structure. The correlation between inclusion and potency is positive but not perfect. The worker who gets his major satisfactions outside his job and is therefore low on the dimension of inclusion may nevertheless be heavily involved in the company for which he works. If for him there are practically no job possibilities outside the one company, his potency of involvement may be high. His job provides the earnings by which he can carry on a satisfactory life outside the organization. The national state functions on a basis of very limited, partial inclusion of most citizens at most times; it would nevertheless rank high on potency of involvement. Most people are partially included in the state when they vote, obey the law, and pay their taxes. Such behavior may occupy little of the total behavior and little of their psychological life space. And yet in terms of potency of involvement the state stands at the apex of all organizational structures; its symbols are the most potent of any institution, and it commands a life-and-death allegiance unduplicated by other organizations.

It may be helpful to supplement the concept of potency of involvement with the term *priority of commitment.* Since individuals belong to many organizations, develop many reference groups, and possess value systems of their own, an operational test of involvement is the priority of these demands if more than one of them is present at the same time. People will handle competing requirements to the extent that they can on the basis of appropriateness of the request both with respect to substance and to time. It is inappropriate for the church to ask a member to change his employment, or for an industrial enterprise to ask a man to change his religion. Nonetheless, many instances of conflict between competing demands occur, and the notion of *cross-pressures* has been used to deal with this phenomenon in political behavior. In addition to the press of situational factors and personal preference, a relative priority of allegiance to institutional symbols has been built in during the childhood socialization process. The political symbols of the state take precedence over all other demands in our day and age, just as the symbols of the church had priority during the Middle Ages. Empirical research on such problems of priority is lacking, although a beginning has been made in some studies of individual behavior during moments of major disaster (Killian, 1952).

TYPE OF ORGANIZATIONAL STRUCTURE

The structural properties of organizations have been described in some detail in Chapters 3 and 4. In any typology of organizations these characteristics must be taken into account as information related and supplementary to their genotypic functions. We shall remind the reader here of three significant structural properties: (1) system openness and differentiation from its environment, (2) elaboration of structure, and (3) separation of the organization into potentially conflicting segments because of the hierarchical differences in power and reward, and because of the differing functional requirements of organizational substructures.

System Openness: Boundaries and Their Permeability

The first aspect of organizational differentiation is the degree to which it has differentiated itself from the surrounding environment. Primitive forms of animal life comprise globular masses of protoplasm through which flow the fluids of their watery environment and from which they cannot be easily distinguished. In contrast to these amorphous structures which lack specialized parts are the structured biological systems of the higher animals forms. Social systems, too, differ in the extent to which they are set apart from their environment. Organizations by definition are specific arrangements of patterned behavior distinct from their social environment, but they differ in the degree to which they are so differentiated. The voluntary organization of firemen in a small community is often an open community activity. Any able-bodied men can join and the central office may be nothing more than the local telephone operator, who has been instructed to call the volunteers on word of a fire. The pattern of voluntary cooperation, involving the members of the force, the local operator, and most of the members of the community, represents little differentiation from other community activities.

The primitive social organization is rooted in a given area of social space such as the community, and its functioning and survival are direct functions of this larger segment of social space. It has no resources or stored energy of its own and little power over its own members or over the larger community. It is more an aspect of community functioning than an independent organization. The large scale organization, though dependent upon the social world, is also a force in its own right. It can influence the surrounding social space and can store the money and the legal contracts which guarantee such influence. It typically lacks the spontaneous or expressive motivation of the primitive organization.

Organizations differ with respect to the permeability of their boundaries. Some organizations are characterized by sharply defined, rigid boundaries. Entrance into such systems and exit from them are not the decisions of the individuals who seek admittance or who seek to leave. The United States Army represents one extreme of a closed organization. At the other extreme would be the major political parties in the United States. Citizens can enter and leave at will and whether they belong or do not belong to the party is largely their own individual decision. Rejection of an applicant or expulsion of a disloyal member is very difficult. So open is the American political party that its very boundaries are not defined. They are determined by whether at any given moment an individual chooses to call himself a member. The major American political parties, in addition to their fringe members, do have a hard core group of supporters who make more stringent demands upon one another than upon the fringe adherents. But these demands have little codification, and admission into the hard core, though it requires some evidence of work for the cause, is generally not difficult.

Between the extremes of the rigid boundaries of the army and the easily penetrated boundaries of the political party exist many degrees of openness and tightness. Applicants for industrial positions must meet the criteria of the company employing them. Their act of entrance is voluntary, however, in the literal and limited sense that they are not drafted. Moreover, while they cannot prolong their membership beyond the organizational decree, they can leave the company at any time, at least in theory. In practice, however, they may have seniority rights in a given concern, and there may be no other company within their own community in which their skills would be wanted. Hence an industrial organization is a semi-voluntary system—more open than the army, more tightly structured than the political party with respect to boundaries. Many civic organizations resemble the political party in the ease of crossing their boundaries.

The continuing and inevitable process of organizational recruitment is one of the most important sources of influence from the external environment. An organization which is completely resolute in its resistance to externally proposed suggestions and ideas may be open to the same substantive inputs when they are imported by new members. As people move into an organization, they bring with them a variety of values and interests from the external environment. It follows that any organization with easy permeability of boundaries is subject to continuing influence from the external environment. Such influence is likely to be varied in content and to affect many aspects of the organization. Indeed, the open organization is subject to transformation by its members and may have difficulty in the single-minded pursuit of given objectives.

An organization which seeks to avoid such influence must make itself less permeable to self-nominating new members. It must screen potential members more carefully and define more broadly the individual characteristics which are relevant in the screening. By so doing the organization will perhaps sharpen its sense of mission and minimize the possibilities of internal disruption. It may pay the price, however, of tending to replicate its current membership characteristics and thus coming to resemble itself more and more closely as time passes. Such organizations can turn into caricatures of themselves. Their thrift becomes miserliness, and their conservatism becomes fearfulness.

There is no prescription for such dilemmas of permeability. That organizational leadership which understands the nature of its exchange with the external environment can choose, however, the forms and degrees of permeability which best meet the contemporary requirements of the organization.

Elaboration of Structure. The more differentiated an organization is from the surrounding environment, the more likely it is to develop a highly differentiated internal structure. In the first place, to maintain its own character, an organization requires boundaries which are not readily permeable by any outside force. It therefore develops its own coding system to screen and filter potential inputs. In the second place, to the extent that it lacks the spontaneous, expressive motivation of voluntary participation, it needs special mechanisms to insure continuing and reliable performance. In the third place, to counteract the rigidity of these mechanisms, it must develop additional structures for permitting some degree of flexibility and adaptability.

The elaboration of organizational structure gets its major impetus from systems in which the maximization principle prevails. To gain a highly favorable ratio of product to energy expended in organizations dealing with the production of physical objects requires a high degree of division of labor. Specialization of function in turn requires subsystems of coordination and control. Moreover, to maximize returns to the organization, it is necessary to develop sensitive regulatory mechanisms which will give feedback not only on overall organizational functioning but on the operations of specific parts of the system.

Elaboration of organizational structure can thus move both in the horizontal direction of routinizing various types of tasks and in the vertical direction of increasing the layers of hierarchical decision-making and control. Some optimum point can be found for efficient operation in most organizations with respect to the degree of both horizontal and vertical elaboration. A simple structure with relatively little role differentiation may prove ineffective for complex tasks involving a large membership. On the other hand, the more the differentiation of structure for task accomplishment, the greater will be the effort required for coordination. The more layers in the hierarchical system and the more control devices, the greater the expansion of nonproductive activity.

Hierarchical Dimension of Organizational Structure: Allocation Mechanisms. Of the many structural differences among organizations a fundamental one has to do with the hierarchical separation within the authority and reward structures. In some organizations the rewards, the privileges, and the power are vested in the top echelons and we have an oligarchical rather than a democratic system. People within any system make contributions of varying effort and value, however, and are likely to be rewarded differentially. Organizations differ with respect to the type of allocation mechanism developed to control the distribution of rewards to various sectors of the organization and to various role occupants.

These mechanisms of allocation comprise subsystems of energic transaction within the larger system, and in Marxian terms are called the social relations of production, in contrast to technology. They are buttressed by the authority and power structure of the organization and often constitute one of the major reasons why an authority structure is necessary. Marxian theory, however, is essentially incorrect in assuming that allocation mechanisms comprise the only major reason for the existence of an authority structure.

Allocation mechanisms are essentially political subsystems within the economic structure. They are less concerned with production per se and more concerned with its distribution. The major mechanism of allocation in early capitalistic enterprise is the private ownership of capital or stored energy. The returns from the use of this invested energy go to those who have legal title to it. The owners or their representatives, in utilizing their capital for turning out a product or rendering a service, enter into transactions with those they seek to employ with the objective of buying their services at some price of optimum advantage to themselves. The differential between the costs of materials and human services and their sales will mean either a profit or a loss for the capital or energy invested. Under this type of allocation mechanism the subsystem of profit making for the owners is an integral part of the total production system and in many respects is the controlling mechanism.

The allocation process in private enterprise is modified in many ways. There are cultural and political forces which influence management away from short-term (and perhaps even long-term) maximization of profit, and urge instead decisions which are complex mixtures of profit-making, community responsibility, and concern for employee welfare. A further modification of allocation takes place by agencies of government, as they exercise the power to tax and as they act to redistribute income by means of social welfare programs. There is also the tendency for ownership to become corporate, with a consequent dispersion of individual owners and a separation of ownership from active management.

The private ownership of capital means then that the profit return to owners can be affected in three ways: (1) by favorable transactions with the external environment, (2) by favorable transactions with employees, and (3) by the internal efficiency of the system. The higher the price for the product and the lower the cost of producing it, the greater the profit. Hence the subgroups within the organization whose services are purchased stand in an ambivalent relation to owners and to the outside public. On the one hand, the owners have a common interest with them in keeping the organization a going concern. On the other hand, the owners find them an opponent much as they do the outside world in that they represent resistances for increasing a favorable return to ownership. In fact, the ownership point of view may be more positively oriented toward its buying public than toward its own employees.

To check still further the allocation subsystem in a private enterprise, the nonowning members organize into a group for the protection of their own interests. This interest type of organization, known as a labor union, is thus a political subsystem within industry which has the primary function of gaining for its members as favorable a portion of the return to the industrial system as possible. It is the counterpart of the political means of reward allocation of private enterprise. It develops other functions, such as giving employees first class citizenship in an organization of their own, thus contributing to potency of involvement.

Organizations then vary with respect to the type of allocation mechanism created by the organizational structure for the system as a whole. Where one segment of the organization is at an advantage in receiving or controlling organizational rewards, as in a privately-owned company, we have a different organizational type than where all members share directly in the profits and losses, as in a cooperative. In the former case, we are more likely to encounter protective organizations for the less privileged groups in the enterprise and institutionalized conflict between the parent organization and its protective offshoot.

Type of authority structure is related to but not synonymous with type of allocation mechanism. Where the legislative function is vested in the membership, members have control over the distribution of rewards. They can still follow various plans for making these decisions; they may vote for a differential return based upon some criterion such as responsibility of office, or they may legislate for uniform rewards or bonuses. Where the legislative function is vested in the top ranks, the same alternatives are available. In general, however, the form of allocation will tend to favor the groups which hold the legislative power. We are so accustomed to the principle of methods and results of reward allocation reflecting the locus of legislative power that we take for granted the outcomes of this principle. We expect that the president of a major corporation shall receive many times the salary of the president of a major union.

Equilibrium versus the Maximization of Energic Return

Organizations differ in the degree to which they follow the maximization principle in obtaining a favorable ratio of return to energic expenditure. At the one extreme are organizations governed by an equilibrium dynamic in which the return to the organization equals the energy expended to turn out the product. Prior to the period of inflation and population explosion, the small college (with a small endowment, the same student enrollment year after year, and the same income ploughed back into operations) approximated this extreme. At the opposite extreme is the industrial firm realizing its growth potential in a highly favorable market.

Most organizations, however, attempt to establish transactional relations with their external environment that furnish energy at a greater rate than it is expended. Even in natural systems, such as the human body, the equilibrium between the energic input and output is not precisely maintained. Where food is available, people will eat in excess of their bodily needs and will tend to store energy in fatty tissue. The biological struggle for survival at the animal level is the attempt of organisms not only to meet the physiological needs of the moment but to secure future satisfactions as well. In this struggle the coping mechanisms for dealing with the environment may involve struggling with and preying upon other animals or finding a habitat favorable to survival.

There are severe limitations to the storing of energy in a natural system like the body or to the ability of a single organism to secure adequate reserves for the future. Social systems, however, as contrived structures, have tremendous capacities for the storage of energy. Moreover, there is less relationship between their energy input and energy output than in the natural system. The dynamic of most social systems is to maximize as favorable a ratio of energic return to energic expenditure as possible. In their attempts to control and even enslave other groups and in their attempts to exploit the physical environment, organizations show forces of struggle and survival similar to those found in the animal world. At the social level, additional mechanisms are brought into play and the organized human effort can multiply by an undetermined factor the possibilities of environmental exploitation. Many organizations had their origin in groups struggling for survival and protection.

RELATIONSHIP BETWEEN GENOTYPIC FUNCTION AND SECOND ORDER CHARACTERISTICS

PRODUCTIVE SYSTEMS

We have defined the economic or productive function as the creation of wealth in direct fashion, either through extracting materials from the environment, transforming objects for consumption, or rendering some services related to these activities. An organization might be privately owned or publicly owned and controlled and still be dominantly economic in function.

Because the economic function as expressed in primary and secondary production activity is directed at the molding of objects rather than people, its structural elaboration is better attuned to things than people. Its immediate adaptive procedures are concerned with research on product development and testing, not on the human beings and relationships comprising the organization. Even its research on its marketing public is extremely limited. Current estimates of the annual expenditure of industry for advertising and related activities run about 16 billion dollars. The same sources estimate the annual budget for market research at only a small fraction of that amount. Clearly the thrust is to shape consumer preference rather than to discover that preference and modify the organization in accordance with it.

Dealing with material things and mechanical services, the economic organization has the criterion of the market place to guide it. This constant pragmatic check reinforces the proficiency dynamic of the system, so that economic organizations have set the pace for the development of other bureaucratic structures, with their elaborate division of labor, systematic controls on operations, and ready institutionalization of new procedures.

The greatest problem of the productive structure is the appropriate handling of maintenance inputs. Since mechanization is the dominant principle of the economic organization, the human tools tend to be adapted to this principle. Rank-and-file members are held in the system by an instrumental cycle rather than an expressive cycle. Economic organizations do have opportunities for binding in their top personnel, both administrative and professional, through intrinsic rewards. And the more simplified, routinized, unsatisfying roles are increasingly being automated. One kind of solution for the future then is to take advantage of the decreasing size of the staff required in some organizations, and to make the remaining members first-class citizens in the operation. Such a solution is more feasible in an automated power plant with twenty technicians than in a nonautomated plant with four hundred workers.

The industrial organization does not stimulate the all-or-nothing loyalty of rank-and-file members that is common in many political groupings. For some segments of the industrial organization the corporation is also a political institution and for them there is more emotional involvement, but in general the economic orientation of the organization permeates its members. If there is a higher paying post in another enterprise, few will hesitate to move into it. Moreover, conflicts between economic organizations competing for the same markets are not fought out by direct attacks upon one another but by reaching the public with product changes, packaging changes, or a persuasive sales appeal. Competition rather than conflict is the basic economic method of controlling the environment for favorable returns. Conflict is direct interference with the other party; competition means greater progress toward the same goal with both parties running roughly parallel courses. Business organizations do engage in conflict activities through their use of pressure groups, but these actions are the political rather than the economic side of the organization.

Profit-making organizations are also characterized by the principle of immediate accountability for operational costs and efficiency. The worth of the junior executive is assessed not by his loyalty to the organization but by his ability to run a tight shop. Immediacy of return as the yardstick of success makes for difficulties in long-range planning and the consideration of distant goals. Even such a revolutionary development for profit-making as automation has been adopted more slowly than efficiency alone would have dictated.

Over a long period, compared to other organizations, industrial enterprises show a greater disposition to change. Even the casual observer of American society remarks the torpid response of non-industrial organizations—schools, agencies of government, and museums, for example—to changing environmental requirements. As this is written, the people charged with the responsibility for setting up training and educational centers for boys and girls of high school age who have "dropped out" are discovering that virtually no universities, colleges, or schools of education are adapting to and experimenting with this new and crucial educational demand. Many industrial organizations are not only willing but are actively bidding to take on such functions, to become in effect agencies of education and in so doing to expand and secure their own functions.

The leading part of the organization will shift from time to time, as different parts represent differential potentials for profit. As Piel (1961) has pointed out, at one time the economically significant industrial property was the machine, then it became the design, and now it is fast becoming "the capacity to innovate design in process and product." Research and development becomes the leading organizational subsystem, and economic organizations have special reasons for responding quickly and appropriately to changes in their situation.

The principle of maximization characterizes economic structures, whether they are publicly or privately owned. The proficiency dynamic means fuller exploitation of an ever expanding technology. Economic systems operate more profitably if they can control their sources of raw materials, if they can produce in quantity, and if they can plan without interference from undercutting competitors. Hence they move in the direction of mergers, cartels, and monopolies. The paradox of the private enterprise type of economic system is that its dynamic reduces the number of competitors and ultimately may lead to public regulation as the enterprise becomes a quasi-public institution.

Some social theorists, and especially the Marxians, have considered the economic structures of a society as the leading subsystems of the societal system. Thus the organization of economic activities is seen as more of an independent than a dependent variable in relation to political, educational, religious, and other organizations. They assert that changes in the economic structure will affect political realignment, the nature of education, and the character of religion much more than changes in the latter activities will affect the economic structure.

A more narrow formulation of the principle of the priority of material change is the generalization that change is more readily accepted in the technological than in the social sphere. There are at least two reasons why this may be so. (1) An improved technique for tilling the soil, and a more efficient machine can be readily demonstrated in terms of the perception of the senses. An atomic bomb is clearly superior to an ordinary explosive; a hydrogen bomb superior to an atomic bomb. A social change is more complex, less observable in immediate effects, and hence is much less compelling.* (2) Through our particular training we have invested more emotion and more personal values in specific political and religious ideas than in specific technical devices. We value our automobiles as an instrumental means for increasing our control of our immediate environment, but we will quickly abandon the old model for a new one or for a helicopter if that would serve our purposes better. Our attachment to political and religious beliefs is less instrumental, however, and more expressive of our own values. In other words, as we have already suggested, economic organizations are based more upon the instrumental than the expressive cycle.

Since it is difficult to effect changes directly in the nonmaterial culture, modifications of political, educational, and religious systems are brought about indirectly through changes in the material culture. This is the thesis of Ogburn (1922), who presented historical evidence of the differential rate of change in the two types of culture. A more current instance of this thesis can be seen in the development of armaments. The technical changes in moving from conventional weapons to hydrogen bombs have profoundly affected our political and international systems.

Though it is plausible to look for the source of change in the developments of material culture, such a search does not encompass all of the major dimensions of societal dynamics. The control of change is often political and the rate and the direction of change may be affected by educational, religious, and other social agencies. Our own approach to the larger problem of causality would emphasize the interactional or field relationship of economic and noneconomic structures. Their interaction is more important for understanding the nature of the social world than is the historical question of which came first.

MAINTENANCE SYSTEMS

The school is the organizational counterpart of the familial institution in training children for their adult roles. It helps build in the patterns of values and norms which facilitate the assumption of roles in adult life. In addition it contributes to the knowledge and skills necessary for adult roles. Increasingly our mass bureaucratic society

---

* Erasmus (1961) cites evidence from a number of anthropological field studies which indicates the importance of the "demonstration effect;" demonstrating the superiority of a new technique in a manner which is readily perceivable markedly increases its chances of acceptance.

depends upon people with a generalized role readiness—an ability to meet the demands of many organizational settings with the proper cooperation. These requirements may shift from situation to situation, but the individual must be able to pick up his cues and play his part. Riesman (1950) has contrasted this other-directedness with the inner-directedness of an earlier period. Such generalized role readiness, however, is essential to the operation of large bureaucracies in a mass society with its norms of reciprocity and mutual helpfulness. Children pick up these patterns in the school situation both through value indoctrination and through assuming the many roles the modern school assigns. Much has been made of the economic and social deprivations of Negroes in northern cities as the causal background of rioting and violence, and rightly so. A contributing factor is the lack of socialization of Negro youth in an adequate school system. Many of the rioters are teenagers, and many of them have not been brought into the social system through a first-rate educational program. In southern communities the social controls were force and fear of force. In northern communities these forms of control have been weakened and have not been fully replaced by the proper educational process. Hence under conditions of frustration these partially socialized citizens do not follow the peaceful and legitimized roles of the civil rights movement, but resort to violence.

Since educational institutions are concerned with the molding of people rather than the transformation of objects, the motivation of their populations presents special problems not encountered in economic organizations—at least with respect to through-put. The same generalization holds, of course, for the restorative organization, whether it be a hospital or social welfare agency. The role of the teacher or of the therapist could be heavily prescribed if one were concerned only with the technical aspects of learning. But learning and reeducation are not only determined by techniques of spacing material and of mechanical reinforcement but also by deeper motivational processes. Therefore, a wider area of discretionary power is necessary for the staff member in the maintenance type of organization. This makes possible an optimum interaction between pupil and teacher, and between patient and therapist. Teaching machines with their programmed learning and television lessons piped into the classroom are important adjuncts to the educational process, but they are not adequate substitutes for the teacher. In the past many students from underprivileged economic groups have gone on to successful college and professional careers because of the special guidance and inspiration of the gifted secondary-school teacher.

The success of the economic model of organization has led many educational and hospital systems to follow the organizational forms of elaborated role structure, mechanization and institutionalization of procedures, control devices, and centralization of power. Nevertheless, these forms have not been simulated faithfully and the gap between the paper blueprint and the empirical system is great. In many universities, for example, the amount of decentralization is much greater than in an industrial firm. Departments are powers in their own right and make many of the decisions in fact which are reserved for the Board of Regents in legal form. Even the individual instructor has considerable autonomy in what he teaches, how he teaches, and what scholarly activity he engages in. The norm of academic freedom and the organizational device of tenure, though not absolute guarantees of autonomy, are relatively effective in giving the staff member a wide range of discretion in his activities.

Hospitals, because of their historical linkage with the military and the church, and because of their special problems of ready mobilization for emergencies and of protecting against the disastrous effects of error, resemble industrial organizations more than do educational institutions. There has been elaborate and rigid role prescription for attendants and nurses, an emphasis upon rules and regulations for predictable performance, and a tendency to treat patients as objects rather than as people. Nevertheless, hospitals do differ from industrial systems in several important respects, two of which are deserving of special mention.

In the first place, there is no single line of authority in many hospitals. The board of trustees, the doctors, and the administrator comprise three centers of authority, so that there is a delicate balance of power rather than a single hierarchical line of command (Georgopoulos and Mann, 1962). In the second place, there is a professionalization of the two principal types of workers, namely, the doctors and the nurses. Professional workers in industry tend to be staff people but in the hospital they represent the major line activities. As professionals they are less subject to lay authority and are part of their own professional system as well as members of the hospital. In Parsons' terms, the break between the managerial and technical systems would occur at a very high level in the organizational structure of the hospital. The professionalization of staff means that the expressive rather than the instrumental cycle characterizes many staff members. They obtain much of their reward from the exercise of their professional skills. Moreover, the objectives of the organization of preserving life and combatting illness are easily assimilated to the corresponding values of the individual organizational member. Professionalization also means that in spite of the potency of involvement in the hospital, the involvement of the individual may be partial or segmented in that he is heavily involved in his profession as the larger system. The medical profession thus takes priority over the hospital administration if there should be any competition between the values of the two systems.

During the past decade fairly radical reforms have been taking place in the administration of some hospitals. The creation of the therapy team and the movement toward an open hospital are indications of the thorough rethinking of organizational structure in this field.

Economic organizations, because of their technological orientation and their feedback from the market place, are generally better equipped to deal with change than are organizations which emphasize the maintenance function. The economic enterprise has its research and development department and its program and planning staff geared to meet immediate changes in input and the reception of output. It is difficult to find an educational institution or a hospital with similar adaptive structures.

Maintenance systems present special problems with respect to the hierarchical separation of power, privilege, and reward, in that there is likely to be a line of cleavage between the staff and the population of subjects to be worked on. This line, moreover, is between the authority to make organizational decisions and the submission to such decisions; to enjoy or be deprived of privileges; to have a fair degree of autonomy in working out one's role and to be assigned specific directives about one's conduct; to administer sanctions and to receive punishments. The older philosophy for molding and influencing people followed the *carrot and stick* principles. The staff, occupying the power positions, meted out rewards for correct behavior and punishments for incorrect behavior to the subordinate subject population. This was the pattern in the school, the old mental hospital, and even the church with its imposition of penances. People can be molded in this fashion under conditions in which the institution has complete control over the behavior of its inmates and is supported by the culture values of the overall society. An additional facilitating condition in schools is the youthfulness of the subject population, in that identification with the aggressor occurs more readily among the weak and helpless.

Today when even children are regarded as having rights of their own, the simple punishment-reward pattern has been altered. The expectation is that people, whether young or old, should cooperate in learning, reeducation, or therapy not on the basis of extrinsic rewards and penalties, but on the basis of intrinsic motivations of their own. Punishment and reward should be cues for the direction or redirection of behavior rather than incentive patterns. School teachers who operate conspicuously on the old principle soon find themselves in conflict with the family, the Parents and Teachers Association, and the community.

The general strategy of involving the subject population in the organization means some obscuring of the line of cleavage of power and privilege. Students will not be eager to accept and enforce rules in which they had no voice. Nor will they be highly motivated to follow narrow prescribed courses of study which stifle their own intellectual interests. On the other hand, subject populations, whether students, patients, or church audiences, are there to be guided by those with superior skills and knowledge. Their resentment of non-directive teaching (and therapy) is considerable and, in our view, justifiable. The appropriate areas of freedom for the second grade student or for the graduate student do not lend themselves to easy definition. In fact, the emphasis upon precise definition of these areas should be replaced by an emphasis upon participation toward common objectives by both staff and subject populations.

Maintenance systems like the school and the church not only impart special skills and knowledge but also teach the values and norms of the society. In a sense, then, their major function is one of preserving the stability of the social structure, of tying people into the normative system. But this is true in general more than in specific terms, i.e., the stability they encourage is for the type of society they operate in rather than for particularistic rules. Thus in a democratic society like the United States the norms inculcated produce less respect for specific laws than respect for law itself as the outcome of a democratic process. Similarly, a church will emphasize the Christian way of life more than its specific theology. Such generalized norms are often an idealized set of values rather than a description of existing practices in the society or a realistic prescription of what they are expected to be. Hence there is the paradox that the maintenance institutions by their emphasis upon general norms furnish some dynamic for social change. By making salient the moral and rational character of a democratic way of life and of Christian ethics, the school and church provide a positive force for changing practices inconsistent with these values. In Russian society as well the ideology of educational systems is rationalized in more idealistic terms than many of the existing practices. Probably this condition had some effect in facilitating changes away from the repression of the Stalinist era. But are these examples too selective to make the point? What of a societal set of norms which justifies slavery, the divine right of kings, or other antisocial goals? Even here the general rule would indicate movement in the direction of a broader, more ethical basis involving the interests of more people than the specific privileged group in power. The divine right of kings went beyond the tyranny of one man; by linking the ruler with religion it also placed on him the responsibility of a demigod for the welfare of his people.

POLITICAL SYSTEMS

In any society the political system has the three functions of handling internal conflict through policy formulation or legislation; implementing such decisions through an executive arm; and mobilizing the society for relations with other nations—whether cooperative, competitive, or conflictual. In a nondemocratic society all three functions are exercised by a single ruler or a small ruling class, whereas in a democratic society the legislative function is directly or indirectly in the hands of the people.

There would be small need for a political system if there were unanimity among people about their goals and the means for reaching them. Any one person could voice the wishes of the group and it would receive immediate assent. The state and its subsystems exist because people are neither homogeneous nor neatly complementary with respect to their roles, their interests, their perceptions, and their values. Homogeneity of interests and goals are not enough to make for automatic solution of problems. There must also be unanimity about the specifics of problem solution. John Paul's example of twelve men marooned on a desert island with one beautiful woman illustrates a conflictual situation precisely because there are common perceptions and common goals. Political scientists use the concept of *scarce resources* to call attention to the basis for political organization. Thus Easton (1961) writes:

> The reason why a political system emerges in a society at all—that is, why men engage in political activity—is that demands are being made by persons or groups in the society that cannot all be fully satisfied. In all societies one fact dominates political life: scarcity prevails with regard to most of the valued things . . . . Only where wants require some special organized effort on the part of society to settle them authoritatively may we say that they have become inputs of the political system. (p. 85)

Political machinery provides the means for reaching some degree of viable consensus among the differing groups, and the political arena is the place where the mutual influencing process goes on before decisions are reached. Marx held that the political state was necessary only in societies with social classes, i.e., conflicting interest groups. In a classless society, the state would wither away because there would be a ready consensus of shared convictions on all issues of importance. The facts are, however, that individual and group differences of opinion do not rest merely on class differences. In Soviet Russia, which is more of a classless society than Czarist Russia, the political state has shown no signs of withering away but has if anything taken a new lease on life.

To achieve a viable consensus, all the means of influencing people are employed in the political arena, from the use of organized force, through debate and bargaining, to persuasion and integrative problem solutions. Within a society, organized force is seldom employed on a significant scale either by those in power or by those out of power, unhappy though they may be with the actions of the power structure. When this does occur we have a riot or a rebellion, a coup d'etat or a revolution. Ordinarily there is a consensus that legitimized decisions (those reached through following the rules of the game) are binding upon all members. This legitimizing of the rules for decision making, so that conflicts can be handled without internal societal strife and anarchy, is at the core of the political system. The only effective way to prevent wars between nations is through international systems that legitimize procedures for handling conflict so that all nations bind themselves to accept the verdict or outcome. To extend political systems in this fashion across national boundaries is extremely difficult because it means a genuine revision in thinking with respect to national sovereignty.

In the modern democracy the principal mechanisms for achieving decisions are accommodation and compromise. In the top decision-making body of elected representatives, differences in interest and ideas are subject to debate, persuasion, and bargaining. The final policy arrived at may not have the enthusiastic approval of the major contending forces, but each major group will have achieved some measure of what it wanted or some assurance of a payment in kind on another issue. Moreover, the whole process is facilitated by the compromises already achieved in the political parties, especially if it is a two party system as in the United States. Each party operates to achieve compromise among the interests of its own subgroups so that not all interest conflicts are reflected to their full extent in the top national decision-making body.

The same logic of compromise extends to the selection of candidates representing a political party at the various levels within the structure. The candidate is often a compromise candidate in the sense that no individual ideally represents all of a given electorate but some one person must be selected. The higher up in the system the official stands, the more he must take into account the compromise nature of his mandate from the electorate. He must see himself as representing the broad electorate which put him in power rather than the narrow sector whose views coincide with his own. This is particularly true at the national level. Otherwise he will be utilizing a system based upon compromise and accommodation to push the views of a small minority. In democratic politics the electorate itself has a check upon this abuse at the very next election. A dictator, however, can take advantage of the system, as Hitler did after he was called to office by President Hindenberg. Once at the head of the state, he violated the implicit mandate of representativeness and corrupted the system so that it became solely the voice of his own Nazi party.

The value systems of political structures reflect the major functional requirements of internal compromise, representativeness, and in-group patriotism toward outsiders. On the one hand, the national government has the ideology of representing all the people, doing something for everybody. Modern political parties seek to be national parties in terms of nationwide appeal to many sectors of the population. Within a system compromise is the order of the day, and politics is recognized as "the art of the possible." On the other hand, the ideology of the political system has a radically different set of values regarding those outside the system. The ideas and interests of outsiders are not to be accommodated within the system. Instead, all system members tend to unite in their loyalty to their own group and to reject the intruder and the foreigner—whether from another party, another state, or another country. The realistic give-and-take conception of internal functioning is in marked contrast to the absolutistic, militant conception of external relations. This dual set of beliefs about the political system can make for confusion and outrage when one political group turns the nationalist values regarding people outside the nation against subunits within the nation. Thus the radical right in the United States defines Americanism in its own image and becomes as militant toward other Americans as if they were outsiders. It is not coincidental that such attacks are bolstered by accusing the target group of being "outside" in some racial or national sense, as well as in political terms. The ultimate in such exclusion, of course, is to define members of the outgroup as literally outside the human race. Any crime against them then loses its criminality. Nazi ideology went to great pains to accomplish this nonhuman definition of Jews, and some contemporary racist propaganda has attempted the same against Negroes.

To the extent that organizations are political in character, they show in more intense form many of the attributes of all organizations. The in-group–out-group dichotomy, for example, becomes sharper in political structures. Members of organizations can and do belong to a variety of groups; but when the organization is basically political, the individual can belong to only one such group, and the members of other political organizations are his enemies. He cannot belong to both the Republican and Democratic parties. The in-group–out-group dichotomy thus accentuates organizational membership and loyalty with an all-or-nothing quality. If one accepts membership, he cannot reserve to himself any decisions or discretion once policy has been decided. He cannot sit this one out. He faces the questions: "Are you with us?" and "Which side are you on?" The resulting affective identification with the political organization means that relations with members of the opposition group are accompanied by heated argument and emotional outbursts.

Actions of an antisocial nature are sanctioned toward members of the outgroup; aggression is countenanced and even encouraged. Unless checked by the larger social structure, such actions will assume the form of physical violence. The labor union members may have highly moral and cooperative attitudes toward other human beings, but scabs or strikebreakers do not fall into this category, and almost any harsh treatment of them is justified. Moreover, the tendency in a political struggle group is to regard all outsiders as members of the opposition. The outgroup is expanded to include not only the formal opposition but all outsiders as well. The neutral category is often dismissed with the view that if you are not for us, you are against us. The great anomaly of the Gandhian movement as a political structure is its attempt to forego violence against the opposition, and to try to define alleged enemies into the movement in the sense that they have some of the same basic humanitarian values and need only to become aware of them. In this sense the Gandhian movement is more religious and ideological than political in nature.

The political organization, which exists primarily to influence and control outside groups, is sometimes assumed to be the pure type of all complex organizational forms. Some students of history maintain that the origin of complex authority structures is to be found in the struggle of one group to maintain its interests against those of another. They assert that much of modern political structure was developed and elaborated as the military forces of one or another tribe became mobilized for purposes of conquest and confiscation. Oppenheimer (1914) and other social theorists hold that the political state itself arose in this fashion and that even today the organizational forms of national states show the character of their struggle origins. In any case, the presence of an authority structure to coordinate all activities of the system and the all-or-nothing involvement of members is seen most clearly in political groupings.

The major or overall political system, the national state, though built upon the segmental involvement of its citizens, has priority in its demands upon them. Most citizens of a modern nation have only peripheral contact with their government during the greater part of their lives. They pay taxes, obey the laws, vote, and on occasion show ritualistic respect for national symbols. The nation state as a functioning system is remote from the pattern of their daily activities.

Nevertheless, there is great potency of involvement in the nation state because it is the one system the individual cannot withdraw from without becoming an outcast, an exile, or a prison inmate. Its legal requests take priority over his membership in any other system—religious, economic, or familial. Not only is this priority established through the early socialization process, it is maintained by the nature of the organization of the state as the one system which embraces all other organizations in the society. The state is both the authority structure and the supersystem of the society. All other organizations must work within its rules. In times of emergency it can even take over its subsystems in direct fashion, incorporating the militia into the armed forces, nationalizing key industries, and the like. The nation state represents the means for maintaining the basic way of life for its citizens. Though individuals belong to many organizations, they all have common membership in the nation state. If it were to be destroyed or overthrown, its people would face a different way of life. We are speaking here, of course, of the established nation state. In newly emerging nations there is often no universal maintenance structure such as the school to inculcate nationalistic ideology and allegiance to national symbols, no political institutions to cut across or integrate tribal organization; in short, potency and priority of involvement have not as yet been achieved.

Political parties as subsystems of the state often have the same segmental character of involvement except that there is less commitment to the subsystem than the state. Admission into the party is of course easier than admission to citizenship, and departure from it not uncommon.

Nevertheless, the majority of people in the United States, which has a very loose party system, remain in the same party throughout their lives. The segmental involvement in the political party belies the strength of allegiance to it. Though not active politically, many people find it difficult to desert their traditional political allegiance in spite of an occasional splitting of ballots. Political activists are bound into the organization at the local and national level in interdependent ways so that even when the party organization is in the hands of their opponents, they tend to stay with it. Campbell and his colleagues (1960) found that two-thirds of American voters who could remember their first vote for president still identified with that party. Indeed a majority of these voters reported that they had *never* crossed party lines. Even the regional transformation of party loyalties in 1964 in the deep south is no more than a ripple on this impressive stability. With a presidential candidate representing a minority faction of the party, the Republican Party had a defection of only 20 per cent of its members in the 1964 election (though as the minority party it could not afford any defection to be successful at the polls).

Perhaps because the political system represents the key decision-making structure of the society, it is generally provided with built-in defenses to preserve its characteristic form—as a constitutional monarchy, an oligarchy, or a democracy. In an authoritarian political society, the state controls not only the military force, but also the political parties or party, the school system, and even the economic structures. Even in a democracy, which legitimizes change, there is a series of checks and balances to prevent rapid change. In the United States the compromise dynamic within political parties and within the national government is aided by the institutional provisions of (1) distribution of powers between federal and local government and (2) separation among the legislative, executive, and judicial branches of government. Part of the pattern of restraints is the legal process whereby law making, administration, and adjudication are public events open to public inspection. In addition, administrative officials must justify their actions by reference to the appropriate enabling legal statutes. To make this even more stringent, some units of government must allocate every expenditure to a specific and appropriate line in the officially authorized budget. Public accountability is thus carried to such a logical extreme that it can become self-defeating in a misplaced emphasis on detail.

The negative aspect of the political system is the penal institution for punishing and confining law breakers. Goffman (1961) has used the concept of total institution to refer not only to prisons but to mental hospitals, to military organizations, and to monasteries. He writes:

Their encompassing or total character is symbolized by the barrier to social intercourse with the outside that is often built right into the physical plant . . . . In total institutions there is a basic split between a large managed group, conveniently called inmates, and a small supervisory staff . . . . Social mobility between the two strata is grossly restricted; social distance is typically great and often formally prescribed. (pp. 4–7)

Goffman's emphasis is thus upon the control exercised by the staff over inmates, and his total institutions are organizations in which there is massive control over all aspects of the inmates' lives by the supervising staff. We shall consider penal institutions, including concentration camps and prisoner-of-war camps, as being the most representative of this control dimension of total institutions. Though the training of the nun or the monk in the monastery does involve complete control over the novice, the person enters of his own accord, can leave of his own accord, and after his indoctrination can move up in the structure. The mental hospital, it is true, was once more of a custodial and penal institution than a rehabilitation center, and some of this older character still persists. Nonetheless, the modern hospital has moved toward openness, with more contact with the outside world and fewer barriers between staff and inmates.

The penal institution often shows some deviation from the official objective of total control over inmates. An empirical system develops in which an informal leadership pattern among the prisoners is tacitly encouraged by prison officials. Transactions occur between leaders and wardens which are of course not officially recognized. Sykes (1958) has used the concept of *inmate cohesion* to refer to the pattern of cooperative getting along which helps to maintain the equilibrium of the prison society. The violent, aggressive, unstable elements are held in check by the informal leaders. The pattern of getting along does not, of course, mean informing on fellow prisoners or accepting the custodial point of view. One factor in prison riots is the undermining of this inmate cohesion by efforts of the custodial force to enforce rules strictly and to crack down on all violations.

Penal systems are organizational devices for handling deviants from the legal order, and their objectives have been traditionally three-fold: (1) to protect society by removing the dangerous offender, (2) to deter potential deviants, and (3) to reform the offender through punishment or more enlightened means of treatment. Partly because the objectives of protection and deterrence have not been adequately realized through punishment and imprisonment, and partly because of a changed cultural ideology, the penal institution is seen increasingly as a rehabilitation agency.

The penal institution is thus supposed to perform two essentially incompatible functions. As part of the political system, it should protect society by isolating deviants who have either a nuisance value or who constitute a threat. As a maintenance subsystem, it should retrain such deviants. The two functions of incarceration and rehabilitation have incompatible elements. An efficient custodial organization would place emphasis upon high walls, electrically charged barriers, and machine guns. Given scarcity of resources, it would place lower priorities on the health and welfare of its inmates so that minimal diets and health standards would be the order of the day. In the most extreme case, the inmates are regarded as expendable, save that the population has to be maintained at some critical point to insure continued appropriations and maintain the institution. The prisoner-of-war camp is the pure case of this sort of custodial institution. The camp fails precisely to the degree that prisoners escape, and succeeds to the degree that escape is prevented at low cost. Other considerations are less relevant or completely immaterial.

Rehabilitation, on the other hand, is the most difficult of educational tasks. It has to do not only with inculcating knowledge and skills but also with change in character habits. To bring about such change requires a different relationship between staff and inmates than is called for by the custodial function (Zald, 1960). Staff members no longer serve as guards but must interact with prisoners in a personal fashion in which their authority is not the dominant factor determining the relationship. Within our prisons, little is attempted in the way of rehabilitation save for occupational training. And partly as a result, our older prisoners comprise a population with records of many previous incarcerations.

The conflict between incarceration and rehabilitation can perhaps be reconciled if a longer temporal frame of reference is accepted by prison authorities, legislators, and the public. The costs of rehabilitation are much heavier in the short run, in requiring more and better trained personnel for prisons; over time, however, they could be assessed against the heavy costs of recidivism. The same long-run time perspective needs to be used with respect to the few inmates who escape the institution concerned with rehabilitation. The tendency is to give undue weight to the exceptional case. In time, rehabilitation may prove more effective in protecting society, and so meet the objective which has so long been used to justify incarceration.

ADAPTIVE SYSTEMS

Adaptive systems are of two types: the research and development adjuncts of the government and of business enterprises; and the independent research agencies and universities. In general, the first type concentrates more on operational research, the second more on basic research. This is a matter of relative emphasis rather than a qualitative distinction. Universities have many contracts with government and business for operational research, and some business organizations carry on basic research in the physical sciences.

Operational research can be systematically organized. Organizations carrying on this applied type of research, however, function better with less separation in the hierarchical dimension of power and privilege than economic or productive systems. Freedom is the factor which has most regularly been discovered to predict research productivity (Meltzer, 1960; Pelz and Andrews, 1964). The break in the line of command between the technical and managerial levels should come high in the structure. The researchers should be making the decisions about research, and management should allow them to translate the problems to be solved on the basis of their technical skill and experience.

There is, of course, the necessity to maintain some linkage between research activities and other organizational subsystems, but this can be done as well by introducing some research people into larger decision-making functions as by permitting managers without research background to enter authoritatively into research activities.

Basic research requires even more freedom than operational research. It is difficult to institutionalize basic research since it deals with yet undiscovered areas of knowledge. An organizational framework, with its role prescriptions and control devices, is based upon existing knowledge. One can program the production of an automobile, since all parts of the productive process and their contribution are well known, but scientific discoveries in the very nature of the case cannot be programmed. This fundamental fact about the nature of the through-put in scientific organizations is often recognized but not as often acted upon because we fall back on the familiar in making organizational decisions.

In research groups we are dealing with an easy maintenance problem for the larger profession of scientists, but with a difficult problem for a specific subsystem. The research scientist gets major rewards from his scientific activity, so that an expressive as well as an instrumental cycle is at work. Moreover, his involvement in his profession is heavy. But his gratifications come less from being a member of a particular university or governmental agency and more from his activities as a scientist. Hence research scientists are fairly mobile people and can be hired from one organization to another by promises of a better laboratory, better equipment, more graduate assistants, and the like.

Colleges and universities were large-scale teaching organizations before they became large-scale research enterprises. Again we have the problem of the single organization, the institution of higher learning, attempting both a socializing or teaching function and an adaptive function. The organizational forms of higher education were built upon teaching rather than upon research. The college professor received his title and his tenure because of his teaching. In the major institutions he was also supposed to give some marginal time outside of his classes to scholarly research. The basic academic budget for a department within a university traditionally has carried little if any funds for research. Hence, to conduct research, the professor had to obtain funds outside the regular budget of the university. The flow of federal funds to support research has become so great that universities are changing their rules to give more status to the research operation. Some schools are even planning to extend academic tenure to their top research personnel.

The inclusion of research in the university structure has made it more of an open system and has increased its relations with the larger society. The ivory tower of scholastic learning is a remote cry from the large scale modern university with its bustling campus, its many research institutes, its conferences for industrial, institutional, and governmental personnel, its ties to professional organizations, and its support from foundations, business, and government. Its many staff members are engaged in a diversity of activities other than teaching, such as serving on the President's Council of Economic Advisers, launching action research on population problems in India, carrying on operational research for state industry, conducting research on the government's space program, cooperating with clinical agencies on problems of training, and placing graduate students in professional jobs in universities, business, and government. To carry on such activities requires freedom of movement, since staff members must spend time away from the campus and take frequent leaves of absence. Thus they serve as members of subsystems other than those of their own university.

The dichotomy between teaching and research as different functions is more of a practical than a logical division. Some of the best training and teaching occurs in the research laboratory. And the college in which teaching is heavily emphasized with a neglect of research soon becomes a dead place even for teaching. Its teachers merely regurgitate the ideas of those whose research is now outmoded. The creative spark of discovery and of scholarship is lost. On the practical side the problems which arise are twofold. Teaching can be geared to mass learning. Research cannot if it is to become a good training vehicle. There is an economy in mass education in inculcating fundamentals before students become apprentices in research. Whether this is a false economy is a debatable issue. The other practical obstacle to combining research and teaching is related to similar considerations, namely that the typical organizational form of the college or university is at the present time not geared to integration of these two functions. It concentrates upon general education and upon professional training, and research experience is not regarded as a basic part of either general education or specific professional training. Moreover, to integrate research experience in these other activities would require a great increase in the freedom allowed both to the teacher and the student.

Apart from the constraints of the educational institution, research in such settings is often handicapped by the organizational requirements of the larger system. In a state university where public accountability of public funds has resulted in an item line budget, the research project must divert time and energy to meeting requirements not appropriate to its activity. An outstanding example of misplaced governmental control is the federal law requiring a budget bureau review and approval of any questionnaire, interview, or research instrument, whether the research is basic or applied or whether it is being conducted by a governmental agency or a university receiving a governmental contract.

How the findings from basic research can be utilized, especially in the behavioral sciences, so that the adaptive function is fully realized is a major problem of our technological society.

ART AND LEISURE TIME PURSUITS

There is an area of life, outside these major organizational structures, where the individual follows his own bent and expresses himself either through hobbies, sports, art, the enjoyment of the art of others, or the vicarious experiences of watching others perform, whether on the stage or in the sports arena. This is the world of leisure time activities.

Even here, however, we have organized structures to meet these individual needs for recreation, for vicarious living, or for enriching experiences. Organized sports operate as a large-scale business. Other areas are not as well organized.

But the world of art by definition does not follow the same rigid codes as other areas. Since this is the world of make believe, of *as if*, there is much more freedom for movement and for the expression of ideas. Moreover, in this less conventional, coded aspect of life not all of the restrictions apply in the same measure as in political and economic affairs. Minority groups barred from any but the lowest positions in other structures traditionally can rise in this field.

And the ideas generated in the world of art can either buttress and rationalize the status quo, as in the more controlled, totalitarian societies, or they can be critical of the existing society, innovative, and a source of change and adaptation. Most significant organizational changes are anticipated by creative artists who help to furnish the rationale for their later acceptance.

SUMMARY

Some of the inherent difficulties of organizational typologies are discussed, including the often-overemphasized uniqueness of individual organizations, and the inability of pure types to account fully for the variability encountered among organizations. Further difficulties include the absence of logical limits to the process of creating categories, and the fact that some organizational properties are readily conceptualized as continuous variables, others as dichotomies, and still others in neither set of terms.

A typology of organizations is proposed, based upon genotypic (first-order) factors and second-order factors. The genotypic function is the function which an organization performs as a subsystem of the larger society. Four such functions are defined, with four types of organizations identified on this basis:

Productive or economic organizations—These organizations are concerned with providing goods and services, and include mining, farming, manufacturing, transportation, and communication.

Maintenance organizations—These organizations are concerned with the socialization and training of people for roles in other organizations and in the society at large. Schools and churches are the major examples of maintenance organizations.

Adaptive organizations—These are organizations intended to create new knowledge, innovative solutions to problems, and the like. The research laboratory is the prototype of such organizations, and universities (as research organizations rather than teaching organizations) would also belong in this category.

Managerial-political organizations—These organizations have to do with the coordination and control of people and resources, and with adjudicating among competing groups. The national state and the agencies of government at lesser levels provide the major examples of this category, although pressure groups, labor unions, and other special-interest organizations would also be classified as managerial-political.

Second-order characteristics can reflect specific aspects of structure, the nature of environmental transactions, internal transactions, and limitless other organizational properties. A discussion of several second-order characteristics is offered in the following terms:

Nature of organizational through-put—a distinction between objects and people as the end products of organizational functioning.

Nature of maintenance processes—a distinction between expressive (intrinsic) rewards and instrumental (extraneous) rewards as ways of attracting and holding members in organizations.

Nature of bureaucratic structure—a distinction in terms of permeability of organizational boundaries (ease of joining and leaving), and in terms of structural elaboration (degree of role specialization and number of echelons).

Type of equilibrium—a distinction between the tendency to a steady state and the tendency toward maximization of organizational return as dominant organizational dynamics.

6

The Concept of
Organizational Effectiveness

There is no lack of material on criteria of organizational success. The literature is studded with references to efficiency, productivity, absence, turnover, and profitability—all of these offered implicitly or explicitly, separately or in combination, as definitions of organizational effectiveness. Most of what has been written on the meaning of these criteria and on their interrelatedness, however, is judgmental and open to question. What is worse, it is filled with advice that seems sagacious but is tautological and contradictory.

In recent years the research evidence of this unsatisfactory state of affairs has begun to accumulate. For example, an attempt to make comparisons in rate of growth among 40 organizations performing similar functions (selling and servicing automobiles) encountered difficulties with the use of growth rate as a criterion of effectiveness. It appeared that the meaning of growth for the health, survival, and overall effectiveness of an organization was very different at different stages of the organizational life cycle. (Seashore, 1962)

A study using expert rankings to determine the effectiveness of 20 successful and 20 unsuccessful insurance agencies developed signs of internal contradiction in the course of analysis. These resulted from the fact that the concept of organizational effectiveness was understood as multidimensional by the expert raters who were in some disagreement with respect to the weighting of the various dimensions. Moreover, they were unaware of their disagreements. A factor analysis of 70 measures of performance obtained from these agencies (independent of the ratings) demonstrated that the effectiveness concept utilized in the research contained no fewer than seven independent factors, and that the expert judgments of effectiveness corresponded very badly to any of them.

A study of 32 operating units of a nationwide service organization was designed to evaluate leadership practices in relation to unit effectiveness, the latter based on managerial rankings. The data for five criteria of effectiveness (overall ratings, productivity as measured by time study, chargeable accidents, unexcused absences, and observed errors) were analyzed separately, after an attempt to predict according to the overall rankings showed an overlarge unexplained variance. The correlations among the five criteria of effectiveness were generally low, with fewer than half of them reaching significant levels. Even more disturbing was the fact that the magnitude of the intercorrelations varied greatly within the 32 organizational units. For example, the relationship between productivity and effectiveness varied from $-.56$ to $+.83$, and the relationships among the other criteria were no less erratic (Seashore et al., 1960).

The existence of the problem of developing satisfactory criteria of organizational performance is clear enough; its solution is much less obvious. Our working assumption is that the difficulty is essentially theoretical and conceptual, and that the remedies must begin with conceptual clarification. Organizational effectiveness has become one of those handy but treacherous pseudo concepts, connoting a sort of totality of organizational goodness—a sum of such elements as productivity, cost performance, turnover, quality of output, and the like. This rudimentary model, as Seashore (1962) states, "is false to most of the data we have examined so far, and more complex models need to be invoked." In earlier chapters we have proposed that open-system theory supplies the elements of such a model for human organization, and we have attempted an elaboration of that theory to fit the phenomena of large-scale human organizations. With this model in mind, let us consider the meaning of organizational effectiveness, beginning with one of its major components, efficiency.

THE EFFICIENCY OF ORGANIZATIONS

As open systems, organizations survive only so long as they are able to maintain *negentropy*, that is, import in all forms greater amounts of energy than they return to the environment as product. The reason for this is obvious. The energic input into an organization is in part invested directly and objectified as organizational output. But some of the input is absorbed or consumed by the organization. In order to do the work of transformation, the organization itself must be created, energized, and maintained, and these requirements are reflected in an inevitable energic loss between input and output. The electric transformer is a relatively efficient machine, but it extracts an energic price (recognizable as heat) in the process of changing alternating current to direct. The vacuum tube must be heated before it can do its work; even the transistor passes on less energy than it receives.

For all open systems, it is appropriate to question the amount of this cost. How much of the energic input from the outside into the system emerges as product, and how much is absorbed by the system? In other words, what is the net energic cost of the transformation? The ideal answer to this question would be provided by a system which exported as intended output 100 per cent of the energy which it received. For such a system the efficiency ratio of output/input would be 1.00 or 100 per cent.

There is a convenient simplicity to examples like that of the electric motor or transformer. They are systems for which the input is a single energic form—electricity—and the output is a single but different energic form—the kinetic energy of a rotating shaft in the case of the motor, and an altered electric current in the case of the transformer. In such cases the efficiency concept (ratio) is relatively obvious in meaning and easy in computation. In all human organizations, however, there are many additional complications, and in private industry there is the special complication of profit and its relation to efficiency.

One of the major and characteristic complications of human organizations lies in the multiple forms in which energy is imported. Almost all organizations take in energy in at least two forms: *people,* as energy sources; and *materials,* which already contain the energic investment of procurement, extraction, or partial manufacture. Many organizations also import energy in other forms such as steam, electricity, or the movement of water.

Rough distinctions are often made among these energic sources and among the uses to which each may be put. For example, it is customary to refer to the energic input of people as *direct* or *indirect,* according to its closeness to the basic transformation in which the organization is engaged. In general, direct labor refers to all energy which acts directly on the materials being put through the organization. (Forming metal, grinding corn, and selling groceries are direct labor.) Energy which acts directly on other members of the organization (supervision or staff services), or on materials not part of the organizational through-put (accounting, running time studies, or planning future requirements), we are accustomed to call indirect labor. It is a long-standing convention of industry, although one which we predict will be shattered by the combined demands of labor unions and automated procedures, to pay for direct labor by the hour and indirect labor by periods of time ranging from a week to a year.

A distinction in some ways similar to that between direct and indirect labor is made with respect to materials. Reflecting primarily their directness of use in the organizational through-put (that is, the rapidity with which they are consumed in the productive process), they are classified as *supplies* or *equipment*. The ideal supply is completely consumed in the process of organizational transformation; it emerges transformed and without waste as product or output. The ideal equipment, on the other hand, is eternal and indestructible; it facilitates the organizational through-put but is not transformed. In practice, of course, the distinction blurs; the electric utility uses up its generators and steam turbines no less than the coal which feeds them —but more slowly.

A further complication in studying the efficiency of human organizations stems from the inadequacy of our methods of accounting and reckoning. The measurement of organizational input and output is not often done in energic terms, nor in any other common denominator which might be translated readily into some energic measure. We speak in tons, board feet, hours, or gallons, according to the material or commodity in question. The nearest we come to a common measure of these diverse units is the dollar (cost), which is not necessarily commensurate with energic input and output. It is interesting, perhaps even ironic, that economists have long recognized the disadvantage of using money as a unit of measure in circumstances that really require measures of energic investment and psychic return. Most economists have nevertheless become so convinced of the elusiveness of such concepts that they have given up trying to make operational their psychic concept of utility and have preferred to be guided by its distant and distorted fiscal echo.

To regard the cycles of organizational life in energic terms does not solve all the conceptual problems of organizational effectiveness. Miller (1963) has proposed that organizations must be regarded both as information-processing and energy-processing systems, and in subsequent chapters on communication and policy-making we will be concerned more with informational than with simple energic processes. Nevertheless, in conceptual terms, if not in terms yet convenient for measurement, we can speak of the efficiency of an organization in a fashion analogous to that of the motor: How much output do we get for a given input? How much input must we invest to assure a given output? And where an absolute answer to such questions may be difficult or impossible, approximations thereto or relative efficiencies of two or more similar organizations are often quite feasible.

Imagine two modest establishments engaged in the manufacture of baseball bats, one producing the bats entirely by hand, and the other making use of a lathe, power saw, and power sander. One immediate measure of the relative efficiency of these two establishments could be had by comparing the energic input required by each to produce a finished bat. It is likely, however, that these quantities would not be readily available, and we might therefore make use of an approximation: the number of man-hours of input required to produce a bat, assuming for the moment that the energic input of the hand-worker during an hour was equal to that of the tool-worker. (We assume, in other words, that the lathe-hand is working as "hard" as the worker using a spoke shave.) If we found that the lathe-hand made one bat during each hour of an eight-hour day, while the hand-worker made only one bat during an entire day, we would conclude that the lathe system was eight times as efficient as the hand system for the manufacture of baseball bats.

The example would have to be elaborated in many respects before it would begin to do justice to the complexities of our subject. The two manufacturing operations do not permit such simple comparisons. They both make direct use of human labor and of wood. But the lathe system uses lathes, and the hand system does not. True, the lathe system does not use up the lathe very fast; it may last, let us say, for the manufacture of 100,000 bats. Nevertheless, it is part of the input, and 1/100,000 part of the energic cost of creating a lathe must be included in the energic cost of each bat. The advantage will still lie with the lathe system over the hand system. But an important principle is involved: our first comparison disregarded entirely the cost of the physical plant; our second comparison at least raised the problem of computing and including such costs. Obviously a complete energic accounting, like a complete cost accounting, would include all inputs—labor, electricity, plant, equipment, and the rest.

The system theorist is not rigid about such matters, however; for him the inclusion or exclusion of any input is a problem of frame of reference. It is permissible (and it is sometimes very useful) to compare the efficiency of two systems with each in a prime ongoing state, without regard to the cost of achieving and maintaining that state. If you do not want to accept the physical equipment of a system as given, or if (which amounts to the same thing) you want to measure efficiency over a period of time longer than the life of the equipment, then the energic cost of replacement must be included in your calculations. Efficiency becomes a matter not only of labor input and materials (direct costs) but also of plant and equipment (indirect costs). For most purposes, any statement regarding efficiency must include both direct and indirect costs, especially in light of the increasing rate at which industrial equipment becomes obsolete.

The problem of defining spatial boundaries for some purpose of organizational analysis is much like the temporal problem. How much space (what activities) are we to include in the system under analysis? The nature of this problem can be readily illustrated by means of the previous example, if we bring into the manufacture of baseball bats the additional issue of wood supply and procurement. Suppose that the Lathe Bat Company is located in New York City and imports its wood from an average distance of 500 miles. The Hand Bat Company is located next to a mature ash grove and brings its wood an average distance of 500 yards. If our comparison of efficiencies is defined solely in terms of the manufacturing process, the facts of location are irrelevant. If we are interested in a larger organizational space of procurement-plus-production, then nearness to source of materials is important. In this example, the relative efficiency of the Lathe Bat Company as compared to its competitor is less because of its location. Analogous arguments with respect to location could be made for any other needed resource, and for any other environmental transaction including marketing.

The spatial and temporal boundaries to system analysis are characteristically interdependent. Suppose we specify that our analysis of bat manufacture is to apply in perpetuity, or at least for a time period of great and indefinite length. To guarantee a permanent supply of the appropriate wood, the bat company may find it necessary (as some large lumber companies do) to extend its boundaries to include operations which will guarantee renewal of major supplies at a rate which balances their consumption in manufacture. Thus the bat company must grow ash trees as fast as it cuts them down and uses them, and a subsystem of reforestation becomes part of the total energic cost of bat manufacture and part of the system for manufacture.

Which frame of reference, or definition of system boundaries in space and time, is appropriate depends on what we want to do. If we want to make an overall comparison between two companies or predict their profitability, the legal boundaries of the establishment may be appropriate for our purpose. But suppose that our efficiency study is intended to determine whether or not the Hand Bat Company should install lathes. For this purpose the comparison of manufacturing operations per se is most appropriate. Similarly, a decision about plant location would involve efficiency comparisons with respect to procurement and marketing, with manufacturing procedures as such largely irrelevant. Empirical studies of industrial mobility have documented the considerations which are dominant in determining the location and re-location of companies (Hoover, 1948; Katona and Morgan, 1950; Mueller and Morgan, 1962).

There is no limit to the extension of time-space boundaries in the study of human systems, since all seemingly independent and separate human systems are linked together into the total system of human life. The human enterprise as a whole, moreover, represents a system of great negative entropy. It persists only by means of massive importation of energy—first of all from the sun, on a continuing basis, and second from other natural processes—some of time long past, like the formation of coal and oil, and some continuing, like the power of rivers and waterfalls.

POTENTIAL AND ACTUAL EFFICIENCY

The efficiency ratio tells us how well the organization utilizes the energy at its disposal, how much energic investment in all forms (labor, supplies, power, and the like) is required for each unit of output. This concept of efficiency, in turn, can be resolved into two distinct components: the potential efficiency of the system design, and the extent to which that potential is realized in practice.

Suppose that two plants identical in technology are set up with different organizational structures, one plan calling for a supervisor for each ten workers and the other calling for a supervisor (putting forth equivalent effort) for each twenty workers. If both plants operate as designed, let us say to produce 1000 television sets in an eight-hour shift, clearly the more efficient system is the organization with fewer supervisory positions. It is achieving the same output with less energic input. Furthermore, its superior efficiency is intrinsic in the organization *design.* Each system is operating as designed, but one design is more efficient than the other.

The example might not work out this way, of course. If the thinness of supervision in the "20:1" plant were reflected in higher scrap loss and lower production, so that this plant produced only 800 working television sets per day, the efficiency comparison between the two plants would be different. One plant would have the more economical (efficient) organizational plan, but would be unable to fulfill in prac-tice the production which the plan called for; the other organization would have a more costly (less efficient) plan, but its operation would meet fully the specifications of the plan. Which of the two plants was more efficient overall would be an empirical question.

This kind of distinction between components of efficiency is com-mon enough. Every automobile enthusiast will assure us that an engine like that of the Jaguar, with its double overhead camshafts and hemi-spherical combustion chambers, is inherently more efficient than a flat-head, side-valve engine of the same displacement. If both engines are in prime condition and properly tuned, the facts of this comparison can be readily demonstrated in terms of speed, developed horsepower, and other criteria of performance and efficiency. One engine is simply a better, more elegant design than the other; it is a superior system for transforming gasoline into transportation. But what if the superior automobile has been badly driven, let out of adjustment, or otherwise abused, so that its actual performance falls far short of its potential efficiency? It may realize so little of its potential that it will in prac-tice be less efficient than its plebeian competitor. There are, in short, two quite separate aspects of the efficiency of any functioning system: the potential or abstract efficiency in the system design, and the extent to which that efficiency is realized in the concrete instance.

The two aspects are not wholly independent, of course. Some or-ganizational designs are more capable of actualization than others, some more fragile or more accident-prone than others. The concept of the socio-technical system as proposed by Trist and his colleagues (Emery and Trist, 1960) and to some extent the concept of man-machine systems represent attempts to bring into the same framework both aspects of efficiency—the ideal efficiency of the system and the practicability of attaining that ideal with human beings and realistic conditions of work. Herman Wouk (1951) offered a more colorful com-ment on the same general issue when he observed in *The Caine Mu-tiny* that the Navy was an organization designed by geniuses to be run by idiots.

PROFIT AND EFFICIENCY

Let us turn to the special but extensive case of the profit-making organization. We said that the efficiency of an organizational system is given by the ratio of its energic output (or product) to its energic input (or cost). We stipulated also that total cost per unit of produc-tion includes procurement, marketing, maintenance, depreciation of plant, and the like. Will this efficiency ratio also define precisely the profitability of the plant? No.

An increase in efficiency will tend to make a plant more profitable, since the greater efficiency means a lesser cost per unit of product and implies no immediate reduction in selling price. Prices tend to be set by what consumers will pay and correspond roughly to the production costs of the least efficient producers. In 1963, for example, the Gen-eral Motors Corporation reported profits of approximately 20 per cent on sales; its competitors reported profit rates of about half that magnitude. No doubt many factors entered into the profit advantage of General Motors, the efficiencies of size and volume prominent among them. A gain in the efficiency of a particular company, then, is likely to mean an increase in profit.

But other considerations must be introduced even into an elementary discussion of profit, considerations which have little to do with system efficiency. Suppose that a manufacturer of television sets has two plants in different parts of the country, and that the plants are technologically identical. The dollar investment in plant and equipment is identical, and the costs of procuring supplies and marketing the finished product are the same. In Plant A, however, the employees work 25 per cent harder than in Plant B, and they produce 25 per cent more sets. As a result, Plant A is certainly more profitable than Plant B, and there is a presumption that it is better managed. Is it also 25 per cent more efficient as a system?

In the energic terms of reference we have employed, it is not. Plant A uses the same number of energy units for each product unit as does Plant B. Plant A is simply getting a greater energic input from each worker. Suppose that employees in Plant A worked ten hours each day instead of eight (an alternative way of obtaining a 25 per cent increase in energic input from each worker). Would this increase in hours of work make Plant A more efficient than Plant B as a producing system? Of course not—at least not in the terms in which we have defined efficiency. Efficiency has to do with the ratio of energic output to input; increasing the output by running the system longer or by increasing the rate of energic input does not per se alter the efficiency ratio.

Only in certain limited respects would such changes in operation tend to affect efficiency. The plant in which workers are suddenly motivated to work 25 per cent harder and produce 25 per cent more has not had a 25 per cent change in the efficiency ratio of output/input, since both numerator and denominator have increased. There will have been some genuine gain in efficiency, however, insofar as the greater output is obtained from the same plant and equipment without a corresponding increase in its rate of depreciation. If the gross increase in product is not cancelled out by the more rapid using-up of plant and equipment, there will be some resultant gain in efficiency. There will be greater differences between these two plants in profitability, however. The company which has induced its employees to increase output by 25 per cent has probably realized a profit increase of much greater magnitude, unless the production increase has been motivated by or rewarded with a corresponding increase in the wage bill. In any case, the important point is that profitability and efficiency are not synomymous, as energic and dollar accounting are not synonymous, although they are certainly related.

EFFICIENCY AND SURVIVAL

The discussion of efficiency has so far made little reference to the dimension of time. The definition of efficiency as an energic ratio can be applied at any instant of time; the cost of the organizational transformation of inputs into product can be computed for any span of time. Short-term analyses are, as is often the case, easier and more obvious. The previous examples of organizations differing in efficiency have stipulated some of the major short-term advantages of the more efficient organization in comparison to its competitors. The more efficient organization can lower prices and thus gain a larger share of the market. Or it can, at a given market price, make more gross profit than its competitors. It can, as a result, increase the return to the members of any or all of its subsystems—managers, stockholders, and wage-earners. The more efficient organization, in short, is in the process of acquiring an energic surplus, because the terms of its input and output transactions are set by its less efficient competitors.

This operating advantage has long-term implications of importance, beginning with the storage of energy. Efficiency gives a margin over the organizational hand-to-mouth condition in which the return from product is barely sufficient to purchase the inputs needed to repeat the productive cycle. This margin can be immediately distributed as wage payments, bonuses, or dividends. In American industry executive bonuses and dividend payments vary sharply with changes in relative efficiency and gross profits; wage payments are more likely to be set by industrywide standards of collective bargaining, although they too respond to increases or decreases in the margin between organizational income and outgo.

It is most unlikely that an organization will distribute all of the surplus of income over cost of production. Some of it is characteristically retained—as reserve funds, as capital funds for expansion, as funds for replacement of equipment and for various kinds of emergencies. All these funds represent the storage of energy by the organization, and the storage process can take other forms than money. The organization can stock-pile materials, as manufacturers who can do so stock-pile steel and coal under threat of a strike. Some part of a surplus over immediate operating needs is typically used for expansion of the enterprise, for additions to plant or for still more efficient equipment, or for extension of organizational activity into new fields or product lines.

The major long-range outcomes of efficiency-generated surpluses are therefore organizational *growth* and an increment in the *survival power* of the organization. The storage of energy permits the organization to survive its own mistakes and the exigencies of its environment. For the organization without such storage, every untoward event, internal or external, is in some degree incapacitating, and mishaps of size can be deadly.

The contribution of efficiency to growth is not a one-way or a one-time organizational event; it is a cycle which continues over a wide span of time and a wide range of organizational circumstances, sizes, and structures. Efficiency begets growth, but growth brings new gains in efficiency. There are limits, of course; for any organization and technology there is some optimum size. But the optimum for technical purposes is apparently very large and the relationship of production costs to size can for many purposes be regarded as a linear function. The auto industry, for example, operates on the basis of substantial annual alterations in style or mechanical specifications, with annual costs of retooling running to the tens and hundreds of millions. The more units produced during the year by a given company, the lower the cost of that retooling which must be borne by each unit. This is an elementary kind of arithmetic, but inexorable. There is, of course, that theoretical point at which size becomes a handicap, and there are environmental changes which can make efficiency irrelevant. In general, however, the long-range effects of efficiency are growth and survival, and the effect of growth is likely to be increased efficiency.

EFFICIENCY IN NONPROFIT ORGANIZATIONS

The foregoing analysis developed in the course of exploring the relationship of two common measures of organizational effectiveness, efficiency and profitability. To what extent is the analysis applicable to other human organizations, organizations which do not sell products and accumulate profits or losses? We can answer this question by posing another: What does profit signify? It means merely that people "want" the organizational product enough to forego other things and choose it, that is, buy it at a price which covers the costs of production, including profit. This is one way by which the larger social environment permits an organization to import energy—that is, hire people, build plants, and buy materials. If there is an overwhelming preference for other organizational products, or if people lack the economic means to signify their wants by buying, then in effect the organization is denied the means to import energy and it must reduce its operations or go out of existence.

Business organizations differ, of course, in the advantageousness of their environmental transactions. As they become more efficient, they require less energic return in order to maintain their operations. There are also the many forms of special advantage bestowed by location, by exclusive production of certain goods, or by reserves built up from past efficiencies. The basic equation remains, however; in the long run the organization must receive its necessary quantum of energy from outside or it must cease to be, and a business receives this input only by selling its product.

For other kinds of organizations, the life-giving or death-dealing energic decisions are made in quite different fashion. A community college does not typically operate at a profit. In a sense, perhaps, the students "buy" its product but they do not pay a tuition high enough to permit the organization to hold its faculty and maintain its plant. The real sale of the college product is to the public, and the decision that the organization shall continue is given by the city council or other legislative body which appropriates the funds for operating the college. The legislature has, in effect, "chosen" the product of the community college in preference to other products which might have been had for the same appropriation. In so doing, the legislature makes it possible for the college to import the energy it requires.

The environmental decision to support the college differs in many respects from the decision to support the business establishment. The decision about the college is made formally and explicitly by a legislative body which has the legitimate power to appropriate funds or refuse them, power which in turn has been given to the legislature by the body politic and which can be withdrawn (at least from specific legislators) at the next election. In the case of a business, no purchaser of goods makes the decision to sustain the establishment or commit it to organizational ruin, and yet the sum of individual consumer decisions adds up to that determination.

For some other kinds of nonbusiness organizations, the picture is still more complicated. The military, for example, is sustained in part as is the college; it is awarded tax funds by legislative act. But it imports human energy in a more direct fashion by conscription. This, too, in our society, requires legislative sanction, but it takes the form of a direct awarding of human energies to the military organization, rather than an awarding of money which enables the organization to attract people. Other inputs are acquired by the military, as by other organizations, through negotiation and purchase.

For some voluntary organizations, the process which determines organizational input is both individually decided and direct. A student weighs the decision to join the Chess Club, wondering whether the psychological return will be sufficiently great and its probability sufficiently high to make it "worth his while" to join and invest some part of his energies in the activities of the club. If he and a sufficient number of other students decide in favor of the club, it will have an organizational existence. If it fails to return enough psychic satisfaction to its members to motivate their continuing investment of energy, it will go out of existence. The "efficiency" of the club and its prospects for survival are given by the amount of such return to members in relation to the demands made on their time and energy.

The concept of efficiency does not have meaning only for business organizations, and the survival benefits of efficiency are not limited to profit-making organizations. These notions are inherent in the characteristics of human organizations as open systems. They remind us that the ultimate decision to give or withhold the needed organizational inputs lies in the environment, and that the larger social environment in this way holds the power of life and death over every organization.

EFFECTIVENESS: MAXIMIZING RETURN TO THE ORGANIZATION

We have seen that efficiency in business organizations produces immediate increases in profits, creates the possibility for energy storage, and is conducive to long-run growth and survival. Certainly the organization which increases its efficiency also increases its effectiveness as a viable system. Nevertheless, the efficiency criterion is insufficient for purposes of a complete organizational analysis; it is only an aspect of organizational effectiveness.

Efficiency is primarily a criterion of the internal life of the organization, and it is concerned with economic and technical aspects of the organization. By itself, it takes inadequate notice of the openness of human organizations. (Especially is this true when the efficiency concept is applied at a single moment of time.) Yet we have defined organizations as open systems, dependent on outside agencies in the environment for making available required energic inputs (labor, materials, and others) and for absorbing the organizational product. This means that the organization is constantly engaged in several kinds of environmental transactions—disposal or marketing, procurement or recruiting, information-getting, and the exertion of influence to accomplish organizational goals. The profitability of a business organization and the survival prospects of all human organizations are not given solely by considerations of efficiency in internal system design and actualization; they are determined also by the advantageousness of the organization-environment transactions.

In our society, as in other industrialized cultures, these transactions are usually carried on by means of money. Profit-making organizations sell their products for money and use the money to buy materials, pay wages, and thus renew the productive cycle. For charitable organizations, educational institutions, and agencies of government, the "sale" of the product may be less obvious but, as we have seen, there is still the problem of persuading some appropriate source in the environment to make operating funds available.

Regardless of the exact forms of the environmental transactions, they are of major significance for the organization. In industry, margin of profit and therefore security and survival are determined in part by such transactions, quite independently of the internal systemic efficiency of the organization. In the discussion of efficiency and profit, we have already considered two of the more obvious examples of such transactional advantage—nearness to supplies and nearness to markets. The location of an organization in relation to agencies in its environment with which it must relate is a clear source of economic advantage or disadvantage. This is true in the absolute reckoning of total costs of production and distribution; it is even more significant in terms of relative costs or the state of the organization in relation to its competitors.

Such advantages of location may be accidental, arising from causes wholly outside the organization and unforeseen within it. They may also come about because of successful planning within the organization. In the latter case, persisting advantage has accrued to the organization because of better information-getting (another form of transaction), or because of superior processing of and inferring from information within the organization.

Location is only one source of advantage in organizational input and output. The getting and sending of information across organizational boundaries are other important sources. Indeed, a key measure of efficiency for a procurement department is the thoroughness with which it scans the potential sources of supply and chooses the source with least organizational cost.

For sales and marketing departments, the analogous function is the discovery of customers who offer greatest organizational advantage. Such transactions, however, are not merely informational; they involve persuasion and exercise of influence. The terms of purchase or sale must be negotiated. We can generalize this point by stating that environmental transactions are in some degree *political;* they involve the making and engineering of choices on grounds other than economics and efficiency in an open market.

The pursuit of organizational goals by political means is most prevalent, and a most natural outcome of the dynamics of organization. The very achievement of internal organizational efficiency promotes growth and, if continued, dominance with some degree of monopolistic control over the terms of procurement and marketing. But even where that degree of internal efficiency has not been attained, a company has much to gain in overall effectiveness by using political tactics. Some of these tactics have been outlawed for almost a century (although the simultaneous existence of anti-trust and "fair-trade" legislation suggests confusion and ambivalence in these matters). Conspiracy in restraint of trade, monopolistic dominance of an industrial field, price fixing among major producers, and the like are illegal. They are nevertheless live legal issues, and few years pass without trials and suits of substantial scope. Political advantages in sale and purchase are pressed, and the number of corporations (and corporate executives) that choose to live dangerously near the legal margin gives testimony to the rewards of doing so.

Many forms of political influence in the service of organizational goals are judged legitimate by the larger society. We are indignant at "payola," and prosecute some forms of bribery. It is considered appropriate, however, for an organization to attempt to bring about advantageous environmental relationships by persuasion of influential people, by lobbying, or even by donations to election funds. These advantages may take the form of subsidies, as in the case of airlines and the merchant marine, or special tax arrangements, as in the case of oil and gas producers. They may take the form of tariffs and duties or even of attacks on unions and legislation to weaken union influence on the conditions under which business is conducted. It is no less an example of political means in the service of organizational effectiveness, of course, when labor unions create their own legislative programs and political campaigns.

Political and economic transactions merge in some instances. A company which has sufficient resources to afford the maneuver may reduce prices below the cost of production for a time, in order to eliminate or make more tractable a competitor who lacks the cushion of stored resources to survive such a program. This is essentially a political tactic, although the immediate means involve economic manipulation.

It is not necessary for our present purposes to attempt a catalogue of political extensions of organizational control over the environment. It is important to recognize such extensions as inevitable outcomes of the organizational dynamic for survival, growth, security, and return to members. The textbook path to organizational survival is internal efficiency: build the better mousetrap or build the old trap less expensively. There is, however, a whole class of alternative or supplementary solutions—the political devices which maximize organizational return at some cost to other organizations or individuals. These alternatives we have called political, in contrast to the economic or technical alternatives.

Economic-technical solutions are reflected as increases in organizational efficiency. They make the organization a more efficient system for the transformation of energy and thereby contribute to its growth and survival. They do not necessarily make the organization more efficient in the acquisition of inputs and the disposal of outputs, although they may contribute to the advantageousness of such transactions by improving the organizational ability to scan the environment broadly and accurately for sources of supply or for markets. Political solutions complement economic ones by dealing with problems of input and disposal in other ways, usually involving direct manipulation of the environment. Both economic and political means contribute to profitability and to organizational effectiveness. We can define organizational effectiveness, then, as the maximization of return to the organization, by economic and technical means (efficiency), and by political means.

The examples of political effectiveness we have offered have dealt entirely with external transactions—with arrangements to maintain price levels, to get subsidies or other preferments, to eliminate or restrict competition, or to get some commitment to obtain inputs on advantageous terms. The use of political means to obtain organizational advantage need not always be directed outside the organization, however, although outside efforts are more conspicuously political. We would also define as political rather than technical most devices for getting more energic investment from the worker for each wage dollar. Extreme cases make the point obvious: slavery is a political institution, a set of political means for guaranteeing labor input to organizations concerned with agriculture and construction. The institution of indenture provides another example.

We would argue also that, if one firm pays lower wages than another, or induces its workers to work longer hours, or to work harder, all these would constitute political increments to organizational effectiveness. And the opposition to such attempts by management takes political forms—in terms of the demand for collective bargaining, for a minimum wage, for a contractual agreement about hours of work and speed of work.

There is admittedly a certain arbitrariness in deciding where to draw the line between efficiency and political effectiveness, and it is tempting to draw it at the organizational boundary. This would have the effect, however, of defining as efficiency all internal arrangements which increased the organizational return—whether by improvements in the energic ratio of input required to create a given amount of product, or by devices for inducing increased energic input from organizational members. We prefer to distinguish between these two kinds of increments to effectiveness, keeping the term efficiency to describe the former and including the latter with other, externally oriented political approaches.

There is in this distinction no implication that to increase organizational return by means of efficiency gains is virtuous and to do so by political means is reprehensible. The value issues involved require separate argument and justification. The neutrality of the political classification can perhaps be illustrated by those programs which are designed to induce greater energic input from organizational members by means which enhance the return to those members. Many human relations programs are frankly intended to increase both energic investment and psychological return to the worker; to the extent that they involve no systemic or structural changes within the organization, they contribute to organizational effectiveness by political means rather than by increasing the efficiency ratio.

Political effectiveness then consists in the short run of maximizing the return to the organization by means of advantageous transactions with various outside agencies and groups, and with the members of the organization as well. Like efficiency, political effectiveness contributes to the immediate profitability of the enterprise and to its growth and survival power for the longer term. It leads also to increased control over the organizational environment, as short-term advantages in external transactions are reinforced and made permanent by precedent and legal recognition.

The preceding exposition of efficiency and political effectiveness in the short term and the longer run is summarized in Figure 5.

FRAME OF REFERENCE AND THE SUPERSYSTEM

We have defined organizational effectiveness as the extent to which all forms of energic return to the organization are maximized. This is determined by a combination of the efficiency of the organization as a system and its success in obtaining on advantageous terms the inputs it requires. We have also distinguished between effectiveness in the short-term and in the long-term sense. The marks of long-term effectiveness we have identified as storage, growth, survival, and control over the environment. This discussion has taken place within the or-

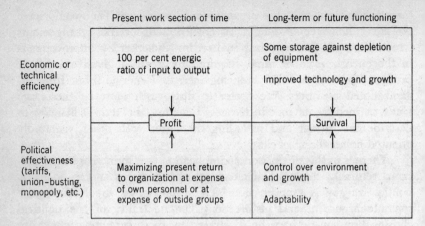

Figure 5   Organizational frame of reference.

ganizational frame of reference—effectiveness from the point of view of the organization.

All frames of reference are arbitrary, however, and there are advantages and disadvantages to the one we have used. In a book on organizations as systems, it is perhaps unnecessary to justify the use of the organizational frame of reference, but we should not leave the issue of organizational effectiveness without reminding ourselves that the single organization is an intermediate level of discourse, and that either a lesser or a loftier frame is appropriate for some purposes. We can discuss organizational effectiveness from the point of view of the individual member, defining as most effective that organization which offers the greatest aggregate return to the member. (The issues of member satisfaction will be more thoroughly discussed in Chapter 12.) We can also consider organizational effectiveness in terms of the super-system, the society of which the organization is a part.

At this level, the effectiveness of the organization would be assessed in terms of its contribution to the efficiency, survival power, and environmental control of the entire societal system. The transactions between the organization and other agencies in the society would be judged effective to the degree that the organization provided maximal return to the society for the energic demands which it made on the society. The test of effectiveness, in other words, would be little changed, but would be applied at the next higher level of social organization. In doing so, the prosperity and survival of the organization becomes secondary.

For example, consider an organization established to discover the causes of cancer. It is most successful and contributes most to the larger society by completing its mission promptly, even if in doing so it terminates its own existence. The agonies of the National Foundation for Infantile Paralysis to convert its March of Dimes and its organizational mission from the cure of polio to the cure of other diseases illustrates this contradiction between organizational survival and societal needs. During wartime, when the needs of the larger society are prominent in the minds of all citizens, the distinction between the organizational and societal frames of reference is obvious and frequently invoked. Organizations are expected to concentrate on meeting the societal need of maximum production and they are criticized if they do "business as usual," that is, operate in such a way as to maximize the gains and survival of the organization as such.

Ordinarily, however, we expect the managers of organizations to act from the organizational frame of reference, and we do not impose on them the strain of acting consistently in the interests of the larger community. We know that what is good for the country may not always be good for the organization, and we expect the concern for the larger society to be concentrated in those roles which are organization-free. Indeed, we are suspicious of conflict of interest on the part of individuals who show themselves to be carrying some of the old impediments into the new role.

Perhaps monopoly is the most obvious example of an organizational form which constitutes high effectiveness in terms of the organizational frame of reference, and reduced effectiveness in terms of the societal or supersystem frame of reference. Monopoly implies extensive control of the environment by the organization; competitors have been eliminated and potential competitors are discouraged by various means. The terms (price, amount of supply) on which the organizational product will be made available to the larger society are determined largely from within the organization. There is typically a restriction of product below the potential levels of output. Monopoly is, in short, a relationship of organization to society characterized by a peculiar degree of political control and effectiveness by the organization. (That effectiveness may have been facilitated by economic efficiency, but it has gone beyond efficiency.)

From the societal view, the political effectiveness of the monopoly is experienced as additional costs in the sense of restricted supply of goods and disadvantageous terms of exchange with the organization (higher prices than are required for organizational sustenance). To risk a generalization which is much more hypothetical than demonstrated, we could say that gains in organizational effectiveness which come about through improved organizational efficiency are likely to be gains also from the societal frame of reference. Gains in overall organizational effectiveness which come about through gains in the political component of effectiveness are more variable in their implications for the larger system. They may be, as in the monopolistic example, losses for the society as a whole.

Examples of discontinuity between the requirements of different systemic levels do not all consist of organizational gains at societal costs. There are times when societal needs, especially in the short term, impose inefficiencies on organizations: the society asks the organization to become less effective in its own terms in order to become more effective in meeting the needs of the supersystem. The sharpest examples can be found in the wartime operation of industry. The short-term demand of the larger society for maximizing gross product takes precedence over all the usual criteria of organizational efficiency. Production costs become almost irrelevant; criteria of employee selection are rewritten. The cost-plus contract is not merely a pressing of organizational advantage for purposes of profit; it symbolizes the abandonment of one set of criteria and frame of reference for another.

We can imagine a similar imposition of supersystem criteria with respect to any goal of great social importance. The identification of such goals is essentially a problem in values rather than organizational theory as such. We might decide, for example, that the importance of discovering causes and cures for cancer in the least possible time is far more important than making such discoveries at the least possible cost, or in ways that conform to the usual signs of organizational efficiency. The indications of such a decision would be the availability of massive inputs for cancer-related research, willingness to support conflicting approaches simultaneously instead of in some sequence of learning, tolerance of duplication, and many other violations of the etiquette of efficiency. It is interesting that the word *war* (war on disease, war on poverty) is in general use to indicate the abandonment of the organizational frame of reference and the launching of a major effort in which the societal frame of reference defines effectiveness.

The conflict between the organizational and societal frames of reference is essentially spatial; it has to do with the number of organizations, roles, and individuals to be considered in applying criteria of effectiveness. An analogous problem arises in connection with issues of time; short-term and long-term frames of reference are no less different than organizational and societal. Like spatial differences, temporal differences may or may not create differences in the criteria and definition of organizational effectiveness. A business may, for example, come into a situation where it must get a product on the market during a certain season or lose the market entirely, get a plant into production during a certain year or lose major initiative to a competitor. In the extreme case, an organization may be faced with attaining some short-run goal for the sake of long-run survival. Under such circumstances, the usual criteria of efficiency and effectiveness are violated in the short-run for the sake of long-term success. The contract is accepted even though the organization will lose money on it; supplies are bought on terms which would otherwise be rejected. Overtime wages are paid; premiums are offered for completion of work ahead of schedule. The short-term criteria of effectiveness, including profit, are sacrificed for that ultimate long-term criterion—survival.

The foregoing section has been a discussion of frames of reference, and the ways in which criteria and judgments of effectiveness are transmuted by changing spatial and temporal frames of reference. It is perhaps appropriate to conclude by considering a frame of reference which has pervaded the entire chapter, which pervades no less the thinking of most people about organizational life, and which is in process of being upset by the changing technology of our time. This frame of reference has as its central assumption the scarcity of energy. It follows that efficiency or energy-conserving modes of production are preferred, that time and energy must be bought, that leisure (time free from outside energic demands) is scarce and precious. The proposition of energic scarcity and its various corollaries probably provide a good and perhaps necessary basis for working toward an affluent, leisure-based society. But do they offer an appropriate basis for maintaining and living in such a society, and especially for understanding the problems and opportunities posed by such a society?

To state in extreme form the argument for a new set of assumptions, we would say that the achievement of real affluence by means of technical success and automated means of production inverts the old assumption of energic scarcity. Real affluence creates a situation in which meaningful outlets for human energy are scarce, while available energy abounds. Under such circumstances, new criteria of organizational effectiveness may be evolved. Organizations of size less than that indicated for maximal efficiency may be chosen for the satisfactions of the social relations they provide. Processes of production less than maximally efficient may be chosen for the intrinsic satisfaction they offer the worker or for the aesthetic satisfaction their variability of product offers to the consumer. These speculations are offered without substantiation or elaboration here, because their accuracy is unimportant for the point of this chapter; they are relevant here only to remind us that virtually every definition and research effort in the area of organizational effectiveness is involved with the unspoken and now shaky assumption of energic scarcity.

SUMMARY

Organizational effectiveness is introduced as a term which has been subject to numerous and conflicting uses. An attempt is made to resolve such conflicts by distinguishing among several components of organizational effectiveness.

Organizational efficiency is the first such component, and is defined as the ratio of energic output to energic input. Efficiency thus tells us how much of the input of an organization emerges as product and how much is absorbed by the system. Further distinctions are made between human energy and materials as organizational inputs, between direct and indirect uses of human energy in organizations, and between the use of materials as supplies and as equipment. The computation of organizational efficiency is shown to be dependent upon the spatial and temporal definitions of organization.

A further distinction is introduced between the potential efficiency of an organization and its actual efficiency. This distinction contrasts the elegance of a given organizational design with the degree to which a given design is realized in organizational practice.

Efficiency is also distinguished from profit, although the two are asserted to be strongly related. The contribution of efficiency to survival is discussed in terms of the storage of energy which efficiency permits and the consequent margin for error which it provides.

The chapter concludes with an explication of organizational effectiveness as the maximization of return to the organization by all means. Such maximization by economic and technical means has to do with efficiency; maximization by noneconomic or political means increases effectiveness without adding to efficiency. Increases in effectiveness by both means are typically observable as storage of energy, organizational growth, organizational endurance and survival, and as organizational control of the surrounding environment. All definitions of effectiveness involve some assumptions with respect to frame of reference. Two such frames are considered, that of the organization as a system in its own right, and that of the larger society or system of which the organization is a subsystem.

7

The Taking of
Organizational Roles

Frame of reference is everything. Macro- and micro-economics appear to the noneconomist as minor subdivisions of a generally homogeneous field. To the dwellers within each of those specialized areas, however, the differences are cosmic and irreconcilable. Psychologists and sociologists also have been guilty of stringing a certain amount of barbed wire along the boundary between their disciplines, each sometimes insisting that there is something slightly suspect if not superfluous about the level of explanation which the other has chosen for his own. On top of this ideological fence sits the social psychologist, striving to look as comfortable as the metaphor will allow. All too often he eases his pain by avoiding the synthesis of sociological and psychological levels of discourse which should be the hallmark of his trade.

To the extent that choice of concepts can contribute to so complex a synthesis, the concept of role is singularly promising. It is at once the building block of social systems and the summation of the requirements with which the system confronts the individual member. Indeed, it has been touted for a generation as the example of a concept uniquely fitted to social-psychological investigation and theory.

Linton (1936) was perhaps the first to give the notion of role a central place in any of the social sciences; Newcomb (1951) brought it from anthropology into social psychology and made it the key concept in his theoretical approach. Parsons (1951) and Merton (1957) consider it essential to understanding social action and social structure. In spite of these and other advocates, however, the role concept has been viewed with justifiable disenchantment by writers who combed the literature seeking in vain the research fulfillment of that conceptual promise (Neiman and Hughes, 1951).

We have given the role concept a central place in our theory of organizations. We have defined human organizations as role systems (Chapter 3), and the psychological basis of organizational functions will be approached in terms of motivation to fulfill organizational roles (Chapter 12). It remains for this chapter to link the organizational and individual levels by making explicit the social-psychological processes by which organizational roles are defined and role behavior is evoked in the ongoing organization. More specifically, we will review briefly the implications of viewing the organization as a system of roles. We will consider role-sending as a continuing cyclical process by means of which each person is socialized into his organizational role, informed about the acceptability of his role behavior, and corrected as necessary. We will examine some of the properties of the organization which determine the nature of specific roles. Finally we will consider the extent to which the process of role-taking is modified by enduring properties of personality and of interpersonal relations.

*The Organization as a System of Roles.** In defining human organizations as open systems of roles, we emphasized two cardinal facts: the *contrived nature* of human organizations, and the unique properties of a *structure consisting of acts or events* rather than unchanging physical components (Chapter 3). There are, of course, many ramifications of these facts. It follows, for example, that human organizations attain constancy and stability in terms of the relationships among their units, rather than in terms of the units themselves. Indeed, one of the chief strengths of formal organization is its constancy under conditions of persistent turnover of personnel. It follows also that, since the units of organization are not linked physically, they must be linked psychologically. Since the organization consists of the patterned and motivated acts of human beings, it will continue to exist only so long as the attitudes, beliefs, perceptions, habits, and expectations of human beings evoke the required motivation and behavior. In short, each behavioral element in the pattern is to a large extent caused and secured by the others. These facts in turn imply that human organizations are characterized by a paradoxical combination of durability and fragility. They remain intact only so long as the intangible psychological cement holds, and yet their intactness and longevity is independent of the life-span of any and all organizational members. There is a variability and flexibility to these social contrivances which free them from the biological cycle of birth, growth, and death.

The emphasis on interdependent acts as the substance of organiza-

* The exposition of role and related concepts draws heavily on Chapter 2 of *Organizational Stress,* Kahn et al., Wiley, 1964.

tion is reminiscent of symbiotic relationships, as we observed earlier (Chapter 3). Formal organizations, however, involve no symbiosis in the strict sense of that term; it is not instinct and immediate biological gratification which motivates role behavior in organizations. Rather, it is a process of learning the expectations of others, accepting them, and fulfilling them—primarily for the extrinsic rewards of membership, although many other motives enter into the taking of organizational roles. There is intrinsic satisfaction in the skillful and successful meshing of our own efforts with those of others, in meeting their expectations as they meet ours, especially if the process affords the expression of valued abilities or the acquisition of new ones.

When we observe an organization in motion, its systemic nature is immediately visible. We have only to look beyond the buildings and grounds, and the individuals present, to see that what is literally organized are acts—people acting on materials, acting on machines, but above all interacting with each other. In any organization we can locate each individual in the total set of ongoing relationships and behaviors comprised by the organization. The key concept for doing this is *office*, by which is meant a particular point in organizational space; space in turn is defined in terms of a structure of interrelated offices and the pattern of activities associated with them. Office is essentially a relational concept, defining each position in terms of its relationship to others and to the system as a whole. Associated with each office is a set of *activities* or expected behaviors. These activities constitute the *role* to be performed, at least approximately, by any person who occupies that office.

Each office in an organization is directly related to certain others, less directly to still others, and only remotely related to some offices in the organization. The closeness of such relationships is defined by the work flow and technology of the organization, and by the lines of authority (managerial subsystem).

Consider the office of press foreman in a factory manufacturing external trim parts for automobiles. The offices most directly related to that of the press foreman might include the general foreman of the trim department and the superintendent of sheet-metal operations. From these offices emanate the work assignments to the office of press foreman, and to these offices he turns for approval of work done. Also directly related to the office of press foreman might be that of the stock foreman, whose section provides sheet-metal blanks for the presses, the inspector who must pass or reject the completed stampings, the shipping foreman whose section receives and packages the stampings, and, let us say, 14 press operators whose work the press foreman directs.

Imagine the organization spread out like a vast fish net, in which each knot represents an office and each string a functional relationship between offices. If we pick up the net by seizing any office, the offices to which it is directly attached are immediately seen. Thus the office of press foreman is directly attached to 19 others—general foreman, superintendent, stock foreman, inspector, shipping foreman, and 14 press operators. These nineteen offices make up the *role set* (Merton, 1957) for the office of press foreman.

Similarly, each member of an organization is directly associated with a relatively small number of others, usually the occupants of offices adjacent to his in the work-flow structure or in the hierarchy of authority. They constitute his role set and typically include his immediate supervisor (and perhaps his supervisor's immediate superior), his subordinates, and certain members of his own or other departments with whom he must work closely. These offices are defined into his role set by virtue of the work-flow, technology, and authority structure of the organization.

Definition of Role Behavior

Generically, role behavior refers to the recurring actions of an individual, appropriately interrelated with the repetitive activities of others so as to yield a predictable outcome. The set of interdependent behaviors comprise a social system or subsystem, a stable collective pattern in which people play their parts.

When we abstract some of the essential persisting features from the specific acts comprising role behavior we speak of roles. For example, we can speak of the role of the quarterback on a football team in general terms of play selection without specifying the particular signals he barks to his teammates or the specific plays with which they respond. This general description applies to roles both within and outside formal organizations. The various members of the family interact in consistent ways in assuming their roles as father, mother, son, daughter, husband, and wife. In formal organizations many of the functionally specific behaviors comprising the system are specified in written and coded presentations. Moreover, in formal organizations the roles people play are more a function of the social setting than of their own personality characteristics. The basic criterion, then, for studying role behavior is to identify the relevant social system or subsystem and locate the recurring events which fit together in converting some input into an output. This can be done by ascertaining the role expectations of a given set of related offices, since such expectations are one of the main elements in maintaining the role system and inducing the required role behavior.

The Process of Role-Sending

All members of a person's role set depend upon his performance in some fashion; they are rewarded by it, judged in terms of it, or require it in order to perform their own tasks. Because they have a stake in his performance they develop beliefs and attitudes about what he should and should not do as part of his role. The prescriptions and proscriptions held by members of a role set are designated *role expectations;* in the aggregate they help to define his role, the behaviors which are expected of him. The role expectations held for a certain person by a member of his role set will reflect that member's conception of the person's office and of his abilities. The content of these expectations may include preferences with respect to specific acts and personal characteristics or styles; they may deal with what the person should do, what kind of person he should be, what he should think or believe, and how he should relate to others. Role expectations are by no means restricted to the job description as it might be given by the head of the organization or prepared by some specialist in personnel, although these individuals are likely to be influential members of the role sets of many persons in the organization.

The mention of influence raises additional issues of definition and theory. Role expectations for any given office and its occupant exist in the minds of members of his role set and represent standards in terms of which they evaluate his performance. The expectations do not remain in the minds of members of the role set, however. They tend to be communicated in many ways; sometimes as direct instructions, as when a supervisor describes to a subordinate the requirements of his job; sometimes less directly, as when a colleague expresses admiration or disappointment in some behavior. The crucial point (for our theoretical view) is that the activities which define a role are maintained through the expectations of members of the role set, and that these expectations are communicated or "sent" to the focal person.* In referring to role expectations as sent, we are following the formulation of Rommetveit (1954). He refers to members of a role set as role senders, and to their communicated expectations as the *sent role.*

The numerous acts which make up the process of role-sending are not merely informational. They are attempts at influence, directed at the focal person and intended to bring about conformity to the expectations of the senders. Some of these influence attempts (for example, those from superiors) may be directed toward the accomplishment of formally specified responsibilities and objectives of office.

* The term *focal person* will be used to refer to any individual whose role or office is under consideration.

Others (perhaps from peers or subordinates) may be directed toward making life easier or more pleasant for the senders themselves, in ways which contravene official requirements.

Thus each individual in an organization acts in relation to and in response to the expectations of the members of his role set, not because those expectations constitute some mentalistic field of forces but because they are expressed in explicit behavioral ways. The expression need not be continuous; human memory can be long, and adults in our society have already graduated from a lengthy period of training and socialization in organizational role-taking. They have learned a quality and technique of role readiness which lets them anticipate many of the role expectations of others with few cues. But let a person stop performing within the range of organizational acceptability, and there will immediately become visible the membership of his role set and the expectations which they hold for him.

As a communicative and influential process, acts of role-sending can be characterized in terms of any of the dimensions appropriate to the measurement of communication and influence. Some of the more important ones proposed by Gross, Mason, and McEachern (1958) include sign (prescriptive or proscriptive), magnitude (strength of the influence attempt), specificity (extent to which the expected behaviors are made concrete and detailed), intensity (extent to which the focal person is allowed freedom of choice in complying or refusing compliance), and range of conditions under which compliance is intended. As our treatment of power, communication, and leadership (Chapters 8, 9, and 11) implies, our interest in the role-sending process centers upon magnitude or strength of the influence attempt. We are interested also in the psychological basis of influence on which different acts of role-sending depend. Every attempt at influence implies consequences for compliance or noncompliance. In organizations, as we have seen, these commonly take the form of sanctions—gratifications or deprivations which a role sender might arrange for the focal person, depending on his having conformed to the sender's expectation or not. The concept of legitimacy, and its acceptance by organizational members, makes the actual use of such sanctions infrequent. Members obey because the source and substance of the command are legitimate. The availability and visibility of sanctions are important, however, whether or not they are used or even threatened. The strengthening of role-sending with the possibility of sanctions is the major basis for gaining compliance with the requirements of formal organization.

The mention of sanctions as necessary to the functioning of formal organizations has become unfashionable, and the word has acquired an unpleasant ring. Yet both the problem and necessity of coercive power in government and in other organizational contexts have been often explored and acknowledged. Such exploration has seldom been carried deeper or carried out with greater effort and anguish than in the formative years of our federal government. With the inadequacies of the confederation still visible, Webster spoke of "the powers of Congress which are perhaps nearly sufficient to answer the needs of our union, were there any method of enforcing their resolutions . . . . A law without a penalty is *mere advice;* a magistrate without the power of punishment is a cypher . . . ." (Hockett, 1939)

The Received Role

To understand the response of any member of an organization to the complex pattern of role-sending addressed specifically to him, we must regard the organization from the vantage point of his office. When we do so, we see that the members of his role set and the influential pressures which they direct to him are part of his objective environment. To consider his compliance with or deviation from his sent role, however, takes us immediately beyond the objective organization and environment. Each individual responds to the organization in terms of his perceptions of it, which may differ in various ways from the actual organization. In the immediate sense, the individual responds not to the objective organization in his objective social environment but to that representation of it which is in his psychological environment.

The objective organization and the psychological organization of a person may or may not be congruent, depending on his ability and opportunity to perceive organizational reality. Thus for each person in an organization there is not only a sent role, consisting of the influential and communicative acts of the members of his role set, there is also a *received role,* consisting of his perceptions and cognitions of what was sent. How closely the received role corresponds to the sent role is an empirical question for each focal person and set of role senders, and will depend upon properties of the senders, the focal person, the substantive content of the sent expectations, the clarity of the communication, and the like.

It is the sent role by means of which the organization communicates to each of its members the do's and don'ts associated with his office. It is the received role, however, which is the immediate influence on his behavior and the immediate source of his motivation for role performance. Each sent expectation can be regarded as arousing in the focal person a motivational force of some magnitude and direction. This is not to say that these motivational role forces are identical in magnitude and direction with the sent influence attempts that evoked them. When sent-role expectations are seen by the focal person as illegitimate or coercive, they may arouse strong resistance forces which lead to outcomes different from or even opposite to the expected behavior. It is such processes, repeated for many persons over long periods of time, that produce the persistent component of unintended effects in organizational behavior. Pressures to increase production sometimes result in slowdowns. Moreover, every person is subject to a variety of psychological forces in addition to those stimulated by pressures from his role set in the work situation. Role-sendings are thus only a partial determinant of his behavior on the job.

Additional and important sources of influence in role-taking are the objective, impersonal properties of the situation itself. In some situations the taking of roles may be aided by the nature of the task and the previous experience of the individual with respect to similar tasks. The soldier in combat seeks cover when under fire not so much because of the expectations of members of his role set as because of the demands of the situation. The man on the assembly line tightens the belt on the passing car both because he has been told that it is his job and because the structuring of his work situation is a constant reminder of what he is supposed to do. People can be conditioned to play their roles by cues other than those of the communicated expectations from other system members. Nevertheless, in most organizations, role behavior is largely dependent upon role sending.

In addition to the motivational forces aroused by sent expectations and other cues, there are important internal sources of motivation for role performance. For example, there is the intrinsic satisfaction derived from the content of the role. The concert pianist has many motives which lead him to give performances; one of them is probably the intrinsic psychological return from exercising a hard-won and valued skill.* But there is, in addition to intrinsic satisfaction in expressing valued abilities, another kind of "own force" important in the motivation of role behavior. In a sense each person is a "self-sender," that is, a role sender to himself. He too has a conception of his office and a set of attitudes and beliefs about what he should and should not do while in that position. He has some awareness of what behaviors will fulfill his responsibilities, lead to the accomplishment of organizational objectives, or further his own interests. He may even have had a major

* The patterns of motivation for role behavior, together with the organizational conditions which evoke them and the organizational outcomes which they produce, will be discussed in Chapter 12.

part in determining the formal responsibilities of his office, especially if he occupies a line or staff position well up in the hierarchy.

Moreover, some of the persisting motives of the individual are likely to include the sector of organizational behavior. Through a long process of socialization and formal training within the organization and in the larger culture of which it and he are parts, he has acquired a set of values and expectations about his own behavior and abilities, about the nature of human organizations and the conditions for membership in them. In short, as Miller (1962), Dai (1955), and others have observed, the person has an occupational self-identity and is motivated to behave in ways which affirm and enhance the valued attributes of that identity. He comes to the job in a state of what we have previously referred to as role-readiness, a state which includes the acceptance of legitimate authority and compliance with its requests, a compliance which for many people extends to acts which they do not understand and which may violate many of their own values. Milgram's recent work (1963, 1964), reporting that two-thirds of the adult subjects in an experiment obeyed an instruction to administer what they believed to be electrical shocks of several hundred volts to groaning and protesting victims, only highlights the phenomenon of compliance in role behavior.

Multiple Roles and Multiple Activities. An organization is a complex arrangement of many collective cycles of behavior, some of which intersect, others of which are tangential to one another, while still others are connected only indirectly. In other words, the organization is made up of many subsystems. The common treatment of *role* and *office* tends to oversimplify this complexity by neglecting the fact that one office can be located in a number of such role subsystems and that one individual can be involved in many organizational subsystems.

Let us examine more closely the meaning and implications of these assertions. The basic unit of organizational life is the *molar unit of behavior,* the behavioral cycle. This is what we mean by *an activity:* a recurring behavior sequence which has organizational relevance, is held in the form of role expectations by some members of the role set, and which affords some sense of closure on completion. For example, taking four bolts out of a barrel and using them to fasten the left rear fender of an automobile to the body is an activity on the assembly line.

A role consists of one or more recurrent activities out of a total pattern of interdependent activities which in combination produce the organizational output. Role, unless otherwise qualified, will refer to a set of such activities within a single subsystem of the organization and within a single office.

An office is a point (location) in organizational space defined by one or more roles (and thereby one or more activities) intended for performance by a single individual. It locates the individual in relation to his fellows with respect to the job to be done and the giving and taking of orders.

The simplest organizational arrangement occurs when one activity defines role and office. Thus, the job of assembly-line operator No. 23 might consist of the one activity described in the previous example, bolting on the left rear fender. That activity defines the role, and the office is merely the point in organizational space associated with that role and activity.

The situation can become more complex in any of several ways:

Multiple activities may be defined into a single role.
Multiple roles may be defined into a single office.
Multiple offices may be held by a single person.

We have suggested that the simplest organizational arrangement occurs when one activity defines role and office. In fact, a general trend in organizations is to move toward such simplification and to fractionate many jobs into their component activities. That, however, is only part of the total story; the more such role specialization develops at one level, the greater is the need for coordination at a higher level. Thus, the very organization which follows the simplified arrangement of one activity, one role, and one office for its assembly line workers must adopt a more complex plan for higher offices, multiplying their activities and roles. The many specialized subsystems must be interrelated and hence offices created in which these various substructures intersect. In fine, the less the coordinative demand within roles, the greater will be the demand for some means of coordination between roles. That means is usually the creation of a new coordinative office.

The inclusion of multiple activities in a single role and multiple roles in a single office is increasingly evident as we move up the hierarchy in most large organizations. The office of first-line supervisor typically involves two roles; the supervisor is a member of two subsystems—the managerial structure and his own immediate task force. Members of middle management may be involved in relations with the various productive, procurement, and marketing subsystems. Top management has an even greater range of roles today.

Recognition of the many roles assumed by a single person is sometimes expressed by his holding more than one office. The Dean of a graduate school may also be University Vice-President for Research. The Secretary of the Communist Party may also be the Premier of the Soviet Union. It is interesting that we generally look upon the holding of multiple offices in an organization as indicating something amiss: a seizure of power, as when a dictator picks up for himself the portfolios of several cabinet ministers; a lack of appropriate manpower; or an inadequacy in the formal organizational plan. There is less tendency, however, to be critical of the same basic process of multiplying the roles played by a single person when all of them are tied to a single office. The essential dilemma is that there is no escape from the coordinative needs resulting from specialized subsystems and fractionated jobs.

It is interesting to speculate on the organizational implications of role definition and office definition within the terms stipulated above. We would offer the following predictions:

1. The more activities contained within a role, the more likely it is to be varied and satisfying, the more likely it is to involve coordination among the activities it comprises, and the less immediate will be the necessity for coordination with other roles and offices.

For example, in a television factory in which each worker (role) builds a complete TV set, there is much coordination of activities within the role but little needed between roles. In a television factory in which the assembly-line system is used, with each worker soldering only a single part or part-cluster into the chassis, there is virtually no intrarole coordination of activities but great need for coordination between roles. If any role is not performed, no workable product is completed. The relationships between roles are multiplicative, not additive.

2. The more interrole coordination an organization requires, the more the achievement of coordination is assigned to offices high in the organizational structure.

The problem of information overload is characteristically built into the top echelons of large organizations with many specialized subsystems. The offices at the upper levels are typically associated with several subsystems and include several roles; the incumbents are subject to information input from all the subsystems in which they have a role, and the likelihood of overload becomes correspondingly great.

3. The more coordinative demands concentrated in a given office, the more the incumbent seeks a generalized, programmed solution —as in the precise, split-second timing of jobs and subassemblies into the final assembly line. Such a programmed solution is sought because it can be set up to hold for a considerable period of time, thus relieving the incumbent of the continuing press of certain types of decisions. Moreover, it affords similar relief to persons who occupy related offices, by presenting them with a set of predictable behaviors to which they can adjust.

4. The greater the programming of interjob coordination, the greater will be the use of organizational authority and sanctions to prevent any failure of role performance.

All this reminds us again of the costs of "efficiency." The gains of Taylorism may be real, but they must be computed in a way which includes Taylor's salary. In short, coordination is not free, and reducing the worker role to subhuman specifications has efficiency limits as well as limits suggested by other values. It often involves relocating coordinative costs rather than eliminating them.

The Role Episode

Our description of role-sending and role-receiving has been based on four concepts: *role expectations,* which are evaluative standards applied to the behavior of any person who occupies a given organizational office or position; *sent role,* which consists of communications stemming from role expectations and sent by members of the role set as attempts to influence the focal person; *received role,* which is the focal person's perception of the role-sendings addressed to him, including those he "sends" to himself; and *role behavior,* which is the response of the focal person to the complex of information and influence he has received.

These four concepts can be thought of as constituting a sequence or role episode. The first two, role expectations and sent role, have to do with the motivations, cognitions, and behavior of the members of the role set; the latter two, received role and role behavior, have to do with the cognitions, motivations, and behavior of the focal person. A model of the role episode is presented in Figure 6.

As the figure suggests, there is symmetry between the two complementary phases of the role episode—the cognitions and behavior of role senders on the one hand, and the cognitions and behavior of

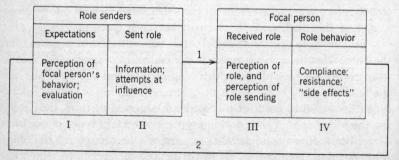

Figure 6 A model of the role episode.

the focal person on the other. There is also a kind of orderliness to the model viewed in another way; boxes I and III represent processes of perception, cognition, and motivation—processes internal to the person, the role sender in box I, and the focal person in box III. Boxes II and IV represent behaviors—acts undertaken in expression of cognitive and motivational processes. These acts are viewed as role-sending when they are the behaviors of members of a role set under our observation, and as role behavior when they are the acts of a focal person (that is, any office occupant whom we have singled out for study).

The designation of an office or person as *focal* is, of course, a matter of convenience; it serves merely to identify our terms of reference for viewing some part of an ongoing organization. A complete study of an organization would require that each office in it be successively treated as focal, its role set identified, the role expectations and sent role measured, and the received role and role behavior similarly described. Every person in an organization receives role-sending from one or more others, and in most organizations each person is also a role sender for one or more others.

The ongoing life of a large organization involves many continuous cycles of sending, receiving, responding, evaluating, and sending again by persons in many overlapping role sets. In Figure 6, arrow 1 represents the process of role-sending, and arrow 2 represents the process by which the role sender (a) estimates the degree of compliance which he has apparently induced on the part of the focal person and (b) prepares to initiate another cycle.

Arrow 2 is thus a feedback loop; the degree to which a person's behavior conforms to the expectations held for him at one point in time will affect the state of those expectations at the next moment. If his response is essentially a hostile counterattack, his role senders are apt to think of him and behave toward him in ways quite different than if he were submissively compliant. If he complies partially under pressure, they may increase the pressure; if he is obviously overcome with tension and anxiety, they may "lay off." In sum, the role episode is abstracted from a process which is cyclic and ongoing: the response of the focal person to role-sending feeds back to each sender in ways that alter or reinforce his expectations and subsequent role-sending. The current role-sendings of each member of the set depend on his evaluations of the response to his last sendings, and thus a new episode begins.

Even this brief description of the process of role-sending and role-receiving indicates that the model presented in Figure 6 is in many respects oversimplified. Three of these are of particular importance:

1. The notion of a role episode—neatly fulfilling the Aristotelian aesthetic requirements of beginning, middle, and end—is an abstraction. It is merely a convenient way of representing what we believe to be a complex ongoing process involving all the members of an organization. The convenience consists of assuming role expectations as a starting point, and presenting them as if the process of interaction were a sequence of discrete episodes.

2. A further simplification is the treatment of role expectations as if there were only a single role sender and he were completely consistent in his expectations, or as if there were consensus among role senders. In fact such consistency and consensus is not attained, and some degree of role conflict is characteristic of human organizations.

3. The third oversimplification inherent in the concept of the role episode is its abstraction from the larger context of organizational events. Every act of role-sending and role-receiving is in part determined by the context within which it occurs.

Of these three limitations, the first requires no further discussion; the second and third we will consider at greater length.

Role Conflict. To assert that some degree of role conflict is characteristic of human organizations does not imply violence as a way of organizational life. We define *role conflict* as the simultaneous occurrence of two (or more) role sendings such that compliance with one would make more difficult compliance with the other. In the extreme case, compliance with one expectation as sent would exclude completely the possibility of compliance with the other; the two expectations are mutually contradictory. For example, a person's superior may make it clear to him that he is expected to hold his subordinates strictly to company rules. At the same time, his subordinates may indicate in various ways that they would like loose, relaxed supervision, and that they will make things difficult if they are pushed too hard. Here the pressures from above and below are incompatible, since a style of supervision which satisfies one set of expectations violates the other set. Such cases are so common that a whole literature has been created on the problem of the first-line supervisor as "the man in the middle," the "master and victim of double-talk."

Several types of role conflict can be identified. One might be termed *intrasender:* the expectations from a single member of a role set may be incompatible, as for example when a supervisor orders a subordinate to acquire material which is unavailable through normal channels and at the same time warns him against violating those channels. A second type of role conflict we can call *intersender:* expectations sent from one sender are in conflict with those from one or more other senders. The earlier example of the foreman urged by his superior to supervise more closely and by his subordinates to allow them greater freedom fits the category of intersender conflict.

If we look beyond the organization, another type of role conflict becomes apparent—conflict between roles. Such *interrole* conflict occurs whenever the sent expectations for one role are in conflict with those for another role played by the same person. Demands from role senders on the job for overtime or take-home work may conflict with pressures from one's wife to give undivided attention to family affairs during evening hours. The conflict arises between the role of the focal person as worker and his role as husband and father.

All three of these types of conflict—intrasender, intersender, and interrole—are conflicts in the content of the role as sent; they exist as conflicts in the objective environment of the focal person. They give rise, of course, to psychological conflicts of some kind and degree within the focal person. Other types of conflict, however, are generated directly by a combination of externally sent role expectations and internal forces or role expectations which the focal person requires of himself. This fourth type of conflict, which we may call *person-role* conflict occurs when role requirements violate the needs, values, or capacities of the focal person. Pressures on an executive to conclude a profitable agreement in restraint of trade, for example, might be opposed by his personal code of ethics. In other cases of person-role conflict the person's needs and values may lead to behavior which is unacceptable to members of his role set; for example, an ambitious young man may be called up short by his associates for stepping on their toes in his haste to advance in the organization.

From these four basic types of conflict other complex forms of conflict sometimes develop. A very prevalent form of conflict in industrial organizations, for example, is role overload. Overload is typically encountered as a kind of intersender conflict in which the sent expectations of various members of the role set are legitimate and are not logically incompatible. The focal person, however, finds that he cannot complete all of the tasks urged on him by various people within the stipulated time limits and requirements of quality. He is likely to experience overload as a conflict of priorities or as a conflict between quality and quantity. He must decide which pressures to comply with and which to hold off. If it is impossible to deny any of the pressures, he may be taxed beyond the limit of his abilities. Thus overload involves a kind of person-role conflict, and is perhaps best regarded as a complex-emergent type combining aspects of conflict between role senders and conflict between senders and focal person.

The major issue with respect to role conflict, however, is not the typology which one chooses or constructs; it is the prevalence of role conflict as a fact. In a nationwide study of male wage and salary workers, Kahn and his colleagues (1964) found nearly half to be working under conditions of noticeable conflict. Forty-eight per cent reported that from time to time they were caught between two sets of people who wanted different things from them, and 15 per cent reported this to be a frequent and serious problem. Thirty-nine per cent reported being bothered by their inability to satisfy the conflicting demands of their various role senders. The hierarchical and depersonalized nature of large-scale organization is also reflected in these data: 88 per cent of all role conflicts reportedly involve pressures from above, and in 57 per cent of these cases the spontaneous description of the source of these pressures was given in such impersonal terms as "the company" or "management."

The Context of Role-Taking. The last of the oversimplifications to which we pointed in our model of the role episode was its abstraction from the context in which it occurs. That context can be thought of as consisting of all the enduring properties, the more or less stable characteristics, of the situation within which a role episode takes place. Some of these will be properties of the organization itself; some will be traits of the persons involved in the process of role-sending and role-receiving; some will be properties of the interpersonal relationships which already exist between the actors in the role episode.

These three additional classes of variables—organizational, personality, and interpersonal—can be conveniently represented in an enlargement and extension of Figure 6. That figure presented a causal sequence: role expectations (I) lead to role-sending (II), which leads to received role (III), which leads to behavior in response to the role as received (IV). That figure and the sequence it represents also forms the core of Figure 7.

The circles in Figure 7 represent not the momentary events of the role episode, but enduring states of the organization, the person, and the interpersonal relations between focal person and role senders. Such enduring properties are for the most part abstractions and generalizations based upon recurrent events and behaviors. For example, characterizing a relationship as supportive means simply that the parties to the relationship have behaved in a supportive manner toward one another on a sufficient number of occasions so that we feel justified in inferring supportiveness as a quality of the relationship. Such repetitions and patterns of events provide the basis and context within each new occurrence can best be understood.

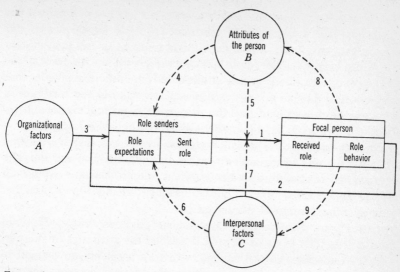

Figure 7 A theoretical model of factors involved in the taking of organizational roles.

To a considerable extent the role expectations held by the members of a role set—the prescriptions and proscriptions associated with a particular office—are determined by the broader organizational context. The technology of the organization, the structure of its subsystems, its formal policies, and its rewards and penalties dictate in large degree the content of a given office. What the occupant of that office is supposed to do, with and for whom, is given by these and other properties of the organization itself. Although human beings are doing the "supposing" and rewarding, the structural properties of organization are sufficiently stable so that they can be treated as independent of the particular persons in the role set. For such properties as size, number of echelons, and rate of growth, the justifiable abstraction of organizational properties from individual behavior is even more obvious.

The organizational circle (A) in Figure 7 represents a set of variables. Some of them characterize the organization as a whole; others describe some part of it. Arrow 3 asserts a causal relationship between certain organizational variables and the role expectations held about and sent to a particular position. For example, there is an almost linear relationship between organizational size and the amount of reported role conflict and tension in the organization (Kahn et al., 1964).

Enduring attributes of the person (circle B) refer to all those variables which describe the propensity of an individual to behave in certain ways—his motives and values, his defense preferences, his sensitivities and fears. Such factors affect the role episode in several ways. First, some traits of the person tend to evoke or facilitate certain evaluations and behaviors from his role senders (arrow 4). Second, the same sent role can be experienced differently by different people; that is, personality factors act as conditioning variables in the relationship between the role as sent and the role as received and responded to. Finally, we propose as a hypothesis that role behavior has effects on personality (arrow 8). This is simply the hypothesis that we become what we do, and in a sense we un-become what we do not do. The man who is required to play a subservient role, for example, cannot do so over an extended time without consequent changes in personality. Most abilities atrophy if unexercised.

As Figure 7 indicates, interpersonal relations (circle C) fulfill functions parallel to those already described for attributes of the person. The expectations held for and sent to a focal person depend to some degree on the quality of interpersonal relations between him and the members of his role set (arrow 6). He will also interpret differently the role-sendings he receives, depending on his interpersonal relations with the senders (arrow 7). Praise and blame have one set of meanings when they come from a trusted source, and another when they stem from untrusted sources. Finally, the behavior of the focal person feeds back to and has effects on his interpersonal relations with members of his role set (arrow 9). If he suddenly and persistently refuses to comply in any respect with their role-sendings, for example, we would predict not only an immediate change in their evaluation of his role behavior (arrow 2), but an enduring change in their liking for him (arrow 9).

The research evidence for this model of role-taking in organizations is substantial in quantity but irregular in quality and in relevance. That distinctive attitudes, values, and points of view are characteristically associated with different roles has been a part of human experience and folk wisdom for time beyond recollection, and within the past twenty years this fact has been well documented.

Stouffer and his colleagues (1949) reported sharp differences between officers and enlisted men in their attitudes toward the army, with officer opinions consistently more favorable. Jacobson (Guetzkow, 1951) showed similar differences among workers, foremen, and stewards in their attitudes toward the company and the union. Research on the differential perceptions of supervisors and subordinates shows consistently that role or position in the organization is related to perceptions no less than to attitudes and values. Mann's findings (Likert,

1961) that 76 per cent of the foremen in a utility report that they "always or almost always get their subordinates' ideas in the solution of job problems" but that only 16 per cent of the workers report being so consulted, is typical of such research.

Most such findings lend themselves to either of two interpretations or perhaps to a combination of both. One can argue that the role shapes the attitudes and perceptions of the individual, or that the individual is selected for his psychological goodness-of-fit to the role requirements. Lieberman (1956) has contributed the most definitive evidence for the former interpretation. He was able to measure the perceptions and attitudes of employees in two appliance plants three times during a period of three years: once when all were rank-and-file workers, a year later when 23 had become foremen and 35 had been elected stewards, and two years later still when about half of the new foremen and stewards had reverted to nonsupervisory jobs and half had continued in their new roles.

In their rank-and-file days, there were no significant differences between future foremen and future stewards, although both groups were more ambitious, more critical, and less unquestioningly loyal to the company than were the workers destined to become neither foremen nor stewards. On becoming foremen, Lieberman's subjects tended to report more favorably about the company as a place to work, to be more favorable in their perceptions of top management, and to endorse the principle of incentive pay. Those men who became union stewards became, according to their responses, more favorable toward unions in general, toward the top officers of their own union, and toward the principle of seniority rather than ability as a basis for wage payments. Those foremen and stewards who subsequently returned to the worker role tended also to revert to the perceptions and attitudes of workers; those who remained as foremen and stewards showed more sharply as time passed the kinds of differences described above. Mean differences between future foremen and future stewards on the numerous scales used were less than one percentage point at the time when all subjects were workers; 48 per cent between the foremen and stewards after one year in role, and 62 per cent after three years in role.

Even these data, however, leave unsupported many of the linkages stipulated in the model. Lieberman's data argue strongly for a causal relationship between the office an individual occupies in an organization (foreman, steward) and his expressed attitudes on job-relevant matters. Whether the characteristic changes in attitude are brought about because of the causal sequence of different role expectations, the sending of these expectations as attempts at influence, the receiving of such communications, and the subsequent response to them remains untested by Lieberman's research. The formulation of such a process with respect to the sending of norms was first proposed by Rommetveit (1954), but he was concerned with the religious attitudes and sex roles of Norwegian adolescents rather than the work situation and the organizational context. Other research, however, can be interpreted as supporting many of the hypotheses specified by the model. Let us consider some of this research, in the order suggested by the numbered arrows in Figure 7.

The Relationship between Role Expectations and Response (Arrow 1). Sarbin and Williams (1953) conducted a laboratory experiment which demonstrated something of the expertise which people acquire in receiving and understanding communications from role senders. The subjects of the experiment listened to 38 sentences, each conveying some role expectation; their task was to determine the age, sex, and role of the sender, the intended receiver, and the action or role behavior which was being requested. Performance of the experimental subjects was so accurate that the resulting distributions showed the typical J-curve of conforming behavior.

Gross, Mason, and McEachern (1958), in their excellent study of school boards and school superintendents, demonstrated a number of significant relationships between the expectations and sending to members of a role set, on the one hand, and the perceptions and responses of the target or focal person on the other. Role-sending from the school board to the superintendent was associated with high job satisfaction on the part of the superintendent when the expectations of the board were consistent with his professional standards, and with low job satisfaction when they were not.

Kahn and his colleagues (1964), in their studies of role conflict and ambiguity, found that objective role conflict (measured by the statements of role senders that they wished for specific changes in the focal person's role behavior) was related to low job satisfaction, low confidence in the organization, and a high degree of job-related tension. The effects of role ambiguity (defined as lack of information regarding supervisory evaluation of one's work, about opportunities for advancement, scope of responsibility, and expectations of role senders) were in general comparable to those of role conflict. Persons subjected to conditions of ambiguity on the job tended to be low in job satisfaction, low in self-confidence, high in tension and in a sense of futility.

Gross and his colleagues (1958) also found that role conflict around such issues as hiring, promotion, teacher salaries, and budgetary matters was associated with low job satisfaction on the part of the superintendent. Getzels and Guba (1954) had previously demonstrated a relationship between role conflict and reduced teaching effectiveness in nine air force training schools.

The Feedback Effect of Role Behavior on the Expectations of Role Senders (Arrow 2). This effect, which is stipulated in the model, has yet to be appropriately tested. The required research would be longitudinal in design, in order to answer the question of whether the performance of the focal person in successive cycles of role-sending and response leads to modifications of the expectations of role senders. Some suggestive findings are available, however. Jackson and his colleagues (1951) found that workers tended to express anti-union attitudes when their stewards failed to involve them in decision-making. Jacobson interpreted this to be the result of the workers' discovery that their initial expectations were unfulfilled, but the data permit other interpretations as well. Kahn and his colleagues (1964) found that role senders expressed fewer intentions to bring about change on the part of focal persons who were high in rigidity, presumably because the intractable performance of the focal person had led to a reduction of expectations on the part of his role senders.

Organizational Factors as Determinants of Role Expectations (Arrow 3). This category of findings reminds us that role expectations and the process of role-sending do not arise as spontaneous and idiosyncratic expressions on the part of role senders nor as simple responses to some previous behavior of the focal person to whom the expectations were sent. Such factors serve only to mediate the major determinants of role-sending, which are to be found in the systemic properties of the organization as a whole, the subsystem in which the role senders are located, and the particular position occupied by each.

Gross, Mason, and McEachern (1958) found that organizational size was a determinant of the pattern of role expectations. Lack of consensus was more frequent in large school systems, and to some extent in communities which utilized complex organizational forms of decision-making rather than the open town meeting. Moreover, members of large school boards were less accepting of any deviation from established lines of authority.

Getzels and Guba (1954) had found earlier that, among the nine air force schools included in their study, strict adherence to military procedure as an organizational norm was associated with lesser role conflict. This finding they interpreted as a problem in normative congruence between system and supersystem, asserting that those schools which maintained strict military procedure were consistent with the norms of the air force and the military establishment as a whole, while those schools which deviated from such procedure created problems of conflict for their staff, who were necessarily members of both the school and the larger military organization.

Kahn and his colleagues (1964) identified five dimensions of normative expectations which appeared to be characteristic of organizations as systems rather than of individual persons or roles. These included the extent to which one is expected to obey rules and follow orders, the extent to which supervisors are expected to show personal interest in and nurture their subordinates, the closeness or generality with which supervision is to be accomplished, the extent to which all relationships are conducted according to general (universalistic) standards, and the extent to which organization members are expected to strive strenuously for achievement and advancement.

Evidence is ample that expectations are shaped by position in organization, as well as by such organizationwide factors. According to the study of Jacobson and his colleagues (1951), almost 70 per cent of the workers held the expectation that the steward should be active in representing the interests of his men rather than waiting until some grievance was presented to him. Only 30 per cent of the foremen took this view of the steward's role, even though the foremen closely resembled the workers in demographic characteristics and had typically been workers in the same plant before their promotion to foreman.

In the studies of role conflict and ambiguity cited above (Kahn et al., 1964) the location of positions within the organization was found to be related to the degree of objective conflict to which the occupant of the position was subjected. In general, positions contained deep within the organizational structure were relatively conflict-free; positions located near the skin or boundary of the organization were likely to be conflict-ridden. Thus jobs involving labor negotiations, purchasing, selling, or otherwise representing the organization to the public were subjected to greater stress. Living near an intraorganization boundary—for example, serving as liaison between two or more departments—revealed many of the same effects but to a lesser degree.

The objective content of the role activities seems also to be related to the pattern of expectations and to the amount of conflict among them. Roles which demand innovative problem-solving are characterized by objective conflict and subjective tension. The occupants of such roles appear to become engaged in conflict primarily with the organizational old guard—men of greater age and power who want to maintain the status quo. Among the major role conflicts of such innovative jobs is the conflict of priority between the nonroutine activities which are at the core of the creative job, and the routine activities of administration or paper work.

Finally, the same research discovered consistent relationships between hierarchical position and the prevalence of conflicting role expectations. The often heard assertion that the lowest levels of supervision are subjected to the greatest conflict is not borne out; rather there is a curvilinear relationship in which the maximum of conflict occurs at the upper middle levels of management. Supervisory responsibility, both direct and indirect, is associated with conflict among role senders with respect to the appropriate style and requirements of the role.

The significant principle reflected by all these specific data is that characteristics of the organization as a whole, of its subsystems, and of the location of particular positions act to determine the expectations which role senders will hold and communicate to the occupant of a particular job. The holding and sending of such expectation is personal and direct; their content is nevertheless shaped by systemic factors.

Personality Factors as Determinants of Role Expectations (Arrow 4). The influence of personality on role-sending is one of those undeniable facts of organizational life which nevertheless awaits measurement and documentation. Anyone who has worked under a number of different bosses has become a student of such personality differences; anyone who has supervised a number of subordinates has discovered how differently they respond to uniform tasks and supervisory behavior. Gross and his colleagues (1958) measured the homogeneity of members of role sets on certain demographic and personality attributes and found some tendency for the degree of such homogeneity to be related to their consensus on expectations for the school superintendent. The combined correlation of political-economic conservatism, religious preference, and motivation to represent some constituent group was .54 with the measure of consensus in role expectations.

Kahn and his coauthors (1964) report similar findings in the industrial context. They found that people who were flexible rather than rigid were subjected to greater pressures to change by their role senders. The behavior of role senders toward extremely rigid focal persons seemed to reflect a judgment of futility and acceptance and the abandonment of continuing attempts to influence behavior in the direction of ideal performance. Role expectations and role-sending were also related to the achievement-orientation of the focal person. The greater the achievement-orientation, especially when such orientation took on a cast of neurotic striving, the more likely were role senders to apply increased pressures to change the style of the focal person.

Personality Factors as Mediators between Role Expectations and Response (Arrow 5). During the past 15 years, the empirical evidence for the mediating influence of enduring properties of the person (demographic, experiential, and personality) has been steadily accumulating. Although such factors are still too often omitted from organizational studies, thus increasing the unexplained variance in organizational behavior, their effects have been reported by dozens of research workers. Stouffer and Toby (1951), in an experiment based on Stouffer's earlier work (1949), found that the chosen behaviors indicated by their experimental subjects in hypothetical situations of role conflict tended to express the predisposition of subjects with respect to the norms of universalism or particularism. Jacobson and his colleagues in the same year (1951) found that the conflict experience of foremen was higher among those who had previously served as stewards, presumably because they had internalized the values of the earlier role.

Sarbin and various colleagues (Sarbin and Rosenberg, 1952; Sarbin and Hardyck, 1952; Albrecht and Sarbin, 1952; Sarbin and Stephenson, 1952) engaged in a series of laboratory experiments showing that the ability of individuals to respond appropriately to role expectations was a function of various personality attributes. The ability to perceive accurately demands of a role was related to a measure of neuroticism based on self-description. Role-taking ability was also related, apparently via the capacity to empathize, to such dimensions as equalitarianism-authoritarianism, and flexibility-rigidity. Extreme inability to take roles was manifested by schizophrenics and psychopaths, a finding consistent with Gough's (1948) earlier theory of psychopathy. He proposed that the characteristic problem of the psychopath is inability to empathize, that is to respond in the focal role *as if* he understood and felt the forces to which the role senders were subjected. Such an interpretation of psychopathy was given some support by Baker's (1954) small comparative study of psychopathic and nonpsychopathic prisoners. Questioning these subjects in terms which others used in appraising and describing them, Baker found that the psychopaths had significantly greater difficulty recognizing in themselves the ascribed traits.

Gross, Mason, and McEachern (1958) found that the effects of role conflict on job satisfaction and expressions of worry among school superintendents were consistently mediated by the characteristic anxiety level of the individual. They also utilized personality variables in attempting to predict the conflict-resolving behavior of the superintendents in four hypothetical situations, involving hiring and promotion, time allocation, salary recommendations for teachers, and budget recommendations. The personality predictor was based on a categorization of the superintendents as moralists, moral-expedients, or expedients—according to their predisposition to emphasize legitimacy or sanctions in response to a series of test items.

Kahn and his coauthors (1964) found that several personality dimensions mediate significantly the degree to which a given intensity of objective conflict is experienced as strain by the focal person. These personality dimensions include emotional sensitivity, introversion-extroversion, flexibility-rigidity, and the need for career achievement.

For example, the effects of objective role conflict on interpersonal bonds and on tension are more pronounced for introverts. The introverts develop social relations which, while sometimes congenial and trusting, are easily undermined by conditions of stress. The preference of such people for autonomy becomes manifest primarily when social contacts are stressful, that is, when others are exerting strong pressures and thereby creating conflict for them. In similar fashion, emotional sensitivity mediates the relationship between objective conflict and tension, with emotionally sensitive persons showing substantially higher tension scores for any given degree of objective conflict. An individual who is strongly achievement-oriented exhibits a high degree of personal involvement with his job, and the adverse effects of role conflict are more pronounced for him than for those who are less involved. (p. 384)

Personality as Affected by Role Behavior (Arrow 8). It is usual for psychologists to treat the characteristics of adult personality as relatively fixed, having been formed during earlier years of life and by earlier experiences. Our approach to personality is more dynamic than that; we believe the personality is essentially the product of social interaction, and that the process of personality formation continues throughout life. More specifically, the model of role-taking which we are proposing treats personality variables in three ways: as a determinant of the role expectations of others, as mediating factors between sent role and the ways in which it is experienced and responded to, and as factors which are affected by experience and behavior in organizational roles. It is the last of these three views of personality to which we now turn.

The empirical evidence for the effects of role experience and behavior on personality is thin, perhaps because it has not been often sought. The truth of the folk saying that "you become what you do" has yet to be put to systematic test. However, Cameron and Magaret (1951) reported that the absence of role-taking skills seemed to contribute to the development of paranoid symptoms. Gough and Peterson (1952) found that the number of roles played by an individual was related to his ability to be self-critical, and that deficiencies in role performance led to an increasing inability to see oneself in objective terms and to identify with the views of others. In an extended experiment involving the manipulation of the level of decision-making in a large clerical operation, Tannenbaum (1957) showed that both the autonomous and the hierarchical conditions produced significant changes in personality. The personality changes were in the direction of increasing congruence between role and person.

Earlier accounts of the effects of role on personality were unsupported by quantitative data, and were concentrated primarily on the dysfunctional effects of bureaucratic requirements. Veblen's discussion of "trained incapacity," Dewey's description of "occupational psychosis," and Warnotte's reference to "professional deformation" are perhaps the major examples of this line of argument. Merton (1957) builds on them in his own exposition of bureaucratic structure and personality, and concludes with a plea for "studies of religious, educational, military, economic, and political bureaucracies dealing with the interdependence of social organization and personality formation . . . ." The conclusion remains appropriate today.

The Significance of Interpersonal Relations in Role-Taking (Arrows 6, 7, and 9). In theory, enduring properties of the interpersonal relationship between a focal person and members of his role set enter into the process of role-sending and response in ways analogous to enduring properties of the person. That is to say, we expect that the interpersonal relations between focal person and role senders will help to determine their role expectations, will intervene between sent role and received role, and will in turn be affected by the role behavior of the focal person. Some evidence for all three of these effects is available from the research on role conflict already cited (Kahn et al., 1964):

The sources of pressure and conflict for a person can be expressed rather fully in terms of his interpersonal relations with these pressure sources (arrow 6). The greatest pressure is directed to a person from other people who are in the same department as he is, who are his superiors in the hierarchy, and who are sufficiently dependent on his performance to care about his adequacy without being so completely dependent as to be inhibited in making their demands known. The people who are least likely to apply such pressures are a person's peers and role senders outside his own department.

The kinds of influence techniques which people are prepared to apply, as well as the degree of pressure they exert, vary with their formal relationship to the potential target of their pressures. To a considerable degree the actual power structure of organizations follows the lines of formal authority. Legitimate power, rewards, and coercive power over an organizational member are largely in the hands of his direct organizational superiors. Although a supervisor has coercive power available to him as a basis for influencing his subordinates, he is likely to refrain from using it where it might impede the performance of these subordinates and perhaps reflect upon the supervisor himself. On the other hand, the techniques used by subordinates to apply coercive power are precisely those which threaten the efficiency of the organization. They include the withholding of aid and information.

The deleterious effects of role conflict are most severe where the network of an individual's organizational relations binds him closely to members of his role set (arrow 7). When a person must deal with others who are highly dependent on him, who have high power over him, and who exert high pressure on him, his response is typically one of apathy and withdrawal—psychological if not behavioral. Under such circumstances the experience of role conflict is intense and job satisfaction correspondingly low. Emotionally, the focal person experiences a sense of futility, and he attempts a hopeless withdrawal from his coworkers. Likewise, the costs of role conflict upon the focal person are most dear where there is a generally high level of communication between the focal person and his role senders.

Since close ties to role senders with regard to functional dependence, power, and communication intensify the effects of an existing conflict, an obvious means of coping with conflict is to sever ties with one's role senders. Symptomatic of this pattern of withdrawal in the face of conflict is the tendency of an individual experiencing role conflict to reduce the amount of communication with his role senders, to derogate bonds with these senders (arrow 9). Although this pattern of coping with stress is common, its logic is questionable. Withdrawal may be successful in alleviating the effects of stress for a time; in the longer run it is likely to prove self-defeating. Withdrawal may not only leave the initial conflict unresolved, but may in addition set off a chain reaction of derivative conflicts. (pp. 382–383)

SUMMARY

The concept of role is proposed as the major means for linking the individual and organizational levels of research and theory; it is at once the building block of social systems and the summation of the requirements with which such systems confront their members as individuals. Each person in an organization is linked to some set of other members by virtue of the functional requirements of the system which are heavily implemented through the expectations those members have of him; he is the focal person for that set. An organization can be viewed as consisting of a number of such sets, one for each person in the organization.

The process by which the expectations of members of a role set are linked to the behavior of the focal person for that set is described in terms of role episodes. The role episode in turn consists of a sequence of events involving members of a role set and the focal person. The sequence begins with the role expectations held by members of the set for the focal person; these are activities which they require of him in order to perform their own roles or to maintain their own satisfactions. The next step in the role episode is the sending of these expectations from the members of the set to the focal person, the communication of role requirements in terms intended to influence his behavior.

With the communication of role expectations from role set to focal person, the first half of the role episode is completed. The second half has to do with the perceptions and behavior of the focal person. He receives, with greater or lesser distortion, the role expectations sent to him. It is the received role which is the immediate source of influence and motivation of his behavior (insofar as it is influenced by members of his role set). Finally, the focal person acts; he behaves in role, showing some combination of compliance and noncompliance with the expectations of his role set. They observe and evaluate his behavior in relation to their expectations and needs, and thus the cycle moves into another episode.

Several complications are considered in connection with the treatment of organizational role in these terms. One role may involve many activities; multiple roles may be incorporated in a single office, that is, intended for performance by a single individual. Moreover, one person may hold a number of offices. Each of these elaborations adds its own complications to the simple situation in which a single recurrent activity comprises a role, which in turn comprises an office occupied by a person without additional organizational commitments.

Three oversimplifications of the role episode are considered: the fact that organizational life is continuous rather than made up of discrete episodes, the fact that members of a role set are often in disagreement among themselves with respect to what the focal person should do, and the fact that the role episode occurs within and is shaped by a matrix of organizational influences. Four basic categories of role conflict are considered: incompatible expectations held by a given member of a role set (intrasender conflict); incompatible expectations held by two or more members (intersender conflict); incompatibilities between two or more roles held by the same focal person (interrole conflict); and incompatibilities between the requirements of a role and the needs or values of the person holding it (person-role conflict).

The chapter concludes with a review of the empirical evidence bearing on the model of role-sending and role behavior which has been proposed.

8

Power and Authority

The exposition of power and authority in human organizations has been forecast to some extent by three themes of earlier chapters: the defining characteristics of such organizations (Chapter 3), the development of organizations from primitive to complex structural forms (Chapter 4), and the nature of organizational roles (Chapter 7). We defined the organization as an open social system, distinguished from other open systems in that is is a structure of events or human acts, rather than of physical components. An array of such acts intended for performance by an individual we defined as a role, and the organization is therefore a system of roles.

It follows that a continuing requirement for all human organizations is the motivation of role behavior, that is, the attraction and retention of individual members and the motivation of those members to perform the organizationally required acts. As Merton (1957) has stated, the reliability of role behavior is the requirement intrinsic to human organizations. To state that requirement in other terms, every organization faces the task of somehow reducing the variability, instability, and spontaneity of individual human acts.

The Reduction of Human Variability. The general success of organizations in achieving this reduction is available to the most superficial observer. Within an organization members behave in ways which they would not do outside the organization. They may wear uniforms or costumes which they would not otherwise wear. They are likely to adopt certain styles and formalities in interpersonal relations which are not elsewhere in evidence. Above all, their behavior in organizations shows a selectivity, a restrictiveness, and a persistence which is not to be observed in the same persons when outside the organization. The most elementary examples of behavior can serve to illustrate this point:

Consider the regularity in the time of arrivals and departures of employees of a company, the synchronization of their pauses for rests or coffee breaks, and the persistence of behavioral cycles which is especially observable among semiskilled or unskilled industrial employees.

F. H. Allport (1933, 1934) called attention to this characteristic of organizations many years ago and gave dramatic expression to it by comparing the normal curve of individual attributes or behavioral acts to the curve of conformity or the J-curve which is characteristic of organizationally determined acts.

Only in the most primitive of organizational forms, however, is the influence of the organization over the member manifest solely in terms of uniformity of behavior. As organizations become more complex, the division of labor and the specialization of tasks prescribe very different patterns of behavior for different roles. The need for reliability of role performance, however, becomes no less; on the contrary, it increases with the complexity and sophistication of the organization. Consider the very simple organizational form of a gang of field hands picking cotton under the supervision of an overseer. In this case, the workers are all doing the same thing, picking the raw cotton and putting it in a sack. The relationship of their individual tasks is little more than additive; each task is in miniature the same as the organizational or gang task of getting cotton off the plant and into the sack. Unreliability in role performance, absence, and turnover merely add to the duration or the required speed at which the others must work.

Contrast this with a different organizational form and task, the manufacture of a washing machine by assembly-line methods. The total task, making a washing machine by manufacturing and assembling the components, is broken down into individual tasks, as was the picking of a field of cotton. But the positions in the manufacturing company differ very much from one another, and none of them resembles very much the organizational task of creating the appliance itself. There are instead specialists in the threading and connecting of electrical wires; there are tub installers, sheet-metal fasteners, polishers, molders, and many more.

The interdependence among these workers is much greater than among the field hands, and the organizational requirements for reliability in role performance are much greater. If the position of tub installer is not filled, even if it is only one position in 1,000, the organizational consequence is not merely a reduction of 1/1000 in total product; the organization will produce tubless washing machines unless that position is filled. To dramatize the situation without overstating its basic character: unless this and each other position is filled, the organization cannot produce washing machines at all.

In certain circumstances a visible and dramatic environmental situation may be enough to stimulate such coordinated effort among people. At other times the values and expectations shared by various individuals may be sufficient to bring them into some state of cooperation. These, however, we have asserted to be more characteristic of ad hoc, voluntary groups than of formal organizations. Members of formal organizations of course respond to visible environmental pressures and are often motivated by shared values; the dominant organizational solution to the problem of achieving reliable performance, however, is to promulgate and enforce rules of conduct. The organizational solution to the problem of achieving lawfulness is to pass laws.

Indeed, that is the meaning behind the definition of an organization as a system of roles. Each role consists of a set of prescriptions or behaviors which are to be performed, and typically includes in addition a set of proscriptions or behaviors which are to be avoided. In the process of creating such prescriptions and proscriptions we have seen the beginnings of the managerial subsystem of an organization.

Some of the organizational prescriptions are very broad and apply to every position in the system. Some apply to subparts of the system, and some apply only to a single role or position. For example, getting to work by 8 o'clock each morning may be a law which applies to all day-shift jobs below the level of superintendent. Keeping the floors clean is an injunction which may apply only to the job of janitor. "Don't steal company property" may be a law which is systemwide in its application. In short, these laws include all of the norms and role requirements of the organization. If foresight were perfect, if incumbents were flawless organization men or automatons, and if the environment of the organization were unchanging, the problems of management might be at an end once the design had been created and the prescriptions communicated. The organization could be given an initial push, and like a mass in motion in theoretical space, it would continue its cycles undiminished in perpetuity. Nor would there be any continuing need for control and coordination; the parts and their functions would be coordinated in the initial statement of functions and relationships. No more would be necessary.

Such a picture has about it the neatness and unreality of a print by Currier and Ives. It is superficially lifelike, but not alive. The characteristics of organizations which demand a more complex and dynamic description are already familiar to us; they can be summarized under three headings.

First, the roles in organizations are filled by people, not by mechanical devices. There is a double consequence to this. For one thing, people vary in strength and intelligence, and these variations will be reflected in their role performance, as deviations from organizational requirements, and as excesses and lacks of various kinds. A second organizational consequence of the use of human components stems from the fact that the life of the person is not wholly comprehended by the organization. The individual has other involvements than his job; he has family, friends, hobbies, and involvements quite apart from his organizational role. His involvement in the organization, in other words, is segmental rather than total. But the person is an entity, and not a collection of segments. His behavior at any moment tends to be, therefore, the product of all his involvements, past and present, not just the result of the input of the point of time and space which he occupies at that moment. His role performance in the organization accordingly is affected by forces which are extraorganizational in their source—by factors of personality and nonorganizational experience. In large degree, it is for these reasons that most acts in the organizational context have unintended as well as intended consequences. Every interpersonal act in an organization has an ultimate individual receiver, who must decode and interpret the message as it comes to him. The product of interpretation has always something of the receiver in it as well as the message.

Second, organizations are not perfect frictionless systems, and their parts wear out. Each role occupant grows old or incapacitated and must be replaced. Each machine and building suffers the same fate. Supplies are consumed. Everything about the organization but the abstract pattern which it embodies is forever in process of being used and used up. The replacement of organization parts, given the basic variability of human beings, means adjustments not only for the new employee, but to some degree for all those others in the organization who must interact with him. In lesser amount, the replacement of non-human elements in an organization imposes some of the same necessity for overall adjustment.

Third, and most important of all perhaps, the organization functions in a changing environment, and each environmental change is received as a demand for some responsive change within the organizational system. The need for appropriate and reliable behavior which led to the emergence of a managerial subsystem in the first place is reiterated with each change in the environment; the organization is in a constant state of redefinition.

Thus, far from approximating the perpetual-motion machine, the organization is engaged in a never-ending process of adaptation, replacement, and attempts to insure role performance, a process which in turn guarantees the product which justifies organizational existence.

We suggested earlier that one organizational means to insuring role performance is to make the role requirements of each position explicit and the fulfillment of them a matter of organizational law. But this solution raises new questions. Why should people become members of the organization and subject themselves to such laws? Why should they obey them? What shall be done if they fail to obey them?

Questions of Obedience and Disobedience. The most general answer to such questions lies in the concept of authority and in the creation within the managerial subsystem of a structure of authority. By *authority* we mean simply legitimate power, power which is vested in a particular person or position, which is recognized as so vested, and which is accepted as appropriate not only by the wielder of power but by those over whom it is wielded and by the other members of the system.

The managerial subsystem and the structure of authority are inseparable. They arise out of the same organizational needs, and they develop interactively and simultaneously. Every organization must have means of insuring role performance, replacing lost members, coordinating the several subsystems of the organization, responding to external changes, and making decisions about how all these things shall be accomplished. For every organization these means include some form of managerial subsystem, some structure of authority, and some roles which have a degree of specialization with respect to these functions.

It is not much of an exaggeration to say that the creation of specialized roles is a generalized solution for all organizational problems; as soon as an unmet functional requirement is recognized, a new role is created, the content of which is to provide for the missing activities. F.H. Allport (1933) recognized this solution as a special case of a still more general tendency: to attempt to cure an institutional defect by a further act of institutionalization. Allport considered this a dangerous and self-destroying practice if carried to the extreme; it seems to us also an unavoidable one in some degree. In any case, it is the modal solution for ensuring that the role requirements of organization are met; a new role (or many) is added to the organization, the requirements of which are solely to see to it that other role occupants are performing in the required manner, at the approved pace, and in the prescribed relation, one to another. In like manner, the organization approaches the continuing problems of adaptation, procurement, and the like, although these are of less concern to us in the present context.

The foregoing description approximates closely the minimal function of the leader or supervisor. He is to observe whether, for some set of roles, the performance of the incumbents conforms to the requirements which the organization has laid down. If it does, well and good. If it does not, he must take corrective action; he must get the occupants to change their behavior to meet the requirements of the role. But how is the supervisor to carry out this crucial part of his role? How shall he get the subordinate to conform more closely to the requirements of the organization?

Again, the generalized solution is employed. The organization stipulates an additional requirement, stating that subordinates shall accede to the legitimate (role-prescribed) requests of their superiors. Indeed, there is no more pervasive law of organization than that the occupants of certain roles shall respond to and obey certain kinds of requests from the occupants of certain other roles. This superordinate requirement may be so taken for granted that it does not appear in the job description which states the requirements of a role. The lathe-hand's job may specify the parts that are to be machined, the number of them to be processed each hour, and the tolerances to be maintained. The job description may even include keeping the machine lubricated and the surrounding area clean. It is unlikely to specify, "Obey the foreman in job-relevant matters, and especially in requests to conform to the role requirements already described," but this remains an essential and binding requirement. In short, the influence of the supervisor over the subordinate is *legitimized*, made a matter of organizational law, and we say that the supervisor has legitimate power solely by virtue of occupying the office.

To say that the occupant of one role has authority over the occupant of another on organizational matters means that the influence of the one over the other is a matter of organizational law; it is legitimate and is so accepted. Compliance with authoritative requests thus becomes a generalized role expectation in organizations; each member of the organization is expected by all others to so comply, and relevant persons and agencies outside the organization agree and on occasion reinforce this view.

Such acceptance of authority is in effect a key clause in the psychological contract (and sometimes, the legal contract) in terms of which each new member accepts membership and enters the organization. He understands these terms at the time of entry; his supervisor assumes the same terms and assumes the new employee's understanding and acceptance of them. His peers agree, and by their agreement reinforce the contractual obligations.

Such a description of authority, the legitimation of influence, does not imply consensus, however; legitimation does not imply that 100 per cent of the employees are in perfect agreement. The organization can run on less than perfection, although how much less is an interesting theoretical and empirical question. No organization can function, however, without substantial recognition and acceptance of authority; the breakdown of such acceptance is precisely what is meant by mutiny, revolution, or more peaceful forms of organizational death.

The specification of certain patterns of influence by leaders as legitimate does not, as we have said, insure consensus. Nor does still broader acceptance of authority guarantee that the accepters will in every instance comply with the requirements of their roles. We are by now accustomed to the imperfection of organizational solutions, and perhaps impressed with the ingenuity and foresight invested in devices for handling contingencies and preventing the potential failures implied by imperfect solutions. The legitimate power of the supervisor, the power of the role, is always backed by the power of punishment and reward. The authority structure, in other words, is bolstered by an ancillary system of rewards and punishments. It is typical for organizations to reward the exemplary fulfillment of role requirements by bonuses, incentive payments, special privileges, and recognition. These rewards are quite apart from the basic wage or other provision for attracting people to the organization in the first place, and keeping them in the system. The special rewards may be given for quality or quantity of work, for regularity of attendance, or for sheer duration of service. The tendency is to reward all organizationally valued role behaviors, and to give special attention to those requirements the fulfillment of which constitutes problems for the organization.

In complementary fashion, failure to meet role requirements is penalized. There is the withholding of rewards; there are fines, suspensions, restrictions of various kinds. An inspection of the roster of penalty-incurring acts in an organization emphasizes the fact that refusal to accept influence from a supervisor on some legitimate matter is invariably defined as a serious failure in role performance. In most organizations, and certainly in business and industry, the ultimate punishment which the organization can impose is expulsion from the system, permanent exclusion from its benefits, and sometimes (by means of the blacklist) exclusion from the benefits of other systems as well. In most organizations, insubordination—the refusal to accept legitimized influence—is a certain cause for punishment, and if it is persisted in, for expulsion. Even organizations whose basic custodial function makes expulsion of members impossible in the usual sense have means for removing the insubordinate from the system. The army has the stockade; the prison has the isolation block; the mental hospital is similarly equipped. Such devices are in part designed to punish past performance failures, and in part are last-ditch attempts at correction; they also perform the vital function of getting the nonperforming, uninfluenceable member out of the system before his performance failure does systemic damage.

The major point of this exposition is to emphasize the central importance of *legitimate power* in organizational life. The organization coordinates and insures the performance of people in different roles, gets correction and compliance, and when necessary implements change in role requirements primarily by making the acceptance of influence in these matters part of one role and the exertion of such influence part of another. Certain types and channels of influence are thus legitimized, and certain relationships of legitimate power, or authority, are established between roles. Finally, the legitimation of power relationships is backed by a system of penalties. In some organizations these are harsh and obvious; in some they may be obscure and appear more as the withholding of rewards. In any case, the establishment of legitimate and illegitimate behavior in organizations presupposes a system of penalty. We cannot conceive of a law without some established consequence for those who break it (or advantage for those who obey it).

To the extent that this line of argument is plausible, we can claim it as an explanation of the need for authority in human organizations and the development of a structure of authority. To say that an organization requires some type and structure of authority, however, by no means explains the rational-legal type and the specific hierarchical form that is conventional in so much of human society.

Forms of Authority. Weber (1947) put this fact in historical perspective by pointing out that modern bureaucratic structures have developed a functional specificity of roles sanctioned by an authority structure of a *rational-legal type*, and that this is in contrast to the feudal system, where authority was vested in *traditional status*, and to systems dependent upon *charismatic authority* or obedience to leaders because of their supernatural or divine qualities.

In traditional authority, people are not observing enacted rules, but the directives of a person occupying a position of authority because he has rightfully inherited his post. In Weber's language, "A system of imperative coordination will be called 'traditional' if legitimacy is claimed for it and believed in on the basis of the sanctity of the order and the attendant powers of control as they have been handed down from the past, have always existed." Where pure types of traditional authority exist, there are no clearly defined spheres of competence for a trained administrative staff whose actions and decisions are determined by impersonal rules. Changes in the requirements of the system to meet changing conditions cannot come from new legislation. To the extent that changes develop at all, they come from the traditional person in authority who justifies them as old values which he wants implemented in these ways. Thus, the only orientation of traditional authority to rules is to the precedents of the group's history.

Charismatic authority is not bound by rules of any kind. The magical qualities of the leader are so unlimited that in pure form charisma would not result in any stable set of role relationships. Over time, charisma moves toward traditionalism as the manner of succession becomes established, e.g., designation of a successor by the leader, or hereditary succession. Or it moves toward legalization as the disciples develop rules for the admission of novices to the group and organizational protocols describing the hierarchy of positions and their rewards.

The legal type of authority asserts that obedience is to be rendered only to the law, that is, to the impersonal order of a person in a position of authority only within the sphere of his defined area of legitimate power. Weber outlined the following characteristics of rational legal authority:

1. A continuous organization of official functions bound by rules.
2. A specified sphere of competence based on a division of labor with authority and sanctions to ensure proper role performance.
3. A hierarchical arrangement of offices in terms of supervision and control.
4. The governing of the conduct of an office by technical rules or by norms and the requiring of specialized training for the incumbents of these offices.
5. Complete separation of the property belonging to the organization and the property belonging to the official. In fact, an official should not be an owner of company property.
6. The lack of rights to his office by the incumbent. He cannot appropriate his official position in his own interests.
7. Administrative acts, decisions, and rules are formulated and recorded in writing . . . . The combination of written documents and a continuous organization of official functions constitutes the "office" which is the central focus of all types of modern corporate action.

Weber's analysis thus emphasizes the diffuseness of roles in systems which emphasize traditional and charismatic authority as against their functional specificity in rational-legal structures. The modern bureaucracy of the industrial corporation represents a good illustration of the working out of rational-legal authority. It is true that organizations, including even the industrial enterprise, will show all types of authority patterns. Some industrial leaders may be obeyed because of charismatic qualities, and traditional status may be found in large-scale corporations. But modern social organizations rest primarily upon rational and legal grounds. Bureaucratic structure in the Weberian sense utilizes role systems in their purest form and they represent the most pliable, the most effective instruments for environmental transactions and exploitation in the evolution of social systems. For maximum utilization of the energy sources in the environment, including man himself, and their transformation into social products, the formal social organization may be the greatest social invention in history.

There is one respect in which Weber's classic analysis combines issues which require separate scrutiny, namely the inclusion of the hierarchical arrangement of offices as a defining characteristic of rational-legal authority. The basic organizational requirement is for dependable role performance; this in turn leads to the requirement that each role be under the surveillance of some other role, in order to assure that performance is delivered. But what structure will suffice for this surveillance?

Some very simple solutions to this problem can be observed. Children at a summer camp frequently make use of the "buddy system" for safety in swimming. The swimmers are paired, and each member of the pair is responsible for the safety and behavior of the other, and for making known to the swimming director any serious problem. Here is a structure of authority which appears to consist of a pairing of peers plus a single supervisor above the peer group. Every member of the group is both supervisor and supervised, and furthermore every member of the group is supervised by the person whom he supervises. All the authority relationships are symmetrical and reciprocal, except for the director who supervises all but is supervised by none of the swimmers. The structure is very flat, with the rudiment of the conventional pyramid appearing only in the role of the director.

Another elementary structure of authority is that which appears in a large family, when the overworked mother makes each child responsible for the next younger in the family. This arrangement resembles the swimmers' system in its simplicity and in its assignment of a "supervisor" to each child; each child has one supervisor and each supervisor is responsible for the behavior of only one child. In this system, too, there is only one overseer of all the roles in the system. The major difference between this system and the summer camp example is that no child in the family is supervised by the same person whom he supervises. All the supervisory relationships are nonreciprocal or asymmetrical. In addition to their simplicity, these two systems of authority share another characteristic; the authority relationships are nontransitive. The oldest boy is responsible for his younger sister, who in turn is responsible for the baby; this does not imply that the oldest boy is responsible for the baby. Similarly, among the swimmers at camp, authority relationships consist of pairs, and there is no connectedness between pairs.

There are inherent limitations and deficiencies in these simple structures of authority once we envision their application in larger and more complex organizations. Some of these problems are well solved by the conventional pyramid of authority. For example, we emphasized the authority structure as an invention to minimize the risk of performance failure in organizations. The simple, flat structure of authority does not offer a protection in depth against this contingency. If one swimmer ventures beyond the prescribed area, what will happen? His buddy is supposed to observe the breach of role performance and bring his companion back. But what if the buddy is not watching as closely as he should and fails to observe the event at all? What, to generalize the question, if the supervisor fails to supervise or is unable to correct his subordinate. The conventional organizational answer applies: create a new role, supervisor-of-supervisors, with direct responsibility for the supervisor and indirect, supervisor-reinforcing responsibility for the object of supervision. Thus the buddy system is likely to be reinforced immediately by the presence of a swimming director, and it may be further elaborated by introducing camp counselors as a level of supervision intermediate between the director and the mutually supervising swimmers.

The proliferation of supervisory levels in order to reduce the risk of performance failures aggravates a problem which is inherent in all supervisory activity: efficiency. The language of organization is rich with reminders of the costs of supervision, and of the fact that the organizational means which are expended in supervision are thereby diverted from roles which contribute more directly to turning out the organizational product. We speak of direct and indirect costs of production, a relatively neutral choice of terminology. But we also speak of supervisory costs as part of the overhead expenditure of the organization, or more simply, as "the burden." The more hours of supervision per man-day of production, the greater is the burden. And the more supervisors who have any responsibility for overseeing a given job, the greater is likely to be the aggregate of supervisory hours invested. Organizations attempt to increase the efficiency of supervision by grouping together under a single supervisor roles which are similar in requirements or closely related in function. A foreman may thus be assigned to supervise twenty workers, all of whom are operating identical machines; or he may be assigned to supervise a subassembly which involves several different kinds of jobs that are in some unifying and meaningful relationship to each other. There is an attempt, in this way, to maximize the number of jobs which can be supervised by one person, and this attempt may persist throughout the several levels of management.

The pyramidal shape is an outcome of such proliferation of supervisory levels in order to reduce the risk of performance failure, and a concomitant effort to minimize the costs of supervision by prescribing for each supervisory office the widest feasible span of control. Much greater gain in efficiency might result from reducing the amount of supervision, perhaps stripping out whole levels of the authority structure. This, however, would require that the organization develop alternative means of insuring role performance, and the alternatives to the hierarchical application of legitimate power are relatively unexplored.

Still another of the forces which shapes the pyramid of authority is the organizational axiom that every required function must be clearly vested in some specific role. Whether this assertion deserves the status of axiom is debatable; that it enjoys that status in our culture is beyond debate. This implies that every organization must have an ultimate leader, a head of state. Suppose, for example, that a small manufacturing company has three major functional departments: manufacturing, sales, and engineering design. The efforts of the three departments must be coordinated if the organization is to produce and sell some article. The designers must create a design which can be mass-produced and sold; the manufacturing department must operate within costs which permit the salesmen to dispose of the product. The need for coordination is obvious, but what are the means for coordination? The usual logic of organization says that since the three departments must coordinate, they must have a coordinator. Hence the organization acquires another level, a supreme commander.

We could object to this deduction. The three departments must coordinate; why should not the three department heads recognize this necessity and work out the necessary agreements? Such a triumvirate could be imagined, although it is easy to see how the need to break occasional deadlocks, resolve disagreements, and represent the organization to the outside world leads away from such a committee structure toward the elaboration of authority levels until the irreducible minimum has been achieved and we have a supreme level of authority with only a single occupant.

A final explanation of the organizational pyramid lies in the pattern of organizational birth and growth. It is convenient for purposes of analysis to presuppose the existence of the direct productive roles in the organization, and then speculate on how this structure might be supervised. This is not the fashion in which organizations are created. Businesses typically begin with the definition of the top of the structure; the would-be founder or president appoints himself and then tries to create the organization. The picture is somewhat different, of course, for voluntary and representative organizations, but so is the resulting structure of authority.

The Democratic Alternative. It is in government and voluntary organizations that there has been developed the major alternative to the pyramidal structure for the administration of complex social organizations. That model we will risk calling democratic, in contrast to hierarchical, in spite of the value-laden nature of the terms. For the most part the subsystems of a democratic organization are the same as those of the hierarchical, other things being equal. The basic difference between the two is in the managerial subsystem, and specifically in the structure of authority.

We have said earlier (Chapter 3) that the managerial subsystem is not separate from the other subsystems of organization in terms of organizational positions (structure of offices); rather, the managerial subsystem interpenetrates the other subsystems. The shape and nature of this interpenetration in a democratic organization is very different from that in the hierarchical model. The pyramid of hierarchical organization represents a fusion of status, prestige, rewards, and power. As we ascend the pyramid, all these increase and reach their maxima at the pinnacle of the hierarchy. The president of a company typically receives the largest salary, enjoys the greatest prestige, can commit the organization to new policies, or veto such commitment. Within the limitations of law and collective bargaining, he can hire a man into any job in the organization or fire a man from any job; on the other hand, he himself cannot be hired or fired by any other person in the organization. (In a public corporation, however, the president's powers may be subject to an outside board of directors.)

Particularly important to the nature of hierarchical organization is the increase in power of different kinds which characterizes each successive level in the hierarchy. Power is not only executive, having to do with the range and importance of acts of implementation; it is also legislative, having to do with the promulgation of organizational law and policy. In short, the hierarchical power includes not only the operation of the organization; it includes the definition of the organization, the power to determine that the organization shall be different tomorrow in policy and structure than it is today. It includes also, by virtue of the prerogative to hire and fire, the power to determine what combination of individuals shall play the stipulated organizational roles.

The democratic organizational model differs from the hierarchical specifically in separating those several aspects of power which are fused in the hierarchy. The distribution of power with respect to certain kinds of decisions is characteristically different in the democratic organization, being shared among the members of the body politic. Specific and crucial to the distinction between democratic and hierarchical structures is the separation of legislative from executive power. Executive power in democratic organizations usually is distributed in accord with the pyramidal structure of authority, which we have examined in detail in our discussion of hierarchy. Legislative power, however, shows a different distribution and is widely shared among the members of the organization. The fullest manifestation of this characteristic is implied in the democratic slogan, "One member, one vote." The major criterion of democratic organizational structure, then, is the extent to which the legislative subsystem includes the entire membership of the organization, all the positions in the structure. The working approach to answering this question would be to ask another: "Who makes the organizational policies?"

The distinction between policy-making (legislation) and policy implementation (execution) is not always made consistently, primarily because the view of the organization depends so much on location in the hierarchy—hence the truism "policy is what my boss decides." We propose that all organizational decisions can be arrayed with respect to three basic dimensions: level of generality, amount of organizational space affected, and extension in time.

Distinguishing between policy-making and policy implementation in terms of these three dimensions implies a continuum of decisions rather than a set of discontinuous categories, with the policy-making component of decisions increasing as there is increase on these three dimensions. In general, policy decisions involve the formulation of substantive goals and objectives, and the formulation of procedures and devices for attaining goals and evaluating goal attainment. Execution involves the application of existing organizational machinery to ongoing operations, in the service of objectives already determined. (For a fuller statement of these definitions, see Chapter 10.) More specifically, if we were looking for policy decisions in the records of an organization, we would attend to decisions about the expansion or contraction of the organization itself, decisions to alter organizational structure in other ways (lines of authority, number of echelons). We would look for decisions to change the nature of the product turned out, to change the location of the organization in the larger environment, or to alter its relationship to the outside environment in other ways. Finally we would look for any decision involving a major disbursement of organizational resources.

A second criterion of democratic structure is the veto, because it identifies the locus of ultimate organizational power. By whom, by what procedures, and under what circumstances can a given decision be overruled? The repeated presentation of an issue to successively higher levels of authority leads ultimately to the office of the president in a hierarchical organization, and to the assembled membership or their representatives in a democratic organization.

The final criterion which we propose for distinguishing hierarchical from democratic organizational forms is the basis on which selection, tenure, and dismissal are determined—especially for key executive positions. It is a characteristic of hierarchy that each level tends to have the power to name the persons who shall hold the positions at the next lower level. Where this power has been lost, its loss is keenly felt and much bewailed. The outstanding example in recent organizational history is the reduction in the hiring and firing power of the firm, and especially of the foreman, by trade unions.

The democratic model, on the other hand, implies in its extreme form that each person shall be named to membership and position by the others. Variations on this theme are many, and not relevant for the present discussion. The crucial issue in the application of this criterion is the mode of selecting (and dismissing) the chief executive officers of the organization. The president-owner of a business is not dismissable by any power within the organization; the president of a corporation can be dismissed only by the board of directors (a quasi-external body). The president of a voluntary organization typically holds office for a stipulated term, is elected by vote of the members, and is subject to recall on the same basis.

All three of these criteria of hierarchy-democracy (the separation of legislative from executive power, the locus of the veto, and the selection of officers) are familiar in political science, although less often invoked in organizational theory. All three reflect the principles of government by the active and expressed consent of the governed.

The appropriateness of democratic and hierarchical structures to different human purposes and conditions is still unsettled. In organizational life, at least, we are inclined to the view that the advantages of hierarchy have been overstated. The military model, adopted in industry and extended with the development of machine-technology, seems to us to be overrationalized and urged by its proponents irrespective of organizational nature, purpose, and surrounding conditions. There are those who demand that every sector of life and every organization be businesslike.

We would propose as hypotheses that the hierarchical system is at its best in terms of survival and efficiency:

1. When individual tasks are minimal in creative requirements, so that compliance with legitimate authority is enough, and identification with organizational goals is not required;

2. When the environmental demands on the organization are clear and their implications obvious, so that information is redundant and can be wasted and the organization need not make use of all the potential receivers and processors of information among its members;

3. When speed in decision-making is a requirement of importance, so that each additional person involved in the process adds significantly to organizational costs and risks;

4. When the organizational circumstances approximate those of closed systems, with minimal change requirements from the environment.

The advantages of democratic organizational structure reach a maximum under an opposite set of conditions, i.e., when the organization is maximally open to environmental demands and when the environment is changing in ways that pose complex and difficult problems of organizational adaptation, so that great value attaches to receiving and using well all available information relevant to such changes and their implications. Democratic organization is particularly advantageous also when the correctness and appropriateness of organizational adaptations are more crucial than the speed with which the adapting decisions are made, and when the nature of individual roles involves creative efforts which require broad understanding of organizational functions and the motivation that comes from identification of one's goals with the aims of organization.

The Logic of Authority. We can sum up rather briefly the underlying logic for the foregoing narrative.

1. For every organization there is a set of activities which must be performed, or the effectiveness and survival of the organization is in jeopardy. The primary organizational means for guaranteeing the performance of these activities is to stipulate them as role requirements,

and to impose a superordinate requirement that the acceptance of role be an initial condition for membership.

2. To forestall the possibility of failure, a set of supervisory roles is created, the essential function of which is to see that the requirements of the basic organizational roles are fulfilled. The elaboration of this sequence produces the conventional pyramid of authority in organizations.

3. To insure that the admonitions of the supervisors shall be obeyed, still another requirement of organization is propounded on a systemwide basis: subordinates shall obey their designated supervisors with respect to matters of role performance.

4. Since this requirement, too, might be disregarded, it is bolstered with a system of rewards and punishments (including expulsion from the system).

It is important to distinguish between those essential problems which every complex human organization must solve in order to attain an existence-insuring degree of efficiency, and those particular solutions which are manifest by certain classes of organizations of our culture and our time. We have proposed the hierarchical and democratic structures as instructive contrasts, not because they are pure types, but because they represent significant differences along several important dimensions.

Some of the limitations of the classical models of organization (Weber, Luther, Gulick) have already been discussed in Chapter 4. It is a further limitation of these models that they focus exclusively on the hierarchical-bureaucratic structure of authority and neglect the exploration of modifications and alternatives. That structure of authority, common to all machine theories of organization, incorporates many deficiencies, of which we have selected four for further examination. It proposes that in an efficient organization, authority and influence must proceed only from hierarchical superiors to their subordinates, that such influence is specifically unidirectional and not reciprocal, that the success of a supervisor in exerting such downward influence is independent of his ability to exert influence upward in the hierarchy, and that the processes of influence in organizations are uniformly applicable (and effective) irrespective of the personalities of the people involved.

We would argue that the empirical research of recent years contradicts each of these assertions, and suggests that the linking of hierarchy with efficiency and authority with authoritarian behavior are errors of great importance and great human cost. In later chapters (11, 12, and 13) we shall discuss some of these research findings.

THE EXERCISE OF AUTHORITY

We have defined authority as the power associated with a position in an organization. Let us turn to a closer examination of the pattern and nature of authority in hierarchical organizations, and the transactions by which it is exercised.

Assume that an organization is already created and ongoing. The division of labor has been accomplished and individuals assigned to specific positions in the organizational structure. For several purposes, but above all in order to see to it that the role requirements are carried out by each member, supervisory positions have been established. The supervisor is to instruct, communicate requirements for change, correct any deviations from required performance; in short, he is to influence. In turn, he is to accede to the influence of his own supervisor, and so on to the top of the hierarchy. The resulting set of role relationships constitutes the *authority structure* and provides for a highly selected and specialized set of influence transactions among the members of the organization.

First of all, the organization stipulates the *persons* who may engage in influence transactions with each other. This is done primarily by specifying the relationship of supervisor and subordinate between pairs of individuals (positions) in such a way that each person except the head of the organization has a supervisor, and each person except those at the very bottom of the hierarchy also have subordinates. The resulting structure of authority can be viewed as a set of dyadic power relationships, or it can be viewed as a set of power relationships between an individual (supervisor) and a collectivity or group (his subordinates). The transactions as they actually occur may be primarily between individuals or between the supervisor and his subordinate group as a whole. Likert (1961) has pointed out some of the differing consequences, for individuals and organization, resulting from these two patterns of interaction. By specifying the sets of actors among whom influence transactions are legitimized, the organization stipulates the *domain* or span of control of each supervisor, the set of persons over whom he has authority.

The resulting pattern of hierarchical relations is by definition *authoritative, asymmetrical,* and *transitive.* If the organization provides that A has authority over B, it follows that B does *not* have authority over A in the same affairs. Organizations need not be hierarchical in this sense, of course. The political model in the United States illustrates a kind of reciprocal power relationship between elected officials and their constituents which is neither perfectly symmetrical nor completely asymmetrical. The senator undoubtedly has certain power over his constituents; he has the indirect power of legislation and the direct power of appointment, for example. But his constituents have certain power over him, including the power to remove him from office under special circumstances, and to keep him from returning to office under any circumstances they choose.

Hierarchy implies *transitive* as well as asymmetrical authority. Each successive level in the hierarchy has authority not only over the echelon immediately below it, but also over *all e*chelons below. There are limitations to this quality of transitivity in most organizations, as we have seen. On the whole, however, a vice-president exerts authority over his department heads and all persons reporting to them, and so on down the line.

Thus the formal, hierarchical organization stipulates *persons* (or agents), *domain*, *asymmetry*, and *transitivity* of authority. All these have to do with the pattern and scope of influence transactions in the organization. The organizational stipulations also include the circumstances, nature, and manner in which influence may be legitimately exerted. Perhaps the most frequent occasion for influence transactions between supervisor and subordinate is the failure of the subordinate to meet fully the requirements of his role, and the nature of the influence attempt is essentially correction. Probably the next most frequent occasion for transactions of influence between supervisor and subordinate is the introduction of change, especially the necessary local adaptation imposed by some decision arrived at higher in the authority structure. In such a transaction there is no fault implied nor any correction; the message is to do something differently because of a change in role requirements.

Influence transactions within the structure of authority are thus *role-relevant*, and the organization specifies the *range* of content which is to be so regarded. A supervisory request to a subordinate to alter his mode of dress, his off-the-job behavior, or his choice of friends would be much resented and resisted. The basis for the resistance would be that the content of such influence attempts is out of the prescribed range, not organizationally defined as role-relevant. The supervisor has exceeded his authority. If the supervisor wishes to put the weight of authority behind such requests, he may go to some pains to show their relevance to the subordinate's role performance. Whether an employee chooses to spend the evening drunk or sober can be defined as his own choice and beyond the organizational interest; the incapacitating morning hangover, however, is another matter.

The strength and form of a specific influence attempt will be affected by many considerations, and there is an extensive colloquial vocabulary for distinguishing among influence transactions in these respects. We speak of suggestions, requests, orders, commands, and the like. In general, however, we would expect the strength of the influence attempt to be coordinated to the organizational significance of the matter at stake, the nature of the interpersonal relationship between supervisor and subordinate, the folkways of the organization itself, and the individual personalities of the agent and recipient of influence.

The assertion that influence within an authority structure must be role-relevant points to the major *motive base* for the exertion and acceptance of influence. The presumption in an organization is that the supervisor is able to exert influence and does so because of the requirements of his own role, not because of any nonorganizational caprice. He exercises his authority primarily because the subordinate is doing something the supervisor is *supposed* to correct, or failing to do something which he is required to do and which the supervisor is required to see that he does. The motive for the influence attempt and for its acceptance have a common root—the acceptance of role in the organization and a desire to remain in that role structure. When the outraged subordinate in many an office joke says, "You can't do that to me; I quit!" he is also saying, "I am out of the system; therefore I no longer accept your authority, and I will not be influenced on that basis."

Some Definitions

The basic concept in our approach is *influence*, which is a kind of psychological force (Cartwright, 1959). The usual basis for inferring influence is an interpersonal transaction in which one person acts in such a way as to change the behavior of another in some intended fashion. A policeman steps into the street and raises his white-gloved hand; a motorist steps on his brakes and brings his car to a halt. We infer, in the absence of other evidence, that the policeman influenced the motorist and that he intended to do so.

We would feel justified in using the term *influence*, however, in much less direct circumstances. If a traffic signal changed from green to red and the motorist brought his car to a stop, we would say that he had been influenced by the traffic signal (and perhaps, more remotely, by the person who decreed that it should be placed there). We could still speak of influence, if the outcome corresponded less well to the intention of the agent. Suppose the policeman raised his hand, and the motorist speeded up. This is influence of a kind; the act of the policeman caused the behavior of the motorist. However, the motorist's response was quite opposite to what the policeman intended. We ecognize this fact by referring to the influence as *negative* or having n effect contrary to the intent of the agent.

It is not necessary for an act to produce overt behavioral change n order to meet our definition of influence. Suppose our motorist finds hat he is being followed closely by a police scout car. He feels ap- rehensive, glances quickly at his speedometer to make sure he is vithin the legal speed limit, and continues down the road, scrupulously naintaining an unvarying speed just under the legal maximum. Again, e has been influenced; his apprehension and careful maintenance of peed, in contrast to his previous mood and variance in speed, give ome measure of the amount of influence. An act of influence is any ehavior which produces an effect whether in behavior, psychological tate, or any other condition.

Every influence attempt is not successful in producing the intended ffect. The effect may be exactly as intended; it may be exactly op- osite to the intent, or it may be nothing at all. If the policeman raised is hand to stop the motorist and the motorist failed to see it and con- inued as before, the influence of the policeman would have been zero. here was an influence attempt, but no receiving of it, and therefore o transaction. A successful influence attempt means not only that he attempt is received in some sense; it means also that the cycle is ompleted by the performance of the desired behavior. The motorist tops his car, or the secretary fills the carafe when asked.

We can define a given act of influence and differentiate it from ther influential acts according to the actors, the direction of influence, e content of the act, the behavior required to complete the cycle, nd so on. It would be unwise to use a different term or concept for ach possible combination, but it is useful to create concepts which mphasize certain important distinctions among acts of influence. Three ıch influence-derived concepts are control, power, and authority.

Control involves the distinction between successful influence at- mpts and those which are unsuccessful (negative or zero in their onsequences, or producing a response in the desired direction but in- dequate in strength). If one person has control over another in some aatter, his influence is sufficiently strong that the cycle of desired ehavior will be completed and any resistance or counterinfluences ill be overcome in the process. This seems very close to the colloquial eaning of control, which is that we can get things (or people) to do hat we wish and request. Lack of control does not imply lack of ttempts at influence; it does not even imply lack of influence. It does nply that other forces in the situation are stronger than the agent's fluence, and that the response he desires is not attained.

Power we shall distinguish from influence in several respects. It refers to potential acts, rather than to transactions actually occurring. It is the capacity to exert influence. This means that power is used to refer to some potential set of influence transactions, and seldom to a single act. We could say that the policeman has the power to stop the motorist. We do not imply by that statement that he has done so, or that he will do so. We mean that he *can* do so if he chooses, and that he has means by which to coerce compliance. We do not specify what those means are nor the circumstances which led to the agent's possession of them. It would be equally appropriate, therefore, to say that an escaped convict, waiting with a gun at the side of the road, has the power to stop a motorist. He has the potentiality for making an influence attempt if he chooses, and the means to coerce compliance or punish noncompliance. He possesses power.

Authority we shall use as the most restricted of this set of related concepts, as influence is the most general. *Influence* includes virtually any interpersonal transaction which has psychological or behavioral effects. Control includes those influence attempts which are successful, that is, which have the effects intended by the influencing agent. Power is the potential for influence characteristically backed by the means to coerce compliance. Finally, authority is legitimate power; it is power which accrues to a person by virtue of his role, his position in an organized social structure. It is, therefore, power which is lawful and socially accepted (at least by the people necessary for the maintenance of the structure). When the policeman in our previous example raised his hand to stop the motorist, he was exercising his authority; when the gangster raised his gun, he was exercising influence, exerting control (assuming the motorist stopped), and demonstrating his power. He was not, however, exercising authority, and his punishment will be precisely for the exercise of unauthorized, illegal power.

Limitations of Legitimacy

The concept of legitimate authority and the general acceptance of such authority in organizations by no means explain all the processes of influence and compliance between supervisors and subordinates in organizations, and legitimate authority has still less to say about processes of influence which do not follow hierarchical lines. In our discussion of leadership (Chapter 11) we will propose a typology of influential transactions in organizations, together with the cognitive and affective characteristics which facilitate such transactions. And in analyzing the psychological basis of organizational effectiveness (Chapter 12) we will consider the patterns of behavior required for organizational functioning, the motivational pattern for generating each of the required behaviors, and the objective means available in organizations to evoke those motivational patterns. Chapters 11 and 12 thus extend the discussion of power and influence which has begun here.

SUMMARY

In this chapter we have sought to explore the relationships between the structural characteristics of authority in organizations and the patterns of interpersonal transactions which comprise this structure in ongoing organizational life. We find that the organization has means and techniques for the exertion of influence, channels for doing so, and organizationally determined content which requires the exertion of influence.

We located the origins of organizational influence and authority in the division of labor, with its stipulation of sequential and interdependent cycles which in combination get the organizational task done. Authority structure is intended to insure the performance of these cycles, and secondarily to introduce necessary changes in their specification. This means that the authority structure must provide for the supervision (or review) of organizationally required acts, and exert corrective or innovative influence as prescribed.

The exercise of authority in an organization should not be confused with authoritarianism. Organizations can have a democratic structure in which the source of legislative power is vested in the membership and the executive directives are an implementation of the wishes of the majority. Members still obey the rules. In an authoritarian system, however, both legislative and executive systems are under the control of the top echelons.

The process of insuring that each person's behavior shall be observed by another person to see that the requirements of organization are met is inevitably a source of great cost. Accordingly there are consistent efforts to minimize these costs, and the shape and process of authority reflects these efforts. The grouping of similar and related jobs under a single supervisor is a major example. This pattern, in combination with the building in of supervisory insurance by means of overlapping areas of authority (each supervisor having authority over his immediate subordinates and also their subordinates, etc.), creates the characteristic pyramidal shape of the authority structure. The organizational tendency to vest each function in a single role and office makes it almost certain that the pyramid of authority will continue to the apex, at which an entire level of authority is represented in only a single office.

We turned from a discussion of authority structure to an analysis of the *interpersonal transactions* which constitute this structure. In addition to the recognized role requirements by means of which the organizational task is achieved, we asserted a superordinate requirement of hierarchical organization—the necessity of accepting the influence attempts of one's superiors. The basis for this acceptance we found in authority, or legitimate power, which in turn depends upon the members of the organization accepting the requirement of obedience to legitimate authority as a condition for continued membership and access to the benefits of organization.

We are led by these analyses to an attitude of great respect for formal, hierarchical organization. It is an instrument of great effectiveness; it offers great economies over unorganized effort; it achieves great unity and compliance. We must face up to its deficiencies, however. These include great waste of human potential for innovation and creativity and great psychological cost to the members, many of whom spend their lives in organizations without caring much either for the system (except its extrinsic rewards and accidental interpersonal relationships) or for the goal toward which the system effort is directed. The modification of hierarchical organization to meet these criticisms is one of the great needs of human life.

9

Communication:
The Flow of Information

The world we live in is basically a world of people. Most of our actions toward others and their actions toward us are communicative acts in whole or in part, whether or not they reach verbal expression. This is as true of behavior in organizations as in other contexts. We have said (Chapter 3) that human organizations are informational as well as energic systems, and that every organization must take in and utilize information. The intake and distribution of information are also energic processes, of course; acts of sending and receiving information demand energy for their accomplishment. Their energic demands, however, are negligible in comparison with their significance and implications as symbolic acts—as acts of communication and control.

When one walks from a factory to the adjoining head-house or office, the contrast is conspicuous. One goes from noise to quiet, from heavy electrical cables and steam pipes to slim telephone lines, from a machine-dominated to a people-dominated environment. One goes, in short, from a sector of the organization in which energic exchange is primary and information exchange secondary, to a sector where the priorities are reversed. The closer one gets to the organizational center of control and decision-making, the more pronounced is the emphasis on information exchange.

In this sense, communication—the exchange of information and the transmission of meaning—is the very essence of a social system or an organization. The input of physical energy is dependent upon information about it, and the input of human energy is made possible through communicative acts. Similarly the transformation of energy (the accomplishment of work) depends upon communication between people in each organizational subsystem and upon communication between subsystems. The product exported carries meaning as it meets needs and wants, and its use is further influenced by the advertising or public relations material about it. The amount of support which an organization receives from its social environment is also affected by the information which elite groups and wider publics have acquired about its goals, activities, and accomplishments.

Communication is thus a social process of the broadest relevance in the functioning of any group, organization, or society. It is possible to subsume under it such forms of social interaction as the exertion of influence, cooperation, social contagion or imitation, and leadership. We shall consider communication in this broad sense, with emphasis upon the structural aspects of the information process in organizations, but with attention also to the motivational basis for transmitting and receiving messages.

It is a common assumption that many of our problems, individual and social, are the result of inadequate and faulty communication. As Newcomb (1947) points out, autistic hostility decreases communication and in turn decreased communication enhances autistic hostility. If we can only increase the flow of information, we are told, we can solve these problems. This assumption is found in our doctrine of universal education. It is fundamental in most campaigns of public relations and public enlightenment. Our democratic institutions, with their concern for freedom of speech and assembly, their rejection of censorship, and their acceptance of the principle of equal time for the arguments of opposing political parties, have extended the notion of competition in the market place to a free market for ideas. Truth will prevail if there is ready access to all the relevant information.

The glorification of a full and free information flow is a healthy step forward in intraorganizational problems as well as in the relations of an organization to the larger social system. It is, however, a gross oversimplification. Communication may reveal problems as well as eliminate them. A conflict in values, for example, may go unnoticed until communication is attempted. Communication may also have the effect, intended or unintended, of obscuring and confusing existing problems. The vogue enjoyed by the word *image* in recent years reflects in part an unattractive preoccupation with communication as a means of changing the perception of things without the expense and inconvenience of changing the things themselves. The television commercials, with their incessant and spurious assertion of new products and properties are the worst of numberless examples. In short, the advocacy of communication needs to be qualified with respect to the kind of information relevant to the solution of given problems and with respect to the nature of the communication process between individuals, between groups, and between subsystems.

Communication needs to be seen not as a process occurring between any sender of messages and any potential recipient, but in relation to the social system in which it occurs and the particular function it performs in that system. General principles of communication as a social-psychological process are fine; they set the limits within which we must operate. But they need to be supplemented by an analysis of the social system, so that they can be applied correctly to given situations.

The discovery of the crucial role of communication led to an enthusiastic advocacy of increased information as the solution to many organizational problems. More and better communication (especially, more) was the slogan. Information to rank-and-file employees about company goals and policies was the doctrine; the means too often were stylized programs and house organs homogenized by the Flesch formula for basic English. Communication up the line to give top echelons a more accurate picture of the lower levels was a complementary emphasis.

Social Systems as Restricted Communication Networks

Though there were and are good outcomes of this simplistic approach, there are also weak, negligible, and negative outcomes. The blanket emphasis upon more communication fails to take into account the functioning of an organization as a social system and the specific needs of the subsystems.

In the first place, as Thelen (1960) points out, an organized state of affairs, a social system, implies the restriction of communication among its members. If we take an unorganized group, say 60 people milling around at random in a large room, the number of potential channels of communication is $n(n-1)/2$ or 1770. If, however, they are organized into a network of twelve combinations of five such that each person on a five-man team has one clearly defined role and is interdependent with four other people, the number of channels within the work group is reduced to *ten* in a completely interdependent condition or to *four* in a serial dependent position.

Without going into such complexities as task-relevant communication, the major point is clear. To move from an unorganized state to an organized state requires the introduction of constraints and restrictions to reduce diffuse and random communication to channels appropriate for the accomplishment of organizational objectives. It may require also the introduction of incentives to use those channels and use them appropriately, rather than leave them silent or use them for organizationally irrelevant purposes. Organizational development sometimes demands the creation of new communication channels. The very nature of a social system, however, implies a selectivity of channels and communicative acts—a mandate to avoid some and to utilize others.

In terms of information theory, unrestricted communication produces noise in the system. Without patterning, without pauses, without precision, there is sound but there is no music. Without structure, without spacing, without specifications, there is a Babel of tongues but there is no meaning.

The same basic problem of selectivity in communications can be considered in terms of Ashby's (1952) conceptual model. Thelen summarizes the Ashby contribution in these terms.[*]

> *Any living system* is an infinitely complex association of subsystems. The complex suprasystem has all the properties of a subsystem plus communication across the boundaries of subsystems. Ashby's brilliant treatment (1952) shows that stability of the suprasystem would take infinitely long to achieve *if* there were "full and rich communication" among the subsystems (because in effect all the variables of all the subsystems would have to be satisfied at once —a most unlikely event). If communication among subsystems is restricted or if they are temporarily isolated, then each subsystem achieves its own stability with minimum interference by the changing environment of other systems seeking *their* stability. With restricted communication, success can accumulate (from successive trials, for example), whereas in the single suprasystem, success is all-or-none . . . . Thus the way an overall system moves toward its equilibrium depends very much on the functional connectedness of its parts. Adaptation of the whole system makes use of two conditions: enough connectedness that operation of one subsystem can activate another so that the contributions of all can contribute to the whole; and enough separation of subsystems that some specialization of function is possible and such that "equilibrium" can be approached in the system as a whole. But no complex suprasystem would ever have equilibrium in all its subsystems at the same time. Each subsystem has the "power of veto" over equilibria in other subsystems, and under a variety of conditions one subsystem can dominate another.

Our loosely organized political system reflects the system requirements of restriction of full and free communication. Chaos in national decision-making is avoided by the device of the two-party system. Instead of representing in clear fashion in Congress all the factional groups and subsystems within the nation, we go through a quadrennial process of successive agreements within the major parties, culminating in the nomination of a presidential candidate by each of them. This is in effect a restriction and channeling of the communication

[*] Mimeographed paper, 1960.

process. Once candidates are selected, the factional groups within each party tend to unite behind one ticket, and the amount of communication to the candidates is restricted. The rank-and-file voter neither communicates up the line nor receives much in the way of communication down the line except for the projected image of the candidate and the general image of the party.

In fact, the average voter is woefully ignorant of the stand of his party on most political issues. On sixteen major issues of the 1956 presidential election, the proportion of people who had an opinion, knew what the government was doing, and saw some differences between the parties never exceeded 36 per cent and for some issues was as low as 18 per cent (Campbell, Converse, Miller, and Stokes, 1960). This is one price we pay for the organizational restrictions of a two-party system and the communication distance between the voters and political leaders. Nevertheless, the two-party system has the advantage of overall political stability and facilitation of national decision-making. If all interested groups and ideological factions had their own parties and their own representatives in Congress, we would have more complete communication between the people and their elected leaders but we would have terrific problems of attaining system stability. We would have many possibilities of veto by coalition of minority groups, of legislative stalemates, and of national indecision. Some European countries with multiple-party systems, with more communication, and perhaps better-informed electorates have had such problems.

The Coding Process

Individuals, groups, and organizations share a general characteristic which must be recognized as a major determinant of communication: the coding process. Any system which is the recipient of information, whether it be an individual or an organization, has a characteristic coding process, a limited set of coding categories to which it assimilates the information received. The nature of the system imposes omission, selection, refinement, elaboration, distortion, and transformation upon the incoming communications. Just as the human eye selects and transforms light waves to which it is attuned to give perceptions of color and objects, so too does any system convert stimulation according to its own properties. It has been demonstrated that human beings bring with them into most situations sets of categories for judging the facts before them. Walter Lippmann (1922) called attention to the coding process years ago in the following famous passages. Even then he was merely putting into dramatic form what had been recognized by the ancient philosophers.

For the most part we do not first see, and then define, we define first and then see. In the great blooming, buzzing confusion of the outer world, we pick out what our culture has already defined for us, and we tend to perceive that which we have picked out in the form stereotyped for us by our culture. (p. 31)

What matters is the character of the stereotypes and the gullibility with which we employ them. And these in the end depend upon those inclusive patterns which constitute our philosophy of life. If in that philosophy we assume that the world is codified according to a code we possess, we are likely to make our reports of what is going on describe a world run by our code. (p. 90)

Most of us would deal with affairs through a rather haphazard and shifting assortment of stereotypes, if a comparatively few men in each generation were not constantly engaged in arranging, standardizing, and improving them into logical systems, known as the Laws of Political Economy, the Principles of Politics, and the like. (pp. 104–105)

Organizations, too, have their own coding systems which determine the amount and type of information they receive from the external world and the transformation of it according to their own systemic properties. The most general limitation is that the position people occupy in organizational space will determine their perception and interpretation of incoming information and their search for additional information. In other words, the structure and functions of a given subsystem will be reflected in the frame of reference and way of thinking of the role incumbents of that sector of organizational space. The different functions and dynamics of the production structure, the maintenance system, and the adaptive system (described in Chapter 4) imply that each of these subsystems will respond to the same intelligence input in different ways and that each will seek out particular information to meet its needs.

All members of an organization are affected by the fact that they occupy a common organizational space in contrast to those who are not members. By passing the boundary and becoming a functioning member of the organization, the person takes on some of the coding system of the organization since he accepts some of its norms and values, absorbs some of its subculture, and develops shared expectations and values with other members. The boundary condition is thus responsible for the dilemma that the person within the system cannot perceive things and communicate about them in the same way that an outsider would. If a person is within a system, he sees its operations differently than if he were on the outside looking in. It is extremely difficult to occupy different positions in social space without a resulting differential perception. Where boundary conditions are fluid and organizational members are very loosely confined within the system (as with people sent abroad to live among foreign nationals for some governmental agency) there will be limited tours of duty, alternation between foreign and domestic service, and careful debriefing sessions to insure that life outside the physical boundaries of the country has not imparted too much of the point of view of the outsider. *and where individuals go out of central govt into private sector!*

The Problem of Translation across Subsystem Boundaries

Within an organization there are problems of clear communication across subsystems. The messages emanating in one part of the organization need translation if they are to be fully effective in other parts. In an earlier chapter, reference was made to Parsons' (1960) specific application of this principle to the chain of command. Instead of a unitary chain from the top to the bottom of an organization, Parsons pointed out that there are significant breaks between the institutional and managerial levels and again between the managerial and technical levels. Communications, then, must be transmitted in general enough terms to permit modification within each of these levels. The same type of translation problem occurs between any pair of substructures having their own functions and their own coding schema. Without adequate translation across subsystem boundaries, communications can add to the noise in the system.

INFORMATION OVERLOAD

Causes of Overload

To view social systems as restricted networks of communication, and as networks which treat communication very selectively even in accepted channels, implies the possibility of information overload—of communication input greater than the organization or certain of its components can handle. In Chapter 7 we called attention to the need for coordination of the many specialized activities in a complex organization, and to the consequent combining of numerous subsystem roles in single offices. The person holding such an office, as a member of multiple subsystems, receives information input from all of them. Incumbents of roles at major intersecting cycles of organizations are often so deluged by the requests reaching them that they respond only to two types of messages—telegrams and long-distance telephone calls. Programmed handling of some types of input with little intervention on the part of the officer reduces his overload so long as the programmed solutions are not outmoded by environmental changes and new inputs of information.

In physical networks the limitations of the communication system with respect to overloading and underloading are readily recognized by the concept of channel capacity. Social systems also exist in a space-time manifold and are also subject to limitations of their communication capacity. The coordination of many cycles of interrelated behavior is necessarily geared to a time schedule. Any given act must be stipulated not only with respect to its adjacencies to other acts in space, but also with respect to its duration and its precedence, simultaneity, or succession to other acts. Temporal planning in the interests of efficiency allows little or no free time in the organization for handling unanticipated information. The receipt, assessment, and transformation of information is geared into the productive process and follows a corresponding time schedule. Even if some decision makers are freed from direct production responsibilities, they still must make their decisions within a limited time period.

Coordination of activity according to a time schedule, however, encounters the difficulty that social organizations do not exist in a constant social environment. Their potential sources of supply may diminish and require additional search or may change in character and require additional selective processes. The markets for their products may grow or decline. To maintain the same proportion of the market may require increased effort. The organizational structure, however, is geared to certain assumed constancies of production input, throughput, and output. Fluctuations overload the system at some point. Decreased input and volume of work, it is true, will create conditions of underload for some units in the organization. For the upper echelons, however, the decline in inputs means more information-seeking both within and without the organization. New inputs have to be found or cuts have to be made in the organizational structure.

Change is not limited to the production system and its adjuncts of procurement and disposal. The maintenance inputs of people to man the organization and to assume its many roles are necessary to keep the system viable. Here again inputs are not a constant. The labor market fluctuates and personnel attrition takes place at differential rates. Moreover, the values and requirements of personnel change with changes in the culture and subcultures in which they live. Any departure from an assumed normal level of operation creates problems of overload for certain echelons within the system. A threatened strike may mean that more demands are made on the production manager and his lieutenants so that they must attend both to production and maintenance problems. An actual strike may give this same group a holiday but may overload top management with other problems.

In summary, since organizational activity must be geared to certain constancies in a time schedule, changed inputs create a condition of overload in one or more of the organizational subsystems.

Inconstancies in the environment of organizations are basically man-made and are largely a consequence of our organized search for knowledge and our technological exploitation of this knowledge. We have developed sources of new input which provide a constantly changing environment for social systems. In Miller's terms (1960), information input overload is a product of the technology and science of our times. Every year over 1,200,000 articles appear in 60,000 books and 100,000 research reports. Scientific and technical publications have doubled in size in the United States approximately every twenty years since 1800.

Miller's Analysis of Reactions to Overload

The responses to information input overload have been classified by Miller (1960) into the following seven categories: (1) omission, failing to process some of the information; (2) error, processing information incorrectly; (3) queuing, delaying during periods of peak load in the hope of catching up during lulls; (4) filtering, neglecting to process certain types of information, according to some scheme of priorities; (5) approximation, or cutting categories of discrimination (a blanket and nonprecise way of responding); (6) employing multiple channels, using parallel channels, as in decentralization; and (7) escaping from the task.

The Miller classification of responses to overload is useful but it treats all seven types of responses as mechanisms of adjustment. In applying this classification to social organizations, however, there are definite advantages in distinguishing between adaptive and maladaptive mechanisms for the functioning of the system. The use of one or more of these types of response will have consequences for organizational functioning and may result in changes in function and structure.

In differentiating between adaptive and maladaptive ways of responding we shall follow the distinction, commonly employed in individual psychology, between coping and defensive mechanisms. Coping or adaptive mechanisms are concerned with solving the problems which the individual encounters. Defensive mechanisms protect the individual from breakdown but do not solve the problem. Denial, for example, is the defense mechanism by which the individual closes his eyes to the objective facts but in so doing protects himself from intolerable anxiety. In similar fashion, the failure to process information may keep a social system from total breakdown, but it is still not the optimal way to handle the problem of overload. Keeping the system functioning even at a low level of efficiency may be considered an adjustive outcome, as Miller does, but there is still the need to examine both the dysfunctional and the coping aspects of the process. Even a "successful" coping response can be evaluated in terms of the duration of the solution, the amount of organizational space to which the solution applies, and the cost to the organization of arriving at and implementing the solution. The shorter the duration, the more limited the area of application, and the greater the cost to the organization, the more dysfunctional do we consider the response.

Both omission and error are dysfunctional types of response to overload. Omission by definition denies information to the organization, and it characteristically does so on an irrational basis. Specifically, omission or failure to process information tends to be selective in terms of the ease with which input can be assimilated, rather than in terms of its importance for the organization. Failure to process critical inputs can magnify the problems with which the organization is sooner or later forced to deal. The grievance case which is not processed because of its ambiguities may be taken to court, and the precedent established there may permit thousands of workers to file suit. Such an actual instance in a large railroad company cost the company millions of dollars because of the failure to process the difficult case early in the game.

Error is also maladaptive by definition, and more or less costly to the organization. The cost often may be minimal, but devices are necessary to check against errors of potential seriousness. One common source of serious error in processing information is the tendency to reverse the meaning of the message. Under certain circumstances, it is easy to omit the *not* in a communication or to add it when it should not be there, and so change the meaning completely. One mechanism in thought association is contrast; we group together concepts at either end of a continuum, like sink or swim, failure or success. This conceptual affinity of opposites results in disastrous errors of the reversal type.

Queuing or delaying the processing of information can be either dysfunctional or adaptive. If the queuing is invoked merely to serve the ease of operation of the individual receiver, it is likely to be dysfunctional. But if it is utilized under circumstances of real overload and with equally realistic anticipation of a future lull, it can be adaptive.

Similarly, filtering or the selective receiving of information can be adaptive if it is set by priorities assigned by the organization and based upon an assessment of organizational needs. But without thoughtfully established guidelines, filtering is likely to be maladaptive. People are likely to process the familiar elements in a message, which they readily understand and which do not constitute major problems for them. Under time pressures the parts of the communication difficult to decode are neglected for the more easily assimilated parts, even though the former may be more critical for the organization. In general, ap-

proximation or cutting of categories under conditions of overload
would be dysfunctional. There are situations, however, in which the
exchange of quality for quantity is justifiable and realistic. Escape from
the task is by definition dysfunctional.

Finally, the use of multiple channels is in many instances highly
adaptive in terms of organizational efficiency and effectiveness. Its
inclusion in Miller's list suggests that he is in fact using two different
criteria in talking about response to overload. On the one hand, he is
referring to the inability of a given system with given capacities to
handle overload (as when a nerve fibre cannot respond to continuous
input in excess of its frequency rate, i.e., during its refractory period),
and on the other hand, he is including system mechanisms which have
been developed for handling overload and now are system structures in
themselves.

Decentralization, which Miller cites as an example of multiple
channels, is not so much the spontaneous dividing up of messages
among parallel channels at times of overflow as it is the deliberate
restructuring of an organization to handle overload. In the same manner, queuing and filtering can become institutionalized as devices for
handling overload. In chain department stores, the priority drilled
into clerks is to take the customers' money and make change first, and
then meet other demands of the task. To the extent that these institutionalized devices handle the problem, we no longer should speak of
information overload save as a causal condition of changes in organizational structures.

A very different approach to problems of overload is to reverse
the usual stance of seeking new mechanisms for handling overload and
to seek instead ways of reducing the input. This is, of course, extremely
difficult with respect to the external environment. Most organizations
cannot control the environmental demands which are made upon
them, except by eliminating some function of their own. To take an
obvious but unlikely example, an automobile dealer might solve his
agency's traffic and parking problems by eliminating certain of its
repair and service functions, but this would be an expensive and risk-
laden approach to the problem of overload. *Within* organizations, however, the planned reduction of input is a more promising possibility.

Part of the overload within organizations is created by the various
subsystems and the various hierarchical levels inundating one another
with information. The premise, as already noted, is the more communication between levels and units the better. What is often needed,
however, is a method for cutting down on the output of information
and of restricting its flow. Some organizations restrict interoffice

memoranda to a single page. The accessibility of all members of the organization to messages at any time during the working day is a technological triumph which has its drawbacks. Research, writing, the pondering of executive decisions, and other phases of creative work require uninterrupted blocks of time. The organization needs to put as much effort into protecting these activities from interruption as it does in facilitating communication where it is functionally required.

Though external demands usually cannot be curtailed at their source, organizations can be more protective of the many roles which their members assume within the interlocking structures of our bureaucratic society. Since universities are now concerned with research as well as teaching, with community and national service as well as maintaining ties with alumni, staff members of universities are subject to an increasing variety of demands as they take on new roles. The same process occurs in other growing organizations.

In his study of a university library, Meier (1961) analyzed the changes which occurred as a result of the increasing demand for books. He noted, among other processes: (1) the setting of priorities, such as giving precedence to the request of a faculty member over that of an undergraduate; (2) destruction of lowest priorities as the queue builds in size (wastebasket policy for communications), the library no longer attempting to preserve everything printed; (3) establishing active files, first the reserve desk and then the closed reserve; (4) creating branch facilities or decentralization; (5) encouraging middlemen or utilizing extraorganizational channels such as publicizing availability of paperback editions in nearby bookstores; (6) creating a mobile personnel reserve, i.e., training people in a variety of skills so that they can be shifted about as the pressures demand; and (7) reducing standards of performance to give legitimacy to actual lowering of performance and thus maintaining morale. Meier (1961) generalizes further about the organizational effects of overload as follows:

The structural effects of being tested up to or even beyond the long run capacity for completing transactions can be expressed in various forms. *Spatially*, the institution becomes decentralized, functionally differentiated in its various branches and *outliers*, develops a complex boundary for the receipt of messages, and evolves a strong headquarters unit. *Economically*, it accumulates deferred maintenance and generally transforms capital assets into a network of interdependencies with individuals and other institutions whose resources can be drawn upon in an emergency. *Status* within the institution depends much more upon functional effectiveness than upon official rank. As a *decision system* it is more complex and adaptive, having developed many alternative sets of rules during the test which can be reapplied as soon as the need arises. The *value* structure is permanently changed because operating at capacity has revealed the importance of conserving resources which were not otherwise scarce. Considered as a *network* of positions and relations, the institution develops a greater variety of relations, adds more positions, and greatly increases the centrality of some positions. Overload causes the destruction of relations more rapidly than they can be rebuilt through experience and instruction (internal communications). (pp. 55–56)

DIRECTION OF COMMUNICATION FLOW AND CHARACTERISTICS OF COMMUNICATION CIRCUITS

We shall discuss communication processes within organizations both with respect to the direction of the flow of information (who communicates to whom) and with respect to the structure of the communication network and the content of the messages carried (how and what is being communicated). The direction of the information flow can follow the authority pattern of the hierarchical positions (*downward communication*); can move among peers at the same organizational level (*horizontal communication*); or can ascend the hierarchical ladder (*upward communication*).

The major characteristics of communication networks which we shall consider are (1) the size of the loop, the amount of organizational space covered by given types of information, (2) the nature of the circuit, whether a simple repetitive pattern or a chain modification type, (3) the open or closed character of the circuit, (4) the efficiency of the circuit for its task, and (5) the fit between the circuit and the systemic function it serves.

1. *Size of loop.* Communication circuits may embrace the entire system, may be restricted to a major subsystem, or may involve only a small unit within a subsystem. Some communication loops may be confined to officer personnel or even to top level echelons. A common organizational problem is the discrepancy between the size of given information loops as perceived by the ranking authorities and the size of the circuit which actually is found. Leaders characteristically overestimate the number of persons reached by their intended communications. Also, the larger the loop, the greater will be the problems of communication, particularly where the penetration of subsystem boundaries is involved.

2. *Repetition versus modification in the circuit.* A large information loop may reach many members of the system through a repetitive pattern of transmitters. For example, a directive may go down the line and be echoed at each level to the one below it. A different pattern of transmission is often used whereby a chain of command will pass along messages with appropriate translation at each level in the system. The

same amount of organizational space is involved in both patterns, so that the size of the loop is the same, but the second pattern calls for some modification of the message. The first pattern has the advantages of simplicity and uniformity. Everyone is exposed to identical information. What is announced publicly topside is the same as what people hear from their own superior. Nonetheless, the simplicity of this system may be advantageous only for simple problems. For complex matters a directive repeated in uniform fashion is not necessarily uniform in its meaning across subsystems. It may need translation in different units to be effective.

3. *Feedback or closure character.* Though the flow of a communication pattern may have a dominant organizational direction (down the line, for example) there is a circular character to communicative acts. There is a reaction to the transmission which can furnish feedback to the transmitter, though it may only be the acknowledgement of the receipt of the message.

Closure of a set of communicative acts can vary from immediate fixed response of acknowledgement and acceptance of the initial message to reports of its inadequacy and attempts to alter its character. In the latter case, though the communication cycle has been completed through feedback about the faulty character of the original communication, the communication process is immediately reactivated. In a larger sense, closure has not been achieved for the organization by the first set of communicative acts. Thus, while almost all processes of communication are cyclical, with a return to the original transmitter, we can characterize some communication circuits as having more of a closed character for systemic functioning than others.

A closed communication loop would be one in which the cycle of transmission acts is not open to change once it has been initiated. In other words, no new information and no radical modifications in the process are provided for by the structural procedures. If the communication process is one of issuing directives and responding to the signal of mission accomplished, we have a closed circuit. The directive cannot be substantially modified. Rigid codes block out sources of information either by definition or practice. There is just no provision for admitting new information at various points in the transmission chain.

4. *The efficiency of communication nets.* A related but somewhat different aspect of communication systems is the efficiency, which can be measured in terms of the number of communication links in a given network. In the beginning of our discussion of communication we pointed out that restriction in the communication process was part of the essential nature of social organizations. Experimental work has

generally supported the hypothesis that the smaller the number of communication links in a group, the greater the efficiency of the group in task performance (Dubin, 1959). There are more links, for example, in the all-channel pattern than in the circle pattern, and more links in the circle than in the wheel pattern (see Figure 8).

Using a sentence construction task, Heise and Miller (1951) found that a two-link system was more efficient than various three-link systems, as measured by the number of words spoken and the time taken to complete the task.

In an extension of Leavitt's earlier work (1951), Guetzkow and Simon (1955) used five-man groups in which the task was to discover which one of six symbols was held in common by all group members. The subjects were seated around a circular table, separated by five vertical partitions. They did not talk to one another, but communicated by passing messages through interconnecting slots. Each person was given a card with five symbols. The missing symbol was different for each subject. The experimenters employed three different networks of communication to which 56 groups were randomly assigned. In the circle net (see Figure 8) subjects could pass their messages to either or both of two neighbors. In the wheel net there is a key man to whom all four colleagues can communicate. In the all-channel pattern everyone can communicate with everyone else. Since messages must flow to some decision center for action and must flow back to the senders to inform them of the decision, the wheel provides a two-level hierarchy and the circle and all-channel nets a three-level hierarchy. In the circle, for example, two neighbors can send information to their opposite neighbors, who in turn relay this information with their own to the fifth member. He can then send the solution back to his group, but three levels are involved in the process.

Leavitt (1951) had found the two-level hierarchy of the wheel to be the most efficient for task accomplishment. Guetzkow and Simon, however, reasoned that this superiority might well be due to the time

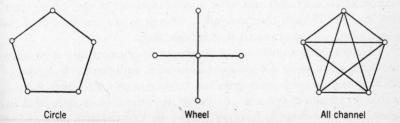

Circle   Wheel   All channel

Figure 8   Types of communication networks.

it took a group to discover and use the optimal organizational pattern for its specific type of net, rather than to the patterns of the networks themselves. For example, a group assigned to the circle might spend considerable time in a more complex interaction than the optimal pattern described above. Hence the experimenters provided a two-minute period between task trials for the groups to discover the best organizational pattern for their situation by allowing them to write messages to each other. The results confirmed the prediction of the experimenters. When groups in the all-channel or circle nets discovered the optimal organizational pattern, they were just as efficient as the wheel groups.

The advantages, then, for the system employing fewer links was not in the efficiency of the simpler network per se, but in the fact that it required little trial and error by the group to use it effectively. Moreover, since the networks with more links allow the possibility for inefficient usage, there is some advantage to ruling out this possibility by means of more restrictive patterns.

These experiments were concerned with task-oriented communications and should not be generalized to socio-emotional or supportive types of communication. In subsequent experiments Guetzkow and Dill (1957) found that groups seemed to prefer a minimum linkage system. Seventeen out of twenty groups which had started with a pattern permitting ten links had, by the end of twenty trials, cut this to four links. Pressures were generated within the groups themselves to move toward the simpler communication networks. The groups that did not follow this pattern, moreover, were less efficient in task accomplishment.

5. *The fit between the communication circuit and systemic functioning.* A circuit may be too large, involving irrelevant people, or too small, omitting key informants. One factor in information overload is the creation of many large communication loops so that people receive frequent messages which have little if anything to do with carrying out their organizational roles. Role incumbents are called upon to decide what is functional and what is nonfunctional in the information they receive. Though they may make wise decisions, the time of decision-making is taken from their own basic tasks.

A common dysfunctional arrangement in organizations is to have communication loops of disproportionate sizes with respect to message-sending and message-receiving. Top echelons issue directives for the whole organization, yet achieve closure from the acquiescence of their immediate subordinates. In other words, the loop involves all levels of the organization on the sending side but only the top two echelons on the receiving side.

Another lack of fit between the communication circuit and the functional needs of the system occurs when closed circuits are used for purposes other than the carrying out of directives in an emergency setting. With complex problems, where time is not highly critical, a communication loop which permits the introduction of new information at various points in the circuit can be highly adaptive. Yet the logic of the closed circuit is carried over into the inappropriate areas of information search. The questions for which information is sought are so formulated by some executives that they predetermine the answers to be supplied. The communication process returns upon itself. For example, a department head concerned about a recent productivity decline calls in his division heads; he wants the problem explored, but it has been his experience, he informs them, that the lax practices of certain types of supervisors are the key factor in this sort of situation. His division heads report back after their exploration that he was indeed right, and they have taken the necessary steps to handle the problem. An open search for the causes of the productivity decline might have furnished a different answer.

Communication down the Line

Communications from superior to subordinate are basically of five types:

1. Specific task directives: *job instructions.*
2. Information designed to produce understanding of the task and its relation to other organizational tasks: *job rationale.* MB 6
3. Information about organizational *procedures and practices.*
4. *Feedback* to the subordinate about his performance.
5. Information of an ideological character to inculcate a sense of mission: *indoctrination of goals.*

The first type of communication is generally given priority in industrial and military organizations and in hospitals. Instructions about the job are worked out with a great deal of specificity and are communicated to the role incumbent through direct orders from his superior, training sessions, training manuals, and written directives. The objective is to insure the reliable performance of every role incumbent in every position in the organization.

Less attention is given to the second type of information, designed to provide the worker with a full understanding of his job and of how it is geared to related jobs in the same subsystem. Many employees know what they are to do, but not why they are doing it, nor how the patterned activities in which they are involved accomplish a given objective. "Theirs not to reason why" is often the implicit, if not explicit, assumption of managerial philosophy. It is often assumed that an emphasis upon information about full job understanding will conflict with strict allegiance to specific task instructions. If the worker thinks he knows why he is to do a certain thing, he may attempt to do it in other than the specified fashion and the organizational leaders may not want to tolerate the variability of behavior this introduces into the system.

Information about organizational procedures completes the description of the role requirements of the organizational member. In addition to instructions about his job, he is also informed about his other obligations and privileges as a member of the system, e.g., about vacations, sick leave, rewards, and sanctions.

Feedback to the individual about how well he is doing in his job is often neglected or poorly handled, even in organizations in which the managerial philosophy calls for such evaluation. Where emphasis is placed upon compliance to specific task directives, it is logical to expect that such compliance will be recognized and deviation penalized. This is necessary to insure that the system is working, and it is a matter of some motivational importance for the individual performer. The frequent complaint, however, by the individual is that he does not know where he stands with his superiors. Often an employee is identified as a major problem for an organization so late in the game that his poor performance or weak citizenship seem beyond remedy, and even transfer or discharge is difficult. There is belated recognition that there should have been an earlier review with him of his performance. Yet systematic procedures for rating and review of the work of employees by their superiors have not proved a panacea.

The reasons are not hard to find. The whole process of critical review is resented both by subordinate and superior as partaking of surveillance. The democratic values of the culture have permeated organizational members so that the superior sees himself as a leader of men, and not as a spy and disciplinarian. The subordinate, in wanting to know how well he is doing, really wants to have his merits recognized and to know how to develop his own talents more fully.

Another major reason for the unpopularity of supervisory appraisal is that many employees have little individual discretion in task accomplishment and little opportunity to excel. Both the company norms and the informal standards of the group set a uniform rate of accomplishment. The performance of workers is often so system-determined that there is little to be gained from evaluating workers as autonomous individuals. The occasional deviant does constitute a problem for the organization, particularly when his deviance is not formally recognized until it is too late. Nevertheless, such slips are probably less costly to the organization than a thorough surveillance system in which the individual does get early and systematic feedback on his performance.

The fifth type of downward-directed information has as its objective the inculcation of organizational goals, either for the total system or a major subsystem. An important function of an organizational leader is to conceptualize the mission of his enterprise in an attractive and novel form. This can be done with particular effectiveness in organizations which are conspicuous for their contribution to societal welfare or for the hazardous character of their activities. For example, a police commissioner may describe the role of his police force as the work of professional officers engaged in a constructive program of community improvement.

Though organizational leaders are quick to recognize the importance of involving their followers in system goals, they are slow to utilize the most natural devices available to them in the form of job rationale. The second type of information in our listing, the understanding of one's role and how it relates to other roles, is a good bridge to involvement in organizational goals. If the psychiatric nurse in a hospital knows why she is to follow certain procedures with a patient and how this relates to the total therapy program for him, it is much easier for her to develop an ideological commitment to the hospital. This is one reason why some hospitals have developed the concept of the therapy team, which permits the doctor, nurse, and attendant to discuss the treatment program for given patients. On the other hand, if the role incumbent receives information about job specifics without job understanding, it is difficult for him to see how his role is related to the organizational objective and hence difficult for him to identify with the organizational mission.

Withholding information on the rationale of the job not only is prejudicial to ideological commitment of the member, but it also means that the organization must bear down heavily on the first type of information—specific instructions about the job. If a man does not understand fully why he should do a thing or how his job relates to the tasks of his fellow workers, then there must be sufficient redundancy in his task instructions so that he behaves automatically and reliably in role performance. This type of problem was dramatically illustrated in the conflict about the information to be given to astronauts about their task in orbit. Some officials were in favor of reducing the astronaut's behavior to that of a robot; others wanted to utilize his intelligence by having him act on his understanding of the total situation. The result was a compromise.

The advantages of giving fuller information on job understanding are thus twofold: if a man knows the reasons for his assignment, this will often insure his carrying out the job more effectively; and if he has an understanding of what his job is about in relation to his subsystem, he is more likely to identify with organizational goals.

Size of the Loop and Downward Communication. The size of the communication loop is an interesting variable in processing information down the line, and has implications for organizational morale and effectiveness. In general the rank-and-file member gets his task instructions from those immediately above him. The loop covers very little of the organizational structure. Upper echelons neither know what the specific task directives are, nor would acquiring such knowledge be an appropriate way for them to spend time and energy. In industry the methods department may have worked out the standard procedures for a job, but these are transmitted to the employee by his immediate boss. On the other hand, communications about the goals of the organization in theory cover a loop as large as the organization itself. The rank-and-file member, however, may in practice be minimally touched by this loop. His degree of effective inclusion within it depends primarily upon how he is tied into the organization. If he is tied in on the basis of being paid for a routine performance, information about the goals and policies of the larger structure will be of no interest to him.

The size of the loop is also important in terms of the understanding of the message. Communications from the top addressed to all organizational members are often too general in character and too remote from the limited daily experiences of the individual to convey their intended meaning. To be effective, messages about organizational policy need to be translated at critical levels as they move down the line, i.e., translated into the specific meanings they have for given sectors of the structure. Katz and Lazarsfeld (1955) demonstrated a two-step process in the flow of communication in a community in which opinion leaders affected by the mass media in turn influenced the rank and file. Within organizations, however, not enough attention has been given to this problem of translation. Communications down the line must be converted to the coding systems of the substructures if they are to register and have impact.

A partial substitute for translation is the ability of some organizational leaders to develop confidence and liking for themselves as personalities among the rank and file. Their position on a policy issue will be accepted not because it is understood, but because people trust them and love them. This is more characteristic of political leadership than leadership in nonpolitical organizations.

The translation problem is related to the fit between the communication cycle and the functional requirements of the organization. The information loop about how a job is to be done should have the immediate supervisor as the key communicant. This does not necessarily mean that a worker should get all his job directives from a single boss, but it does mean that additional bosses should be introduced only if they have an expertness about a clearly demarcated function. The research worker, in addition to listening to his project director, can also listen with profit to the sampling and statistical expert. Where the functional lines are fuzzy, the rule of a single boss has much to be said for it.

Transmitting information down the line may partake of a closed-circuit character if there is little opportunity for clarification of directives from above. Two things occur when directives remain limited and unclear because people down the line have no way of getting a fuller explanation. People will give minimal compliance so as to be apparently observing the letter of the law, or they will test out in actual behavior their own ideas of what can be done. If there is inadequate feedback up the line, this behavioral testing out can produce real deviations in organizational practice. Such deviations can run from constructive actions in support of organizational objectives to actions crippling and destructive to the organization.

Horizontal Communications

Organizations face one of their most difficult problems in procedures and practices concerned with lateral communication, i.e., communication between people at the same hierarchical level. The machine model would be highly restrictive of lateral communication. A role incumbent would receive almost all his instructions from the man above him, and would deal with his associates only for task coordination specified by rules. Though such a plan neglects the need for socioemotional support among peers, it is still true that unrestricted communication of a horizontal character can detract from maximum efficiency. What are the conditions under which lateral communication is desirable?

We shall start with the proposition that some types of lateral communication are critical for effective system functioning. Many tasks cannot be so completely specified as to rule out coordination between peers in the work process. The teamwork by which a varsity team beats an alumni group of greater prowess has many parallels in other organizations. (In fact, there is something to be said for not mechanizing coordination devices for a group task unless the whole process can be mechanized.)

Communication among peers, in addition to providing task coordination, also furnishes emotional and social support to the individual. The mutual understanding of colleagues is one reason for the power of the peer group. Experimental findings are clear and convincing about the importance of socio-emotional support for people in both unorganized and organized groups. Psychological forces always push people toward communication with peers; people in the same boat share the same problems. *Hence, if there are no problems of task coordination left to a group of peers, the content of their communication can take forms which are irrelevant to or destructive of organizational functioning.* Informal student groups sometimes devote their team efforts to pranks and stunts or even to harassing the administration and faculty.

The size of the communication circuit and its appropriateness to the function of the subsystem are important considerations for horizontal communication. By and large the nature and extent of exchanges among people at the same level should be related to the objectives of the various subsystems in which they are involved, with primary focus on their own major task. Thus there are real disadvantages in lateral communication that cuts across functional lines and that nevertheless attempts to be highly specific. For example, if divisions with differentiated functions are part of a department, the communication between peers in different divisions should be on departmental problems and not on divisional matters. Peer communication on divisional matters can better be conducted within divisional boundaries.

Horizontal communication implies a closed circuit in that it satisfies people's needs to know from their own kind without taking into account other levels in the organization. In hierarchical structures it can mean that people overvalue peer communication with a neglect of those below them. Cabots talk only to Cabots, and vice-presidents only to vice-presidents. It is interesting to observe how often organizational leaders, when going outside their own structures for information, will seek their own status level, i.e., their counterparts in other organizations. Sometimes, however, the really critical information is at levels below them.

It is important to look at lateral communication in terms of the control function in organizations. Horizontal communication, if in operation at various levels in an organization, is a real check on the power of the top leaders. The more authoritarian and hierarchical the system, the more information is a secret property of select groups, and the more it can be utilized to control and punish people at lower levels. In such a system there is little horizontal communication across levels of equal rank. The department chief knows about his ten division heads and their respective divisions, but each one of them knows only about himself and his own division. Hence the department chief is in a powerful position to manipulate them as he will.

The simple paradigm of vertical funneling up the line with no horizontal flow of information is a fundamental basis of social control in most social systems. As systems move toward greater authoritarian structure, they exert more and more control over any flow of horizontal information. This is done by abolishing institutional forms of free communication among equals and by instilling suspicion of informers, so that people will be restricted in their communication even to friends. Without such communication there can be a great deal of unrest without organized revolt. People cannot organize cooperative efforts when they cannot communicate with one another.

Totalitarian regimes have shown ingenuity in their use of techniques to restrict and direct the flow of information. By blocking out the channels of horizontal communication and other sources of information, they have made their people dependent solely upon communication from above. This channeling works to strengthen the hierarchical structure, but in modern society it is impossible to maintain such tight control of the communication processes over time.

Communication Upward

Communication up the line takes many forms. It can be reduced, however, to what the person says (1) about himself, his performance, and his problems, (2) about others and their problems, (3) about organizational practices and policies, and (4) about what needs to be done and how it can be done. Thus the subordinate can report to his boss about what he has done, what those under him have done, what his peers have done, what he thinks needs to be done, his problems and the problems of his unit, and about matters of organizational practice and policy. He can seek clarification about general goals and specific directives. He may under certain circumstances bypass his own superior and report directly to a higher level. Or he can utilize the suggestion system of the company (an approved institutional method of bypassing). Grievance procedures represent another institutional pattern of getting problems referred to a higher level. In addition, systematic feedback and research may develop as formal processes in the system. They constitute such an important form of communication about organizational functioning that they will be considered in a separate section of this chapter.

The basic problem in upward communication is the nature of the hierarchical administrative structure. The first role requirement of people in executive and supervisory positions is to direct, coordinate, and control the people below them. They themselves are less in the habit of listening to their subordinates than in telling them. The subordinates also fall into this role pattern and expect to listen to their bosses rather than be listened to. Moreover, information fed up the line is often utilized for control purposes. Hence there are great constraints on free upward communication. The boss is not likely to be given information by his subordinates which will lead to decisions affecting them adversely. It is not only that they tell the boss what he wants to hear, but what they want him to know. People do want to get certain information up the line, but generally they are afraid of presenting it to the most relevant person or in the most objective form. Full and objective reporting might be penalized by the supervisor or regarded as espionage by peers. To these difficulties must be added the fact that full and objective reporting is difficult, regardless of the organizational situation; no individual is an objective observer of his own performance and problems.

For all these reasons the upward flow of communication in organizations is not noted for spontaneous and full expression, despite attempts to institutionalize the process of feedback up the line. Suggestions for improvement of work procedures and company practices are also limited in quantity and quality in most organizations. The more top-heavy the organizational structure and the more control is exercised through pressure and sanctions, the less adequate will be the flow of information up the line. It is not a matter of changing the communication habits of individuals, but of changing the organizational conditions responsible for them.

The typical upward communication loop is small and terminates with the immediate supervisor. He may transmit some of the information to his own superior, but generally in a modified form. The open-door policy of some high-level officers extends the theoretical size of the circuit to include all levels below them. It generally contributes more to the self-image of the officer as an understanding, democratic person, however, than to adequacy of information exchange. The closed nature of the upward circuits has already been indicated and resides both in the restricted communication passed upward and in the limited codes of the recipients.

Obstacles to vertical communication occur in both industrial organizations and democratic structures. Labor unions, in which the membership possesses the formal power to elect officers and command referenda on basic issues, manifest striking gaps in understanding between top echelons and local leaders closer to the rank and file. In the fall of 1964 officials of the United Auto Workers concluded negotiations for a contract with General Motors and were ready to announce the outcome as a main accomplishment, only to have the pact rejected by their local unions. The top leaders were apparently not in effective communication with lower levels of leadership and the rank and file.

The Longshoremen's Union came to terms with shipping companies in January, 1965 in a contract which the top union people regarded as favorable. It was promptly rejected by the membership. The officials responded with all sorts of measures to reach their men by way of the mass media and by a broadside of letters. In other words, the information channels between leaders and membership were closed over before and during the contract negotiations and the public demonstration of this phenomenon led to desperate efforts on the part of officials to restore communication. It is typical that the attempted solution was not only delayed, but took the form of communication *downward*.

Asymmetry of Communication Needs and Communication Flow

There are no studies of the distinctive types of communication which characteristically flow horizontally, upward, or downward in organizations, although such research is much needed. The information requirements of superior and subordinate are not symmetrical. What the superior wants to know is often not what the subordinate wants to tell him; what the subordinate wants to know is not necessarily the message the superior wants to send. The greater the conflict between the communication needs of these two hierarchically situated senders and recipients of information, the more likely is an increase in lateral communication. Among peers there will be greater complementarity of information needs. Where a foreman finds little reception from his superior, he will readily turn to fellow foremen to talk about his problems. Horizontal exchange can be an escape valve for frustration in communicating upward and downward; and sometimes it can operate to accomplish some of the essential business of the organization.

Another type of communication flow, thus far not considered, is criss-crossing, in which a subordinate in one unit talks to the boss of another unit or vice-versa. Again, this process is furthered by blockages in communication up and down the line. A department head perceived as a sympathetic person may be sought out by people in other departments as an audience for their problems because they feel they cannot talk to their own department head.

INFORMATION AND RESEARCH STRUCTURES

Organizations cannot rely on communication processes which develop naturally both for internal coordination and feedback from the external world. Hence formal structures are devised to protect against the idiosyncratic perceptions and systematic biases of people in different subsystems, as well as to increase the total amount of relevant information. These structures make explicit the search process, the coding categories to be employed, and the procedures for processing and interpreting information according to these categories. Three types of informational procedures can be distinguished: (1) direct operational feedback, (2) operational research, and (3) systemic research. Operational feedback is basically a process of immediate routine control; systemic research, to use the distinctions employed by Rubenstein and Haberstroh (1960), is a process of delayed evaluation. Operational research is a mixture of these two processes.

Operational Feedback

Operational feedback is systematic information-getting which is closely tied to the ongoing functions of the organization and is sometimes an integral part of those functions. For example, the number of units turned out by any division of an organization and the number of units marketed are necessary items of record-keeping for everyday operations. Earlier, reference was made to the regulatory mechanisms which distinguish organizations from primitive groups (Chapter 4). These regulatory devices are based upon built-in intelligence circuits which are parts of the operating mechanism itself or are close adjuncts to the mechanism. Information provided in this fashion can be readily systematized so that its reporting follows standard rules and includes detailed specifications about elements of time and quality. It is readily converted into terms of cost accounting and can be compared in many respects with similar figures of competing companies. In most organizations direct operational feedback is available for the performance of the total organization and for its major subsystems. It is frequently not informative about the performance of work groups or of individuals, and it does not deal with the effectiveness of social-psychological practices of the organization in carrying out its mission, e.g., the value of given types of leadership procedures, of morale-building practices, or of training programs.

The major function of operational feedback is to provide routine control over operations. It is thus similar to the negative feedback of the servo-mechanism which keeps the subsystem on course. This type of control information involves relatively short loops in the communication system. Information is generated by the operating unit involved and the backflow of information is directly to that unit. It follows that this type of operational feedback is a continuous rather than a delayed process. It is a form of routine control which permits decisions without lengthy consideration of a variety of inputs. The latter process involves a delayed evaluation (Rubenstein and Haberstroh, 1960).

Direct operational feedback is limited to reporting of current operations. It is not concerned with an assessment of trends in the external environment nor with a detailed analysis of the functioning of subsystems or the total system. It is less a search for new information than a utilization of existing operational records. For this utilization, little additional organizational structure is required beyond existing managerial, production, and maintenance structures. A small unit is sometimes attached to the managerial structure to study the company records in relation to the records of competitors, but for the most part we are dealing with information-processing that is built into the ongoing operations.

The major limitations of this type of intelligence have already been noted: its coding categories are restricted to existing practices, and hence can report how well they may be working but not the reasons for their success or failure. The impact of environmental change may be felt by the organization, but the nature of such change is not revealed by direct operational feedback. The basic determinants of organizational functioning are hardly touched by the knowledge such feedback supplies. Nevertheless, this is still the basic institutional form of information upon which many organizations rely. They will supplement it in various ways; i.e., through the insight, observations, and wisdom of men in leadership positions; through the use of consultants; or even through an occasional special investigation or research project.

Though these supplementary means of intelligence gathering may prove of great value in critical situations, they do not provide an organization with a reliable means for getting adequate information about its prospects for survival and effectiveness in a changing world. So long as the coding categories and information processing are confined to the regulatory mechanisms of ongoing operations, there is a closed circuit informational system—a circuit, moreover, whose circular enclosure covers a small area of the relevant universe.

Operational Research

Organizations in a changing world develop adaptive structures, and within these structures may be housed departments of research and development. The most common type of intelligence activity which takes on an institutionalized form is operational research. It actively institutes search for new information and it seeks explanations as well as descriptions, but its focus is upon two targets: the improvement of specific products, and the improvement of methods for turning them out. It is technologically oriented, and its achievements are in depth, not breadth. Operational research examines various problems in the production system and supplies information on the basis of which efficiencies can be effected. It supplements the inadequate descriptive function of operational feedback and logically derives from this more central organizational process.

The great limitation of operational research is that it deals so sparingly with the problems of the managerial structure, the maintenance structure, and the institutional relations with the larger environment. Since these structures are based upon human interaction rather than upon the technological transformation of materials, they are not seen as affecting productivity in a measurable way. When operational research ventures into the field of human relationships, it deals more with ecological patternings and with personnel measures than with the social structure of the organization. It is concerned with the improvement of technical operations and not with the relations of the organization to the external social world.

The coding categories of operational research provide a circuit of information which has no ready way of dealing with intelligence of a nontechnological type; for example, the causes of such events as workers threatening to strike, the legislature in the state increasing its taxes on local business, consumers boycotting a certain type of product, the production department at loggerheads with the sales department, or the personnel department having problems with the line production people about personnel procedures. In other words, the information loops of operational research, though larger than those of operational feedback, do not embrace the organization as it functions in its environment. Though there is more evaluation than in immediate routine control, the questions raised and the answers sought by such research are largely in terms of control.

Systemic Research

Organizations can and do extend their information resources by moving towards systemic research. Systemic research, like operational research, seeks new information, but its target is the functioning of the total system in relation to its changing environment. The objectives of systemic research include study of environmental trends, long-term organizational functioning, the nature of organizational structure, the interrelationship of the subsystems within the total system, and the impact of the organization on its environment. Where operational research concentrates upon improving technical aspects of production, systemic research explores the organizational changes which technical improvement would produce, including both the intended and the usually unanticipated consequences of the technical change. Operational research would be governed by the *satisficing* principle, to use the terminology of March and Simon (1958), whereas systemic research would be governed by an optimizing principle. This distinction refers to the difference between finding some minimally acceptable answer and seeking for an optimal answer.

Stated in these sweeping terms, systemic research seems Utopian in organizations with limited financial resources and with limited, fallible human beings to initiate and carry out such research. The concept, however, is critical and of great practical importance. In some organizations the thinking of top leaders is systemic; they utilize whatever intelligence is available about the present and future relationship of their system to its environment, and they initiate research to guide them on central problems. For example, some oil companies with foreign holdings and foreign markets have economists and political experts on their staffs to study the development of the European common market, social forces in the developing African nations, and similar problems. The approach here is systemic even though the program of research to support it is tiny in relation to the firm's needs and resources. Another device of systemic research is the occasional study by a concern of its institutional relations with society, e.g., the corporate image held by various sectors of the public or the public response to corporate bigness. Sometimes the organization may ask its own research unit to ascertain how a training program for supervisors is affecting the whole organization.

Various compromises are attempted by organizational leaders to provide some degree of systemic intelligence without an adequate allocation of resources and manpower to this function. Research units are set up to bring together and analyze data already available from other sources, such as governmental agencies, other companies, and university institutes. Outside consultants are hired not only for expert opinion, but for their knowledge of what is happening in the research world. These compromises may be of considerable value in giving top leadership guidance in their decision-making. The greatest weakness in using them is the reliance upon data gathered in another context and sometimes for a different purpose. The specific determinants of the organization's own problems may be slighted, and the existing data may not dig deep enough into causes.

Disaster may lead to a specific investigation of a systemic type. After the collaboration of some American soldiers in the Korean War, the Army instituted an investigation, not only of the incidence of various kinds of behavior in captivity, but also of the causes of collaboration and the capacity to resist brainwashing. The President's code for captured soldiers was the outcome of this investigation, but the procedural lesson of the intelligence failure was not learned in that no steps were taken to provide the armed services with continuing research on the relation of its members to their mission.

Organizations will also attempt the compromise of using market research in place of more systematic investigation of the relationship of the organization to its environment. Though market research is concerned with consumer demand, which is an important aspect of system survival, its characteristic frame of reference comes from operational feedback. The search for new data will not go much beyond the sales figures of the organization. Additional surveys may pick up consumers' reactions to a form of packaging or the more obvious properties of the product. Thorough studies of the basic psychology of the consumer, with adequate samples, field experiments, and continuing panels, are the exception rather than the rule.

Motivation research had its brief period of popularity because it was supposedly a cheap short cut to people's motives as buyers and consumers. What was subsumed under motivational research, however, was essentially idea research in which a few individuals' reactions were interpreted according to various theories of personality. Motivational research helped copy writers who had run out of ideas, but it was not research in the scientific sense of the term. The Ford Motor Company lost heavily in attempting to produce and market a new model, the Edsel, in part because it was not willing to do genuine research on the marketing side and accepted the ersatz of motivational research. In summary, market research is much more of a control process than an evaluation process.

Systemic research then is limited by three factors. The first is the amount of resources available to an organization to carry on a continuing research operation concerned with systemic variables. The second factor is the conception of management held by the top leaders of an organization. If they do not think in system terms, or if they think in system terms only when confronted with disaster, then the coding of whatever systemic information is available will be fragmentary and inadequate. In our discussion of leadership (Chapter 11) we call attention to the importance of *systemic perspective* for the leader who is an innovator and creator of policy. The third factor which encourages or limits systemic research is the jolting of the organization as it pursues its course in the environment. A series of reverses in which successive *satisficing* moves have been only temporarily ameliorative may lead to a more *optimizing* search.

The Organizational Locus of Informational Subsystems

Informational processes can have their primary locus at any level in the organization or in any one of its substructures. Operational feedback is received first by the appropriate operating unit and then filtered up the line as overall summaries of operations at each level to the managerial level just above. Thus the head of each production unit knows the number of pieces turned out by his unit at the end of a given time period. The superintendent of production has summary figures for all the units reporting to him, and he again makes a summary for the echelons above him.

Since this kind of feedback is tied closely to actual operations, little distortion is possible over time, though some filtering may result in an oversimplified picture at top levels. The units with poor records may not be pinpointed in average figures covering all units. Interpretations of these figures may be supplied by the heads of units or divisions, but such interpretations tend to be coded by their transmitters as favorable to their own way of operating. If the forge shop is below expectations in productivity for any given month, the head of the forge shop will furnish reasons which do not suggest poor management on his part. He may assert that the materials were not up to par or absenteeism due to illness was great. But the major distortion is probably not the defensive explanation; it is the selective bias of each unit head, who will utilize as his basis of judgment the specific frame of reference of the operations in which he is daily involved.

Operational research is generally geared into some part of the production system. Its reports, however, can go beyond the production system to top management. Since the changes its information may suggest for organizational functioning require some degree of acceptance by the production structure, there is some advantage to tying operational research closely to the operations under investigation. A common procedure is to have the group conducting the operational research report to one level higher than the specific operation being researched. This helps to protect its results from being ignored.

Information, however, that has direct relevance for system functioning, as in all cases of systemic research, should be reported to top management. This is even true of market research, which is often placed very low in the sales structure. The locus of market research thus does not provide the organization with information about the success of its product. Rather, it supplies the sales department with ideas for promotional campaigns. What may be necessary for organizational success is an actual change in product. This cannot be achieved through a research unit serving the sales department, since the function of the sales department is to sell what is being produced, and not to tell the production people what to produce. The information of the market research unit follows the general principle of being coded by the sales department as sales information, and it fails to be coded with its proper implications for the production structure.

Another common failing is to assign to a given substructure whose primary function is noninformational the secondary mission of providing information about the relations of the organization with the external world. The primary task determines the types of information which will be received and its mode of processing. For example, the State Department has traditionally utilized its diplomatic personnel abroad to report on the political, economic, social, and psychological conditions of the foreign country. In their primary roles as diplomats, State Department personnel move in very limited circles; they meet primarily with their counterparts in the diplomatic corps of that nation. They are not necessarily expert in the subject about which information is sought; they seldom have training or knowledge of research procedures; and their major motivation is to carry out their function in the implementation of State Department policy. It is no wonder then that we have been consistently misinformed about the structures of foreign countries and the prevailing currents within them. Reliance upon the impressions of exclusively upper-class informants, refugees from disaffected elements, and émigrés from dispossessed groups has aggravated the problem. A reverse situation occurred in the Cuban fiasco in which the Central Intelligence Agency, supposedly an information structure, became absorbed in overthrowing the Castro regime rather than in obtaining accurate information about it. In both cases, however, we are dealing with closed intelligence circuits which are not open to relevant information.

Two points are involved in the above examples. One concerns the necessity of a system of information with its own staff to carry on its own function and develop its own norms, standards, and expertness. The other concerns the place in the system to which intelligence should be reported.

The first problem has so far been presented as if there were only one answer. When information concerning the system as a whole and its relations to its environment is involved, there are genuine advantages in a subsystem which has this information-gathering as its major responsibility. This can mean that specialized expertness is made possible, that the coding limitations of an irrelevant function are obviated, and that standards of accurate prediction and valid assessment develop as in a scientific research organization.

These advantages do not inevitably follow. The major values of the system still operate to affect the subsystem; directives of top management control the freedom of the subsystem and may indicate receptivity to only certain types of information. Cigarette manufacturers, for example, could set up a research agency reporting to top management with the task of investigating the relationship of cigarette smoking to lung cancer, heart disease, and related health problems. They could hire competent researchers (though perhaps not top scientists) with an adequate budget to pursue a research program. It is not likely, however, that the researchers would furnish top management unambiguous reports on the injurious effects of the use of tobacco and recommendations that the company change its goals and turn to the use of nicotine as a poison against insects or some such alternative.

To avoid the corruption of information by the system of which it is a part, it is necessary to guarantee to the researcher within an organization some of the same freedoms he would enjoy in a university setting. Some of the big electric and utility companies have actually done this in the natural sciences, and the resulting discoveries have more than justified the policy. With the exception of one or two token units, no industrial concern has ever done this in the social sciences even though it is in this area that management needs information most desperately. One type of freedom absolutely essential for such research is that the directives of top management do not pose specific questions they want answered. General problem areas can be indicated, but once the lines of inquiry are restricted in particularistic fashion, we are back to a closed system of intelligence. Answers are easily predetermined by the questions asked, especially when these questions originate at the top of a power structure. This applies both to an intelligence system which is conducting basic research and to one which is gathering information at a more descriptive level. A narrow definition of the mission of an information-gathering agency means that the answers it furnishes will also be extremely limited and frequently erroneous.

Another means by which an organization can avoid corrupting or being corrupted by its own information service is the astute use of multiple channels as check procedures. Multiple channels, if based upon the same sources of information, can merely duplicate error. But they can be set up so as to utilize various sources of information and process it in similar enough fashion to produce a consistent or inconsistent picture for decision makers.

The problem of the latitude to be permitted to an intelligence operation is an extremely difficult one for top management. On the one hand, the organization needs useful information, and if it gives researchers a completely free hand, the relevance of their findings for organizational functioning is not insured. To this rational consideration is added the irrational fear of the incomprehensible techniques and language of a suspect group of "longhairs." On the other hand, there is not much advantage to management in setting up an intelligence agency if it merely reflects management's coding processes.

The critical question is whether the task of the intelligence or research unit is system research or operational research. If the former is the case, then management has to be able to tolerate the differences in values, methods, and approach of specialists in information-gathering. In fact, these differences are among the major reasons for hiring specialists. Some restriction on their activities can nevertheless be imposed in terms of the general objectives assigned to them. And even if no specific and immediate answers are demanded, over time the information agency must provide some useful information to the organization or forfeit its right to organizational support. An important factor working toward organizational control of information specialists (and often working too well) is the natural tendency for specialists to take on the coloration of the system and behave too much as conforming members rather than as objective outsiders.

Outside research agencies are occasionally called in to provide the types of information which organizational leaders think cannot be readily supplied by their own personnel. The more research-oriented outside agencies will seek to obtain a broader definition of the problem than management generally presents. In other words, the tendency of organizational leaders is to narrow the problem to the visible and troublesome symptoms, whereas adequate intelligence about it has to probe into the causes. The process of redefining the problem for management is often easier for the outside group than for the captive agency.

The question of the optimal place for reporting the results of systemic research becomes complicated in large organizations. Though top echelons should be the recipients of information about the functioning of the total system, it is difficult for them to find the time to take adequate note of it, let alone absorb it and give it some weight in their decisions. Hence there is generally more relevant information in an organization than its top leaders utilize. Several changes are necessary in organizational structure to achieve reform in this respect. One is the elevation of the head of the information agency in status, so that he not only reports to top levels but also can command a hearing when he and his aides believe they have some vital intelligence. The second is the perfecting of translation mechanisms, so that critical pieces of information can be transmitted up the line in the information agency itself and finally to the top echelons of the organization. A third is the restructuring of the top jobs to reduce the component of routine administration; this will not guarantee the acquisition and use of systemic information, but it will have a powerful facilitating effect.

SUMMARY

Human organizations are informational as well as energic systems, and both the exchange of energy and the exchange of information must be considered in order to understand the functioning of organizations. Information exchange is itself energic, of course, but its energic aspects are of minor significance compared to its symbolic aspects. In other words, information transmission is significant for what it implies, triggers, or controls. In general, the closer one gets to the center of organizational control and decision-making, the greater is the emphasis on information exchange and transmittal.

The importance of information processes to organizational functioning does not imply, however, a simple relationship between amount of communication and organizational effectiveness. The advocacy of communication as a desideratum of organization needs to be qualified with respect to the kind of information required for the solution of given problems, and with respect to the nature of the communication process between individuals, groups, and subsystems of organization. Indeed, social systems can be defined as *restricted* communication networks; unrestricted communication implies noise and inefficiency.

Every organization thus must solve the problem of what pattern of communication shall be instituted, what information shall be directed to what offices. One issue in establishing such a pattern is information overload. There are limits to the amount of communication which can be received, coded, and effectively handled by any individual. The tendency to overload certain executive offices with communications is strong, and the responses of individuals to information overload are often maladaptive. Miller has identified seven categories of response to information overload, each of which can be assessed in terms of its adaptive or maladaptive implications for the individual and the organization. These categories include omission, error, queuing, filtering, approximation, multiple channels, and escape.

Five dimensions are proposed for characterizing communications circuits in organizations:

(a) The size of the loop; that is, the amount of organizational space encompassed by the communication circuit;

(b) The nature of the circuit;

(c) The openness of the circuit; that is, the extent to which messages can be modified once the communication process has been initiated;

(d) The efficiency of the circuit for task completion; that is, the speed and accuracy with which the circuit permits the completion of specified tasks; and

(e) The goodness of fit between the circuit and its systemic function.

Further distinctions are made between communications in a hierarchical organization directed upward, those directed downward, and those directed horizontally. Each of these directions implies characteristic content in messages.

The chapter concludes with a discussion of formal communication devices, such as operational feedback, operations research, and systemic research. The hypothesis is offered that communication and information subsystems are often located disadvantageously in organizations, both in terms of accessibility to top leaders and in terms of contamination of the information-getting process.

10

Policy Formulation and Decision-Making

Organizational policies are abstractions or generalizations about organizational behavior, at a level which involves the structure of the organization. This definition is in contrast to the notion that policies are behavior itself, or that they are official statements regardless of their relation to organizational structure and behavior.

As abstractions about organizational behavior, policy statements may be either prospective or retrospective. If the latter, we are dealing merely with a process of recognition; the pattern was there but was not previously stated or formally acknowledged. The more interesting process, however, and the one around which this chapter is constructed, is policy-*making:* prospective generalizations about what organizational behavior shall be, at a level implying changes in organizational structure. Such prospective statements of policy comprise a category of decisions: those decisions within an organization which affect the structure of the organization. Policy-making is therefore an aspect of organizational change—the decision aspect. Policy-making is also the decision aspect of that level of leadership which involves the alteration, origination, or elimination of organizational structure.

Decision-making can be considered in terms of three basic dimensions: the level of generality or abstraction of the decision; the amount of internal and external organizational space affected by the decision; and the length of time for which the decision will hold. For example, suppose that the manager of a manufacturing plant announces that "every employee is to punch in at 8:30 a.m., without exception, and for the duration of operations in this plant." This is a policy which is low on the dimension of abstraction, but extremely high on the dimensions of time and internal organizational space. On the other hand, consider the following statement of a dean to the members of his faculty. "Gentlemen, our policy is to contribute our very best to facilitate student self-development." This policy is abstract and general, both with respect to the principle being enunciated and the means for its implementation.

The combination of these three dimensions enables us to distinguish among (1) policy-making as the formulation of substantive goals and objectives, (2) policy-making as the formulation of procedures and devices for achieving goals and evaluating performance, (3) routine administration, or the application of existing policies to ongoing operations, and (4) residual, ad hoc decisions affecting organizational space without temporal implications beyond the immediate event.

The first two categories of decision-making are clearly in the area of policy formulation, and represent the major content of this chapter. The third category, routine administration, is not policy determination in any sense of the term; it includes the many small decisions which implement existing policies by prescribed means. The residual class of ad hoc decisions represents policy only in a negative sense. Decisions without acknowledged implications for the future imply a lack of continuity in organizational direction; they are policy-making only in the sense that the organization has no policy. The warning cliche, "don't take this as a precedent," is the hallmark of a policy-shy management. That most organizational decisions have precedent value nevertheless, reflects a need for policy which is inherent in the nature of organizations.

THE FORMULATION OF GOALS AND OBJECTIVES

The formulation of organizational goals would be represented by substantial positive positions on all three dimensions of decision-making; such positions, in fact, are the criteria for classifying actions in this category of policy determination. The goal-formulating decisions of members of the executive or the legislative system must be general enough to transcend the specific case; they must hold over time for many cases; and they must affect a substantial part of organizational space or structure.

The mere announcement of an official that the policy of the organization will be thus and so is not in itself proof of policy-making. To take a hypothetical case, it is possible for the president of a company to issue a pious statement that the policy of his company does not countenance discriminatory hiring practices. But this statement may have no effect upon the operations of the company, and many other actions of the management of the company may be supportive of such practices. On the other hand, if the statement is not merely a public relations matter but does affect the activities of organizational members as they function in their roles, it can be regarded as a policy-making statement. A borderline case would be a conscious and explicit formulation of objectives which attempts no shift in operations but merely a recognition of current practices as official policy. If this formulation has no effect upon the system apart from satisfying the needs of some officials for cognitive neatness, it would not be policy-making. If, on the other hand, the conscious recognition of some current operation as expressing an organizational goal leads to structural changes to reinforce this mode of operation, the act of recognition would fall in the area of policy-making.

The major point is that we can easily be misled by teleological fictions presented by organizational spokesmen. The organization is a social system and the consciously expressed intent of some of its members is not to be confused with the functioning of the system. Hence, when officials announce a change in policy to embrace new objectives, we should look at the actual systemic changes taking place rather than accepting the statement at face value. We should follow such a procedure not because there may be insincerity in official pronouncements, but because the functioning of a system is not necessarily given in the statements of its leaders no matter how sincere they may be.

Changes in organizational objectives as stated by officials, however, provide a good starting point for determining whether changes in the system have taken place. We must recognize here the implications of a general social-psychological law. Men act first and then rationalize their actions, but over time they acquire understanding of how and why certain behavior has been successful. This understanding is then systematically exploited through deliberate and conscious planning.

Such a process has occurred more often and more successfully with respect to technological exploitation of the natural environment than to management of the social world. Social systems have not been understood to the same degree. Increasingly, however, knowledge and awareness of the nature of bureaucratic structures have been developing. Much of this knowledge is in the heads of operating officials rather than in academic disciplines. At the operating level of individual organizations there is a great deal of conscious effort to utilize social structure to accomplish given objectives. Programs for executive training and management development are flourishing, and in some of them an insightful mixture of academic and operating wisdom about social organizations is formulated and imparted to junior executives. Such deliberate use of knowledge of social organizations still is confined within narrow limits; moreover, few men of major position in the national structure, for example, are making any consistent attempt to apply the existing knowledge of social systems to the prevention of international war. Nevertheless, the self-conscious character of organizational management implies continuing effort to examine alternative courses of action, to consider carefully their probable effects on organizational structure, and to choose specific means of change on the basis of such analysis. We need therefore to take account of the rational processes of decision-making on the part of organizational leaders.

Policy-making, however, is not only the product of deliberate consideration of long-run problems facing the organization. Policy is also created by day-to-day decisions, often made on an ad hoc basis and often made by administrators rather than by designated policy makers. The criterion again is whether systemic change in the organization has been produced by a cumulation of administrative decisions, even though their makers were not consciously trying to determine policy. Political theorists from Woodrow Wilson (1887) on have created a false distinction between policy-making and administration because they have restricted policy-making to deliberate attempts at decision-making by the formal groups assigned such functions. This definition implies that policy must be sought in the pronouncements of a legislature or a head executive, in contrast to the decisions of people in administrative positions. This legalistic approach has confused the issue and diverted attention from the facts of organizational life.

The real distinction between policy-making and administration is not to be found in the formal separation of functions nor in the official titles of positions, but in the significance of decisions for organizational structure and functioning. The president of an organization may devote himself to routine administration while his administrative assistants make policy. Actually, of course, in most organizations, there is some correlation between policy-making and position in the hierarchy. The relationship is so imperfect, however, that some political scientists have tended to reject the distinction between policy-making and administration completely.

Friedrich (1940) came to the conclusion that the policy-administration dichotomy had become "a fetish, a stereotype in the minds of theorists and practitioners alike." And Gulick (1937) suggested that modern theory should be concerned not "with the division of policy and administration but with the division between policy veto on the one side and policy planning and execution on the other." The fact that government, like other social structures, does not conform too well to the organizational blueprint, however, does not relieve us of the need for distinguishing decisions of a high level of generality with consequences extended in organizational space and time from decisions which are highly specific and have no effect upon organizational structure.

Some examples of policy-making may show the necessity of maintaining the concept to refer to decisions which affect the system as a system. The city colleges of New York a few years ago made a policy change which affected the system of higher education for that municipality. They announced the inauguration of programs to grant the doctoral degree. Previously, they had participated in graduate training in a very marginal manner, with limited programs awarding the master's degree in some fields and in some colleges. Doctoral training, however, requires research facilities of a different character than undergraduate instruction, and requires different skills from the staff. The appropriate model is seminar discussion and individual guidance in the laboratory, rather than large groups of students in the classroom or lecture hall. The teaching load must be adjusted to provide opportunity for faculty members to conduct research. In short, this policy decision had serious implications for the whole system of higher education in New York as the city colleges became comparable in some respects to the private universities which have long granted the doctorate.

The officials of a corporation, to take another example, may decide to set up a plant overseas in order to meet competition in the foreign market more effectively. The effects of this decision may not reverberate quickly through all parts of the organization, but the decision will result in significant changes in the larger system. Top management will devote time to the foreign branch, will become more concerned with international affairs, and will have to set up new coordinating machinery. Some local plants may be cut back or their products altered. The legal, accounting, and research and development departments will be affected. The personnel department will encounter new problems in the rotation of management personnel in overseas assignments, or in the appointment and promotion of men to take the place of those going abroad.

The practical criterion for identifying a policy decision is the novelty and readjustment which will result in many parts of the organization as a consequence of the decision. At the Baltimore shipyards during World War II, management took action to slow the production of Liberty ships and to start the production of invasion barges in response to changing military requirements. The novelty which this change introduced into plant operations was not fully anticipated when the decision was made. Technological changes had been foreseen but

the impact upon the social system of the workers had not been anti
cipated. Skilled workers saw their most valuable personal assets, ex
perience and skill in building big ships, suddenly devalued an
liquidated. Workers who had identified with the product of their wor
on Liberty ships took no pride in producing "row boats." Since th
purpose of these barges was labeled classified information, worker
could not be told they were turning out the craft to be used in th
invasion of the European continent. In the absence of information
about these technological and threatening changes, the shipyard be
came a rumor factory, morale and productivity declined, and a disas
trous strike was narrowly averted. Policy changes were substantial
unanticipated, and unexplained.

On the other hand, expectations about policy change are ofte
unfulfilled. For example, a change in political control of a city, a state
or even the nation may create expectations of policy changes of
sweeping sort. Often, however, no novelty in the functioning of th
system can be detected as a result of the political change. Old gov
ernment employees who entered the civil service in the Hoover ad
ministration may not have changed their role performance in any per
ceptible manner during six successive presidencies. They themselve
will observe with satisfaction that while their departmental heads com
and go, they go on forever.

The consideration of organizational goals by policy makers may
move in the direction of (1) sharpening and clarifying organizationa
purposes and excluding irrelevant activities, (2) adding new objec
tives, (3) shifting priorities among objectives, or (4) shifting the mis
sion of the organization.

The last alternative is the least likely of these possibilities. Many
policy decisions come about to clarify the major organizational mission, or to achieve consistency between it and subgoals which have
developed in the organizational structure. Subparts of the organization may have developed too far on a logic of their own, and the system moves to redress the imbalance in its functioning. For example,
a university finds that its program of competitive intercollegiate athletics has achieved a degree of professionalism which is in blatant
conflict with its educational objectives. It is faced with a policy decision of reaffirming its basic mission and bringing athletics into line,
or having its goals altered by the deviant subsystem. Or a labor union
is faced with policy decisions about the elimination of racketeering in
some of its locals. Imbalances within an organization may not in themselves compel a policy decision. Persistent imbalance leads, however,
to external difficulties which do precipitate organizational action.

CENTRAL QUESTIONS FOR POLICY-MAKING WITH RESPECT TO SUBSTANTIVE GOALS

Decision-making in organizations with respect to substantive goals is sooner or later confronted with two types of critical questions: (1) clarity and consistency of objectives versus the pressures of expediency, and (2) broadening of goals versus the narrow self-interest of the organization.

Expediency and Organizational Objectives

Organizations face the problem of adjusting to environmental change without losing their basic character and distinctive contributions and capabilities. On the one hand, if the objectives around which the structure has been built are adhered to strictly in spite of environmental change, there may be losses in input or even threats to survival. On the other hand, if the goals are modified over time, there is the risk of eventual defeat in carrying out the original mission of the organization. Decisions which compromise the principles upon which the organization is based may cause it to lose its distinctive character, its members, and its clientele. (The Social Democratic Party in Germany, for example, furnished very weak opposition to the Nazis. It had followed the dictates of expediency so much in the past that its members no longer knew what their principles were and when they should take a stand in their support.)

On the other hand, in a dynamic world an organization cannot maintain its goals in pristine purity without the risk of becoming ineffective or even extinct. The American scene has had a radical political party which has maintained a pure Marxian position over the last sixty years or more—the Socialist Labor Party. It would not compromise its stand by advocating political reforms such as social security legislation, because it was interested in changing the capitalist system and not in repairing its inequities. Hence, the Socialist Labor Party has remained a doctrinaire group of no consequence in American politics. The Catholic Church, with its unparalleled depth and breadth of experience, has combined idealism and realism in its policy-making. Its leaders have been opportunistic when they saw real gains, but they have also insisted upon the preservation of ideological convictions about basic goals. The present ecumenical movement is only the most recent example of such flexibility.

Since any organization must survive in order to carry out its basic functions, survival becomes a salient goal for organizational decision makers. We have described in Chapter 4 the dynamic forces generated by maintenance structures which have as their implicit, and sometimes explicit, goal the survival of present organizational forms. For many administrators and officials, concern with the preservation of the bureaucracy assumes primary significance. Indeed, the term bureaucracy is often used, not in the Weberian sense, but in the sense of an officialdom absorbed only in the preservation of its own structure and in the ease of its own operation. Thus Drucker (1946) comments: "If the organization has become too bureaucratic, the top people will have lost flexibility too—in the same way in which bureaucratic dry rot extended through the French Army in 1939." When bureaucratic survival becomes paramount, there is an abdication of policy-making with respect to the major substantive goals of the organization. And paradoxically this form of concentration on survival leads readily to organizational disaster.

Another issue in the definition and maintenance of organizational goals concerns multiplicity as against singleness of purpose. The labor union which attempts to combine political action with its established economic activities may become a stronger organization if it succeeds, but to succeed as a multiple purpose organization is a difficult task. The success of Samuel Gompers in organizing skilled workers in the early days of American unionism, when more radical leaders were failing, can be attributed in part to the simplicity and consistency of his objective. He preached pure and simple trade unionism, the organization of skilled workers to achieve a better economic bargain for themselves. There was no militant ideology of social change, no political objective save a personal rewarding of friends and a punishing of enemies at the polls. The American Federation of Labor was a business union striving for a good business bargain and not concerned with broad social objectives. The success of the A. F. of L. was due in part to its ideological compatibility with the larger patterns of American society, but in part also to its singleness of purpose and simplicity of organizational objective.

Broadening of Organizational Goals

A radically different question about the formulation of organizational goals has to do with their breadth, their relation to societal welfare. This issue is characteristically bypassed in behavioral science because it is so heavily laden with value judgments. Yet the sociologist or social psychologist who accepts the policies of the organization as *givens* is merely accepting the value judgments of the immediate social environment and is less objective than if he had explored the problem more thoroughly. A study of the relationship between the ideological goals of an organizational system, the motivation of its members, and the effectiveness of its functioning can yield valuable knowledge about he nature of the undertaking. For example, an organization devoted to public welfare, such as the American Cancer Society or the Red Cross, has special motivations upon which it can draw. In contrast, an essential requirement of a business enterprise is to make profit; otherwise it cannot stay in business. To this extent its goal is narrowly defined as protecting and furthering the interests of one group, its owners.

Though there are many instances of the survival of narrow-interest organizations concerned solely with the making of profit, the general trend has been for business officials to broaden their policies to take account of some aspects of the public interest. The private enterprise of classical economics has been modified by the collectivistic ideology which grows naturally out of the common interests of an interdependent society. Private business will dip into its profits to make donations to charities, will contribute to foundations in the public interest, will make substantial grants to education and the support of research. And the higher its profits, the more it must by law pay out in taxes to the support of collective and national purposes.

It is true that such policy changes can be interpreted as attempts to insure profits over time and to create a favorable public image rather than to maximize public service. Yet it is easy to be too cynical about such matters. During World War II private industry contributed over one hundred times as much as the federal government to carry on the domestic information campaigns of the government, some of which were often against their own immediate interests, e.g., urging people to prevent inflation by buying government bonds rather than consumer goods. The business enterprises making these contributions received little credit for their efforts. Even the naive statement of Charles Wilson that what was good for General Motors was good for the nation had a grain of social truth in that Wilson saw the mass production of cars as not only profit-making but as contributing to the public good. The essential point is that the acceptance by large business structures of some responsibility for the national welfare does result in policy change from the individual enterprise system of the robber barons.

The general trend in organizations as they grow is toward a broadening of their social goals. In his study of a federal agency for law enforcement, Blau (1955) reported a succession of goals through which officials moved in extending the limited directives of their original mission. In opposition to the thesis of Michels (1949) that bureaucratic personnel become obsessed with administrative detail, Blau proposed the hypothesis that ". . . internal bureaucratic conditions, except in atypical cases where insecurity prevails, generate increasing concern with objectives that formerly appeared Utopian." Expressions of concern for societal welfare, even if initially rationalization can contribute to actual changes in policy. Our political state and our political parties have finally moved toward including as first-class citizens people of all religions and all skin colors. To their theological goal of the doctrinal salvation of the individual, many churches have added the objective of improving social conditions in the here and now. Churches of all denominations have been prominent in current efforts to achieve racial equality in education, housing, economic opportunity, and civil rights throughout the United States.

The recognition of some responsibility for the national welfare by the church or business enterprise is an illustration of the general principle that organizations obtain their legitimation through their acceptance of the values of the larger society. The interdependence of an advanced technological society increases the significance of cooperation toward common goals. The overriding values of such a society will therefore be reflected in the policy formulation of many organizations and subsystems.

POLICY-MAKING AS THE DEVELOPMENT OF GENERAL PROCEDURES AND STRATEGIES

In addition to substantive decisions about the nature of objectives, policy is also made by decisions about the general procedures for attaining objectives. Whereas decisions about organizational goals meet clearly the policy-making criteria of generality and spatial and temporal effects, decisions about procedures can vary from questions of what the constitutional rules should be to question of revising some detail in the method of time and motion study. We are concerned here with the former type of procedural decision, decisions about the general strategy for attaining organizational goals. Once such a strategy has been adopted, it can be applied to problems as a routine matter of administration. But setting up new procedures or changing existing ones are matters of policy.

By procedures we do not refer to the role prescriptions which specify how each person is expected to do his job. We refer to the general rules or strategies which commit the organization to follow one path toward achieving its goals rather than another, rules according to which it handles external problems, and meets internal ones, and assesses its progress.

For example, two hospitals may have the same objectives of patient care; yet one may be committed to the open-hospital strategy of maximum freedom for patients and for teams of staff members of differing occupational and professional status, while the other may follow the traditional rules of medical hierarchy. Two industrial enterprises may have the same objectives of producing cars and making profits;

yet one may decentralize its divisions, while the other follows a procedure of heavy control from the top of the organizational structure. As a matter of policy, one company may handle the adjudication of internal conflicts through the immediate intervention of top management; another may attempt to have such conflicts worked out at lower levels, with the conflicting parties heavily involved in the solution of difficulties. One organization may have developed clear criteria for the evaluation of performance which become the guidelines to everyday decisions about operations and personnel; another may have as its criterion of performance only the occasional protest from some articulate member of its public.

Procedural decisions thus vary in generality from those which affect the basic structure of the organization to those which provide rules for the solution of very minor conflicts. At the most general level, procedural decisions constitute policy with respect to where and how various types of policy decisions should be made in the organization.

The Development of Objective Criteria for Decision-Making

Procedures or strategies can emphasize the development and use of criteria for the evaluation of organizational functioning and success. Or, the strategy of the organization may be to give little attention to assessment and to throw all its energies into the self-fulfilling prophecy. For example, a manufacturing concern may not explore the psychological market for a new product but may rely instead upon creating such a market through a huge advertising campaign. In general, however, the trend is toward the development and utilization of yardsticks for the measurement of performance and progress toward organizational goals.

March and Simon (1958) have distinguished between *operational* and *nonoperational* organizational goals. The distinction is based upon whether means of testing actions can be employed to choose between alternative courses of action with respect to an objective. Thus the goal of promoting the general welfare is nonoperational and can be related to specific actions only through the intervention of subgoals. Subgoals are often substituted for the more general goals of an enterprise in order to gain the advantages of operationality. In general, restricted objectives and subgoals lend themselves more readily to the employment of operational criteria in making decisions. March and Simon argue further that where there are shared operational goals, differences about the course of conduct are more likely to be resolved by rational, analytic processes. Where the shared goals are not operational (or where the operational subgoals are not shared), differences are more likely to be adjusted through a qualitatively different process, that of bargaining. In other words, if shared goals are operational, the problem of differential perceptions of the optimal course of action has a logical solution. If the goals are nonoperational, there is no logical and testable answer to such differences of judgment. The probable outcome is therefore a compromise based upon concessions and trading, and more attuned to achieving internal harmony than organizational objectives.

Though there is a trend in technological society toward making organizational goals operational, there is some counteracting of this tendency because of organizational growth. As an organization increases in size and complexity, the goals of the overall system become increasingly difficult to operationalize, though the goals of the subsystem remain operational. This is a basic argument in favor of decentralization; it gives autonomy to organizational units in which goal operationalization is possible. In fact, decentralization takes advantage of one important criterion by which the goals of business organizations are made operational—the yardstick of the market place. The effectiveness of a division, which is often difficult to assess within the total system, is readily measured if it must compete for its share of the market.

The yardsticks for measuring performance and progress toward organizational goals are measures of feedback from organizational transactions with the environment or from cycles of internal operations. Assessment of organizational functioning can be built around any of the major import-export relations of the organization with its environment. Its three types of export to the environment (product or service, image in the outside world, and ideological output) are all capable of measurement. In fact, however, only the assessment of product sales compared to other organizations, the yardstick of the market place, has been widely used.

Criteria of internal functioning can also be developed for the different substructures within the organization. The less the dissension and conflict within the organization, the better job the maintenance structure is doing. The more numerous the new ideas and the better their quality, the better job the research and development groups are doing. A more general criterion of internal functioning is the development of capable leaders to solve the difficult problem of managerial succession.

Finally, cost accounting is commonly employed to give some measure of the total input of energy in relation to output. Though theoretically a good approximation to energic exchange, the practical difficulties of accurate, reliable, and adequate cost accounting are such that it needs to be combined with other devices for the evaluation of performance of the various substructures within the organization.

Profitability and growth are two additional indicators of overall organizational success that are widely used. Both these measures are complex outcomes of many interacting factors, including properties of the organization and of its immediate environment. They are feedback of a kind, but the feedback loop is so long and the information reflects so many causes that they are less than satisfactory as criteria for organizational functioning. The company whose profits plunge is in trouble, but management still requires measures of internal and external functioning which will indicate the nature and locus of the trouble. Rate of growth is still more complicated and ambiguous in meaning.

Criteria for assessing organizational effectiveness are discussed more fully in Chapter 6. They are summarized here because of their dual relevance and importance for policy-making. In the first place, the policy of an organization may favor certain criteria and pay little attention to others. Thus, a business enterprise may put all its eggs into the basket of the market criterion and pursue a policy of maximizing immediate return without attention to such long-range factors as its image in the minds of the general public, its ability to innovate, or its capacity to develop leaders.

In the second place, criteria of effectiveness, when they are actually put to use, provide material for the development of policy itself. Significant decisions for the future of an organization depend upon adequate intelligence about present functioning and possible consequences of alternative patterns of action. Before a company moves toward decentralization, for example, it needs to examine the possible effects of the move upon costs, productivity, the potential for innovation, the potential for the development of leaders, and other relevant criteria. There are both theoretical and practical limits for collecting and analyzing information. Yet the uses of research for improving the quality and quantity of information have barely been tried, except in the traditional field of sales and cost accounting. Even in the hard-headed business world, top management operates with little information about the psychological nature of its market. And few organizations have any systematic information about the effect of policy decisions on the development of leaders or the encouragement of innovations.

Coordination for Tomorrow: the Problem of Planning

A basic issue of strategy for large organizations in modern industrial societies concerns their policy with respect to planning. Industrialized societies are dynamic in character. Once past a critical point in the accumulation of scientific knowledge, technology grows at an ever accelerating pace. Through its development, luxuries not available to royalty a century ago have become necessities for American society. Moreover, technology moves in many directions: toward improving the material way of life, toward conquering disease and extending the span of life, toward the conquest of space, and toward unbelievably efficient devices for the destruction of the human race.

The rapidity of change and the diverse potential uses of technology put a premium upon the anticipation and direction of these changes through systematic planning. Any organization which does not have a four-, or five-, or ten-year plan is risking destruction or a series of continuing crises in its operations. In his description of one of the largest and most successful of industrial corporations, Drucker (1946) writes, "Of all the functions of central management, this responsibility to think ahead is perhaps the most important as it more than anything else makes General Motors a unified institution with but one purpose."

The generic policy decision in organizations with respect to planning has to do with the extent to which there will be programing for innovation. At one extreme would be the policy of leaving to top management the task of coping with problems as they arise. At the other extreme would be systematic institutionalization of the planning process. March and Simon (1958) contend that under the former policy the rate of innovation would be more sensitive to environmental changes, but that the average rate of innovation would be higher under a policy of institutionalization of innovation given a relatively stable environment.

Programed planning can be implemented through two auxiliary or staff functions, one to develop specific alternative courses of action for anticipated changes in the environment, the other to gather intelligence about environmental changes and reactions to organizational programs. Both these functions are generally combined in a single staff group, to the great neglect of the intelligence function. Guesswork replaces exact knowledge of environmental trends.

The planless extreme is currently illustrated by many universities and hospitals which lack a planning staff and have been overwhelmed by the tremendous increase in demand for their services (trends which everyone knew about but which were not anticipated in building or staffing programs). Many municipalities have been in the same situation, and have not planned for zoning, traffic, water, and sewage services. They are now paying the price for the old policy of day-to-day opportunism.

Partial programing for change, which emphasizes planning but eglects the intelligence function, is illustrated at the national level by ederal agencies concerned with foreign policy. The State Department nd the armed services are much more involved in action programs o meet enemy attacks than in systematic staff research and adequate ntelligence to feed information into the planning for future contin- encies.

Policy decisions concerning general procedures can profoundly ffect planning possibilities and planning decisions. Our governmental tructure at the local, county, state, and national levels is geared to perating on a fiscal budget for a single year. No governmental agency an legally make commitments beyond a twelve-month period. Con- ress is elected on a two-year basis and no congress can make fiscal lecisions legally binding on its successors. Informal arrangements have elped to bypass these restrictions on planning, but public account- bility in terms of yearly budgets is a severe handicap to planning olicy.

Two specific types of planning problems plague many organiza- ions in a technological society. One is the rapid growth of demand for ertain types of service, already suggested by the example of colleges and universities, of institutions providing medical care, and of munici- palities providing public service. If an organization is to double in size in a short period, it may have to change its essential character. Its policy makers need to face all the implications of such rapid growth and either attempt to control the growth or to make appropriate pro- visions for expansion so as to maintain the nature and quality of the organizational product. By failing to plan, they merely postpone prob- lems which will intensify and multiply over time. Individual problems sometimes disappear if we ignore them, but ignoring problems is a risky policy for an organization.

The other type of policy problem which technology creates is potential overproduction, the reverse of an expanding market. Produc- tive industries are confronted recurrently with capacities so well de- veloped that their full use would soon flood the available market. The steel industry in peacetime seldom runs at one hundred per cent of its capacity. Our agricultural productive capacities so far outrun the market that no governmental administration has been able to solve the problem of agricultural surpluses, even with subsidies to farmers for holding down production. The oil industry is threatened with the same type of problem.

The overexpansion in the primary and secondary industries, in contrast with the underexpansion of the tertiary industries of service, illustrates a third need in planning, the coordination of related subgroups in a society. Though the need for such coordination exists, ther is little evidence about the priority to be assigned it in relation to othe societal needs. Nor are there ready answers to questions concernin the extent to which such planning is socially desirable, the mecha nisms for achieving it, the types of decentralized structures whicl should be preserved and fostered, and the additional political device necessary for maximizing individual freedom in a bureaucratic world

THE DECISION-MAKING PROCESS

Organizational decisions of a policy-making character, though they may be more complex than decisions made outside organizations, are still made by individuals. Organizational procedures are set up to guard against the more common errors of individual judgment, and the latest development of this sort is the programming of the decision process for electronic computers. An adequate model for understanding policy-making must start with the individual and his many types of fallibility, but it must also take account of the collective situation in which executives function.

We shall follow the classical account of Dewey (1910) in describing four stages in the process of problem solution, and shall relate these stages to the way in which individuals function in an organizational context. We can distinguish among (1) immediate pressures on the decision maker (Dewey's old felt difficulty), (2) the analysis of the type of problem and its basic dimensions, (3) the search for alternative solutions, and (4) the consideration of the consequences of alternative solutions, including the anticipation of various types of postdecisional conflict and the final choice.

These stages in the process of reaching a decision are affected by (a) the nature of the problem, (b) the organizational context, (c) the basic personality characteristics of the policy maker, and (d) the cognitive limitations of human beings stemming both from situational and personality factors.

Not all policy decisions involve all four stages in any thoroughgoing sense. Immediate pressures may result in an immediate solution with little analysis of the problem, no search for alternative solutions, and little attempt to weigh the consequences. Or the analysis stage may be short-circuited and a great deal of attention conferred on the anticipation of certain possible types of consequences.

Immediate Pressures

The immediate forces which induce the felt difficulty may stem from the executive's own encounter with the problem, from the requests of others in the organization, or from demands made by individuals or groups outside the organization. The immediate pressures not only call attention to a problem; in many instances they also suggest a strategy of solution or even a specific solution. Thus the executive is confronted with demands which vary from "something has to be done" to "unless the salaries of our electronic engineers can be raised by thirty per cent we will lose at least half of these men."

Some of these pressures will develop as it becomes known that management is considering a change in policy. As the executive discusses the situation within and without the organization, he may find himself committed, or urged to become committed, to some of the views generated in these discussions. The strength of these pressures depends upon the power and influence of the group pushing for a given solution, the unanimity within the group, the clarity of their proposal, and often the degree of immediate personal contact. The lieutenants surrounding the executive may exert more influence than a powerful group of stockholders more remote in time and place.

Immediate pressures often seem so overriding to executives that they will accept some hasty solution and bypass a thorough analysis of the problem and a careful weighing of the likely major consequences of their action. The objective circumstances may be of such an emergency nature that decisive actions must be embarked upon immediately. Often, however, specific organizational pressures and personality considerations are responsible for decisions being reached without an adequate analysis of the problem or an intelligent assessment of the consequences. And action may give momentary relief to the decision-maker whether or not it really solves the problem. Sometimes the urgency is induced by the perception that hostile outside forces can be halted by organizational anticipation of their direction.

An example of a poor assessment of a problem and its consequences, made under such conditions of urgency, can be found in the actions of the Chancellor and the Board of Regents at a state university some years ago in a controversy over the loyalty oath for its faculty. These decision makers were faced with a possible witch hunt by a legislative committee. By imposing a special loyalty oath on all members of the faculty, the top university administration hoped to forestall the investigation and prevent more repressive measures from the state legislature. But they failed to analyze the nature of the problem and to anticipate the consequences of this decision. Though the immediate faculty revolt which ensued was squelched, the divisionism within the university community and the reaction of the academic and scientific world seriously damaged the university for a number of years.

In general, organizations develop policies and procedures for change which are designed to guard against such short-circuiting of the process of problem solution. Nevertheless, immediate pressures can lead to bypassing the necessary stages in problem solution, either through the creation of a feeling of urgency or through the heavy weighting given a particular course of action by the forces creating the pressure. In the example cited above, both factors were at work. It seemed to the policy makers important to anticipate legislative action, and it is probable that they were more concerned with placating reactionary elements in the legislature than with the morale of their own faculty.

Identification and Analysis of the Problem

The immediate pressures experienced by executives are not necessarily synonymous with the basic problem confronting the organization. The identification of the nature of the problem and an analysis of its dimensions may call for a different type of solution than that dictated by the immediate pressure. In an older period of our industrial history, management in many companies reacted to the threat of unionism by attempts to smash unions. The problem was identified in terms of the immediate pressures, namely the move by union organizers to organize a given plant. The basic problem of the need of workers for first-class citizenship in a structure affecting their lives was not recognized. The direct attempts to solve the problem by expelling the organizers, by force if necessary, and intimidating the workers were successful in some instances. By and large, however, efforts directed at such symptoms probably stimulated rather than hampered the growth of unionism in a democratic society.

One basic element in the analysis of difficulties confronting the decision maker has been suggested by Anatol Rapoport (1960), who distinguishes between *problems* and *dilemmas*. The problem type of difficulty is one which can be solved in the frame of reference suggested by its nature, by past precedents for dealing with it, or by the application of existing policy. A dilemma, on the other hand, is not soluble within the assumptions explicitly or implicitly contained in its presentation; it requires reformulation. Many types of mechanical puzzles or trick problems are dilemmas in this sense of the word. If we approach a puzzle with all our customary preconceptions about the nature of the problem, we can never solve it. We must abandon our habitual set and find a new way of looking at the puzzle. Policy makers in organizations encounter similar situations. While many organizational difficulties are problems of the variety which can be solved in their own erms of reference, other difficulties call for innovation in the very ormulation of the problem.

For example, the organizations seeking an end to racial discrimiation in the southern states faced the dilemma of achieving their egalitarian goals in areas where the local forces of law and order, as vell as other power structures, were arrayed against them. The strategy hey adopted was based on a novel conceptualization of the problem. They adopted the Gandhian philosophy of a vigorous but nonviolent oursuit of goals, and they envisaged their opponents not as enemies out as misguided people to whose ideals they could appeal. Their infringement of local laws of segregation in lunch rooms and in churches vas carried out peacefully and in a nonthreatening manner. When subected to violence, they reacted in a dignified, even Christlike fashion. Such strategy imposed difficulties upon the white local groups in favor of law and order, who had to choose between white hoodlums resorting o illegal violence and well-behaved Negroes quietly asserting their rights to be seated in a lunch room, or to kneel in a church.

The facts of organizational life often preclude the recognition of dilemmas and their requirements for a radical restructuring of the very basis of the problem. The decision maker at lower levels in the organization often lacks the power to reformulate the problem. It comes to him with the givens of previous policy decisions which he must accept. At top levels in the organization, there are also constraints upon the recognition of dilemmas and the development of innovative solutions. These constraints may come from the public upon which the organization depends or from other structures with which it is interdependent.

The organizational context is by definition a set of restrictions for focusing attention upon certain content areas and for narrowing the cognitive style to certain types of procedures. This is the inherent constraint. To call a social structure organized means that the degrees of freedom in the situation have been limited. Hence organizations often suffer from the failure to recognize the dilemma character of a situation and from blind persistence in sticking to terms of reference on the basis of which the problem is insoluble. Just as a person can persist in the same series of fruitless manipulations in trying to solve a mechanical puzzle, so too can management try a series of related efforts which are doomed to failure because the problem as conceived is insoluble.

For example, management may persevere in attempting to get a kind of dedication from its hourly employees which logically is to be expected only from first-class citizens in the organization. Managers may hope to do away with group norms restricting productivity or to imbue workers with a sense of organizational mission. They will try

new communication methods; they will single out certain men fo
rewards; they will give their foremen courses in human relations. Bu
none of these approaches goes outside the conventional manageria
frame of reference, the conception of employees as hourly worker
without tenure or prospects for major advancement, participating i
the labor but not in the legislation of organizational life. Nor has man
agement seriously considered what might be done to bring hourl
workers into first-class citizenship in the organization. In addition t
the situational constraints which prevent the decision maker fron
breaking out of the customary framework for the analysis of sucl
problems, there are more personal reasons for staying with the con
ventional assumptions.

The failure to distinguish between problems and dilemmas ca
take a curious reverse form. Under certain circumstances some execu
tives try to find an outlet for their creativity and innovative ability b
turning problems into dilemmas. Many problems easily capable o
solution in their own terms of reference are reformulated to admit o
novel solutions. Novelty and originality become values in their ow
right, whether or not they are appropriate to the organizational prob
lem. Some executives are bored by routine solutions to routine prob
lems, and their frustrated artistic creativity finds outlet in change fo
the sake of change, which is then rationalized as having virtue becaus
"it keeps the animals stirred up."

To aid in the analysis of problems and dilemmas, the organization
develops resources in its research and planning departments and in its
intelligence operations. Both the basic data and the interpretations of
their organizational implications are fed to top policy makers by
operational intelligence or by the research staff. Operational intelligence alone can be a weak informational reed because of the vested
interests which develop in the substructure. Hence it needs to be
checked by staff research and by outside experts. The executive in a
complex organization must utilize more than one system of information
so that he will not become a captive of one sector of his own organization.

Search for Solutions

The identification of a difficulty as a dilemma or as a problem will
determine the type of search conducted for an appropriate solution. If
there is recognition of the dilemma character of the situation facing
the organization, then the search will be directed in an imaginative
fashion toward all sorts of conceivable answers. If the difficulty is more
problemlike in character, the dictates of organizational precedent and
policy will determine the direction and limits of the search.

In general the search for a solution begins at the specific level of past precedent and may stop there if a satisfactory answer is found. If not, the search goes on to a more general level of existing policy, and perhaps to the most general statement of organizational purpose. In other words, the search proceeds on the principle of conservation of organizational and individual energy. Old policies will be redefined and sharpened before attempts are made to change them or to develop new policy.

Research and staff groups may be instructed to institute a search for desirable solutions but often the injunction is added that search be rapid and practical and not seek final answers. The urgency of immediate pressures as experienced by executives places limits upon the depth and breadth of the search process. During World War II psychologists were asked to devise selection procedures for various types of personnel, but could not be given time to develop the most valid instruments for such selection. They had to adapt available measures on the basis of educated guesswork, for scientifically constructed and validated instruments would have come too late to be of any use.

In the search process one of the first lines of inquiry is directed at the experience of other organizations with the same type of problem. A university president or dean will turn to the solutions reached by the leading universities in the country. The perplexed industrial executive will attempt to find out how executives in other companies are handling the same sort of problem confronting his organization. Political parties will copy each other's techniques, especially when they seem successful. In the absence of more thorough research on the organization's own problems, the experience of others is a natural type of resource to be utilized. Policymakers can of course be betrayed by slavish imitation of more illustrious organizations. They can fail to take account of the differences between their own situation and that of their model, and so misapply a solution. This is another way in which the emotional and intellectual attributes of leaders affect organizational decisions.

Anticipation of Consequences of Alternative Solutions

The policy maker facing a decision, pressured by his colleagues and by outside interests, and influenced by the staff analysis and their suggested solutions still must weigh the probable costs and gains of alternative courses of action. If he is at all close to the operational problems of his organization, his first consideration is likely to be in terms of the difficulties of getting the new plan to function. *Will it work* is often his first question, and this question does not mean: *Is this the best solution,* nor even, *is this a desirable solution,* but *can we put it into acceptable operation easily.* Considerations of the practical problems of implementing a plan, including the difficulties it may raise for the decision maker, may arise even before its potential value as a solution is weighed. Many good ideas may fail to get an adequate hearing because the obstacles to their implementation raise questions about their practicality.

The logical model of a four-stage process in reaching a decision, in which analysis of the problem and identification of alternative solutions precede a consideration of consequences for the organization, does not fit the actual sequence of many organizational decisions. Short-circuiting of various types may occur, including the dismissal of solutions without regard to their intrinsic merits, because they involve difficulties for administrators and hence are ruled impractical. Excellent long-run plans for the solution of organizational problems may be summarily dismissed on trivial grounds. If the merits of the plan as a solution are considered fully and found to be outstanding, means usually can be found for its practical implementation.

Considerations of practicality can also be underestimated, of course. The policy makers of some organizations are so remote from everyday operations that they make decisions in terms of desirable goals with little regard for their translation into practical operation. Top management may adopt a new safety plan for reducing accidents in its factories with no consideration for the psychological acceptance of the cumbersome equipment to be worn by workers or the troublesome routines to be followed. They find subsequently that, in spite of the cost of the program, no appreciable reduction in accidents has taken place. Or to take an example from recent history, our federal government took action to save China from the Communists by furnishing military aid to Chiang Kai-shek. But the decision was made at such a distance from the operational scene that it was not only impractical; it actually boomeranged, sending some of the aid into communist hands.

This then is one of the dilemmas of large-scale organizations. On the one hand, policy decisions cannot be made purely on the basis of their theoretical desirability. Such a tendency may occur when decision makers are at a great distance, in terms of experience and psychological understanding, from the area in which their decisions are to apply. Human intelligence and insight are not so godlike that they can divorce desirable ends from the concrete experiences for achieving them. On the other hand, the administrators closest to a problem are likely to overestimate the practical difficulties which loom large in their everyday mode of functioning. Their frequent answer to any radical plan for policy change or structural reorganization is to point out that the eggs are already scrambled. They argue that we are not starting *de novo* with the possibility of imposing a new blueprint for the organization. We are dealing with long established patterns and must work within this framework. This view leads to defeatism with respect to desirable policy change.

One solution to this organizational problem may be to bring together the top decision maker concerned with long-range objectives and the middle or lower level administrators with practical experience relevant to the alternative under consideration. This solution seems so simple and so obvious to the naive outsider that students of organizations have a difficult time in explaining why the complexities of organizational life so often prevent problem-solving activities across hierarchical lines.

An executive convinced of the desirability of a course of action but aware of the practical difficulties of launching it will often avoid the major issue and make the smaller decisions which lead to the outcome he is seeking. Franklin Roosevelt probably was committed in his own thinking to a war against the Axis powers long before Pearl Harbor. He realized, however, that a message to Congress to this effect would be premature. Hence he did everything in his power to support the Allies and to persuade Congress to give all possible aid short of war. His refusal to give the Japanese a free hand in the Far East helped to precipitate their attack on Pearl Harbor, and his instructions to the Navy to employ warlike tactics against German submarines helped to produce the German declaration of war when the Japanese called for help from their Axis partner.

Where the probability of success is fair and the gains for the organization outweigh the costs but slightly, the crucial factor in an executive decision may be the executive's own potential gains and losses. Policy makers are human; it is difficult for them to divorce their own fate from the fate of the organization, and there is more than a grain of truth in their equating of individual and organizational interests. The power and rewards of the executive grow as his organization prospers. Both personal and organizational factors enter into the judgmental process, and they tend to become fused. The legal doctrine of conflict of interest has been developed precisely because individuals do not easily divorce their own interests from those of the organization. The personal interests of the official cannot be relied upon to dictate the same type of decision as the interests of the organization. Any analytic scheme for identifying the forces involved in decision-making must take into account the ambitions and motives of the individual for his own career as well as his perceptions of systemic outcomes for the organization.

The consideration of the consequences of alternative solutions may be very restricted or may range widely through the sectors of organizational space and into the extraorganizational environment. Immediate pressures from outside may lead to a neglect of the probable effects of a course of action upon the internal structure. And the converse is also true. Side effects and long-range consequences may be difficult to assess. For example, the introduction of automation may have the direct consequences of increasing organizational efficiency and creating problems in the employment of displaced workers, and these effects may be carefully considered before the automation program is launched. The problems of moving to shift work because of the need to keep the expensive automated plant operating twenty-four hours a day are also likely to be foreseen. Consequences less direct and less likely to be foreseen might include problems of overproduction and the need for entering into industrywide agreements to alleviate it.

The executive will often be profoundly affected by his anticipation of the many postdecisional conflicts in which a policy action may place him. Janis (1959) has outlined a schematic balance sheet for dealing with the various types of factors affecting decisional conflicts. He calls attention to the utilitarian gains and losses, the social approval and disapproval, and the self-approval or disapproval which the decision maker may anticipate. These factors are affected by the conscious goals, the preconscious affective charge, and the unconscious charge which they have for the decision maker. The usual rational model of man is inadequate for describing policy-making in part because the executive's rational assessment of the objective merits of a proposal may be affected by his emotional forebodings about his own postdecisional conflicts.

The objective and complete assessment of probable consequences of a policy decision can be aided by research on a pretest of the contemplated change, on the resistance or readiness to change of various affected groups, or on some of the assumptions underlying the proposed change. The effective use of research for such purposes requires a commitment to long-range planning on the part of top management.

RATIONALITY AND ORGANIZATIONAL DECISION-MAKING

It is apparent that the evaluation process in reaching a decision on an organizational problem is not readily reduced to the total and simplistic rationality of the economic man. March and Simon (1958) have employed instead the concept of a bounded rationality or *the cognitive limits of rationality*, and have written cogently about the realities of organizational decision-making in these terms. There are always limitations with respect to knowledge of alternative courses of action, of the relative utility of these alternatives, and of the consequences of these courses of action. March and Simon reject the older model of rationality because it does not examine its own crucial premises.

The organizational and social environment in which the decision maker finds himself determines what consequences he will anticipate, what ones he will not; what alternatives he will consider, what ones he will ignore. In a theory of organization these variables cannot be treated as unexplained independent factors, but must themselves be determined and predicted by the theory . . . . Choice is always exercised with respect to a limited, approximate, simplified "model" of the real situation . . . the chooser's . . . "definition of the situation." (p. 130)

The complexities of the problems facing organizations are so great that the executive as a limited human being must attempt to deal with matters by simplifying the dimensions of the problem and the possible alternatives. He will seek to retain the major features of a problem without all of its complexities.

The simplifications have a number of characteristic features: (1) Optimizing is replaced by satisficing—the requirement that satisfactory levels of the criterion variables be attained. (2) Alternatives of action and consequences of action are discovered sequentially through search processes. (3) Repertories of action programs are developed by organizations and individuals, and these serve as the alternatives of choice in recurrent situations. (4) Each specific action program deals with a restricted range of situations and a restricted range of consequences. (5) Each action program is capable of being executed in semi-independence of the others—they are only loosely coupled together. (p. 169)

In other words, executives deal with problems in piecemeal fashion; they tend to handle one thing at a time, and they tend to follow an established repertory of programs for dealing with immediate problems. They do not consider all possibilities of problem solution because it is of the very nature of organizations to set limits beyond which rational alternatives cannot go. The organization represents the walls of the maze and, by and large, organizational decisions have to do with solving maze problems, not reconstructing the maze walls.

March and Simon carry their concept of bounded rationality into decisions of planning and innovation. They point out, for example, that theories of rational choice tend to ignore the distinction between deciding to continue existing programs and deciding to initiate new ones, and that such theories are particularly weak with respect to innovation. Rational theory might well predict more innovative change than actually occurs, because it would expect innovations to be adopted whenever their costs and organizational return compared favorably with those of present operations. Yet the chances are that this rational optimization is less likely than the maintenance of existing operations so long as they yield a satisfactory return.

These authors suggest also that the rational process followed by organizations in a search for programs to achieve organizational goals is not one of objective logic but of limited psycho-logic. Attention will be given first to the variables under control of the decision maker or his organization, and if this attempt is unsuccessful, then to variables not under organizational control. If this does not work, the criteria for a successful program will be reexamined with the possibility of relaxing them so that a satisfactory program can emerge. In other words, the ease of the administrator is an important consideration, and the assumption is that people will move toward a thorough and full exploration of all possibilities in terms of successive efforts from a series of frustrations. They will not usually move to a new stage of search and appraisal if they can work out some satisfactory adjustment at a prior stage. Objective rationality would call for full evaluation of all possibilities, limited only by the objective organizational costs of the search. Psychological rationality means the acceptance of the most immediate and painless solution.

Predisposing Factors in Decision-Making: Psychological Aspects of the Thought Process

A discussion of the cognitive limits of rationality would be incomplete without a more specific description of the psychological factors which determine the nature of the thought process. The human mind, though an amazingly complex apparatus for problem solving, operates according to known principles which make for fallible judgments. Seven such principles are discussed in the following pages.

Determination of Thought by Position in Social Space. It is a truism that we all stand somewhere in social space and time, and that our standards for judgment are accordingly affected. The ethnocentrism of the unugly American is paralleled by the ethnocentrism of the citizens of every nation.

Sherif (1936) has used the term community centrism to refer to more limited effects of social space, the effects of the norms of subgroups in a culture on values and frames of reference of group members. Similarly we need to take account of the system centrism of the members of any social organization; their position in organizational space will affect their knowledge, their experiences, their attitudes and their judgments. Such determination of thinking applies both to the information and knowledge people possess, and to their standards of judgment for evaluating that information. To the inhabitants of Britain a storm over the English Channel, disrupting communications, means that the Continent is isolated. We are all affected by national, class, and organization centrism to some degree; organizational leaders are particularly prone to system centrism, a tendency to evaluate everything from the frame of reference of their own organizational milieu. Drucker (1946) writes of this problem as follows:

The executive of a big business affects society by every one of his moves and is affected by it. Yet he inevitably lives in an artificial environment and almost as isolated as if he were in a monastery. This isolation is necessary. The executive of a big corporation—like the executive of any big organization—is too busy to see people except on business . . . . His contacts of people outside of business tend to be limited to people of the same set, if not to people working for the same organization. The demand that there be no competing outside interest and loyalty applies to the corporation executive as it does to the army officer. Hence, executive life not only breeds a parochialism of the imagination comparable to the "military mind" but places a considerable premium on it.

In our present-day society this isolation is emphasized far beyond the necessary. It is, for instance, made practically impossible for the corporation executive to find out anything about the ideas, concerns, approach and mentality of labor in his frequent contacts with union leaders—or for union leaders to find out anything about management and managers. For those two never meet except as antagonists trying to defeat each other. (p. 81)

The system centrism of the executive is prominent in his choice of subordinates and successors. As a result, the managements of some organizations come to resemble themselves more and more closely, a form of inbreeding which is likely to sap the vitality of the organization rather than to increase it.

The problem of system centrism applies to all organizational leaders, though some are more closed in their thinking than others. Some of Hitler's success stemmed from his ability to perceive the weaknesses in social structure of his own country as well as neighboring countries, and to act accordingly. On the other hand, he never could grasp some of the strategic concepts of a world conflict. He remained preoccupied with his landlocked armies in spite of the many attempts of his naval chief, Admiral Raeder, to brief him on the overall problems of naval strategy and of the dimensions of the world conflagration he had started. (Shirer, 1960)

Identification with Outside Reference Groups. The executive not only follows the norms of his own organizational family; he is also affected by outside groups with which he identifies. Such groups tend to be at his own level of power and status, or somewhat above it. The information and values of these outside groups are given more weight

than similar inputs from groups of lower status and power. The parochialism described above refers primarily to cognitive limitations due
to the executive's way of life. The process of identification refers to his
emotional ties with groups of the same or superior power to which he
turns and to which he may defer. There is rational justification for
giving full consideration to power groups, since they may be helpful
to the organization. The irrational element enters when they are consulted even though they have little to contribute in the way of knowledge or of other help, and when more lowly groups with relevant
knowledge are ignored.

In setting up programs for our various international policies, the
State Department has often ignored the people with field experience
abroad, both in its own staff and in other organizations. Instead it has
organized conferences of top industrialists, university presidents, and
other key leaders apparently chosen more for position than for relevant
experience and expertise. Many poor organizational decisions are made
on the basis of overweighting information from powerful and illustrious
sources irrelevant to the problem. It is a truism that organizational
leaders frequently make important policy decisions without obtaining
relevant information from within the organization.

The tendency toward selective perception through identification
with reference groups is exaggerated by the very nature of organized
group meetings. People are placed together in organizational space
and play similar roles. Hence they reinforce one another in maintaining
a common frame of reference toward problems. March and Simon
(1958) describe this process as follows:

> Within the organizational unit there is reinforcement through the *content
> of in-group communication*. Such communication affects the *focus of informa
> tion* and thereby increases subgoal persistence. The vast bulk of our knowl
> edge of fact is not gained through direct perception but through the
> second-hand, third-hand, and nth-hand reports of the perceptions of others
> transmitted through the channels of social communication. Since these per
> ceptions have already been filtered by one or more communicators, most of
> whom have frames of reference similar to our own, the reports are generally
> consonant with the filtered reports of our own perceptions, and serve to
> reinforce the latter. In organizations, two principal types of in-groups are of
> significance in filtering: in-groups with members in a particular organizationa
> unit, and in-groups with members in a common profession. Hence, we may
> distinguish *organizational* identifications and *professional* identifications
> There are others, of course, but empirically these appear to be the most
> significant.
> Finally, there is reinforcement through selective exposure to environ
> mental stimuli. The *division of labor in the organization* affects the informa
> tion that various members receive. This differentiation of information con

tributes to the differentiation of subgoals. Thus perceptions of the environment are biased even before they experience the filtering action of the frame of reference of the perceiver. Salesmen live in an environment of customers; company treasurers in an environment of bankers; each sees a quite distinct part of the world [Dearborn and Simon, 1958]. (pp. 152–153)

Division of labor and the restricted communication within subgroups narrows the focus of the information received. This leads to differentiation and persistence of subgoals, with a resultant narrowing of the focus of attention. Time pressures also contribute to restricting the focus of attention (Figure 9).

Projection of Attitudes and Values. Reciprocal to the process of identification is that of projection. In the former case, people see themselves as similar to those of greater prestige and power; in the latter, they see others as similar to themselves. Projection is the attribution to others of our own feelings and beliefs. The term is often used to describe the defense mechanism by which we project our own unrecognized faults and *id* impulses on to other people, in whom we can then attack these undesirable qualities. We are referring here, however, not to the unconscious mechanism for dealing with internal conflict but to the tendency to see other people as sharing our ideas and values.

When decision makers are not confronted directly by realities and objective research data are not introduced, they will often assume that groups within their own organization or outside their organization

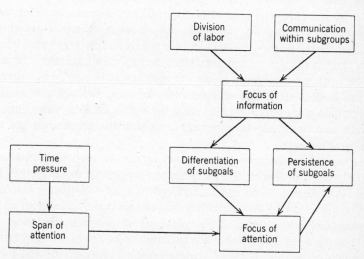

Figure 9 Some factors affecting selective attention to subgoals. (From *Organizations,* James G. March and Herbert A. Simon, New York: Wiley, 1958, p. 154.)

share the same values as they do. Heads of many industrial enterprises have often been surprised by the success of unionization among their own employees. They could see why unions might gain a footing in other companies, but, after all, they had treated their own workers very well and could see no reason for such employee defection. What they did not appreciate was that workers did not share their frame of reference about good treatment nor their beliefs about company objectives and policies. Attributing to others our own attitudes operates most freely in the absence of factual information about the psychology of other groups.

Global or Undifferentiated Thinking. Instead of grasping the many differentiations in the world about us, we move toward a simplified cognitive structuring of external realities. We tend to see other groups and other peoples as homogeneous entities.

The more remote the group in terms of psychological contact, the more we tend to regard it as an undifferentiated entity. We think of Russia as a communist nation and do not recognize the differentiations within that structure of its various ethnic groups and occupational groups, or the differences between party members and nonparty members.

Dichotomized Thinking. Another common form of simplification in human thought is to view the world in terms of opposing categories (good and evil, black and white, good guys and bad guys). The oversimplified dichotomy of free enterprise versus collectivism has led many of our industrial leaders to contradictory actions. Some of their decisions reflect their interdependence with other industrial structures; in other decisions they are moved by appeals to free enterprise which deny any collective or cooperative action. Our dichotomies of east versus west and communism versus democracy have long been resented by the leaders of nations who see themselves as belonging in neither camp. They are eastern in geography but not in alliance with China or Russia, and politically they belong in neither the communist nor the democratic camp.

Political leaders are especially vulnerable to such simplifications. They have to deal with the dichotomous aspects of social reality; the creation of issues which can be reduced to a for-and-against choice is their stock in trade. Moreover, they win or lose at the polls on an all-or-nothing basis. Yet many of the problems with which they deal are multidimensional and involve a continuum of positions. Having talked in dichotomous terms, these leaders become prisoners of their own propaganda. The present administration faces this dilemma with respect to the recognition of Red China and its admission to the United

Nations. To recognize and admit Red China would be regarded as a reversal of the anticommunist position of the last campaign and, even more important, might become the basis of charges in the next campaign that the Democrats were not vigorously anticommunist. Yet it is not possible to negotiate adequately in the arms race or in other important matters if one of the major parties to the negotiations is unrepresented at the conference table.

Cognitive Nearsightedness. People characteristically respond to the immediate, the visible, and the palpable and neglect the dimensions of the problem which are more remote in time and place. A concrete demonstration means more than the presentation of the scientific principles upon which it is based. The spatial and temporal frame of reference of human beings is limited. The immediate situation looms greater than problematic events several months removed. This immediacy has many advantages but it militates against a long-run, intelligent course of conduct. Successful organizational policy requires a larger frame of reference both spatially and temporally than comes readily to most people. This human limitation results in the overweighting of immediate pressures in organizational decision-making. Moreover, the leader who can free himself from cognitive myopia must face the further problem of persuading his shorter-sighted colleagues to support the implications of his vision.

Oversimplified Notions of Causation. In the analysis of organizational problems and in the assessment of alternative courses of action, decision makers must guard against the common fallible notions of causation. We tend to be animistic and to attribute causes to personal agencies. We tend to accept the exciting event as the major cause. We are given to faculty thinking or the tendency to attribute the cause of an observed action to a faculty for that activity on the part of the actor. Faculty thinking is thus a form of tautology which consists essentially of using a name or synonym to account for the process observed (as we think we have an explanation for a disease if we can find a name for it). We are frequently guilty also of linear thinking, in which we see only a one-way sequence of cause and effect, whereas we are really dealing with a cycle in which cause and effect are mutually interacting.

Most of these errors are forms of nondialectical thinking about the causal process. The dialectical approach of modern physics has departed from the class thinking of Aristotle, with its attribution of cause to the class of properties of which the object is an example, and with its assumption of simple and constant correlations between factors. The modern scientific approach is to view causation as an aspect of a mutually interacting field of forces. A given factor is not a constant but is influenced by the pattern in which it is found. The events in a field of forces are thus determined both by the elements in the field and by the structure of the field, i.e., the transformation of those elements resulting from their relationships.

Many problems of industrial management are incorrectly analyzed as a result of oversimplified notions of causation. The problem of informal restrictions of productivity is one example. The linear, simple-cause approach may attribute the restrictive standards to the work of a few agitators; a more sophisticated but still Aristotelian type of thinking will relate them to irrational fears of workers stemming from past and outmoded management practices of cutting rates. A more complex view, which sees such standards as a viable compromise between top management demands and worker needs, accepted by workers, by stewards, and by supervisors in immediate charge of operations, is rarely presented in the councils of management.

Factors in Decision-Making: Personality Determinants

In addition to the general cognitive limitations of human thinking, organizational decisions are affected by deep-seated orientations of personality, those attributes which individual decision makers bring with them because they are what they are.

The personality determinants of decision-making are overplayed by psychoanalysts and underplayed by social determinists. The psycho-analytic approach neglects the field in which the leader operates, the component of rationality in his thinking, and the fact that different substantive decisions can express the same personality need. Social determinists overlook the differing patterns within a broad trend of social events which a given personality can effect. Without the personality of Adolph Hitler the Weimar republic in Germany would in all probability have been replaced by a military autocracy, but the excesses of the Hitler regime might well have been avoided.

Social psychologists have asserted consistently that characteristics of personality act in combination with situational factors to cause behavior. Lewin's summary statement that behavior is a function of personality and environment has been reiterated almost to the point of banality. Like many worthy principles, however, this one has been honored in speech and neglected in deed. Few research studies have dealt simultaneously with situational and personality determinants of decisions and behavior. As such studies are conducted, we can expect that they will examine the relationship between the organizational situation and the consequent response, taking into account the variations in response among individuals in the same situation and explaining those variations in terms of individual personality. In other words, characteristics of personality will be treated as mediating or conditioning factors, which alter the relationship between organizational environment and individual response. The relevant dimensions of personality to be utilized for such purposes will depend in part upon the kinds of situations and the kinds of responses we wish to understand.

Among the more important personality dimensions of policy makers which may affect their decisions are: (1) their orientation to power versus their ideological orientation, (2) their emotionality versus their objectivity, (3) their creativity versus their conventional common sense, and (4) their action orientation versus their contemplative qualities.

Ideology versus Power Orientation. The extremes of this dimension are represented by the fanatic and the broker. The fanatic has internalized the ideology of the organization so thoroughly that he is constitutionally incapable of compromise. Any deviation from organizational objectives he sees as treason. Social movements are much more likely to have leaders of this type than are established formal organizations. The broker can work skillfully within different organizational frameworks. He is the politician less concerned with the platform of his party as a statement of compelling ideals for which he should work, and more given to the practical realities of getting elected and staying in power. He could serve either political party, and it is an accident or a pragmatic choice that he represents one rather than the other.

Few organizational leaders are pure types, either crusading warriors for their ideas or power-actuated political manipulators. Most decision makers represent combinations of these value orientations, and often view practical compromises to achieve power as a way of achieving their ideological goals. How much they salvage of their ideology after they take office, and how much they can rationalize any behavior which promises personal success are the significant questions to ask.

The head of a state university must make some concessions to popular pressures and political forces in his state, but he must also be firm in his allegiance to some basic educational goals or he may damage his institution seriously. The leaders of political parties are often under great pressure to consider only the power factors in their decisions and to neglect ideological considerations. Nonetheless, the popular notion of the political leader as a pure power type is often wrong because it takes into account only those decisions motivated by expediency and gives no weight to more idealistically motivated decisions. Woodrow Wilson persisted in his espousal of the League of Nations despite its growing unpopularity in political circles. Margaret Chase Smith deserted her party to attack Senator McCarthy when such action was tantamount to political suicide (as was demonstrated in the case of Senator Benton). And six Congressmen were courageous enough to vote against an appropriation for the continuance of the House Committee on un-American Activities in 1960.

An organization dominated by power-driven leaders will find its policy decisions moving in the direction of the survival and aggrandizement of those leaders rather than toward its healthy development. There may be times when the power interests of leaders and the organizational welfare coincide, but this coincidence is often short-lived. The question to be answered is how permanent are the contributions of the leader to the organization; what is left for the structure when he has moved on.

A company may have a remarkable executive whose brilliant rise in the company structure is accompanied by new organizational developments which are part of his own empire. He moves on to a larger rival organization and leaves behind nothing of substantial benefit to the organization. The correlation between the motivational orientation of leaders and their organizational contribution is less than perfect, but it is positive. The educators who have left a permanent effect upon their institutions, such as Eliot and the elective system at Harvard, Wilson and the preceptorial system at Princeton, Hutchins and the great-books approach at Chicago, have all been men with definite ideological orientations.

Emotionality versus Objectivity. As Janis (1959) points out, there are two types of emotionality which may affect organizational leaders and the objectivity of their judgments. One is the load of preconscious affectivity, the emotional impulses which can move into the conscious sphere; the other stems from deeper defensive needs of which the individual has no awareness. The second would consist both of chronic emotional biases and of momentary emotional impulses.

Janis cites a number of decisions of President Truman which were apparently based upon his immediate, conscious emotional arousal; for example, when he dismissed General MacArthur in part because he became angered by a MacArthur press release in open defiance of administration policy. Defensive needs refer to weaknesses in basic character structure which are such a threat to the ego that they are not consciously recognized by the person but nevertheless overdetermine his behavior. Time after time in World War II Hitler made military decisions reflecting his need for the strength of a superman. Armies, though outflanked, were never to withdraw but were to fight to the death. The Germans suffered unnecessary losses on the Russian front, in Egypt, and finally on the western front because decisions were made not only on the basis of objective military strategy and tactics, but also on the basis of Hitler's unconscious needs to avoid any display of weakness.

Defensive needs can operate at any stage of the problem-solving process. They can block out or distort the analysis of the problem, or the assessment of consequences, or they can overweight a given type of solution. Experimentation has demonstrated the intervention of defense mechanisms even in the perception of incoming information. Threatening and unpleasant facts are often denied, ignored, or distorted. The organizational executive whose defensiveness results in his avoiding certain types of unpleasant information may be reinforced in his blindness by subordinates who keep such facts from him.

One great weakness in an autocratic structure is that defense mechanisms among its top leaders will receive institutional support rather than correction. Subordinates protect their own positions by screening facts to accord with the emotional biases of the chief. The whole institutional environment may become modified to confirm the pathological tendencies of the men on the top. The realities of the immediate social environment are ordinarily a good check on fictitious views of the universe and delusional systems. But in the autocratic organization so modified, social realities now reinforce fictions, false perceptions, and erroneous beliefs. Criteria for the evaluation of organizational performance will be avoided under these circumstances, because they threaten the present comfortable way of life of the authorities by intruding with objective facts. Its leaders become incapable of changing policy, and unless these leaders can be replaced, the organization faces disaster. Any organization which is unable to adapt to environmental forces will be destroyed by them. Even democratic organizations are not wholly exempt from such problems. They do, however, have the advantages of internal criticism and of provision for orderly change of leaders after a specified term.

Creativity versus Common Sense. People differ not only in general intelligence (Spearman's g factor), but in two rather contrasting types of ability. Some individuals are gifted in originality; they are able to see new relationships and to impose new structure upon old facts. Others may have marked ability in making common-sense judgments requiring the assessment of many relevant factors and accurate prediction of likely outcomes. Though not logically antithetical, these two abilities do not often occur in the same person. The idea man, by virtue of his enthusiasm, originality, and creativity, does not examine his flow of ideas with searching criticism. Such an attitude would inhibit his creativity. On the other hand, the person seeking to make a balanced judgment and concerned with giving the appropriate weight to competing plausible notions is unlikely to produce a new solution. Occasionally, the two abilities are combined in a person who can move from a phase of creativity to a phase of criticism.

In general, organizational policy-making is in the hands of the men of good judgment, rather than men of creativity. The executive of good judgment can take on subordinates to perform the innovative function. The creative executive can supplement his talent by surrounding himself with men of good sense but he still has the problem of making the final judgment. It is understandable, then, that the most original minds in any organization are rarely found in top executive positions. The complexities of organizational life with its many conflicting demands on executives mean that critical and judgmental abilities are the essential requirement at this level.

Action Orientation versus Contemplation. Another personality characteristic relevant to organizational functioning is the capacity for action, the ability to act upon judgments. Many people have excellent ideas; not nearly as many translate their ideas or even their decisions into the required implementing actions. Most of us make that translation and write what the group dynamicists have called the action paragraph, only under the compulsion of the situation. As a result the opportunity for action is sometimes lost entirely.

German generals had plotted to overthrow Hitler long before the outbreak of World War II. Hitler was successful, however, in getting rid of the men of action, and the rest lacked that decisive quality of personality so necessary for a successful coup. Hitler himself possessed this quality of immediately moving to decisive action, and it contributed heavily to his meteoric rise and to the early success of German arms. While others talked and debated or reached intellectual decisions, Hitler acted. Moreover, his pace of action was always ahead of his opponents' gait. Information was often available to his enemies in advance of his moves, but it did not seem to help them. The Norwegian government knew of the impending invasion but moved with incredible slowness compared to the pace of the German attack.

INDIVIDUAL AND ORGANIZATIONAL FLEXIBILITY: SYSTEMIC CHECKS ON IRRATIONALITY

We have discussed the psychological basis of the cognitive boundedness which March and Simon (1958) find in organizational decision-making. Devices are built into organizations to facilitate the rational solution of problems in spite of personal limitations. These devices may not work perfectly nor do they necessarily work in all situations. Moreover, they entail certain recognized and unrecognized costs. Nonetheless, they help in the prevention of error and they avoid risks as the organization plays "percentage ball."

Specific procedures and general programs have been developed in many organizations to counter immediate pressures in problem-solving, to insure more penetrating analysis of problems, to increase the search for alternative courses of action, and to assess more adequately the utility functions of such alternative courses. Automation and the use of computers will strengthen this development. Thus far the contribution of the computer is most easily appreciated in the fields of memory and of complex calculation. The fallibilities of human memory are well known and they often affect decision-making. The computer has a perfect memory not only for specific items of information stored within it, but for the weights assigned to these items in relation to their significance for outcomes. It can perform in fantastically rapid fashion complex computations about courses of action and, for certain types of problems, can actually test alternative solutions in experimental settings.

The process of casting organizational problems into the language of the computer is itself an exercise in the direction of rationality. The creation of a decision-making program requires that one be very clear about the variables and parameters to be taken into account, the sequence or priority with which different criteria of decision-making are to be invoked, and the process of inference by which decisions are to be made. The procedure requires the elimination of undefined terms, and builds in complete stability from one decision-making situation to another. In short, *if* the essential data and procedures for decision-making can be programmed, many of the erratic and fallible elements in organizational decisions are eliminated.

General procedures for protecting against some types of individual and organizational fallibility can be formulated and used whether or not they are programmed into computers. The following practices are often employed by organizations for this purpose.

Checks against Immediate Pressures

Formal periods of waiting or deliberation are often required before decisions can be made with respect to policy changes. In many legislative systems, policy proposals cannot be voted upon during the meeting at which they are introduced. In many organizations, proposals involving constitutional revision or other fundamental change must receive more than the usual majority of votes in order to be enacted. This device also gives the system more time to consider the new plan. Rules of this sort prevent precipitous action and provide the organization with the opportunity to get more information and to consider the matter more fully. Delay also gives some realistic measure of the strength of the pressures for change, which may dissipate over time or become more powerful.

Devices to Increase the Adequacy of Search Procedures

A major limitation in the search for solutions is the restricted cognitive range of the policy maker, whose views must be influenced in some degree by his position in social space and by his reference groups. A common device to overcome this limitation is the use of the expert both within and without the organization. Though this is not a sovereign remedy, it does help to achieve an objective, fact-finding orientation in the search for solutions and to broaden the courses of action under consideration. A major error in the use of experts is the lack of precise identification by the organization of relevant experts. A psychiatrist, for example, may have expertise in the treatment of individual patients, but his specialized knowledge of neuroses may have little relevance to the problems of worker disaffection with organizational policies. The calling in of experts requires some discrimination with respect to fields of knowledge and the source of experience and research in these fields.

A second error in the use of experts is to call in men who are so similar to the executive in experience and point of view that they can only give the illusion of broadening the search for alternatives. Consultants from a conservative school of business administration, with a staff recruited from the business world, are more able to offer social support to management than new ideas. The research scientist may offend management with his unconventional views and his inability to act or talk like a businessman. And yet it is this very difference in point of view that can make him valuable; if management merely wanted a playback of its own selections and cognitive style, there would be no point in calling in the outside expert.

Another device to broaden the search for solutions is to take advantage of direct experience, to seek out people who have been in direct contact with the problem. These people may be in other organizations or they may be in the organization considering the problem. They may not always have good answers or their answers may already be available to the policy makers. It is surprising, however, to find that in large complex structures people who are most knowledgeable and most directly involved in a problem are often not consulted.

A related device is to make sure that problem-solving suggestions are obtained from more than one subsystem in the total structure. Search procedures (not necessarily the final decision-making choice) should cut across organizational lines both horizontally and vertically, and policy can require that they do so.

Devices for Evaluating Alternative Solutions

The use of computers provides a ready mechanism for evaluating courses of action, provided that data are available for putting the computers to work. They can of course generate some of their own data, but usually research is required to provide original data.

A significant step in the direction of rational evaluation is taken when organizational procedure calls for advance quantitative specifications in terms of which alternative solutions will be evaluated, and provides resources for obtaining data to make such evaluations. There has been considerable development of such procedures with respect to materials, products, and machines, but relatively little recognition of the potential contribution of quantitative measurement to the human aspects of organization. And yet the human factor within and without the organization is no less important when choosing among solutions.

Another requirement for improving the evaluation of different solutions is some provision for considering side effects. Though it is difficult to anticipate side effects, which are by definition the unintended consequences of an action, there are two frames of reference which can be invoked. One is the temporal frame, in which consideration is given to how the plan will operate in six months, a year, or even several years from the time of its initiation. Another framework is that of the socio-technical nature of the organization. If the new policy is to change the social-psychological patterning of the system, then the effects upon technical processes and task accomplishment should be considered. In fact, this is commonly done. But the converse is not; the impact of a change in the technical system is not necessarily evaluated in terms of its effect upon the social system. In assessing the effects of technical change upon the social system, attention should be directed at the people in the subsystem for whom the technical innovations produce the greatest movement and disturbance.

The possibility of such procedures and the greater resources of organizations make possible more rationality in system decision-making than in individual decision-making. The great gains in productive enterprise and collective services furnished by large-scale organizations are due in part to the greater rationality of such system decision-making. There are, however, occasions when decision-making in systems can be more irrational than individual decision-making.

The system multiplies the characteristic strengths and weaknesses of human beings and can fragment their moral responsibility. The defense mechanism which handicaps the individual in his social adjustment may have powerful social effects when reinforced in an organizational setting. The colossal irrationality of the Third German Reich in the extermination of allegedly inferior racial groups illustrates horribly this phenomenon of the exaggerated error in organizations. Similarly, wars are system decisions which in an age of nuclear weapons represent the height of irrationality.

The decision-making of organizations may be highly rational within the frame of reference of the objectives of the particular organization, but these objectives may be so irrational in larger terms that the net result is systemic and human destruction. As individuals, some people like alcohol enough to make health problems for themselves; others are not affected by their casual drinking, and still others do not drink. If we organized ourselves into a group dedicated to the pursuit and use of alcohol, we could bring about a greater amount of physical and personality deterioration in a shorter space of time. Organizations are more efficient than individuals, whether concerned with good or evil, sense or nonsense.

SUMMARY

An organizational policy is an abstraction or generalization about organizational behavior, at a level which has structural implications for the organization. Such generalizations can be made retrospectively, as recognitions of existing practice; the more interesting process, however, is policy-*making*, the making of general statements of what organizational behavior shall be. The making of policy in this sense is at once a category of decision-making, an aspect of organizational change, and perhaps the most significant expression of leadership.

Organizational decisions can be characterized on three dimensions: level of generality or abstraction, amount of organizational space affected, and duration. Two major categories of policy-making are proposed, based upon these dimensions: the formulation of organizational goals and objectives, and the formulation of strategies and procedures for achieving and assessing progress toward such goals.

The formulation of organizational goals includes sharpening and clarifying present organizational purposes, adding new objectives or relinquishing old ones, shifting priorities among objectives, and altering the major mission of the organization. Examples of all these policy-making activities are considered. Least in evidence are major shifts in organizational mission, which are opposed by all the stability-seeking machinery of the organization itself.

That form of policy-making which deals with strategy and the assessment of performance in relation to accepted goals involves somewhat different activities. These include the development of criteria for decision-making, and the development of feedback measures which provide information about the adequacy of present organizational functioning. Feedback measures in principle can be constructed around any internal organizational process and around any continuing transaction between an organization and its environment. In practice these potentialities for guiding data are little developed. Only cost accounting, sales, profitability, and growth are in general use as feedback mechanisms established and maintained as matters of policy. The limitations of these devices are considered, particularly under conditions of rapid and continuing technological change.

To define policy-making as a category of decision-making raises very general questions about how decisions are made, what situational factors affect the making of them, and what inherent limitations in rational decision processes are implied by the nature of human beings as decision-makers. The latter sections of the chapter deal with these issues. Decision-making is described in terms of four stages, in accordance with the schema first proposed by John Dewey. In sequence these include immediate pressure or felt difficulty experienced by the decision-maker, analysis of the presenting problem and its basic dimensions, search for alternative solutions, and consideration of the consequences of these alternatives.

In any specific instance movement through these stages and the decisional outcome itself will be affected by the nature of the problem, the organizational context, the personality characteristics of the decision-makers, and the cognitive limitations of human beings. These include the determination of thought processes by position in social space, identification with outside reference groups, projection of one's own values and attitudes, the tendency toward undifferentiated or dichotomized thinking and toward cognitive nearsightedness, and the reliance on oversimplified notions of causality. The chapter concludes with a review of several systemic checks on such tendencies which can be built into formal organizations.

11
Leadership

The concept of leadership has an ambiguous status in organizational practice, as it does in organizational theory. In practice, management appears to be of two minds about the exercise of leadership. Many jobs are so specified in content and method that within very broad limits differences among individuals become irrelevant, and acts of leadership are regarded as gratuitous at best, and at worst insubordinate. Nevertheless, management typically responds to instances of organizational success by rewarding the formal leader, and to instances of organizational failure by blaming the person so designated. There is an almost universal assumption that even a small subpart of an organization can operate successfully only if some person has been formally designated as leader. Difficult assignments are often awarded with the injunction to "make it work," a kind of implicit recognition that something more than the formal prescriptions of organization is required for the system to function successfully. Managerial practice acknowledges to some extent the needs of the organizational system for continuing creative elaboration, revision, and improvisation; and management expects every member of the organization to exercise such creativity on occasion—some more than others, according to their position in the structure.

Organizational theory is no less ambivalent. Many people who have studied organizations intensively explain organizational effectiveness and survival primarily in terms of the behavior of formal leaders. McGregor (1960) and Likert (1961) provide recent and notable examples of this approach. On the other hand, March and Simon (1958) wrote a major book on formal organization in which the word *leadership* appears neither in the table of contents nor in the index.

Among social scientists who emphasize the concept of leadership there is no close agreement on conceptual definition or even on the theoretical significance of leadership processes. On the one hand, the great-man school views history as the study of biography. The Protestant reformation is the story of Luther, of Calvin, and of Zwingli; the French revolution, the story of Voltaire, Robespierre, Danton, and Napoleon; and our own period, the tale of Hitler, Roosevelt, Churchill, Stalin, and Gandhi. On the other hand, the cultural determinists see history in terms of social patterns relatively unaffected by the intervention of leaders. In the recent past several writers have acknowledged this unsatisfactory state of affairs and have attempted to make sense of the differences by proposing some schema or paradigm which encompasses them (Gibb, 1954; Bass, 1960; Stogdill, 1959; Cartwright and Zander, 1960; Tannenbaum, Weschler, and Massarik, 1961).

Leadership appears in social science literature with three major meanings: as the attribute of a position, as the characteristic of a person, and as a category of behavior. To be a foreman is to occupy a position of leadership, and to be a company president is to occupy a position of greater leadership. Yet it may be said that a certain foreman exercises considerable leadership, and that the presidents of some companies exercise very little. Moreover, leadership is a relational concept implying two terms: the influencing agent and the persons influenced. Without followers there can be no leader. Hence, leadership conceived of as an ability is a slippery concept, since it depends too much on properties of the situation and of the people to be "led." If the powerfully leading foreman were catapulted into the president's office, would his leadership abilities still be manifest? And if he could not lead as president, what would have become of his leadership abilities?

One common approach to the definition of leadership is to equate it with the differential exertion of influence. Thus we would not speak of a leader in a group of people all of whom were equally effective or ineffective in influencing one another in all areas of the group's functioning. Even where one individual has more effect upon his fellows than another, we do not ordinarily speak of his leadership if the effect derives almost entirely from his position in the social structure rather than from his special utilization of that position. The sergeant who passes along the order "forward march" when the whole company is on the move is close to the zero end of the continuum of leadership. The same sergeant, however, in charge of his platoon in combat may deploy them effectively and energize them to hold their position against odds. His behavior would then fall far toward the positive end of the leadership continuum. This is not to equate leadership with the exertion of influence at the informal level (which would rule out acts of institutional leadership). We maintain that leadership does occur in formal structures, and indeed that every act of influence on a matter of organizational relevance is in some degree an act of leadership. To the extent that such influential acts are prescribed for certain positions in the organization, even the routine functioning of the role system involves acts of leadership.

When we think of leadership in contrast to routine role performance, however, we become particularly interested in the kinds of individual behavior which go beyond required performance and realize more fully the potential of a given position for organizational influence. In other words, *we consider the essence of organizational leadership to be the influential increment over and above mechanical compliance with the routine directives of the organization.* Such an influential increment derives from the fact that human beings rather than computers are in positions of authority and power.

With respect to the legitimate power of office and the rewards and sanctions which go with it, all supervisors at a given level in the hierarchy are created equal. They do not, however, remain equal. Some of them are much more knowledgeable about the technical aspects of production than others; some have a better understanding of organization. Some have a better understanding of people, and the character traits of some are more acceptable to superiors and subordinates. French and Raven (1959) have suggested five types of power: legitimate power, reward power, punishment power, referent power, and expert power. (Referent power refers to influence based upon liking or identification with another person.)

The organization does provide equal legitimate power to all supervisors at the same level and the same access to the use of organizational rewards and punishments. But one supervisor may utilize his legitimate power in appropriate and telling ways to maximize his influence in the structure, whereas another may fail conspicuously to use the organizational structure to get the job done. Such differences are cryptically summarized (and exaggerated) in the old dictum, "You can't delegate power." Moreover, both the particular utilization of legitimate power and the actions of the supervisor outside his use of formal power have a marked effect upon his referent power, i.e., his influence based upon the affection and respect people accord him.

A person's expertise in technical matters and in organizational lore also provide increased acceptance of his suggestions and directives. Neither referent power nor expert power can be readily conferred by the organization and yet both are important in getting organizational work done. Even the appropriate use of legitimate power cannot be spelled out in the organization rule book for the higher and more complex officer positions. Detail, contingencies, and ramifications make such efforts self-defeating.

The concept of influential increment has relevance for organizational effectiveness in several ways. First, expert and referent power, to the extent that they develop within a group, represent additions to the power available from the organizationally given stock of rewards and punishments and from the legitimizing acceptance of organizational policies. There is literally an increase in the total amount of control which such a group can exert over its members, and this has been shown to be a persistent factor in increased organizational performance (Tannenbaum, 1962).

Secondly, expert and referent power can be substituted for other bases of power. As substitutes for power based on punishment especially, expert and referent power are relatively free of unintended and undesirable organizational consequences. The man who complies for fear of punishment plans and longs for the day when he can escape or overpower the person whom he obeys. The man who complies for external rewards is likely to ponder how he can obtain the reward without the circuitous and strenuous business of compliance. Even legitimate power, if unaccompanied by referent and expert power may produce a sullen and grudging performance. To the extent that referent and expert power are substitutable for, or can be added to these other bases, they offer clear organizational advantages. The whole human relations emphasis in organizational leadership can be thought of as an attempt to promote referent power in addition to, and to some extent instead of, power based on rewards, punishments, and the acceptance of organizational law. Likert's (1961) *new patterns,* McGregor's (1960) *theory Y,* and Argyris's (1962) *interpersonal competence* have this emphasis in common.

Finally, referent and expert power represent potential additions to total organizational control and effectiveness because they are available to all members of the organization. They depend much more on personal and group properties than on the formal definition of organizational roles. They can be utilized by peers as well as by supervisors and formal leaders. Peer influence has been shown in many situations to be more readily accepted than influence from organizational superiors, and as such has a unique contribution to make to organizational effectiveness.

The Need for Leadership

We may ask why an organization, once it has attained a state of maturity, has any requirement for leaders, leadership, and influential increments. Does not the exertion of influence in the organization automatically flow from its structural properties rather than from the particular people who happen to be the role incumbents in the officer echelons? Why will the organizational system not roll on unchanged and unchanging in social space?

There are several answers to this question, including the necessary imperfections and incompleteness of the organization as a formal, abstract design; the changing external conditions under which every organization must operate; the changing internal state of the organization produced by separate dynamics of the several substructures of the organization; and finally, the special characteristics of human beings as occupants of organizational positions and fillers of organizational roles.

The Incompleteness of Organizational Design. The characteristic incompleteness and imperfection of organizational design is obvious whenever the organization chart and charter or the written policies of the organization are compared with the ongoing cycles of behavior which define the pattern of the "real" organization. For one thing, the actual behavior is infinitely more complex, inclusive, and variable than the plan. Everyone knows this. The new worker, after receiving from the personnel division the official version of his job and the policies which will affect his life, is brought to the group with which he will be working. His first concern is to learn from the other members of the group how "things are really done," the unwritten but all-important facts of organizational life.

Another, and equally familiar, evidence of the insufficiency of the formal organizational plan is provided by a form of legal insubordination and sabotage which is occasionally employed by organization members. It consists merely in following the letter of organizational law, doing what is formally stipulated, but no more nor less. The jokes and comedies which present this theme in the military and in industry are numberless, and no audience misunderstands them.

Earl Brooks * describes an episode which is a vivid example of such behavior. In the course of a study which he was doing of a railroad, he spent some time one afternoon observing and interviewing a man in a switching tower, who was separating and recombining trains of freight cars. The electrical controls and relays were so worn that they failed to slow the cars appropriately, and the violence with which they coupled led the researcher to inquire whether the cargo might not be seriously damaged. The switchman agreed that it might. "And shouldn't some of the equipment be replaced?" continued the researcher. The switchman agreed that it ought. "Then," said the researcher, "why don't you tell the regional office about it?"

* Personal communication to authors.

The switchman's reply was oblique. "About how hot would you say it was in this tower?"

"It must be over 100," said the researcher, looking at the afternoon sun beating in the west bank of windows, "but what has that got to do with it?"

"I've been trying for six months to get a Venetian blind for that window," said the switchman. "They told me that my job was to switch trains, and they would make decisions about equipment. When they get around to that blind, I may get around to telling them about the relays in those braking controls."

Changing Environmental Conditions. A second source of the organizational requirement for leadership stems from the openness of the organization as a system, and from the fact that it functions in a changing environment. Every open system is affected by the environment in which it functions and with which it engages in energic exchange. Since this environment is subject to technological, legal, cultural, climatic, and many other kinds of change, the organization is characteristically confronted with demands that it change, too, in order to maintain its relationship with the environment or establish a new one on the terms now available. Thus a systemic state or environmental relationship which was optimal initially may become inefficient or completely unfeasible.

The history of organizations (and of nations) is littered with the corpses of enterprises which failed to respond appropriately to the demands of the environment for change. The required changes may stem from market fluctuations, or from long-term alterations in technology or culture which make a whole product obsolete. The Studebaker organization began as a manufacturer of wagons. Early in the century it changed to the manufacture of automobiles, in response to signs that the demand for wagons was vanishing without prospect of return. Such an event could hardly have been anticipated when the organization was founded, and decisions of such magnitude are typically unpredicted. As a result, there is nothing in the built-in stabilizing devices of organization for coping with change demands of this magnitude, as the more recent history of the company has demonstrated.

Many aspects of the relationship of organization to environment are well represented in Lewin's (1951) concept of quasi-stationary equilibrium. It is consistent with Lewin's exposition of such equilibria that environmental fluctuations of certain kinds and amplitudes are handled by the organization without any change in the organization itself as a system. It absorbs and adjusts to the external change and returns to the previous level of equilibrium. When an environmental change exceeds this amplitude, the organization may nevertheless adjust to it, but it will undergo systemic change itself in the process and a new level of equilibrium will be established with the environment. It is adaptation of such scale which demands invention and creativity beyond the performance of role requirements; it requires leadership of a high order.

The Internal Dynamics of Organization. A third source of developing organizational imbalance and consequent need for system change stems from the internal dynamics of organizations as systems. At the level of the organization as a whole, one of the most important tendencies is the growth dynamic. Organizations as open systems show characteristic striving to insure survival by extending their sovereignty over those parts of the outside world which impinge on them. Those who have the greatest stake in the organization seek to secure it as a system. Yet this effort, paradoxically enough, leads to demands for organizational change. When an organization extends its control over the environment, new functions are added within the organization itself; new complexities of structure are created to provide for these functions; new needs for coordination with existing structures arise, and new policies must be invented.

At the level of organizational substructures, the internal tendency toward imbalance (and recovery) can also be observed. We have noted earlier the different dynamics of the several subsystems which make up the organization as a whole. (See Chapter 4.) For example, the efficiency dynamic of the production structure is in some opposition to the characteristic attempts of the maintenance structure to bind members into the organization and prevent them from leaving. A characteristic observation by production men is that the people in the personnel department would "give away the front gate" if they were not prevented from doing so by wiser heads, that is, by members of a substructure dedicated to a different organizational subgoal and permeated by a different dynamic (immediate efficiency in the productive process).

The result of such internal differences and organizational tendencies is not merely a continuing need for coordination and adjudication. It is persisting organizational change, internally and in relation to the environment, and a consequent need for additional complementary changes, in order to achieve a new balance and working structure.

The Nature of Human Membership in Organizations. A fourth and final reason why organizations, once launched, do not continue to spin unmodified in social space lies in the nature of human membership in organizations. The energic cycles which constitute organizational life are not free-floating, but of human origin and human embodiment. The organization is an open system with respect to its human maintenance aspects as well as to its production inputs. From this fact stem several characteristics of organizations, all of which mitigate against the maintenance of equilibrium without structural modification.

Only people can be members of an organization, but people are not only members of organizations, and above all not members of only one organization. Human membership in an organization is segmental in nature; it involves only a part of the person. Other activities and affiliations fill his other hours, make demands on his energies, gratify his needs. These extraorganizational and other-organizational aspects of his life affect the behavior of the person in the organization which employs him, and changes in these aspects of his life produce changes in his behavior on the job. If such changes disrupt the organizational patterns of required behavior, they will necessitate some kind of complementary and adaptive change within the organization (modifications in rewards, penalties, and work content, for example).

We can also view the requirements for organizational change introduced by members of the organization in terms of individual change and development. People mature, age, and otherwise assimilate the continuing experience of living. In so doing they undergo changes in the pattern and intensity of their needs, motives, and characteristic responses. Each such change has organizational ramifications and represents a kind of extraorganizational source of demand which cannot be wholly predicted from organizational properties.

Closely related to such changes is the inevitable wearing out of the human part. Every organization member must be replaced at some time, and every replacement brings to the organizational role his unique experience and personality. Despite attempts to define organizational roles in such a way as to minimize the effects of turnover and replacement, these effects persist. Especially in the complex, demanding, and maximally influential roles in organization will the formal prescriptions necessarily stop short of the needed behavior and the unique attributes of the person effect ramifying organizational changes.

When the president of a large company retires and his successor is about to be named, what interest is generated over the specialty from which the new man will come! This is a rational concern, a recognition that a former salesman will have a concept of the job and of the organization different from that of a former engineer or accountant. In some degree every event of departure and replacement has its effects and requires adaptation on the part of the organization as well as the person who accedes to office.

Still another way in which the segmental nature of organizational membership is encountered is as a lack of fit between the role requirements and the needs of the person. Responses to such a situation are various. If the person has low influence within the organization and few alternatives for need gratification (including the getting of a living for himself and his family), he may comply with the demands of the organizational role at almost any cost to himself and others with whom he affiliates. If his situation is stronger within the organization, his needs and motives become an internal force toward organizational change.

For all these reasons (systemic incompleteness of the formal organization, changing external conditions, the diverse dynamics of organizational subsystems, and the segmental nature of organizational membership) the organization functions under continuing demands for systemic change and under the continuing necessity of motivating the behavior required of its human members. Tools, machinery, equipment, the nonhuman components of organization, share with the human components a kind of mortality. They too wear out and must be replaced. But their specifications render them truly interchangeable; mass production was impossible until this condition was achieved. The processes of teaching and learning the organizational role, of mutual accommodation, and the property of performing only when motivated are peculiarly human. Much of leadership has to do with these processes and properties.

THE NATURE OF ORGANIZATIONAL LEADERSHIP

A consideration of the nature of organizational functioning clearly shows the sources of demand for leadership practices and the degrees of freedom for their exercise. In fact, organizational leadership, like other cases of the exertion of influence in complex social settings, is always a combined function of social structural factors and of the particular characteristics of the individuals making up the structure. And yet, social-psychological literature has been strangely silent in describing the operation of leadership processes in the real social world, i.e., within social systems; the literature of leadership has a disembodied, nonorganizational quality.

Three basic types of leadership behavior occur in organizational settings: (1) the introduction of structural change, or policy formulation, (2) the interpolation of structure, i.e., piecing out the incompleteness of existing formal structure, or improvisation, and (3) the use of structure formally provided to keep the organization in motion and in effective operation, or administration.

The origination of structure, or the initiation of structural change, is the most challenging of all organizational tasks and rarely occurs without strong pressures outside the organization. Changes in market and competition can necessitate such changes. Selznick (1957) describes well the conversion of the Ford organization from the Model T to the Model A. This organizational change was a grudging and delayed response to a disastrous decline in sales. Retooling was extensive; whole factory interiors were altered as the huge single-purpose machines of the Model T era were removed. Turnover was tremendous; the conversion required eighteen months and cost (in 1927) $100,000,000. In Selznick's view, the changes in human organization continued for a decade and a half, and only during the period of World War II did the Ford Company complete a reorganization in depth. Such changes in the formal structure of organization, the addition or elimination of major departments and the like, are easily observed.

Less apparent, and continuous rather than occasional, is the piecing out or interpolation of the existing formal structure. Every statement of organizational policy is by definition general and every problem is in some aspects unique. As a result, the formal structure of organization must be continuously and creatively embellished or pieced out. Every supervisor functions within the limits of formal policy, but within these limits he adds and improvises. For example, during World War II, sergeants in the United States Army were notorious for their skill in developing their own structures for supplementing, bypassing, or cutting through bureaucratic procedures for getting a job done. Such improvisation of structure is a second organizational means for preventing systemic failure.

Third, there is the use of already existing structure, the response of the organization as a system to some potential disruption which has been so fully foreseen that the corrective mechanisms and procedures are prescribed and built into the organization. This is the category of acts which are often seen as so institutionalized as to require little if any leadership. Nevertheless, existing organizational devices can be employed with varying degrees of frequency and intensity, with degrees of consistency and inconsistency, and with degrees of appropriateness to differing situations. Such differential uses of available organizational means will have consequences for the behavior and attitudes of rank-and-file members relevant to organizational functioning and thus constitute acts of leadership.

Every instance of leadership involves the use, interpolation, or origination of organizational structure to influence others. When people are influenced to engage in organizationally relevant behavior, leadership has occurred. When no such attempt at influence is made, there has been no leadership. We are not content to know, however, when the definition of leadership has been met. We want to know whether the influence transactions of leadership, when they occur, have the effects which the leader intended. We want also to compare the effectiveness of different acts and styles of leadership, and of different persons as leaders.

The effectiveness of any act of leadership must be assessed in terms of some specific criterion of organizational functioning; for example, growth rate, ability to attract members, efficiency in use of resources, gross productivity, and the like. (See Chapters 6 and 12). Under most circumstances, leadership acts which are maximally effective for some of these criteria are less effective for others. For example, national policy during World War II subordinated efficiency to gross productivity. In the more contemporary international competition for space exploration, we make the same value judgment, and would condemn as shortsighted and overcautious a leadership which weighted efficient use of resources more heavily than gross accomplishment.

Moreover, the effects of an act of leadership must be stipulated not only with respect to specific criteria of organizational functioning, but also with respect to some specific period of time. The short-range effects of harshness and threats may be compliance; in the long run the major effect may be an organizational inability to maintain staff. Thus, for any specified criterion and period of time, the effects of an act of leadership can be measured in quantitative terms, and may assume values which are positive, negative, or zero. The "overall" effect of a leadership act on the organization is a meaningful phrase only insofar as the criteria of organizational functioning to be included in the overall index and the relative weight of each criterion have been previously stated. Such actual effects can always be compared to the effects intended by the actor. Each act of leadership in an organization can have both intended and unintended effects, and both types of outcomes should be assessed.

PATTERNS OF ORGANIZATIONAL LEADERSHIP
AND HIERARCHICAL POSITION

The distribution of leadership acts is by no means random. Some positions (offices) are defined very largely in terms of expectations involving such influential acts. The presidency of a company is an example, and so is the office of first-level supervisor. The exercise of leadership by persons who occupy such positions is facilitated by the organizational resources (rewards, punishments) which are made available to them, and above all by the power of legitimacy, the implicit contract which each member makes to accept influence in prescribed matters from designated "leaders." The distribution of information in organizations follows a similar pattern, so that positions designated formally as offices of leadership receive information that increases the expertise of the occupants relative to those they are expected to lead.

There is a relationship between the three patterns of leadership we have described and the hierarchical levels of positions in the organization. Except in democratically constituted systems, only the top echelons of line and staff officers are really in a position to introduce changes in structure. The piecing out of structure is found most often in the intermediate levels of the organization. And the lowest supervisory level has open to it mainly the exercise of leadership by the skillful use of existing structure. In other words, the degree of freedom to supplement existing structure is not as great at the lowest officer level as it is at the second and third levels of command. And the freedom to originate, eliminate, and change organizational structure is not as extensive at the intermediate as at the top levels. It is true, of course, that the top level can exercise all three patterns of leadership, so that as we ascend the hierarchy we find more types of action available to the officer groups.

The exercise of these three patterns of organizational leadership also calls for different cognitive styles, different degrees and types of knowledge, and different affective characteristics. Hence the leadership skills appropriate to one level of the organization may be irrelevant or even dysfunctional at another level. The consistent and equitable employment of devices characteristic of the good administrator at the lowest level may be of little use to the policy maker at the top level.

This observation is congruent with the existing literature on personal factors associated with leadership. Personality traits related to leadership in one situation will not necessarily be predictive of leadership in other situations (Stogdill, 1948; Gibb, 1947). The logic of this relational approach, although proposed in the past (Likert, 1958), has not been extended to organizations. We shall turn then to a more careful examination of the cognitive and affective requirements of the three patterns of organizational leadership. (See Table 2.)

COGNITIVE AND AFFECTIVE REQUIREMENTS OF THE THREE PATTERNS OF ORGANIZATIONAL LEADERSHIP

In general, our attempt to show some of the differences between the cognitive orientation and the affective style of the leader is congruent with the experimental findings that the two basic dimensions of the leader-follower relationship are task direction and socio-emotional supportiveness. In studying groups without formal leaders, Bales

Table 2 LEADERSHIP PATTERNS, THEIR LOCUS IN THE ORGANIZATION AND THEIR SKILL REQUIREMENTS

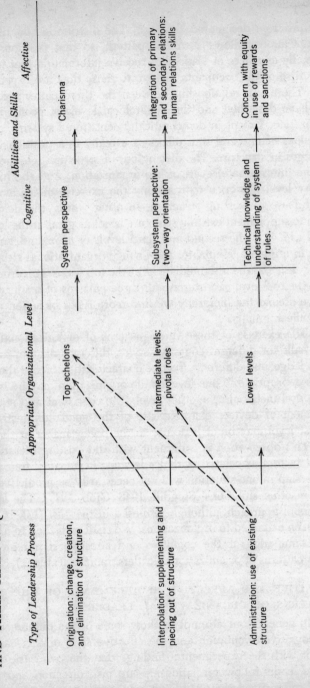

Type of Leadership Process	Appropriate Organizational Level	Cognitive	Affective
		Abilities and Skills	
Origination: change, creation, and elimination of structure	Top echelons	System perspective	Charisma
Interpolation: supplementing and piecing out of structure	Intermediate levels: pivotal roles	Subsystem perspective: two-way orientation	Integration of primary and secondary relations: human relations skills
Administration: use of existing structure	Lower levels	Technical knowledge and understanding of system of rules.	Concern with equity in use of rewards and sanctions

(1958) found that these two functions of progress toward the task goal and social support for members of the group invariably appeared, sometimes in the person of a single leader, but more often in separate people. Carter (1949, 1950, 1951) and other experimenters have confirmed these results. Moreover, Fiedler's (1958) enigmatic finding that the socially distant leader is more effective is readily understandable if his research investigations are scrutinized in terms of these two dimensions. In organized groups his task-directed and socially distant leaders were influential provided that the supportive function was handled by other means or through other leaders. In describing the methods of leadership associated with our three basic patterns, we shall examine first the cognitive or more task-oriented skill requirements, and second the appropriate affective orientation of the leader in relation to his followers.

Origination: Change, Creation, and Elimination of Structure

The major cognitive requirement for the origination or modification of organizational structure is *systemic perspective* and the major affective requirement is *charisma*.

Systemic Perspective. We have in mind two aspects of systemic perspective. One of these is external perspective, and has to do primarily with the complex which we may call organization-in-environment. We have earlier defined an organization as an ongoing, open system, in a state of dynamic equilibrium with its environment. This environment is made up in part of other organizations (agencies of government, competing organizations, labor unions, and the like) and in part of individual persons. Everyone who has lived the organizational life has experienced the differences among individuals in their ability to see, conceptualize, appraise, predict, and understand the demands and opportunities posed to the organization by its environment. Yet the intellective aspect of leadership has been neglected in research. Persuasiveness, warmth, and interpersonal skills are frequently urged as the essentials of leadership, but to what end? If a leader is seriously mistaken about the systemic requirements of his organization or the demands of its environment, his interpersonal abilities may become organizational liabilities. To use an already overworked example, the Ford executive who pressed for the manufacture of the large and expensive Edsel when the public was waiting for the more compact and economical Falcon, was *wrong*, and to be wrong and influential is organizationally worse than being merely wrong. It is better to be wrong and beloved than wrong and hated to boot, but interpersonal skill and organizational perspective are different attributes of leadership and largely independent of each other.

External perspective is thus in part a sensitivity to environmental demands, to the requirements which the organization must meet in order to maintain a state of equilibrium with its environment. In part external perspective involves a sensitivity to environmental opportunities, to the possibilities of achieving a more advantageous relationship with the environment. Finally, external perspective requires sensitivity to trends and changes in the environment, which is characteristically in a state of movement both with respect to the demands it makes on organizations and the opportunities it affords to them.

To some extent, then, external perspective is a matter of obtaining information about the organizational environment. At least as important, however, is the understanding of environmental factors, the successful relating of facts in the environment to facts about the organization. This process in turn permits forecasting the probable effects of different courses of action and consequent choosing among them. The formal leader of the organization or any subpart of the organization is, of course, not the sole source of external perspective. Indeed, he may depend heavily on others in the organizational unit for achieving it. In this his interpersonal skills will be of crucial importance, and in this sense interpersonal skills may substitute in part for direct information and understanding of the organizational environment. The basic requirement for external perspective remains, nevertheless, and the importance of such perspective increases as one ascends the hierarchy of organization. Mann (1964), whose trilogy of technical, interpersonal, and conceptual skills emphasizes some of the same points as our discussion of system perspective, has proposed that in the upper managerial levels the conceptual abilities of the manager considerably overshadow in importance his technical skills and his skills in human relations.

In most organizations a review of the major executive decisions of any year makes immediately apparent the importance of external perspective. The decision to merge or to resist merger, to make a major change in location or to maintain a present position, to launch an entirely new line of products or to stay with the traditional items, to be the first with a new manufacturing process or to wait until others attempt it—these are the kinds of issues which demand the greatest understanding of the environment on the part of management. They are the kinds of issues also which will make the difference between successful and unsuccessful competition, between growth and stagnation, survival and failure. Lack of such perspective has led once successful companies to persist in the production of conventional washing machines when the whole market was about to become automatic, or to persist in the use of slow and elegant letterpress printing when the techniques of photo-offset were about to create entire new markets.

It is, of course, easy to speak of the organization in relation to its environment when such appraisals are made in retrospect. The test of external perspective is the ability to make appraisals on a predictive basis. This predictive test cannot be rejected by the leadership of any organization. To reject it is to fail it, and in the long run every leadership group is judged by the criterion of external perspective.

The concept of internal system perspective is analogous in many ways to the notion of external perspective. Every organization, itself a system, consists in turn of subsystems. These subsystems have different needs, and the people in them manifest characteristically different kinds of strivings. It is an unavoidable function of leadership to attempt to integrate and harmonize these subsystem differences; indeed, coordination and control of subsystems are essential functions of the managerial subsystem as described in Chapter 3. To perform these functions successfully requires constant awareness and perceptiveness of the changing requirements of the subsystems and their populations.

Consider, for example, the production structure and the ancillary structures of a typical business organization (sales, engineering, personnel, and others). It is inherent in the conditions of the private market and in the division of labor represented within the organization that these subsystems shall have somewhat different needs and goals. Thus the manufacturing division judges a product design very largely on the efficiencies of production it permits. The sales division, on the other hand, is in direct touch with the consuming public and will be more concerned with meeting the preferences of consumers than with conforming to production requirements about which its members are likely to be very little informed. For the management which must integrate the different strivings of these and other subsystems, interpersonal skills are useful, but somewhat more than interpersonal skills is required. The management will be more effective if it understands the dynamics, needs, and potential of these subsystems, and if it can express that understanding in terms of organizational structure. Interpersonal abilities may help management to get the appropriate data into its hands, but this function is additional to and separable from internal perspective on the nature of the system.

The leader with systemic perspective about the internal functioning and the external relations of his organization understands the nature of the symbols and values both of the larger organization and of its subsystems. Many of these symbolic values are associated with sacred prerogatives such as the right to manage in industry or academic freedom within a university. Effective leadership takes account of these symbols and avoids their arousal when dealing with issues internal to the organization. Threats to symbolic values can lead to bitter conflict between parts of the organization. Hence the wise course is to deal with the practical realities and skirt the symbolic issues. The organizational statesman avoids ideological struggles within the system, except as a last resort. Such conflicts are not only divisive, but are difficult to mediate and lasting in their effects. Issues of practical interest can be handled more readily through compromise and negotiation. This avoidance of symbolic struggle, however, refers only to feuds within the organization. The values of the system may be involved effectively in mobilizing the structure against the outside world.

Among theorists of leadership, the importance of systemic perspective, external and internal, has been best recognized and explicated by Selznick (1957). It is at the heart of his distinction between institutional leadership and mere administrative efficiency.

For Selznick, the institutional leader is the unique possessor of system perspective, and it is this quality which distinguishes him from the leader who is merely an interpersonal adept. The institutional leader is concerned with policies as well as with persons; he is concerned with content as well as with process. He is concerned, as Selznick puts it, with the dynamic adaptation of the total organization to its own internal strivings and to its external pressures. There may be only two or three decisions in the course of a year which demand perspective on this level, but Selznick argues that they are crucial, and that their quality is quite independent of the human relations skills of the manager and of the psychological glamor which he may possess. These are decisions which insure the survival of the organization and avoid unintended corruption of organizational aims. Management which is unable to rise to the challenge of such decisions retreats either to technology or to the uninformed practice of human relations. By contrast, Selznick argues, the leadership which deals successfully with the dynamic adaptation of the total organization to internal striving and external pressures is alone truly creative. It is, in his terms, "beyond efficiency." Such leadership is characterized by "an institutional embodiment of purpose, by a clear definition of organizational mission, and by the adaptation of organizational policy to take into account the achievement of that mission in the context of the conditions presented by the environment and by the internal life of the organization."

The Subordination of Structure. One measure of systemic perspective is the ability of the management to act on such perspective, to change the organizational clientele, its own personnel, or its policy if the demands of the environment require these things. In terms of the three basic functions of leadership which we described earlier—the use, interpolation, and origination of structure—the emphasis of effective leadership is away from the unvarying use of existing structure and toward the origination of structure. Such leadership manifests the ability to change in response to external demands for change. To put it another way, the subordination of structure means that leaders assert freedom from the requirements of existing structure; they propose to use structure for the achievement of organizational goals, rather than to be used by it.

Perhaps the outstanding example of the subordination of structure in our time was provided by Franklin Delano Roosevelt. His creation of new agencies of government produced an alphabet of bureaucracy and became a joke in the hands of his friends and enemies. The central truth, however, was that the government was taking on new functions, especially during the early years of the New Deal, and that it had an overwhelming mandate to do so. To have attempted the accomplishment of these functions entirely within existing structures of government would have been extremely difficult, given the background and ideologies of the old-line government agencies. It was far wiser to permit the old-line agencies to remain in their mausoleums while new agencies of government, lodged in temporary quarters of all sorts, got on with the new and crucial jobs.

We are not advocating the subordination of structure as an unvarying good in the practice of leadership. We are asserting that one mark of effective leadership is the ability to subordinate structure when situational requirements are clear and popular support is adequate. The subordination of structure, in other words, is the behavior which flows reasonably from an adequate attainment of system perspective. Even Franklin Roosevelt, whom we have proposed as an effective exemplar of this principle, on occasion found himself on the wrong side of the boundary between a structural change which was needed and wanted and one which was inadequately supported. It is difficult to select political examples which are beyond controversy, but it seems likely that the enlargement of the Supreme Court can serve as a case where Roosevelt's subordination of structure may have been questionable in terms of support if not in terms of organizational necessity.

The importance of what we have called subordination of structure —a willingness to interpolate, alter, and originate structure—can be highlighted by imagining an organization led by people with the complete inability to make structures subordinate to the needs and mission of the organization. Such a leadership group would be destined forever to use the structure of the organization only as they had inherited it. The inability to alter and originate structure is perhaps an inconspicuous disease of leadership. Indeed, on most days the failure to subordinate structure to organizational needs would be superficially unobservable, and the leadership group might appear competent and blameless. Nevertheless, in the long run the disease is absolutely and certainly fatal to organizations.

As with other aspects of effective leadership, the importance of the ability to subordinate structure varies with the echelon of leadership. It is of particular importance at the apex of the organization. It varies also with the stability of the organizational environment and with the stage of the organization in its total life cycle. During periods of rapid environmental change or rapid development of the organization itself, the ability to modify and originate structure is of the greatest importance. During times of environmental stability and organizational maturity, the requirements for structural subordination will be minimal.

Charisma. Even the top organizational leader, with his possession of legitimate power and his control of rewards and sanctions, can mobilize more support for his policies if he can generate charisma, that magical aura with which people sometimes endow their leaders (Weber, 1947). Charisma derives from people's emotional needs and from the dramatic events associated with the exercise of leadership. The critical period of a war and the dependence of people upon their military leaders is productive of charisma. In less strenuous times bold and imaginative acts of leadership help to create a charismatic image of the leader.

Charisma is not the objective assessment by followers of the leader's ability to meet their specific needs. It is a means by which people abdicate responsibility for any consistent, tough-minded evaluation of the outcome of specific policies. They put their trust in their leader, who will somehow manage to take care of things. Charisma requires some psychological distance between leader and follower. The immediate superior exists in the work-a-day world of constant objective feedback and evaluation. He is very human and very fallible, and his immediate subordinates cannot build an aura of magic about him. But the leader in the top echelons of an organization is sufficiently distant from the membership to make a simplified and magical image possible. Thus between the upper echelons of a system and its rank-and-file membership there may develop an emotional tie which is not accessible to the lower echelons of supervision.

The formulation of policy and the origination of structure represent the kind of leadership acts most appropriate to charismatic leadership. The great majority of people are not in a position to evaluate proposals for major organizational change in any detail. They may or may not want to see social changes, and they may be sound in their judgment of overall goals, but they will not often be knowledgeable about specific programs to attain these goals. Hence they will turn to the great man whose character, strength, and skill give assurance that he will handle the problem.

This charismatic idealizing of the remote general in contrast to the realistic evaluation of the top sergeant does not mean that the top leader has only to emphasize his distance from his followers in order to achieve charisma. On the contrary, to achieve maximum emotional identification the leader must have what Brown (1936) called membership character in the group he is leading. He must be like his followers in some readily perceptible ways so that a common bond can be formed.

Adlai Stevenson had charisma only for the intellectuals who could identify with him, whereas Eisenhower, for all his military honors, talked and acted in his television appearances like the common man. But the charismatic leader not only must provide a shared emotion between himself and his followers, he must also rise above them in some quality of greatness so that identification will permit them to participate vicariously in some of his greatness.

Interpolation: Supplementing and Piecing Out of Structure

Origination of organizational structure refers to policy changes directly affecting formal structure. Interpolation or piecing out of structure refers to the development of ways and means for implementing existing policies and reaching existing organizational goals. As we leave the first line of supervision and move into the intermediate level of a hierarchy, we find that managerial roles often prescribe objectives without specifying every detail of the route to the objectives. Even where there is considerable prescription of the means, alternative courses are sometimes possible.

The critical task of the intermediate levels of management is to piece out the organizational structure, or guide subordinates to do so, in ways which optimize organizational functioning. On the cognitive side this involves some degree of internal system perspective, specifically technical know-how about tasks of the relevant subsystems and knowledge of their relationships with immediately adjacent subsystems. In terms of affective orientation, the basic requirement is the ability to integrate primary and secondary relationships. This type of orientation has been associated with human relations skills. The difficulty with the human relations concept, however, is that it is frequently used without reference to an organizational context. It does require some skill in human relations for a supervisor to become a father figure to female employees, and such a relationship can be therapeutic in part for both parties. These facts do not in themselves imply organizational value; the relationship may be irrelevant for organizational functioning or may even impair organizational effectiveness. In referring to human relations skills we shall assume an organizational context and organizational goals and shall be mainly concerned with the integration of primary and secondary patterns, i.e., personal relationships and role-prescribed relationships.

Subsystem Perspective: Two-Way Orientation of Leader. The middle ranges of management, to develop supplementary structure successfully, must face two ways in the organization. They must understand how those above them are likely to act because of their organizational position and how those below them are similarly motivated and limited by their placement in organizational space.

The area of freedom open to the middle management operator is neither as broad as his superiors sometimes define it, nor as narrow as they view it when something goes wrong. He must understand the functioning of his subsystem and its contribution to the larger organization, so that he can work out the appropriate degrees of freedom for his operations. If his division is counted upon heavily to raise productivity and he gets results in these terms, he is not likely to meet with much censuring from above even if he pieces out existing structure in new and unconventional ways. Another important criterion in setting the degrees of freedom for middle management is the avoidance of organizational embarrassment with the outside world. This criterion is more difficult of assessment and generally has lower priority than getting results. A football coach is likely to be more concerned with winning games than with the possible unfavorable image of his university arising from overzealous recruiting practices or questionable procedures for keeping his men eligible.

In addition to assessing the area in which his superiors will permit movement, the middle manager must face toward the people below him. He must depend upon subordinates for the efficient accomplishment of the subsystem task, and modifications in structure must be acceptable to them. The echelons above may not inquire into tough and repressive measures, for example, but the astute middle level officer will realize that such procedures are better for tightening existing organizational structure than for elaboration and improvisation. If he seeks the productive advantages of reform rather than the tightening of controls, he needs the ingenuity and sustained extra effort of those below him. Such behavior is not easily elicited by external pressure but flows from internalized motivations.

Another aspect of the two-way role of the middle manager is his function of representing the needs of the people below him to his superiors. In the first Michigan study of the Detroit Edison Company, Pelz (1951) found that supervisors following good human relations practices had no better morale and motivation in their units than supervisors following less desirable practices. When Pelz examined the supervisors in terms of their effectiveness in representing their men up the line, and controlled on this factor, then the anticipated correlation between worker morale and good supervisory relations was clear. The man in the middle, to be effective, must realize that he is in the middle and must relate effectively in both directions. Likert (1961) has emphasized the significance of this principle and has made it one of the foundation stones of his theory of management. According to this theory, every member of the organization, except at the very highest and lowest levels, should act as a linking pin between two levels of the organizational structure.

Our observations about the intermediate levels of management have been made in part by other writers about the first level supervisor, the man in the middle between the officers and the workers. Often, however, in large organizations the real men in the middle stand higher in the organizational structure. The first level supervisor in many firms has too restricted an area of freedom to supplement structure or to deal effectively with superiors. We are directing our analysis to the levels in the organization where the major emphasis in role definition is on objectives rather than upon the means for accomplishing objectives—in Morse's terms, the pivotal organizational roles (1956). In some companies, of course, this will take us to first level foremen.

Integration of Primary and Secondary Relationships. The essence of good human relations practices in an organizational context is the integration of primary and secondary relationships, and the integration of the primary group with the larger secondary structure. Where such integration occurs, the norms of the work group are congruent with the norms of the organization, the paths for organizational success are the paths for individual achievement, and the organizational requirements are in themselves productive of member satisfaction, rather than an indirect means to such satisfaction. Obviously these achievements have little to do with such superficialities as calling men by their first names or remembering the birthdays of workers' children. Let us define more closely what we mean by primary and secondary relations and consider their significance in organizational life.

Secondary relations in an organization are those interpersonal transactions required by organizational role. For example, the division of labor in most organizations makes the creation of the organizational product a highly coordinated, sequential business. The polisher in a washing machine factory cannot proceed with his task until the grinder has smoothed the aluminum casting and handed it on. The grinder must wait for the shake-out man, who knocks off some of the larger protuberances and disposes of the debris of molding and casting.

For each pair of roles so related, there are formal prescriptions in terms of which the interdependence is defined. This is equally true for formal leaders (foremen, supervisors, managers, and the like) and the people under their supervision. The relationship is defined by the prescriptions of the supervisory role and each complementary subordinate role. Typically the job description of the supervisory role will state the content areas in which the supervisor is to have jurisdiction over the subordinate, the activities which he will supervise, and the means (rewards and sanctions) by which his legitimate authority may be enhanced. The subordinate is given complementary information; the supervisor's legitimate rights appear as the subordinate's obligations. Such secondary relationships are in large part the stuff of which formal organizations are constructed; the properties of each office are defined in part in terms of obligations, expectations, and rights in respect to other offices. These relationships tend to be rational when viewed in the frame of reference of the defining organizational cycle of input-transformation-output and the intended organizational product.

Secondary relationships tend also to be universalistic rather than particularistic. The organizational presumption is that any occupant of a given office will be treated like all others who might occupy that office or similar ones. The military here, as in so many other respects, epitomizes the bureaucratic characteristic: salute the uniform, not the man. The supervisor who violates the universalistic aspect of role relations in organizations is accused of playing favorites, or worse. As for the subordinate whose behavior toward the supervisor becomes particularistic, there is a whole vocabulary—largely unprintable—in terms of which his colleagues characterize him, his behavior, and his relation to the supervisor.

Perhaps the most telling property of the secondary relationship is its alleged affect-free quality. The common assumption of organizational theory is that the role relationships in organizations imply no fear or delight in interdependence, no pleasure in giving rewards, no hatred in receiving punishment. In our institutional society this aspect of human relationships is carried to extremes. The executioner is not required or expected to feel for the criminal either hatred or sympathy. His job is to pull the switch. Even the making of war partakes of the bureaucratic transformation. It was not required of the pilot over Hiroshima that he hate the Japanese nor even the then government of Japan. It was his job to drop the bomb, a role. Indeed, when the pilot of that historic aircraft later found himself severely ridden with guilt, he was considered to be neurotically incapacitated.

The providing of help is no less transformed. We create roles and even entire social agencies to provide economic assistance, without any implication of affective bonds between helpers and helped, nor among those engaged in the common task of providing assistance. It must be said that the perfection of organizational role-taking as rationalistic, universalistic, and affect-free is more to be found in organizational theory than in organizational practice, and fortunately so. Nevertheless, practice and theory agree in this area to some extent. It follows from this definition of the secondary role relationship that the motivation for engaging in such relationships must be largely instrumental (for example, to earn wages) and not primarily intrinsic to the relationship. Indeed, the development of personally meaningful relationships in the work situation (significantly designated "informal") is a kind of triumph over bureaucratic requirements.

Primary relationships involve direct face-to-face interaction rather than remote organizational connections. They tend to be person-specific (particularistic) rather than universalistic, and they are affectively connected rather than rationalistically role-related. The relationships within families or among friends provide examples of what we mean by primary. In such cases the motivation to sustain the relationship is largely intrinsic to the activities jointly engaged in and the personal satisfactions derived therefrom.

The dichotomy between primary and secondary relationships, however, is a conceptual distinction which though useful is less than clear in the life situation. All roles are in some degree segmental, asking only a part of the person (part of his time, part of his skills, part of his interests). But people, despite their ability to compartmentalize and despite the schizoid character of modern life, are not essentially segmental. In a physical sense the segment of the person corresponding to his job role cannot report for organizational duty. The whole person is either present or absent, and with his physical self necessarily arrive all his psychological properties, potentialities, and uniquenesses. Organizations (as systems of rational-legal authority) operate specifically by controlling and reducing that variability of human behavior which directly expresses idiosyncratic motives and needs.

The inherent conflict between individual needs and organizational requirements is handled in part by emphasizing the separation of the requirements of organizational roles from the nonrole motives of affective, moral, or other origin. The vocabulary of bureaucracy is rich with the disavowals of primary motives in secondary relationships. "Nothing personal, but . . . . " "I am sorry to have to do this, but . . . . " "Business is business." "I have my job to do too, you know." The common meaning of these and similar expressions is: your primary needs are about to be disregarded. As we have said, the separation of primary from secondary relationships works in part. Some people even resent in organizational life the invoking of values which they would approve outside. Outside the organization, for example, we do not necessarily consider it immoral that a person should be given some special financial assistance simply because he needs it, nor that we should behave differently toward people according to the affection which we bear toward them.

Even in formal organizational roles, however, people respond affectively to support and approval, as they do to punishment and restriction. Their behavior in role therefore is always a mix of role-determined and other-determined characteristics. We have already noted that a persistent characteristic of effective leadership is the use of referent power, a kind of power which depends upon a bond of liking and respect (primary relationship) and which is not a role-given characteristic.

There is ample evidence also that informal relationships in the work situation may be powerful enough to enhance greatly the performance of the organization or to impede substantially its ability to accomplish the formal mission. The classic and perhaps the first quantitative demonstration of this phenomenon was provided by Roethlisberger and Dickson (1939) in the course of experiments at the Western Electric Company. They found systematic, group-determined restriction of individual production in the manufacture of telephone equipment, a type of finding which has often been corroborated in the subsequent research literature. (Coch and French, 1948; French and Zander, 1949; Dubin, 1951; Viteles, 1953; Whyte, 1955; Argyris, 1957).

Roethlisberger and his colleagues also discovered at Western Electric an outstanding example of informal group structure acting to enhance production. Under a variety of physical circumstances the experimental groups at the Hawthorne Plant showed increases in pro-

ductivity which were at first baffling but were ultimately interpreted
as an experimental side-effect of great importance. The tendency of
experimentally chosen groups to show heightened morale and productivity has come to be referred to as the Hawthorne effect, and is certainly one of the best known findings of social science.* In the years
since the Hawthorne experiments a long line of research has added to
the evidence that group solidarity and loyalty is sometimes associated
with productivity and effectiveness. (Katz and Kahn, 1952; Stouffer
et al., 1949; Merton and Lazarsfeld 1950; Argyris, 1957).

More recently several studies have been conducted which bring
into the same schema and situation both kinds of group effects—enhancement and impedance of larger organizational goals. Seashore's
(1954) research demonstrates that the most direct and consistent effect
of group cohesiveness (attraction of the individual to the group) is on
the *variance* of the behavior of members, rather than on the energic or
productive level of that behavior. Members in cohesive groups adhere
more closely to group norms, and other factors (the behavior of leaders, the structure of rewards, and the degree of supportiveness in the
organization as a whole) determine whether those group norms will
exceed, equal, or fall below the formal production demands of the
organization. Similar findings are reported by Zaleznik (1958) and his
colleagues.

The conclusion urged on us is that the most effective leader in a
pivotal organizational role is not the perfect bureaucrat (rational, role-
actuated, heedless of primary bonds), but rather the successful integra-
tor of primary and secondary relationships in the organizational situation. This means not only that the successful leader mediates and
tempers the organizational requirements to the needs of persons; he
does so in ways which are not organizationally damaging and, indeed,

* The term *Hawthorne effect* has come to be widely misused in the literature
to refer to any favorable effect upon the performance of an experimental group
resulting not from the specifics of the experimental treatment but merely from the
special recognition and attention of being selected as an experimental group. In the
Hawthorne experiments, however, the type of treatment was the significant factor.
The girls selected for the experiment were (1) assigned the best supervisor in the
plant, (2) accorded special privileges of genuine importance to them, and (3) made
into a cohesive group by encouragement of patterns of interaction. Anyone familiar
with organizational change knows how difficult it is to produce lasting changes in
an organizational unit merely through the special attention it receives as an experimental group. French (1960) and his colleagues were not able to achieve such
changes in their experimental groups in a Norwegian factory, nor were researchers
at Western Electric (Roethlisberger, 1941) able to achieve comparable changes in
a group of male workers whose cohesion around their own norms was already
strong.

are organization-enhancing. He promotes group loyalty and personal ties. He demonstrates care for persons as persons. He relies on referent power rather than on the power of legitimacy and sanctions alone. He encourages the development of positive identification with the organization and creates among his peers and subordinates a degree of personal commitment and identification. He does these things by developing a relationship with others in the organization in which he introduces what might be termed primary variations on the secondary requirements of organization. Within limits he adapts his own interpersonal style to the needs of other persons. In so doing, he generates among members of his group a resultant strength of motivation for the achievement of group and organizational goals which more than compensates for occasional bureaucratic irregularities. The secondary role requirements remain the dominant figure in his behavior, but they appear on a background of, and are embellished by, an attention to primary interpersonal considerations. According to Kahn (1964) and his colleagues, when people are asked how they themselves would like to be treated by those above them in the hierarchy, they reply in terms consistent with the pattern of primary-secondary integration, rather than in the impersonal language of secondary relationships.

The motivational effects of such an integration of primary and secondary requirements will be made clearer when we consider the motive patterns important in leading a person to enter an organization, remain in it, and perform satisfactorily the requirements of the role to which he has been assigned (Chapter 12). One of these patterns has to do with acceptance of legitimate authority and fear of sanctions. Another stems from the fact that the performance of the organizational role is instrumental to need gratification in the life of the person both inside and outside the organization.

Still other possibilities for motivating a person to membership and role performance depend upon the satisfactions inherent in the performance of the task itself. Traditional theories of organization, with their emphasis on external rewards and control, and their relative disregard for informal interpersonal relations and for the intrinsically rewarding properties of the job, represent a clear and restricted emphasis on the first two of these motivational patterns. More recently, the literature of management has paid some attention to the intrinsically satisfying aspects of the job, although this attention has for the most part taken a perverse form. The perversion consists in making an ideology of the importance and psychological rewardingness of work, rather than considering what definition of the job might make it directly experienced as satisfying and rewarding. Concern with image has been greater than concern with structural reality.

The most effective formal leaders bridge the gap between primary and secondary relationships in many ways, and in so doing enhance all three of the motive patterns described above. With respect to the instrumentality of the job for other groups and affiliations, the effective leader is positive and accepting. In dealing with his subordinates he acknowledges these primary relations to which the job is secondary. He manifests interest in his subordinates' off-the-job life, without insisting on information which he has not earned.

With respect to the instrumentality of the job for gratifying social needs in the work situation, the effective supervisor is accepting and constructive. He regards the value of the group to each individual as a potential asset rather than a bureaucratic irrelevancy or a threat to authority. As a result, he devotes a good deal of effort to creating a cohesive work group, a group in which each member finds the fact of membership rewarding. He permits, encourages, and may even model informal interaction. He uses task-relevant decisions as opportunities to build the group. In short, he deviates from the bureaucratic ideal by endowing the relationships in the work group with a primary quality, making them valuable and valued for themselves.

This is admittedly a difficult feat within a conventional bureaucratic structure, since it implies some conflict with the depersonalized, affect-free ideal of the bureaucratic relationship. The conflict, however, is more with the petty requirements of organizational life than with the overall goals of organizational effectiveness, and many leaders manage a tolerable compromise. The human-relations fraud, of course, is the bureaucrat who professes primary concerns for members of his group without feeling them and without any willingness to acknowledge their modifying claims on bureaucratic protocol.

Finally, the effective pivotal leader makes the task requirements themselves more satisfying by permitting greater autonomy and influence by members of the group. This constitutes a revision in some degree of the requirements themselves. In all these ways the effective leader merges the secondary aspects of organizational life with the primary qualities of "chosen" interpersonal relationships. The construction of cohesive, close, informal relationships built around the achievement of organizational goals adds materially to worker motivation and organizational effectiveness.

Administration: Use of Existing Structure

In discussing the initiation of structure and the piecing out of structure we have emphasized major acts of organizational leadership, attempts to meet challenges to organizational functioning and survival. Much more common, particularly as we move down the organizational hierarchy, are those lesser acts of leadership which utilize existing organizational devices and follow established organizational rules.

Routine directives and routine compliance fall near the zero point on the continuum of leadership, but for the most part they meet the definition; they involve influence on matters of organizational relevance. Only when the influence attempt is completely ineffective, or redundant because compliance is forthcoming anyway, does administration lose all its leadership properties. Moreover, the utilization of existing rules and regulations for exercising influence is never wholly mechanical; it can be judged in terms of consistency and appropriateness. Administration is the least of the levels of leadership, but administration can be sloppy or efficient, helpful or saturated with officiousness.

Because such distinctions are possible, the concept of influential increment is appropriate with respect to administration, as it is to those levels of leadership which we have called interpolation and origination of structure. The use of legitimate structure to produce an influential increment depends upon the supervisor's technical knowledge of the tasks, his understanding of the rules, and his concern with fairness, consistency, and equity in their application. Technical know-how and understanding of the legal system are primarily cognitive attributes; concern with equity is an affective orientation.

Knowledge of the technical aspects of the job to be done enables the administrator to make judicious use of the personnel and resources under his command. Part of his responsibility is to see that his people have an adequate flow of materials, proper tools for doing the work, and appropriate directives on how to apply their energies. In their study of railroad section gangs, Katz, Maccoby, Gurin, and Floor (1951) found that the foremen whose work groups were superior in productivity were the foremen with greater technical competence in the relevant task. They supplied expert technical direction to the work of the group. A later study in heavy industry (Kahn and Katz, 1960) corroborated this finding, as do the studies in power plants done by Mann (1962) and Mann and Hoffman (1960).

In addition to technical skills the administrator must also understand the system of rules and be concerned with the effects of their application. The strength of a legal system depends in practice upon two factors: (1) equity or the use of rewards and penalties in a clear, consistent, fair manner and (2) a reasonable consideration of the law in terms of spirit as well as letter.

Equity in the application of rules does not mean that the rules themselves must be completely equitable; it does mean that it is not the individual as an individual who is rewarded or penalized.

Suppose that a rule of seniority accords extra vacation to employees after five years in the organization. The rule may seem inequitable from some points of view because one man may have put in five years of outstanding service and another man five years of marginal performance. Nevertheless, once such rules exist, they must be applied consistently, so that people will know where they stand and what they can expect. Personal favoritism and prejudice of superiors thus will not affect their fortunes. Moreover, even where the rules do not provide specifically for equity with respect to a given treatment, the good administrator acts in accordance with this principle. A new employee may be brought in at a high salary because of the competitive labor market. The administrator must then fight for higher salaries for older employees of equal competence.

The importance of adherence to rules as a matter of equity is borne out by current research of Kahn (1964) and his colleagues on role conflict. In a study of six industrial organizations they found extremely widespread convictions that each member of the organization "should obey the rules of his organization and follow orders . . . . He should treat other members of the organization according to generally acceptable standards (universalistically), rather than according to their individual relationship to him (particularistically)." These convictions were particularly strong among people of supervisory responsibility and long tenure. Moreover, in those situations in which the norms of rule orientation and universalism were relatively weak, role conflict and job-related tensions were almost twice as prevalent.

People must be able to rely on administrators for a clear and stable set of actions consistent with organizational protocol. Systemic rewards, for reasons which we will consider in Chapter 12, are not calculated to insure the highest levels of performance but are a reliable means of insuring adequate role behavior in large organizations. Administration as we are using the term (utilizing structure in contrast to changing or supplementing it) depends heavily upon system rewards.

The second requirement for the successful use of structure concerns a contextual rather than a literal interpretation of rules. Administrative decisions should take into account not only the sentence in the book but the context in which it appears. The meaning of the rule is furnished by the larger framework, which often includes rule relevance to organizational functioning. Literal interpretations lead to ritualism and officiousness. The traffic officer in a crowded urban center, for example, cannot afford such practices. He has to keep traffic moving and to do so he must be less concerned with minor, irrelevant infractions of the traffic code than with positive directives to avoid traffic snarls.

PROBLEMS OF CONCENTRATION UPON A SINGLE PATTERN OF LEADERSHIP

Because of the contradictory character of organizations, with their needs for rule enforcement and their needs for spontaneous and internally motivated actions in the interests of the organizational mission, there is a good deal of ambivalence about administration and administrators. On the one hand administrators are regarded as bureaucrats and administration as the uninteresting performance of household chores in contrast to policy-making and creative leadership. Our own description of organizational leadership follows this line of thought. On the other hand, the administrative arts are sometimes glorified as the major forms of organizational control, and some top managers preoccupy themselves with administrative chores and eschew genuine policy-making and origination of structure. Running a tight ship becomes more important than accomplishing a mission.

Either extreme may lead to the neglect of important organizational functions. If the emphasis upon administration becomes the major concern of the top echelons, they may give too little time to critical issues of change, policy formulation, and planning. The increasing recognition of the organization as an open system carries with it an increasing understanding of this problem. But it is also possible to observe the neglect of the administrative function in organizations in which the top leaders spend almost all their time discussing policies, plans, and crises and are out of touch with the daily requirements of organizational life. Under such circumstances the household chores just may not get done, and appalling inefficiencies may characterize the system. It is true that man does not live by bread alone but it is also true that without bread he perishes. Organizations do not achieve greatness on the basis of their adequacy in handling daily administrative chores, but unless these are taken care of, the organization deteriorates. If there is no office space for the new professor, no research laboratory for the researcher, poor telephone service, and inadequate arrangements for assigning classrooms and duplicating reading lists, the university has increasing difficulty in holding together its staff of scholars and scientists. When administration is neglected, many people are forced into a grudging, costly, and inadequate effort to compensate for it. Alternatively, disregard for administration at higher levels in an organization may lead to the administrative function being carried out independently of policy-making. Administration thus develops a rigidity and a life of its own which may have many dysfunctional elements for the larger system. Some rapidly growing universities illustrate well the first type of neglect; some governmental bureaucracies, the second.

The relative emphasis upon the three forms of organizational leadership—origination, interpolation, and use of structure—should reflect the relationship of the system to its environment. An organization in a relatively stable environment with some assurance of inputs into the system will require less attention to changes in structure than an organization in a rapidly changing environment. Different patterns of leadership are also appropriate to different periods in organizational history. After a period of change an organization may require a period of stability, with consolidation of the changes and concomitant emphasis on the use of structure rather than further origination.

At any time, however, the relative importance of originating, interpolating, or using structure will be different for different echelons of organization, as we suggested earlier in this chapter. The recent work of Mann (1964), although it does not employ the conceptual scheme here proposed, is concerned with the different *skill-mix* which seems to be appropriate at different levels of organization and at different times in the organizational life cycle. Mann and his colleagues report, for example, that department heads in hospitals are satisfied or dissatisfied with their superiors primarily according to the superiors' coordinative and integrative abilities. The measures and descriptions of these abilities fit well our concepts of systemic perspective and origination of structure. People at lower levels in the organization, however, are more concerned with their supervisors' fairness and supportiveness and speak in terms that fall within our category of the equitable use of structure.

A study of an organization during a period of profound technological change (e.g., conversion of major clerical and billing operations to electronic data processing) shows, as one would expect, that the sharp differentiation of required *skill-mix* at different echelons is temporarily reduced, and that there is a heightened emphasis on systemic perspective and the origination of structure throughout the managerial structure. Mann suggests that during a period of major change this emphasis moves like a wave through the organization, beginning at the top and spreading rapidly downward as the top executives formulate major objectives and policy changes and then expect the next echelon to make the complementary changes which will create a new organizational state of equilibrium.

Distribution of Leadership Function

Perhaps the most persistent and thoroughly demonstrated difference between successful and unsuccessful leadership at all three levels has to do with the distribution or sharing of the leadership function. We have defined leadership as the exertion of influence on organizationally relevant matters by any member of the organization. By and large, those organizations in which influential acts are widely shared are most effective. The reasons for this are in part motivational, having to do with implementation of decisions, and in part nonmotivational, having to do with the excellence of decisions.

The motivational argument is familiar. People have greater feelings of commitment to decisions in which they have a part, or in which they act autonomously. This has been demonstrated repeatedly in small-group research and in organizational studies. Less evidence is available for our second assertion—that the wide distribution of the leadership function is likely to improve the quality of decisions. The argument depends essentially on the notion that the group utilizing its informational and experiential resources most fully will be most effective. All the knowledge of the world within and outside the organization is not located in the formal chain of managerial command, much less at the upper end of that chain. Few indeed are the organizational disasters which occurred unforeseen—by someone. The sharing out of the leadership function means using more fully the resources of the organization. It means, incidentally, avoiding some of the crucial problems of overload which are so common in large-scale organizations, especially in the managerial structure.

There are many ways in which the distribution of the leadership function may be manifest. Even a broad categorization would distinguish among delegation, participative decision-making, accessibility to influence, and communication of organizationally relevant information. In formal organizations of business and government all of these appear often as voluntary modifications in the formal structure of organization by some designated leader. He may change the official distribution of the leadership function by ceding directly to his subordinates duties for which he is formally responsible. This is what we mean literally by delegation, and the extent of delegation has proved to be one of the better predictors of productivity in organizations of many kinds.

Another way in which the formal leader of a group in a hierarchical organization may broaden the distribution of leadership is by including his subordinates in the making of decisions affecting the group itself or the larger organization. Suppose that the manager of a trucking depot is told that an unusually heavy shipment of packages will arrive the following day, and that it must be given home delivery within one day thereafter. The drivers are paid on a complicated basis reflecting hours worked and rate of performance. If the manager insists on the completion of the extra work within the usual eight hours, the drivers will receive incentive pay; if he allows them extra hours of work, they will receive overtime pay. He can make this decision himself, since it is within the limits of his formal authority, or he can involve his drivers in the decision and attempt some degree of joint decision-making. This is another area in which the evidence of studies of small groups and large organizations is generally consistent. We would confidently predict higher performance in those cases where the drivers were involved in the decision.

Less conspicuous than the formal delegation of leadership functions or the interpolation of group decision-making is the voluntary openness of the supervisor to influence from his subordinates. The leader may exercise his legitimate powers in a way that permits neither questions nor suggestions from others in the group. For example, if he has been given the responsibility for determining the kinds of equipment required for his unit, he may not tolerate discussion of the wisdom of his requisitions (nor need he listen to the suggestions of subordinates in such matters). Another supervisor may tolerate suggestions, discuss them, sometimes even act on them. Tannenbaum (1962) and others have shown that such accessibility to influence is consistently associated with higher performance at the group and organizational levels.

Perhaps the least way in which a formal leader initiates the distribution of the leadership function is by providing information to those in his group regarding resources, processes, problems, external demands, and the like. This principle is well understood and often given a kind of inverse demonstration: the leader who wishes to keep his powers unshared covets information, permits exchange of information within the group only through himself, and maintains his subordinates without potential influence by keeping them without data on which to base a course of action or an influence attempt. It is perhaps more accurate to view the sharing of information by the formal leader as a preliminary to the distribution of the leadership function rather than as constituting in itself any functional change. Again, the empirical evidence relating increased communication from formal leaders to increased performance within groups is substantial and consistent.

The principle of distributing broadly the functions of leadership cannot be extended indefinitely, however. An organization in which all members had equal access to all information, equal share in all decisions, would not be maximally effective. On the contrary, it would be deprived of much of the efficiency stemming from that basic invention of organization—the division of labor. The point, however, is of theoretical rather than pragmatic interest. Most organizations in our culture, at least outside the voluntary sector, show no signs of sharing the functions of leadership beyond the limits of efficiency. Gains in organizational effectiveness are still the predicted effect of broadening the base of leadership, whether by means of change, interpolation, or use of structure.

SUMMARY

In the description of organizations, no word is more used than leadership, and perhaps no word is used with such varied meanings. Leadership is sometimes used as if it were an attribute of personality, sometimes as if it were a characteristic of certain positions, and sometimes as an attribute of behavior. The last of these seems to us to offer distinct conceptual advantages, and we define leadership in behavioral terms as *any act of influence on a matter of organizational relevance.*

This definition of leadership includes many routine acts of supervision; the essence of leadership, however, has to do with that *influential increment* which goes beyond routine and taps bases of power beyond those which are organizationally decreed. These include *referent power*, which depends upon personal liking between leader and follower, and *expert power*, which depends upon the knowledge and ability of the leader. In contrast to these are the organizationally given powers of reward, punishment, and legitimate authority.

One may question the need for leadership so defined, and ask why an organization properly designed for its purpose will not function adequately without acts of leadership. The answer lies in four inescapable facts of organizational life: necessary incompleteness of organizational design, changing environmental conditions, internal dynamics of organization, and the nature of human membership in organizations.

No organizational chart and no book of policies and procedures can specify every act and prescribe for every contingency encountered in a complex organization. To attempt such specification merely produces an array of instructions so ponderous that they are ignored for the sake of transacting the business of the organization. Moreover, even if such specifications could be provided, they would soon be out of date. Organizations are open systems and exist in ever-changing environments. Each change in the environment implies a demand for change within the organization. To some extent such demands are foreseeable and the appropriate responses can be programed; to some extent they require leadership beyond such responses. Additional factors which mitigate against organizational stability and create a continuing need for leadership are the uneven development and different dynamics of the several organizational subsystems, and the segmental nature of human membership in organizations.

To analyze leadership behavior, we propose three categories or levels of leadership acts, differentiated in terms of their effects on organizational structure: the *origination of structure*, or policy formulation; the *interpolation of structure*, or the piecing out of policies to meet immediate problems; and the *use of structure*, or the routine administration of applying prescribed remedies for predicted problems. Each of these categories of leadership behavior is characteristically encountered at a different organizational level, and each requires for successful use a different cognitive style, different kinds of knowledge, and different affective characteristics.

Finally, no pattern of leadership is appropriate for all phases of organizational life. There is evidence, however, that the broad sharing of leadership functions contributes to organizational effectiveness under almost all circumstances.

12

The Psychological Basis of Organizational Effectiveness

Organizations may function at a high level of effectiveness for various reasons (Chapter 6). Technically, they may possess the finest machinery and the most modern automated equipment. Ecologically, they may be strategically placed between their sources of input and the market for their output. Organizationally, they may have worked out an unusually appropriate type of role system for their tasks. In this chapter we shall be concerned with another reason for the level of organizational functioning: the motivations of the people within the organization.*

Though knowledge about motivational principles has been growing as a result of psychological experimentation and research, there has been little systematic application of this body of knowledge to the specifics of organizational functioning. In brief, the approach taken in dealing with organizational problems has been oversimplified and too global. People have either assumed that the organization was like a single individual, or that there was a single problem of motivation for the entire organization with a single answer, or that organizational structures and processes could be ignored in dealing with the psychology of the individual. The use of rewards in blanket fashion for all organizational members is an instance of the first type of oversimplification, the concept of a global morale an example of the second. Examples of the third type are provided by the research on small groups and the human relations approach, both of which neglect the formal structure of organization. While the older theory of scientific management looked at the organization and forgot about the people in it, some recent psychological approaches look closely at people and forget their structured interdependence in the organizational context.

* The theoretical analysis in this chapter is adapted from "The Motivational Basis of Organizational Behavior," by Daniel Katz. (1964)

The complexities of motivation in organizations can be understood if we develop an analytic framework comprehensive enough to identify the major sources of variance and detailed enough to predict differences among different organizational units. The framework we propose calls for the formulation of answers to three types of analytic questions:

1. What are the types of behavior required for effective organizational functioning? From most of its members any organization will require not one but several patterns of behavior, and the motivational bases of these various behavioral patterns may differ.

2. What different motivational patterns are used and can be used in organizational settings? How do they differ in their logic and psychologic? What are the differential consequences of the various motivational patterns for organizational functioning? A given motivational pattern may be very effective in bringing about one type of necessary behavior and completely ineffective in producing another.

3. What are the conditions for eliciting a given motivational pattern in an organizational setting? We may be able to identify the type of motivation we think most appropriate for producing a given behavioral outcome, but we still need to know how this motive can be aroused or produced in the organization.

BEHAVIORAL REQUIREMENTS

In Table 3 are listed the major types of activity which the organization must engender in its members if it is to survive.

Table 3   PATTERNS OF INDIVIDUAL BEHAVIOR REQUIRED FOR ORGANIZATIONAL FUNCTIONING AND EFFECTIVENESS

1. Joining and staying in system
   (a) Recruitment
   (b) Low absenteeism
   (c) Low turnover
2. Dependable behavior: role performance in system
   (a) Meeting or exceeding quantitative standards of performance
   (b) Meeting or exceeding qualitative standards of performance
3. Innovative and spontaneous behavior: performance beyond role requirements for accomplishment of organizational functions
   (a) Cooperative activities with fellow members
   (b) Actions protective of system or subsystem
   (c) Creative suggestions for organizational improvement
   (d) Self-training for additional organizational responsibility
   (e) Creation of favorable climate for organization in the external environment

First of all, sufficient personnel must be kept within the system to perform its essential functions. People must be induced to enter the system at a sufficiently rapid rate to counteract the amount of retirement and defection. They must also be induced to remain within the system. The optimum period of tenure will vary for different individuals and situations, but high turnover is almost always costly. Moreover, while people are members of a system they must validate their membership by regular attendance. Thus turnover and absenteeism are both measures of organizational effectiveness, albeit partial measures. People may, of course, be within the system physically but be psychological absentees. The child may be regular and punctual in school attendance and yet daydream in his classes. It is not enough, then, to hold people physically within a system.

Secondly, there must be dependable activity. The great range of variable human behavior must be reduced to a limited number of predictable patterns. In other words, the assigned roles must be carried out in ways that meet some minimal level of quantity and quality. A common measure of productivity is the amount of work turned out within some stipulated period by an individual or by a group. Quality of performance is not as easily measured, and the problem is met by quality controls which set minimal standards for the pieces of work sampled. In general, the major content of the member's role is clearly set forth by organizational protocol, observable characteristics of the situation, and instructions of leaders. The man on the assembly line, the nurse in the hospital, the teacher in the elementary school all know what their major job is. To do a lot of it and to do it well are the most conspicuous behavioral requirements of the organization. It may be, of course, that given role requirements are not well conceived or functionally related to organizational accomplishment. This is a problem in organizational structure which does not contradict the fact that some major role requirements are necessary.

A third and often neglected set of requirements includes those actions not specified by role prescriptions but which facilitate the accomplishment of organizational goals. The organizational need for actions of an innovative, relatively spontaneous sort is inevitable and unending. No organizational planning can foresee all contingencies within its own operations, can anticipate with perfect accuracy all environmental changes, or can control perfectly all human variability. The resources of people for innovation, for spontaneous cooperation, for protective and creative behavior are thus vital to organizational survival and effectiveness. An organization which depends solely upon its blueprints of prescribed behavior is a very fragile social system.

The patterned activity which makes up an organization is so intrinsically cooperative and interrelated that it tends to resemble habitual behavior of which we are unaware. Within every work group in a factory, within any division in a government bureau, or within any department of a university are countless acts of cooperation without which the system would break down. We take these everyday acts for granted, and few of them are included in the formal role prescriptions for any job. One man will point out to another that his machine is getting jammed, or will pass along some tool that his companion needs, or will borrow some bit of material he is short on. Men will come to the aid of a fellow who is behind on his quota. In most factories specialization develops around such informal giving of help. One man will be expert in first aid; another will be expert in machine diagnosis. We recognize the need for cooperative relationships by raising specific questions about a man's capacity for them when he is considered for a job. How well does he relate to his fellows; is he a good team man; will he fit in?

Another subcategory of behavior beyond the formal requirements of role has to do with the protection of the organization against disaster. There is nothing in the role prescriptions of the worker which specifies that he be on the alert to save life and property in the organization. Yet the worker who goes out of his way to remove the boulder from the railway spur, or to secure a rampant piece of machinery, or even to disobey orders when they are obviously wrong and dangerous, is an invaluable man for the organization.

Acts beyond the line of duty also take the form of creative suggestions for improving methods of production or maintenance. Some organizations encourage their members to feed constructive suggestions into the system, but coming up with good ideas for the organization and presenting them to management is not the typical job of the worker. An organization that can stimulate its members to contribute ideas for organizational improvement is likely to be more effective, since people who are close to operating problems can often furnish informative suggestions about them which would not occur to those more distant. The system which does not have this stream of contributions from its members is not utilizing its potential resources effectively.

Still another subcategory of behavior beyond the call of duty includes the self-educative activities of members who learn to do their own jobs better and prepare to assume more responsible positions in the organization. There may be no requirement that men prepare themselves for better positions, but the organization whose members spend their own time to master knowledge and skills for more responsible jobs in the system has an additional resource for effective functioning.

Finally, members of a group can contribute to its operations by helping to create a favorable climate for it in the community which surrounds the organization. Employees talk to friends, relatives, and acquaintances about the qualities of the company for which they work. A favorable climate helps in problems of recruitment and, sometimes, product disposal.

In short, for effective organizational functioning many members must be willing on occasion to do more than their job prescriptions specify. If members of the system were to follow the precise letter of job descriptions and organizational protocol, things would soon grind to a halt. Many acts of spontaneous cooperation and many anticipations of organizational objectives are required to make the system viable. The ritualistic bureaucracy becomes inefficient partly because the prescribed behavior of role requirements is virtually the only form of behavior which remains. Clerks react to cases which cross their desks on the basis of the rules provided for their disposition. Cases occur, however, which are too complex or too difficult to handle within the existing rules. Instead of making the extra effort to meet such problems, the bureaucratized clerk, who is not sticking his neck out, pushes the atypical cases to one side of his desk for his supervisor to look at in the weekly checkup. In turn, the supervisor may accumulate his own set of exceptional cases to be pushed into a drawer for future consideration with the head of the department. Memoranda are exchanged, precedents are invoked, and an already overspecified book of rules is enlarged yet again. The organization moves in a costly and inefficient way.

The foregoing categories and subcategories of behavior, though related, are not necessarily motivated by the same drives and needs. The motivational pattern that will attract and hold people to an organization is not necessarily the same as that which will lead to higher productivity. Nor are the motives which make for higher productivity invariably the same as those which sustain cooperative interrelationships in the interests of organizational accomplishment. Hence, when we speak about practices and procedures which will further the attainment of the organizational mission, we need to specify the type of behavioral requirement involved.

TYPES OF MOTIVATIONAL PATTERNS

It is profitable to consider the possible motivational patterns in organizations under four major headings: legal compliance, instrumental satisfaction, self-expression, and internalized values.

Table 4   MOTIVATIONAL PATTERNS FOR PRODUCING VARIOUS TYPES OF REQUIRED BEHAVIORS

A. Legal compliance. Securing acceptance of role prescriptions and organizational controls on the basis of their legitimacy. The rule enforcement approach of simple machine theory. Controlling production through the speed of the assembly line.

B. The use of rewards or instrumental satisfactions for inducing required behaviors. The approach of modified machine theory.

   (1) System rewards earned through membership or seniority in system such as fringe benefits, cost-of-living raises, or other benefits across the board.

   (2) Individual rewards such as pay incentives and promotion on the basis of individual merit.

   (3) Instrumental identification with organizational leaders in which followers are motivated to secure the approval of leaders.

   (4) Affiliation with peers to secure social approval from own group.

C. Internalized pattern of self-determination and self-expression. The satisfactions from accomplishment and the expressions of talents and abilities.

D. Internalized values and the self-concept. The incorporation of organizational goals or subgoals as reflecting values or self-concept.

Type A. The first pattern is the acceptance of role prescriptions and of organizational directives because of their legitimacy. The group member obeys the rules because they stem from legitimate sources of authority and because they can be enforced by legal sanctions. This is the basic pattern of motivation in simple machine theory. Motivation bears no relation to the activity itself. Any rule or directive from the proper authority must be obeyed because it is the law of the nation, of the organization, or of the group.

The working of legitimacy to secure compliance rests upon two motivational sources. One is the external force which can be mobilized to compel obedience, and the second is an internalized acceptance of legitimate authority. The two sources have been illustrated by the contrast between the English police, who carry no guns and seldom use clubs, and the American police who frequently seem to need guns, clubs, and fire hoses. Internalized respect for the law is a generalized acceptance of all relevant legal norms and does not necessarily imply the internalization of specific laws as part of the individual's own value system.

The concept of legitimacy was introduced by Weber, as we have seen, and has been properly employed by sociologists to refer to the fact that a great deal of behavior can be readily predicted once we know the rules of the game. It is not always necessary to take extensive representative samplings of the behavior of many people to know how most of them will conduct themselves in certain situations. All we need are a few informants who can tell us the legitimate norms for given types of behavioral settings. In most European countries the simple norm of giving the right of way to the driver on the right accounts for a great deal of driver behavior. The same principle holds for all social structures. If the traveler from Mars is informed about the rules of the game in any social situation, he can predict and understand a great deal of what goes on. In a baseball game he can predict that the batter after hitting the ball will run to first base, not to third, and not around the grandstand.

Psychologists have tended to ignore the concept of legitimacy and its meaning for the individual. It is basically a social-psychological concept in that it refers both to social situations in which widespread compliance occurs and to the psychological processes within individuals which account for their compliance. Acceptance of the legal rules of a system is a necessary condition for participation in that system by the individual. His acceptance of them is in part a recognition of the objective social realities and in part an outcome of the socialization process in which a generalized acceptance of legal rules is developed. The objective social realities are that organized group effort cannot take place if people behave as anarchists. Rousseau's doctrine of the social contract, according to which people voluntarily exchange some of their individual rights for the benefits of social cooperation, is not necessarily an accurate description of the origin of social systems. It does, however, contain the profound truth that the involvement of people in social systems entails generalized obligations to follow systemic demands.

Involvement in any social structure thus means that its symbols of authority and its rules, promulgated in the prescribed manner, are accepted as binding. It is typically an all-or-nothing affair. The person cannot become involved in a system and make himself the arbiter of what he will accept or reject in its requirements. He can attempt to influence or alter the system decisions but, once made, these decisions are binding upon him regardless of his own views. Even in such loosely structured organizations as American political parties, factions which were violently antagonistic at the nominating convention subsequently close ranks and accept some measures of party discipline. In more tightly organized groups there is no question about compliance with legitimately derived decisions. When they enter an organization, individuals often assume that they can control their degree of involvement and retain the right of discrimination with respect to organizational requirements. Before they are aware of it, however, they are acting like other organizational members and complying with the rules and authorized decisions.

Some very loose voluntary organizations show less of this all-or-nothing pattern. Such organizations often make only minimal demands on most members, who are really marginal to the group. This large marginal group is asked only to give verbal and financial support, and to maintain a favorable climate of opinion in which the small core of activists can function. For the activist, however, the demands are heavy, and failure to meet them relegates him to the inactive marginals.

To assert that involvement in a structure means acceptance of its legitimate authority raises interesting problems of individual responsibility. If the individual must comply with the legitimate norms of his group, how can he be held responsible for his actions while carrying out his prescribed duties. Executioners are not guilty of murder. As members of social systems, we do not assume full responsibility for our actions in carrying out our prescribed roles, nor is such responsibility usually imposed on us. In practice, however, we do hold people responsible for their actions as members of organizations under any of several circumstances: (1) when on their own volition they have entered a structure whose norms run counter to the political state, e.g., joining the Communist Party; (2) when they have failed to exert all the influence they could muster to affect decisions in the structure, e.g., the guilt of the German people in accepting the Nazi regime; (3) when they possess considerable power and latitude in formulating and implementing policy, usually as occupants of some position of formal leadership.

The nature of the commitment to the legal norms of a system is recognized by anarchists and by their nonideological cousins, "the angry young men." These rebels refuse to vote or to participate in the political system because they would then be bound by the decisions reached. They see clearly the all-or-nothing character of system involvement though they do not follow their own logic by withdrawing completely from organized society.

Type B. The military ideal of commanding any required behavior from its soldier membership is also the theoretical ideal of machine theory. The characteristic limitation of this approach is its inability to motivate people for anything but routine compliance with role requirements. A second form of motivation is thus attempted—the linking of rewards to desired behaviors, with the expectation that as rewards increase, motivation for performance increases. In other words, the actions become instrumental to the achieving of specific rewards.

Four subtypes of such instrumental rewards are often employed in social systems. In the first place, rewards can be earned merely through membership in the system and increased through seniority in it. For example, government, industry, and educational institutions offer retirement pensions, sick leave, health examinations, and other forms of fringe benefits. They furnish cost-of-living raises and other across-the-board wage increases. They may provide attractive working conditions and recreational facilities. Many of these benefits are available without differentiation to any member of the system; others are apportioned according to status or seniority. But they are all system benefits, rewarding a whole category of persons for staying in the system.

In addition to these general system rewards are the individual rewards of pay increases, promotion, and recognition accorded to people on the basis of individual merit. They may take the form of a piece-rate system in which each individual is paid according to the amount he produces. They may take the form of giving outstanding workers some priority with respect to promotion. Or a suggestion system may reward individuals in proportion to the value of their suggestions to the company.

Another form of instrumental motivation for group members derives from the approval they receive from their leaders. This category does not refer to the approval of the superior interpreted by the employee as a promise of promotion. It refers to the gratification a person may find in the praise of a powerful and respected figure. Such a person wants to do things which will insure continued approbation from his superior, even without the implication of upgrading and higher pay.

A similar type of individual reward is social approval of one's own group. The potency of the peer group in influencing behavior is a continuing source of surprise to parents. Social approval of the immediate work group motivates members toward organizational requirements, however, only to the extent that those requirements are congruent with the norms of the group. This type of motivation can facilitate or prevent attainment of organizational objectives, depending upon the nature of the group norms.

The motivational sources for these patterns of instrumental activities are varied. We shall not attempt to push them back to some ultimate physiological cause. For our purposes it is enough to recognize that many human actions are the means to the satisfaction of utilitarian drives or ego needs, and are performed for no other reason. Between a need and its satisfaction may be interposed almost any behavioral demand. Fulfilling the behavioral requirement is made a condition for the satisfaction of the need. The behavioral requirement may be otherwise unrelated to need satisfaction and, except for the rewards placed upon it, might seldom occur.

The third and fourth types of motivational pattern differ significantly from the two just discussed. The first (Type A) reminded us that people meet organizational requirements because it is their duty to obey, and because they will run afoul of organizational law if they do not. Type A involves external reminders of the rules and sufficient policing to reinforce internal acceptance of legitimacy. The second (Type B) dealt with activities that are instrumental to the attainment of positive rewards. In Type B such rewards are the sine qua non for performance.

Now we are concerned with activities that are rewarding in themselves. In Types C and D gratifications derive directly from the behavioral expressions of the role. Motivation is so internalized that performance is autonomous. The supervisor does not have to be present to wave a stick or offer candy. The activities carry their own rewards; they are so much a part of the pattern of motive satisfaction that they need no additional incentive. Years ago Gordon Allport (1937) observed that activities supposedly undertaken in the service of other motives became functionally autonomous. His observation of the reward character of many forms of expressive behavior was undoubtedly correct but his analysis of the reasons why some activities are self-motivating and others are not was inadequate.

We shall not examine all the reasons why activities become self-rewarding but shall concern ourselves with those forms of behavior that are expressions of the ego or its central values. These include: self-determination, or the satisfaction of making decisions about one's own behavior; self-expression, or gratification derived from expressing one's talents and abilities; value expression, or the satisfaction of expressing one's central values; and self-identification and idealization, the motivation to establish and maintain a satisfying self-concept. Self-determination in a sense is a precondition for the other three forms of ego motivation. The individual must feel that he has responsibility for his own actions and feelings. Self-expression refers to his opportunities for showing what he can do; value expression refers to his saying what he feels and thinks, and self-identification to asserting and expressing what he is like.

Type C. Self-expression and self-determination are the basis for *job identification*, that is for satisfactions deriving directly from role performance. The scientist derives gratification from scientific inquiry, the musical composer from creating his symphony, the craftsman from the exercise of his skill in a job well done.

Type D. Value expression and self-idealization lead to the *internalization of organizational goals*. The goals of the group become incorporated as part of the individual's value system or as part of his conception of himself. As a result, satisfactions accrue to the person from the expression of attitudes and behavior reflecting his cherished beliefs and self-image. The reward is not so much a matter of social recognition or monetary advantage as of establishing his self-identity, confirming his notion of the sort of person he sees himself to be, and expressing the values appropriate to this self-concept. A man who considers himself an enlightened conservative, an internationalist, a prudent, hard-headed business executive, or a devoted union man will be motivated to actions which are overt manifestations of these values.

The expression of values not only gives clarity to the self-image but also brings that self-image closer to the aspirations of the individual. He derives satisfaction from seeing his self-concept approach his self-ideal. Added to the need to know *who I am* is the need to realize that *I am the type of person I want to be.*

The socialization process during the formative years sets the basic outlines of the individual's self-concept. Parents do not train children only by the use of reward and punishment; they also utilize a mediating notion, the model of the good character they want their children to be. A good boy eats his spinach, does his homework, and does not clobber girls. Children do not accept every parental injunction but they do acquire the concept of character models. In a play, a political contest, or an international conflict they want to know who are the "bad guys" and who are the "good guys." And they apply the same type of character role to themselves. In play they can quickly take over a part and become another person, but again in terms of a character model.

As adults our self-concept becomes more integrated and stable, and we can no longer move back and forth so readily between various models. Just as the kind, considerate person will cover over his acts of selfishness, so too will the ruthless individualist become confused and embarrassed by his acts of sympathetic compassion. One reason why it is difficult to change the character of an adult is that he is not comfortable with the new "me." Group support for such changes is almost a necessity, as in Alcoholics Anonymous, so that the individual is aware of approval of his new self by people who are like him.

Type D then refers to internalized motivation by which an individual is activated toward the goals of the group because these goals represent his own personal values or are appropriate to his own self concept. People so motivated are usually described as having a sense of mission, direction, or commitment. In most organizations there is a small core of such committed members who have internalized the values of the system.

CONDITIONS AND CONSEQUENCES OF DIFFERENT
MOTIVATIONAL PATTERNS

The preceding analysis of the various types of behavior required for organizational effectiveness and the different motivational patterns available for energizing and directing such behavior strongly suggests that there will be costs and gains in emphasizing any single desired outcome. Maximizing dependable role performance may involve motivational conditions that inhibit spontaneous and innovative behavior. Attracting people to a system and holding them in it may not lead to a high level of productivity. We need to examine in detail the differential effects of the four patterns of motivation upon organizational behavior, and to analyze the conditions most likely to arouse these patterns.

Type A. Legal Compliance. Organizational and legal controls will not be generally effective for attracting people into a system or holding them there, except in cases where recruitment and tenure can be legislated. Military service and attendance at school can be organizationally compelled because the apparatus of government and the acts of legislatures stand behind the organizational demand for compliance. Absenteeism can be reduced through legal rules in all organizations, but the legalistic control of absence may be reflected in a high rate of turnover.

Emphasis on legal compliance can bring about acceptable levels of individual performance both in quantity and quality. The more routine the activity, the more likely this is to be true. Creativity is difficult if not impossible to legislate. Legality, moreover, needs the reinforcement of situational reminders. The time clock, the use of mechanical "speeds and feeds" beyond the control of the worker, and the occasional policing of rules and regulations are characteristic of the legal motif in organizations.

Emphasis on the legalities of organizational control tends in practice to mean that the minimal acceptable standard for quantity and quality of performance becomes the maximal standard. If it is legitimate and proper according to company and union standards to turn out 40 pieces on a machine, then there is no point in exceeding this standard. One cannot be more legal or proper than the norm, though there are degrees of nonconformity in failing to meet it. Of course, individuals may be motivated to exceed the norm for various rewards but not for the satisfaction of properly meeting the rules.

Another reason for the minimal standard becoming the maximum is that an organization geared to rules and regulations can find the overachiever just as much a problem as the underachiever. The eager beaver who turns out more work than the minimal standard requires is a problem to his boss and his fellow workers alike. His boss has problems in speeding up materials to keep the enthusiast supplied or in explaining to his own superiors why all the jobs in the section should not be retimed.

Finally, the legal basis of influencing people is notoriously deficient in affecting performance beyond the narrow role prescriptions for quantity and quality of work. What is not covered by rules is by definition not the responsibility of the organizational member.

The attempt is usually made to extend the rules to cover more and more of the behavior required for good overall organizational performance. But several considerations argue against such extension. Acts of creativity or spontaneous, mutual helpfulness cannot be legislated. Major role requirements will be obscured if the legal specifications become too numerous. Finally, building up the role of every member would entail some upgrading of even the lowliest positions and would run counter to the machine-theoretical basis of many hierarchial organizations. Machine theory holds that the organizational task can be broken down into its component parts, each of these small parts can be assigned to a given worker, and his performance can be governed wholly by a simple set of rules and prescriptions.

Conditions Conducive to Legal Compliance. Four conditions activate legal compliance: (1) the use of recognized sources of authority, (2) the clarity of legal norms, (3) the use of specific sanctions and penalties, and (4) the threat to the individual's staying in the system.

Table 5 CONDITIONS AFFECTING THE ACTIVATION OF PATTERN A, LEGAL COMPLIANCE

Objective Conditions	Mediated by Psychological Variables	Outcome
1. Use of appropriate symbols of authority	1. Recognition and acceptance of symbols	Produces minimally acceptable quantity and quality of work
2. Clarity of legal norms and requirements	2. Lack of subjective ambiguity permitting wishful interpretations	Can reduce absenteeism
3. Use of specific penalties	3. Individual expectation of being caught	May increase turnover
4. Expulsion of nonconformers	4. Desire to stay within system; dependence on system for way of life	Affects innovative and other behavior beyond the call of duty adversely

The acceptance of directives on the basis of legitimacy requires the use of symbols and procedures that identify an appropriate source of authority in the system under consideration. The worker may grumble at the foreman's order but he recognizes the right of the foreman to give an order. Particular directives are accepted as legitimate when they conform to the authority structure of the system. In a representative democracy the policy decision of an administrator may be rejected because it lacks the legislative stamp required in that system. A company may have a union contract stating that changes in the speed of the assembly line must be agreed to by both organizations. The workers accordingly will accept a speedup in the line if it is sanctioned by union-management agreement, but not if it is the work of a general foreman attempting to impress his superiors.

The acceptance of legal rules is also restricted to their appropriate realm of activity. Union policy as formulated in its authority structure is binding upon its members only when it specifies relations with the company. The edicts of union officials on matters of desegregation or support of political parties are not seen as legal compulsions by union members. In similar fashion, employees do not regard the jurisdiction of the company as extending to their lives outside the plant. Areas of private behavior and personal taste are generally regarded in our democratic society as outside the realm of coercive laws. The most spectacular instance of the violation of a national law occurred in the case of the Volstead Act. While people were willing to accept laws about the social consequences of drinking, such as reckless driving, many of them were not willing to accept the notion that their private lives were subject to federal regulation.

A related condition for the acceptance of legal decisions is clarity —of authority symbols, of procedure, and of the content of the decision itself. Lack of clarity can be due to vagueness of the stimulus-situation or to conflict between stimulus cues. In some organizations, symbols of authority are sharply enough defined but the relationship between competing symbols lacks clarity. The armed services make visible in conspicuous fashion their authoritative symbols, but conflicts between branches of the service occur because of difficulties in unification of command. Confusion can also occur when different types of authority structure are introduced in the same social system. One difficulty of using group decision in certain parts of an otherwise authoritarian structure is that group members may not perceive the democratic procedure as legitimized by the larger structure. They will question the compelling effect of any decisions they reach, and often they may be right. Another kind of conflict arises when the exercise of power is not consistent with its substantive purpose. The classic case is that of *ordering* people to be democratic.

Procedures as well as symbols may be ambiguous. Where there are many interrelated channels for the formulation of legal rules, people may be confused as to what interpretation of the law to follow. The doctrine of interposition, used in the South to justify resistance to the Supreme Court decision on desegregation, had the sole function of giving apparent legal support to the segregationists. Laws are promulgated at local, state, and national levels, and are interpreted by state and federal courts in various ways. The procedural complexity created confusion for many Southern citizens. If they complied with the Supreme Court decision, they would in fact violate local laws. And the doctrine of interposition, which set the sovereignty of the state above that of the nation in certain areas of life, gave legal support to setting the legal structure on its head.

Specific laws can also be ambiguous in their substance. They can be so complex, so technical, or so obscure that people will not know what the law is. The multiplication of technical rulings and the patchwork of legislation with respect to tax structure motivates people to pay as little as possible without risking legal prosecution, but leaves them confused as to how little that is. Such ambiguity generates a counter dynamic to the tendency to comply with legal requirements, namely, the use of legal loopholes to defy the spirit of the law. Any complex maze of rules in an organization will be utilized by the guardhouse lawyers in the system to their own advantage.

In brief, legal compliance rests upon the belief that there are specific imperatives which all good citizens obey. If there is doubt about what the imperative is, or if there are many varying interpretations, then the law is not seen as having a character of its own but as a means for obtaining individual advantage. To this extent, the legitimate basis of compliance is undermined.

To maintain the internalized acceptance of legitimate authority requires reinforcement in the form of penalties for violation of the rules. If there is no policing of laws governing speeding, speed limits will lose their force over time for many people. Penalties can take the form of social disapproval as well as legal action. But the very concept of law as binding upon everyone in the system requires penalties for violation either from above or below. Where there is no enforcement by authorities and no sanctions against infractions from the group itself, the rule in question becomes a dead letter.

Finally, a basic condition for legal compliance is the individual's involvement in a social system. The systems in which he participates are part of his way of life. To reject the authority and rules of the system is to reject the system. The naturalized citizen takes an oath of allegiance to his new country, and many groups require similar formal commitments. Even without such formalities, there is the understanding that serious failure to accept legitimized norms will result in expulsion from the system. At some point, denial of the authority of the system becomes psychological if not legal treason. The relevant consideration is the conditions under which involvement in the system is threatened by acts of nonconformity. The Catholic Church, for example, makes clear that excommunication will follow overt defiance of authority as well as certain types of heresy, whereas other violations of its code can be atoned for. Political states define some category of acts as treasonable.

There is a wide range of behaviors that are subject to varying interpretations. External threat to a system extends the concept of disloyalty to forms of legal infraction which are normally tolerated. A sentry who falls asleep during a peacetime maneuver will be disciplined; during war he will be subjected to a court-martial. Even where external threat is not objectively documented, a climate of opinion can develop to produce the same effects—hence the well-known technique of creating a sense of systemic danger in order to destroy one's opponents by accusing them of disloyalty. In general, infractions of legal norms central to the major objectives of organizations or to the authority structure itself are most likely to lead to expulsion. In the Catholic Church one does not flaunt the authority of the Pope. In a plant devoted to defense production one does not violate security regulations. In a research organization the faking of results would be a cardinal sin.

Another way of stating the relationship between involvement in an organization and the acceptance of its legal norms is to say that such acceptance is a sign both to the individual and to his fellows of his membership. His acquiescence to the authority structure is a symbol of his belonging. By the same token, any act of conspicuous violation of system norms is tantamount to giving up one's way of life in the structure.

The individual is often unaware of the full significance of his involvement in a social system and the strength of the compliance demand. Only when his own actions or the actions of others create the possibility of expulsion does the real meaning of withdrawal and membership come home to him. He may then do a great deal to insure his membership in the system. This is why the phenomenon of McCarthyism reached such irrational limits. People did not dare take the risk of opposition, when it was likely to be defined as disloyalty and to threaten their way of life. To oppose unsuccessfully meant loss of membership in many occupational, professional, political, and social structures. It is not surprising that most revolts in social structures are easily quelled by invoking the symbols of authority, or that rebels make rejection by certain social systems tolerable by building their own alternative structures.

Type B. Instrumental Satisfaction. The first extension of machine theory beyond the rules is the addition of rewards to motivate performance. It is important to distinguish between rewards administered in relation to individual effort and performance and the system rewards which accrue to people by virtue of their membership in the system. In the former category are piece-rate incentives, promotion for outstanding performance, or any special recognition bestowed in acknowledgement of differential contributions to organizational functioning. The category of system rewards includes fringe benefits, recreational facilities, cost-of-living raises, across-the-board upgrading, job security, and pleasant working conditions.

Table 6 CONDITIONS AFFECTING THE USE OF INDIVIDUAL MONETARY REWARDS

Objective Conditions	Mediated by Psychological Variables	Outcome
1. Amount of reward for individual effort	1. Frame of reference in evaluating reward: what standards are used for comparison purposes	Possible reduction in turnover
2. Immediacy of reward	2. Temporal frame of reference of individual	Some reduction in absenteeism
3. Constancy of reward	3. Perception of dependability and no cutting back of rates;	Possible increases in productivity
	Other consequences of reward striving such as disapproval of peers	No necessary increase in cooperative or protective behavior
		Possible increases in creative suggestions

Individual rewards properly administered help attract people to the system and hold them in it. A major factor in their effectiveness is the extent to which they are competitive with individual reward systems in other organizations. Individual rewards can also be effective in motivating people to meet and exceed the quantitative and qualitative standards of role performance. This effectiveness is limited, however, when large numbers of people are performing identical tasks, so that superior individual performance threatens the rewards and security of the majority. In other words, differential individual rewards are difficult to apply effectively to masses of people doing the same work and sharing a common fate in a mass production organization. It is no accident that large organizations have moved in the direction of converting individual rewards into system rewards.

Individual rewards are also difficult to apply to contributions that go beyond the formal requirements of role. Spectacular instances of innovative behavior can be singled out for recognition, of course, and heroism beyond the call of duty can be decorated. But the everyday cooperative activities which keep an organization from falling apart are more difficult to recognize and reward. Creative suggestions for organizational improvement are sometimes encouraged through financial rewards. In general, however, singling out of individuals for their extra contributions to the cause is not the most effective and reliable means of evoking high motivation for the accomplishment of organizational objectives.

Conditions Conducive to Effective Individual Instrumental Rewards

If rewards such as pay incentives are to work as they are intended they must meet three primary conditions. (1) They must be clearly perceived as large enough in amount to justify the additional effort required to obtain them. (2) They must be perceived as directly related to the required performance and follow directly on its accomplishment. (3) They must be perceived as equitable by the majority of system members, many of whom will not receive them. These conditions suggest some of the reasons why individual rewards can work so well in some situations and yet be so difficult of application in large organizations. The facts are that most enterprises have not been able to use incentive pay, or piece rates, as reliable methods for raising the quality and quantity of production (McGregor, 1960; Marriott, 1957).

In terms of the first criterion many companies have attempted incentive pay without making the differential between increased effort and increased reward proportional from the point of view of the worker. If he can double his pay by working at a considerably increased tempo, that is one thing. But if such increased expenditure means a possible 10 per cent increase, that is another. Moreover, there is the tradition among workers, and it is not without some factual basis, that management cannot be relied upon to maintain a high rate of pay for those making considerably more than the standard and that their increased efforts will only result in their "being sweated." There is, then, the temporal dimension of whether the piece rates which seem attractive today will be maintained tomorrow.

More significant, however, is the fact that a large-scale organization consists of many people engaging in similar and interdependent tasks. The work of any one man is highly dependent upon what his colleagues are doing. Hence individual piece rates are difficult to apply on any equitable basis. Group incentives are more logical, but as the size of the interdependent group grows, we move toward system rather than toward individual rewards. Moreover, in large-scale production enterprises the role performance is controlled by the tempo of the machines and their coordination. The speed of the worker on the assembly line is not determined by his decision but by the speed of the assembly line. An individual piece-rate just does not accord with the systemic nature of the coordinated collectivity. Motivational factors about the amount of effort to be expended on the job enter the picture not on the floor of the factory but during the negotiations of the union and management about the manning of a particular assembly line. Heads of corporations may believe in the philosophy of individual enterprise, but when they deal with reward systems in their own organizations they become realists and accept the pragmatic notion of collective rewards.

Since there is such a high degree of collective interdependence among rank-and-file workers the attempts to use individual rewards are often perceived as inequitable. Informal norms develop to protect the group against efforts which are seen as divisive or exploitive. Differential rates for subsystems within the organization will be accepted much more than invidious distinctions within the same subgrouping. Hence promotion or upgrading may be the most potent type of individual reward. The employee is rewarded by being moved to a different category of workers on a better pay schedule. Some of the same problems apply, of course, to this type of reward. Since differential performance is difficult to assess in assembly-type operations, promotion is often based upon such criteria as conformity to company requirements with respect to attendance and absenteeism, observance of rules, and seniority. None of these criteria is related to individual performance on the job. Moreover, promotion is greatly limited by the technical and professional education of the worker.

It is true, of course, that many organizations are not assembly-line operations, and even for those which are, the conditions described here do not apply to the upper echelons. Thus General Motors can follow a policy of high individual rewards to division managers based upon the profits achieved by a given division. A university can increase the amount of research productivity of its staff by making publication the essential criterion for promotion. In general, where assessment of individual performance is feasible and where the basis of the reward system is clear, instrumental individual rewards can play an important part in raising productivity.

System rewards differ from individual rewards in that they are not allocated on the basis of differential effort and performance but on the basis of membership in the system. The major basis for differential allocation of system rewards is seniority in the system. A higher pension for thirty years of service than for twenty years does not violate the principle of rewarding membership. Management often overlooks the distinction between individual and system rewards, and operates as if rewards administered across the board would produce the same effects as individual rewards.

System rewards are most effective for holding members within the organization. Since these rewards are often distributed on the basis of length of service, people will want to stay on to receive them. The limiting factor is competition with attractions in other systems. As the system increases its attractions, other things being equal, it should reduce its problems of turnover. In fact, it may sometimes have the problem of too little turnover, with many poorly motivated people staying on until retirement.

Table 7 CONDITIONS AFFECTING THE USE OF SYSTEM REWARDS

Objective Conditions	Mediated by Psychological Variables	Outcome
1. Alternative system available to the individual	1. Perception of alternatives and law of least effort	Reduction in turnover
2. Relative advantages of system rewards in other available organizations	2. Perception and meaning to the individual of these differences	Some reduction in absenteeism Minimal quantity and quality of role performance
3. Uniformity of system rewards for all members or for major categories	3. Perception of equity	No creative contribution but some degree of cooperative and protective behavior and creation of favorable external environmental climate

System rewards will not lead to work of higher quality or greater quantity than is required to stay in the organization. Since rewards are given equally to all members or differentially in terms of seniority, people are not motivated to do more than meet the standards for remaining in the system. It is sometimes assumed that the liking for the organization created by system rewards will generalize to greater productive effort. Such generalization of motivation may occur to a very limited extent, but it is not a reliable basis for the expectation of higher productivity. Management may expect gratitude from workers because it has added some special fringe benefit or some new recreational facility. Employees will be motivated to remain in an enterprise with such advantages, but are unlikely to express gratitude by working harder for the company.

System rewards do little to motivate performance beyond the line of duty, with two possible exceptions. As people develop a liking for the attractions of the organization, they may be more likely to engage in cooperative relations with their fellows toward organizational goals. They may be more likely also to contribute to a favorable climate of opinion for the system in the external environment. It may be easier for a company to recruit personnel when employees have described it as a good place to work.

The effective use of system rewards requires their uniform application for all members of the system or for plausible major groupings within the system. If rewards are to be given by virtue of membership in the system, any allocation favoring some individuals over others is suspect. Management is frequently surprised by resentment over differential system rewards when there has been no resentment of differential individual rewards.

One public utility, for example, inaugurated an attractive retirement system for its employees before such fringe benefits were common. Its employees were objectively much better off because of the new benefits, and yet the most hated feature of the whole company was the retirement system. Employee complaints centered on two issues: years of employment in the company before the age of thirty did not count toward retirement pensions; and company officials, because of their higher salaries and correspondingly higher pensions, could retire on livable incomes. The employees felt intensely that, if they were being rewarded for service to the company, it was unfair to rule out years of service before age thirty. The service of a man who started to work for the company immediately after high school graduation was unrecognized for a dozen years. Moreover, workers felt that a lifetime of service to the company should enable them to retire on a livable income just as it enabled company officials to do so. The company house organ devoted considerable space over a few years to showing how much the workers actually benefited from the plan, as in fact was the case. On the occasion of a companywide survey, this campaign was found to have had little effect. The most common complaint was still the patent unfairness of the retirement system.

The critical point then is that system rewards have a logic of their own. Since they accrue to people by virtue of their membership or length of service in an organization, they will be perceived as inequitable if they are not uniformly administered. The perception of the organization member is that all members are equal in their access to organizational benefits. Office employees will not be upset by differences in individual rewards that recognize differences in responsibility. However, if their organization gives them free meals in a cafeteria and sets aside a special dining room for executives, many of them will be upset. In our culture we accept individual differences in income but we do not readily accept differences in classes of citizenship. To be a member of an organization is to be a citizen in that community, and all citizens are equal in their membership rights. Universities which do not extend to research workers the same tenure rights and fringe benefits accorded to the teaching staff have a morale problem on their hands.

The Citizenship Meaning of Membership in an Organization. There has been little systematic inquiry as to what it means for an individual to be a member of an organization or social system. By membership we do not necessarily mean that the individual pays or carries a card. We only mean that he is part of the system's operations, that he fulfills certain role obligations. Membership in this sense can be discussed in terms of the input a person regards as his due as a member of the system, and the output or behavior required of him to support the organization.

We have described the input side of this exchange in discussing system rewards. People in a democratic society feel that any system in which they are involved should accord them certain citizenship rights by virtue of their membership in the system. One such right is uniformity and equity in the distribution of system rewards. Another is equality of opportunity to earn the differential individual rewards available in the system. There should not be arbitrary discrimination against a worker because of race, religion, or social origin. Another right is that of due process of law, the right of the individual to be dealt with through established legal procedures and not through arbitrary, whimsical actions. Even though people are working for industrial organizations in which the power structure is oligarchical, they increasingly expect that their citizen rights in those organizations will be handled on the basis of democratic principles. Management in general also recognizes these citizen rights, and flagrant departures from them are not condoned. In fact, management goes even further in some instances and avoids the language of authority even though the citizen expectations of members do not demand a democratic authority structure.

There are many implications for organizations in the citizenship demands of members. The basic problem is the distribution of system rewards and privileges to different levels of workers, to different functional groups, and to the incumbents of different hierarchical positions.

The simple solution of uniform privileges and rewards for all organizational members regardless of position, type of work, or function would horrify the upper echelons. It would mean in a university, for example, that faculty members, research workers, clerks, and custodians would be entitled to the same provisions of tenure, retirement benefits, and vacations. When research workers and faculty members take ten days of vacation at Christmas, secretarial and administrative staffs would not be required to stay on the job. Though many would find this simple solution upsetting, the general trend is in this direction. Cost-of-living increases, which in many institutions are an important part of system rewards, are applied in a uniform fashion. Recreational facilities may be open to all members, and even parking permits, those coveted symbols of utility and prestige, are sometimes accorded to all.

A second solution is to translate inequitable system rewards into individual rewards. Instead of giving officials one plan of retirement and workers another, the retirement system can be the same for all, but the officials, by virtue of their individual positions and their unusual effort and achievement in those positions, can be given individual bonuses.

Another solution would be to find some acceptable rationale for distinguishing between functions and classes of citizens within an organization. In the university, the faculty perform a different function than clerical and custodial staff. Apart from meeting classes and conforming to other institutional requirements, faculty members can decide for themselves whether to work a thirty or a seventy hour week. Their Christmas vacation may in reality mean that they take less time from their professional duties than do their secretaries. In general, this distinction of functions is the major solution followed by most organizations in allocating system rewards. It has the merit of recognizing some of the realities of the situation, and encouraging a clear formulation of visible differences in functions, responsibilities, and obligations of different groups within the organization. On the other hand, this solution works against unification of all groups around the common goals of the organization, and it often encourages in-group loyalties and identifications at the expense of the total organization.

The problem of allocating system rewards is complicated by the functional subdivisions of the organization and the division of the total structure into sectors of organizational space. If system rewards are distributed differentially according to the status, responsibility, and power of subgroups, the identity of these subgroups will be reinforced and their goals will tend to become more important than organizational goals. If system rewards are distributed uniformly, the people whose positions carry more responsibility and require more effort and more investment in preliminary training will say that numerical equality is not genuine equality. Equal pay for equal work has the corollary that unequal pay should go with unequal work. The terms of the relations should not be lost.

The tendency of differential allocation of system rewards to intensify subgroup identification is greatest in an organization where the subgroup functions are in fundamental opposition. A university needs scientists who can pursue the search for knowledge with maximum freedom. It also needs security police to protect its laboratories from theft and destruction. The conventional arrangement makes the security police a subsystem of the university which ties directly to the top administrative structure and has no direct organizational tie to the functional units of the university whose premises the police are "protecting." As a result, none of the system rewards which accrue to the individual policeman—pay, promotion, timing and duration of vacation, and the like—are determined by the university units in which he physically performs his job. He patrols the premises at times when members of these subunits are for the most part not present and he is in the odd position of having physical occupancy without membership. Thus, he has little knowledge of the mission of the research group and little commitment to it. He may be just as suspicious of those he is protecting as he is of malicious intruders. An alternative arrangement would locate the security police in the subunit which they were protecting or at least would allocate some of the system rewards on the basis of their performance as evaluated by the members of those subunits. This could lead to an embracing of the subsystem's mission by the security unit.

System rewards uniformly distributed will lead some people to identify with the larger organization, but more fundamental changes in organizational structure and roles make identification with the larger organization more likely. Specifically, this means broadening the role of members of the subgroup and giving them membership in some subsystem which is central to the mission of the organization. This could mean complete reorganization on the basis of teams concerned with problems rather than on the basis of functional specialization; it could mean assignment of a specialist to a team for limited periods, or it could mean maintaining the old groupings of functional specialists with additional organization along task lines.

Hospital administrators have attempted reforms exemplifying the last of the above-mentioned alternatives. Attendants and nurses in mental hospitals tend to become more concerned with their custodial duties than with the major objective of improving the health of patients. The creation of teams involving doctors, administrators, nurses, and attendants to discuss individual cases and alternative methods of dealing with them can help immeasurably in changing the conception of the job of the attendant and the nurse. One cannot make the security policeman a member of the scientific research team in the same sense, but he can be assigned to a particular laboratory and placed under the supervision of its director for the discharge of many of his duties. Thus he can learn that one of his functions is not to throw the scientist who has forgotten his identification card out of the laboratory, but to issue a new card for him. He can be given more responsibility rather than less in contributing to the mission of the organization.

The revision of organizational arrangements to involve peripheral and low-status groups in organizational goals has implications for system rewards. To the extent that the lowly member is now part of the team, it becomes more difficult to treat him as a third-class citizen in the distribution of organizational rewards. Professional baseball teams recognize this principle when they vote shares of the World Series bonus to players who have spent most of the season on the bench, to trainers, and to other nonplaying personnel. Football coaches follow the same principle by getting many of their first-squad members into a minute or more of playing in criterion games so that they can earn their varsity letters. Joint authorship, in which the names of all research workers are listed as responsible for a research report, is becoming a common practice. Where an obvious differentiation of individual contribution to the group product can be ascertained, it is feasible to set up individual rewards for differential effectiveness and effort. Where there are no palpable criteria for the determination of individual effort and where the emphasis is upon teamwork, system rewards are more feasible and lead to higher identification with the organization.

Though system rewards maintain the level of productivity not much above the minimum required to stay in the system, there still may be large differences *between* systems with respect to the quantity and quality of production as a function of system rewards. An organization with substantially better wage rates and fringe benefits than its competitors may be able to set a higher level of performance as a minimal requirement for its workers and still hold its employees. System rewards can be related to the differential productivity of organizations as a whole though they are not effective in maximizing the potential contributions of the majority of individuals within an organization. They may account for differences in motivation between systems rather than for differences in motivation between individuals in the same system. They operate through their effects upon the minimal standards for all people in the system. They act indirectly in that their effect is to make people want to stay in the organization; to do so people must be willing to accept the legitimately derived standards of role performance in that system. The direct mechanism for insuring performance is legal compliance, but the legal requirements of the organization will not hold members if demands are too great or rewards too meager in comparison to other organizations. The mediating variable in accounting for organizational differences based upon system rewards is the relative attractiveness of the system for the individual compared to other systems accessible to him.

The Rewards of Approval. Another instrumental satisfaction for group members derives, as we have mentioned earlier, from the approval and support of their leaders. This category has to do with the psychological rewards of leader approval and is distinct from the leader's use of more tangible rewards. The use of approval by organizational leaders is nevertheless subject to the same limitation as is use of other reward forms. He can avoid inequity and make his approval part of the system reward by speaking words of encouragement to every member meeting standards. Or he can single out for special approval the very few who perform above standard. In the former case, he may merely contribute to the feeling that this is a pleasant place to work. In the latter case, he may strengthen the motivation of a few "company" men and add to the resistance of the majority.

The actions of the superior in ministering to the dependency needs of his followers, moreover, may develop a satisfying interpersonal relationship which has, if anything, a negative effect upon organizational performance. The dependent employee may gravitate to the officer who can give him some psychological assurance in coping with personal problems. The support of the father figure, understandably

enough, may not be given to the person who does the job well but
to the dependent person on the basis of his needs. In turn, the superior
may derive gratification from playing this supportive role. Though both
individuals profit from the relationship, it may be so unrelated to the
tasks to be performed that it merely subtracts from the productive
time of both people. Kaye (1958) has provided data consistent with this
interpretation.

Another type of reward is the approval of peers in the organization.
Social support from peers can add to the attractiveness of the subsystem
and can be a factor in the reduction of absenteeism and turnover. It will
lead to increased productivity and quality of work, however, only if the
norms of the peer group sanction such performance. In many industrial
organizations, the norms of the peer group set informal standards for
production which are not optimal from the company's point of view. In
voluntary organizations, however, the norms of the group are often an
important source of increased individual activity.

Table 8   CONDITIONS AFFECTING THE USE OF PEER-
GROUP APPROVAL

Objective Conditions	Mediated by Psychological Variables	Outcome
1. Group cohesion	1. Individual's own attraction to group	Decreased turnover and absenteeism
	2. The relevance of group norms with respect to organizational objectives	Possible increases or decreases in productivity
		No necessary relations with behavior beyond the call of duty

Behavior beyond the formal requirements of role may be fostered
or discouraged by the need for approval from peers. The norms of
the local group generally sanction productive cooperation and support
actions which protect the organization against disaster. The values of
the work group seldom approve, however, of the eager member who
wants to save the company money through some brilliant suggestion,
or of the ambitious employees who seek to train themselves for better
jobs. The work group tends to value seniority as the best principle
for allocating privileges and benefits, and to be protective of the group
rather than the organization.

Type C. Self-Expression and Self-Determination. The motivational
pattern of self-expression (Type C) is the most conducive to the

achievement of high quantity and quality of role performance. When this pattern is successfully evoked, the pathway to high productivity and to high quality production affords intrinsic job satisfaction. The man who finds the type of work he delights in doing will not worry about the fact that the role requires a given amount of production of a certain quality. His gratifications accrue from accomplishment, from the expression of his own abilities, from the exercise of his own decisions.

Craftsmanship is the old term for the work of the skilled performer who enjoys intrinsic job satisfaction. This type of worker is not the clock watcher, nor the shoddy performer. On the other hand, such a person is not necessarily tied to a given organization. As a good carpenter or a good mechanic, it may matter little to him where he does work, provided that he is given ample opportunity to do the kind of job he is interested in doing. He may, moreover, contribute little to organizational goals beyond his specific role.

Table 9   CONDITIONS AFFECTING THE USE OF SELF-EXPRESSION

Objective Conditions	Mediated by Psychological Variables	Outcome
1. Complexity and skill requirements of job	1. Appropriateness of individual's own skills	No necessary relationship with turnover
2. Responsibility and autonomy of job	2. Degree of normal self-development vs. stunted personalities	Decreases in absenteeism
3. Other job alternatives	3. Perception of alternative job possibilities	High productivity
		Some increase in co-operative activity but in general little direct relation with behavior beyond the call of duty

If such intrinsic job satisfaction or identification with the work is to be aroused and maximized, then the job itself must provide sufficient variety, sufficient complexity, sufficient challenge, and sufficient exercise of skill to engage the abilities of the worker. If there is one confirmed finding in all the studies of worker morale and satisfaction, it is the correlation between the variety and challenge of the job and the gratifications which accrue to workers. There are cases of people who do not want more responsibility and of people who become demoralized by being placed in jobs which are too difficult for them. But these are the exceptions. By and large, people seek more responsibility, more skill-demanding jobs than they hold, and as they are able to attain these more demanding jobs, they become happier, better adjusted, and suffer fewer health complaints.

Obviously, the conditions for securing higher motivation to produce and to produce quality work involve changes in organizational structure—job enlargement rather than job fractionation. Yet the tendency in large scale organizations is toward increasing specialization and routinization of jobs. Workers would be better motivated toward production and higher quality work if we discarded the assembly line and moved toward the craftsmanlike operations of an older time. Industry has demonstrated, however, that it is generally more efficient to produce via assembly line methods with lowered motivation and job satisfaction than with highly motivated craftsmen with a large area of responsibility. The preferred path to the attainment of production goals in turning out cars or other mass physical products is the path of organizational control and not the path of internalized motivation. The quality of production and the joys of craftsmanship may suffer somewhat, but it is still cheaper to buy several mass-produced cars than a single Rolls Royce.

In the production of physical objects for mass consumption, the assembly line may furnish the best model. This may also apply to service operations in which the process can be sufficiently simplified. But when we consider organizations which have the modification or treatment of human beings as their product (as in educational institutions, hospitals, or remedial institutions) we do not want to rely solely on organizational controls which guarantee only a minimum effort of employees. We want employees with high motivation and high identification with their jobs. Jobs cannot profitably be fractionated very far, or standardized and coordinated to a rigorous time schedule, in a research laboratory, in a medical clinic, in an educational institution, or in a hospital. An educational system which routinizes learning so that throughout an entire state all fourth-grade students will be memorizing the same paragraph from page 146 of a standard text on American History is simply not an educational system. Hospital administration, which modeled itself after the machine theory of organization, is beginning to move to a more appropriate managerial model with emphasis upon "open" hospitals permitting greater freedom to patients and hospital personnel. The ideal is no longer to wake up every patient with a wet washcloth at five in the morning.

In addition to recognizing the inapplicability of the organizational devices of factory and army to all organizations, we should recognize that not all factory operations can be left to institutional controls without regard to the motivation of employees. Job fractionation can be pushed to the point of diminishing returns even in industry. The success of the Tavistock workers in raising productivity in the British coal mines through job enlargement was due to the fact that the specialization of American long-wall methods of coal mining did not yield adequate returns when applied to the difficult and variable conditions under which British miners had to operate (Trist et al., 1963).

The question of whether to move toward greater specialization and standardization in an industrial operation or whether to move in the opposite direction is generally an empirical one to be answered by research. One rule of thumb can be applied, however. If the job can be so simplified and standardized that it is readily convertible to automated machines, then the direction to take is that of further institutionalization until automation is possible. If, however, the overall performance requires complex judgment, differential weighing of factors which are not markedly identifiable, innovation and creativity, then the human mind is an instrument far superior to the most elaborate electronic brain.

The paradox is that where automation is feasible, it can actually increase motivation among the employees left on the job after the change-over. Mann and Hoffman (1960) conclude from their study of automation in an electric power plant that the remaining jobs for workers can be more interesting, that there can be freer association among colleagues, and that the elimination of some supervisory levels brings the top and bottom of the organization closer together.

Type D. Internalization of Organizational Goals. The pattern of motivation associated with value expression and self-identification (Type D) has great potentialities for the internalization of system goals and thus for the activation of behavior not prescribed by specific roles. It is generally confined to the upper echelons or to the officer personnel. In voluntary organizations it extends into the rank and file and in fact most voluntary organizations depend almost entirely on a core of dedicated people.

The complete internalization of organizational goals is not as common as two types of partial internalization. The first has to do with general organizational purposes which are not unique to the organization. A scientist may have internalized the research values of his pro-

Table 10 CONDITIONS AFFECTING THE INTERNALIZATION
OF ORGANIZATIONAL GOALS

Objective Conditions	Mediated by Psychological Variables	Outcome
1. Hazardous character of organizational goals	1. Individual's own sense of the heroic and dramatic	Reduced turnover and absenteeism
2. Organizational goals expressive of cultural values	2. Appropriateness for individual's own values	Increased productivity
3. Organizational leader as model	3. Identification with model	Spontaneous and innovative behavior
4. Sharing in organizational decisions	4. Perception of being important part of organization	
5. Sharing in organizational rewards		

fession but not necessarily of the specific institution to which he is attached. As long as he stays in that institution, he may be a well-motivated worker. But he may find it just as easy to work for the things he believes in another institution.

A second type of partial internalization concerns the values and goals of a subsystem of the organization. It is often easier for the person to take over the values of his own unit than of the larger organization. We may be attached to our own department in a university more than to the university as a whole.

Internalization of organization objectives can come about through the utilization of the socialization process in childhood or through the adult socialization which takes place in the organization itself. In the first instance, a selective process initiated either by the person or the organization matches personality with system. A youngster growing up in the tradition of one of the military services may have always thought of himself as a military officer. The crusader for civil liberties and the American Civil Liberties Union find one another.

The adult socialization process in the organization can build upon the personal values of its members and integrate them around an attractive organizational model. People can thus identify with the organizational mission. If the task of an organization has emotional significance, the organization enjoys an advantage in the creation of an attractive image. If the task is attended by hazard (as in the tracking down of criminals by the FBI) or by high adventure (as in the early days of flying) or by service to humanity (as in the case of a cancer research unit), it is not difficult to develop a convincing model of the organization's mission.

The imaginative leader can help in the development of an attractive picture of the organization by some new conceptualization of its mission. Policemen entrusted with the routine and dirty business of law enforcement can be energized by seeing themselves as a corps of professional officers devoted to the highest form of public service. Even though reality factors limit the innovative use of symbols for the glorification of organizations, occupational groups constantly strive to achieve a more attractive picture of themselves. Press agents have become public relations specialists, and undertakers have become morticians.

The image of the organization is aided appreciably by personalization or casting the model in the form of present leaders or past heroes. General Patton of the Third Army, with his military posture, his silver pistols, and his standards of discipline, presented such a personal model for his troops. Political parties glorify their past warriors, and institutions constantly attempt to create charisma about their leaders. This identification with personal models may produce only partial internalization of organizational purposes. People may identify with the great figure in order to participate in a compensatory manner in his greatness. Nonetheless, some of the virtues he represents become their own ideals.

Internalization of subgroup norms can come about through identification with fellow group members who share the same common fate. People take over the values of their group because they identify with their own kind. They see themselves as good group members, and as good group members they model their actions and aspirations in terms of group norms. This subgroup identification can work for organizational objectives only if there is agreement between group norms and organizational objectives. In industry the norms of the work group are often much closer to union objectives than to company objectives.

This suggests three additional factors which contribute to internalization of group objectives: participating in important decisions about group objectives; contributing to group performance in a significant way; and sharing in the rewards of group accomplishment. When these three conditions are met, the individual can regard the group as his, for he in fact has helped to make it.

The trouble with group decision, as the term is so often used, is that it fails to meet these criteria. To meet them would mean genuine changes in the role structure of the organization. The power and authority system would have to be altered, with new legitimacy attached to group decision-making.

STUDIES OF MOTIVATION IN ORGANIZATIONS [*]

Our theoretical analysis of the motivational basis of organizational performance is much more an application of general principles of social psychology than a summary of empirical findings from organizational studies. Quantitative investigations of organizational effectiveness are surprisingly few in spite of the voluminous literature on organizations. We shall call attention to some of these studies in relation to the analytic framework just presented.

Determinants of Job Satisfaction

The clearest and most consistent body of findings in industrial social psychology has to do with the determinants of intrinsic job satisfaction. Studies corroborate one another in demonstrating that the more varied, complex, and challenging tasks are higher in worker gratification than less skilled, routine jobs.

Comparisons of occupational groups show that the more skilled the vocation, the more its members enjoy their jobs. Hoppock (1935) reported that more than 90 per cent of a group of 500 teachers liked their work, whereas Bell (1937) found that 98 per cent of young people working in canning factories and textile mills hated their jobs. In another study by Hoppock (1935), of 309 people in a small Pennsylvania town, the greatest dissatisfaction with work occurred among the unskilled laborers. Satisfaction increased with occupational level, with the greatest satisfaction among professional groups. The relationship between job satisfaction and occupational status has also been confirmed in studies by Hull and Kolstad (1942), Thorndike (1935), Super (1939), and by Uhrbrock (1934).

A more recent study further documents this finding and adds to its generalizability since the research was based upon a national sample of the population. Gurin, Veroff, and Feld (1960) report that the greatest amount of job satisfaction occurs among the professional, technical, and managerial personnel, and the least amount among unskilled workers. The groups intermediate in gratification are the clerical, sales, and manually skilled and semiskilled. No differences were found between these intermediate groups, either because the manually skilled job is as challenging as clerical work or because white-collar workers have higher levels of aspiration and are therefore less easily satisfied.

[*] Some of the material in this section is adapted from "Satisfactions and Deprivations in Industrial Life," by Daniel Katz (1954).

	Professionals, Technicians	Managers, Proprietors	Clerical Workers	Sales Workers	Skilled Workers	Semiskilled Workers	Unskilled Workers	Farmers
Job Satisfaction								
Very Satisfied	42%	38%	22%	24%	22%	27%	13%	22%
Satisfied	41	42	39	44	54	48	52	58
Neutral	1	6	9	5	6	9	6	4
Ambivalent	10	6	13	9	10	9	13	9
Dissatisfied	3	6	17	16	7	6	16	7
Not Ascertained	3	2	—	2	1	1	—	—
TOTAL	100%	100%	100%	100%	100%	100%	100%	100%
Number of men	(119)	(127)	(46)	(55)	(202)	(152)	(84)	(77)
Sources of Satisfaction								
Mention only ego satisfactions	80%	68%	39%	60%	54%	40%	29%	58%
Mention both ego and extrinsic satisfactions	16	20	35	29	28	31	26	17
Mention only extrinsic satisfactions	2	9	24	7	14	24	29	17
Mention no reasons for liking job	—	—	2	2	2	3	8	1
Not ascertained	2	3	—	2	2	2	8	7
TOTAL	100%	100%	100%	100%	100%	100%	100%	100%
Number of men	(119)	(127)	(46)	(55)	(202)	(152)	(84)	(77)

* From Gurin, Veroff, and Feld, 1960, pp. 159 and 163.

In most of these studies, job satisfaction is used loosely to cover overall liking for the job situation as well as intrinsic job satisfaction deriving from the content of the work process. Hence the greater gratification of the higher occupational levels can be due to the higher pay, the greater prestige of the calling, the hours, or working conditions, and the like. It is important, therefore, to hold constant factors other than the nature of the work in comparing the satisfaction derived from jobs varying in level of skill and complexity. This is, of course, not possible in dealing with broad occupational groupings where wages and conditions of work are tied to type of occupation. Within a single company, however, it is possible to make meaningful comparisons of intrinsic job satisfaction within a restricted range of differential skill level. The company may have the same working conditions and the same program of employee benefits for all workers within this range. Moreover, the wages may take account of seniority as well as of skill level. Hence it is possible to find workers at more complex tasks earning no more than workers at less skilled jobs.

Such a situation was true for clerical workers in the home office of a large insurance company, where the tasks vary from routine filing through correspondence with policy holders to moderately complicated mathematical computations. The Survey Research Center of The University of Michigan conducted a survey of employee morale in this company in which 580 employees were intensively interviewed (Morse, 1953). Intrinsic job satisfaction was measured by an index which summarized the answers to four qestions: How well do you like the sort of work you are doing? Does your job give you a chance to do the things you feel you do best? Do you get any feeling of accomplishment from the work you are doing? How do you feel about your work; does it rate as an important job with you?

In this study employees were grouped into four classes on the basis of job level: high-level technical, semi-supervisory, varied clerical, and repetitious clerical. In the high-level technical group only 7 per cent of their members fell into the category of low intrinsic job satisfaction, compared with 41 per cent of the group doing repetitive clerical work. Moreover, this relationship was not reduced when length of service or salary was held constant. These results suggest strongly that the greater gratifications found among high-level occupational groups are not wholly a function of wages and conditions of work. People do derive important satisfaction in the expresssion of their skills, in interesting and challenging work, and in the sense of accomplishment from successful performance.

In the same study, the employees who were higher on intrinsic job satisfaction tended to be the people who described their jobs as having variety and as giving them some chance to make decisions. In other circumstances, this could be interpreted as a subjective phenomenon, that is, a manifestation of the ability of some people to find variety in even the most routine tasks. In this instance, however, the people who found their work varied and containing opportunities for some decision-making were in fact doing more skilled and varied work. The old contention that people do not like to make decisions is also answered by the findings of this study. Only 24 per cent of the employees were satisfied with the amount of decision-making in their jobs, as the following figures indicate:

Employees making no decisions who would not like to make any	11%
Employees making some decisions who would not like to make more	13
Employees making no decision who would like to make some	30
Employees making some decisions who would like to make more	46

Total	100%
$N =$	537

A similar finding, though not so pronounced, comes from the Survey Research Center's 1950 study of the production workers in a plant representative of heavy industry. These factory workers do not represent as high an educational level as the home-office employees of the insurance company. Nevertheless, 51 per cent of 5700 workers, in response to the question, "Would you like to have more or less to say about the way your work is done?" wanted to have more to say. And the majority of workers (68 per cent) felt that they had little or nothing to say about how their jobs should be carried out. Moreover, the majority (65 per cent) thought the work would be performed better if the men had more chance to make suggestions about such things as design, setups, and the layout of the work. When pressed further on the problem of why the men did not make suggestions on how the work should be done, the following reasons were given:

Men don't get credit for suggestions	50%
Top management won't use suggestions men make	28%
Foremen won't use suggestions men make	23%
Other men don't think a man should make suggestions	11%
Men don't know where to make suggestions	10%
Men don't know what suggestions to make	7%

The implication of these results is clear: in spite of the deadening of expectations about participation in the work process in large-scale mechanized production, many workers still feel deprived of the opportunity to apply their skill and knowledge in a full measure to their jobs. Vroom (1962), for example, obtained a correlation of .59 between job satisfaction and the perceived opportunities for self-expression for 489 blue-collar workers in an Candian oil refinery. Self-expression was measured by a series of nine questions, such as, "How much chance do you get to use the skills you have learned for this job?" and "How much chance do you get to do the kinds of things you are best at?"

Other evidence is available which analyzes the nature of the work in relation to its gratification potential. Walker and Guest (1952) investigated the factor of repetitiveness versus variety in an automobile plant in terms of the number of operations the worker carried out. Of those performing more than five operations, a clear majority (69 per cent) found their tasks interesting or fairly interesting. Of the workers carrying out two to five operations, only 44 per cent gave similar reports on the interest of their work, and of those performing a single operation, the percentage fell to 33 per cent. Many workers themselves complained about the repetitive character of the work in the groups performing few operations. Another measure of the repetitive character of work was used by Baldamus (1951) in timing the length of the work cycle. He found that the labor turnover rates for the men with a short work cycle (less than thirty minutes) was twice as great as the men in longer work cycles (though the sample in this study was very small).

Studies of job enlargement also report greater satisfaction with an increase in the meaningful cycle of activities. Trist and his colleagues (1963) found this to be true in their investigation of British coal miners, and Rice (1958) has contributed to the generality of this finding across cultures in his experimental work with Indian textile workers. Similarly, Walker (1950, 1954) has noted the results of job enlargement in a factory making calculating machines. The fractionation of work whereby three different groups of employees were assigned to setting up the job, operating the machines, and inspecting the product was replaced by a system in which the worker performed all three functions. The outcome was that feelings of boredom and frustration characteristic of the older system diminished and in some cases disappeared. Guest (1957) and Elliott (1953) have also conducted investigations of job enlargement, the former in an insurance company and a manufacturing concern, the latter in a public utility. The results of these studies support the generalization that more varied and demanding tasks produce greater job satisfaction than routine, repetitive activity.

The study of Mann and Hoffman (1960) of the automation of a power plant in a large public utility also constitutes substantiating evidence. In the new automated plant with many fewer employees, workers were given more duties and more rotation in different types of jobs. One hundred per cent of the workers questioned reported that their new, enlarged jobs were much more interesting than their old jobs. Moreover, the general level of job satisfaction was much higher in the automated plant than in another plant in the same company where the jobs followed a more repetitive and less varied pattern.

In spite of a culture which emphasizes speed and mechanization to a degree which makes for robotlike performance, the old values of craftsmanship, of creativity, of individual initiative, and of self-determination are very much alive in millions of American workers. Men still prefer jobs which challenge their skill and which give them some measure of decision-making and responsibility. The fact that the great majority of jobs offer a routinized work content is a constant source of frustration to the man who still has some craftsmanship and enterprise in his make-up.

Job Satisfaction and Productivity

Since job satisfaction is definitely related to challenging work calling for skill and responsibility, the expectation is that it would also relate to productivity, i.e., that higher job satisfaction would also be found in conjunction with better performance. This prediction would also be made from a theoretical analysis in which we assume that involvement in task activity, i.e., craftsmanship, would result in greater quantity and better quality of productive work. Empirical studies show, however, that measures of job satisfaction among workers on the same type of job are far from being reliable indicators of productivity. An extensive review of the research literature by Brayfield and Crockett (1955) called attention to the general disagreement of studies on this point. These authors stated: "In summary, it appears that there is little evidence in the available literature that employee attitudes of the type usually measured in morale surveys bear any simple—or, for that matter, appreciable—relationship to performance on the job." In a more recent review Vroom (1964) further documents this research outcome. He analyzed twenty correlational studies and found the median correlation between satisfaction and performance to be $+.14$ with a range of $+.86$ to $-.31$.

In many of these studies, job satisfaction was loosely defined and represented many factors other than involvement in the task itself, e.g., liking for the supervisor, or identification with the company. Even where measures of intrinsic job satisfaction have been employed (questions relating to the opportunities for expression of abilities in the task), the anticipated relationship with productivity has not appeared with any degree of consistency. In fact, two of the studies specifically concerned with intrinsic job satisfaction have reported negative relationships. In a study of clerical employees, Katz, Maccoby, and Morse (1950) found that there were more employees satisfied with their jobs in low producing groups than in high producing groups. Katz, Maccoby, Gurin, and Floor (1951) replicated this finding among maintenance of way crews on a railroad.

The reasons for this failure to confirm the expectation that intrinsic job satisfaction is positively related to productivity are not difficult to find in a post hoc analysis. On the basis of the types of dissatisfactions expressed by the clerical workers in the above-mentioned study, Morse (1953) suggested that the levels of aspiration of the workers were affecting the relationship. Workers with higher job involvement were probably setting higher levels of aspiration for themselves and hence reacted more negatively to blocks in their progress than less motivated workers. Thus an intrinsic job satisfaction measure which does not take into account the aspirations of the worker is an inadequate measure of his degree of job involvement. Likert (1961) has pointed out that in routine and repetitive work there is little opportunity for differential task involvement and hence little chance for a positive relationship between intrinsic job satisfaction and performance to appear. Where tasks are more varied and require more skill, Likert maintains that the expected positive correlations do occur.

Our own interpretation follows the Likert thesis in that our theoretical model would require certain specifications before job involvement would predict to productivity. Productivity is a measure of role performance and for most production workers such performance has been almost completely standardized. Hence it relates very little to individual variables of motivation and satisfaction and much more to system determinants of the flow of materials, the organization of the work process, the speed of the flow process (e.g., speed of the assembly line), and the like. Individuals have little opportunity to express their craftsmanship with the result that the basic motivation is to maintain an acceptable level of performance rather than to excel.

We are suggesting that both performance and task involvement vary little for hourly workers assigned to the same types of jobs in many organizations. The studies to which reference has been made were restricted to comparisons within the organization, all the members of which performed the same routine operations. Comparisons across organizations might show more of a relationship but they have generally not been made because of the difficulty of equating productivity measures for the different tasks. The wartime study of Katz and Hyman (1948) showed a significant positive relationship between morale and productivity for five shipyards varying greatly in productivity where comparisons were between shipyards as the major units of analysis.

Where individual piece rates are employed, the expectations for a positive relationship between task involvement and performance should be higher provided that there is room for the individual worker to show his ability. There is suggestive evidence that this in fact is the case. One of the highest relationships between job satisfaction and productivity was reported by Brody (1945)—a correlation of .68 and his subjects were production workers on piece rates. In this study, however, it was possible that higher earnings might have affected the responses to the questions on intrinsic job satisfaction.

Job Satisfaction and Motivation to Remain in the System: Absenteeism and Turnover

The preceding analysis would suggest that job satisfaction would not relate to productivity except in special cases but that it would relate to staying in the system, i.e., to a low rate of absenteeism and a low rate of turnover. The reason is that job satisfaction as generally measured is not so much an index of direct gratification from the type of work as a reflection of satisfaction with all aspects of the job. The attractions of the job are less a matter of furnishing differential opportunities for the worker to show his skills and abilities and more a matter of system determinants of working conditions, wages, and company treatment. Liking for the job as operative in many industrial settings is not so much an intrinsic satisfaction with the content of the work as the reflection of the attractiveness of the system. Hence this more generalized job satisfaction should hold the individual in the system.

Vroom (1964) states essentially the same hypothesis:

> If we assume that measures of job satisfaction reflect the valence of the job to its occupant, then it follows from our model that job satisfaction should be related to the strength of the force on the person to remain in his job. The more satisfied a worker, the stronger the force on him to remain in his job and the less probability of his leaving it voluntarily. (p. 175)

The available evidence confirms this expectation. Vroom summarizes the research literature as follows.

> There are seven studies dealing with the satisfaction-turnover relationship, four of them using individuals as the unit of analysis and three using groups. All studies indicate the expected negative relationship between these variables although the magnitude and significance of this relationship varies considerably from study to study.

Weitz and Nuckols (1953) assumed that job satisfaction would be negatively related to turnover and consequently sought to determine the relative validity of indirect and direct job satisfaction measures by seeing which one best predicted future turnover. They mailed questionnaires containing both direct and indirect measures of job satisfaction to 1200 insurance agents representing a single company in the southern states. Forty-seven per cent of these replied. The authors related the satisfaction data obtained in this manner to subsequent information they received about terminations. The satisfaction scores obtained by the direct method correlated .20 with survival (significant at the 1 per cent level). The scores obtained through the indirect method (in which agents were asked to estimate the attitudes of other agents toward their jobs) correlated only .05 with survival. The latter correlation was not significant.

Webb and Hollander (1956) obtained three different measures of morale from each of 210 cadets enrolled in a preflight curriculum in a naval air training situation. The three measures were: (1) a questionnaire pertaining to "interest in and enthusiasm for the naval air program" (p. 17); (2) peer nominations of interest and enthusiasm for naval aviation; (3) self-rankings on interest and enthusiasm for naval aviation. Subsequent to the morale measurement, 16 of the 210 cadets voluntarily withdrew from the program. All three of the measures had some relationship to withdrawal, with peer nominations and self-evaluations being the better predictors. Fourteen of the 16 persons who withdrew were below the median on these two measures, whereas 10 were below the median on the questionnaire. . . .

In group analyses, Giese and Ruter (1949) found a correlation of −.42 between the morale and turnover rates of 25 departments in a small mail-order company; Fleishman, Harris, and Burtt (1955) found a correlation of −.21 between the turnover rates and morale of production and nonproduction departments at International Harvester; and Kerr, Koppelmeir, and Sullivan (1951) found a correlation of −.13 between the average job satisfaction scores and turnover rates of 20 departments in a metal fabrication factory. (pp. 176–177)

Essentially the same prediction would be made concerning a negative relationship between job satisfaction and absenteeism, namely the more attractive the job the lower the absence rate. By and large, research studies support the hypothesis though not every investigation provides clear confirmatory evidence. Kornhauser and Sharp (1932) provided some suggestive findings for women factory workers in which lost time was related to unfavorable attitudes toward the job. In a study of 18 plants during World War II, Katz and Hyman (1947) found significantly more job dissatisfaction among absentees than among nonabsentees. This comprehensive investigation included interviews taken in the homes of some 1800 workers based upon a random sample of 100 employees from each plant. Kerr, Koppelmeir and Sullivan (1951) used group measures for 29 departments in a metal fabrication factory and obtained a correlation of −.44 between mean job satisfaction for a department and unexcused absences. The correlation was revised, however, when total absences were the criterion measure (which suggests that long illnesses can obscure the relationship). Mann and Metzner (1953) found that blue-collar workers in a large public utility had better attendance records if they liked their jobs. Of the workers who were absent less than three times during a six month period, 27 per cent were high in finding self-expression in their work compared to only 6 per cent of the men with over five absences. And of those who had less than three absences in the half-year period, some 33 per cent liked the type of work they were doing as against 13 per cent of those with more than five absences.

Three other correlational studies furnish confirming evidence. Van Zelst and Kerr (1953) reported a correlation of .31 between good attendance records and job satisfaction for 340 employees in some 14 firms. A study conducted at International Harvester by Fleishman, Harris, and Burtt (1955) showed a correlation of −.25 between morale and absence rates. Harding and Bottenberg (1961) employing eight measures of satisfaction obtained a multiple correlation of −.38 between these measures and absence rates. Three other studies do not, however, yield similar results. An investigation by Vroom (1962) gave a correlation of only −.07, another by Bernberg (1952) correlations of .00 and .06, and a third by Mann, Indik, and Vroom (1963) correlations of .14 for drivers and −.32 for package-sorters in a large delivery company.

The critical factor, as Vroom (1964) suggests, may be the amount of involuntary absence due to long illness which is often included in the absence rate. Where this can be factored out, as in the Kerr, Koppelmeir, and Sullivan and the Mann and Metzner studies, the predicted relationship does appear.

Group Cohesion as Related to Productivity and System Attraction

Industrial social psychology received its major impetus from the work of Elton Mayo (1931) and his colleagues in their studies at the Western Electric Company. These investigators demonstrated that the norms of informal work groups could affect productivity positively or negatively depending upon the relationship of the informal norms to the goals of the organization. In their famous Hawthorne study they set aside a group of girls under an excellent supervisor, gave them special privileges, and in general encouraged an informal organization favorable to the company. The result was a clear and sustained increase in productivity. The same methods, however, produced no rise in performance among a group of men whose informal norms for restricting productivity were too strong to yield to the manipulations of the experimenters.

Likert's (1961) review of the research in this area concludes:

Work groups which have high peer-group loyalty and common goals appear to be effective in achieving their goals. If their goals are the achievement of high productivity and low waste, these are the goals they will accomplish. If, on the other hand, the character of their supervisor causes them to reject the objectives of the organization and set goals at variance with these objectives, the goals they establish can have strikingly adverse effects upon productivity. (p. 30)

The most impressive demonstration of this principle in an ongoing organization comes from the study of Seashore (1954) in a company manufacturing heavy machinery. Seashore used as his measure of group cohesion an index based upon questions of how much workers felt a part of their group, how much they wanted to stay in the group, and how much they helped each other. His findings were (1) that highly cohesive groups showed much less within-group variation on productivity than low cohesive groups; but (2) that the production variation between groups was greater for the more cohesive than the less cohesive groups. Further, the high cohesive groups were above average in performance when they accepted company goals and below average when they rejected company goals, whereas the low cohesive groups tended to be more average in performance (Figure 10).

Though the relationship of cohesion with productivity can go in

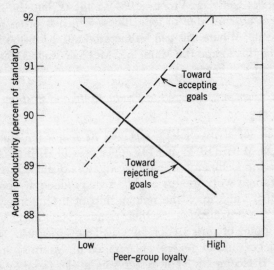

Figure 10 Relationship of peer-group loyalty to productivity when motivation is toward accepting versus rejecting company goals. (From *New Patterns of Management*, Rensis Likert, New York: McGraw-Hill, 1961, p. 32.)

either a positive or negative direction, the relationship is more often positive than negative in the studies conducted to date. Though there is a risk to the larger system as subunits develop their own solidarity, the risk has been exaggerated. The leading values of the larger system are not readily ignored by cohesive units which have to come to terms with the overall system.

This was even true within the prison studied by Sykes (1958) in which the informal organization of the inmates, though protective of their welfare, also served the interests of the institution. We are not dealing here with the basic problem of integrating cohesive units into the larger structure but are suggesting that the divisive effect of sub-group loyalty is not the whole story. Likert (1961) has suggested that these groups can be tied into the larger organizational system through membership in a structure of overlapping organizational families. Integration is also facilitated by a fuller participation in the tangible rewards of organization and in the making of policy decisions.

Though solidarity of peer groups does not always make for superior performance, it should make for increased motivation to stay within the system. If the individual's colleagues form an attractive group for him, it should make the organization more attractive and there should be less absenteeism and less turnover.

Mayo and Lombard (1944), in their study of the aircraft industry in California during World War II, reported that absenteeism was lowest in those groups regarded as clannish and highest among the workers who were not team workers. There was a marked contrast between one department in which there were well-knit teams, and other departments in which there was little group spirit in the working units. Mann and Baumgartel (1953) confirmed this finding in their study of workers in a public utility. Figure 11 illustrates the fact that the greater the group solidarity of the white-collar workers, the lower the absenteeism. Blue-collar workers followed the same pattern. These results were based on questions having to do with how workers felt about their group sticking together and getting a job done. Similar findings emerged from an analysis of questions of group belonging-ness, i.e., how much the men felt they were really a part of their group. These investigations help to explain the relationships reported by Revans (1957) between absence, accidents, and sickness, and the size of the total enterprise and the size of work groups. His data cover such varied enterprises as coal mines, quarries, hospitals, and telephone exchanges. In general, the larger the size of the unit, the greater Revans found the rate of absences and accidents to be. The inference is that large units interfere with the formation of informal cohesive groups.

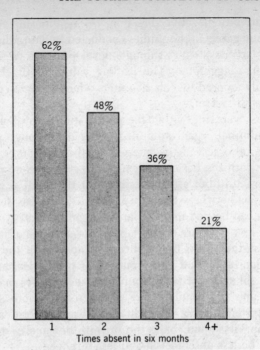

Figure 11 Relation of group solidarity to absence (white-collar men). (From *New Patterns of Management*, Rensis Likert, New York: McGraw-Hill, 1961, p. 35.)

Georgopoulos and Mann (1962) in their study of community hospitals found absenteeism to be more a function of organizational units than of individual personality factors.

Internalization of Organizational Goals

The involvement of the individual in a system so that he regards its goals as his own personal objectives has seen little study. Such involvement should result in a variety of behaviors supportive of the organizational mission (higher productivity, lower absenteeism and turnover, and many spontaneous actions on behalf of the organization). The basic condition for producing internalization of system objectives is the self-realization of the individual in furthering these objectives. As has already been indicated, the values the individual brings to the organization are one determining factor. Another major factor is the degree to which the individual can see the organization as his own creation. By participating in its decisions and sharing in its rewards, it becomes part of himself and he is a part of it.

Participation has become something of a shibboleth in our society and everything from consultative management to group decision is therefore seen through rosy glasses. There are, of course, degrees and types of participation. We refer here, however, to the engagement of the individual in the system so that he is involved in decisions which affect him as a system member. In effect, he has both a voice and a vote in the subsystem in which he functions and a voice and a vote in the representation of that subsystem in the larger structure. And this type of participation also guarantees him an opportunity to share in the rewards of the group cooperation that constitutes the system.

The boldest attempt at such participation in American industry is the Scanlon Plan. The Scanlon Plan has been variously defined and much written about, although in the last five years there has been a significant and ominous reduction in the output of Scanlon literature. The titles in the earlier bibliography ring with phrases of optimism —enterprise for everyman, industrial democracy, every man a capitalist, and the like. To be more specific and less extravagant, we may say that the Scanlon Plan consists of a set of very general principles, a set of specific and crucial structural changes, and some procedural suggestions for introducing such changes into an ongoing organization.

Scanlon himself saw four principles as basic to the Plan: major participation by the workers in the solution of production problems and other ongoing decisions of the enterprise; most of the direct gains in productivity (75 to 100 per cent) to be paid as wage bonuses to the workers, with all such bonuses depending on the success of the total enterprise; these two principles to be implemented within the context of the collective bargaining agreement between management and union, and in no way to substitute for that agreement or its provisions; and finally, the importance of "a genuine sense of partnership by both parties" (a principle which seems to us to express an outcome of the Plan at least as much as a requirement for its initiation).

To some extent the means by which a particular company moved to implement these principles were locally decided. There are, however, several structural changes which are universal requirements for the Scanlon Plan.

The first of these is a major change in the power structure of the company. The initial act, following immediately the agreement between union and management that the Scanlon Plan shall be attempted, is the election of production committees by the workers. A production committee is elected in each department of the organization and these committees are empowered to put into practice any change in productive technique which does not involve changes in the activities of other departments or major outlays of money. (The exact limit on expenditure is agreed upon formally by management and union.) The workers also elect representatives to a companywide committee which is given the mandate of performing at the company level functions comparable to those in the production committees at the level of the individual departments. Usually there are management representatives as well as representatives of the workers on the departmental production committees and also on the companywide screening committee or advisory board. At the departmental level management usually appoints as its member the supervisor of the department or some person in a comparable position. The departmental committees meet at least once a month and their agenda consist of proposals for the elimination of waste and for improved ways of performing individual jobs and the departmental function. The committee must also consider every suggestion for change in methods and setup of the work made by any employee or by the union. The issue in every case is whether the specific suggestion under consideration should be adopted, at least on a trial basis.

From our point of view the outstanding characteristic of these procedures of representative election, initiation of suggestions, and review and decision-making is the tremendous change in the power structure of the organization which they represent. New organizational units (departmental committees and screening committee) have been created and major decisions are being made by these units. The total effect is to move downward in the organization many decisions relating to its specific operations; moreover, this delegation or downward movement of authority and decision-making is carried out by means of formal changes in the organizational structure.

No less drastic are the changes in reward structure which are an explicit and formal part of the Scanlon Plan. Indeed, the first formal task of the new committee structure, before the flow of suggestions has begun, is to agree on "the formula." This agreement determines the conditions of production under which workers will begin to earn bonuses in excess of the wage rate set by collective bargaining, and it determines also the basis on which management and workers will share in the results of any production gains which are achieved.

The specific arrangements have varied among the different companies in which the Scanlon Plan has been instituted, but a typical formula might be worked out along the following lines. The committees would agree upon that percentage of the value of the finished product of the company which can properly be regarded as a normal labor cost, that is a proportion of the total value of the product which can normally be allocated as wage costs rather than other costs. Such agreement might be based, for example, on the actual costs of labor during the twelve month period preceding the institution of the Plan.

Suppose that it is agreed upon that 38 per cent is the normal labor percentage. This percentage figure now becomes the "bogie" for the future operation of the Scanlon Plan. Since the agreed upon percentage for normal labor costs is 38, it follows that 38 per cent of the value of the finished product of the company during any future month will be available for the payment of "normal" wages. To the extent, however, that workers and management are able to achieve increases in productivity (without capital investment), they will be turning out product for which the actual labor cost is less than 38 per cent of the finished value. To make the arithmetic apparent, if unrealistic, suppose that during the first month after the institution of the Scanlon Plan a work force unchanged in number were to produce double the amount of product which it had turned out during the base period. Since the value of the product would now be double the amount for the base period, and the base wages would have been unchanged, it follows that wages would represent only 19 per cent of the value of the present product, as contrasted to the earlier figure of 38%. According to the requirements of the Scanlon Plan, if this were to have occurred, the total amount of money available and agreed upon for allocation to workers, however, would continue to be 38 per cent of the value of the finished product. In this highly inflated example, therefore, workers would receive a bonus under the Plan which would in effect double their wages for the month in question.

A more realistic experience under the Plan is that the amount available as bonus earnings runs to approximately 25 per cent of wages after the Plan has been in operation for a period of perhaps two years. Whatever the amount of the bonus, however, it is a requirement of the Plan that there be a computation each month to determine whether the workers have been able to produce at a labor cost which is a lesser proportion of the total value of the product than that which is permitted by the agreement. Whatever amount is indicated as productive gains in terms of this computation is immediately available as bonus payments to the workers and is immediately paid by separate check.

In one report Scanlon (1948) presented three case studies of profit sharing under collective bargaining, only one of which met the criteria for his Plan. The first company installed a profit-sharing plan to forestall organization by the Steelworkers' Union. For six years it accomplished this objective, but the workers knew they were getting a bonus for staying out of the union. According to the report, every year before the Board of Directors met,

> a synthetic organizing threat developed within the ranks of the employees . . . . The Board of Directors always decided that the company had experienced a good year and the bonus was paid . . . . No sense of partnership, no joint participation in an effort to increase efficiency, no effort to improve the profit-making possibilities or the competitive position of the company had been developed. The plan was founded in hypocrisy and bad faith and had degenerated into a subtle game of wits. (p. 60)

Finally the workers did vote to join the union in a National Labor Relations Board election. A strike followed and the compromise settlement made a constant bonus dependent not upon a decision of the Board of Directors, but upon whether or not the company fell below a certain minimum profit. The bonus was not geared to the amount of profits and the workers did not know from month to month whether the company would achieve the required profit level at the end of the fiscal year. From Scanlon's point of view, the failure of the company to motivate its workers cannot be chalked up as a failure of profit sharing in that employees had no chance to share in the profits of the company and accept responsibility for enhancing those profits.

The second case study reported by Scanlon of an unsuccessful attempt to install a profit-sharing plan occurred in a steel fabricating plant with a fair earnings record. The plan was instituted by management in unilateral fashion with a sudden announcement to the union that 50 per cent of company profits over a 4 per cent net worth level would be placed in a pool for distribution to employees. This action came some four weeks after a strike settlement as an indication of a changed attitude of management toward the workers. The earlier strike, which lasted for three weeks, had begun with a refusal of management to deal directly with the union and had engendered bitterness among employees. Though the profit-sharing plan represented a sincere change of philosophy by management and was so interpreted by local union officials, the rank and file were suspicious and did not understand the details of the management proposal. The plan failed to provide an incentive for increased productivity and cooperation between officers and men. The failure was due to the timing of the proposal, to its unilateral character, and to the lack of a stable relationship of mutual confidence.

In contrast, another small steel fabricating plant with a long history of good labor relations developed a profit-sharing plan cooperatively with workers' representatives that was based upon a background of experience with labor-management committees during World War II. A joint committee was set up to study existing profit-sharing plans in August, 1944 and to formulate a model adapted to their own particular needs. The plan, so developed, was a straight profit-sharing arrangement and ran afoul of national wage stabilization rules. The committee went to work again and, after a thorough study of the procurement and productive processes, suggested a plan based upon the ratio of labor costs to production values. The War Labor Board approved the plan and the first year's results showed a 2 and one-half times increase in profits with workers sharing in the outcome with a 41 per cent increase in their earnings. After the war, union and management agreed upon changing the plan to a new straight profit-sharing arrangement by which employees were paid 50 per cent of the profits on a monthly basis. To keep the employees informed of their progress, the records of the current month were set up against preceding months on a huge clocklike instrument inside the factory entrance. Again, company profits doubled the 1945 figure and an employee's earnings were boosted some 54 per cent. The production committee members of the local union voluntarily voted the company president an annual salary to supplement his previous income based entirely on a profit percentage even though half of this came out of their own share of the profits.

The changes in the reward structure required by the Scanlon Plan are thus no less dramatic than those in the power structure. Workers typically experience an important increase in take-home pay as a result of the Plan, and they are protected against reductions in pay by the collective bargaining agreement. Their pay increases are earned in accordance with a formula agreed upon by the union and the departmental committees, and the bonuses are paid in cash as earned, each month. Finally, the payments reward not the efficiency of the individual or the group, but the gains in the overall efficiency of the company as a procurement-production-marketing system. For a worker to increase his own output in a way that handicaps the man on the next shift or in the next position on the assembly line would be absolutely self-defeating. In contrast to individual incentive systems, piece-rate payments, and the like, the Scanlon Plan offers little or no motivation for such intramural competition.

Although these changes in the structure of power and rewards are the hallmarks of the Scanlon Plan, the process of change ramifies into other subsystems of the organization. For example, to reach initial agreement on the formula and to implement the suggestions of the departmental committees implies and requires important changes in the communications structure. Workers, through the departmental committees, have access to information about costs of production, the competitive acts of other firms in the same field, and the like. Thus the downward channels of communication are carrying data which would previously have been restricted to management; the upward structure of communication is enlarged and transformed by the creation of the departmental committees and the companywide screening committee.

Such ramifications in communications, however, are no greater than the changes in policy-making and decision-making. The creation of the committee structure, the completion of the agreement, and the setting of the formula are themselves great changes in policy and in the procedures of decision-making. The changes in these areas enlarge and persist as the committees do their work, as their members become increasingly knowledgeable, and as the total system moves toward a new set of internal balances. The four basic changes which initiate the plan (joint request by management and union; memorandum of agreement; election of departmental and screening committees; and agreement on the formula of reward) create within the organization a complex set of further change demands; the organization which works these through successfully is likely to have undergone a major transformation in many of its subsystems.

It is perhaps clear from the foregoing description that the Scanlon Plan is an interesting innovation in the management of privately owned complex organizations. Many questions persist, nevertheless, about the inherent limitations of the plan. Among the more important of these questions are the issues of company size, company success, the element of charisma in the initiation of the plan, and the effects of automation and cybernation on the appeal of the plan to management.

With respect to size, we must admit that the Scanlon experience is concentrated in companies of small labor force. Although there is at least one instance of a successful installation of the plan in a company of several thousand employees, the typical successes are in plants of only a few hundred, and there is no instance of a major American corporation converting to the Scanlon operation. We are inclined to think that this fact is significant, but liable to misinterpretation. Certainly the Scanlon Plan, like other forms of representative government (or of nonrepresentative government, for that matter) becomes increasingly complex and difficult to administer as the body politic increases in size. It is likely, however, that the reluctance of large companies to experiment with the Scanlon Plan is due also to their relations with stockholders and to their fiscal success.

This last point brings us to the next question most frequently put as a challenge to Scanlon enthusiasts: must a company be in financial difficulty before its management is likely to turn to so drastic a remedy? History permits no easy answer to this question. In the early years of the plan, the companies which pioneered in its application were often searching for solutions to acute problems of competition or lagging sales. There are cases, however, in which managements have been motivated more by the hope of improving an already tolerable operation than by the hope of saving an operation which was becoming intolerable.

Nevertheless, we must be skeptical of what the effects of the plan would be on a large, well-managed company with a strong staff of innovative engineers and technicians. Would the Scanlon Plan add as much to the productivity of General Motors as it did to the Adamson or LaPointe companies? And if the Scanlon ground rules were maintained in General Motors or its hypothetical equivalent, to what extent would the resulting changes improve the position of stockholders as well as employees? The answers to these questions are not necessarily negative; they are, however, yet to be supplied.

A third issue still unsettled lingers from the early successes of Scanlon himself. It is not clear how much of personal expertise and charisma is required to launch the plan, how much the name of the plan itself identifies at least one of the crucial ingredients. Finally, we must ask to what extent the second industrial revolution, the revolution of automation and cybernation, renders obsolete some of the appeal of the plan to management. It is not that the principles of cooperation, reward, and self-determination are in danger of becoming outmoded. However, as the processes of production become machine-determined and machine-guided, as well as machine-executed, labor costs become an ever smaller fraction of the total costs of production and management concern with them is correspondingly reduced.

Despite these unresolved issues, the Scanlon Plan is an innovation of the utmost importance and interest for students of organization. Where it succeeds, it does so by producing an internalization of organizational objectives among all members including the rank-and-file. Increased earnings for increased effort is not the critical factor, for this process operates for individual incentive systems. In the case of the Scanlon Plan the increased effort is not only to achieve higher earnings but to contribute to the carrying out of the shared purposes of the group members. The opportunities for participation in decision-making about vital matters of concern to the individual permit the engagement of his ego motives of self-determination.

The job itself ceases to be a routine role performance, for now the worker is concerned with all activities that facilitate a good group outcome. Hence his motives of self-expression are activated. The performance of the organization now represents his own achievement and gives positive feedback to his ego involvement. Internalization of organizational objectives not only contributes to increased quantity and quality of role performance and to reduced absenteeism and turnover, it also carries the individual on to the many specific spontaneous actions necessary for organizational survival and the highest level of system performance. On the negative side such internalization can result in too much variability of behavior and to lack of organizational concentration as suggested by the phrase "all chiefs and no Indians." The Scanlon Plan may produce internalization without a breakdown in organizational integration by its devices for continuing communication and by its involvement of members as subgroups.

In short, the Scanlon Plan appears as a creative solution to many of the problems which have become traditional in large organizations. It adds strong positive factors to the usual arsenal of "motivators," and it adds no penalties. There is a formal enlistment of the peer group via the representative committee structure, and such groups are strengthened through the close linkage of reward to group and supergroup contributions to system efficiency. The job of the individual worker is enlarged and enhanced by the recognition and encouragement of innovative contributions, and the model of leadership which is called for comes much closer to the values of democratic practice as they exist in our culture and institutions outside industry.

SUMMARY

This chapter attempts to develop a comprehensive framework for predicting the effectiveness of organizations in terms which specify the types of behavior required for organizational effectiveness, the different motive patterns which can evoke such behavior, and the organizational conditions which elicit these motive patterns.

Three categories of behavior are required to achieve high levels of organizational effectiveness. People must *join and remain* in the organization; they must *perform dependably* the roles assigned to them; and they must *engage in occasional innovative and cooperative behavior* beyond the requirements of role but in the service of organizational objectives. More specific behaviors are described within each of these broad categories.

Four motive patterns are proposed as characteristics of organizations and as capable of producing the required behaviors in varying degrees. These are *legal compliance, instrumental satisfaction, self-expression,* and *internalization of organizational goals.*

The complex sequences which link these and other mediating variables can be summarized for each of the four motive patterns, as follows:

Legal compliance is evoked by the use of unambiguous symbols of authority, backed by the use or threatened use of penalties. It tends to produce performance at the minimum acceptable level, and to generate no particular willingness to remain in the organization when alternatives are available.

Instrumental satisfaction is evoked by the use of rewards, and is more strongly evoked as the rewards are immediate, constant, and adequate. The behavioral patterns produced by reliance on rewards vary according to these factors, and also depend heavily on whether the rewards are systemwide or tied more specifically to performance. In general, system rewards hold people in the system but do not necessarily encourage more than minimally acceptable performance and are ineffective for stimulating innovative behavior. Individual rewards for performance are difficult to apply in large-scale organizations but under the proper conditions of immediacy, constancy, and adequacy can lead to increased productive effort.

The motive of self-expression depends primarily on objective attributes of the job itself. As the job increases in complexity, variety, and responsibility, the individual has increased opportunity to express his skills and abilities through performance on the job. High productivity and strong attraction to the occupational system are characteristic of this motive pattern.

The internalization of organizational goals is at once the most effective of motive patterns and the most difficult to evoke within the limits of conventional organizational practice and policy. The extent of internalization depends upon the character of the organizational goals themselves, and their congruence with the needs and values of the individual. It depends also on the extent to which the individual shares actively in the determination of organizational decisions and in the rewards which accrue to the organization. High internalization of organizational goals tends to result in low absence and turnover, high productivity, and maximal spontaneity and innovativeness in the service of those goals.

This chapter concludes with a review of the empirical research findings which bear upon the preceding framework. They are too few and too scattered to test it fully, but the major patterns of research results are compatible with the framework as proposed.

13
Organizational Change

The major error in dealing with problems of organizational change, both at the practical and theoretical level, is to disregard the systemic properties of the organization and to confuse individual change with modifications in organizational variables. It is common practice to pull foremen or officials out of their organizational roles and give them training in human relations. Then they return to their customary positions with the same role expectations from their subordinates, the same pressures from their superiors, and the same functions to perform as before their special training. Even if the training program has begun to produce a different orientation toward other people on the part of the trainees, they are likely to find little opportunity to express their new orientation in the ongoing structured situation to which they return.

Almost all psychotherapy, including group therapy, suffers from this same weakness. Its immediate target is improved insight by the individual into his motivations. Even if individuals and small groups emerge from the therapeutic sessions with improved understanding of themselves and others, the effects of such individual change on social structures tend to be minimal. With respect to the supersystem of the nation-state the same confusion of individual and system functioning is often apparent. It was conspicuous, for example, in the objections to changing Negro-white relations by law. A common point of view was that individuals would have to change their attitudes and habits first. The fallacy in this position has been demonstrated by the revolution created by changes at the top of the legal structure, specifically the Supreme Court decision of 1954.

The confusion between individual and organizational change is due in part to the lack of precise terminology for distinguishing between behavior determined largely by structured roles within a system and behavior determined more directly by personality needs and values. The behavior of people in organizations is still the behavior of individuals, but it has a different set of determinants than behavior outside organizational roles. Modifications in organizational behavior must be brought about in a different manner.

Let us examine the individual approach in more detail. Its essential weakness is the psychological fallacy of concentrating upon individuals without regard to the role relationships that constitute the social system of which they are a part. The assumption has been that, since the organization is made up of individuals, we can change the organization by changing its members. This is not so much an illogical proposition as it is an oversimplification which neglects the interrelationships of people in an organizational structure and *fails to point to the aspects of individual behavior which need to be changed.*

Some psychoanalysts, for example, assume that wars are caused by the aggressive impulses of man and that if we can lessen frustrations and redirect aggressive impulses, we can change the belligerent character of the state and eliminate war. Reasonable as this sounds, it has very little to do with the case. The finger that presses the button unleashing a nuclear warhead may be that of a person with very little repressed hostility, and the cabinet or state directorate behind the action may be made up of people who are kind to their families, considerate of their friends, and completely lacking in the psychopathology of aggression. They are merely carrying out their roles in a social system, and unless these roles and the social structure which gives them definition are changed, we will still have wars. Yet we persist in attempting to change organizations by working on individuals without redefining their roles in the system, without changing the sanctions of the system, and without changing the expectations of other role incumbents in the organization about appropriate role behavior.

In short, to approach institutional change solely in individual terms involves an impressive and discouraging series of assumptions—assumptions which are too often left implicit. They include, at the very least: the assumption that the individual can be provided with new insight and knowledge; that these will produce some significant alteration in his motivational pattern; that these insights and motivations will be retained even when the individual leaves the protected situation in which they were learned and returns to his accustomed role in the organization; that he will be able to adapt his new knowledge to that real-life situation; that he will be able to persuade his coworkers to accept the changes in his behavior which he now desires; and that he will also be able to persuade them to make complementary changes in their own expectations and behavior.

The weaknesses in this chain become apparent as soon as its many links are enumerated. The initial diagnosis may be wrong; that is, the inappropriate behavior may not result from lack of individual insight or any other psychological shortcoming. Even if the initial diagnosis is correct, however, the individual approach to organizational change characteristically disregards the long and difficult linkage just described. This disregard we have called the psychological fallacy. In warning against it, however, we do not propose to commit a complementary sociological fallacy. We do not assert, in other words, that *any* alteration in human behavior can be brought about in organizations provided the process of change is initiated with due attention to organizational structure. The problems of change are too complex for such simplistic generalizations and require further specification.

Perhaps the best way of introducing such specification into problems of social change is to examine two separate aspects of the matter: the methods employed to bring about change, and the targets at which such methods are directed. Although a single method may be directed at different targets or at a sequence of targets, it can be argued that there is inherent in each method a primary or preferred target and a hypothesized linkage by which other targets may be reached. We shall discuss a primary target in relation to our presentation of each method of change.

These methods for bringing about organizational change include the direct use of information, skills training, individual counseling and therapy, the influence of the peer group, sensitivity training, group therapy, feedback on organizational functioning, and direct structural or systemic alteration. The primary target of change may be the individual as an individual personality, the interpersonal relationships between members of peer groups, the norms of peer groups, the interpersonal relationships between members of an organizational family, the structure of a role, the role relationships of some segment of organizational space, or the structure of the organization as a whole. The difficulty with many attempts at organizational change is that the changers have not clearly distinguished their targets and have assumed that the individual or group-level target was the same as the social-structure target.

INFORMATION AS A METHOD OF CHANGE

The use of information (merely supplying additional cognitive input) has a supplementary and supportive function for other methods of change, no matter what their target. It can give the rationale for an anticipated program of change and make clear what is expected of the individual, the group, or the organization as a whole. But it requires the use of other methods to produce the basic modification desired. The target of information may be a change in the individual's role; unless this change is legitimized with the invoking of penalties and rewards, the mere explanation of his new role is not likely to bring about new behavior. Information capitalizes upon the existing forces in a situation, and is not itself a prime mover. It produces change, therefore, only if the necessary motivation is forthcoming from other sources. One of the studies of the Survey Research Center (Kahn, 1964), conducted in a company manufacturing household appliances, investigated the effects of the communication skills of foremen in presenting and explaining changes in methods and incentive rates. The initial and discouraging finding was that differing communication skills of foremen produced no significant differences in the response of workers. Further analysis revealed that the communication practices of the foreman made a difference in the behavior of the men, if the foreman possessed a significant amount of power in the organizational structure. Among foremen who lacked such power, communication practices were negligible in their effects.

One exception to the statement that informational techniques are effective only in combination with some other motivational source should be noted. Techniques relying primarily on information-giving are effective in ambiguous situations, where lack of information is the obstacle to appropriate performance. The individual accepts suggestions which clarify matters for him and give him a feeling that things are under control. In organizational settings, however, the patterns of expected behavior are more often clear than not.

INDIVIDUAL COUNSELING AND THERAPY

The realization that information can reinforce rather than redirect behavior has led to utilization of therapeutic devices for bringing about personality changes at a deeper level. Theory and research suggest the importance of dealing with basic motives in attempting to change the individual. Gordon Allport (1945, 1946, 1954) suggested that giving people insight into the psychological dynamics of prejudice toward other races and nations might be an effective way of restructuring their attitudes. Katz, Sarnoff, and McClintock (1956) demonstrated that prejudices toward Negroes could be changed momentarily by information, but that more lasting change resulted from giving people insight into their own motivation about prejudice. A number of industrial organizations have utilized consulting firms for therapeutic counseling of middle management personnel. Often the practice has not been to select out problem cases but to give all supervisory personnel at the intermediate level the benefits of a series of long sessions with a professional counselor.

The logic of therapy leads to social change by a long and doubtful route, as we have already implied. The assumption is that if the individual is to change, he should first be removed from the social situation reinforcing his present behavior. In isolation from his former associates he can learn about himself, then learn to relate to his therapist, and finally to his former colleagues. Since there has been no corresponding change occurring in his colleagues, the changed personality of the subject encounters a series of shocks in attempting to try out his new *me* on his old colleagues. Even if he himself can maintain his personality change, it is unlikely to make a dent on the pattern of the organization.

The target of therapy is basically the personality of the individual. If he gains new insights, overcomes his insecurities, experiences his world as a less threatening place, and hence perceives it more objectively, he should be able to relate to his fellows more effectively. The secondary target then of changing an individual's personality structure is the restructuring of his own role and his relationships with others in the organization. In extreme cases, such individual changes may help the functioning of the organization; sick people, or people with particular blind spots or psychological weaknesses, may no longer impede organizational functioning. The semiparanoid character after therapy may be capable of being integrated into his group, or into his organizational family. In less extreme cases, it is difficult to predict the carryover of individual change to organizational targets. Nor is every organization so structured that it can absorb healthy, well-integrated personalities who express rather than inhibit their aggressions. Other things in the organization must change, too, or the rehabilitated individual may find himself outside the organization because of his rehabilitation.

There is, however, the occasional case in which personality conversion is achieved in the individual who is either the most powerful figure in the organization or who is close to the top in power position. Here, of course, the change achieved through individual therapy may have reverberations in the organization as a whole. Since such a person is in a position to introduce legitimized change in the organization through utilizing its authority structure, any real changes in his personality can have important organizational consequences. This is especially true in small organizations, where the other social forces maintaining a steady state are less imposing in their weight.

In summary, the difficulty with the use of personality conversion in changing organizations is twofold: (1) In general, the top officers of an organization tend to see counseling and therapy as more appropriate for their subordinates than for themselves. They do not have the time for it, nor, as successful operators, do they see the need. (2) Other organizational forces will tend to maintain the organization in a steady state. The manager who returns to his organization a relaxed and secure individual may still not be able to change the many subsystems and their mutually reinforcing relationships which tend to preserve the operating mode of the enterprise. A more precise theoretical statement would be that organizational properties are by definition systemic and their change calls for system change. The personality of the manager is not a system property or variable save in a small group which is organized around the idiosyncratic traits of the leader.

To these difficulties must be added the fact that therapy is not yet a very predictable tool for personality change. It varies in effectiveness, depending upon the patient and his problems, the therapist, the relation between the two, and the type of therapy utilized. Many people have undoubtedly benefited in some degree from therapy; others have not been changed appreciably, and some have changed for the worse. Research evidence on the effectiveness of therapy and the conditions under which it is effective is only now beginning to be gathered.

THE INFLUENCE OF THE PEER GROUP

A third approach to producing individual change is through the influence of the peer group. This method has three advantages. (1) The behavior of associates does exert tremendous power over the individual. (2) Changing several people at the same status level in the organization introduces the possibility of continuing reinforcement of the behavioral changes. (3) The possibility of discovering an acceptable solution calling for change is greater in groups not inhibited by authority figures. Maier and Hoffman (1961) have demonstrated that the production of creative solutions to a problem increased when subjects' orientation to authority relations was low. There are serious limitations, however, in the organizational change which can be accomplished through peer group discussion and decision.

The target of group influence may be any one of a number of peer groups. It may be a group of first-line foremen or a cabinet of vice-presidents and managers. As with therapy, the creation of better relations in the peer group may not lead to the desired organizational change. A stronger peer group at the rank-and-file level may become more resistant to organizational needs, as the study of Seashore has demonstrated (1954). Moreover, the lower the group in the organizational structure, the less likely is any significant movement in the total structure. Maier (1952) has suggested the concept of area of freedom to indicate the amount of decision-making possible at various hierarchical levels in the organization. The method of group discussion has been used predominantly at those levels where the area of freedom for decision-making is smallest.

The peer group is a promising vehicle for intragroup processes of influence because equal status and power encourage full discussion, free decision-making, and the internalization of the resulting decisions. Research evidence clearly establishes the effectiveness of such group discussion and decision-making in changing behavior and attitudes where the individual is the target of the attempts to produce change.

Kurt Lewin and his followers were the first to demonstrate systematically the superiority of the group method over the usual informational approach in modifying individual behavior. Lewin's (1952) first experiment in changing food habits during World War II was directed at getting housewives to use unpopular foods such as beef hearts, sweetbreads, and kidneys instead of the more conventional cuts of meat. Six groups of Red Cross volunteers organized for home nursing were the subjects. Three groups received the usual lecture and three were involved in group discussion and decision. A followup of the women showed dramatic differences, with only 3 per cent of the lecture groups serving the unpopular foods as compared with 32 per cent of the discussion groups.

Similar results were obtained by Radke and Klisurich (1947) in two additional experiments aimed at changing food serving habits. The subjects were housewives of low economic status, and they were visited two and four weeks after the experimental inductions to check on the effectiveness of the methods. Though only small numbers were involved in the experiments, the group discussion proved to be significantly superior to both an individual instruction technique and to the lecture method. Moreover, the followup four weeks after the experimental treatments showed greater contrast than after two weeks. There was some tendency for the group method to increase in effectiveness over time more than the lecture method, although this was not clearly the case in all groups.

In a later experiment by Betty W. Bond (1956) using longer time intervals for the checkup, the continued superiority of the group method over time was confirmed. In this investigation larger numbers of subjects were employed, longer time intervals for the persistence of effects were utilized, and, in general, the experimental controls and procedures were more rigorous than in previous studies. The objective was the early detection of signs of breast cancer. Group discussion helped to allay fears of the hopelessness of the disease and to show that many supposedly unique feelings about the problem were shared by many other women.

Follow-up interviews were conducted seven and thirteen months after the lecture and discussion treatments. Three criteria were used as measures of the effectiveness of the health education attempted. (1) Had the women actually gone to their physician for a breast examination since the cancer education meeting? (2) Had the women routinely conducted breast self-examinations after the cancer education meeting? (3) Had the women demonstrated their breast self-examination technique to the physician or the physician's assistant after the cancer education meeting? On all three criteria there were significant differences between the two methods both after seven months and after thirteen months in the expected direction. Moreover, the superiority of the discussion method over the lecture method was greater after thirteen than after seven months. The women in the lecture group who became convinced of the need for examination tended to have known someone who had recovered from cancer or to have discussed cancer with someone after the meeting. In the discussion group neither of these factors was necessary for women to follow the agreed-upon practices. The sharing of experiences through group discussion took the place of other knowledge and contact.

An interesting application of group discussion and decision-making to industrial problems is found in the work of Levine and Butler (1952). These experimenters were interested in getting supervisors to rate employees on the basis of performance alone. Previous studies had shown that such ratings were colored by knowledge of the grade and pay scale for the job. One group of supervisors was given information about the pitfalls of ratings in a lecture, followed by a question and answer period. In a second group the discussion method was employed, and a third group served as a control. The performance of employees was rated by an outside group of experts and these expert evaluations comprised the criterion against which the supervisors' ratings were compared. Improvement in ratings occurred only in the group in which the discussion procedure had been utilized.

In all of the above experiments the group method was used to influence the individual without respect to his further involvement in the group. Most of the individuals involved never saw one another again, though the group influence persisted over time. In other experiments, however, the group method has been used to change the norms of groups which continue as groups. Here the primary target is group norms rather than individuals. Bavelas (Lewin, 1947), for example, tackled the difficult problem of changing the informal norms of a work group with respect to productivity. Employees in a garment factory were given the problem of their production standards for group discussion and decision. Two other groups used as control groups also had discussion but were under no constraint to come up with a group decision about a solution. The group which reached a decision about production goals was the only one to increase its productivity.

Coch and French (1948), also working in the Lewinian tradition, employed the method of group discussion to gain acceptance for changes in work methods in the garment factory where Bavelas had conducted his action research. A change in work methods generally meets with resistance among workers, who feel threatened by it. It tends to be accompanied by lowered morale, a decline in productivity persisting beyond a reasonable period for relearning, and an increase in turnover. In the factory in question, turnover was significantly higher among operators whose jobs were changed than among those who continued in the old pattern. Moreover, experienced operators not only showed a decline in productivity during the period of learning their modified assignments, but they took much longer to learn these assignments than newly hired workers.

In the Coch and French experiment a control group of employees was introduced to the job changes in the conventional manner. They were informed in a group meeting of what was now required of them, what the new piece rates would be, how they had been arrived at, and why the company had to institute these changes to meet competitive conditions. A question and answer period followed the announcement. Two experimental treatments involved three other groups of workers. In one treatment, the workers were given the problem facing the company, invited to discuss it, and after they had reached agreement about the need for change, were asked to name the workers who would first be given special training. The last provision was especially important because the work of these selected operators during relearning would be the basis for the new piece rates. Workers are always concerned that new time standards should not be set by the performance of the fastest man in the group and in this experimental situation they had control over the problem. In the second experimental treatment, the participation technique was pushed even further, and all members of the two experimental groups were involved in the training for the revised job assignments.

It should be added that the initial presentation of the problem to the experimental groups was much more dramatic than to the control group. Two garments were shown to the workers, one of which sold for 100 per cent more than the other. Each group was asked to indicate which garment was cheaper but could not do so. This demonstration effectively shared with the group the need to reduce production costs. The members reached a general agreement that a savings could be effected by removing the "frills" from the garment without affecting individual efficiency ratings. It can be argued that such a dramatic demonstration gave a genuine advantage to the experimental group discussion method without being an intrinsic part of it. It is an open question whether the demonstration would have been as effective in the control group, where the company spokesman would have picked a few representatives of the group to decide which was the better garment. The main point is that the experimental treatment moved in the direction of group participation and the control treatment did not.

At any rate, the results of the treatment were spectacular, even though the number of workers was small. The control group showed hardly any improvement over its earlier efficiency ratings after the change and displayed marked hostility toward management and its representatives. Moreover, 17 per cent of this group left the company within the first forty days. The groups in the first experimental treatment demonstrated quick relearning; they were back at their pre-change level within fourteen days and showed some improvement thereafter. The groups in the second experimental treatment relearned even more quickly, were back at their prechange level after the second day, and went on to show a 14 per cent improvement over that level. (Even a return to the old level of 60 units a day with the improved work methods represented a great gain for the company.) Under both participation treatments, morale was high, with only a single act of aggression against a supervisor under this regime and with much evidence of cooperation. And not a single employee in the experimental groups quit his job during the forty days of the experimental observation. It is not surprising that this action experiment has been so widely quoted, in spite of the small number of cases.

Coch and French (1948) also ran a second experiment in which they reassigned the members of the control group to new jobs after thirty-two days of the older treatment. This time the workers were introduced to their new jobs through group participation. They responded as the other experimental groups had done, with rapid re-learning, an increase in productivity, and a modification from their previous pattern of hostility to one of cooperation.

The dramatic results of the Coch-French experiment were not replicated, however, when French and some Scandinavian colleagues

(1957) attempted a similar experiment in the footwear department of a Norwegian factory. Again the problem was one of getting workers to accept changes in work methods with as much organizational effectiveness as possible. Two groups were subjected to the experimental treatment of group discussion and decision about allocation of articles to be produced, length of training, division of labor, and assignment of jobs within groups. Three groups were given the experimental treatment of participation only with respect to the allocation of articles, and four groups in the control condition did not participate in any of these four types of decisions. Though more members of the experimental than of the control groups felt that they had had greater influence over the change in work methods than in previous years, there were no significant differences in production as a result of the participation procedures. All groups kept fairly close to the standard level of production, although the two experimental groups participating in all four types of decisions reached this standard more quickly than other groups.

The failure to affect the informal standards of the work groups is reminiscent of the studies at Western Electric. Mayo and his colleagues were able to improve the productivity of a group of girls who were removed from the floor of the factory; subsequent efforts to improve the productivity of men by setting them apart in a Test Room were unavailing, however. Though the wage incentive scheme contained a complicated group piece rate by which the faster workers contributed more to the earnings of the group than the slower workers, the pressures within the group were brought to bear on the faster rather than the slower workers. In the Norwegian factory the same fears were expressed about increasing productivity as in Western Electric. Specifically some 64 per cent of the workers in the Norwegian study said they knew that if they exceeded a certain standard, piece rates would be cut.

The degree of objective truth behind such workers' fears has too often been dismissed as unimportant, and emphasis has been placed upon the psychological fact that workers believe management to be capable of such behavior. It should be recognized that reductions in piece rates are not unusual and that historically workers, like other groups, have had to rely upon themselves for the preservation of their own interests. All groups tend to resort to protective devices for that purpose.

The failure of the group-decision method to raise productivity in the Norwegian experiment is explained by the investigators as the weakness of the experimental manipulations and the factor of the legitimate expectations of the Norwegian worker. The manipulations were weak in that they dealt with allocation of articles and of men rather than production standards and piece rates. The latter were not manipulated because the workers already had the power to set the production rate, and their union representatives had the right to bargain about the piece rate. The legitimate expectations of the Norwegian workers were that their participation in such issues would be mediated through their elected union representatives and not through the intervention of a management research team. The latter explanation gives implicit recognition to a central fact of social change, namely, that group discussion is very limited in its effect upon group norms if it neglects the organizational structure and the legitimizing of organizational change.

The major factor conditioning the success of group discussion and group decision in changing group norms and individual behavior is the significance of the decisions for the people involved. One reason for the efficacy of the method is the involvement of people, the degree to which they can work out problems of importance to themselves and make decisions about their own fate. Workers are not generally as involved in making higher profits for management as they are in their own problems of making a living, achieving job security, and doing interesting work under good working conditions. The group discussion method, to be successful with hourly employees, must offer something of importance to them for decision-making. Unless the area of freedom in the organization gives them some scope, the method may be ineffective or may actually boomerang. To be asked to invest time and energy in discussing trivial matters, while important issues are forbidden, can be infuriating.

Besides the major factor of influence in significant decisions, there are other factors which account for the effectiveness of group process. Discussion and decision about problems of importance invoke powerful individual forces of self-expression and self-determination. Not only are people discussing important matters, but each individual is given a chance to express his own views and to persuade others. Ideas that come from the outside, even if significant for personal welfare, are not as satisfying as the expression of a person's own ideas on the problem.

The peer group, especially without the presence of authority figures, can develop a warm, permissive atmosphere in which spontaneity is encouraged. People can not only contribute constructive suggestions but can express specific grievances or ventilate their feelings about things in general. Such complaints can mutually reinforce one another and produce a negative organizational outcome. This generally does not happen if the group has freedom to make decisions of consequence to themselves. Less aggrieved individuals will bring the discussion around to a positive orientation and even the more offended, having unburdened themselves of some of their troubles, may move in upon problems in a constructive fashion.

Since the solution emerging from group discussion is a group product, the individuals experience the satisfaction of being part of something greater than themselves. They have had a hand in creating it, but it is bigger than they, and knowing they are a part of it heightens their self-esteem.

Group interaction, as it reaches the point of decision, makes salient the group norm or consensus. Norms imposed from without may vary in clarity, visibility, and psychological nearness. After a discussion has finally reached consensus, the group norms are abundantly clear and psychologically real to the members.

Since the group has to come up with a decision if it is to be successful, members have to reach a point of crystallization in their own thinking and hence a self-commitment on the issues. Often when outside views are presented to us we may assent without reaching that genuine crystallization of our own views which represents self-commitment.

The self-commitment embodying the group decision is a public commitment. At the end, all members have stood up to be counted. This public visibility of their individual positions helps to freeze the outcome of the group process. It may account for the fact that the changes produced in the cancer education groups persisted for more than thirteen months. Public commitment should be even more potent in a group with a continuing life in which members mutually reinforce one another.

Finally, group discussion and decision is more powerful when its decision outcome is clearly stated in terms of a course of action. The changed beliefs are removed from the area of good intentions to the realities of everyday behavior. When the individual steps out of the group setting and is subjected to other sources of influence, he may not act on his newly acquired beliefs and attitudes unless they have been structured with a commitment to specific forms of behavior.

In spite of the complexity of variables which interact to make up the process of group discussion and decision, there has been little experimentation to assess the relative weighting of these factors, their interaction effects, or the conditions optimal for any given factor or combination of factors. The lone experiment of an analytic nature in this area is that by Bennett (1955). Her subjects were college students in an introductory psychology course and the problem presented was the need for volunteer subjects in social science research. The design of the study permitted independent manipulation of each of four factors in group discussion: lecture versus group discussion, whether or not members made a decision to perform a specified action, public versus private commitment to the decision, and the degree of consensus in the group. Thus, bringing the individual to a decision point, whether through lectures or group discussion, could be examined as a factor in its own right, as could each of the other three variables. The criterion of effectiveness of the various influence procedures was the number of students who several days later climbed the four flights of stairs to the appointed office and offered to serve as volunteers. Two of the variables were found to be effective—bringing the individual to a decision point, and achieving a perception of high group agreement. Group discussion in itself contributed nothing to the criterion of action, nor did the degree of public commitment.

These results are not in contradiction with the findings of the Lewinian experiments since those experiments typically required complete agreement in the group for a decision, as well as the self-commitment of the individual. The Bennett experiment does raise the question of whether the main effects of the Lewinian studies might not be achieved through the lecture method followed by a request for information about individual opinions and a report to the lecture group of what the majority think. To some extent this is an academic question because the perception of group norms which emerges from a natural process of reaching group agreement is probably more effective than feeding the group information about the nature of the consensus among them.

Several other qualifications must be made about the Bennett findings. The groups were not given problems of salience to them, about which they could work out a solution of importance for their own interests. Many variables of significance in group process were not studied. The conditions which might make a given factor of especial importance could not be varied in a single experiment. For example, it made no difference in this particular experimental setting whether the individual had publicly commited himself to volunteering or not. In other settings, where the desired action is related to group membership or where failure to act in the promised manner carries some social stigma, the factor of public commitment could be of genuine importance. In spite of the problems of generalization of results, the Bennett experiment suggests the value of systematic experimentation for a more precise understanding of the forces involved in group decision-making and the contingent conditions under which it is most effective.

The determinants of the quality of group problem-solving have been systematically studied by Maier and Hoffman. These investigators found that homogeneous groups (composed of members similar with respect to personality characteristics) produced fewer high-quality solutions than did heterogeneous groups (Hoffman and Maier, 1961; Hoffman, 1959). Presumably, diversity of approach among group members facilitates problem-solving. In another experiment diversity of opinion was produced by strengthening the original position of rank-and-file members in opposition to their leaders (Hoffman, Harburg, and Maier, 1962). Moreover, some of the leaders were instructed to play their roles as foremen in a fashion considerate of group members; others were instructed to play a dominating role. The greatest number of integrative solutions occurred in groups led by considerate leaders with strongly convinced members; the fewest occurred in those groups led by considerate leaders and composed of members with weak convictions. The authors conclude that the conflict generated between the subordinate members and their leaders was productive of high-quality solutions because it made differences of opinion visible and stimulated consideration of several points of view. Pelz (1956) has also shown that scientific productivity is facilitated by an environment in which the scientist has contact with some people who do not resemble him closely in values and orientation toward problems.

When groups with formally designated leaders discuss problems, as in the experiments cited above, the character of the leadership is a significant factor in determining the quality of the solution. Maier (1950) has demonstrated that groups with leaders trained in democratic approaches achieve more inventive solutions than groups with untrained leaders. The training in this instance emphasized (1) having the group identify the nature of the problem; (2) keeping the discussion task-oriented rather than personally oriented; (3) considering all suggestions; and (4) stimulating the group to analyze and evaluate completely all suggested solutions. In a further experiment Maier (1953) employed industrial groups and obtained similar results. Groups in which leaders had had eight hours of training in democratic methods achieved integrative solutions in 36 per cent of the cases, whereas groups with untrained leaders attained no such solutions.

Two basic assumptions in the original Lewinian method of group discussion and decision are not always made explicit but have profound implications: (1) The technique has been essentially limited to the peer group, to people who come together as equals with respect to formal authority and formal status. (2) People come into the group because of common interests of their own and not as formal representatives of other groups. They can disagree or even leave the group, without ramifying consequences.

The first assumption is important with respect to the power of the group influence generated. If authority or status figures are present, the spontaneous interaction of group members is inhibited. People are less free to work through their own feelings and ideas, and the resulting group decision may reflect less of their own constructive solutions and produce less internalization. A peer group does not lend itself readily to organizational structure in which the hierarchical principle is dominant. In fact, decision-making by peer groups could not be carried out fully without genuine modification of the hierarchical principle. The dynamic of the peer group is in contradiction to the hierarchical principle.

The second assumption has received even less attention in Lewinian theory, which has been little concerned with the distinction between people playing formal roles and people acting as individual personalities. In many group situations, however, people represent the wishes of their constituents, or in some fashion serve as role representatives of other groups. Every legislative group is, of course, of this character, as is the mediation group composed of representatives from management and union.

The heads of departments in an industrial company, or in a university, or in government may have equal status in their group meetings, but each department head is constrained by the interests of his own constituency. University committees are frequently set up as peer groups and given problems of common university interest. Their members are supposed to act as citizens of the university. But often the member from the history department will have in the back of his mind the reactions of people in his own department, and the classical scholar will think in terms of how well he is representing the humanities. Organizational life means that many group meetings will bring together people from different sectors of organizational space, each subject to the influences of the particular sector from which he comes. A continuing problem in organizations is to produce a true peer group situation in which members leave behind their other role involvements and function only as citizens of the organization.

There are many situations in which the role of the individual is and should be paramount because of the nature of organizational structure. In such situations, the group meeting is a means by which needs and wishes of subgroups are given vigorous expression and compromises are achieved. The Lewinian group method presumes a solution which integrates rather than compromises the needs of the members; hence the demand that the final decision be unanimous. With the representative group, the usual requirement is a majority vote and the commitment of the minority to abide by the majority decision until the next round of decision-making. Representative groups may be legislative, mediative, executive, or administrative in character, and their common techniques are logrolling, trading concessions, bargaining, and compromise. This is the realm of *real* politics, and politics has been defined as the great art of compromise.

No substitute for this type of group process has been devised. The pure democracy of the small Lewinian group discussion and decision is not directly applicable to systems composed by many subgroups with distinctive functions, values, and interests. On the other hand, a monolithic authority structure which eliminates all group process is undesirable and for that matter impossible to achieve. The art of politics and of group process has not been eliminated from Soviet Russia. The solution to the dilemma of representative group process is not to abolish it, but to make it more truly representative and in so doing to establish the central membership character of citizenship in the organization.

SENSITIVITY TRAINING: THE BETHEL APPROACH

The group process of Lewin for achieving agreement among peers on their own problems has been extended by his students to the technique of sensitivity training. Just as the individual has to be isolated from ongoing influences to learn about himself, so too must the group be separated from its usual environment. As the therapist leads the individual to express his own emotional conflicts, to become aware of them, to explore and to attain insight into his own motivations, so too is the group encouraged to express its emotions, to examine its activities, and to become aware of group process.

Since 1947 the National Training Laboratories has held sessions every summer at Bethel, Maine for leaders from industry, government, universities, and other institutions. On this cultural island people leave behind their organizational roles and enter as peers, unrepresentative of their group memberships, into an exploration of group process and leadership. The frustrations in dropping their usual role supports and ingrained organizational techniques lead to a reexamination of methods of participating in groups and influencing other people.

The major device for such learning is the T-group (training group). Each such group consists of approximately ten to sixteen people, including one or two trainers. The group is scheduled for one or two meetings each day over a period of two or three weeks. The meetings typically last for an hour and a half or two hours.

Each group begins without agenda, structure, division of labor, or rules of procedure. The people in each group are strangers to each other, brought together only by the common goal of learning more about themselves, the impact which they have on others, and the ways in which groups can become effective instruments for meeting the needs of their members. The absence of the usual props of officers, agenda, and Robert's Rules of Order creates an initial vacuum which is often quite uncomfortable. As the members struggle to fill this vacuum with meaningful activity and relationships, the trainer attempts to observe problems of communication, attempted seizures of power, misunderstandings, and other phenomena of interpersonal life. He communicates these observations to the group, whose members gradually begin to attend to such matters themselves and to check the accuracy of their own observations by describing them and asking for corroboration or correction from others. By this method (which is difficult to describe but most exciting and rewarding to experience) the members of the group attain increased sensitivity to their own behavior, the actions of others, and the nature of group development. Group members often emerge with a restructuring of their values about people and about their operations in group settings.

Powerful as this method is, its target is essentially the individual and not the organization. When the individuals return to their old structures, they step back into the same definitions of their roles. What is more basic, these roles are intimately related with a number of other organizational roles; the converted returnees may want to redefine their own way of functioning, but the expectations of superiors, subordinates, and colleagues have not changed, nor has there been a change in organizational sanctions and rewards.

If the person who has undergone change happens to be the head of an organization or a major unit of an organization, then organizational change may ensue. But there is no guarantee of significant organizational change even in such an instance. The old methods of operation have forces behind them other than the personal style of the leader, and these too must change to insure system change. Sometimes such changes are beyond the power of the organizational head. Sometimes they are possible but require skills and methods beyond those the chief learned in the laboratory training experience.

In recent years the activities of the National Training Laboratories have greatly expanded, and the methods pioneered by Bradford and his colleagues have been adopted by many organizations and individuals. Laboratory or sensitivity training sessions are conducted under various auspices on a continuing basis in many different locations throughout the country. In addition, many innovations have been introduced and given some research evaluation (Bradford, Benne, and Gibb, 1964). The most important of these, for our present purpose, is the closer linking of the T-group to the realities of specific organizations. This is achieved in part by dealing specifically with problems of organizational change as adjunct curriculum. A more dramatic innovation has been the use of the T-group procedure with people who are members of the same organization, whether company, school, or labor union. Such a group may consist entirely of peers, or of people at different levels in the organizational family, such as a superior and his immediate subordinates.

It is perhaps too early to attempt an evaluation of these variations on the T-group theme. Certainly they offer increased power with respect to generating organizational change, and to the maintenance of changes begun within the group. On the other hand, the role relationships which members bring into the T-group setting add to the initial difficulties of launching the training process, and may continue to impede it. The organizational T-group, in short, is a promising development, but its properties and potentialities require continuing exploration and research evaluation.

The relationship of sensitivity training to group therapy has often been discussed (and as often left unresolved). There is sufficient variation among practitioners of the laboratory method of training and among group therapists to make difficult any estimation of the degree of relationship or separation between the two.

Our own view is that laboratory training is not basically therapeutic in theory or in practice. Laboratory training does not aim at the resolution of unconscious conflicts within the individual but at a fuller perception of his behavior and the behavior of others. The content of the discussion in the T-group, and especially of the comments of the trainer, is consistent with these aims. The comments are strongly oriented toward interpersonal processes as they are directly observable in the group; inferences about the motives and internal conflicts of others are not encouraged. Each member comes to understand that he is expert and can talk well about how he feels or what he sees, but that he is on questionable ground when he attempts to make inferences about the motives of others.

As we have noted, the differences among trainers are great and the distinction between cognitive learning and therapy is not absolute. The distinction is easy to observe, however, if we contrast the training procedures of the National Training Laboratories with those of Elliott Jaques and his former colleagues at the Tavistock Institute. Jaques emphasized the analogy between individual therapy and organizational change. His underlying hypothesis is that many organizational problems are rooted in unconscious motives and their solution opposed by unconscious resistances. The excavation and working through of such material becomes the major means to organizational change, in his view. The basic assumption of the laboratory training method, on the other hand, is that the major problems of human organization are not unconscious and irrational, or at least that they can be successfully attacked at the conscious level and in terms of behavior observable and understandable by the members of the group themselves.

GROUP THERAPY WITHIN ORGANIZATIONS

An interesting attempt to produce organizational change through group therapy introduced into the organization itself has been utilized by the Tavistock Institute in England and is reported by Elliot Jaques (1951). The factory in question is an engineering and metals concern, the Glacier Company. The essence of the procedure is to have the organization change itself by means of group processes occurring at every level in the organization. The immediate target in this approach is the improvement of people's understanding of their organizational interrelationships and their own personal motives. The remote target is organizational restructuring by responsible organizational members themselves. The basic philosophy flows from individual therapy. The research team of outsiders is only one change agent; the major agents of change are the organizational members themselves. To quote Jaques, the research team is "to act only in advisory or interpretive capacity. The team is not here to solve problems for Glacier. They may, however, be able to help with the continuing development of methods of getting a smoother organization."

In accordance with this philosophy the research team began its program only after gaining acceptance from the Director, the Works Council (a body composed of management and elected union representatives), and the factorywide committee of shop stewards. Instead of applying the therapeutic approach in literal fashion, the Tavistock researchers focused upon organizational problems. Their preliminary move was a historical investigation of the plant, followed by an organizational study to establish the role structure of the system. This latter study included "an examination . . . of how far the social structure of the factory had proved effective in coping with the forces which affected production and group relations."

After the presentation of these background reports to the Works

Council, various sections of the organization began to ask the research team for cooperation on specific problems. The procedure of the research team was to direct the groups with which they worked toward the discovery of underlying causes and the expression of partly unconscious motives. Resistances emerging in group sessions were sometimes interpreted by the research teams; in other instances the group was left to make its own discoveries. To use Jaques' words:

> The method used was to draw attention to the nature of the resistance on the basis of the facts known to those concerned. Opportunities were taken to illuminate in the specific situation the meaning of the feelings (whether of fear, guilt, or suspicion) that constituted the unpalatable background to anxieties that were present about undergoing changes that were necessary. When successful, interpretations of this kind allowed group members to express feelings which they had been suppressing sometimes, for years, and then to develop an altered attitude to the problem under consideration. Even awkward or over-blunt comments often came as a relief. (p. 306)

And in the same context Jaques observes:

> The process of helping a group to unearth and identify some of the less obvious influences affecting its behavior is one borrowed from medical psychotherapy, from which is borrowed also the technical term *working-through*. It presupposes access by a consultant trained in group methods to a group accepting the task of examining its own behavior as and while it occurs, and a group able to learn, with the aid of interpretive comment, to recognize an increasing number of forces, both internal and external, that are influencing its behavior. The expectation, then, is that the group will acquire a better capacity to tolerate initially independent insights into phenomena such as scapegoating, rivalry, dependency, jealousy, futility and despair and thence a greater ability to deal effectively with difficult reality problems. When we speak of a group working through a problem we mean considerably more than is ordinarily meant by saying that a full discussion of a problem has taken place. We mean that a serious attempt has been made to voice the unrecognized difficulties, often socially taboo, which have been preventing it from going ahead with whatever task it may have had. (p. 307)

The Tavistock researchers regard two factors as necessary for successful working-through, and a third is desirable though not always essential. The first factor is similar to Dewey's old initial condition for problem-solving, the existence of a felt difficulty. The group must be hurting; its members must recognize a severe and painful problem. The second factor is group solidarity or cohesiveness. Members must have commitment to the group and its objectives. Otherwise they will not have the motivation to overcome the additional anxieties involved in problem solution. The third condition is a state of frustration created by the failure of denial and other mechanisms of defense to function in their accustomed manner. Groups tend to avoid facing up to the basic causes of their problems through various devices of avoidance and denial. When group members, through the help of a consultant or by other means, find that running away from the problem gives them no relief, they are ready for more realistic exploration.

The group-therapy procedure had an interesting outcome in the Glacier Company, an outcome illustrative of the strengths and weaknesses of the approach. No fundamental restructuring of the organization took place, but inconsistencies and ambiguities were resolved and the pseudo-democratic stance of management was replaced by a clearer authority structure. The Works Council was reorganized to include representatives of various levels of management in addition to top management and union stewards, and its function as an advisory rather than a decision-making body was explicitly formulated. The executive system was clearly separated from the functions of the Works Council so that the line of authority was not interfered with in everyday operations.

The target of change and the nature of the changes attempted and achieved in the Glacier project deserve careful consideration. The group therapy was nondirective in the sense that the research team did not propose specific answers to problems in organizational functioning. Instead, they emphasized a method by which organizational members could discover their own solutions. The focus was upon procedures for enabling groups to gain better understanding of themselves and others. Essentially the approach was aimed at the removal of unrecognized and unconscious forces which impede the rational functioning of people in group relationships.

To the extent that there is a commonality of interests and goals among all subsystems and groupings within an organization, much can be accomplished by aiding people to make full use of their rational faculties in problem solution. The result should be more efficient organizational functioning and improved morale and interpersonal relations. Many of the anxieties of people, whether about their personal lives or about their roles in a social system, are crippling in their effects and often groundless in relation to objective facts. These irrational worries and emotional difficulties can gain group reinforcement and so be more potent in their undesirable consequences. The insecurities of one group can lead to scapegoating and uncooperative behavior toward another group in the same organization and so make the task of the second group unusually difficult.

The great limitation in the use of group therapy is that all conflicts and problems in organizational functioning are not irrational in nature. Many difficulties are based upon genuine conflicts of interest, and the more the irrational anxieties are stripped away, the more clearly these interest conflicts come into focus. In the early history of American industrialism some employers exploited the antagonism of one nationality group against another. To have the Irish at odds with the Poles obscured their common interests and made unionization more difficult. Group therapy in this situation could have reduced the tensions between the different nationality groups, but it would not have solved the basic conflicts between workers and management.

In the Glacier Company, then, the organizational changes should not be construed as a basic restructuring of the organization and a democratic resolution of competing interests within the organization. It is true that the Works Council was to some extent revitalized as a policy-making body, but the broadening of its representative character revitalized the management representatives on the Council more than the workers. Previously management had appointed all its representatives to the Council; now the various echelons of supervisory and management personnel elected their own representatives. In his own account of the later functioning of the company, the Director, Brown (1960), is honest and straightforward in describing the changes which took place. The changes essentially clarified and made consistent the basic philosophy of management and its operational procedures. Some degree of employee representation does not mean that the organization is a democratic political system. In such a system the constituent members elect their officers and legislators, who in turn appoint executive officers; policy on all matters is determined by the constituents or their duly chosen representatives.

The Glacier Company, according to its stated policy as an industrial enterprise concerned with profits, is not governed basically by its Works Council. The Company recognizes three other influential systems: the executive system, the shareholders and their board of directors, and the customers. The representative system comprising both managerial and nonsupervisory employees is only one system, and very limited in the decisions it can make. Neither the written policies of the Company nor its philosophy as described by its Director define an area of discretionary judgment for the Works Council, except to assert that its decisions should not interfere with what the stockholders think desirable in terms of costs and profits, what the customers want in terms of services and products, or what the executive system should handle as the implementation of policy. Moreover, the Director, who is chairman of the Works Council, speaks with several voices in the deliberations of that body. He is the chief representative of the executive system, he speaks for the stockholders and their interests, and he also is the self-admitted spokesman for the customers or clientele of the organization. If the discussion should enter an area which he regards as belonging within the province of the stockholders, or of executive management, or of the customers, he can merely say, "Gentlemen, that is not the legitimate concern of this group" or "Gentlemen, the *given* in this situation by which we must abide is the following wish of our stockholders." Small wonder that few crucial decisions are made by the Works Council.

The Company formula frankly states that the area of discretion or contribution to policy by the employees is defined by their willingness to mobilize whatever power they possess to oppose or support a proposal. If management proposes changes which are likely to lead to rebellion among the employees, this can be tested out in the Works Council. If the representatives of the employees rise up in their wrath and predict that a given change will lead to a strike, management may then back down. The wise use of Council meetings by management can avoid widespread discontent in the company, since management will be guided by what they gauge the opposition forces to be. On the more positive side, management has an opportunity to gain the assent and sanctioning power of the Works Council for those proposals accepted by the Council after discussion.

Fundamentally the representation of employees on one of the policy-making boards of the Company gives the workers a feeling that they will not be pushed too far or too fast by management. Precedents will be followed, people will be heard if drastic changes are contemplated, and management probably will accept a veto which the employees are ready to implement by a strike or a slowdown. Employees are confident that they will have some voice in any change that would fundamentally alter their way of life in the organization, and they have a means of getting a hearing for proposals of their own.

Though the representative system must rely on the power it can mobilize to affect decisions, the full power of the employees is not lodged in it. The trade union and the shop stewards constitute the organized power with which management negotiates, and the union is outside the representative system, though there are relations between the two. In fact, the Works Council includes union men, though they are not elected as such, who can informally represent the point of view of the union and in turn carry back to the union the views of management. This division keeps clear the struggle between management and union over contracts and does not involve the employees in negotiations with the company as representatives in the Works Council. By the same token it reduces the power of the representative system in the overall legislative process.

The group therapy process at Glacier thus helped management

clarify its policies and procedures with respect to management responsibility, make unambiguous the character of the executive structure as an order-giving system, and stipulate the part to be played by the representative system and by the union. In the past management had suffered from confusion about the use of consultative democratic procedures, the pretense of democratic participation, and the abdication of management from some of its responsibilities. The Director was reluctant to assert his authority among the divisional managers. At times he refused to take the chair and lead the group, and wanted to appear merely as one of the group members. The role of middle management was weakened because it saw itself as being bypassed. The workers' representatives sat in council with top management and were in fact closer to top management than managers down the line. The very concept of role with its clear demarcation of duties was avoided. The assumption was made that if management and workers could get along amiably, all problems would be solved. The group processes instituted by the Tavistock research team enabled members of management to see clearly what they had been doing and what was necessary for effective operation as the sort of organization they wanted to be.

As leaders of a marginal operation in a competitive industry, top management probably made a correct assessment of the situation with respect to survival. It was not, however, the only possible course of action. They could have attempted to clear up the contradictions of democratic and authoritarian philosophy and practice by moving toward a cooperative enterprise, with employees sharing in the profits and policy decisions and electing the company officials. One difficulty with this solution is that the workers themselves may not have wanted it. To have become true partners in production with management would have meant breaking with the trade union structure and losing the security of long-standing membership in the union, for the sake of becoming members of an unusual partnership which the next turn of the market might wipe out. Moreover, the investment of the stockholders and their legal control of the company also represented a limiting factor in organizational change. Finally, top management was not willing to turn over the direction of the company to employees and perhaps to throw away its years of experience and its special competence in running the company. Management saw itself as dependent upon stockholders and the consuming public, no less than upon employees. As a marginal enterprise the company was very much an open system, and management had been trying to reconcile the demands from outside the organization with the internal needs of the employees. For all these reasons, the Glacier management rejected a democratic political model as inappropriate for the organization. They did not, however, want to move toward the other logical extreme of machine theory, in which the organization is seen solely as a mechanism for task accomplishment and the people in it as objects to be molded to their job assignments. Management, though giving priority to the nature of the task as determined by the customer system and the stockholder system, also recognized the needs of employees. They hit upon the Glacier formula as an excellent means of preserving the best in machine theory with a clear enough concession to the democratic trend of the times to avoid serious discontent in the plant. This formula swept democratic consultative practices in everyday task decisions out of the door. The executive system was given full and complete authority for getting the job done within the scope of policy decisions made by the Board of Directors and the Works Council. The employees could be heard in the Works Council and when they felt very strongly about a given policy, could get it modified. Moreover, they had their own union to fall back upon for the protection of their interests. Management's recognition of the veto power of employees and its willingness to listen in advance to their wishes helped to sanction the workings of the executive system and to give psychological security to the members of the organization. Clarity of responsibility and authority in the executive system enabled the organization to get the most out of hierarchical authority.

The solution achieved in the Glacier Company is thus a viable compromise, probably well suited both to its immediate situation and to the larger context of British industrial society, with its well established trade union movement and its value emphasis upon gradualism and precedent. The compromise arrangement, however, does not permit the full use of the democratic process with all its potentialities for problem solution, for the development of people, and for motivating them to use their full abilities. Two of the traditional difficulties of machine theory remain unsolved at Glacier: (1) The conflicts of group interest still persist. The deep-seated problems of restriction of production, of worker reliance upon the seniority principle, and of resistance to mechanization and automation have not been touched by the Glacier formula. Such problems do not yield to the use of group therapy. They can be solved only through the internalization of organizational goals by employees, which in turn requires accepting them as real partners in production. (2) The clear change of authority and responsibility in the executive system makes for precise allocation of duties but in so doing loses the advantages of group responsibility and of innovative and cooperative behavior beyond the line of duty.

The use of group therapy in the Glacier Company was, however, a landmark in the theory and practice of organizational change. The Mayo tradition with its emphasis upon informal groups, the Lewinian approach with its use of group process for organizational reform, and the extension of that approach to the sensitivity training of individuals apart from the organizational context had neglected the facts of organizational structure and the properties of organizations as social systems. Individual change was equated with organizational change and small groups were equated with large organizations. It was the genius of the Tavistock workers to combine a knowledge of therapy with a knowledge of the social psychology and sociology of organizations. Their theoretical approach took account of the systemic character of the situation with which they were dealing, even though the method for modifying social structure was that of group therapy. Their first step to gain access to the company was to gain acceptance from the component subsystems of the organization. Their next step was a background study of the system as a whole and its functioning. In working through problems for various sections of the enterprise they were guided by their awareness of the relations of one subsystem to the other subsystems of the organization. Finally, they were perceptive of the high degree of the openness of the company to related systems in the environment which helped to determine its input and the market for its output.

Recently there have been promising attempts to adapt small-group approaches, especially sensitivity training and its variants, to account of the organizational context. The work of Schein and Bennis (1965), Argyris (1964), and Blake and Mouton (1964) are outstanding examples. The final pages of the work by Bradford, Gibb, and Benne (1964) speak of the "extended use of T-groups and laboratory methods in nonlaboratory (i.e., organizational) settings." The Tavistock work deserves to be recognized, however, as the first purposeful and successful fusion of the therapeutic and organizational approaches.

THE SYSTEMATIC USE OF FEEDBACK AND GROUP DISCUSSION: THE APPROACH OF FLOYD MANN

Most organizations have at least one kind of feedback from the environment to guide their operations and indicate the need for organizational change. This feedback is from the reception of their product accorded by the clientele or market. When an automobile company cannot sell its cars it must make changes in the nature of its product. But there is another kind of feedback to the organization which derives from its own internal functioning. Two types of such internally generated information are frequently used by organizations. One concerns the technical side of internal functioning and implies an accounting for each production job in the organization. Some factories still follow the Taylor system in this respect, and at the close of every day report forms are passed up the line from each level of the organization describing the number of pieces produced, the utilization of materials, the amount of scrap and waste material, and the number of hours each employee spent on the various aspects of his job.

The second type of internal information concerns the human side of the productive and production-supportive processes of the organization. Typically such feedback reaches the upper echelons only when some problem has become acute. Top management learns that there has been a disastrous slowdown in the foundry and that castings are not reaching the assembly line on schedule, or that some key engineers and research people have resigned to take jobs with competing companies.

Suggestion systems are sometimes employed both to get ideas about technical improvement and to get feedback on the human problems of organization. Surveys of morale and of employee feelings, attitudes, and beliefs are also conducted by companies to give the latter type of feedback. If there were full and accurate communication up the line such surveys would not be needed, but the barriers to such upward communication are too numerous and too strong to ignore. Nor are these barriers only to peripheral data about employee attitudes. A sharp distinction between information about technical and human processes is false. The concept of the socio-technical system of Emery and Trist (1960) rightly gives emphasis to the complex interrelationships of social and technical processes. An adequate morale survey will furnish information both about the feelings of people and the actual operations of the technical or work system.

The great weakness in the use of surveys of employees' ideas and feelings is the inability of management to utilize this type of feedback about the internal functioning of the organization. Sometimes top management feels that it has done the proper thing just by conducting a survey, and proceeds to file the reports in the personnel office; at other times it will pass the findings along to lower echelons with no specific directives about their use. If the results of the survey are read by these subordinates, the natural tendency is to select the items that reinforce their present biases and to discount findings that run contrary to their own ideas.

Employees have two reactions to such unutilized surveys. The first and perhaps the dominant one is satisfaction in having been asked to express their views and in actually ventilating their feelings. The other reaction, which arises particularly when they have been led to expect positive action, is one of frustration in that nothing happens after all their efforts to tell the company what was wrong and what should be done.

To make the survey an effective form of feedback for organizational change Floyd Mann and his colleagues at the Survey Research Center developed a plan for group discussion of survey results by appropriate "organizational families." Mann's approach was first used in a fairly large company in which there had been a thorough survey by questionnaire and interview of all officers and workers. The concept of the organizational family refers to a supervisor at any hierarchical level and the employees reporting directly to him. Any supervisor thus would have membership in two organizational families. He would be involved in the group he supervises and he would also be a member with his coordinate supervisors of the family reporting to the officer above him. Thus the concept of organizational family takes account of the linking of subgroups in an organizational structure through the dual membership of their top men.

Mann's use of group discussion by such organizational families is like the Tavistock approach in taking into account the realities of organizational structure. Moreover, the hierarchical character of an enterprise is recognized by starting the feedback process with the top organizational family, for example the president and the vice-presidents reporting to him. The next series of feedback discussions might include each vice-president and the department heads who report to him. Starting at the top of the structure means that the serious examination of survey results is sanctioned or legitimized by the executive system. Every supervisory officer who calls a meeting of his subordinates has already been through a comparable discussion session with his coordinate officers and their chief.

The feedback material prepared for each session by the research team is, moreover, of special relevance for the particular organizational family into which it is introduced. The branch chief meeting with his department heads will be given companywide totals of employee ideas and feelings about all issues as well as branch totals, but, in addition, the branch totals will be broken down for the departments represented at the meeting. Thus, at the meeting the participants can see how their branch compares with the company as a whole as well as the strong and weak points of the departments within the branch. In turn, when the department head meets with his supervisors, they will have before them data to show how their department compares with the branch of which it is a part and how the sections within the department, manned by the supervisors present, compare with one another. In general then each organizational family is presented feedback about its own problems in detail and comparative information about the company as a whole or the larger part of the company to which it belongs.

For example, in one company studied by Mann, the top echelons of one department could immediately see that they compared very unfavorably with the company as a whole on certain aspects of employee morale. A much higher percentage of workers in that department than in the rest of the company had thought about quitting their jobs during the past year and were apparently waiting for the first good opportunity to leave; identification with the company was much lower in that department and dissatisfaction with supervision was higher. These findings brought home forcibly to the departmental officers and to their superiors what they had long been aware of to some degree, namely that top management had at times considered the department as expendable, its services always replaceable by contractual arrangements with outside firms. That company policy had affected rank-and-file employees so deeply was, however, something of a surprise.

The presentation of survey findings to the various organizational families sometimes brought new problems to light. More often it gave an objective and factual basis to problems that had either been brushed aside or dealt with by some opinionated gesture. Not only had vague reports about the perceptions and feelings of employees been reduced to facts and figures, but comparisons could be made among similar groups and the findings could be related to possible causal factors. In this objective atmosphere questions could be raised about the data, many of which could be answered by further analysis of the same data. And this was the emphasis of the Mann feedback procedure—group discussion of facts and figures in a task-oriented atmosphere where people were seeking to analyse the problem, identify possible causes as objectively as possible, and agree upon possible solutions. The reason for utilizing organizational families and presenting to them the relevant data about their operations thus becomes clear. The members of a specific organizational family have been involved in these very problems, already know a good deal about them, and know what questions should be asked to dig deeper into the available data for answers. Moreover, the group members are the immediate agents for implementing any policy changes with respect to problems at their own level. If they understand the causes, have been involved in a discussion of solutions, and perhaps have proposed the new policy, they will be more effective agents for achieving change.

The feedback technique, utilizing group discussion and group

420   THE SOCIAL PSYCHOLOGY OF ORGANIZATIONS

involvement, must be used under certain conditions if it is to realize its potential strength. Mention has already been made of the need for a factual, task-oriented atmosphere. A second necessity is the discretion of each organizational family to consider the implications of findings at its own level. Again, an area of freedom is required to utilize group process. General problem areas may be designated at higher echelons, but the detailed answers must be worked out by people closer to the problem.

For example, when the top management family looks at departmental comparisons they may become immediately aware of the low morale in a given branch. They may also note that there is more dissatisfaction with supervision in this branch and may want to attribute its morale problems to the practices of its first-line supervisors. This, however, is something the branch head can look into more definitively when he meets with his own department chiefs. At this meeting they will have a more complete breakdown of survey findings by sections and type of work, and it may become apparent that discontent with supervision is concentrated among the unskilled laborers.

Suppose problems of supervision are revealed to be specific to certain sections and independent of the general disaffection in the department. It becomes apparent that supervisors of unskilled laborers were not helped by the supervisory training program as much as other supervisors. The men under them are more accustomed to authoritarian methods than were other workers. Supervisory training in human relations had confused rather than helped these foremen, in that they were not really enabled to use more consultative methods and yet were made insecure in their use of older authoritarian approaches. They are also of lesser education and ability than the other groups of foremen, and feel the double insecurity of being men in the middle in a marginal department. It is difficult to imagine the revelation and discussion of such material except in the organizational family of its greatest relevance, acting according to its own discretion.

A third requirement for the effective use of the feedback procedure is a reporting back up the line of the outcome of meetings at the lower organizational level. When a department was satisfied that it had some answers to its problems and some recommendations about them, its head could present these findings at a subsequent branch meeting. He could report to the branch meeting to what extent various difficulties could be met at the departmental level and to what extent they seemed to arise from branch and company policies which would have to be changed at higher levels in the organization. The branch then could discuss all departmental reports and could attempt a summary report to go to the sessions of top management. At any point in the procedure the research team might be asked to bring back further breakdowns of relevant data.

One great advantage in this type of feedback with group discussion is its utilization of existing organizational structure. The executive line is not bypassed in securing information and implementing policy. Effective working relationships between supervisory levels are improved and two-way communication facilitated. Management policy is better understood and more fully put into practice, and the special knowledge and competence of all levels is more fully utilized. Mann (1957) recognizes that improving organizational functioning means dealing with the systemic properties of organizational structure:

> Organizations, as systems of hierarchically ordered, interlocking roles with rights and privileges, reciprocal expectations, and shared frames of reference, contain tremendous forces for stability or change in the behavior of individuals or subgroups. Change processes need to be designed to harness these forces for creating and supporting change. (p. 162)

Mann also points out five other related sets of facts which make for the efficacy of systematic feedback of survey data through organizational families.

Participation in the interpretation and analysis of research findings leads to the internalization of information and beliefs. When ideas are a person's own, they are much more likely to be translated into meaningful practices than when they are the suggestions of an outside expert.

The feedback of information and its discussion by the appropriate organizational family makes it highly relevant to the functioning of the subgroup and its members. Principles taught at a general level of abstraction are more difficult to apply than the discovery of principles from a person's own immediate experience.

Knowledge of results can in itself motivate people toward improving their performance. Level-of-aspiration studies indicate that individuals tend to raise their sights when they see the outcome of their efforts. If there is continuous feedback on the basis of some objective criterion of behavior, people will be motivated to attain better scores.

Group support is especially effective where there is continuing membership in a particular group. The members of an industrial organization during most of their waking hours are part of one or two organizational families. If the other members of these permanent groupings also change, there is a continuing reinforcement for individual change. More remote and fleeting group memberships are occasionally significant but one cannot escape the constant pressures of the here and now.

Finally a hierarchical ordering of roles with respect to authority is characteristic of most organizations, or at least of their executive systems. Hence the introduction of feedback starting at the top of the structure not only gives organizational legitimacy to the process but insures that for every individual in the organization there will be expectations from his immediate superior about his behavior. The changes will have been worked out in part by lower levels in the organization but in their final implementation will have the authority of the organizational line of command.

The effectiveness of this type of feedback program was demonstrated in the accounting branch of an industrial enterprise. All employees of the company had been included in a companywide study in 1948, and the results had been fed back to all branches of the organization. In 1950 a similar questionnaire was filled out by all employees of the accounting branch and these returns furnished the basis for the feedback experiment. Four accounting departments participated in the feedback process, which was initiated with a meeting of the accounting executive and his eight department heads. Two of the eight departments were eliminated from the research design because of changes in their key personnel since the 1948 survey was conducted. Two other departments were held out of the feedback process to serve as controls. In the four experimental departments the feedback activities varied somewhat, especially in the extent to which the nonsupervisory employees were involved. The basic pattern was essentially as described above, however, with meetings of organizational families down the line at which were also present a member of the research team and a member of the personnel department of the company. These latter two individuals were not active participants in the discussions except when called upon as resource people for certain types of information.

After an 18-month period in which the natural variations of the feedback programs in the four departments had run their course, a new survey was conducted in the accounting branch. The before and after measures indicated that more significant changes had occurred in the four experimental than in the two control departments. As Mann (1957) states:

Two measures of change were employed: a comparison of answers to sixty-one identical questions which had been asked in the previous surveys and a comparison of answers to seventeen questions dealing with changes perceived by the workers since the 1950 survey. In the experimental group (comprising four departments), a fourth of the sixty-one items showed relative mean positive changes, significant at the .05 level or better; the change for another 57 per cent of the items was also positive in direction, but not statistically significant. Major positive changes occurred in the experimental groups in how employees felt about (1) the kind of work they do (job interest, importance, and level of responsibility); (2) their supervisor (his ability to handle people, give recognition, direct their work, and represent them in handling complaints); (3) their progress in the company; and (4) their group's ability to get the job done. The seventeen perceived-change items were designed specifically to measure changes in the areas where we expect the greatest shift in perceptions. Fifteen of these showed that a significantly higher proportion of employees in the experimental than in the control departments felt that change had occurred. More employees in the experimental departments saw changes in: (1) how well the supervisors in their department got along together; (2) how often supervisors held meetings; (3) how effective these meetings were; (4) how much their supervisor understood the way employees looked at and felt about things, etc. These findings indicate the extent to which the feedback's effectiveness lay in increasing understanding and communication as well as changing supervisory behavior.

Comparisons of the changes among the four experimental departments showed that the three departments which had two feedback sessions with their employees all showed positive change relative to the control departments. The change which occured in the fourth was directionally positive, but it was not significantly different from the control departments. In general, the greatest change occurred where the survey results were discussed in both the departmental units and the first-line organizational units. The greater the involvement of all members of the organization through their organizational families—the department heads, the first-line supervisors, and the employees —the greater the change. (pp. 161–162)

The procedure of feedback to organizational families as developed by Floyd Mann is similar in many ways to the group therapy approach of the Tavistock Institute. It has the same objective of clarification and improvement of organizational functioning through an objective assessment of problems by the organizational members themselves. It differs in four respects:

Mann had the considerable advantage of providing objective feedback on organizational functioning through detailed data furnished by his comprehensive survey. This made possible a task-oriented atmosphere where facts and figures were the guiding criteria. It also made possible the setting of performance norms, and insured a representation of the views of all employees in the consideration of problems by the various levels of management.

Mann's technique covered the entire organizational structure in systematic fashion. The Tavistock research team entered only those sections and groups of the organization to which they were specifically invited, and tended to spend more time with top management than with the lower echelons.

The Tavistock investigators were more active participants in the change process than were Mann and his colleagues. Though the Glacier people were not presented with solutions, they were led persistently to reexamine their thinking and to become aware of unrecognized and unconscious forces in the situation.

This meant that the focus in the Glacier study was more upon irrational sources of difficulty and in the Detroit Edison Company more upon reducing areas of ignorance through the acquisition of facts and modifying vague opinions with documented beliefs. It would be interesting to have a research comparison of the amount of personal and organizational change produced by the two methods and of the mediating processes responsible for whatever changes did occur.

Both methods by choice avoid identifying in advance desired changes in organizational structure and functioning. The objective is to induce the organization to change itself. This has a tremendous advantage in removing from the researcher the onus of deciding what needs to be changed. It has the possible disadvantage of making an organization more vigorous in its present mode of operation even when there may be basic defects in its operating philosophy. For example, a non-union factory, if subjected to the Tavistock group therapy, might emerge with a management clearer in its conception and more ingenious in its pursuit of ways to prevent union organization. In general, the organizational change attained by either the therapy or the feedback technique is likely to be in the direction of more efficient functioning but not in the direction of basic structural change. The oligarchy will still remain an oligarchy, the autocracy still an autocracy. These methods represent the philosophy of mild and bland reform, not radical change.

To state it more precisely, the primary target of the feedback technique employed by Mann is improvement of both personal and role relationships within the organizational family. The objective is not to introduce a systemic change but to improve the relationships among the members of each organizational family and between organizational families, through their discussion of their common problems. The specific changes which occur may vary from one sector of organizational space to another and they may all add up to better understanding and clearer communication in the organization as a whole. But the target has not been to change the system as a system.

This approach thus raises the question of the effective limits of change which is not systemwide in its character. Lippitt, Watson, and Westley (1958), in their incisive analysis of planned change, point out the problems raised by interdependence among the subparts of a system with respect to change processes. Change in one subpart can generate forces in other parts to produce related modifications, but interdependence can also mean that more sources of resistance are mobilized against any alteration of established procedures. Hence these authors emphasize the need for defining the unit in the organization appropriate to the change attempted. They write:

> If the subpart is too small to cope with a given problem, it will be unable to change because of resistance originating outside the subpart, coming either from the larger systems in which it is embedded or from parallel systems to which it is related. If the unit is too large and includes semiautonomous subsystems which are not directly involved in the change process, it may be unable to change because of resistance originating within the system. On the other hand, if the size of the unit selected as a client system is appropriate for a particular change objective and if several subparts of this system all become committed to achieving the same objective, the motivation and energy available to the system for working on change will be intensified by the interdependence and interaction among the subparts. (p. 77)

SYSTEMIC CHANGE: CHANGING ORGANIZATIONAL VARIABLES (THE MORSE-REIMER EXPERIMENT)

Most of the experimental attempts to produce change in organizations have been directed at individuals and not at the organization itself. This is true of the typical psychological approach with its emphasis upon individual training programs and of the group dynamics movement with its concentration on the small group irrespective of its organizational dependence. The group therapy approach of the Tavistock team recognized the organizational structure but made no direct attempt to change it. Similarly the feedback procedure of Mann recognized the interlocking organizational families but left all change to these families themselves. In everyday life, however, attempts are made to change an organization as a social system, i.e., to deal directly with organizational characteristics as properties of the organization rather than as the outcome of group and individual properties. Such an attempt involves the legitimation of changes in the role relationships making up the system. It is sometimes done by executive order, as when two companies merge and large sectors are reorganized or even eliminated. It can come about from revolution from within, as when young reformers capture a state or local political organization, oust the old guard from control, and reorganize the functioning of the political party. Systemic change can come about from pressures from without, as when the government orders the reorganization of an industrial empire which has achieved something of a monopolistic position in a given field of enterprise. Or the outside pressure can be the power of a labor union, which moves in on some of the old management functions of employee discipline, lay-off, and dismissal.

There have been very few attempts at the experimental manipulation of organizational variables by social scientists, partly because of the practical difficulties of attaining sufficient power to introduce organizational changes or of persuading organizational leaders already planning a change program to carry it out with experimental controls and measurements. To these difficulties must be added one which is self-imposed: research workers in this field have taken organizational variables as given, as the walls of the learning maze in which experiments on learning are to be run. Moreover, the individualistic bias of psychologists has prevented them from recognizing organizational variables as basic determinants of the social process.

One major experiment in which there was a direct and deliberate attempt to change an organizational variable was conducted by Morse and Reimer (1956) in one department of a large business enterprise. The organizational variable selected for modification involved the authority structure of the system, or more specifically the degree of organizational decision-making at various levels in the company. The experimenters, following the theorizing of F. H. Allport, conceptualized this variable as the degree of *axiality*, since organizations can be described as having an *axis* of control and regulation of their processes extending from the person or persons in the highest authority position down to the rank-and-file members of the organization. In the words of Morse and Reimer (1955):

> The hierarchical location of the regulation and control processes on this axis is the degree of *axiality* of the organization. A description of the degree of axiality of an organization as a whole can be obtained by examining, for each hierarchical level in turn, the degree to which the organization is controlled and regulated by people at higher levels in the organization compared to the degree to which it is controlled and regulated by individuals at a given level or lower in the hierarchy. (p. 1)

In this experiment the objective was to change the role structure with respect to decision-making and its accompanying activities so that the lower hierarchical levels in the structure would have more power and responsibility for carrying on the work of the organization. The essential idea was that all the advantages of small group democracy are lost in an organization in which the group has virtually no power to make decisions of any importance. Unless a given person or group in the legitimized authority structure is assigned responsibility for decision-making, all the training of individuals or of small groups to utilize group process and group decision are likely to be transitory or even abortive in their outcome.

We do not change organizations by occasional demonstrations of the value of the democratic process. The ongoing forces are structurally fixed in the system and the legitimate authority will not be affected to any appreciable degree without a direct attack upon its permanent structure. Hence the experimenters worked with the top echelons in the company to attain a legitimized change in organizational structure, so that the rank-and-file employees would be given the authority and responsibility for carrying out not only their own previous assignment but also the previous functions of the first-line supervisors. The first-line supervisors were to give up their previous decision-making for the people under them and were to take over the running of the division. In turn, the division managers gave up their former divisional responsibilities and were made responsible for the department. This left the department head without a major function and so he was asked to assume some of the executive vice-president's duties of coordination between the production department in question and the methods and personnel departments.

In other words, axiality, or the degree of control and regulation of the activities of the organization, cannot be changed at one level without affecting the whole organization. In fact, this is characteristic of any systemic property. If we are really dealing with an organizational or system variable, its manipulation will involve the entire organization. To achieve organizational change we have to deal with these systemic variables. Individual or group change applies only to specific points in organizational space and is more likely to be vitiated by the enduring systemic properties than to change them.

Change of organizational characteristics is regarded as inherently difficult to bring off because it means changing so much, and, of course, this is correct. What is overlooked, however, is that modification of major organizational processes by working with less relevant variables is infinitely more difficult to attain, even though working with such variables may entail less effort on the part of the change agent. For example, it is relatively easy to persuade many individuals to sign petitions renouncing war as a way of settling disputes between nations. Pacifist pledges of individuals have always been meaningless, however, when the latent war-making structure of the nation becomes its manifest structure in times of crisis. Unless national structures become modified to accept the jurisdiction of a larger international structure like the United Nations, war is inevitable.

The target of experimental change in the Morse and Reimer experiment was the variable of control and regulation of organizational processes. The proposed change was to shift the locus of control downward in the structure. To accomplish this purpose a variety of procedures was employed.

First in sequence was the persuasion of the executive vice-president and his assistants of the desirability of the change. Part of the persuasion was accomplished through group sessions of his own staff and the research team, part through the presentation of findings from a previous survey in his own company, the implications of which supported downward delegation. The results of the survey showed that the higher producing sections in the organization were less closely supervised and had more group involvement of their members than the lower producing sections. In the higher producing sections, for example, the clerks did not confine themselves to their own narrow job assignments but would help one another out. Supervisors in these sections gave the clerks more freedom in their tasks and gave extra time to training any clerk interested in moving up to a better job in the company.

A second procedure was the use of group discussion at various levels in the organization to prepare the employees for the anticipated change. This method of preparation also included the training of supervisors for their new roles.

The third procedure was the official introduction of the change as the new policy of the company, in a presentation by the executive vice-president himself to the employees. In other words, the change was legitimized as new role requirements by the proper authority structure. Finally, group discussion and decision-making was the mode of operation by which the rank-and-file employees and first-line supervisors implemented the new program.

Some nine months were spent in preparation for the experimental changes, including the early meetings for securing the approval of top management. The experiment itself ran for a year, with before and after measurements of productivity and morale. In all, four parallel divisions of one department were involved. Two of the divisions were assigned to the experimental treatment described above. The other two were placed in a change program which also involved manipulation of the axiality variable, but in the direction of tighter control and increased regulation from the upper echelons. In a field experiment the classical notion of a control group which operates as usual is not appropriate, since the experimental group has the advantage of special treatment no matter what the treatment. Accordingly, the design in this experiment called for the two opposed experimental treatments, to control for the effects of special attention. The divisions in the two programs were matched in productivity on the basis of their performance during the previous year. The program of downward delegation was called the *Autonomy Program;* the program of tighter control from above the *Hierarchically Controlled Program.* In the latter program of hierarchical control, decisions formerly made by first-line supervisors and by division heads were now made at the departmental level.

Some 33 supervisors and 204 nonsupervisory employees constituted the four divisions in the two programs. Each division processed contractual forms and had separate sections dealing with lapses, cash surrenders, new business, and the like. Each was identical or similar to the other three in every respect which the company could control. Productivity was measured by the number of employees required to complete a given volume of work. The volume of work accomplished by a given section was not under its control, but what did vary was whether the section needed more or fewer clerks to get the job done. Increased productivity thus could be achieved only by out-placing some of the clerks, or not replacing those who left of their own accord. Decreased productivity would result from calling in extra workers (or floaters, in the company's terminology).

The experimental manipulations were successful in creating two different social subsystems for the two sets of divisions. In the Autonomy Program the clerical work groups did in fact make a variety of group decisions on matters of importance to them, such as recess periods, the handling of tardiness, work methods, and work processes. Some work groups were more active than others in getting together to discuss and decide on how their section should operate, but all groups in this program assumed group responsibility for the operations of the section. In the Hierarchically Controlled Program, on the other hand, the employees were less involved than before in the regulation and control of their own activities. Previously they had little direct influence on decisions, but they did have some degree of influence on their supervisors and division managers with whom they had direct contact. Now decisions were made at the departmental level, and employees were completely removed from affecting the control process. The measurement of the changes perceived by the employees in the two programs corroborates the effectiveness of the experimental manipulations. In the Autonomy Program the clerks saw decision-making activities as less a function of higher organizational levels than before the experiment, whereas in the Hierarchical Program the clerks now perceived all policies and procedures as determined to a very high degree at levels above their own.

It was hypothesized that the Autonomy Program would improve the morale of the employees in the following attitudinal areas: (1) self-actualization, (2) satisfaction with supervision, (3) liking for working for the company, (4) job satisfaction and (5) liking for the program.

Correspondingly it was predicted that there would be a decrease in favorable attitudes in these areas in the Hierarchically Controlled Program. It was also hypothesized that over time there would be an increase in productivity in the Autonomy Program and a decrease in productivity in the Hierarchically Controlled Program.

Self-actualization was measured by combining answers to the following five questions into an index score. (1) Is your job a real challenge to what you think you can do? (2) How much chance does your job give you to learn things you are interested in? (3) Are the things you are learning in your job helping to train you for a better job in the company? (4) How much chance do you have to try out your ideas on the job? (5) How much does your job give you a chance to do the things you are best at? Significant differences were found in the predicted direction, with an increase in self-actualization in the Autonomy Program and a decrease in the Hierarchically Controlled Program.

The programs also had differential effects on attitudes toward supervision. Relations with the assistant manager and the division manager improved significantly in the Autonomy Program and deteriorated in the Hierarchically Controlled Program. Similarly, attraction to the company increased in the former program and decreased in the latter program. The results on intrinsic job satisfaction were less clear cut. As predicted, there was a significant decrease in the Hierarchically Controlled Program, but contrary to prediction there was no significant change in the Autonomy Program, though there was some slight improvement. Morse and Reimer speculated about this one failure of their predictions on attitudinal change as follows.

The lack of change in the Autonomy Program may be due to the fact that the job content remained about the same. It is also possible that the increases in complexity and variety of their total work were offset by a rise in their level of aspiration, so that they expected more interesting and varied work. (p. 126)

There were marked differences between the two experimental groups in their liking for the programs to which they had been assigned.

The clerks in the Autonomy Program typically: wanted their program to last indefinitely, did not like the other program, felt that the clerks were one of the groups gaining the most from the program and described both positive and negative changes in interpersonal relations among the girls. The clerks in the Hierarchically Controlled Program, on the other hand, most frequently wanted their program to end immediately, liked the other program and felt that the company (rather than the employees) gained the most from their program. Not one single person in the Hierarchically Controlled Program mentioned an improvement in interpersonal relations as a result of the program. All of the noted changes were for the worse, with increases in friction and tension being most frequently mentioned. (p. 126)

For example, whereas 24 per cent of the Autonomy group reported more cooperation and 18 per cent more friendliness among the girls than had existed prior to the program, not a single employee in the Hierarchically Controlled Program gave such a positive response.

Unfortunately there were no good overall measures of productivity, or total costs to the company in relation to amount produced by the two programs. Both experimental groups showed significant increases in productivity on the basis of company figures for the costs of clerk time to get the job done, whereas the original predictions called for an increase in the Autonomous Program and a decrease in the Hierarchically Controlled Program. As a matter of fact, the increase in the Hierarchical Program was greater than that in the Autonomy Program on the clerk-time measure of productivity.

On the other hand, the costs in terms of clerk time do not cover the costs of turnover. Of the 54 girls who left the company from the four divisions during the course of the experiment, 23 made unfavorable comments in their exit interviews with members of the personnel department about pressure and too rigorous work standards. Of these 23, nineteen were from the Hierarchically Controlled Program. There is no doubt, however, that the productivity of the employees was increased by the direct expedient of assigning fewer girls to handle the same amount of work in the Hierarchically Controlled Program. This was achieved, however, at the cost of employee morale and may have been a short-run solution. What would have happened had the experiment run for a longer period can only be conjectured. A major reorganization, which had nothing to do with the experimental programs, but which called for decentralization of the whole clerical operation to divisional geographical offices, meant the end of the experimental groups.

Two other factors in extrapolating the results of this experiment to other situations should be kept in mind.

The first of these is the character of the employees. The overwhelming majority of clerks were girls recently graduated from high school who intended to stay only a few years with the company before getting married. They had little commitment to their jobs as a permanent occupation. Hence they were probably less responsive to either experimental treatment than men with more involvement in their occupation. Though they disliked the Hierarchically Controlled Program, these young, unorganized girls were not as likely to quit, go on strike, or rebel in an overt manner as more involved people might do. Management in the Hierarchical Program was able to increase productivity by tightening the screws. In other situations, management may not be able to overpower its workers in this fashion because of the presence of unions, or the presence of outside job opportunities for skilled workers, or the active resentment of a more occupation-conscious worker.

The second limiting factor in this experiment was the constant rate of work flow to all sections. This meant that the cooperative group spirit engendered in the Autonomy Program could not be fully expressed in increased productivity without disrupting the group. In effect the girls would have had to tell their superiors that they were asking for the transfer of a group member because she was not vitally necessary for handling the volume of work. Increased productivity actually came about in the Autonomy Program when the girls decided not to replace a member who was leaving to get married or to have a baby. But they could hardly be expected to dismember their group if no one was willing to leave, and they showed no inclination to do so. If the girls themselves could have determined their quotas of work, there would have been more opportunity for increases in productivity, as in the Bavelas experiment, in which workers raised their sights about what was an acceptable, fair day's work. Under these circumstances, the Autonomy Program might well have showed larger gains in productivity. Alternatively, as Likert (1956) suggests, the continuation of the experiment might have produced continued gains in the productivity of the Autonomy Program and reversal of gains in the Hierarchical Program. However plausible these possibilities, they are only that, and await confirmation or rejection in future research. Meanwhile, the increases in productivity in the Hierarchical Program constitute a clear disconfirmation of the original prediction, and a reminder of the effective power of hierarchy under conditions favorable to it.

Field experiments of the Morse-Reimer pattern, which attempt to change an organizational variable and measure the outcome upon the functioning of the organization, are desperately needed to advance our knowledge of organizational dynamics and effectiveness. The great difficulty with the therapy and feedback approach is that, in the first place, we do not know if any significant organizational change will occur and in the second place, if change does take place, what precisely has occurred. What is necessary in studies of this sort is a wide net of measures continued over time to discover the central change and its impact. Any organizational change which experimenters want to bring about to increase knowledge in this field must, of course, gain acceptance from the authority structure of the organization, and this itself imposes great limitations on scientific manipulations. Nonetheless, on many occasions organizations are open to modification and organizational leaders contemplate change programs themselves. Within this framework researchers can introduce the controls and measurements, and sometimes stipulate the means or sequence of change to yield more documented knowledge about social systems than we now possess.

THE TARGET OF CHANGE AS THE FIT BETWEEN THE TECHNICAL AND SOCIAL SUBSYSTEMS

Organizational structure as the direct target for change includes all types of patterned relationships which comprise a system or subsystem. It is useful, however, to consider two dimensions of any production system, the technical system and the accompanying social-psychological system, and the fit between these two interlocking arrangements. Trist (1963) and his Tavistock colleagues have developed the concept of the socio-technical system to take account of these two related dimensions of the organization of work:

> The concept of a socio-technical system arose from the consideration that any production system requires both a technological organization— equipment and process layout—and a work organization relating to each other those who carry out the necessary tasks. The technological demands place limits on the type of work organization possible, but a work organization has social and psychological properties of its own that are independent of technology . . . . (Rice, 1958, p. 4)

Some technical systems may make imperative a particular type of social arrangement; for others there may be alternative social-psychological systems possible within the technical requirements of the machines and tools for getting the task done. And yet one social-psychological system may be far superior to another, both with respect to member satisfaction and organizational productivity. The target for Trist and his research group has been to find the best fit between the technical and social systems, and to introduce into a given industry the reforms needed to attain that fit. Priority is accorded the technical requirements of task accomplishment but this does not mean that any so-called technical improvement imported from another industry is accepted uncritically as an appropriate modification of an existing work structure.

The assumptions of this approach as presented by Rice (1958) start with the following proposition:

> The performance of the primary task is supported by powerful social and psychological forces which ensure that a considerable capacity for co-operation is evoked among the members of the organization created to perform it. (p. 33)

The sources of gratification in getting the job done are: (1) closure or a sense of completion in finishing a meaningful unit of work,

(2) some control over their own activities by those engaged in a task, and (3) satisfactory relationships with those performing related tasks.

(1) The completion of a whole task by an individual is of course difficult to achieve in many types of industry, but this feeling of completing a meaningful cycle of activities can be provided by the group assignment rather than the individual job. This necessitates, however, a group organization in which individuals share in some perceptible fashion a meaningful task. It has been shown in the experimental laboratory that there is a group Zeignarik (1927) effect. Zeignarik originally demonstrated that an interrupted task results in frustration and leads to perseveration of the interrupted activity. People seek closure or completion of a process once begun. Moreover, if two or more people are given a common task, the logic of the Zeignarik effect carried over to their joint activities. One member may achieve closure through the activities of his fellow member or may be stimulated to complete a task begun by his comrade. This is not conjecture. The experimental findings of Lewis and Franklin (1944) demonstrated that partners on a group task would remember the task if not allowed to complete it. If, however, one partner was allowed to finish the task, the other partner would also experience a sense of closure. And Horwitz (1954) found that groups of five college women experienced less tension for the tasks their groups had decided not to finish than for unfinished tasks which the group was committed to complete. The usual application of machine theory to the development of a technical work system overlooks the possibilities of worker motivation to perform a meaningful part of a cycle of activities which is completed by a group.

(2) The need for autonomy in the control of one's own activities has already been discussed in relation to the need for self-determination and self-expression (Chapter 12). The autonomy need can find genuine expression at the group as well as the individual level. Not every person has to make all the decisions about his work in order to experience a feeling of autonomy or self-determination. If his own immediate group has some degree of decision-making, this can satisfy his needs very adequately. Moreover, it has the advantage of not overwhelming him with responsibility for which he is not prepared.

(3) The need for satisfactory work relationships with others has been discussed (Chapter 12). All that need be added here is the negative side of the coin. If the socio-technical system is not properly organized, workers may blame others indiscriminately, form cliques, and engage in reciprocal scapegoating activities.

To achieve better work organization Rice makes the following additional assumptions:

Group stability is more easily maintained when the range of skills required of group members is such that all members of the group can comprehend all the skills and, without having, or wanting to have them, could aspire to their acquisition. (pp. 37–38)

In other words the greater the differences in skill the more difficult it is for members to communicate and the harder it is to develop group cohesiveness. Similarly,

The fewer the differences there are in prestige and status within a group, the more likely is the internal structure of a group to be stable and the more likely are its members to accept internal leadership. (p. 38)

And finally,

When members of small work groups become disaffected to the extent that they can no longer fit into their own work group, those disaffected should be able to move to other small work groups engaged in similar tasks. (p. 39)

These assumptions describe the conditions under which a social-psychological system can operate to further organizational goals and to increase member satisfaction. An ideal arrangement for a socio-technical system would be one in which the technical aspects of the work could be organized in such a manner that the immediate work group would have a meaningful unit of activity, some degree of responsibility for its task, and a satisfactory set of interpersonal relationships. And the greater the differences in skills, prestige, and status among members of the work group, the more difficult it will be to establish and maintain satisfactory interpersonal relationships.

The Trist Studies of British Coal Mines

The relationship between the technical and the social systems in British coal mines has been studied by Trist and Bamforth (1951) and other Tavistock researchers, with respect to problems of technological change in the industry. The production side of coal mining includes three different types of operations: (1) the winning of the coal by hand or machine from the coal face, (2) the loading and transportation of the coal from the face, and (3) the supportive and preparatory activities of advancing the roof supports and of bringing up the conveyor system as the mining cuts deeper into the coal face. The early organization of these technical operations in many British mines was a simple system of small, self-contained units working independently. For example, in some pits the primary work group would consist of six men, two to a shift. Each man would be a complete miner, i.e., would have all the skills for carrying out the three types of operations described above. The two men working during the day would go through that part of the cycle of activities which the work demanded. The two men who succeeded them on the next shift would take up the task at whatever stage in the cycle their predecessors had left it, and so on through the three shifts. All six men would be on the same paynote, i.e., they would be paid the same wages, the amount being based upon the productivity of the six-man group. The composition of the group was based on self-selection, with men selecting their own mates. Any primary work group tended, therefore, to have six men fairly equal in overall performance. The earnings and performance of different mate or marrow groups, however, varied greatly, with differences of two hundred and three hundred per cent between the most productive and least productive of them. Each work group enforced its own standards of production and had considerable autonomy in its task. This simple system of working had advantages in mines in which irregularities of coal seams put a premium upon the adaptability of work groups. Each team could set its own work pace as the conditions required, and each worker as a complete miner could adapt to the changing situation. Moreover, there were many psychological advantages in the system. Workers gained satisfaction from being engaged in meaningful cycles of activity, in having considerable autonomy and variety of work, and in being part of a group of their own choosing.

This traditional system of single place working was replaced in Britain by the longwall method of mining, partly because of the intro-duction of the face conveyor. As reported in the Trist studies:

> The longwall system made possible by the face conveyor has a com-pelling economic advantage in that the proportion of stonework necessary for roadways in relation to extraction area is considerably reduced compared with what is necessary in single place layouts . . . . There is also the question of extraction at greater depth where the lateral effects of pressure often crush short pillars and longwall faces are preferred even under high seam condi-tions. (p. 41)

These technical changes in the coal mining process were accompanied by a reorganization of jobs and of work relationships. The model was the machine theory of the mass production industries. Division of labor in which each worker was limited to a single task replaced the inte-grated task and complete miner of single place working. The three basic types of operations were separated, so that the first shift had the task of cutting into the coal face, the second shift the task of shoveling the coal into the conveyor, and the third shift the task of advancing the face and enlarging the gateways. Moreover, within each of these phases there was further job specialization. When mechanical cutters were used in the first phase, five different work roles were specified. In place of the single work group of the older system six or more task groups were established. Though the longwall technology clearly required some modification of the older social system of single place working, the kind of job fractionation introduced and the neglect of the motivational forces of the primary work group were mistakes of the first order.

The justification for job fractionation is the economy in training a worker to exercise only a single skill, and the greater efficiency of the person performing a single operation over the person performing a number of functions. But the skills which were separated out for specialization in the longwall system were not of such complexity or variety that their performance by a single worker prevented the attainment of a high level of efficiency. Moreover, the artifical distinctions between jobs failed to recognize a common underlying ability required of all miners. In addition to their direct role in the production process miners must have the ability to contend with the dangers, threats, and interferences which are part of the business of working underground. This is in fact a more basic skill than the separate acts of cutting, drilling, hewing, or shoveling coal; it is, moreover, an ability which miners have in common. It is buttressed by involvement in a cohesive group, and it develops from the actual experience of working underground. It is essential for maintaining a high level of performance when difficulties arise. The conventional longwall system, because it failed to develop a work system appropriate to the utilization of this common experience and ability, depressed the productive performance of the miners.

A further difficulty with the conventional longwall system was its failure to maintain the natural or spontaneous coordination of the work cycle which had existed prior to its introduction. The longwall system organized work groups around task specialties, and each specialty had its own pay rate. Formerly each work group of six men had carried through all three phases of the mining operation, had taken joint responsibility for the amount of coal turned out, and had been paid accordingly. Now the fillers, the men who shovel the coal onto the conveyor, were given responsibility for this function alone, although they were dependent upon the previous shift for an adequate amount of work and in turn could hold up the succeeding shift if they did not make the expected progress. Each group was made pseudo-independent in its function, and was separated psychologically and socially from the other groups. The performance of the three phases of the cycle, which comprise an interdependent whole, is no longer a worker responsibility. To management fell the burden of coordination, and the longwall supervisor added for this purpose had a continual struggle meeting the crises which threatened the smooth flow of the continuing work process.

The institutionalization of the work system around specialized tasks carried over into the method of payment and produced further problems for management. Since miners were no longer paid according to the amount of coal turned out by their own group, each main task and its related subtasks became subject to negotiation. The result was a long list of itemized prices to cover all subtasks and related activities. Since objective measures were difficult to apply to many of these items, there was haggling on every payday and a constant flow of grievances from the miners. Moreover, the different specialized work groups were now in competition to increase their earnings, and anxious to put the blame for slowdowns on the other groups. Such competition does not mean greater production, because energy is channeled into making one's own task easier or better rewarded, at the expense of other jobs.

The psychological separation between work groups under the longwall system was increased by distinctions of status. The men who shoveled coal were doing a less skilled job and a less desirable job than the cutters or the hewers. New men were assigned to handling shovels in the filler group, and many of the older men in the group were resentful at not having moved to a more desirable status. They were not strongly motivated to cooperate with more privileged miners in insuring a coordinated work cycle. An indication of the low morale of the fillers was the high rate of absenteeism found among this group.

Finally, the miners found the fractionation of their jobs distasteful. Under the old system there was variety and challenge in their work. They much preferred being multiskilled complete miners to being hewers or cutters or fillers. In some mines where short conveyor faces made conversion to the conventional longwall system less urgent for technological reasons, the men exerted pressure to maintain the older form of group organization with the variety of tasks it entailed. There was no question that one of the most disliked features of the conventional longwall system was its tieing the worker to a single, narrowly defined task.

A Comparison of Two Different Social Systems for Dealing with the Same Technical Problems of Production: The Conventional Longwall versus the Composite Longwall Systems

The Tavistock researchers found that not all pits had moved to the conventional longwall method with its job specialization and machine theory applications. Especially in pits in which coal was found in short faces, the traditions of the single place system had sometimes been carried over into the new technological system, with its new face conveyors and its new cutters. A systematic comparison was therefore possible between two pits, one of which had taken over the conventional longwall method and the other of which had adapted the composite method of the older system to the new technology.

The Composite Longwall System. The composite method of the single working place originally had involved groups of six men, two on each of three shifts, with each group of six carrying major responsibility for completing the three basic phases of the production cycle. The adaptation of this system to longwall operation in the pit under observation involved 41 men, divided among three shifts. The requirement of additional skills for handling the new machines was met, not by tieing each worker to a specific job, but by the movement of the team from one task to another as the work demanded. The group would bring one phase of the operation to completion, then reassign its members for the next phase. It was not necessary for every member of the team to be completely multiskilled; it was necessary for each team to contain enough skill in its total man power to handle any tasks that might arise. The major difference between the composite system in the single working place and in longwall mining was that in the former system there was complete rotation of tasks, while in the latter not all men were necessarily rotated through all the specialized tasks required by the new machines. There was still, however, variety in the work in that all men were rotated through a number of different jobs.

The composite work method applied to longwall mining thus restored the continuity of task effort so lacking in the conventional system. In the composite system little external coordination of activity is required because the men move naturally from one task to the next as part of the requirements of their overall role. There is no lag between phases and no group conflict over the difficulties created by one group for the succeeding group.

The cohesiveness of the composite group stems from several sources. The group selects its own members and so the marrow, or mate, relationships traditional in British coal mining are preserved. This is an especially important factor for difficult and hazardous occupations. Moreover, the group assumes responsibility both for the overall task and for the allocation of members to the various jobs. It provides not only for ready job rotation but for shift rotation as well.

Finally, the method of payment recognizes and increases the interdependence of the group members. Their monetary rewards are tied directly to their performance. To the base rate of payment is added incentive pay based upon the productivity of the group. This pooling of earnings does not require that each member draw exactly the same pay. The basic assumption, however, is that every miner in the group is a multiskilled worker, interchangeable with his mates according to the requirements of the unfolding task, and hence entitled to the same reward. In short, the composite longwall system mobilizes the social-psychological forces of the immediate work group for maintaining a high level of production. Moreover, it saved management the cost of an external system of coordination and of the bickering each payday over payments for the itemized list of subtasks.

The observations of the Tavistock researchers on the functioning of the two longwall systems and their theoretical analysis of the superiority of the composite system were put to test by a factual comparison of the two systems in operation. Two panels of 41 workers each were studied, one panel organized on the conventional longwall pattern, the other according to the composite method. Though the panels were in different pits, the conditions of work were basically the same—both coal faces were in the same seam; the geological conditions were very much alike; similar haulage systems were employed; and the same cutting technology was used.

One measure of the effectiveness of group functioning is the rate of absenteeism, both voluntary and involuntary. Absence rates usually are not sensitive measures, because the total rate of absenteeism under normal industrial conditions tends to be very low. Yet the differences between the conventional and the composite systems are striking; total absence rates in the conventional panel are two and a half times as great as in composite panels, and voluntary absence is ten times as great. A plausible explanation for these differences would emphasize two points: (1) the competitive, distrustful relations between workers on different tasks in the conventional system make the work situation less attractive psychologically than the composite system, with its supportive relationships among all workers on the panel; (2) the stresses produced by the work are greater in the conventional than in the composite method of operation. If some workers encounter heavy and difficult tasks in the conventional system there is no relief, whereas in the composite mode of operation the load can be spread among other members of the panel.

The productivity measures also implied clearly the superiority of the composite to the conventional method. Production was much more regular in the composite system. As Trist says,

. . . the conventional longwall with conditions quite normal ran for only twelve weeks before it lost a cut, and during these twelve weeks it needed reinforcement to enable it to complete its cycles. The composite longwall, on the other hand, ran for sixty-five weeks before it lost a cut, and never needed any reinforcement. (p. 125)

Table 12   PRODUCTIVITY AS PER CENT OF ESTIMATED
FACE POTENTIAL *

	Conventional Longwall	Composite Longwall
Without allowance for haulage system efficiency	67	95
With allowance	78	95

* Trist et al., 1963, p. 125.

Productivity as measured by output per man-shift was 3.5 tons for
the conventional longwall, which was very close to the national norm;
for the composite system it was 5.3 tons. When allowances were made
for possible differences in seam sections and other factors, the composite
system was found to be operating at 95 per cent of its potential and the
conventional system to be operating at 78 per cent of its potential
(Table 12). Finally, a measure of organizational effectiveness must go
beyond output per worker and include other costs such as supervision.
It should be noted, therefore, that the greater need for external coordination in the conventional longwall method necessitated the assignment of a supervisor not required by the composite system. Not only
were the 41 men in the composite panel turning out more work than
the conventional panel, but they were doing it without costing management the salary of a supervisor.

One reason offered for the greater productivity of the composite
group corresponds closely to one of the types of behavior required,
according to our analysis, for a high level of organizational functioning.
That is the behavior which goes beyond specified role requirements
and yet advances the organization toward its goals. In the conventional
system men did their work without regard to the effects which their
way of operating might have upon other groups.

Fillers, concentrating on tons of coal filled, were not greatly worried by
the consequences for the pullers of how they put in their supports. Pullers, in
their turn, were not very concerned to stack withdrawn supports behind the
belt, and tended to leave them in the cutting track. For men in all groups,
their view of the work of the face is limited to their own task. There is,
therefore, a good deal of *unnecessary work* created by one group for another.
On the composite longwall, on the other hand, where there is only one team
all of whom share a single primary task and a single paynote, the effect of
the work done by any shift group on their mates who will follow them on
later shifts, was anticipated, and anything likely to cause extra work later
was avoided. The standard of workmanship, therefore, tended to be better.
The effect of these differences was very striking to the observer. On the

composite face the coal was completely cleared off the face, with no band of coal left lying; the timber was always in a straight line; and the face gates and equipment were kept in very tidy order. On the conventional face, timber was badly set and out-of-line; the face always had a good deal of spillage left on it; and the gates and equipment were in noticeably less well-kept condition. (p. 120)

The Tavistock research team extended its investigation to the socio-technical systems emerging in other British coal fields with the introduction of new technology. For example, they compared two composite longwalls which varied in the degree to which the ideal of the composite system was approximated. One embodied all the features of the composite system, the other only some of them. This latter longwall system was organized as two face teams. Each worker was assigned one main task, supplemented by occasional involvement in other work roles. There was little movement of workers from one task group to another, and responsibility for each given task was on an individual rather a group basis. The other longwall group resembled much more closely the composite system described earlier, with multi-task jobs, rotation of work, and free movement of workers within the panel. Both the modified and the composite systems operated in the same seam, under similar technical conditions, and with workers very much alike in qualifications and experience. Again the "pure" composite panel was definitely superior to the modified composite panel; it had a lower absence rate, a lower accident rate, higher productivity, and a more successful regulation of cycle progress.

The research team was not able to work directly with top management, government, and union officials to introduce a change program in the industry as a whole. They worked at the local level in those mines where local officials were willing to have research conducted and were interested in research outcomes. In some cases the research findings and the concepts of the researchers had an effect upon the ongoing change process. The availability of new machines had plunged the coal fields into a process of technological change, and the way was partly open to seek the most appropriate change in the accompanying social-psychological system. Nevertheless, the thrust of the Tavistock group toward developing the best fit between the technological system and the social system met with only partial success. Its efforts were limited by its inability to gain entry to the top-power circles in the industry, the difficulty of communicating the research results to groups who had not themselves been involved in the experimental comparisons, and the threat to the larger social system of the implications of a thorough rational reform.

Rice's Studies of Indian Textile Mills

The impact of a behavioral science approach, with its emphasis upon adequate theory and hard-headed experimental findings, should not be discounted. An inroad was made in the British mining industry, and the follow-up studies of Rice (1958), another Tavistock researcher, in the calico mills of India attest to the validity of their conceptualization of a productive organization as a socio-technical system in which the subsystems must be articulated for effective group performance. Rice's action research was conducted in a single company with two textile mills in Ahmedabad, employing some 8000 workers as of December, 1955. The research was undertaken at the invitation of the chairman of the mills. The consultant-client relationship was unusually broad, in that Rice as the representative of Tavistock was not committed to specific projects which management might want. Moreover, the company agreed that any of its workers or officers might discuss in private with the investigators any problems about their work, their roles, or their relationships. The general objective of the project was to help in the solution of social and psychological problems arising from changes in methods of work and managerial practice.

The first major problem of the research team had to do with the failure of the introduction of automatic looms to improve productivity. Though the morale of workers appeared good, and the supervisors and workers seemed to get along well, neither the quantity nor the quality of cloth was higher than that woven on the old nonautomatic looms. Observation of the work process revealed that twelve different occupational roles had been assigned individual workers to assure continuous operation of the looms. Workers had been assigned to these different specialized operations in accordance with American and British standards for machine production. The twelve job roles were: *battery fillers* to keep the batteries full of new bobbins, *weavers* to keep the machines in operation by mending broken warp threads and the like, *cloth carriers* to cut and remove the finished cloth from the machines, *smash hands* to deal with such major entanglements as the breaking of a large number of warp threads at the same time, *gaters* to remove exhausted beams and gate in new ones, *jobbers* and *assistant jobbers* to adjust, tune, and maintain the looms, an *oiler* to keep all moving parts oiled, a *feeler-motion fitter* to maintain the automatic device for ejecting empty bobbins, a *humidification fitter* to keep the plant at the humidity level necessary for the yarn to hold up in the weaving process, a *bobbin carrier* to remove empty bobbins, and a *sweeper* to remove the fluff from the shed and to clean under the looms during gating. In all, 29 men were distributed over these roles for the operation of 224 automatic looms.

With the exception of the jobbers and assistant jobbers who did comprise a group, the 29 workers constituted an aggregate of individuals with a confused pattern of interrelationships. Though the three smash hands served the eight weavers, the priorities of the eight weavers for their services had not been clearly established. Similar ambiguities in relationships existed among the other types of workers. Moreover, the task demands varied in that the thickness of the yarn for the different types of cloth changed the work load differentially for the various types of workers. A weaver might drop from operating 32 looms to 24 if given finer yarn because there would be more frequent warp breaks. On the other hand, a change to yarn of a higher count would increase the number of looms serviced by battery fillers and gaters, because the greater quantity of finer yarn wound on bobbins and beams would last longer. No rigid specifications could therefore be set down for the timing of the interdependent activities of the workers, nor did the technical system with its job fractionation and individual role responsibility encourage any internal group structure making for cooperation. Moreover, there was no psychological reward in the accomplishment of a whole task either by the individual alone or by his participation in the group.

If productivity was to be raised to take advantage of the new automatic looms, management faced two alternative courses of action. One was to retain the present technical system and to police it with more supervisors. The other was to reorganize the socio-technical system to provide internal group structure related to task accomplishment. The first alternative would add to personnel costs and would risk resistance by the workers to more external controls. "The workers would not only continue to experience the discomfort of their unstructured confusion but would feel further coerced and policed."

The researchers therefore proposed to management, after further study of the problem, a reorganization by which a group of workers would be responsible for a group of looms, with some sharing of the previously fractioned job assignments and with an overall group leader. Management accepted the proposal and planned to introduce it in one section of the weaving shed through a series of group meetings and discussions with successive levels of supervision, and finally with workers. There was such spontaneous acceptance of the plan, however, that the supervisors and workers immediately took over the scheme and proceeded to implement it. Through a process of mutual choice the workers formed four groups of seven men each, four in the weaving subgroup and three in the gating and maintenance subgroup. Moreover, they agreed to take over the ancillary services previously allocated to workers performing only a particular service.

By and large the history of the effects of the experimental plan is an amazing success story. This does not mean that all problems were automatically solved, that quantity and quality of production continuously soared, and that no new problems confronted management or workers. The amount of cloth woven did rise sharply during the first eleven days for the reorganized groups, fell during the next three days, then rose again and remained at a high level for four months, regressed to the preexperimental levels for two months, but then recovered and maintained its high rate for the next year and a half. For the two years and three months of measurement, productivity averaged some 95 per cent of potential, as compared to 80 per cent before the experimental reorganization. Quality of production, measured in terms of amount of damaged cloth, improved remarkably over the course of the 27 month period. In the first few days of the experiment damage actually rose, but it fell from 32 per cent in the preexperimental period to about 25 per cent during the next fifteen months, 20 per cent for the six months thereafter, and to about 15 per cent for the final six months of the experiment. The ups and downs in quantity and quality indicate that difficulties did arise in the new system and that they were resolved successfully by an alert management working with employees motivated to maintain the new system. Some of the adjustments required to make the new system work at high levels of performance were: allowing adequate time for the training of new workers, providing spare workers for increased stoppage rates with increased speed of production, keeping a group on the same type of yarn as long as possible, and confining experimental sorts (or types of yarn) to whole groups rather than spreading them over all groups.

The success of the experimental program led to its extension to the entire weaving shed, a change which the workers under the old system themselves pressed for. The motivational lift of the new system was palpable to any observer in its initial stages. Weavers ran to looms which had been stopped by a break in the yarn to get them back in operation. Some gaters carrying beams weighing over two hundred pounds trotted rather than walked. Indian industrial legislation to prevent exploitation of workers does not permit employees to stay in the working place during a meal break. As the experiment progressed, the men did not stop their looms at the beginning of the meal period but left them running until they were stopped automatically by a yarn break. And a supervisor had to remain in the shed during the meal period to keep members of the team from returning to the looms to insure that they be kept running. A third shift previously regarded as impossible because of climatic conditions was successfully inaugurated.

In spite of the great difference in culture between India and western societies, the same psychological findings in worker motivation are apparent. When people have a meaningful task and have membership in a satisfactory primary work group organized meaningfully for task accomplishment, they work harder and are more satisfied with their work. In other experiments in the same calico mills, the sociotechnical system for nonautomatic looms was changed by integrating workers into a group with responsibility for performing a whole task on a group of looms. Efficiency was improved and the new system spread to other sheds in the plant using nonautomatic looms. Though the cost of the original experimental shed was 13 per cent higher than other sheds because of higher worker earnings, the output was 21 per cent higher and the number of damages 59 per cent less.

CHANGE AND STABILITY

Though organizations are always in some degree of flux and rarely, if ever, attain a perfect state of equilibrium, major changes are the exception rather than the rule. They can be attributed to two sources: (1) changed inputs from the environment including the organizational supersystem, and (2) internal system strain or imbalance.

Changed Inputs

Changes in information or energic input into the organization are of two types. The first, new or modified production imports, has to do with modifications of quantity or quality in the inflow of materials and messages. These changes may be due directly to environmental changes, such as the discovery of new resources and the depletion of old ones, or to changes in the transactional process through which the organizational output provides energic return and reinforcement. The saturation of a market with a given type of product is a case in point; it demands a search for new markets, a change in product, or a revival of demand. Changes in input may also come from the supersystem which legitimizes various aspects of organizational functioning, as when new laws are enacted affecting taxes, labor relations, or restrictive trade agreements.

A second type of change has to do with maintenance inputs, which represent the values and motivations of the organizational members. In general this type of change is evolutionary. For example, in the

United States the growth in intensity and extensity of the democratic ethic has slowly affected the character and expectations of the American people. When they assume their organizational roles today in industry, in government, or in school, they expect, and if necessary demand, more democratic rights and privileges than most people asked or aspired to a hundred years ago. Such changes in maintenance inputs can be facilitated by outside systems, as labor unions have facilitated democratic developments within industry. Slower, more evolutionary changes in norms and values may go unnoticed until they accumulate at some critical point or threshold area and are consolidated around some precipitating event.

Internal Strain and Imbalance

Organizations function by means of adjustments and compromises among competitive and even conflicting elements in their structure and membership. These diverse elements produce system strain of two kinds: (1) the competition between different functional subsystems, or horizontal strain, and (2) vertical strain, the conflict between various levels in the hierarchy of power, privilege, and reward.

We have already described horizontal strain in Chapter 4, in pointing out the different dynamics of the various subsystems, each with its own essential functions. Thus the research and development people, with the task of innovation and adaptation, may want to move the entire organization in a different direction than seems reasonable to people in the production subsystems. Or two divisions of a single subsystem—two departments in a university, for example—may be in competition for the same resources. Each represents to the dean the greater importance of its particular program.

In addition to conflicts engendered by differences in function, subsystems may be in conflict because of their differential rates of growth. One subsystem may for a variety of reasons show a very rapid rate of growth. It becomes a leading subsystem and other subsystems move to adjust to it, either by following its pattern or attempting to check its development. The interdependence of all units in producing a stable overall system means that no one subsystem can move very far out of line without evoking strain. Other subsystems catch up by acquiring more momentum, or the leading subsystem is checked in its expansion, or the entire organization undergoes some degree of restructuring to find a new equilibrium.

For example, suppose that the professional and technical schools of a university accept large increases in enrollment while the liberal arts college attempts to hold constant the number of new students accepted. The liberal arts college now finds its stable position threatened by the demands of the other schools of the university for more space and more resources. Moreover, service teaching of the college for other schools increases relative to its use of resources for its own students, since it must admit to its classes all qualified students in the larger university of which it is a part.

Hierarchical or Vertical Conflict. Every organization requires some communality of goals which transcends the differential loyalties of subunits and binds the organization together. Such communality is difficult to achieve, particularly when there are large differentials in rewards and power between hierarchical ranks. The conflict evoked by such distinctions is made sharper if the different levels in the organization are defined more in terms of ascribed than achieved status. If the worker on the floor of the factory can never move up the rungs of the hierarchical ladder because of his limited education, he and his fellow workers have a common set of interests not identical with those occupying the officer positions or those eligible for them. This source of strain takes on greater significance in a democracy than a tradition-oriented society, since the values of the democratic society emphasize equality of opportunity.

It is our thesis, however, that these sources of internal strain are not the most potent causes of organizational change. The set of conditions which we have called changed inputs from without are the critical factors in the significant modification of organizations. Often the changes from without interact with internal strains to promote organizational revolution. The Marxian theory that change arises from basic internal contradictions that become aggravated as the system develops seems to us disproved by the facts of history. Systems develop many mechanisms for handling internal conflict. Though they change in this process, the change is slow and generally does not alter the basic character of the system. The highly developed capitalistic countries in which internal contradictions were to have led to revolution, according to Marx, have been able to compromise their internal conflicts and maintain their essential systemic character. On the other hand, the countries which have experienced revolutions are those which suffered changed inputs. The blows of World War I destroyed the social structure of czarist Russia and only then were the revolutionists able to come to power. Similarly the Chinese regime of Chiang Kai-shek was weakened by years of assault from without before it was overcome by internal revolution. The overthrow of the ancient Manchu dynasty in the earlier years of this century illustrates the same pattern of decisive external defeat as the predecessor of internal revolution.

The basic hypothesis is that organizations and other social structures are open systems which attain stability through their authority structures, reward mechanisms, and value systems, and which are changed primarily from without by means of some significant change in input. Some organizations, less open than most, may resist new inputs indefinitely and may perish rather than change. We would predict, however, that, in the absence of external changes, organizations are likely to be reformed from within in limited ways. More drastic or revolutionary changes are initiated or made possible by external forces.

A large-scale business organization set up along hierarchical lines and pursuing a policy of profit maximization, will not become a producers' cooperative or some other kind of democratic collectivity unless it collides with important environmental obstacles and is subjected to new inputs. A trade union with protective policies for its own members, including discriminatory hiring practices and restrictive apprentice training, becomes more open and democratic primarily as it meets obstacles to its way of operating in the larger society. A university is transformed from a teaching institution into a research-teaching complex primarily because outside funds are made available for the research function.

Two qualifications to our emphasis on external events remain to be made. First, we recognize that every organization, as a unit in a supersystem, not only is influenced by events in that supersystem but also contributes to those events. We have, for example, spoken of the ways in which American industry has been influenced by the spread of democratic doctrine and values in the larger culture. It is no less true that life within the organization feeds into that culture as members of the organization move back and forth across the organizational boundary. The contribution of any single organization may be impossible to trace, but the relation of the organization to the outside world is nevertheless a two-way transaction.

The second qualification has to do with the cumulative effects of small internal changes. Until we have evidence from longitudinal studies of a more ambitious kind than have yet been attempted, the profundity of such cumulative changes in organizations remains a subject of speculation. It seems a logical possibility that a succession of such internally generated changes might in time produce organizational transformations of great depth without the advent of external forces. Our reading of organizational history nevertheless argues the primary role of external forces in major organizational change.

SUMMARY

The study and the accomplishment of organizational change has been handicapped by the tendency to disregard systemic properties of organizations and to confuse individual change with change in organ-

izational variables. More specifically, scientists and practitioners have
assumed too often that an individual change will produce a corresponding organizational change. This assumption seems to us indefensible.
To clarify the issue this chapter analyzes seven approaches to organizational change, and considers their characteristic strengths and weaknesses.

Information—The supplying of additional cognitive input has real
but limited value as a way of creating organizational change. It can
support other methods, give the rationale for proposed changes, and
explain what will be expected of individuals. It is not, however, a
source of motivation; other methods are required to provide the necessary motive force to change. Moreover, the target of information is
necessarily the individual and not the organization.

Individual counseling and therapy—These methods represent attempts, in part successful, to avoid the limitations of mere information-
giving and to bring about individual change at a deeper level. It is
true that the production of new insight can lead to deeper and more
enduring changes in attitudes, and therefore to tendencies toward
altered behavior. The target of such attempts is still the individual,
however, and the translation of his new insights to organizational
change is left wholly to him.

Influence of the peer group—A third, and in many ways a more
potent, approach to organizational change is through the influence of
the peer group. It is based on the undeniable fact that peers do constitute strong influences on individual behavior, and that a process of
change successfully initiated in a peer group may become self-energiz-
ing and self-reinforcing. A dilemma is encountered, however, in trying
to maximize the relevance of the peer group approach to organizational
change. If the peer group consists of strangers without a common organizational affiliation, they face the same problems of transferring
their insights and individual changes that we have already noted for
individual approaches. If on the other hand the peer group is taken
intact from the organization, it is likely to be inhibited in its change
efforts by the role and authority structure which characterize it in the
organizational setting.

Sensitivity training—This technique is essentially an ingenious
extension of the peer-group approach to individual and organizational
change. The primary target of change remains the individual, although
recent variations of this training technique deal specifically with the
problem of adapting individual change to the organizational context.

Group therapy in organizations—This approach is best illustrated
by the work of Jaques, and some of his colleagues in the Tavistock

Institute. It has shown significant results, and represents an original and important fusion of individual therapy and the social psychology of organizations. Its most serious limitation is the assumption that organizational conflicts are primarily the expression of individual characteristics and neuroses, for the most part unrecognized by the individual.

Feedback—This approach to organizational change developed out of the attempt to make survey research results more usable by management. It has evolved into a well-defined procedure which relies on discussion of relevant findings by organizational families, each consisting of a supervisor and his immediate subordinates. The organization-wide use of feedback begins with the president and his executive vice-presidents, and works through the hierarchy of organizational families in order. The targets of this demonstrably effective technique are personal and role relations within the organizational family.

Systemic change—In our view this is the most powerful approach to changing human organizations. It requires the direct manipulation of organizational variables. One example of this approach is the work of Morse and Reimer, in which the target of change was the hierarchical distribution of decision-making power in a large clerical organization. Other examples are provided in the work of Trist and Rice, in mining and textile industries respectively. The target of change in their work is the goodness of fit between the social and the technical systems which comprise the organization.

The concluding sections of this chapter deal with the broad issue of change and stability in organizations, and consider the relative significance of inputs from the environment and internal strains as sources of organizational change. The argument is made that changed inputs of various kinds are the most important sources of organizational change.

14

Conclusion

In this book we have attempted to apply and extend open-system theory to human organizations. In making this attempt we have confronted the following questions:

What is open-system theory?
What elaboration of it is required to make it a theory of human organizations?
How does such an elaboration deepen our understanding of the long-recognized problems and processes of such organizations—of communication and influence, policy-making and leadership, organizational effectiveness and organizational change?

We intend this last chapter as a brief summary of our answers to these questions, which have been discussed at greater length throughout the book. We intend it also as a statement of a few of the chief dilemmas of organization which await solution, and which in solution will shape the future of man.

ORGANIZATIONS AND OPEN-SYSTEM THEORY: A SUMMARY

The Nature of Open-System Theory. In some respects open-system theory is not a theory at all; it does not pretend to the specific sequences of cause and effect, the specific hypotheses and tests of hypotheses which are the basic elements of theory. Open-system theory is rather a framework, a meta-theory, a model in the broadest sense of that overused term. Open-system theory is an approach and a conceptual language for understanding and describing many kinds and levels of phenomena. It is used to describe and explain the behavior of living organisms and combinations of organisms, but it is applicable to any dynamic, recurring process, any patterned sequence of events.

It is such a recurrent pattern of events, differentiated from but dependent on the larger stream of life in which it occurs and recurs, that constitutes an open system. All such systems involve the flow of energy from the environment through the system itself and back into the environment. They involve not only a flow of energy but a transformation of it, an alteration in energic form the precise nature of which is one definition of the system itself.

The functioning of any open system thus consists of recurrent cycles of input, transformation, and output. Of these three basic systemic processes, input and output are transactions involving the system and some sectors of its immediate environment; transformation or through-put is a process contained within the system itself. The transactions by which agencies in the environment accept the systemic product typically are linked to the transactions by which new inputs are made available to the system. To locate a system, to specify its functions, and to understand its functions, therefore, requires that this cyclical energic process be identified and traced. An open system is defined by its boundaries for the selective reception of inputs (a coding process) and for its typical transmission of outputs. It is further characterized by such properties as negentropy to counteract the tendency of all systems to run down; by feedback or responsiveness to information provided by its own functioning; homeostasis, the tendency to maintain a steady state; by equifinality or the use of different patterns to produce the same effect; and by differentiation, i.e., the tendency toward elaboration of structure.

An Open-System Approach to Organizational Theory. Some advocates of the open-system approach believe that a theory can be devised that will comprehend all levels of life. For the general-system theorists this is an article of faith. Our view is that theoretical progress can best be made by attempting instead to adapt the open-system model to each genotypic category of phenomena to which it is to be applied, adding specification to the meta-theoretical framework in order to maximize its explanatory power for the population category under study. This we have attempted for human organizations.

For human organizations, as for other open systems, the basic systemic processes are energic and involve the flow, transformation, and exchange of energy. Human organizations have unique properties, however, which distinguish them from other categories of open systems. Perhaps the most basic of these unique properties is the absence of structure in the usual sense of the term—an identifiable, enduring, physical anatomy which is observable at rest as in motion and which in motion generates and performs those activities which comprise the systemic function. The human organization lacks structure in this anatomical sense; its land and buildings are trappings; its members come and go. Yet it has structure; it is not a formless aggregate of interacting individuals engaged in the creation of some random combination of events.

We have argued that the resolution of this paradox lies in the patterns of the events of organizational life themselves. The events are structured, and the forms they assume have dynamic properties. Social organizations as contrived systems are sets of such patterned behavioral events. They consist of such events and have no anatomical structure analogous to that of physical and biological systems. In the most generic sense the structure of a social organization is contained in its various functions. In small subsystems the functions may be directly observable in the human activities involved; in dealing with larger sectors of organizational activity the patterns and functions are inferred from observable events.

This primary structural-functional quality of human organizations is closely linked to others that can be derived from it. The fact that organizational structure is created and maintained only as the members of the organization interact in an ordered way suggests a high degree of openness, a persistent and inherent vulnerability to forces in the organizational environment. It suggests also a continuing necessity to maintain the organizational structure against such forces or to adapt it to them. Much of the theorizing and empirical work about organizations has assumed explicitly or implicitly a closed system, in which the inputs into the system are regarded as constants. The open-system approach reminds us that organizational inputs are neither constant nor guaranteed. In particular, the organization lives only so long as people are induced to be members and to perform as such.

One way of giving theoretical recognition to this organizational characteristic is to distinguish between that energic flow which goes into procuring, transforming, and exporting the organizational product, and, on the other hand, that energic flow which goes into overcoming the centrifugal and permeable qualities inherent in the unique function-structure of the human organization. We have done so by proposing an essential dichotomy between production inputs and maintenance inputs. Production inputs are the materials and energies directly related to the through-put or the work that comprises the activity of the organization in turning out a product. Maintenance inputs are the energic and informational contributions necessary to hold the people in the system and persuade them to carry out their activities as members of the system. No social organization can exist without habitual acceptance by its members of their expected activities, understanding and skill needed for the performance of those activities, and motivation to engage in that performance.

Another theoretical problem in the treatment of organizations as open systems arises from the characteristics just described. How can this function-as-structure system of influenced, motivated, interdependent events be described and conceptualized? Moreover, how can it be conceptualized in terms which are not only meaningful at the systemic level but which have meaning as well for the individual processes of cognition and motivation which create the system? Our answer to these questions depends upon the concept of role and on role theory.

The set of activities required of an individual occupying a particular position in an organization constitutes a role. The requirements may be obvious to him because of his understanding of the technical process and the larger task of the organization or suborganization. They will also be communicated to him by those other members of the organization who require and depend upon his role behavior in order to meet the expectations for their own jobs. The entire organization can thus be viewed as consisting of roles or clusters of activities expected of individuals, and of role sets or overlapping groups, each consisting of persons who hold such expectations for a given individual. At one level of conceptualization, then, the organization is a structure of roles.

This is not to say that the particular array of roles which gives form to an organization is a constant. Though role systems and subsystems can be abstracted from their human carriers for anthropological or historical study, a full understanding of them must be predicated upon the continuing motivational and cognitive processes which keep (or fail to keep) the individuals performing their roles.

In the early chapters we have attempted some specification of the subsystems which arise to give continuity to and to provide developmental opportunities for the organization. The most generalized description of the various substructures at a social-psychological level, however, is that of the role system. A role system is a set of functionally specific, interrelated behaviors generated by interdependent tasks. Their role enactments are appropriate to the system requirements and not necessarily to the personality expression of the individual. The forces which maintain the role system are the task demands, the shared values, and the observance of rules. Organizations develop out of more primitive groupings in which these first two forces may have been dominant, but they grow by formal elaboration of the third factor of rule enforcement. The formulation of rules and the sanctions of rewards and punishments result in an authority system for the organization. Though the authority system invokes sanctions, it is also supported by the nature of the task demands and the shared values of the group. Thus organizational norms and values continue to be supportive of the role system. The values of the system are a justification and idealization of its functions. The most generic norm is that of legitimacy, i.e., an acceptance of the rules of the game because people acquiesce in the belief that there must be rules. Increasingly in contemporary organizations the values emphasize an ethic from below based upon social experience rather than an ethic from above deriving its force from divine revelation. Legitimacy in the organization thus takes on the pragmatic meaning of observing traffic rules rather than obeying a moral imperative.

Types of Structure as Functional Subsystems. As organizations develop the various functions of carrying on the work of the system, insuring maintenance of the structure, obtaining environmental support, adapting to environmental change, and of coordinating and controlling activities, they become differentiated into appropriate subsystems. Thus the technical or productive subsystem grows around the major type of work that gets done. The maintenance subsystem insures the survival of organizational forms through the socialization of new members and the use of penalties and rewards in rule enforcement. The supportive functions of procurement and disposal are directed at transactions with agencies in the external environment. The most critical supportive task of relating to the larger society and of legitimizing the part played by the organization is carried by the institutional subsystem. The anticipation of changing forces which may affect the organization is carried on by an adaptive subsystem with its research and planning activities. Finally cutting across all subsystems is the managerial structure which adjudicates conflicts within the organization and coordinates the activities of the subsystems both in relation to one another and to the external world.

To some extent, each subsystem has its own norms, its own set of coding categories, and its own dynamic. The people in the boundary subsystems are moved by the dynamic of securing environmental support and of adapting to change, and face out toward the external world; the production and maintenance people face in upon the organization and develop different values. The overall dynamic of the whole organization is one of growth and maximization.

The maximization dynamic means a reformulation of the equilibrium principle at the level of bureaucratic organizations: the push toward growth and expansion. The proficiency dynamic of the production system leads to increased volume of through-puts; to insure continued inputs the supportive subsystems attempt to control or ingest more environmental space; the adaptive subsystems move toward adjustments which place the organization in a position of advantage. Finally, bureaucratic structure as a set of functionally related roles can readily create new roles in an attempt to handle all problems. Hence bureaucratic organizations are characterized by a push toward expansion and growth. The equilibrium that is maintained is a dynamic one in which many of the relationships between the parts are reestablished after periods of growth.

Organizations differ, of course, in many respects but we have suggested a basic typology which follows from our analysis of the four major functions of a single large-scale organization. If we shift to a societal frame of reference it is apparent that most organizations are predominantly concerned with one major function. Thus from the point of view of the larger society, the productive or technical function is carried out by economic organizations, the managerial function by political structures and penal institutions, the maintenance function by socialization agencies, such as schools and churches, or rehabilitation agencies, such as hospitals, and the adaptive function by research groups and universities.

Processes of Organization. In human organizations the cycle of energy transformation operates at two levels: the direct utilization or modification of energy as energy, and the use of an energic input as information exchange between people interacting with one another. We have treated these interpersonal transactions at three levels of generality. At the most general level we have discussed communication with respect to the ways in which information flows through an organization, including the restrictions of the flow. Here the concern is with such problems as closed circuits, the direction of the flow, information overload, and the utilization of feedback.

At a more intermediate level of generality we have considered interaction in terms of influence. To a large extent the expected activities in terms of which individual roles are defined are expressed in terms of communicative acts of an influential character. The role prescriptions specify the persons from whom one is to accept influence and expect role-related communications, as well as the persons over whom one is expected to exert such influence and from whom such information is to be provided. The authority structure of an organization is nothing more than the pattern of such legitimized and influential communicative acts.

At a more specific level we have dealt with problems of leadership as differential acts of influence, differential in the sense that some individuals contribute much more to the outcome of the social process than do others. Within the organizational framework the exercise of authority contributes heavily to influence process. Nonetheless, the fact remains that individuals in the same authority positions differ in the increments of power they exert. Indeed, we have asserted that the essence of leadership consists in the expansion of influence to such other bases as expertise and personal liking. Leadership is most effective when it is based on these modes of influence as well as or instead of the organizational forces of legitimacy and the associated stock of rewards and punishments.

Like other phenomena of organization, leadership can be viewed at the systemic level as well as the interpersonal. In systemic terms we have distinguished three categories of leadership acts—those which involve alterations in organizational structure, those which involve minor extensions or interpolations of structure to fit particular cases, and those which involve merely the mechanical application of existing structural provisions.

Our discussion of policy-making is built around the same basic concepts. Policy is defined as an abstraction or generalization about organizational behavior, at a level which has implications for organizational structure. A proposed policy describes some set of transactions which will be required. It is thus a set of multiple role prescriptions, and it is also the highest of the three forms of leadership which we have proposed (acts involving changes in organizational structure). As a policy is carried out, it is expressed by means of influential and communicative acts.

The concept of organizational effectiveness is treated in terms of the same basic processes of communication, influence, and energic exchange. A distinction is made between organizational effectiveness as an inclusive measure of the ongoing state of the organization in relation to its environment, and organizational efficiency as one component of effectiveness. Efficiency is defined in terms of the energic ratio of organizational output to input. An organization is most efficient when, without any incapacitation of its resources over time, all of its inputs emerge as product. As increasing proportions of organizational input are utilized to maintain and energize the organization itself, and are therefore absorbed rather than transformed into product, the organization becomes less efficient.

Organizational effectiveness is a more inclusive concept. It is defined as the maximization of return to the organization by all means. Such maximization by economic and technical means has to do with efficiency, the more ingenious use of given amounts of input. Maximization by political means or other noneconomic means increases the inputs available to the organization without a corresponding commitment of output; it therefore increases effectiveness without adding to efficiency.

Increases (or decreases) in organizational effectiveness are viewed at several levels of abstraction—as transactions between the organization and its own subsystems or individual members, as changes in the internal structure of the organization, and as changes in the pattern of transactions between the organization and the larger environmental system of which it is a part.

Seven approaches to organizational change are considered—information, individual counseling and therapy, peer-group influence, sensitivity training, group therapy, survey feedback, and direct systemic change. Each is analyzed as a starting point of choice, given that any significant and enduring change implies not only individual motivational changes, but structural changes within the organization and in its relationship to the environment. Failing the attainment of such new equilibria, the change effort is absorbed and the organization returns to its previous level of functioning.

At the individual level, organizational effectiveness is discussed in terms of three generic requirements—joining and remaining in the organization, performing dependably the assigned activities, and engaging in occasional innovative and cooperative behavior in the service of organizational objectives. The motive patterns for maximizing these three requirements are not the same, nor will the same conditions necessarily arouse all of these motive patterns. Organizations thus face the problem of what mix of conditions they seek to create for what sectors of the organization in order to achieve given types of effectiveness.

DILEMMAS OF AN ORGANIZATIONAL SOCIETY

The characteristic properties of bureaucratic structures, which we have just summarized, are responsible for some of the major dilemmas of our society. In the first place, the maximization dynamic with its push toward organizational growth has, on the one hand, made possible a richer material life and, on the other, created corporate bigness and the nightmare of totality. In the second place, the use of role systems as a rational device for handling all problems has given us certain efficiencies but at the expense of some impoverishment of personal relations and loss of self-identity. In the third place, the moral integration of a society based upon a universally accepted ethical code seems to be threatened by the many roles of a bureaucratic system which emphasizes conformity rather than internalization and which, moreover, emphasizes empirical outcomes and compromises rather than rigid moral standards. Finally, the complexity and specialization of large-scale structures makes more difficult the involvement of its rank and file in decision-making. Information about policy problems is restricted to a small number of decision makers who have the time, the background, and the position to use it. And this tendency grows at the same time that all members have their expectations of democracy raised by being included as first-class citizens in the system.

Corporate Bigness and the Nightmare of Totality

Robert Presthus (1962) has nicely documented the trend of bureaucratic structure in our society toward bigness and toward ever increasing inclusion of all areas of human existence. Both world wars were followed by a consolidation movement in which thousands of individual firms disappeared to be replaced by mergers; some 2100 such mergers occurred between 1919 and 1930. Already in 1925 over fifty per cent of the total national generating capacity was controlled by sixteen public utilities.

Fortune magazine estimated that during the period from 1945 to 1953 there were 7,500 mergers important enough to be noted by the financial journals. (p. 72)

Labor, too, followed the merger pattern and the American Federation of Labor and the CIO joined forces in 1955. In the communication field today three networks determine what 180,000,000 Americans will see on television.

The merger trend not only works toward the domination of a single industry by one or two corporate giants, but it also cuts across industries, agencies of communication, the entertainment field, and others. As more areas of life are included under the organizational tent and as that tent becomes part of a larger societal covering, we may approach the situation which George Orwell (1949) described in 1984—the nightmare of totality.

The condition of organizational totality is met when all paths lead to the same source of authority. Dictatorship, absolute monarchy, totalitarianism—all have this common meaning. The separation of church and state, the persistent suspicion and opposition to monopolistic growth which characterize the earlier years of this country give testimony to the sensitivity of American statesmen in former times to the problem of organizational totality. This is a theme which has been eloquently presented in various art forms, including the work of Franz Kafka.

It may be worthwhile to distinguish at least two forms of organizational totality—totality in a role, as when a subordinate must obey in every detail the commands of an authoritarian supervisor; and a totality of roles, when an organization assumes possession of what would ordinarily be many separate roles of the individual. The army and the prison provide perhaps the outstanding examples of totality in this sense.

The advocates of political pluralism have dealt with this second form of organizational totality in which all the roles of people are under the control of a monolithic structure. Their answer has been a direct and frontal attack urging competing and conflicting structures within the same society—strong labor unions to counter strong industrial organizations, a strong Tennessee Valley Authority to check monopolistic power companies privately owned, vigorous private enterprises to offset governmental business activities, privately controlled universities to balance state universities. This approach limits the sovereignty of the national state by legitimizing the power position of other organizations within given spheres of operation. The competition and conflict which necessarily occur within a pluralistic society are costs well justified by the gains, since such conflicts can be adjudicated, negotiated, and compromised. In the past this has indeed been the pattern of American society but there is a growing fear that as we move toward more centralized planning, more governmental involvement in all areas of life, and more coordination across organizations, pluralism will be undermined. There are those, moreover, who see totality as less a governmental hegemony than an unholy alliance of the military-industrial complex.

What has preserved political pluralism in the past and what continues to be its hope in the future is both a democratic form in government and in nongovernmental structures and an active exercise of that democratic form by the people. Where the source of power in an organization is an electorate of all members, the totality of control from above can be effectively checked, though there are conditions which militate against the exercise of democratic rights by the membership. In his classical account of political parties, R. Michels (1949) formulated the iron law of oligarchy according to which it was claimed that the bureaucratic leaders possessed fairly complete control of a party in spite of its nominal democratic form. They did this, he maintained, by virtue of their monopoly of critical information and their use of it to maintain their own power positions, by a vertical structure which maintained lines of communication to those below them without adequate horizontal lines of communication for those in the lower ranks, by their long experience in bureaucratic positions, and by the inability of the rank-and-file members to acquire the organizational skills to permit them to challenge the leaders. Though Michels pointed out the weaknesses of a democratic structure, empirical studies of political parties show that the iron law of oligarchy is not an accurate account of their functioning. Leaders do rise from the ranks, lower levels do communicate with one another, and the control of information from above is far from complete and is also subject to the reality test of what the leaders are able to accomplish (Valen and Katz, 1964).

There are at least three basic conditions which can prevent a nominal democracy from becoming a functioning oligarchy. First, the democratic structure should be an open structure with respect to people entering it, participating in it, and moving up in the ranks. Membership should not be restricted by sizeable fees, by accident of skin color, or religious creed, or sex. Leadership roles similarly should not be limited by ascribed status but should be a matter of achieved status. Second, the level of education of all citizens should be raised so that groups are not excluded from participation through lack of knowledge of the opportunities to participate or lack of verbal skills required for some degree of participation. Finally, the most important requirement is that of involvement, of willingness to take part in the political opportunities available. Motivation is generally the most difficult variable in social problems. We do know, however, that it is not independent of the factors of openness of structure and of increased educational level. As education increases so too do the standards the individual sets for himself, and so too does his political participation. (Campbell et al., 1960)

Moreover, political apathy in our society tends to be greatest among the groups most poorly integrated into the reward structure of the society, i.e., Negroes, the unemployed, and the economically under privileged.

For a pluralistic society political democracy is, however, not enough. Other organizational structures should also follow democratic forms. By democratic forms we do not mean that the leaders merely consult their followers but that the source of legislative power is vested in the rank-and-file membership. Thus the leadership of professional societies, labor unions, and educational institutions should have to validate their positions by a vote of the members and by referenda on new policies. Even industrial enterprises should reserve some areas of decision-making for their lowest echelons.

If industry and executive government as central sectors of modern life are to contribute significantly to democratic and pluralistic values, they can scarcely deny such values in their own operations for the sake of efficiency. The degree and form of functional democratic procedure, the degree of establishment size and local autonomy most appropriate for various human purposes, is still being learned. It is paradoxical that the standard justification for autocratic practice in industry is its alleged efficiency, since the empirical research results do not support that conclusion. In fact, increased rank-and-file responsibility, increased participation in decision-making, and increased individual autonomy are associated with greater personal involvement and productive results.

The reason for extending democratic organizational form to nongovernmental structures is to make totality highly improbable if not impossible. In the days when democracy was reserved for the political sector, industrialists had the possibility of dominating a state legislature through their economic power and their control of the press. With the growth of labor unions, whose leaders were responsible to their members, this possibility decreased. With the growth of the democratic principle in other organizations, political pluralism was further assured. We have emphasized the distinction between the democratic and the authoritarian bases for an authority structure in our discussion of the exercise of power in organizations because we think it has been glibly passed over in much of the theorizing and writing about organizations. We view it as a central factor in understanding any social system and we see it as the only answer to the nightmare of totality.

Depersonalization and Fragmentation

A second dilemma of our organizational society is the depersonalization and fragmentation demanded by bureaucratic systems. A fundamental requirement is the assumption of roles, the relating to others not as personalities but as members of a role set. The individual must play many roles, no one of which is likely to express his total personality. Moreover, the returns from his role performance may be less in the direct expression of that role than in the extrinsic and indirect rewards of his role enactment. In an organizational culture, we develop a role readiness to move into any role the situation requires. Such role readiness implies a lack of internalized values and produces the other-directed person, in Riesman's (1950) formulation, or the hollow man of T. S. Eliot. To the extent that the individual possesses specific values of his own he may experience genuine personal role conflict. It has been suggested, for example, that Adlai Stevenson found his role as United Nations ambassador something of a torture when he had to defend the decision of the President to intervene in the Dominican Republic—a role requirement that conflicted with his own personal convictions. To the extent that a person has been socialized so that role readiness supplants internal standards he is handicapped in achieving self-actualization. It is interesting that the psychological literature as well as the popular press have in recent years become concerned with problems of self-identity. In an earlier society the issue never arose because it never would have occurred to people to ask who they were. Their personalities were developed around their positions in society. They may not have liked the patterns of their lives but they knew who they were.

Though personality integration around a core of central values may be more difficult in an organizational society as compared with an entrepreneurial or a traditional society, we should not assume without detailed analysis that the past was something of a Golden Age. It should be remembered that the lot of the average man in an older period was impoverished economically, psychologically, and culturally. Comparisons are often made by taking the population as a whole today and a tiny elite group of an older period. The great majority of men and women of an older day lived lives of enslavement to physical and economic necessity, to the rigid constraints of an oppressive social order, and to the hopelessness of problems beyond their control. Under these conditions they were brutalized in their relations to their fellow men and stunted in their personality development.

In other words, there is another side to the picture of the rise of bureaucratic structures with its depersonalization of people. The very fact that roles do not demand all of the individual's personality, that there are many roles to play, that the roles themselves change, means more freedom for the person. Since the organization does not require a marriage of the individual with the subsystem, the individual has many more degrees of freedom in patterning his life as he chooses. The entrepreneurship of earlier American society was limited to a small minority and was largely confined to the making of fortunes. Today the entrepreneur operates within a different framework—that of the bureaucratic structures. Within this framework more possibilities of individual choice are available in more areas of life and for more people than ever before. The workweek, which formerly occupied most of a person's waking hours, has been drastically reduced. The chains which bound a man to the same locality and the same job for all of his life have been broken. Geographical and occupational mobility have increased, as have the opportunities for participation in noneconomic roles. The woman of the last century had but one role, that of housewife and mother, and she had to come to terms with that role no matter how much enslavement and impoverishment of personality was involved. Today a woman may be in conflict about the many roles open to her but she leads a richer psychological life than her predecessor.

The literature of the last century deals with the problems of people caught up in rigid structure from which there was no escape. Many of these problems now seem ridiculously easy of solution. The dependence of children upon parents well into adulthood, the lack of economic opportunity, the restriction of the expressive satisfactions of art, play, and personal interests to the privileged few created barriers against which the individual was forever beating his head, and the simple expedients of deserting the tyrannical family, of leaving the repressive small town, or of giving up the hateful job were bold and unusual solutions.

Bureaucratic development in a democratic society has extended the scope of choices available to the average citizen and has thus given reality to the concept of freedom. Most of the organizations in the United States are voluntary organizations. A man can enter into political party activity to the extent he wishes, subject to the time demands of his job. He can change his place of employment within limits. He can elect to increase his education and skill if he has certain minimum ability. He can find time for his hobbies and find like-minded colleagues to join him whether it be to bowl, to bird watch, to collect rocks, to breed a certain species of dog, to watch ball games, to tour the United States or other countries, to improve his community, or to combat juvenile delinquency. In one small midwestern town of 50,000 people, for example, there are some 400 organizations. For the great majority there are more choices, more opportunities to express the multitudinous variety of human interests than ever before. Many of course do not take advantage of the elections available to them, and others are troubled by the conflicting demands upon their time. There is perhaps more risk in our type of society for individual peace of mind but there is also more chance of a richer psychological life.

Another aspect of the depersonalization of bureaucratic society is the fragmentation produced in interpersonal relationships. The depth of such relationships is affected by their role character, by the many roles, and by the geographical and social mobility of the population. We know more people but we know them less well; we have more social contacts but they are for specific purposes and not for developing personal ties. We do not know who we are because we are so many things to so many people. We have many more friends than did our

fathers and grandfathers, but the level of the friendship is less involve
and can be met by exchanging mimeographed accounts of the year'
happenings at holiday time.

Although it is true that bureaucratization is responsible for a les
personalized way of life than traditional society, the specific effect
of the tendency have still to be documented by research. And researcl
on this problem must take into account both the highly involved citi
zens in bureaucratic structures, who are a minority, and the partiall
and minimally involved, who are a majority. The minority can achiev
some personality integration and some degree of depth in persona
relationships through the reinforcing effects of similar roles in simila
organizations. The member of the Civil Liberties Union meets himsel
coming when he assumes his role as a member of the N.A.A.C.P.
the American Veterans Committee, and the Americans for Democratic
Action. His many memberships contribute to the integration of hi
value system. And he establishes continuing contact with his friends
since there is a high degree of overlap in the membership of related
organizations. The exact numbers of those who achieve such a consistent patterning in their lives have yet to be ascertained by empirical
investigation, but there is no doubt that the opportunities are there for
the achievement of such patterning.

The great majority, it is true, belong to very few organizations
(Axelrod, 1956; Wright and Hyman, 1958). Relatively few Americans
are joiners in spite of the common belief to the contrary. Most of their
contacts outside the job are limited to the family and larger kinship
groups. Those people occupying the less rewarding occupational roles
are also less likely to be members of voluntary organizations. The reduced workweek has given them a freedom which may be spent as
passive spectators before television sets, at movies, and at ball games.
And there are critics of our mass culture who see a deterioration in
aesthetic and intellectual standards as the various entertainment, informative, and artistic media seek the common denominator of the
large audience. The fruitful use of leisure time, as automation makes
possible further reductions in hours of employment and longer vacations, is seen as one of the challenging problems of our society.

Pessimism about its solution may, however, be based upon too
short-term a view of historical trends. As the level of education rises
(in another 25 years a majority of the American people will have at least
some college training) the degree of participation in meaningful activities may also increase. And it is possible that the problem as originally conceived may not be solved but merely reformulated. The
Protestant ethic which demanded hard work, constant striving, and

ndividual accomplishment may no longer furnish the criteria for the
uccess of personality realization. The reduced emphasis upon an economic career may open up many other possibilities of personality expression in noneconomic fields. At present the older ideology may
actually inhibit new lines of development, and the ferment of the
younger generation may lead to constructive forms.

Moral Integration

A third major dilemma of a bureaucratic society is the problem
f the moral integration of the system. In an earlier chapter we called
attention to the thesis of Durkheim that in a simpler society with little
ole differentiation, social solidarity was based upon a common set
f moral values—a collective internalized conscience. Criminal law was
merely the formal expression of the universally held ethical code. With
he growth of a society based on division of labor people moved away
rom a simple moral code and were tied together more through func-
ional interdependence and a spirit of mutual cooperation. As people
eparate into many subgroups with their own parts to play ethics become more relative to given situations and an absolutistic moral code,
based on rigid notions about good and evil, becomes weaker. Bureau-
ratic structures, in coordinating subsystems, employ negotiation and
compromise; and adaptive, coping mechanisms replace fixed moral
positions.

The decline in traditional morality is a common complaint of some
f our older citizens, who cite the apparent rise in juvenile delinquency,
he payola in government and business, the open appropriation of tools
and materials by workers, the difficulties which libraries have in keep-
ng their books, the vandalism of youngsters, the increase in illicit sexual
behavior, and higher divorce, etc. The Gallup Poll questioned people
n seven countries (release October 9, 1963) about their satisfac-
ion with the moral standards of people in their own countries. They
ound the greatest dissatisfaction in the two most advanced industrial
bureaucracies, West Germany (65 per cent dissatisfied) and the United
States (63 per cent dissatisfied), and the least dissatisfaction in Norway
(23 per cent dissatisfied)—findings clearly consistent with the thesis
f Durkheim.

The major issue at stake, however, is not the matter of morality
as such, but how a society is held together if there is no longer agreement about a common moral code and willing observance of it. We
believe that critics are correct in pointing to the deterioration of the
older traditional morality. But we believe that societal integration has
not suffered. Rather its basis has shifted and is now maintained by two

major factors: (1) a cooperative interdependence within a nation state which can legitimize direct and indirect forms of coordination, and (2) the growth of the democratic ethic.

We have already commented on the role readiness of bureaucratic society with its norms of cooperation. This psychological force is channeled through the various subsystems of the society and utilized by the ultimate legitimizing agency, the nation state, in the compromising of conflicts. The democratic ethic has received less attention both in our own treatment and in related discussions of the integrating values of social systems. The commitment to the values of equality of opportunity, the dignity of the individual, and the involvement of people in decision-making about their own fate has seen remarkable growth in the past sixty years but it has been gradual and cumulative and so has not been adequately recognized. The authoritarian training characteristic of the last century survives only in scattered sections of society. In industry where authority is still exercised by the upper echelons its mode of operation is sensitive to the perceptions of those below. Even in the most authoritarian structure, the military, the sergeant is less often the model of the martinet. Indeed, in formal organizations there has grown up a new etiquette of authority which is characterized by a kind of diffident, pseudo-participative behavior on the part of formal, appointed leaders. Limited as some of this behavior is, it should be noted that leaders in hierarchical organizations tend increasingly to act *as if* they were the elected representatives of the people whom they supervise.

There are other evidences of the infusion of democratic norms into hierarchical organizations, one of the most important having to do with the distribution of tangible rewards. Increasingly, the allocation of such rewards is on a system basis rather than on an individual or incentive basis. System rewards we have defined earlier as those rewards which accrue to the individual merely because of his membership in the organization. Retirement and pension plans, surgical and hospitalization benefits, vacation privileges, even stock options are increasingly available to all members of industrial organizations or at least to broad classes of members rather than to a small elite. Although those at the apex of the pyramid are still the most heavily rewarded, some of the qualitative distinctions between classes of membership in the system have been breached. The concept of first-class citizenship in an organization has been formulated and is receiving attention even in industry.

Another indication of the growth of the democratic dynamic can be seen in the outmoding of the once sacred prerogatives of authority.

Management's right to manage and the invoking of authority as the privilege of the person in authority are being replaced by a search for consensus.

The democratic ethic, moreover, has expanded beyond political equality to embrace ideas of social justice, of equality of opportunity, and of access to education, employment, and social life. In this connection it is instructive to look at changes in religious institutions. The doctrines of the Church were once concerned with the nature of original sin and with theological problems. Today most churches address themselves to the problems of man's relations to his fellows. Religious leaders have been in the forefront of the civil-rights movement and in general have been concerned with the practice of Christianity rather than with theological issues. Though we can bewail the passing of the traditional morality, we must also recognize that we have seen a strengthening of a practical morality. An ethics from below has replaced the ethics from above. The basic agreement throughout our society about the rights of the individual and about the acceptance of democratically achieved decisions furnishes a type of moral integration of society not envisioned by Durkheim.

Restricting Information about Decision-Making

Perhaps the greatest organizational dilemma of our type of bureaucratic structure is the conflict between the democratic expectations of people and their actual share in decision-making. Though the great majority of decision have to be made by leaders, their followers can participate in the process psychologically if they can share in the information about decision-making. By being informed, individuals, moreover, can mobilize public opinion to affect the decision process, and even if given groups are unsuccessful in achieving all they want, they may experience satisfaction in having meaningfully participated. The need for such involvement has been stimulated by democratic teaching in the home and the school and reinforced by the values of the culture. Increasingly, the level of expectation has been raised so that people in all organizations from the local recreation club to the nation state want to feel some relationship to the policy formulation which affects their lives.

As organizations grow in size and complexity, however, the decision centers become more removed from the people and the information needed to make decisions becomes more the exclusive property of the leaders. There is the further difficulty, described in Chapter 10, of individuals at the top of the hierarchy talking mostly with a small group at their own level and reinforcing each other in their views.

Often these people are under constraints of time in informing their followers and bringing them along to view things from the leadership point of view. But there are other constraints as well. Officials often believe that to share information would tie their hands in that the public or specific, interested groups would press for certain alternatives. Such public dissemination of information might also give competing outside structures too much knowledge of an organization's plans. Finally, even where there is the desire to communicate fully to followers, the means of reaching people effectively are not always available. Not only are appropriate mechanisms for sharing information often weak but the audience, remote from the specifics of the problem, may lack the cognitive basis for receiving the message and often the motivation to listen.

The effects of the conflict between rising expectations of involvement and the difficulties of communication and participation in a complicated structure of decision-making can have three maladaptive effects: (1) It can produce apathy or alienation among certain elements, who see themselves hopelessly outside the system. (2) It can produce blind conformity among those who accept the system and its normative requirements as demands external to themselves and for which they have no responsibility. (3) It can result in ferment without form, rebels without a cause, demonstrations with no appropriate target. Students, for example, can riot in aimless fashion because they feel frustrated by the system but do not know what is wrong or what the possible remedies are.

Adaptive solutions to this conflict have been discussed throughout this volume. They include some of the following changes: (1) Most organizations can profitably move toward some decentralization of decision-making in substructures. (2) Democratic forms can be introduced not so much through consultation of leaders with followers as through a shift in the source of authority from the officials to the members. (3) Distinctions between classes of citizenship can be broken down. (4) The Likert principle of overlapping organizational families can improve communication. (5) Feedback from organizational functioning can include systematic communication from organizational members. (6) Closed circuits of information which make captive their own initiators can be opened up through operational research. (7) Role enlargement is often possible within existing structures and, with automation, may be a significant trend of the future. Such enlargement increases the sense of participation of members. (8) Group responsibility for a set of tasks can insure greater psychological involvement of individuals in organizations. (9) More explicit recognition is needed of the nature of bureaucratic systems. They are by nature open systems and the tendency to act as if they were closed, rigid structures makes people their servants rather than their masters. We have not as yet fully exploited the true character of the bureaucracy—namely its openness as a social form.

The development and dominance of bureaucratic organizations has many meanings and many ramifications. Bureaucratic development has been stimulated by the growth of science and science-generated technologies, and they in turn have been stimulated by the creation of bureaucracies devoted to science-making and technological innovation. Bureaucracy assumes somewhat different expressions in different cultures and in the service of different goals, but its defining characteristics remain identifiable and seem to possess a universality which survives economic and political boundaries.

Perhaps the crucial quality of the bureaucratic era in human society is that organizations and individual response to them are made secular rather than sacred considerations. Certainly the treatment of organizations as secular, instrumental objects rather than as sacred entities is part of the bureaucratic transformation. It is, moreover, an aspect much criticized by social observers who long for the simplicity of a world where the requirements of organizations were not merely legitimate but supernaturally compelling.

We would urge instead that the transformation from sacred to secular is unsatisfactory only in that it has not gone far enough. The welfare of man is best served when organizational forms are regarded with a tentative, questioning—even experimental—eye.

Too often changes in the social arrangements of organizations are lagging and fragmentary adjustments to technical changes already accomplished. We automate the equipment first and repair the social dislocations afterwards. The same rational considerations, however, that operate within the framework of technology can be utilized to determine social objectives and thus make the technical system the means rather than the master of social organization. The revolution introduced into the functioning of the economy by the Keynesians is one example of the application of bureaucratic intervention for the sake of desired social outcomes. More serious organizational experimentation, more trial-and-evaluation sequences, and more data on the effects of organizational alternatives are much needed.

It is common today to honor competition and pragmatic outcomes as desirable bases for choosing among organizations producing similar products by means of similar structural arrangements. But the principles of competition and pragmatic judgment can be extended. One of the great competitions is among alternative ways of organizing human behavior for productive tasks and the accomplishment of social goals. One of the great pragmatic tests is the determination of what organizational forms produce and accomplish most, enhancing rather than depleting meanwhile the resources of the society they serve. This implies measures of organizational effectiveness which comprehend the needs of leaders and followers, shareholders and workers, consumers and citizens at large.

One of the great dangers of this historical period is the dominance of an opposite doctrine. To advocate major organizational innovations in control, patterns of reward, or nominal ownership is dangerous in some parts of the world and unpopular in most. The coincidence of national boundaries and economic systems has moved part of the great organizational debate out of the realm of science and pragmatism and into the realm of sacred and patriotic matters. This seems to us unfortunate.

As an end state, the perfectibility of human society must perhaps remain an article of faith; nevertheless, some of the conditions necessary to give the perfectibility notion reality as a social process are known. They include an increased understanding of human organizations and a concomitant willingness to test that understanding by trial, experiment, and the scrutiny of research. It is in that spirit and in the hope of contributing to that end that this book has been written.

Bibliography

Albrecht, R., and T. R. Sarbin. 1952. Contributions to role-taking theory: annoyability as a function of the self. Unpublished manuscript.

Allport, F. H. 1924. *Social psychology*. Boston: Houghton Mifflin.

Allport, F. H. 1933. *Institutional behavior*. Chapel Hill, N. C.: University of North Carolina Press.

Allport, F. H. 1934. The J-curve hypothesis of conforming behavior. *Journal of Social Psychology*, **5**, 141–183.

Allport, F. H. 1954. The structuring of events: outline of a general theory with applications to psychology. *Psychological Review*, **61**, 281–303.

Allport, F. H. 1962. A structuronomic conception of behavior: individual and collective. I. Structural theory and the master problem of social psychology. *Journal of Abnormal and Social Psychology*, **64**, 3–30.

Allport, G. W. 1937. *Personality: a psychological interpretation*. New York: Holt.

Allport, G. W. 1945. Catharsis and the reduction of prejudice. *Journal of Social Issues*, **1**, 1–8.

Allport, G. W. 1954. *The nature of prejudice*. Cambridge, Mass.: Addison-Wesley.

Allport, G. W., and B. M. Kramer. 1946. Some roots of prejudice. *Journal of Psychology*, **22**, 9–39.

Argyris, C. 1957. *Personality and organization*. New York: Harper.

Argyris, C. 1962. *Interpersonal competence and organizational effectiveness*. Homewood, Ill.: Irwin-Dorsey.

Argyris, C. 1964. *Integrating the individual and the organization*. New York: Wiley.

Asch, S. 1952. *Social psychology*. Englewood Cliffs, N. J.: Prentice-Hall.

Ashby, W. R. 1952. *Design for a brain*. New York: Wiley.

Ashby, W. 1958. General systems theory as a new discipline. *General Systems Yearbook*. Vol. 3, 1–17.

Axelrod, M. 1956. Urban structure and social participation. *American Sociological Review*, **21**, 13–18.

Baker, B. 1954. Accuracy of social perceptions of psychopathic and non-psychopathic prison inmates. Unpublished manuscript.

Baldamus, W. 1951. Type of work and motivation. *British Journal of Sociology,* **2,** 44–58.

Bales, R. F. 1958. Task roles and social roles in problem-solving groups. In Eleanor Maccoby, T. M. Newcomb, and E. L. Hartley (Eds.) *Readings in social psychology,* 3rd ed., New York: Holt, Rinehart, and Winston, 437–447.

Barnard, C. 1938. *The functions of the executive.* Cambridge, Mass.: Harvard University Press.

Bass, B. A. 1960. *Leadership, psychology, and organizational behavior.* New York: Harper.

Bavelas, A. 1950. Communication patterns in task-oriented groups. *Journal of the Acoustic Society of America,* **22,** 725–30.

Bell, D. 1960. *The end of ideology.* New York: Free Press.

Bell, H. M. 1937. *Youth tell their story.* Washington, D. C.: American Youth Commission.

Bendix, R. 1956. *Work and authority in industry, ideologies of management in the course of industrialization.* New York: Wiley.

Bennett, E. B. 1955. Discussion, decision, commitment, and consensus in "group decision." *Human Relations,* **8,** 251–273.

Berkowitz, L. 1963. Responsibility and dependency. *Journal of Abnormal and Social Psychology,* **66,** 429–436.

Bernberg, R. E. 1952. Socio-psychological factors in industrial morale. *Journal of Social Psychology,* **36,** 73–82.

Blake, R. R., and Jane S. Mouton. 1964. *The managerial grid.* Houston, Tex.: Gulf.

Blau, P. 1955. *The dynamics of bureaucracy.* Chicago: University of Chicago Press.

Blau, P., and W. Scott. 1962. *Formal organizations.* San Francisco: Chandler.

Bond, Betty W. 1956. The group-discussion-decision approach: an appraisal of its use in health education. *Dissertation Abstracts,* **16,** 903–904.

Boulding, K. 1953. *The organizational revolution.* New York: Harper.

Boulding, K. E. 1956. General systems theory: the skeleton of science. *General Systems.* Yearbook of the Society for the Advancement of General System Theory, **1,** 11–17.

Bradford, L., J. Gibb, and K. Benne (Eds.) 1964. *T-group theory and laboratory method: innovation in re-education.* New York: Wiley.

Bradley, D. F., and M. Calvin. 1956. Behavior: imbalance in a network of chemical transformations. *General Systems.* Yearbook of the Society for the Advancement of General System Theory, **1,** 56–65.

Brayfield, A. H., and W. H. Crockett. 1955. Employee attitudes and employee performance. *Psychological Bulletin,* **52,** 396–424.

Brody, M. 1945. The relation between efficiency and job satisfaction. Unpublished Master's thesis, New York University.

Brown, J. F. 1936. *Psychology and the social order.* New York: McGraw-Hill.

Brown, W. 1960. *Exploration in management.* London: Heinemann.

Browne, C. G., and B. J. Neitzel. 1952. Communication, supervision, and morale. *Journal of Applied Psychology,* **36,** 86–91.

Cameron, N., and A. Magaret. 1951. *Behavior pathology.* Boston: Houghton Mifflin.

Campbell, A., P. E. Converse, W. E. Miller, and D. E. Stokes. 1960. *The American voter.* New York: Wiley.

Carter, L., W. Haythorn, and M. Howell. 1950. A further investigation of the criteria of leadership. *Journal of Abnormal and Social Psychology,* **45,** 350–358.

Carter, L., W. Haythorn, B. Shriver, and J. Lanzetta. 1951. The behavior of leaders and other group members. *Journal of Abnormal and Social Psychology,* **46,** 589–595.

Carter, L., and M. Nixon. 1949. An investigation of the relationship between four criteria of leadership ability for three different tasks. *Journal of Psychology,* **27,** 245–261.

Cartwright, D. 1959(a). A field theoretical conception of power. In D. Cartwright (Ed.) *Studies in social power.* Ann Arbor, Mich.: Institute for Social Research, 183–220.

Cartwright, D. (Ed.) 1959(b). *Studies in social power.* Ann Arbor, Mich.: Institute for Social Research.

Cartwright, D., and A. Zander (Eds.) 1960. *Group dynamics: research and theory,* 2nd ed. Evanston, Ill.: Row, Peterson.

Cattell, R. B. 1951. New concepts for measuring leadership, in terms of group syntality. *Human Relations,* **4,** 161–184.

Coch, L., and J. R. P. French, Jr. 1948. Overcoming resistance to change. *Human Relations,* **1,** 512–533.

Cohen, A. M. 1964. Predicting organization in changed communication networks. II. *Journal of Psychology,* **57,** 475–499; **58,** 115–129.

Cohen, E. 1954. *Human behavior in the concentration camp.* London: Jonathan Cape.

Coser, L. 1956. *The functions of social conflict.* New York: Free Press.

Dahl, R. 1957. The concept of power. *Behavioral Science,* **2,** 201–215.

Dahrendorf, R. 1958. Toward a theory of social conflict. *Journal of Conflict Resolution,* **2,** 170–183.

Dai, B. 1955. A socio-psychiatric approach to personality organization. In A. Rose (Ed.) *Mental health and mental disorder.* New York: Norton, 314–324.

Dalton, M. 1959. *Men who manage: fusions of feeling and theory in administration.* New York: Wiley.

Dearborn, D. C., and H. A. Simon. 1958. Selective perception: a note on the departmental identifications of executives. *Sociometry,* **21,** 140–144.

Dewey, J. 1933. *How we think.* New York: D. C. Heath.

Dornbusch, S. 1955. The military academy as an assimilating institution. *Social Forces,* **33,** 316–321.

Drucker, P. F. 1964. *The concept of the corporation.* New York: Mentor (c. 1946).

Dubin, R. 1951. *Human relations in administration.* Englewood Cliffs, N. J.: Prentice-Hall.

Dubin, R. 1958. *The world of work.* Englewood Cliffs, N. J.: Prentice-Hall.

Dubin, R. 1959. Stability of human organizations. In M. Haire (Ed.) *Modern organization theory.* New York: Wiley, 218–253.

Durkheim, E. 1947. *Division of labor in society.* New York: Free Press.

Easton, D. 1961. The analysis of political systems. In R. C. Macrides and B. E. Brown (Eds.) *Comparative politics.* Homewood, Ill.: Dorsey, 81–94.

Eliot, T. S. 1926. The Hollow Men. In *Poems 1909–1925.* London: Faber Gwyer.

Elliott, J. D. 1953. Increasing office productivity through job enlargement. In *The human side of the office manager's job.* New York: American Management Association, Office Management Series, **134,** 3–15.

Emery, F. E., and E. L. Trist. 1960. Socio-technical systems. In *Management sciences models and techniques.* Vol. 2. London: Pergamon Press.

Erasmus, C. J. 1961. *Man takes control.* Minneapolis: University of Minnesota Press.

Etzioni, A. 1961. *A comparative analysis of complex organizations*. New York: Free Press.

Evans, C. E. 1957. Supervisory responsibility and authority. *Research Report*, No. 30, American Management Association.

Evans, C. E., and L. N. Laseau. 1950. *My job contest*. Personnel Psychology Monograph No. 1. Washington, D. C.: Personnel Psychology Inc.

Festinger, L. 1954. A theory of social comparison processes. *Human Relations*, 7, 117–140.

Festinger, L. 1957. *A theory of cognitive dissonance*. Evanston, Ill.: Row, Peterson.

Fiedler, F. E. 1958. *Leader attitudes and group effectiveness*. Urbana, Ill.: University of Illinois Press.

Fleishman, E. A. 1961. *Studies in personnel and industrial psychology*. Homewood, Ill.: Dorsey.

Fleishman, E. A., E. H. Harris, and H. E. Burtt. 1955. Leadership and supervision in industry. *Ohio State Business Educational Research Monograph*, No. 33.

French, J. R. P., Jr., J. Israel, and D. Aas. 1960, An experiment on participation in a Norwegian factory. *Human Relations*, 13, 3–19.

French, J. R. P., Jr., and B. H. Raven. 1960. The bases of social power. In D. Cartwright and A. Zander (Eds.) *Group dynamics: research and theory*, 2nd. ed., 607–623.

French, J. R. P., Jr., and A Zander. 1949. The group dynamics approach. *Psychological labor-management relations*, Industrial Relations Research Association, 71–80.

Freud, S. 1928. *Future of an illusion*, (tr. by W. D. Robson-Scott). London: Hogarth Press.

Friedrich, C. J. 1940. Public policy and the nature of administrative responsibility. In C. J. Friedrich and E. S. Mason (Eds.) *Public policy, Yearbook of the Graduate School of Public Administration*. Cambridge, Mass.: Harvard University Press.

Georgopoulos, B. S., G. Mahoney, and N. Jones. 1957. A path-goal approach to productivity. *Journal of Applied Psychology*, 41 (6), 345–353.

Georgopoulos, B. S., and F. C. Mann. 1962. *The Community general hospital*. New York: Macmillan.

Getzels, J. W., and E. G. Guba. 1954. Role, role conflict and effectiveness: an empirical study. *American Sociological Review*, 19, 164–175.

Gibb, C. A. 1947. The principles and traits of leadership. *Journal of Abnormal and Social Psychology*, 42, 267–284.

Gibb, C. A. 1954. Leadership. In G. Lindzey (Ed.) *Handbook of social psychology*, Vol. II. Cambridge, Mass.: Addison-Wesley, 877–920.

Giese, W. J., and H. W. Ruter. 1949. An objective basis of morale. *Journal of Applied Psychology*, 33, 421–427.

Goffman, E. 1961. *Asylums*. Garden City, N. Y.: Doubleday.

Gough, H. G. 1948. A sociological theory of psychotherapy. *American Journal of Sociology*, 53, 359–366.

Gough, H. G., and D. R. Peterson. 1952. The identification and measurement of predispositional factors in crime and delinquency. *Journal of Consulting Psychology*, 16, 207–212.

Gouldner, A. W. 1954. *Patterns of industrial bureaucracy*. New York: Free Press.

Gouldner, A. W. 1960. The norm of reciprocity: a preliminary statement. *American Sociological Review*, 25, 161–179.

Gross, B. 1964. *The managing of organizations.* New York: Free Press.

Gross, N., W. Mason, and A. W. McEachern. 1958. *Explorations in role analysis: studies of the school superintendency role.* New York: Wiley.

Guest, R. H. 1957. Job enlargement, a revolution in job design. *Personnel* Administrator, **20**, 9–16.

Guetzkow, H., and W. R. Dill. 1957. Factors in the organizational development of task-oriented groups. *Sociometry,* **20**, 175–204.

Guetzkow, H., and H. A. Simon. 1955. The impact of certain communication nets upon organization and performance in task-oriented groups. *Management Science,* **1**, 233–250.

Gulick, L., and L. Urwick (Eds.) 1937. *Papers on the science of administration.* New York: Institute of Public Administration.

Gurin, G., J. Veroff, and Sheila Feld. 1960. *Americans view their mental health.* New York: Basic Books.

Haire, M. 1959. Biological models and empirical histories of the growth of organizations. In M. Haire (Ed.) *Modern organization theory,* New York: Wiley, 272–306.

Harding, F. C., and R. A. Bottenberg. 1961. Effect of personal characteristics on relationships between attitudes and job performance. *Journal of Applied Psychology,* **45**, 428–430.

Heise, G. A., and G. A. Miller. 1951. Problem solving by small groups using various communication nets. *Journal of Abnormal and Social Psychology,* **46**, 327–335.

Hersey, J. 1959. *The war lover.* New York: Alfred Knopf.

Herzberg, F., B. Mausner, and B. Snyderman. 1959. *The motivation to work,* 2nd ed. New York: Wiley.

Hockett, H. C. 1939. *The constitutional history of the United States.* New York: Macmillan.

Hoffman, L. R. 1959. Homogeneity of member personality and its effect on group problem-solving. *Journal of Abnormal and Social Psychology,* **58**, 27–32.

Hoffman, L. R., E. Harburg, and N. R. F. Maier. 1962. Differences and disagreement as factors in creative group problem-solving. *Journal of Abnormal and Social Psychology,* **64**, 206–214.

Hoffman, L. R. and N. R. F. Maier. 1961. Quality and acceptance of problem solutions by members of homogeneous and heterogeneous groups. *Journal of Abnormal and Social Psychology,* **62** (3), 401–407.

Hoffman, L. R., and N. R. F. Maier. 1964. Valence in the adoption of solutions by problem-solving groups. *Journal of Abnormal and Social Psychology,* **69**, 264–271.

Homans, G. C. 1958. Social behavior as exchange. *American Journal of Sociology,* **63**, 597–606.

Hoover, E. M. 1928. *The location of economic activity.* New York: McGraw-Hill.

Hoppock, R. 1935. *Job satisfaction.* New York: Harper.

Horwitz, M. 1954. The recall of interrupted group tasks: an experimental study of individual motivation in relation to group goals. *Human Relations,* **7**, 3–38.

Hull, R. L., and A. Holstad. 1942. Morale on the job. In G. Watson (Ed.) *Civilian morale.* New York: Reynal and Hitchcock.

Hyman, H., and D. Katz. 1947. Industrial morale and public opinion methods. *International Journal of Opinion and Attitude Research,* **1**, 13–30.

Jacobson, E., W. W. Charters, Jr., and S. Lieberman. 1951. The use of the role concept in the study of complex organization. *Journal of Social Issues,* 7, 18–27.

Jacobson, E. 1951. Foremen-steward participation practices and work attitudes in a unionized factory. Unpublished doctoral thesis. Ann Arbor, Mich.: University of Michigan.

Janis, I. 1959. Decisional conflicts: a theoretical analysis. *Journal of Conflict Resolution,* 3, 6 27.

Janowitz, M. 1960. *The professional soldier: a social and political portrait.* New York: Free Press.

Jaques, E. 1951. *The changing culture of a factory.* London: Tavistock Publications.

Kahn, R. L. 1958. Human relations on the shop floor. In E. M. Hugh-Jones (Ed.) *Human relations and modern management.* Amsterdam, Holland: North-Holland Publishing Co, 43–74.

Kahn, R. L. 1964(a). Field studies of power in organizations. In R. L. Kahn, and Elise Boulding (Eds.) *Power and conflict in organizations.* New York: Basic Books, 52–66.

Kahn, R. L., and Elise Boulding (Eds.) 1964(b). *Power and conflict in organizations.* New York: Basic Books.

Kahn, R. L., and D. Katz. 1960. Leadership in relation to productivity and morale. In D. Cartwright and A. Zander (Eds.) *Group dynamics: research and theory,* 2nd. ed. Evanston, Ill.: Row, Peterson, 554–571 (c. 1953).

Kahn, R. L., D. M. Wolfe, R. P. Quinn, J. D. Snoek, and R. A. Rosenthal. 1964(c). *Organizational stress: studies in role conflict and ambiguity.* New York: Wiley.

Katona, G., and J. Morgan. 1950. *Industrial mobility in Michigan.* Ann Arbor, Mich.: Institute for Social Research.

Katz, D. 1954. Satisfactions and deprivations in industrial life. In A. Kornhauser, R. Dubin, and A. M. Ross (Eds.) *Industrial conflict.* New York: McGraw-Hill, 86–106.

Katz, D. 1964. The motivational basis of organizational behavior. *Behavioral Science,* 9, 131–146.

Katz, D. and H. Hyman. 1947. Morale in war industry. In T. M. Newcomb and E. L. Hartley (Eds.) *Readings in social psychology.* New York: Holt.

Katz, D., and R. L. Kahn. 1952. Some recent findings in human relations research in industry. In G. W. Swanson, T. M. Newcomb, and E. L. Hartley (Eds.) *Readings in social psychology,* 2d. ed. New York: Holt, 650–665.

Katz, D., N. Maccoby, G. Gurin, and L. Floor. 1951. *Productivity, supervision, and morale among railroad workers.* Ann Arbor, Mich.: Institute for Social Research.

Katz, D., N. Maccoby, and Nancy Morse. 1950. *Productivity, supervision, and morale in an office situation.* Ann Arbor, Mich.: Institute for Social Research.

Katz, D., I. Sarnoff, and C. McClintock. 1956. Ego-defense and attitude change. *Human Relations,* 9, 27–45.

Katz, D., and R. L. Schanck. 1938. *Social psychology.* New York: Wiley.

Katz, E., and P. Lazarsfeld. 1955. *Personal influence: the part played by people in the flow of mass communication.* New York: Free Press.

Kaye, Carol. 1958. Some effects on organizational change of the personality characteristics of key role occupants. Unpublished doctoral dissertation. Ann Arbor, Mich.: University of Michigan.

Kerr, W. A., G. K. Koppelmeier, and J. J. Sullivan. 1951. Absenteeism, turnover, and morale in a metal fabricating factory. *Occupational Psychology*, 25, 50–55.

Killian, L. M. 1952. The significance of multiple-group membership in disaster. *American Journal of Sociology*, 57, 309–314.

Kohler, W., and D. Emery. 1947. Figural after-effects in the third dimension of visual space. *American Journal of Psychology*, 60, 159–201.

Kohler, W., and H. Wallach. 1944. Figural after-effects: an investigation of visual processes. *Proceedings of the American Philosophical Society*, 88, 269–357.

Kornhauser, A. W. 1965. *Mental health of the industrial worker: a Detroit study.* New York: Wiley.

Kornhauser, A. W., and A. A. Sharp. 1932. Employee attitude: suggestions from a study in a factory. *Personnel Journal*, 10, 393–404.

Krech, D., and R. Crutchfield. 1948. *Theory and problems of social psychology.* New York: McGraw-Hill.

Kroeber, A. L. 1952. *The nature of culture.* Chicago: University of Chicago Press.

Leavitt, H. J. 1951. Some effects of certain communication patterns on group performance. *Journal of Abnormal and Social Psychology*, 46, 38–50

Leavitt, H. J. 1958. *Managerial psychology.* Chicago: University of Chicago Press.

Leavitt, H. J. (Ed.) 1963. *The social science of organizations.* Englewood Cliffs, N. J.: Prentice-Hall.

Levine, J., and J. Butler. 1952. Lecture vs. group decision in changing behavior. *Journal of Applied Psychology*, 36, 29–33.

Lewin, K. 1947. Frontiers in group dynamics. *Human Relations*, 1, 5–41.

Lewin, K. 1951. *Field theory in social science.* D. Cartwright (Ed.) New York: Harper.

Lewin, K. 1952. Group decision and social change. In G. E. Swanson, T. M. Newcomb, and E. L. Hartley (Eds.) *Readings in social psychology*, rev. ed., New York: Holt, 459–473.

Lewis, H. B., and M. Franklin. 1944. An experimental study of the role of ego in work. II. The significance of task orientation in work. *Journal of Experimental Psychology*, 34, 195–215.

Lieberman, S. 1956. The effects of changes in roles on the attitudes of role occupants. *Human Relations*, 9, 385–402.

Likert, R. 1956. Developing patterns of management II. *General Management Series*, American Management Association, No. 182, 3–29.

Likert, R. 1958. Effective supervision: an adaptive and relative process. *Personnel Psychology*, 11, 317–352.

Likert, R. 1961. *New patterns of management.* New York: McGraw-Hill.

Linton, R. 1936. *The study of man.* New York: Appleton-Century.

Lippitt, R., J. Watson, and B. Westley. 1958. *The dynamics of planned change.* New York: Harcourt, Brace.

Lippmann, W. 1922. *Public opinion.* New York: Harcourt, Brace.

Luce, Clare B. 1964. Address to the Detroit Economic Club.

McClintock, C. 1958. Personality syndromes and attitude change. *Journal of Personality*, 26, 479–593.

McGregor, D. 1960. *The human side of enterprise.* New York: McGraw-Hill.

Maier, N. R. F. 1950. The quality of group decisions as influenced by the discussion leader. *Human Relations*, 3, 155–174.

Maier, N. R. F. 1952. *Principles of human relations.* New York: Wiley.

Maier, N. R. F. 1953. An experimental test of the effect of training on discussion leadership. *Human Relations*, 6, 161–173.

Maier, N. R. F., and L. R. Hoffman. 1961. Overcoming superior-subordinate communication problems in management. In N. R. F. Maier, L. R. Hoffman, J. G. Hooven, and W. H. Read (Eds.) *Supervisor-subordinate communication in management*. American Management Association Research Study, No. 52.

Malinowski, B. 1926. *Crime and custom in savage society*. New York: Harcourt, Brace.

Mann, F. C. 1957. Studying and creating change: a means to understanding social organization. *Research in Industrial Human Relations*, Industrial Relations Research Association, No. 17, 146–167.

Mann, F. C. 1964. Toward an understanding of the leadership role in formal organizations. In R. Dubin, G. Homans, and D. Miller (Eds.) *Leadership and Productivity*. San Francisco: Chandler.

Mann, F. C., and H. J. Baumgartel. 1952. *Absences and employee attitudes in an electric power company*. Ann Arbor, Mich.: Institute for Social Research.

Mann, F. C., and L. R. Hoffman. 1960. *Automation and the worker: a study of social change in power plants*. New York: Holt.

Mann, F. C., B .P. Indik, and V. H. Vroom. 1963. *The productivity of work groups*. Ann Arbor, Mich.: Survey Research Center.

Mann, F. C., and H. Metzner. 1953. Employee attitudes and absences. *Personnel Psychology*, 6, 467–485.

March, J. G., and H. A. Simon. 1958. *Organizations*. New York: Wiley.

Marriott, R. 1957. *Incentive payment systems*. London: Staples Press.

Mayo, E. 1933. *The human problems of an industrial civilization*. New York: Macmillan.

Mayo, E., and G. Lombard. 1944. Teamwork and labor turnover in the aircraft industry of Southern California. Business Research Studies, No. 32. Cambridge, Mass.: Harvard University.

Meier, R. L. 1961. *Social change in communication-oriented institutions*. Ann Arbor: Mental Health Research Institute, Univ. of Michigan.

Meier, R. 1963. Information input overload: features of growth in communications-oriented institutions. *Libri*, International Library Review, 13, 1–44.

Meltzer, L. 1956. Scientific productivity in organizational settings. *Journal of Social Issues*, 12, 32–40.

Melzack, R., and W. Thompson. 1956. Effects of early experience on social behavior. *Canadian Journal of Psychology*, 10, 82–90.

Merton, R. K. 1957. *Social theory and social structure*, rev. ed. New York: Free Press.

Merton, R. K., and P. F. Lazarsfeld (Eds.) 1950. *Continuities in social research*. New York: Free Press.

Michels, R. 1949. *Political parties: a sociological study of the oligarchical tendencies of modern democracy*. New York: Free Press.

Milgram, S. 1963. Behavioral study of obedience. *Journal of Abnormal and Social Psychology*, 67, 371–378.

Milgram, S. 1964. Group pressure and action against a person. *Journal of Abnormal and Social Psychology*, 69, 137–143.

Miller, D. R. 1963. The study of social relations: situation, identity, and social interaction. In S. Koch (Ed.) *Psychology: a study of a science*, Vol. 5. New York: McGraw-Hill, 639–737.

Miller, J. G. 1955. Toward a general theory for the behavioral sciences. *American Psychologist*, **10**, 513–531.

Miller, J. G. 1960. Information input, overload, and psychopathology. *American Journal of Psychiatry*, **116**, 695–704.

Miller, N. E., and J. Dollard. 1941. *Social learning and imitation*. New Haven: Yale University Press, (reissue, 1962).

Moore, W. E. 1963. *Man, time, and society*. New York: Wiley.

Morse, Nancy. 1953. *Satisfactions in the white collar job*. Ann Arbor, Mich.: Survey Research Center.

Morse, Nancy, and E. Reimer. 1955. Mimeographed report on organizational change. Survey Research Center, Univ. of Michigan.

Morse, Nancy, and E. Reimer. 1956. The experimental change of a major organizational variable. *Journal of Abnormal and Social Psychology*, **52**, 120–129.

Mueller, Eva, and J. Morgan. 1962. Location decisions of manufacturers. *American Economic Review*, Proceedings of the American Economic Association. May, **52**, 204–217.

Neiman, L. J., and J. W. Hughes. 1951. The problems of the concept of role—a re-survey of the literature. *Social Forces*, **30**, 141–149.

Newcomb, T. M. 1943. *Personality and social change: attitude formation in a student community*. New York: Dryden.

Newcomb, T. M. 1947. Autistic hostility and social reality. *Human Relations*, **1**, 69–86.

Newcomb, T. M. 1950. *Social psychology*. New York: Dryden.

Ogburn, W. F. 1922. *Social change with respect to culture and original nature*. New York: Huebsch.

Oppenheimer, F. 1914. The state: its history and development viewed sociologically (translated by J. M. Gitterman). Indianapolis: Bobbs-Merrill.

Parkinson, C. N. 1957. *Parkinson's Law*. Boston: Houghton Mifflin.

Parsons, T. 1951. *The social system*. New York: Free Press.

Parsons, T. 1960. *Structure and process in modern societies*. New York: Free Press.

Patchen, M. 1961. The choice of wage comparisons. Englewood Cliffs, N. J.: Prentice-Hall.

Peabody, R. 1964. *Organizational authority*. New York: Atherton Press.

Pelz, D. C. 1951. Leadership within a hierarchical organization. *Journal of Social Issues*, **7**, 49–55.

Pelz, D. C. 1956. Some social factors related to performance in a research organization. *Administrative Science Quarterly*, **1**, 310–325.

Pelz, D. C. 1957. Motivation of the engineering and research specialist. Improving Managerial Performance, AMA General Management Series, No. 186, 25–46.

Pelz, D. C., and F. M. Andrews. 1962. Organizational atmosphere, motivation, and research contribution. *American Behavioral Scientist*, **6**, 43–47.

Piel, G. 1961. End of toil: science offers a new world. *The Nation*, **192** (24), 515–519.

Presthus, R. 1962. *The organizational society*. New York: Knopf.

Radke, M., and D. Klisurich. 1947. Experiments in changing food habits. *Journal of the American Dietetic Association*, **23**, 403–409.

Rapoport, A. 1960. *Fights, games, and debates*. Ann Arbor, Mich.: University of Michigan Press.

Revans, R. W. 1957. The analysis of industrial behavior. In *Automatic production—change and control*. London: Institution of Production Engineering.

Rice, A. K. 1958. *Productivity and social organization: the Ahmedabad experiment.* London: Tavistock Publications.

Rice, A. K. 1963. *The enterprise and its environment.* London: Tavistock Publications.

Riesman, D. 1950. *The lonely crowd.* New Haven: Yale University Press.

Roethlisberger, F. J. 1941. *Management and morale.* Cambridge, Mass.: Harvard University Press.

Roethlisberger, F. J., and W. J. Dickson. 1939. *Management and the worker.* Cambridge, Mass.: Harvard University Press.

Rommetveit, R. 1955. *Social norms and roles.* Minneapolis: University of Minnesota Press (c. 1954).

Rosen, B. C. 1955. Conflicting group membership: a study of parent-peer group cross-pressures. *American Sociological Review,* 20, 155–161.

Rubinstein, A. H., and C. H. Haberstroh. (Eds.) 1960. *Some theories of organization.* Homewood, Ill.: Dorsey.

Sarbin, T. R., and C. Hardyck. 1953. Contributions to role-taking theory: role-perception on the basis of postural cues. Unpublished manuscript.

Sarbin, T. R., and B. G. Rosenberg. 1955. Contributions to role-taking theory. IV. A method for a qualitative analysis of the self. *Journal of Social Psychology,* 42, 71–82.

Sarbin, T. R., and R. W. Stephenson. 1952. Contributions to role-taking theory: authoritarian attitudes and role-taking skill. Unpublished manuscript.

Sarbin, T. R., and J. D. Williams. 1953. Contributions to role-taking theory. V. Role perception on the basis of limited auditory stimuli. Unpublished manuscript.

Sarnoff, I. 1962. *Personality dynamics and development.* New York: Wiley.

Scanlon, J. N. 1948. Profit sharing under collective bargaining: three case studies. *Industrial and Labor Relations Review,* 2, 58–75.

Schanck, R. L. 1932. A study of a community and its groups and institutions conceived as behaviors of individuals. *Psychological Monographs,* 43, (2).

Schein, E. H., and Bennis, W. G. 1965. *Personal and organizational change through group methods.* New York: Wiley.

Scudder, K. 1954. The open institution. *The Annals.* American Academy of Political and Social Science, 293, 79–87.

Seashore, S. E. 1954. *Group cohesiveness in the industrial work group.* Ann Arbor, Mich.: Institute for Social Research.

Seashore, S. E. 1962. *The assessment of organizational performance.* Ann Arbor, Mich.: Survey Research Center (multilith).

Seashore, S. E., and D. G. Bowers. 1963. *Changing the structure and functioning of an organization.* Monograph No. 33, Ann Arbor, Mich.: Survey Research Center.

Seashore, S. E., B. P. Indik, and B. S. Georgopoulos. 1960. Relationships among criteria of job performance. *Journal of Applied Psychology,* 44, 195–202.

Selznick, P. 1949. *TVA and the grass roots.* Berkeley: University of California Press.

Selznick, P. 1957. *Leadership in administration.* Evanston, Ill.: Row, Peterson.

Sherif, M. 1936. *The psychology of social norms.* New York: Harper.

Shirer, W. L. 1960. *The rise and fall of the Third Reich.* New York: Simon and Schuster.

Simon, H. 1957. *Administrative behavior,* 2nd ed. New York: Macmillan.

Singer, D. 1961. The level of analysis problem in international relations. *World Politics*, 14, 77–92.

Sloan, A. P. 1964. *My years with General Motors*. J. McDonald (Ed.) with C. Stevens. Garden City, N. Y.: Doubleday (c. 1963).

Solomon, P., et al. (Eds.) 1961. *Sensory deprivation*. Cambridge, Mass.: Harvard University Press.

Spitz, R. A. 1945. Hospitalism: an inquiry into the genesis of psychiatric conditions in early childhood. *Psychoanalytic Study of the Child*, 1, 53–74.

Stagner, R. 1951. Homeostasis as a unifying concept in personality theory. *Psychological Review*, 58, 5–17.

Stagner, R. 1956. *The psychology of industrial conflict*. New York: Wiley.

Stanton, A., and M. Schwartz. 1954. *The mental hospital*. New York: Basic Books.

Statistical abstract. 1963. Washington, D. C.: U. S. Bureau of the Census.

Stogdill, R. M. 1948. Personal factors associated with leadership. *Journal of Psychology*, 25, 35–71.

Stogdill, R. M. 1959. *Individual behavior and group achievement*. New York: Oxford University Press.

Stouffer, S. A., et al. 1949. *The American soldier*. Vols. 1 and 2 of Studies in Social Psychology during World War II. Princeton, N.J.: Princeton University Press.

Stouffer, S. A., and J. Toby. 1951. Role conflict and personality. *American Journal of Sociology*, 56, 395–406.

Super, D. 1939. Occupational level and job satisfaction. *Journal of Applied Psychology*, 23, 547–564.

Survey of current business. 1964. Washington, D. C.: U. S. Department of Commerce, September.

Survey Research Center. 1950. Attitudes and opinions of hourly employees. Ann Arbor, Michigan.: The University of Michigan.

Sykes, G. M. 1958. *The society of captives*. Princeton, N. J.: Princeton University Press.

Tannenbaum, A. S. 1957. Personality change as a result of an experimental change of environmental conditions. *Journal of Abnormal and Social Psychology*, 55, 404–406.

Tannenbaum, A. S. 1962. Control in organizations. *Administrative Science Quarterly*, 7, 236–257.

Tannenbaum, A. S., and M. N. Donald. 1957. *A study of the League of Women Voters of the United States. Factors in League functioning*. Ann Arbor, Mich.: Institute for Social Research (mimeograph).

Tannenbaum, A. S., and R. Kahn. 1958. *Participation in union locals*. New York: Harper, Row.

Tannenbaum, R., I. Weschler, and F. Massarik. 1961. *Leadership and organization*. New York: McGraw-Hill.

Taylor, F. W. 1923. *The principles of scientific management*. New York: Harper.

Thelen, H. A. 1954. *Dynamics of groups at work*. Chicago: University of Chicago Press.

Thelen, H. A. 1960(a). Exploration of a growth model for psychic, biological, and social systems. Mimeographed paper.

Thelen, H. A. 1960(b). Personal communication to authors.

Thorndike, E. L. 1935. Workers' satisfactions: likes and dislikes of young people for their jobs. *Occupations*, 13, 704–706.

Trist, E. L., and K. W. Bamforth. 1951. Some social and psychological consequences of the long-wall method of coal-getting. *Human Relations*, **4**, 3–38.

Trist, E. L., G. W. Higgin, H. Murray, and A. B. Pollock. 1963. *Organizational
choice*. London: Tavistock Publications.

Urbrock, R. 1934. Attitudes of 4,430 employees. *Journal of Social Psychology*, **5**,
365–377.

Valen, H., and D. Katz. 1964. *Political parties in Norway*. Oslo, Norway: University of Oslo Press.

Van Zelst, R. H., and W. A. Kerr. 1953. Workers' attitudes toward merit rating.
Personnel Psychology, **6**, 159–172.

Viteles, M. S. 1953. *Motivation and morale in industry*. New York: Norton.

von Bertalanffy, L. 1940. Der organismus als physikalisches system betrachtet.
Naturwissenschaften, **28**, 521 ff.

von Bertalanffy, L. 1950. The theory of open systems in physics and biology.
Science, **111**, 23–28.

von Bertalanffy, L. 1956. General system theory. *General systems*. Yearbook of
the Society for the Advancement of General System Theory, **1**, 1–10.

Vroom, V. 1960. *Some personality determinants of the effects of participation*.
Englewood Cliffs, N. J.: Prentice-Hall.

Vroom, V. 1964. *Work and motivation*. New York: Wiley.

Walker, C. R. 1950. The problem of the repetitive job. *Harvard Business Review*,
28, 54–58.

Walker, C. R. 1954. Work methods, working conditions, and morale. In A. Kornhauser, R. Dubin, and A. M. Ross (Eds.) *Industrial conflict*, New York:
McGraw-Hill.

Walker, C. R., and H. Guest. 1952. *The man on the assembly line*. Cambridge,
Mass.: Harvard University Press.

Wall Street Journal. January 31, 1961.

Webb, W. B., and E. P. Hollander. 1956. Comparison of three morale measures:
a survey, pooled group judgments, and self-evaluation. *Journal of Applied
Psychology*, **40**, 17–20.

Weber, M. 1930. *The Protestant ethic and the spirit of capitalism* (translated by
T. Parsons) New York: Scribner.

Weber, M. 1947. *The theory of social and economic organization* (translated by
A. M. Henderson, and T. Parsons) T. Parsons (Ed.) New York: Free Press.

Weiss, R. 1956. *Processes of organization*. Ann Arbor, Mich.: Survey Research
Center.

Weitz, J., and R. C. Nuckols. 1953. The validity of direct and indirect questions
in measuring job satisfaction. *Personnel Psychology*, **6**, 487–494.

White, L. A. 1949. *The science of culture*. New York: Farrar, Strauss and Cudahy.

Whyte, W. F. (Ed.) 1955. *Money and motivation*. New York: Harper.

Wilson, Woodrow. 1887. The study of administration. *Political Science Quarterly*,
197–222.

Worthy, J. C. 1950(a). Factors influencing employee morale. *Harvard Business
Review*, **28**, 61–73.

Worthy, J. C. 1950(b). Organizational structure and employee morale. *American
Sociological Review*, **15**, 169–179.

Wright, C. R., and H. Hyman. 1958. Voluntary association memberships of American adults. *American Sociological Review*, **23**, 284–294.

Wouk, H. 1951. *The Caine Mutiny*. Garden City, N. Y.: Doubleday.

Zald, M. N. 1962. Organizational control structures in five correctional institutions. *American Journal of Sociology*, 68, 335–345.

Zaleznik, A., C. R. Christensen, and F. Roethlisberger. 1958. *The motivation, productivity, and satisfaction of workers: a predictive study*. Boston: Harvard Graduate School of Business Administration.

Zeigarnik, B. 1927. Das Behalten erledigter und unerledigter Handlungen, III. The memory of completed and uncompleted actions. *Psychologische Forschung*, 9, 1–85.

Index